BEHAVIOR IN ORGANIZATIONS SIXTH EDITION

We have included in this book several key features designed to help students find and understand the most important aspects of the material. To help you get the most out of this book, we thought it would be useful to introduce some of these features here.

LEARNING OBJECTIVES
Your guide to what you should know after reading this chapter.

Key Terms
Definitions of the most important terms appear in the margins near where they are introduced.

Cross References
Other chapters where related material may be found are identified in the margins.

Summary and Review
A simplified recap of all the most important ideas in the chapter, divided into major heading.

Questions for Discussion
Useful questions for both reviewing the material and thinking about it further.

Take It to the Net
Internet addresses where Web–based information about many of the companies identified within the chapters can be found. This section also leads to the book's own home page.

PART 4 GROUP PROCESSES

CHAPTER **Eight**

GROUP DYNAMICS AND TEAMWORK

OBJECTIVES

After reading this chapter you should be able to:

1. Define what is meant by a *group*, and explain why it is not just a collection of people.
2. Identify different types of groups operating within organizations and understand how they develop.
3. Describe the importance of *norms*, *roles*, *status*, and *cohesiveness* within organizations.
4. Explain how individual performance in groups is affected by the presence of others (*social facilitation*), the cultural diversity of group membership, and the number of others with whom one is working (*social loafing*).
5. Define what *teams* are and how they may be distinguished from groups in general.
6. Describe the various types of teams that exist in organizations and the steps that should be followed in creating them.
7. Understand the evidence regarding the effectiveness of teams in organizations.
8. Explain the factors responsible for the failure of some teams to operate as effectively as possible.
9. Identify things that can be done to build high-performance teams.

Special Sections
Close-up looks at some of the most fascinating aspects of the field, focusing on such themes as ethics, quality, globalization and diversity, and future trends.

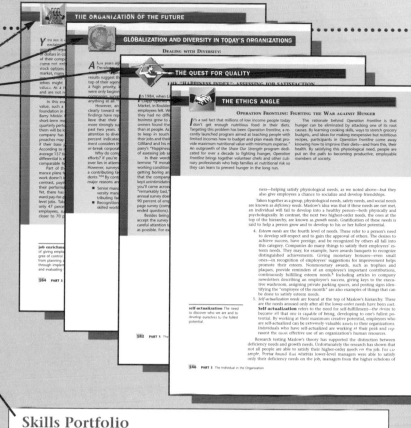

Skills Portfolio
Exercises that help you to learn about yourself as an individual (Experiencing Organizational Behavior) and to experience key ideas first hand together with others (Working in Groups).

You Be the Consultant
Questions designed to get you to think about how the material may be applied to solving a typical organizational problem.

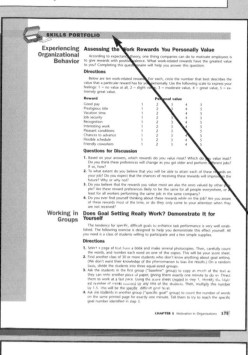

Case Studies
To demonstrate how organizational behavior is put to use, each chapter contains two cases describing actual organizations—one to help you understand the importance of the topic (Preview Case) and one to highlight how key concepts are used in practice (Case in Point). A Video Case from ABC News appears at the end of each major part of the book.

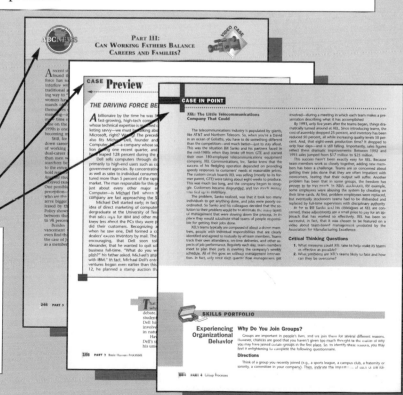

BEHAVIOR IN ORGANIZATIONS

UNDERSTANDING AND MANAGING THE HUMAN SIDE OF WORK

sixth edition

Jerald Greenberg
The Ohio State University

Robert A. Baron
Rensselaer Polytechnic Institute

PRENTICE-HALL INTERNATIONAL, INC.

Acquisitions Editor: Natalie Anderson
Development Editor: Ronald S. Librach
Associate Editor: Lisamarie Brassini
Editorial Assistant: Crissy Statuto
Editor-in-Chief: James Boyd
Director of Development: Steve Deitmer
Marketing Manager: Sandy Steiner
Project Manager/Liaison: Lynne Breitfeller
Production Editor: York Production Services
Production Coordinator: Renee Pelletier
Managing Editor: Carol Burgett
Manufacturing Supervisor: Arnold Vila
Manufacturing Manager: Vincent Scelta
Senior Designer: Ann France
Design Director: Patricia Wosczyk
Cover Interior Design: Lorraine Castellano

This edition may be sold only in those countries to which it is consigned by Prentice-Hall International. It is not to be re-exported and it is not for sale in the U.S.A., Mexico, or Canada

ISBN 0–13–724189–5

Prentice-Hall International (UK) Limited, *London*
Prentice-Hall of Australia Pty. Limited, *Sydney*
Prentice-Hall Canada, Inc., *Toronto*
Prentice-Hall Hispanoamericana, S.A., *Mexico*
Prentice-Hall of India Private Limited, *New Delhi*
Prentice-Hall of Japan, Inc., *Tokyo*
Simon & Schuster Asia Pte. Ltd., *Singapore*
Editora Prentice-Hall do Brasil, Ltda., *Rio de Janeiro*
Prentice-Hall, Upper Saddle River, New Jersey

Printed in the United States of America

10 9 8 7 6 5 4 3

To my best pal, for giving me strength, serenity, and sustenance.

J.G.

To three of the people who truly matter in my life:
   Jessica—who shares my optimism
   Richard—who shares my love of good food, and
   Randy—who shares so many of my views

R.A.B.

BRIEF CONTENTS

CONTENTS

PART II

BASIC HUMAN PROCESSES

PART III

THE INDIVIDUAL IN THE ORGANIZATION

PART V

INFLUENCING OTHERS

CHAPTER 12   INFLUENCE, POWER, AND
POLITICS IN ORGANIZATIONS   400

ON COMING OF AGE IN A CHANGING WORLD

When some people see that this book is in its sixth edition they take it as a sign that we must be doing something right—or so they tell us. We gratefully accept the compliment. To others it is a warning sign that the book must be getting stodgy and overly comfortable as it ages. We respectfully disagree. In fact, we contend that textbooks need not get stale as they mature. Rather, it is quite possible for them to be as current and dynamic as the fields on which they report. Nowhere is this more important than in the case of organizational behavior. Although we admit to our share of graying, this applies more to the color of the hair around our temples than, we believe, to our account of organizational behavior. Specifically, our goal in preparing this revision has been to stay at the cutting edge of the field by highlighting the ever-changing nature of organizations and people's involvement in them. Capturing this dynamic has precluded any opportunity to rest on our laurels. If you think about it, keeping things the same is hardly a luxury one has when dealing with an ever-changing field. The result: On these pages we present a fresh look at the field of organizational behavior.

By taking a "fresh look," we do not mean to imply that we have abandoned totally the approach that has led so many of our colleagues to favor this book. To the contrary, one thing that has remained unchanged is the field's dual allegiance to both research and practice, and with it, our attention to both these activities. If anything, our commitment to balancing the field's complementary orientations to research and theory is greater than ever. Specifically, we have continued the research focus that has been so well received in previous editions. Indeed many new studies were used to broaden the book's research base.

At the same time, we continue to augment our coverage of the practical, applications-oriented side of OB—that is, the many ways in which its findings and principles are put to use in organizations. In fact, we have widened our quest to provide updated examples showing how OB practices and principles are used in today's organizations. Not surprisingly, our special Company Index is brimming with many new entries. To give readers a good sense of the wide variety of organizations that exist, we purposely refer to a broad range of real companies—ones both large and small, some offering products and others providing services, and those with domestic operations as well as those whose reach is more global.

In recent years, the balance between OB research and practice has been brought to the forefront by rapid changes in the nature of organizations and their relationships with the people who work within them. As a result, many new topics have become the focus of systematic study, and many well-established ones have received increased attention. We have carefully monitored these changes and have tailored our coverage accordingly. The result, we believe, is a book that closely reflects the state of OB as it is studied and practiced today. We will now point out some of the specific improvements that can be found in this sixth edition of *Behavior in Organizations*.

Special New and Revised Features

We have included several new features in this edition that, we believe, will make it our most useful book yet.

"You Be the Consultant" Sections

The matter of how organizational research can be applied to solving organizational problems is a special concern in the field of OB. Our new feature, **You Be The Consultant,** provides students with opportunities to make these connections. Brief sections inserted within each chapter ask students questions that require them to apply creatively the material covered to a typical organizational problem. These exercises are designed to help students sharpen their analytical skills while appreciating the complexities involved in making the leap from theory to application.

"Skills Portfolio" Sections

We now include a special section at the end of each chapter in which various types of exercises are provided to help develop students' managerial skills and their appreciation of OB phenomena. They are called the **Skills Portfolio.** Two types of exercises are included in each portfolio.

1. **Experiencing Organizational Behavior** exercises are designed to help students learn about themselves as individuals. Some examples include:

- Measuring Your Own Self-Monitoring (Chapter 4)
- Are You Committed to Your Job? (Chapter 6)
- What is Your Personal Decision Style (Chapter 10)
- Personal Styles of Conflict Management (Chapter 11)

2. **Working in Groups** exercises are designed to help students learn about group and organizational phenomena by working together with others. Some examples include:

- Role Play: The Disciplinary Interview (Chapter 3)
- Recognizing Organizational Politics When You See It (Chapter 12)
- Identifying Great Leaders in All Walks of Life (Chapter 13)
- Recognizing Impediments to Change—And How to Overcome Them (Chapter 16)

"Take it to the Net" Sections

Internet-savvy readers will find the **Take it to the Net** sections appearing at the end of each chapter to be useful sources of relevant Internet addresses. These include an address containing supplementary material for this book, as well as the addresses of various companies cited in the text. Readers interested in learning more about the organizations mentioned will surely find this a helpful resource.

Cross-References to Other Material

Too often, when people study new material they fail to recognize the connections between concepts. This problem can be quite serious in the case of OB, where many concepts are inter-related and do not fit into unique categories. To overcome the appearance that key concepts are really as isolated as any textbook structure suggests, each chapter contains several references to other places in the text where related material may be found. These cross-references, appearing in marginal annotations, are designed to highlight the connections between various OB concepts and to identify the several major categories of knowledge into which they belong.

Easier Access to Key Terms

Our students tell us that learning definitions is an important way in which they use the text to study the material. With this in mind, we have changed in two ways the manner in which we present definitions. First, we now provide formal definitions of key terms in the margins, next to where they are introduced in the text. Second, we now have a master Glossary at the end of the text to provide ready access to definitions. To make them especially useful, the definitions appearing in the glossary include indications as to the exact pages in the text they may be found.

More, and New, Cases

In our quest to highlight the involvement of OB in the latest business activities, we have revised all of the chapter-opening **Preview Cases,** and many of the chapter-summarizing **Case-in-Point** sections. The Case-in-Point sections contain follow-up questions designed to elicit critical thinking on the part of students. Also, at the end of each major part of the book are new **Video Cases.** These written cases are coordinated with video clips from various ABC News programs that are available on VHS cassettes to professors adopting this book. Some of the new cases included are as follows.

- Shooting for the Moon at Intel (Chapter 4)
- Workplace Equality Yields High Interest at the Bank of Montreal (Chapter 6)
- Baby Superstore: All Grown Up (Chapter 10)
- Bill Gates: He Doesn't Run the World—Yet (Chapter 12)
- Zales Becomes a Gem of a Chain (Chapter 16)

Enhanced Attention to Major Themes

We have gone out of our way to highlight the major themes cutting across various aspects of the field of organizational behavior and to incorporate these throughout the text. This mission begins in a new **Chapter 2, Work in the Twenty-First Century: The Changing World of People and Organizations,** in which we identify five key themes that have had profound effects on OB in recent years. These are:

- Globalization and Culture: The International Nature of Organizational Behavior
- The Shifting Demographics of the Workforce: Trends Toward Diversity
- Trends in Working Arrangements: New Organizational Forms and Jobs
- The Quality Revolution: Total Quality Management and Reengineering
- Corporate Social Responsibility: The Ethical Organization

We pay attention to these themes through this book, both in the text itself, and in four different kinds of special boxed sections appearing in the chapters.

Globalization and Diversity in Today's Organizations

Many of the most pressing issues faced by organizations today center around the growing *internationalization* of all business activities, and the increasing *cultural diversity* of people in today's workforce. OB, as a field, is deeply concerned with such issues. To reflect this fact, and to illustrate the many ways in which OB can help modern organizations in their efforts to deal with these matters, we have included a special section called **Globalization and Diversity in Today's Organizations.** A few examples:

- Saving Face in Japan: Where Renting Acquaintances is Big Business (Chapter 3)
- Breaking Down the Barriers to Cross-Cultural Communication (Chapter 9)

- Trust: Does it Differ Around the World? (Chapter 11)
- Men and Women: Comparing their Leadership Styles (Chapter 13)

The Organization of Tomorrow

Now that we are poised at the threshold of the twenty-first century, it is tempting to consider what organizational life might be like in the years to come. Our special section, **The Organization of Tomorrow,** focuses on future trends in technology and the nature of organizations themselves that are likely to influence the practice of OB. Some examples:

- The Hottest Careers of the Twenty-First Century (Chapter 7)
- Videoconferencing: Groups in Cyberspace (Chapter 8)
- Decisions at 30,000 Feet: Training Pilots to Avoid Fatal Errors (Chapter 10)
- Internal Markets: Design for the Information Age (Chapter 15)

The Quest for Quality

Whether it's part of a strategic commitment to a *total quality management* philosophy, or simply an effort to gain a competitive edge, many of today's organizations are more committed than ever to improving the quality of their products, services, and the lives of their employees. Because these efforts are such an important part of organizational life today, we have highlighted them in special sections called **The Quest for Quality.** Some examples include:

- Sabbaticals: Time Off the Job Satisfies Many Needs Simultaneously (Chapter 5)
- ServiceMaster Uses Incentives to Create a Safety-Conscious Culture (Chapter 14)
- The Joint Venture Between Universal Card and TSYS: Lessons Learned (Chapter 15)
- Competitive Intelligence: Planning Change by Learning About the Competition (Chapter 16)

The Ethics Angle

As in previous editions, we continue to highlight the growing concern over matters of ethical behavior that have permeated the workplace in recent years. Brief sections in each chapter, entitled **The Ethics Angle,** highlight ethical practices and controversies that are relevant to OB. Some of these include:

- Valuing Differences at DEC (Chapter 6)
- Sears Installs the "Ethics Assist" Line (Chapter 9)
- Northrop Keeps Tabs on Leaders' Ethics (Chapter 13)
- NYNEX's "GuideLine" to Ethical Culture (Chapter 14)

Coverage of New Topics

In our quest to stay at the cutting edge of the field of OB, we have updated many sections of the text. As a result, dozens of new topics are now covered. Here is just a partial listing of these topics.

- Hofstede's cultural dimensions (Chapter 2)
- cultural pluralism versus the melting pot (Chapter 2)
- contingent workforce (Chapter 2)
- expatriates and culture shock (Chapter 2)
- telecommuting (Chapter 2)
- voluntary reduced work-time (V-time) programs (Chapter 2)
- corporate image (Chapter 3)
- first-impression error (Chapter 3)
- selective perception (Chapter 3)
- 360° feedback (Chapter 3)

IS THIS ANY WAY TO RUN AN AIRLINE? HERB KELLEHER THINKS SO

When you conjure up the image of the CEO of a major airline, chances are good that it's not someone who has ever dressed up in public as Elvis and the Easter Bunny, or who has stood up in the company cafeteria and led the crowd in cheers. Yet, at the age that many of his fellow CEOs are retiring, Southwest Airlines' CEO Herbert D. Kelleher has done these things—and has encouraged even zanier antics among his employees. But Kelleher is more than outrageous; he is an executive who has been hailed as the "principal driving force for changes occurring in the airline industry." In fact, he has made Southwest the most profitable airline in the business, the only major airline in recent years not to suffer losses.

Southwest does things differently than other airlines. It doesn't rely on travel agents, it includes only one type of aircraft—Boeing 737s—in its fleet, and it avoids using major airports. There are no assigned seats and, with the exception of peanuts or crackers, no meals. What Southwest does do is get you between point A and point B with a crew that goes the extra mile when needed. During slow periods, pilots might staff boarding gates and ticket agents might move luggage. One Southwest reservations clerk even flew to another city with a frail, elderly passenger just to put her at ease and make sure she made her connection. And when Southwest acquired Morris Air in 1993, Southwest employees welcomed their new colleagues with hundreds of cards, candy, and company T-shirts.

If you asked any of Southwest's 12,000 employees where this "rah rah" company spirit comes from, they'd probably all point to Kelleher. Unlike an ordinary CEO who might not stray too far from the executive suite, Kelleher gets involved in his employees' lives. He explains: "I feel that you have to be with your employees through all their difficulties, that you have to be interested in them personally." And that he does. Kelleher has been described by one industry analyst as "the sort of manager who will stay out with a mechanic in some bar until four o'clock in the morning to find out what is going on. And then he will fix whatever is wrong."

This attention to people has made Kelleher's employees very loyal. Southwest has one of the lowest turnover rates in the industry. And to date, Southwest has never laid off any of its employees—a claim few of its competitors can make. Unlike most other airlines, Southwest has been on very good terms with labor unions. Instead of treating unions as adversaries, Southwest's management thinks of them as partners for reaching mutual goals. Instead of the traditional "us versus them" mentality that characterizes so many airlines, Southwest employees think of themselves as being part of a family. At the head of that family is surely Herb Kelleher. One airline industry spokesperson captured Kelleher's secret: "At other places, managers say that people are their most important resource, but nobody acts on it. At Southwest, they have never lost sight of the fact."

There are doubtless many factors responsible for the success of Southwest Airlines. Its unique reservation system, the uniformity of its equipment, and its use of less expensive, secondary airports certainly all play a part. But what stands out most is Herb Kelleher's special relationship with the people who make up the company. It is the unique way that Kelleher and his employees behave that sets Southwest apart from the competition.

If you think about it, however, there is really nothing so magical about the spell Kelleher has cast on Southwest's workforce. He is perhaps a far more gifted leader and manager of people than a sorcerer. But if there is any secret to Kelleher's wizardry, it is his keen awareness of one essential fact: People are key to the success of organizations! There can be no organizations without people. And so, no matter how sophisticated a company's mechanical equipment may be, and no matter how healthy its financial status, people problems can bring an organization down very quickly. Thus it makes sense to realize that "the human side of work" (not coincidentally part of the subtitle of this book) is a critical element in the effective functioning—and basic existence—of organizations. It is this people-centered orientation that is taken in the field of *organizational behavior* (OB for short)—the field specializing in the study of human behavior in organizations.

OB scientists and practitioners study and attempt to solve problems by using knowledge derived from research in the **behavioral sciences**, such as psychology and sociology. In other words, the field of OB is firmly rooted in science. It relies on research to derive valuable information about organizations and the complex processes operating within them. Such knowledge is used as the basis for helping to solve a wide range of organizational problems. For example, what can be done to make people more productive and more satisfied on their jobs (see Figure 1-1)? When and how should people be organized into teams? How should jobs and organizations be designed so that people best adapt to changes in the environment? These are just a few of the many important questions that are addressed by the field of organizational behavior.

As you read this text, it will become very clear that OB specialists have attempted to learn about a large variety of issues involving people in organizations. In fact, over the past few decades, OB has developed into a field so diverse that its scientists have examined just about every conceivable aspect of behavior in organizations.[1] The fruits of this labor already have been enjoyed by people interested in making organizations not only more productive, but also more pleasant for those working in them.

In the remainder of this chapter, we will give you the background information you will need to understand the scope of OB and its potential value. With this in mind, this first chapter is designed to introduce you formally to

behavioral sciences Fields such as psychology and sociology that seek knowledge of human behavior and society through the use of the scientific method.

■ **FIGURE 1-1**
Enhancing Employee Performance and Satisfaction: An Important Organizational Issue
Although the scientific study of behavior in organizations doesn't go back as far as the era depicted here, concerns about enhancing performance and satisfaction have long been quite prevalent in organizations.

(**Source:** THE FAR SIDE © 1985 FarWorks, Inc. Distributed by Universal Press Syndicate. Reprinted with permission. All rights reserved.)

"Excuse me, sir, but Shinkowsky keeps stepping on my sandal."

safe to say that the scientific approach is a central defining characteristic of modern OB.

OB Focuses on Three Levels of Analysis: Individuals, Groups, and Organizations

To best appreciate behavior in organizations, OB specialists cannot focus exclusively on individuals acting alone. After all, in organizational settings people frequently work together in groups. Furthermore, people—alone and in groups—both influence and are influenced by their work environments. Considering this fact, it should not be surprising to learn that the field of OB focuses on three distinct levels of analysis: individuals, groups, and organizations.

The field of OB recognizes that *all three levels of analysis* must be used to comprehend fully the complex dynamics of behavior in organizations (see Figure 1-2). Careful attention to all three levels of analysis is a central theme in modern OB and will be fully reflected throughout this text. For example, at the individual level, we will be describing how OB specialists are concerned with individual perceptions, attitudes, and motives. At the group level, we will be describing how people communicate with each other and coordinate their activities between themselves in work groups. Finally, at the organizational level, we will examine organizations as a whole—the way they are structured and operate in their environments, and the effects of their operations on the individuals and groups within them. We're optimistic that you will come to appreciate the value of all three approaches long before you finish reading this book.

Organizational Behavior Today: Characteristics of the Field

Now that we have defined what is meant by organizational behavior, we believe it is useful and important to summarize some of the major characteristics of the field as it exists today. This overview will prepare you for appreciating our presentation of the work of OB scientists in the chapters ahead.

OB Seeks to Improve People's Quality of Life at Work

In the early part of the twentieth century, as railroads opened up the western portion of the United States and the nation's population rapidly grew (it doubled from 1880 to 1920), the demand for manufactured products was great. New manufacturing plants were built, attracting waves of new immigrants in search of a living wage and laborers lured off farms by the employment prospects that factory work offered. These men and women found that factories were gigantic, noisy, hot, and highly regimented—in short, brutal places in which to work (see Figure 1-3). Bosses demanded more and more of their employees and treated them like disposable machines, replacing those who quit or who died from accidents with others who waited outside the factory gates.[3]

Obviously, the managers of 100 years ago held very negative views of employees. They assumed that people were basically lazy and irresponsible and treated them with disrespect. This negativistic approach, which has been with us for many years, reflects the traditional view of management—what Douglas McGregor called a **Theory X** orientation.[4] This philosophy of management assumes that people are basically lazy, dislike work, need direction, and will only work hard when they are being pushed, goaded into performing (i.e., because there is a carrot at the end of the stick).

Today, however, if you asked a diverse group of corporate officials to describe their basic views of human nature, you'd probably find some more optimistic thoughts. Although some of today's managers still believe that people are basically lazy, many others would disagree, arguing that it's not that sim-

■ **FIGURE 1-3**
Factory Work a Century Ago
Compared to the relatively safe and comfortable conditions encountered in today's factories, manufacturing plants at the beginning of the twentieth century were highly unpleasant places in which to work. The field of OB is concerned with improving the quality of people's lives on the job.

Theory X A traditional philosophy of management suggesting that most people are lazy and irresponsible and will work hard only when forced to do so.

ple. They would claim that most individuals are at least as capable of working hard as they are of "goofing off." If employees are recognized for their efforts (such as by being appropriately paid) and are given an opportunity to succeed (such as by being well trained), they may be expected to work very hard without being pushed. Thus, employees may put forth a great deal of effort simply because they want to. Management's job, then, is to create those conditions that make people want to perform as desired.

The approach which assumes that people are willing to work hard when the right conditions prevail is known as the **Theory Y** orientation. This philosophy assumes that people have a psychological need to work and seek achievement and responsibility. In contrast to the Theory X philosophy of management, which essentially demonstrates distrust for people on the job, the Theory Y approach is strongly associated with promoting the betterment of human resources (for a summary of the differences, see Figure 1-4).

As you might suspect, the Theory Y perspective currently prevails among those interested in organizational behavior. This approach assumes that people are highly responsive to their work environments and that how they are treated will influence how they will act. OB scientists are very interested in learning exactly what conditions will lead people to behave in the most positive ways. As you will learn in reading this book, conditions in which employees are treated favorably will help them become more committed to their organizations and to go above and beyond the call of duty. In contrary fashion, those who are exploited will act more negatively—slacking off, behaving antisocially (e.g., stealing), or eventually quitting. In short, modern OB assumes that there are no intrinsic reasons why work settings cannot be made both pleasant and productive.

OB Recognizes the Dynamic Nature of Organizations

Thus far, our characterization of the field of OB has focused more on behavior than on organizations. Nonetheless, it is important to point out that both OB scientists and practitioners *do* pay a great deal of attention to the nature of organizations themselves. Under what conditions will organizations change? How are organizations structured? How do organizations interact with their environments? Questions such as these are of major interest to specialists in OB. But before we can consider them—as we will later in this book—we must first clarify exactly what we mean by an "organization."

Although you probably have a very good idea of what an organization is, you might find it difficult to define. Thus we offer the following definition.

Theory Y A philosophy of management suggesting that under the right circumstances, people are fully capable of working productively and accepting responsibility for their work.

As we will see in Chapter 15, Theory X and Theory Y philosophies are reflected in the way organizations are designed.

■ **FIGURE 1-4**
Theory X versus Theory Y: A Summary
The traditional Theory X orientation toward people is far more negativistic than the more contemporary Theory Y approach that is widely accepted today. Some of the key differences between these management philosophies are summarized here.

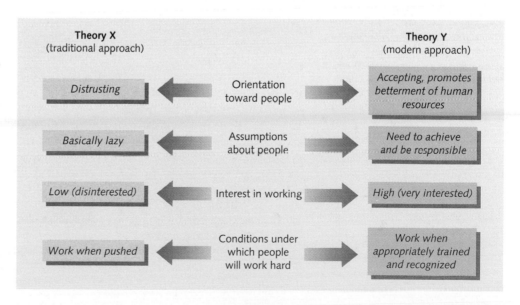

organization A structured social system consisting of groups and individuals working together to meet some agreed-upon objectives.

open systems Self-sustaining systems that transform input from the external environment into output, which the system then returns to the environment.

An **organization** is a structured social system consisting of groups and individuals working together to meet some agreed-upon objectives. In other words, organizations consist of structured social units, such as individuals and/or work groups, that strive to attain a common goal, such as to produce and sell a product at a profit.

In studying organizations, OB scientists recognize that organizations are not static: Rather, they are dynamic and ever-changing entities. In other words, they recognize that organizations are **open systems**—that is, self-sustaining systems that use energy to transform resources from the environment (such as raw materials) into some form of output (for example, a finished product).[5] Figure 1-5 summarizes some of the key properties of open systems. As this diagram makes clear, organizations receive input from their environments and continuously transform it into output. This output gets transformed back to input, and the cyclical operation continues.

Consider, for example, how organizations may tap the human resources of the community by hiring and training people to do jobs. These individuals may work to provide a product in exchange for wages. They then spend these wages, putting money back into the community, allowing more people to afford the company's products. In turn, this exchange creates the need for still more employees, and so on. If you think about it this way, it's easy to realize that organizations are dynamic and constantly changing. In a sense, then, they are like the operations of the human body. As people breathe, they take in oxygen and transform it into carbon dioxide. This, in turn, sustains the life of green plants, which in turn, emit oxygen for people to breathe. The continuous nature of the open system characterizes not only human life, but the existence of organizations as well.

OB Assumes There Is No "One Best" Approach

What's the most effective way to motivate people? What style of leadership works best? Should teams be used to make important organizational decisions? Although questions such as these appear to be quite reasonable, there is a basic problem with all of them: They all assume that there is one simple answer. That is, they suggest that there is one best approach—one best way to motivate, to lead, and to make decisions.

■ **Figure 1-5**
Organizations as Open Systems
The open systems *approach assumes that organizations are self-sustaining— that is, they transform inputs into outputs in a continuous fashion.*

(**Source:** Based on suggestions by Katz & Kahn, 1978; see Note 5.)

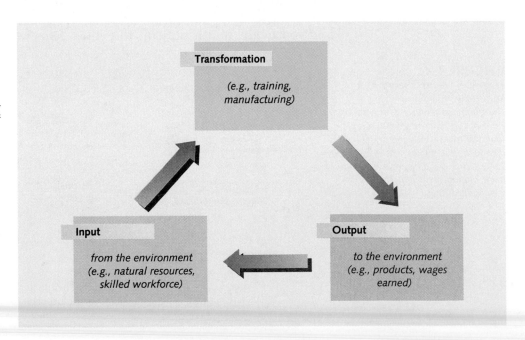

contingency approach A perspective suggesting that organizational behavior is affected by a large number of interacting factors. How someone will behave is said to be contingent upon many different variables at once.

A popular theory of leadership presented in Chapter 13 explicitly uses a contingency approach to identify the conditions under which certain styles of leadership bring about the best group performance.

Specialists in the field of OB today agree that there is no one best approach when it comes to such complex phenomena. To assume otherwise is not only overly simplistic and naive, but, as you will see, grossly inaccurate. When it comes to studying human behavior in organizations, there are no simple answers. The processes involved are too complex to permit such a luxury. Instead, OB scholars recognize that behavior in work settings is the complex result of many interacting forces. This fact is recognized in what is known as the **contingency approach**, an orientation that is a hallmark of modern OB.[6]

Consider, for example, the broad array of factors that may determine how productive someone is on the job. Clearly important are various personal characteristics, such as an individual's work values, skills, and motives to work hard. But these factors alone tell only part of the story. We also must consider various situational factors, such as the nature of the organization (e.g., the social relations between co-workers). As if all these considerations are not enough, we also need to take into account numerous characteristics of the environmental context in which work is done. For example, how strong is the economy? How competitive is the industry in which the organization operates? Not only may all these variables play separate roles when it comes to influencing how a particular individual is likely to behave on the job, but they may combine to paint a very complicated picture. It is such complexities that come to the forefront in the contingency approach to OB (see Figure 1-6).

When we teach OB to our students, we often find ourselves answering their questions by saying, "It depends." As our knowledge of behavior on the job becomes more and more complex, it becomes difficult, if not impossible, to give "straight answers." Rather, it is usually necessary to report that people will do certain things "under some conditions" or "when all other factors are equal." Such phrases provide a clear indication that the contingency approach is being used. They tell us that a certain behavior is *contingent upon* the existence of certain conditions.

■ **Figure 1-6**
The Contingency Approach to Organizational Behavior
By adopting a contingency approach, the field of OB recognizes that behavior in organizations is influenced by a wide variety of factors in combination with each other.

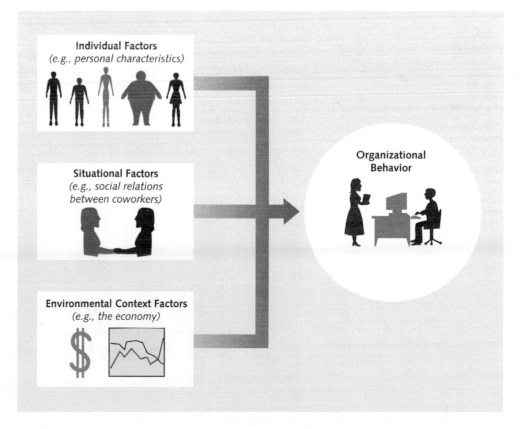

Individual Factors
(e.g., personal characteristics)

Situational Factors
(e.g., social relations between coworkers)

Environmental Context Factors
(e.g., the economy)

Organizational Behavior

Although this approach may frustrate and disappoint some people because it makes the use of simple cookbook formulas impossible to predict and explain behavior, we believe that such a complaint is unjustified. After all, *accuracy*, and not simplicity, is the ultimate goal of our studies of behavior in organizations. In the chapters that follow, you will see how this approach prevails with respect to various aspects of the field. In presenting this material to you, we will attempt to walk the fine line between being so complex as to be incomprehensible and so simplistic as to be misleading.

OB Confronts Challenges Created by the Changing Nature of Work

It's no secret that the world is constantly changing, and this phenomenon includes the world of work. Consider, for example, the dynamic nature of the workforce itself. In fact, if we had to characterize today's labor force using only one word, it would be *diversity*. The demographic characteristics of the workforce have been changing over the past few decades, and such shifts have not gone unnoticed in the field of OB.[7]

For example, there are more women working today than ever before, and they are more highly educated and better trained for a wider variety of positions. In addition to gender diversity, racial and cultural diversity is another potent demographic trend in the workforce (see Figure 1-7). The relative proportion of white native Americans in the workforce has been steadily shrinking as growing numbers of African Americans, Hispanic Americans, Asian Americans, and foreign nationals enter the workforce.[8] As you will see throughout this book, these trends are of considerable interest to OB scientists and practitioners. Indeed, they are closely connected to such topics as prejudice and stereotypes (Chapter 6), organizational culture (Chapter 14), stress (Chapter 7), communication (Chapter 9), conflict (Chapter 11), and career development (Chapter 7).

When the study of behavior in organizations first emerged, it was a time in which the United States was the world's predominant economic power. As a result, much of what was learned about organizations came from a uniquely American middle-class perspective.[9] Today, however, it is clear that the economy is much more global in scope and orientation. There exist strong economic forces all over the world and organizations operating within many different cultures. Even formerly Communist nations, such as Russia, are developing into economic powers. Moreover, many organizations have operations in several different countries. Considering these trends, it would be seriously limiting—not to mention very misleading—to ignore the possibility that behavior in organizations is affected by cultural differences. Indeed, there are clear signs that the field of OB is rapidly becoming increasingly international in its approach to the study of organizations.[10]

In Chapter 2, we will describe the challenges associated with the introduction of capitalism in the nations comprising the former Soviet Union.

■ FIGURE 1-7
Diversity: An Important Trend in the Workplace
Major demographic trends, such as growing levels of diversity with respect to race, culture, and gender in the workforce, have important implications for the field of OB. For example, special efforts are needed to coordinate the work of Solectron Corporation's 3,200 employees—people from 30 different nationalities who speak 40 different languages.

Today's organizations do not confront only challenges related to the nature of the workforce, but also to the rapidly changing nature of the work that people do—changes stemming largely from sophisticated computer technology. For example, advances in automation and computers have to a great extent been responsible for eliminating many jobs and creating others. As we will see later in this book (Chapters 2 and 14), jobs that used to take many people to complete may now take only a few—if people are needed at all. And the work people are doing in those new jobs is generally cleaner, safer, and more high-tech. Computer technology has made it possible for people to do more work with less effort, and with greater flexibility, than ever before.

In summary, the world of work is constantly changing in many ways. With these changes come a variety of interesting issues and special challenges for the field of organizational behavior.

Organizational Behavior: A Capsule History of the Field

Although today we take for granted the importance of understanding the functioning of organizations and the behavior of people at work, this was not always the case. In fact, it was not until the early part of the twentieth century that the idea first developed—and only during the last few decades that it gained widespread acceptance.[11] So that we can appreciate how the field of OB got to where it is today, we will now briefly outline its history and describe some of the most influential forces in its development.

Scientific Management: The Roots of Organizational Behavior

The earliest attempts to study behavior in organizations came out of a desire by industrial efficiency experts to improve worker productivity. Their central question was straightforward: What could be done to get people to do more work in less time? It's not particularly surprising that attempts to answer this question were made at the turn of the century. After all, this was a period of rapid industrialization and technological change in the United States. As engineers attempted to make machines more efficient, it was a natural extension of their efforts to work on the human side of the equation—making people more productive, too. Given this history, it should not be too surprising that the earliest people we now credit for their contributions to OB were actually industrial engineers.

Frederick Winslow Taylor worked most of his life in steel mills, starting as a laborer and working his way up to the position of chief engineer (see Figure 1-8).[12] In the 1880s, while a foreman at Philadelphia's Midvale Steel Company, Taylor became aware of some of the inefficient practices of the employees. Noticing, for example, that laborers wasted movements when shifting pigiron, Taylor studied the individual components of this task and established what he believed was the best way—motion by motion—to perform it. A few years later, while a consulting engineer at Pittsburgh's Bethlehem Steel, Taylor similarly redesigned the jobs of loading and unloading rail cars so they, too, could be done as efficiently as possible. On the heels of these experiences, Taylor published his groundbreaking book *Scientific Management*. In this work, Taylor argued that the objective of management is "to secure the maximum prosperity for the employer, coupled with the maximum prosperity of each employee."[13]

Beyond identifying ways in which manual labor jobs can be performed more efficiently, Taylor's **scientific management** approach was unique in its focus on the role of employees as individuals. Taylor advocated two ideas that hardly seem special today but were quite new 85 years ago. First, he recommended that employees be carefully selected and trained to perform their

■ FIGURE 1-8
Frederick Winslow Taylor (1856–1917)
Regarded as the founder of the scientific management movement, Frederick Winslow Taylor pioneered an approach to management that focused on maximizing efficiency so that both employers and employees would benefit.

scientific management An early approach to management and organizational behavior emphasizing the importance of designing jobs as efficiently as possible.

As we will describe in Chapter 5, different theories suggest different ideas about the role of money as a motivator in the workplace.

time-and-motion study A type of applied research designed to classify and streamline the individual movements needed to perform jobs with the intent of finding the most efficient way of doing them.

human relations movement A perspective on organizational behavior that recognizes the importance of social processes in work settings.

jobs—helping them become, in his own words, "first-class" at some task. Second, he believed that increasing workers' wages would raise their motivation and make them more productive. Although this idea is unsophisticated by today's standards—and not completely accurate—Taylor may be credited with recognizing the important role of motivation in job performance. It was contributions like these that stimulated further study of behavior in organizations and created an intellectual climate that eventually paved the way for the development of the field of OB. Acknowledging these contributions, management theorist Peter Drucker has described Taylor as, "the first man in history who did not take work for granted, but who looked at it and studied it."[14]

The publication of *Scientific Management* stimulated several other scientists to pick up on and expand Taylor's ideas. For example, the psychologist Hugo Münsterberg worked to "humanize" the jobs of people by explaining how the concepts of learning and motivation are relevant to the behavior of people at work.[15] Similarly, management writer Mary Parker Follet claimed that organizations could benefit by attempting to recognize the needs of employees.[16] However, the scientists most closely influenced by Taylor were the industrial psychologists Frank and Lillian Gilbreth. This husband-and-wife team pioneered an approach known as **time-and-motion study**, a type of applied research designed to classify and streamline the individual movements needed to perform jobs, with the intent of finding the most efficient way of doing them.[17] Although this approach appears to be highly mechanical and dehumanizing, the Gilbreths, parents of 12 children, practiced Taylorism with a human face in their personal lives. In fact, you may even recall the story of how the Gilbreths applied the principles of scientific management to the operation of their household as told in the classic book and film *Cheaper by the Dozen*.

The Human Relations Movement: Elton Mayo and the Hawthorne Studies

Despite the important contributions of scientific management, this approach did not go far enough in directing our attention to the wide variety of factors that might influence behavior in work settings. To be sure, the efficient performance of jobs and monetary incentives are very important. Emphasizing these factors, however, tends to make people feel like cogs in a machine. In fact, many employees and theorists alike rejected Taylorism, favoring instead an approach that focused on employees' own views and emphasized respect for individuals.

At the forefront of this orientation was Elton W. Mayo, an organizational scientist and consultant widely regarded as the founder of what is called the **human relations movement**.[18] This brand of management philosophy rejects the primarily economic orientation of scientific management and focuses instead on noneconomic, social factors operating in the workplace. Mayo and other proponents of the human relations movement *were* concerned with task performance, but they realized that it was greatly influenced by the social conditions which existed in organizations—the way employees were treated by management and the relationships they had with each other.

In 1927, a series of studies was begun at the Western Electric's Hawthorne Works near Chicago. Inspired by scientific management, the researchers were interested in determining, among other things, the effects of illumination on work productivity. How brightly or dimly lit should the work environment be for people to produce at their maximum level? Two groups of female employees took part in the study. One group, the *control room* condition, did their jobs without any changes in lighting; the other group, the *test room* condition, worked while the lighting was systematically varied, sometimes getting brighter, sometimes dimmer. The results were baffling: Productivity increased in *both* locations. Just as surprising, there was no clear connection between illumination and performance. In fact, output in the test room remained high even when the level of illumination was so low that workers could barely see what they were doing!

In response to these puzzling findings, Western Electric officials called in a team of experts headed by Elton Mayo. Attempting to replicate these results, Mayo and his colleagues examined the effects of a wide variety of different variables on productivity. Among these were the length of rest pauses, the duration of the workday and workweek, and the presence or absence of a free midmorning lunch. How would these factors influence the amount of work performed? To answer this question, Mayo and his colleagues studied female employees working in the company's Relay Room. As shown in Figure 1-9, the results were once again quite surprising: Productivity improved following almost every change in working conditions.[19] In fact, performance remained extremely high even when conditions were returned to normal, the way they were before the study began.

Not all of Mayo's studies showed that Hawthorne employees were highly productive, however. In fact, in another study conducted at the company's Bank Wiring Room, male members of various work groups were observed during regular working conditions and then interviewed at length after work. In this investigation, no attempts were made to alter the work environment. What Mayo found here was also surprising: Instead of improving their performance, employees deliberately restricted their output. Not only did the researchers actually see the men stopping work long before quitting time, but in interviews the men admitted that they easily could do more if they desired.

Why did this occur, especially in view of the increased performance noted in the Relay Room studies? Eventually, Mayo and his associates recognized that the answer resided in the fact that organizations are *social systems*. How effectively people worked depended, in great part, not only on the physical aspects of their working conditions, but also on the social conditions that prevailed. In the Relay Room studies, Mayo noted, productivity rose simply because people responded favorably to the special attention they received. Knowing they were being studied made them feel special and motivated them to do their best. Thus, it was these social factors, more than the physical factors, that had

■ **FIGURE 1-9**
The Hawthorne Studies: Some Puzzling Results
In one part of the Hawthorne studies, female employees were exposed to several changes in working conditions. Surprisingly, almost every one of these alterations produced an increase in productivity.

(**Source:** Based on data from Roethlisberger & Dickson, 1939; see Note 21.)

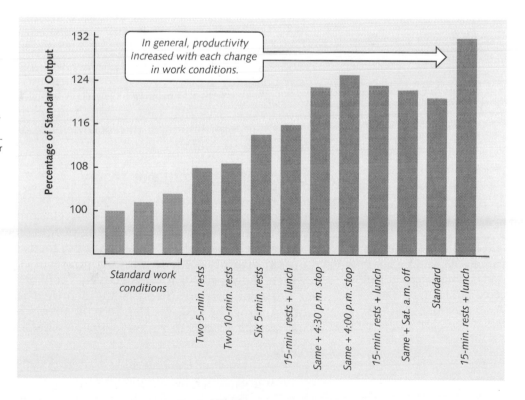

These informal social rules, known as norms, *play an important role in shaping the behavior of people in work groups, as we will describe in Chapter 8.*

such profound effects on job performance. The same explanation applied in the Bank Wiring Room study. Here, the employees feared that because they were being studied, the company was eventually going to raise the amount of work they were expected to do each day. To guard against the imposition of unreasonable standards (and, hopefully, to keep their jobs), the men agreed among themselves to keep output low. In other words, informal rules were established about what constituted acceptable levels of job performance. These social forces at work in this setting proved to be much more potent determinants of job performance than the physical factors being studied.

This conclusion, based on the surprising findings of the Hawthorne studies, is important because it ushered in a whole new way of thinking about behavior at work. It suggests that to understand behavior on the job, we must fully appreciate people's attitudes and the processes by which they communicate with each other. This way of thinking, so fundamental to modern OB, may be traced back to Elton Mayo's pioneering Hawthorne studies. In contrast with the scientific management views that prevailed at the time, this perspective was quite novel.

This is not to say, however, that the Hawthorne studies were by any means perfect. Indeed, by modern standards, the research was seriously flawed. As we will describe later in this chapter, the research violated several important rules. For example, no effort was made to assure that the rooms used in the study were identical in every way except for the variables studied (i.e., the level of illumination and the scheduling and duration of the rest pauses), making it possible for factors other than those being studied to influence the results. (Interestingly, research on the topic of illumination is still being conducted today, although it is far more sophisticated and carefully conducted.[20]) Furthermore, because no attempt was made to assure that the employees chosen for study were representative of all those in their factory (or all manufacturing personnel generally), it is difficult to generalize the results of the study beyond those individuals studied.

Clearly, although the Hawthorne studies are imperfect, their impact on the field of OB is considerable. This contribution lies *not* in what the research tells us about the effects of illumination, but what it reveals indirectly about the importance of human needs, attitudes, motives, and relationships in the workplace. In this respect, the work established a close link between the newly emerging field of OB and the behavioral sciences of psychology and sociology—a connection that persists today. Although the human relations approach was gradually replaced by more sophisticated views, several of its ideas and concepts contributed greatly to the development of the field of OB. Little would those workers in that long-vanished plant outside of Chicago have guessed that their contribution to the social science of organizational behavior would have been so enduring.

Classical Organizational Theory

During the same time that proponents of scientific management got people to begin thinking about the interrelationships between people and their jobs, another approach to managing people emerged. This perspective, known as **classical organizational theory**, focused on the efficient structuring of overall organizations. This is in contrast, of course, to scientific management, which sought to organize effectively the work of individuals.

Several different theorists are identified with classical organizational theory. Among the first was Henri Fayol, a French industrialist who attributed his managerial success to various principles he developed.[21] Among these are the following:

- A *division of labor* should be used because it allows people to specialize, doing only what they do best.

classical organizational theory An early approach to the study of management that focused on the most efficient way of structuring organizations.

- Managers should have *authority* over their subordinates, the right to order them to do what's necessary for the organization.
- Lines of authority should be uninterrupted; that is, a *scalar chain* should exist that connects the top management to the lower-level employees.
- There should exist a clearly defined *unity of command*, so that employees receive directions from only one other person so as to avoid confusion.
- Subordinates should be given *initiative* to formulate and implement their plans.

Although many of these principles are still well accepted today, it is widely recognized that they should not always be applied in exactly the same way. For example, whereas some organizations thrive on being structured according to a unity of command, still others require that some employees take directions from several different superiors. We will have more to say about this subject when we discuss various types of organizational designs in Chapter 15. For now, let's say that current organizational theorists owe a debt of gratitude to Fayol for his pioneering and far-reaching ideas.

Probably the best-known classical organizational theorist is the German sociologist Max Weber.[22] Among other things, Weber is known for proposing a form of organizational structure well-known today—the **bureaucracy**. This is a way to design organizations in a way that makes them efficient by having a clear hierarchy of authority in which people are required to perform well-defined jobs. Weber's idea was that the bureaucracy is the one best way to organize work in all organizations—much as proponents of scientific management searched for the ideal way to perform a job. The elements of an ideal bureaucracy are summarized in Table 1-1.

When you think about bureaucracies, negative images probably come to mind of lots of inflexible people getting bogged down in lots of red tape. (By the way, the phrase "red tape," is said to have become popular during World War I, when red tape was used on documents from the British government. Given the tendency for national governments to be bureaucratic in structure, it is not surprising that the term *red tape* came to refer to bureaucracies of all

bureaucracy An organizational design developed by Max Weber that attempts to make organizations operate efficiently by having a clear hierarchy of authority in which people are required to perform well-defined jobs.

■ TABLE 1-1   CHARACTERISTICS OF AN IDEAL BUREAUCRACY

According to Max Weber, bureaucracies must possess certain characteristics. Here is a summary of the major defining characteristics of bureaucratic organizations.

Characteristic	Description
Formal rules and regulations	Written guidelines are used to control all employees' behaviors.
Impersonal treatment	Favoritism is to be avoided, and all work relationships are to be based on objective standards.
Division of labor	All duties are divided into specialized tasks and are performed by individuals with the appropriate skills.
Hierarchical structure	Positions are ranked by authority level in clear fashion from lower-level to upper-level ones.
Authority structure	The making of decisions is determined by one's position in the hierarchy; people have authority over those in lower-ranking positions.
Lifelong career commitment	Employment is viewed as a permanent, lifelong obligation on the part of the organization and its employees.
Rationality	The organization is committed to achieving its ends (e.g., profitability) in the most efficient manner possible.

types.[23]) Weber's "universal" view of bureaucratic structure lies in contrast to the more modern approaches to organizational design (see Chapter 15) in which it is recognized that different forms of organizational structure may be more or less appropriate under different situations. Although the bureaucracy may not have proven to be a perfect structure for organizing all work, organizational theorists owe a great deal to Weber, many of whose ideas are still considered viable today.

Organizational Behavior in the Modern Era

Based on the pioneering contributions noted thus far, the realization that behavior in work settings is shaped by a wide range of individual, group, and organizational factors set the stage for the emergence of the science of organizational behavior. By the 1940s, clear signs appeared that an independent field had emerged. For example, in 1941 the first doctoral degree in OB was granted (to George Lombard at the Harvard Business School).[24] Only four years later, the first textbook in the field appeared.[25] By the late 1950s and early 1960s, OB was clearly a going concern. By that time, active programs of research were proceeding—research into such key processes as motivation and leadership and the impact of organizational structure.[26]

Unfortunately—but not unexpectedly for a new field—the development of scientific investigations into managerial and organizational issues was uneven and unsystematic in the 1940s and 1950s. In response to this state of affairs, the Ford Foundation sponsored a project in which economists R. A. Gordon and J. E. Howell carefully analyzed the nature of business education in the United States. They published their findings in 1959, in what became a very influential work known as the *Gordon and Howell Report*.[27] In this work, it was recommended that the study of management pay greater attention to basic academic disciplines, especially the social sciences. This advice had an enormous influence on business school curricula during the 1960s and promoted the development of the field of organizational behavior. After all, it is a field that draws heavily on the basic social science disciplines recommended for incorporation into business curricula by Gordon and Howell.

Stimulated by this work, the field of OB rapidly grew into one that borrowed heavily from other disciplines. In fact, the field of OB as we know it today may be characterized as a hybrid science that draws from many social science fields. For example, studies of personality, learning, and perception draw on psychology. Similarly, the study of group dynamics and leadership relies heavily on sociology. The topic of organizational communication networks obviously draws on research in the field of communication. Power and politics is studied by political scientists. Anthropologists study cross-cultural themes. And OB scientists look to the field of management science to understand ways to manage quality in organizations. Taken together, it is clear that modern OB is truly a multifaceted field (see Figure 1-10).

In recent years, the study of OB has added a few new characteristics worth noting. Although there are too many new developments to mention, a few current trends deserve to be pointed out.

- The field of OB has been paying increased attention more than ever to the *cross-cultural aspects of business*, recognizing that our understanding of organizational phenomena may not be universal. Today, research that considers the international generalizability of OB phenomena is considered key to understanding organizational competitiveness in a global society.
- The study of *(un)ethical behavior in organizations* is considered more important than ever before. Indeed, OB scientists are fascinated by understanding the factors that lead people to make ethical or unethical decisions and by their willingness to engage in such antisocial behaviors as lying, cheating, stealing, and acting violently.

■ FIGURE 1-10
OB: A Hybrid Science
*The field of OB may be characterized
by the fact that it draws upon several
different social science disciplines.*

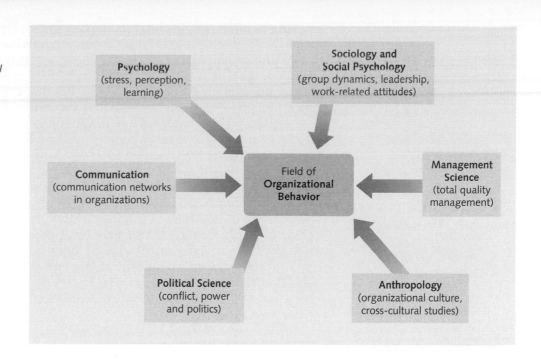

■ Today's OB scientists and practitioners recognize the importance of the *external environment* on organizational behavior. That is, they do not consider organizational behavior in a vacuum. Instead, they investigate how factors such as laws, governmental regulations, and international affairs affect behavior in organizations.

■ The traditional emphasis on manufacturing has been expanded to include studies of the *service and information sectors* of business. As more people move into these lines of work, the study of OB follows right behind them.

■ Few developments have changed the world of work more than *advances in technology*. Many people do different jobs, and perform them in different ways, than they did just a few years ago. Naturally, such developments are important to the field of OB.

As you read this book, you will learn more not only about the traditional interdisciplinary nature of OB, but also about these rapidly developing topics.

Theory and Research: Tools for Learning about Behavior in Organizations

Because organizational behavior is a science, it should not be surprising to learn that the field relies heavily upon the scientific method. As in the case of other scientific fields, OB uses the tools of science to achieve its goals—in this case, to learn about organizations and the behavior of people working in them. With this in mind, it is essential to understand the basic tools scientists use to learn about behavior in organizations. In this section, we will briefly describe some of these techniques. Our goal here is not to make you an expert in scientific methodology, but to give you a solid understanding of the techniques you will be encountering as you venture further into this book.

Isn't It All Just Common Sense?

Maybe you're not a top executive of a large business firm with decades of experience in the work world (or, at least, not yet!). Still, you no doubt know *something* about the behavior of people on the job. After all, you may already have learned quite a bit from whatever jobs you have had yourself or from talking to other people about their experiences. This isn't surprising, given that we can all observe a great deal about people's behavior in organizational settings just by paying casual attention. So, whether you're the CEO of a *Fortune* 500 firm or a part-time pizza-delivery driver, you probably have a few ideas about how people behave on the job. Besides, there are probably some things about behavior in organizations that you take for granted.

For example, would you say that happier employees tend to be more productive? If you're like most people, you would probably say, "Yes, of course." It's logical, right? Well, despite what you may believe, this is generally *not* true. In fact, as we will see in Chapter 6, people who are satisfied with their jobs are generally no more productive than those who are dissatisfied with their jobs. This contradiction of common sense is not an isolated example. This book is full of examples of findings in the field of OB that you might find surprising. To see how good you may be at predicting human behavior in organizations, we invite you to take the brief quiz appearing in the EXPERIENCING ORGANIZATIONAL BEHAVIOR section at the end of this chapter (see pp. 30–31). If you don't do very well, don't despair. It's just our way of demonstrating that there's more to understanding the complexities of behavior in organizations than meets the eye.

If we can't trust our common sense, then on what can we rely? This is where the scientific method enters the picture. Although social science research is far from perfect, the techniques used to study behavior in organizations can tell us a great deal. Naturally, not everything scientific research reveals contradicts common sense. In fact, a considerable amount of research confirms things we already believe to be true. Is research therefore useless? The answer is emphatically no! After all, scientific evidence often provides a great deal of insight into the subtle conditions under which various events occur. Such complexities would not have been apparent from only casual, unsystematic observation and common sense. In other words, the field of OB is solidly based on carefully conducted and logically analyzed research. Although common sense may provide a useful starting point for getting us to think about behavior in organizations, there's no substitute for scientific research when it comes to really understanding what happens and why.

Now that you understand the important role of the scientific method in the field of OB, you are prepared to appreciate the specific approaches used to conduct scientific research in this field. We will begin our presentation of these techniques with a discussion of one of the best-accepted sources of ideas for OB research—*theory*.

Theory: An Indispensable Guide to Organizational Research

What image comes to mind when you think of a scientist at work? Someone wearing a white lab coat surrounded by microscopes and test tubes busily testing theories? Although OB scientists typically don't wear lab coats or use microscopes and test tubes, it *is* true that they make use of theories. This is the case despite the fact that OB is, in part, an *applied* science. Simply because a field is characterized as being "theoretical," it does not follow that it is impractical and out of touch with reality. To the contrary, a theory is simply a way of describing the relationship between concepts. Thus, theories help, not hinder, our understanding of practical situations.

theory Efforts by scientists to explain why various events occur as they do. Theories consist of basic concepts and assertions regarding the relationship between them.

Formally, a **theory** is a set of statements about the interrelationships between concepts that allow us to predict and explain various processes and events. As you might imagine, such statements may be of interest to both practitioners and scientists alike. We're certain that as you read this book, you will come to appreciate the valuable role that theories play when it comes to understanding behavior in organizations—and putting that knowledge to practical use.

To demonstrate the value of theory in OB, let's consider an example based on a phenomenon we'll describe in more detail in Chapter 5—the effects of task goals on performance. Imagine observing that word processing operators type faster when they are given a specific goal (e.g., 75 words per minute) than when they are told to try to do their best. Imagine also observing that salespeople make more sales when they are given quotas than when they are not given any quotas. By themselves, these are useful observations: They allow us to predict what will happen when goals are introduced. In addition, they suggests ways to change conditions so as to improve performance among people in these groups. These two accomplishments—*prediction* and *control*—are major goals of science.

Yet there's something missing—namely, knowing that specific goals improve performance fails to tell us anything about *why* this is so. What is going on here? After all, a phenomenon was observed in two different settings and among two different groups of people. Why is it that people are so productive in response to specific goals? This is where theory enters the picture. In contrast to some fields, such as physics and chemistry, where theories often take the form of mathematical equations, theories in OB generally involve verbal assumptions. In the present case, for example, we might theorize as follows:

- When people are given specific goals, they know exactly what's expected of them.
- When people know what's expected of them, they are motivated to work hard to find ways to succeed.
- When people work hard to succeed, they perform at high levels.

This simple theory, like all others, consists of two basic elements: concepts (in this case goals and motives) and assertions about how they are related.

In science, the formation of a theory is only the beginning of a sequence of events followed to understand behavior. Once a theory is proposed, it is used to introduce *hypotheses*—logically derived statements that follow from the theory. In our example, it may be hypothesized that specific goals will only improve performance when they are not so difficult that they cannot be attained. Next, such predictions need to be tested in actual research to see if they are confirmed. If research confirms our hypotheses, we can be more confident about the accuracy of the theory. However, if it is not confirmed after several well-conducted studies, our confidence in the theory is weakened. When this happens, it's time to revise the theory and generate new, testable hypotheses from it. As you might imagine, given the complexities of human behavior in organizations, theories are rarely—if ever—fully confirmed. In fact, many of the field's most popular and useful theories are constantly being refined and tested. We have summarized the cyclical nature of the scientific endeavor in Figure 1-11.

It will probably come as no surprise to you to learn that the process of theory development and testing we have been describing is very laborious. In view of this fact, why do scientists bother constantly to fine-tune their theories? The answer lies in the very useful purposes that theories serve. Specifically, theories serve three important functions—organizing, summarizing, and guiding. First, given the complexities of human behavior, theories provide a way of *organizing* large amounts of data into meaningful propositions. In other words, they help us combine information so diverse that it might be difficult to grasp without the help of a theory. Second, theories help us to *summarize* this knowledge by making it possible to make sense out of bits and pieces of information that otherwise would be difficult—if not impossible—to understand. Finally, theories provide an important *guiding* function. That is, they help scientists identify important areas of needed research that would not have been apparent without theories to guide their thinking.

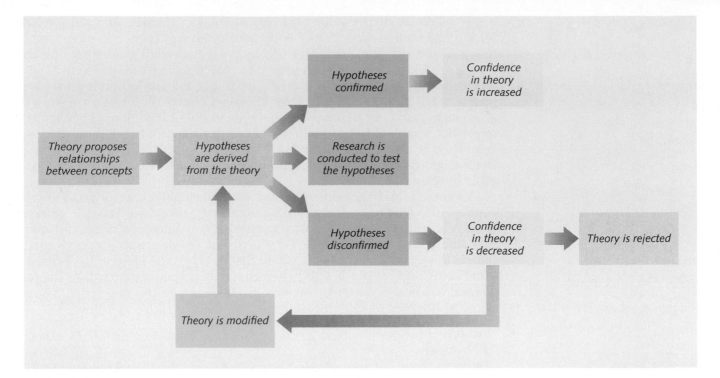

■ FIGURE 1-11
Theory Testing: The Research Process
Once a theory has been formulated, hypotheses derived from it are tested through direct research. If these are confirmed, confidence in the theory is increased. If they are disconfirmed, confidence is diminished. At this point, the theory is either modified and retested or completely rejected.

As you read this text, you will come across many different theories attempting to explain various aspects of behavior in organizations. When you do, we think you will appreciate the useful organizing, summarizing, and guiding roles they play—in short, how theories help provide meaningful explanations of behavior. In all cases, the usefulness of any theory is based on the extent to which it can be confirmed or disconfirmed. In other words, theories must be *testable*. A theory that cannot be tested serves no real purpose to scientists. Once it's tested, a theory—or at least part of it—must be confirmed if it is to be considered an accurate account of human behavior. And of course, that's what the field of OB is all about.

How are theories tested? The answer is by conducting *research*. Unless we do research, we cannot test theories, and unless we test theories, we are greatly limited in what we can learn about behavior in organizations.[28] This is why research is such a major concern of specialists in OB. Thus in order for you to fully appreciate the field of OB, it's critical for you to understand something about the techniques it uses—that is, how we come to know about the behavior of people at work. As a result, throughout this book, we will not only be explaining *what* is known about OB, but in many cases also *how* that knowledge was derived. We are confident that the better you understand OB's "tools of the trade," the more you will come to appreciate its value as a field. With this in mind, we will now describe some of the major research techniques used to learn about organizational behavior.

Survey Research: The Correlational Method

The most popular approach to conducting research in OB involves giving people questionnaires in which they are asked to report how they feel about various aspects of themselves, their jobs, and their organizations. Such questionnaires, also known as **surveys**, make it possible for organizational scientists to delve into a broad range of issues. This research technique is so very popular because it is applicable to studying a wide variety of topics. After all, you can learn a great deal about how people feel by asking them a systematic series of carefully worded questions. Moreover, questionnaires are relatively easy to administer (be it by mail, by phone, or in person), and—as we will

surveys Questionnaires designed to measure people's perceptions of some aspect of organizational behavior.

note shortly—they are readily quantifiable and lend themselves to powerful statistical analyses. These features make survey research a very appealing option to OB scientists. Not surprisingly, we will be describing quite a few survey studies throughout this text.

The survey approach consists of three major steps. First, the researcher must identify the variables in which he or she is interested. These may be various aspects of people (e.g., their attitudes toward work), organizations (e.g., the pay plans they use), or the environment in general (e.g., how competitive the industry is). They may be suggested from many different sources, such as a theory, previous research, or even hunches based on casual observations. Second, these variables are measured as precisely as possible. As you might imagine, it isn't always easy to tap precisely people's feelings about things (especially if they are uncertain about those feelings or reluctant to share them). As a result, researchers must pay a great deal of attention to the way they word the questions they use. For some examples of questions designed to measure various work-related attitudes, see Table 1-2. Finally, after the variables of interest have been identified and measured, scientists must determine how—if at all—they are related to each other. With this in mind, scientists analyze their survey findings using a variety of different statistical procedures.

correlational research An empirical research technique in which variables of interest are identified and carefully measured. These measures are then analyzed statistically to determine the extent to which they are related to one another.

hypothesis An unverified prediction concerning the relationships between variables. These propositions may be derived from previous research, existing theory, or informal observation.

The theories and research to which we allude here are described in Chapters 5 and 6.

Scientists conducting surveys typically are interested in determining how variables are interrelated—or, put differently, how changes in one variable are associated with changes in another. This approach is known as **correlational research**. This is an empirical research techique in which the variables of interest are identified and carefully measured. These measures are then analyzed statistically to determine the extent to which the variables are interrelated.

Let's consider an example. Suppose that a researcher is interested in learning the relationship between how fairly people believe they are paid and various work-related attitudes, such as their willingness to help their co-workers and their interest in quitting. Based on various theories and previous research, a researcher may suspect that the more people believe they are unfairly paid, the less likely they will be to help their co-workers and the more likely they will be to desire new jobs. These predictions constitute the researcher's **hypothesis**—the untested prediction the researcher wishes to investigate. After devising an appropriate questionnaire measuring these variables, the researcher would have to administer it to a large number of people so that the hypothesis can be tested.

Once the data are collected, the investigator must analyze them statistically and compare the results to the hypothesis. Suppose a researcher obtains results like those shown in the left side of Figure 1-12. In this case, the more fairly employees believe they are paid, the more willing they are to help their co-workers. In other words, the variables are related to each other such that the more one variable increases, the more the other also increases. Any vari-

■ TABLE 1-2	SURVEY QUESTIONS DESIGNED TO MEASURE WORK ATTITUDES
Items such as these might be used to measure attitudes toward various aspects of work.	■ Overall, how fairly are you paid? Not at all fairly 1 2 3 4 5 6 7 Extremely fairly
	■ Imagine that one of your office-mates needs to stay late to complete an important project. How likely or unlikely would you be to volunteer to help that person, even if you would not receive any special recognition for your efforts? Not at all likely 1 2 3 4 5 6 7 Extremely likely
	■ How interested are you in quitting your present job? Not at all interested 1 2 3 4 5 6 7 Extremely interested

■ FIGURE 1-12
*Positive and Negative
Correlations: What They Mean*
*Positive correlations, such as the one
shown on the left, exist when more of
one variable is associated with more of
another variable. Negative correlations,
such as the one on the right, exist
when more of one variable is associated
with less of another variable.*

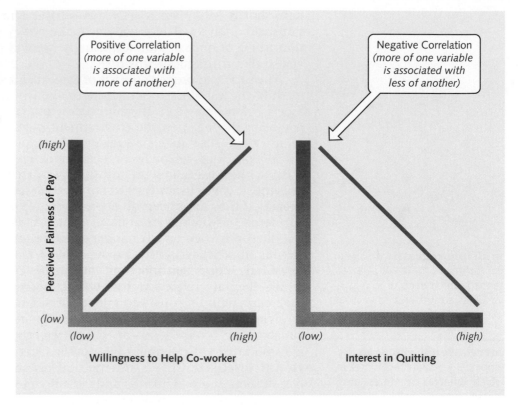

positive correlation A relationship between variables such that more of one variable is associated with more of another.

negative correlation A relationship between variables such that more of one variable is associated with less of another.

correlation coefficient A statistical index indicating the degree to which two or more variables are related.

ables described in this way are said to have a **positive correlation**. Now, imagine what will be found when the researcher compares the workers' perceptions of pay fairness with their interest in quitting their jobs. If the experimenter's hypothesis is correct, the results will look like those shown on the right side of Figure 1-12. In other words, the more people believe their pay is fair, the less interested they are in looking for a new job. Any such case—in which the more one variable increases, the more another decreases—is said to have a **negative correlation**.

OB scientists are not only interested in the direction of the relationship between variables—that is, whether the association is positive or negative—but also in how strong that relationship is. To gauge this, researchers rely on a statistic known as the **correlation coefficient**. This is a number between −1.00 and +1.00 used to express the strength of the relationship between the variables studied. The closer this number is to 1.00 (either −1.00 or +1.00), the stronger the relationship—that is, the more closely the variables are related to each other. However, the closer the correlation coefficient is to 0, the weaker the relationship between the variables—that is, the less strongly they are associated. When interpreting correlation coefficients, therefore, there are two things to keep in mind: its *sign* (in keeping with algebraic traditions, positive correlations are usually expressed without any sign) and its *absolute value* (that is, the size of the number without respect to its sign). For example, a correlation coefficient of −.92 reflects a much stronger relationship between variables than one of .22. The minus sign simply reveals that the relationship between the variables being described is negative (more of one variable is associated with less of another variable). The fact that the absolute value of this correlation coefficient is greater tells us that the relationship between the variables is stronger.

When variables are strongly correlated, scientists can make more accurate predictions about how they are related to each other. Using our example, in which a negative correlation between perceptions of pay fairness and intent to quit, we may expect that, in general, those who believe they are unfairly paid will be more likely to quit their jobs than those who believe they are fairly paid. If the correlation coefficient were high, (say, over −.80) we would be more confident that this would occur than if the correlation were low (say, under −.20). In fact, as correlation coefficients approach 0, it's impossible to make any accurate predictions whatsoever. In such a case, knowing one variable would not allow us to predict anything about the other. As you might imagine, organizational scientists are extremely interested in discovering the relationships between variables and rely on correlation coefficients to tell them a great deal.

Although the examples we've been using involve the relationship between only two variables at a time, organizational researchers are frequently interested in the interrelationships between many different variables at once. For example, an employee's intent to quit may be related to several variables besides the perceived fairness of pay—such as satisfaction with the job itself or liking for one's immediate supervisor. Researchers may make predictions using several different variables at once, using a technique known as **multiple regression**. Using this approach, researchers may be able to tell the extent to which each of several different variables contributes to predicting the behavior in question. In our example, they would be able to learn the degree to which the several variables studied, both together and individually, are related to the intent to quit one's job. Given the complex nature of human behavior on the job, and the wide range of variables likely to influence it, it should not be surprising to learn that OB researchers use the multiple regression technique a great deal in their work.

Even though the analysis of surveys using correlational techniques like multiple regression can be so valuable, conclusions drawn from correlations are limited in a very important way. Namely, *correlations do not reveal anything about causation*. In other words, although correlations tell us about how variables are related to each other, they don't provide any insight into their cause-and-effect relationships. So, in our example, although we may learn that the less employees feel they are fairly paid the more interested they are in quitting, we cannot tell *why* this is the case. In other words, we cannot tell whether or not employees want to quit *because* they believe they are unfairly paid. Might this be the case? Yes, but it also might be the case that people who believe they are unfairly paid tend to dislike the work they do, and it is this factor that encourages them to find a new job. Another possibility is that people believe they are unfairly paid because their supervisors are too demanding—and it is this factor that raises their interest in quitting (see Figure 1-13). Our point is simple: Although all these possibilities are reasonable, knowing only that variables are correlated does *not* permit us to determine what causes what. Because it is important for researchers to establish the causal relationships between the variables they study, OB researchers frequently turn to another technique that *does* permit such conclusions to be drawn—the experiment.

Experimental Research: The Logic of Cause and Effect

Because both scientists and practitioners not only want to know the degree to which variables are related, but also how much one variable causes another, the **experimental method** is sometimes used in OB. The more we know about the causal connections between variables, the better we can explain the underlying causes of behavior—and this, after all, is one of the major goals of OB.

To illustrate how experiments work, let's consider an example. Suppose we're interested in determining the effects of social density (the number of people per unit of space) on the job performance of clerical employees—that is, the degree to which the crowdedness of working conditions in an office influences how accurately word processing operators do their jobs. Although this topic might be studied in many different ways, imagine that we do the following. First, we select at random a large group of word processing operators

multiple regression A statistical technique indicating the extent to which each of several variables contributes to accurate predictions of another variable.

experimental method An empirical research method in which one or more variables are systematically varied (the independent variables) to determine if such changes have any impact on the behavior of interest (the dependent variables).

Correlations: What They Don't Reveal about Causation

Just because there may be a strong negative correlation between pay fairness and the desire to leave one's job, we cannot tell why this relationship exists. As shown here, there are many possible underlying reasons that are not identified by knowledge of the correlation alone.

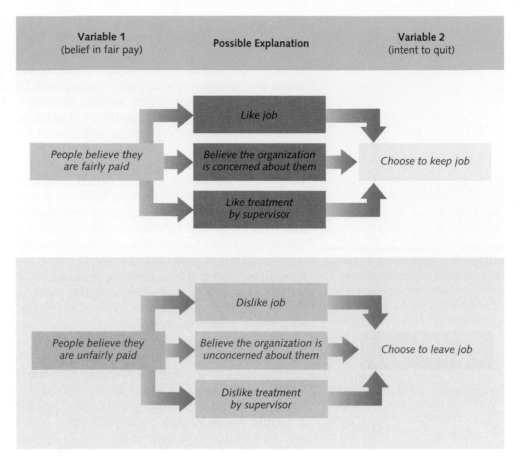

working in a variety of different organizations—the participants in our study. Then, we prepare a specially designed office, the setting for the experiment. Throughout the study, we would keep the design of the office and all the working conditions (e.g., temperature, light, and noise levels) alike with one exception—we would systematically vary the number of people working in the office at any given time.

For example, we could have one condition—which we could call the "high-density" condition—in which 50 people are put into a 500-square-foot room at once (allowing 10 square feet per person). In another condition—the "low-density" condition—we could put 5 people into a 500-square-foot room at once (allowing 100 square feet per person). Finally, we can have a "moderate-density" condition in which we put 25 people into a 500-square-foot room (allowing 20 square feet per person). Say that we have several hundred people participating in the study and that we assign them at random to each of these three conditions. Each word processing operator is then given the same passage of text to type over two hours. After this period, the typists are dismissed, and the researcher counts the number of words accurately typed by each typist, noting any possible differences between performance in the various conditions. Suppose that we obtain the results summarized in Figure 1-14.

Let's analyze what was done in this simple hypothetical experiment to help explain the basic elements of the experimental method and its underlying logic. First, recall that we selected participants from the population of interest and assigned them to conditions on a *random* basis. This means that each of the participants had an equal chance of being assigned to any one of the three conditions. This is critical because it is possible that differences between conditions could result from having many very good operators in one condition and many unproductive ones in another. To safeguard against this possibility, it is important to assign people to conditions at random. When this is done, we can assume that the effects of any possible differences between people would equalize over conditions.

Thus, by assigning people to conditions at random, we can be assured that there will be just as many fast operators and slow operators in each. As a result, there is no reason to believe that any differences in productivity that may be noted between conditions can be attributed to systematic differences in the skills of the participants. Given "the luck of the draw," such differences can be discounted, thereby enhancing our confidence that differences are solely the result of the social density of the rooms. This is the logic behind *random assignment*. Although it is not always feasible to use random assignment when conducting experiments in organizations, it is highly desirable whenever possible.

Recall that word processing operators were assigned to conditions that differed with respect to only the variable of interest—in this case, social density. We can say that the experimenter *manipulated* this aspect of the work environment, systematically changing it from one condition to another. A variable altered in this way is called an **independent variable**. An independent variable is a variable that is systematically manipulated by the experimenter so as to determine its effects on the behavior of interest. In our example, the independent variable is social density. Specifically, it may be said to have three different *levels*—that is, degrees of the independent variable: high, moderate, and low.

The variable that is measured, the one influenced by the independent variable, is known as the **dependent variable**. A dependent variable is the behavior of interest that is being measured—the behavior that is dependent upon the independent variable. In this case, the dependent variable was word processing performance, the quantity of words accurately typed. Besides studying this variable, we could have studied other dependent variables, such as satisfaction with the work or the perceived level of stress encountered. In fact, it would be quite likely for OB researchers to study several dependent variables in one experiment. By the same token, researchers also frequently consider the effects of several different independent variables in a given experiment. The matter of which particular independent and dependent variables are being studied is one of the most important questions researchers make. Often, they base these decisions on suggestions from previous research (other experiments

independent variable The factor in an experiment that is systematically varied by the experimenter to determine its impact on behavior (the dependent variable).

dependent variable The variable in an experiment that is measured, affected by the impact of the independent variable.

■ **FIGURE 1-14**
Example of Simple Experimental Results

In our hypothetical example, word processing operators were put into rooms that differed with respect to only one variable—social density (i.e., the number of people per unit of space). The results summarized here show that people performed best under conditions of lowest density, and worst under conditions of highest density.

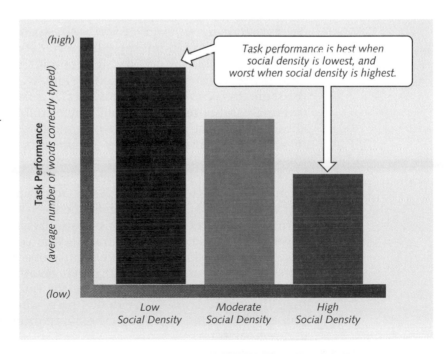

suggesting that certain variables are important) and existing theory (conceptualizations suggesting that certain variables may be important).

The basic logic behind the experimental method is quite simple. In fact, it involves only two major steps. First, some variable of interest (the independent variable) must be systematically varied. Second, the effects, if any, of such variations must be measured. The underlying idea is that if the independent variable does indeed influence behavior, then people exposed to different amounts of it should behave differently. In our example, we can be certain that social density caused differences in processing performance because when all other factors were held constant, different amounts of density led to different levels of performance. Our experiment thus follows the same basic logic of all experiments—namely, it is designed to reveal the effects of the independent variables on the dependent variables.

For the conclusions of experiments to be valid, it is critical for them to hold constant all factors other than the independent variable. Then, if there are differences in the dependent variable, we can assume that they are the result of the effects of the independent variable. By assigning participants to conditions at random, we already took an important step to ensure that one key factor—differences in the ability levels of the participants—would be equalized. But there are other possible factors that also may affect the results. For example, it would be essential to hold constant environmental conditions that might influence word processing speed. In this case, more people would generate more heat, so to make sure that the results are influenced only by density—and not heat—it would be necessary to air-condition the work room so as to keep it the same temperature in all conditions at all times. If you think about it, our simple experiment is really not that simple at all—especially if it is conducted with all the care needed to permit valid conclusions to be drawn. Thus, experiments require all experimental conditions to be kept identical with respect to all variables except the independent variable so that its effects can be determined unambiguously.

As you might imagine, this is often easier said than done. How simple it is to control the effects of extraneous variables (i.e., factors not of interest to the experimenter) depends, in large part, on where the experiment is conducted. In the field of OB, there are generally two options available: Experiments can be conducted in naturalistic organizational settings, referred to as the *field*, or in settings specially created for the study itself, referred to as the *laboratory* (or, *lab* for short).

The study in our example was a lab experiment. It was conducted in carefully controlled conditions specially created for the research. The great amount of control possible in such settings improves the chances of creating the conditions needed to allow valid conclusions to be drawn from experiments. At the same time, however, lab studies suffer from a lack of realism. Although the working conditions can be carefully controlled, they may be relatively unrealistic, not carefully simulating the conditions found in actual organizations. As a result, it may be difficult to generalize the findings of lab studies to settings outside the lab, such as the workplace.

However, if we conducted our study in actual organizations, there would be many unknowns, many uncontrollable factors at work. To conduct such a study, we would have to distinguish between those who worked in offices differing with respect to social density and later compare people's performance. If we did this, we would be sure that the conditions studied were realistic. However, there would be so little control over the setting that many different factors could be operating. For example, because people would not be assigned to conditions at random, it might be the case that people work in those settings they most desire. Furthermore, there would be no control over such factors as distractions and differences in environmental conditions (e.g., noise and temperature).

In short, field studies, although strong in the level of realism they offer, are weak with respect to the level of control they provide. By contrast, lab experiments permit a great deal of control, but tend to be unrealistic. In view of these complementary strengths and weaknesses, it should be clear that experiments should be conducted in *both* types of sites. As researchers do so, our confidence can be increased that valid conclusions will be drawn about behavior in organizations. Figure 1-15 summarizes the trade-offs involved in conducting research in each setting.

Qualitative Research: Naturalistic Observation and the Case Method

In contrast to the highly quantitative approaches to research we have been describing thus far, we should also note that OB researchers sometimes use a less quantitative approach. After all, probably the most obvious ways of learning about behavior in organizations are to observe it firsthand and to describe it after it occurs. Organizational scientists have a long tradition of studying behavior using these nonempirical, descriptive techniques, relying on what is known as *qualitative research*.[29] The qualitative approach to research relies on preserving the natural qualities of the situation being studied, attempting to capture the richness of the context while disturbing naturalistic conditions only minimally, if at all. The two major qualitative methods used by OB scientists are *naturalistic observation* and the *case method*.

Naturalistic observation. There's probably no more fundamental way of learning about how people act in organizations than simply to observe them—a research technique known as **naturalistic observation**. Suppose, for example, that you wanted to learn how employees behave in response to layoffs. One thing you could do would be to visit an organization in which layoffs will be occurring and systematically observe what the employees do and say both before and after the layoffs occur. Making comparisons of this type may provide very useful insights into what's going on. As a variation of this technique, you could take a job in the organization and make your observations

naturalistic observation A qualitative research technique in which an investigator observes events occurring in an organization while attempting not to affect those events by being present.

■ FIGURE 1-15
Trade-offs between Lab and Field Experimentation
Organizational behavior researchers may conduct experiments in laboratory or field settings, each of which has its own relative advantages and disadvantages. Generally, the lab offers more control but less realism, whereas the field offers less control but more realism.

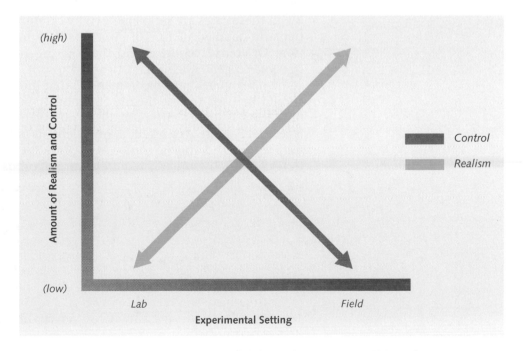

participant observation
Naturalistic observations of an organization made by individuals who have been hired as employees.

case method A qualitative research method in which a particular organization is studied in detail, usually in the hopes of being able to learn about organizational functioning in general.

as an insider actually working there—giving you a perspective you might not otherwise gain. This technique, often used by anthropologists, is known as **participant observation**.

It's not too difficult to think of the advantages and disadvantages of observational research. It's major advantage is that it can be used without disrupting normal routines, allowing behavior to be studied in its natural state. Moreover, almost anyone—including people already working in the host organization—can be trained to use it. However, observational research also suffers from several important limitations. First, the potential for subjectivity among researchers is considerable. Even among the most diligent of researchers, it's inevitable that different people will make different observations of the same events. Second, being involved in the daily functioning of an organization will make it difficult for observers to be impartial. Researchers interpreting organizational events may be subject to bias due to their feelings about the people involved. Finally, because most of what goes on in an organization is fairly dull and routine, it's very easy for researchers to place a great deal of emphasis on unusual or unexpected events, possibly leading to inaccurate conclusions. Given these limitations, most OB scientists consider observational research to be more useful as a starting point for providing basic insight into behavior than as a tool for acquiring definitive knowledge about behavior.

The case method. Suppose that we conducted our hypothetical study of reactions to layoffs differently. Instead of observing behavior directly, we might fully describe the company's history leading up to the event and some statistics summarizing its aftermath (e.g., how long people were unemployed, how the company was restructured after downsizing, and the like). We might even include some interviews with people affected by the event, and quote them directly. The approach we are describing here is known as the **case method**. More often than not, the rationale behind the case method is *not* to teach us about a specific organization as such, but to learn what happened in that organization as a means of providing cues as to what may be going on in other organizations. The case method is similar to naturalistic observation in that it relies on descriptive accounts of events. However, it is different in that it often involves using subsequent accounts of events from those involved as opposed to firsthand observations by scientists.

As you might imagine, a great deal can be learned by detailed accounts of events in organizations summarized in the form of written cases. Especially when these cases are supplemented by careful interviews, cases can paint a particularly detailed picture of events as they unfolded in a particular organization. Of course, to the extent that the organization is unique, it may not be possible to generalize what is learned to others. To get around this limitation, some researchers have recommended that multiple, as opposed to single, cases should be used to test theories.[30] Another problem with the case method—a limitation it shares with naturalistic observation—is that the potential for bias is relatively high. As a result, many scientists believe that while the case method may serve as a valuable source of hypotheses about behavior on the job, fully testing those hypotheses requires more rigorous research methods.[31]

The Field of Organizational Behavior

Organizational behavior (OB) seeks knowledge of all aspects of behavior in organizational settings through the systematic study of individual, group, and organizational processes. It uses this knowledge to promote basic understanding of human behavior and to enhance the effectiveness of organizations and the well-being of individuals working in them. Because it relies on scientific methods, the field of OB provides much more accurate knowledge about work behavior than simply relying on common sense.

In contrast to the traditional view that people are basically lazy and uninterested in working (the **Theory X** approach), modern OB is characterized by the belief that under the right combination of conditions people are responsive to their work environments and are highly committed to work (the **Theory Y** approach). The field also recognizes that organizations are dynamic, self-sustaining units known as **open systems**. In view of the complex nature of human behavior at work, OB generally takes a **contingency approach**, recognizing that behavior depends on the complex interaction of many different variables. OB also confronts various challenges brought on by the changing nature of work, such as growing diversity in the workforce, globalization, and rapidly advancing technology.

Historical Development of the Field of Organizational Behavior

The roots of OB can be traced back to the early twentieth century work of Frederick W. Taylor on **scientific management**—a management philosophy that attempted to find the most efficient ways for people to perform their jobs. Around this same time, **classical organizational theory** attempted to discover the most effective ways of designing organizations. Among these was the **bureaucracy**—a form of organizations identified by Max Weber that advocated clear organizational hierarchies and well-defined jobs. The field was also greatly influenced by the **human relations approach**, an orientation highlighting the impact of complex social systems on job performance. Elton Mayo's Hawthorne studies represented the pioneering efforts in this area. In the second half of the twentieth century, the field of OB grew dramatically to become the diverse, multidisciplinary field it is today.

Research Methods in Organizational Behavior

Although much of what OB studies appears to be commonsensical, casual observations are often misleading and fail to reveal the complex nature of behavior. Accordingly, the field of OB is based on knowledge derived from scientific research. Research is often guided by **theories**, testable explanations as to why various events occur as they do.

Correlational research is among the most popularly used techniques in the field. In this approach potentially important variables are identified and then systematically measured using **surveys** to determine how they are related to one another. The **correlation coefficient** is the statistic used to summarize the degree and direction of the relationship between variables.

Because the correlational method does not allow us to draw conclusions about cause and effect, researchers often rely on the **experimental method**. Using this approach, researchers systematically vary one or more variables (**independent variables**) while holding other factors constant so as to determine the effects on the behavior of interest (**dependent variables**).

In contrast to these empirical techniques, OB researchers often rely on qualitative approaches, such as **naturalistic observation**, in which trained observers make systematic observations of behavior in an organization, and the **case method**, in which detailed accounts are given of events that occurred in a particular organization.

1. How can the field of organizational behavior contribute to both the effective functioning of organizations *and* to the well-being of individuals? Are these goals inconsistent? Why or why not?
2. Explain the following statement: "People influence organizations, and organizations influence people."
3. What is the "contingency approach" and why is it so popular in the field of OB today?
4. Explain how the field of organizational behavior stands to benefit by taking a global perspective. What would you say are the major challenges associated with such a perspective?
5. Kurt Lewin, a famous social scientist once said, "There is nothing as applied as a good theory." Explain how this statement is applicable to the study of organizational behavior.
6. Under what conditions would it be advisable to learn about organizational behavior by using survey research as opposed to experimental research?
7. The Hawthorne studies inadvertently revealed a great deal about behavior in organizations despite flaws in the way the research was conducted. Using your knowledge of the experimental method, describe some of the weaknesses of the Hawthorne studies and ways they may have been alleviated.

CASE IN POINT

● ●

GE's New Washer Cleans Up Appliance Park

Domestic appliances such as clothes washers and dryers, refrigerators, and ranges—known in the trade as "white goods"—comprise some $6 billion in annual sales for General Electric. At the heart of this empire is GE's Appliance Park, in Louisville, Kentucky: 15 million square feet of manufacturing space in five factories over 1,500 acres in which 9,000 employees work. But in the fall of 1992, facing losses of $45 million a year at this 40-year-old complex, GE management was getting ready to pull the plug on the operation and purchase its washers from other companies.

Around this same time, GE appliance executives came to realize that the future of their line of washing machines required scrapping its basic design (which had been upgraded and improved little by little over two decades) and coming up with an entirely new product. It would have to be a big improvement—larger capacity, much quieter, no vibration, and free of defects. And its retail price would have to be about average, $399. The head of manufacturing and engineering at Appliance Park at the time, Dick Burke, convinced GE officials that they should try to build the new washer at his facility instead of taking the project outside the company.

At the heart of the plan was an agreement with the labor union that represented most of the facility's employees. To save the Park—and thousands of jobs—management and labor worked closely together as partners, hammering out ways to produce the new washers more efficiently. Among the changes was the elimination of individual piecework and the combining of employees into teams that could work together as units. The new assembly lines were redesigned so that workers could more easily and safely move as required to do their jobs. For example, overhead work was eliminated, as was the movement of forklifts that often makes factory work so hazardous. Toxic operations, such as painting, were completely automated. The new plant is cleaner and quieter.

In all, 43 initiatives were put into place that would save GE $60 million over three years, and that improved the quality of life for GE's workforce.

To help ensure that the new washers were designed properly, GE sought input from throughout the company. Not only did this include engineers who specialized in such matters as noise and metallurgy from GE's aircraft engine operations, but also the very people who worked with GE washers every day: service technicians, installers, and retail salespeople. To help these specialists understand the new product (which went into production during the summer of 1995 and was introduced in the fall of that year), special interactive computer programs and videos were developed.

From all early signs, the new operation is a success. Information from spot checks at the end of the assembly line is fed back to the workers so they can see how well they have done. The numbers have been good. In addition, GE's employees are quite pleased with their new facility. In the words of company veteran Bill Hamilton, "The employees and management used to be pulling in opposite directions. People are proud to work back here now. They listened to us."

Critical Thinking Questions

1. Would you say that GE was using a Theory X or Theory Y approach at Appliance Park? What is the basis of this assessment?
2. How might a proponent of scientific management attempt to increase efficiency at Appliance Park? What would be the strengths and weaknesses of this approach?
3. How could scientific research be conducted to determine the impact of the newly designed jobs on GE's employees? Identify a specific research question and an approach that could be taken to answer it.

SKILLS PORTFOLIO

Experiencing Organizational Behavior

Testing Your Assumptions about People at Work

What assumptions do you make about human nature? Are you inclined to think of people as primarily lazy and disinterested in working (a Theory X approach) or that they are willing to work hard under the right conditions (a Theory Y approach)? This exercise is designed to give you some insight into this question.

Directions

For each of the eight pairs of statements below, select the one that best reflects your feelings by marking the letter that corresponds to it.
1. **(a)** If you give people what they need to do their jobs, they will act very responsibly.
   (b) Giving people more information than they need will lead them to misuse it.

2. (c) People naturally want to get away with doing as little work as possible.

(d) When people avoid working, it's probably because the work itself has been stripped of its meaning.

3. (e) It's not surprising to find that employees don't demonstrate much creativity on the job because people tend not to have much of it to begin with.

(f) Although many people are by nature very creative, they don't show it on the job because they aren't given a chance.

4. (g) It doesn't pay to ask employees for their ideas because their perspective is generally too limited to be of value.

(h) When you ask employees for ideas, you are likely to get some useful suggestions.

5. (i) The more information people have about their jobs, the more closely their supervisors have to keep them in line.

(j) The more information people have about their jobs, the less closely they have to be supervised.

6. (k) Once people are paid enough, the less they tend to care about being recognized for a job well done.

(l) The more interesting work people do, the less likely they care about their pay.

7. (m) Supervisors lose prestige when they admit that their subordinates may have been right while they were wrong.

(n) Supervisors gain prestige when they admit that their subordinates may have been right while they were wrong.

8. (o) When people are held accountable for their mistakes, they raise their standards.

(p) Unless people are punished for their mistakes, they will lower their standards.

Scoring

1. Give yourself 1 point for having selected b, c, e, g, i, k, m, and p. The sum of these points is your Theory X score.

2. Give yourself 1 point for having selected a, d, f, h, j, l, n, and o. The sum of these points is your Theory Y score.

Questions for Discussion

1. Which perspective did this questionnaire indicate that you endorsed more strongly, Theory X or Theory Y? Is this consistent with your own intuitive conclusion?

2. Do you tend to manage others in ways consistent with Theory X or Theory Y ideas?

3. Can you recall any experiences that may have been crucial in defining or reinforcing your Theory X or Theory Y philosophy?

Working in Groups

Common Sense about Behavior in Organizations: Putting It to the Test

Even if you already have a good intuitive sense about behavior in organizations, some of what you think may be inconsistent with established research findings (many of which are noted in this book). So that you don't have to rely on your own judgments (which may be idiosyncratic), working with others in this exercise will give you a good sense of what our collective common sense has to say about behavior in organizations. You just may be enlightened.

Directions

Divide the class into groups of about five. Within these groups, discuss the following statements, reaching a consensus as to whether each is true or false. Spend approximately 30 minutes on the entire discussion.

1. People who are satisfied with one job tend to be satisfied with other jobs, too.

2. Because "two heads are better than one," groups make better decisions than individuals.

3. The best leaders always act the same, regardless of the situations they face.

4. Specific goals make people nervous; people work better when asked to do their best.

5. People get bored easily, leading them to welcome organizational change.

6. Money is the best motivator.

7. Today's organizations are more rigidly structured than ever before.

8. People generally shy away from challenges on the job.

9. Using multiple communication channels (e.g., written/spoken) tends to add confusion.

10. Conflict in organizations is always highly disruptive.

Scoring

Give your group one point for each item you scored as follows: 1 = True, 2 = False, 3 = False, 4 = False, 5 = False, 6 = False, 7 = False, 8 = False, 9 = False, and 10 = False. (Should you have questions about these answers, information bearing on them appears in this book as follows: 1 = Chapter 6, 2 = Chapter 8, 3 = Chapter 13, 4 = Chapter 5, 5 = Chapter 16, 6 = Chapter 5, 7 = Chapter 15, 8 = Chapter 5, 9 = Chapter 8, 10 = Chapter 11.)

Questions for Discussion

1. How well did your group do? Were you stumped on a few?
2. Comparing your experiences to those of other groups, did you find that there were some questions that proved trickier than others (i.e., ones where the scientific findings were more counterintuitive)? If you did poorly, don't be frustrated. These statements are a bit simplistic and need to be qualified to be fully understood. Have your instructor explain the statements that the class found most challenging.
3. Did this exercise give you a better understanding of the sometimes surprising (and complex) nature of behavior in organizations?

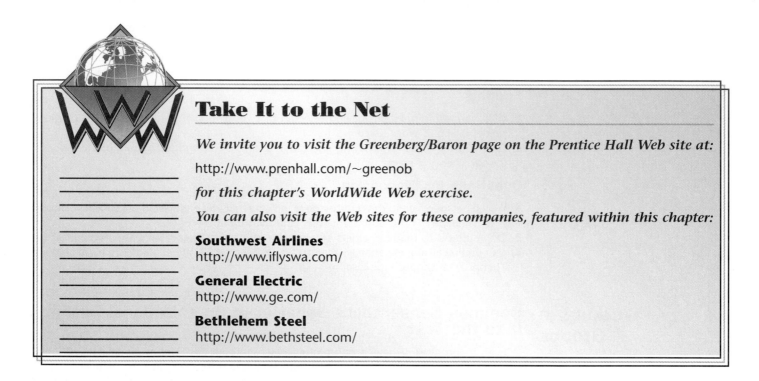

Take It to the Net

We invite you to visit the Greenberg/Baron page on the Prentice Hall Web site at:

http://www.prenhall.com/~greenob

for this chapter's WorldWide Web exercise.

You can also visit the Web sites for these companies, featured within this chapter:

Southwest Airlines
http://www.iflyswa.com/

General Electric
http://www.ge.com/

Bethlehem Steel
http://www.bethsteel.com/

Two

WORK IN THE TWENTY-FIRST CENTURY: THE CHANGING WORLD OF PEOPLE AND ORGANIZATIONS

■ OBJECTIVES

After reading this chapter you should be able to:

1. Describe the impact of *globalization* of the economy on the operation of organizations.
2. Explain how cultural differences between people from various nations may account for different organizational behaviors.
3. Understand the nature of *diversity* in today's organizations and things that are done to capitalize on it.
4. Appreciate the impact of various trends in working arrangements,

including *downsizing, outsourcing,* the *contingent workforce, virtual corporations,* and *telecommuting.*

5. Describe various approaches that today's organizations are taking to improve the quality of their goods and services, such as *total quality management,* and *reengineering.*
6. Explain why unethical behavior occurs in organizations and what can be done to prevent it.

FOSTERING DIVERSITY AT TEXAS INSTRUMENTS: MISSION ACCOMPLISHED

When you're a multibillion dollar company with facilities in 30 nations around the world, you have a special opportunity to draw on the skills and talents of a broad group of people—a potential that may provide a considerable advantage in a competitive business environment. Texas Instruments (TI) is such an organization. And, any company like TI, operating in the rapidly changing, highly competitive world of high technology, can use all the help it can get from its human resources. Jerry Junkins, TI's President and CEO, was well aware of this in 1989 when he developed this mission for his top management team: By the year 2000, make TI the kind of company that values people as individuals and that treats them with dignity, respect, and equality.

Working toward this end, TI launched several programs designed to help women and minorities become more involved in its operations. For example, the *Minority Business Development* initiative was created to help minority-owned businesses successfully compete as business partners with TI and other companies. TI is also involved in the *Dallas Women's Covenant,* pledging to meet specific goals for hiring women and doing business with organizations owned by women.

These efforts hardly scratch the surface of TI's deep commitment to diversity. TI also has formed about 20 different grassroots networks to help its associates from various racial and ethnic groups (e.g., African Americans, Hispanics, people from China and India, and women) deal with the unique issues facing them. At the core of these activities is the *TI Diversity Network*—a forum through which representatives from these various "initiatives," as they are known, gather to share ideas, and to build networks of resources that can help them function more effectively on and off the job.

TI also has made policy changes to accommodate the needs of its diverse workforce. For example,

the company has reinforced its stance against discrimination and sexual harassment and even offers programs to train employees on ways to avoid these problems. Some such efforts have been initiated by company officials and some by employees themselves. Other efforts have resulted from research examining employees' attitudes toward various aspects of their workplace.

One such survey of over 16,000 TI employees found that efforts to help employees balance their work and personal responsibilities would be highly effective in attracting and retaining the best employees, and it would also help current employees reach their potential. Indeed, TI's *Work and Family Program* provides family-friendly benefits to employees so they do not have to leave their jobs permanently when family needs arise. For example, the company provides flexible scheduling options and leaves of absence. There are also rooms provided where new mothers can care for their infants and seminars on topics such as how to care for the elderly. Taking these matters seriously, TI even has a full-time "Work/Life Programs Coordinator" who is responsible for developing strategies for dealing with such issues.

In all, TI's efforts at capitalizing on the diversity of its workforce have paid off in many tangible and intangible ways. For example, the Minority Business Development program helped TI do business with 750 minority-owned suppliers in 1994 alone. In addition, TI's efforts have been recognized by civic groups throughout Dallas (e.g., the Greater Dallas Hispanic Chamber of Commerce named TI its "Corporation of the Year"). Although the direct financial impact of such goodwill is difficult to assess, TI officials are pleased with the kind of corporation these diversity-enhancing efforts have created—one that is true to the mission that CEO Junkins articulated.

Texas Instruments is clearly a company that has gone out of its way to capitalize on the strengths of its diverse workforce and to be a pleasant and productive place in which to work. As reasonable as this strategy would appear to be, it represents a departure from the past ways many people have been treated in organizations in general. So, just as TI's high-tech world is rapidly changing, so too is the world of its primary resource—its people.

Living at the close of the twentieth century, we have seen more changes in our daily lives than people at any earlier times. If what the experts are saying is correct, this is only the beginning. The twenty-first century, almost upon us, promises to be even more complex and to bring change at an even more rapid pace.[1] As you might imagine, this state of affairs has important implications for the study of behavior in organizations. After all, as the world changes, so too does the nature of work. In this chapter we will describe some of the major forces bringing change to the world of organizations. As you will realize after reading this chapter, understanding such trends provides crucial insight into the dynamic nature of the field of organizational behavior.

Specifically, in this chapter we will focus on several major themes that will be reflected throughout this book—both in the main text and in various *special sections*. To begin, we will examine the rapidly growing trend toward *globalization*—the highly international nature of today's organizations. Then, we will describe changes in the composition of the workforce—the trend toward *diversity*. These themes, focusing as they do on cultural differences between and within organizations, will be highlighted in special sections called GLOBALIZATION AND DIVERSITY IN TODAY'S ORGANIZATIONS.

We also will describe various trends in the basic nature of the way work is conducted. Such changes stem primarily from rapid advances in the development of *technology*, which affect the design of jobs and organizations. Throughout this text we will focus on changes in technology and work itself in a special section called THE ORGANIZATION OF THE FUTURE. As the name implies, we will describe the latest trends in the world of work and what the experts predict as they look into their crystal balls.

Third, we will examine the strong *emphasis on quality* that has permeated many of today's organizations. We are thinking not only of improvements in the quality of goods and services that organizations offer, but enhancements in the quality of people's work lives as well. After providing essential background on this trend in this chapter, we will showcase some of these developments throughout this book in special sections called THE QUEST FOR QUALITY.

Finally, we will pay attention to the ethical aspects of behavior in organizations. Given that the headlines of our newspapers frequently contain stories about scandals in organizations, it is easy to appreciate the importance of studying the ethical and unethical aspects of people's behavior. We will highlight the determinants of ethical behavior in this chapter. Then, throughout the text we will provide examples of ethical issues tackled by organizations in special sections called THE ETHICS ANGLE.

In short, this chapter will focus on several key aspects of the changing nature of the world of work, themes that also will be highlighted throughout this book. For a summary of these various topics and the special sections to which they are linked, see Figure 2-1. If you are beginning to think that we are singling out certain themes for special attention, you are correct. After all, there is no better way to emphasize the dynamic nature of the field of OB than to focus on the broad array of factors responsible for the ever-changing world of work.

Globalization and Culture: Today's International Organizations

Chances are good that the car you drive is constructed of parts made in various countries and may even be assembled in several of them. The bank on the nearest corner may be owned by a large Japanese conglomerate headquartered halfway around the world. Your personal computer with the well

The Changing Nature of the World of Work: The Theme of This Chapter and This Text
Several special themes, reflecting the changing nature of the world of work, are described in this chapter. These various themes are highlighted within special sections appearing throughout this text.

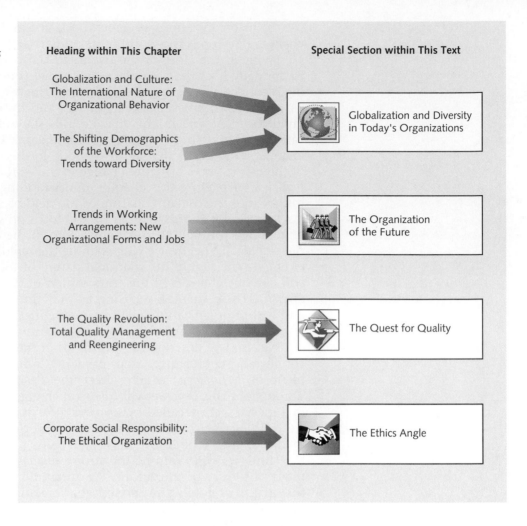

Heading within This Chapter

Globalization and Culture: The International Nature of Organizational Behavior

The Shifting Demographics of the Workforce: Trends toward Diversity

Trends in Working Arrangements: New Organizational Forms and Jobs

The Quality Revolution: Total Quality Management and Reengineering

Corporate Social Responsibility: The Ethical Organization

Special Section within This Text

Globalization and Diversity in Today's Organizations

The Organization of the Future

The Quest for Quality

The Ethics Angle

known American nameplate may be assembled in Mexico using chips made in Korea. Your clothes may be sewn by people in Taiwan using fabric woven in India. We could go on, but by now our point should be clear: The world of business is an international world. As you might imagine, this fact has important implications for the study of organizational behavior. With this in mind, we will highlight the global nature of organizations throughout this book in special sections called **GLOBALIZATION AND DIVERSITY IN TODAY'S ORGANIZATIONS.** To set the stage for these discussions we will begin this section of the chapter by taking a closer look at the international nature of today's organizations. We also will examine the important role of culture in organizations and then describe a major framework for organizing cultural differences between people.

Organizations in the Global Arena

To fully understand behavior in organizations we must appreciate the fact that organizations operate within an economic system in which resources such as information, goods, and money are constantly flowing. In recent decades, economic transactions have not been restricted to those occurring within countries, but with growing frequency, between countries as well. As one expert has put it, "By a wide margin . . . global competition is the single most powerful economic fact of life in the 1990s."[2] Consider these facts:

■ Whereas only 7 percent of U.S. companies were influenced by foreign competition in the 1960s, the comparable figure stands at over 70 percent today.[3]

- Either directly or indirectly, international trade accounts for approximately 20 percent of all jobs in the United States.[4]
- For every $1 billion exported by U.S. companies, approximately 20,000 new jobs are created.[5]

International trade. Commerce between nations of the world has grown from $308 billion in 1950 to $3.8 trillion in 1993.[6] Several factors account for such dramatic growth. First, technology has drastically lowered the cost of transportation and communication, thereby enhancing opportunities for international commerce. Second, laws regulating trade have generally become less restrictive throughout the world (e.g., in the United States and other heavily industrialized countries, free trade policies have been advocated). Third, developing nations have sought to expand their economies by promoting exports and opening their doors to foreign companies seeking investments. This trend has expanded opportunities for economic growth and competition throughout the world. The impact of such worldwide trade can be seen in the rapid growth of international lending. For example, whereas banks loaned companies in other countries $324 billion in 1980, the figure rose to $7.5 trillion in 1991.[7] Money flows rapidly into and out of nations, creating a situation in which the countries of the world are highly interdependent on each other economically and politically.

To illustrate this point, consider the following example.[8] The decline of Communism in Europe led to the unification of the wealthy capitalist nation of West Germany and the poorer, formerly communist nation of East Germany in October 1991. To finance this effort and to control inflation, in July 1992 the German Bundesbank raised interest rates to attract investors. At the same time, the United States required an influx of foreign investments to help meet its huge debt obligations. To prevent money from flowing out of the United States and into Germany, the U.S. Federal Reserve Board had to keep U.S. interest rates at a competitive level. As such, it failed to respond to President George Bush's pleas to help end the U.S. recession by lowering interest rates. The American people, harmed by the recession and what was perceived as President Bush's inability to improve the economy, declined to reelect him in November 1992. Thus, it may be said that the election of Bill Clinton to the U.S. presidency was at least the partial result of a seemingly unrelated situation that occurred thousands of miles across the Atlantic Ocean. Although it is certainly true that the election of a U.S. president is the result of many factors, our analysis highlights an important point: The people of the world are highly interconnected in complex ways. This is part of the growing trend toward **globalization**—the process of interconnecting the world's people with respect to the cultural, economic, political, technological, and environmental aspects of their lives.[9]

globalization The process of interconnecting the world's people with respect to the cultural, economic, political, technological, and environmental aspects of their lives.

multinational corporations (MNCs) Organizations that have significant operations spread throughout various nations but are headquartered in a single nation.

Multinational corporations. If international trade is the major driver of globalization, then the primary vehicles are **multinational corporations (MNCs)**—organizations that have significant operations spread throughout various nations but are headquartered in a single nation. MNCs are greatly responsible for direct investment in foreign nations: The 300 largest MNCs account for a quarter of the world's productive assets, with the 100 largest valued at $3.1 trillion. For a listing of the ten largest nonfinancial MNCs, and some vital statistics about them, see Figure 2-2. If upon examining this list you observe that many MNCs consistently call the same few countries home, you are not mistaken. Indeed, approximately half of all MNCs are headquartered in only four nations—the United States, Japan, Germany, and Switzerland.[10]

There are now approximately 35,000 MNCs throughout the world, and their numbers are growing—particularly in high-tech fields.[11] MNCs generally have very large proportions of their total assets invested in foreign countries

■ **Figure 2-2**
The Ten Largest Nonfinancial Multinational Corporations
The largest MNCs in the world are in the automotive and oil businesses. These are most frequently headquartered in the United States and Japan, although they come from all over.

(**Source:** Based on data from the United Nations as reported in Lodge, 1995; see Note 8.)

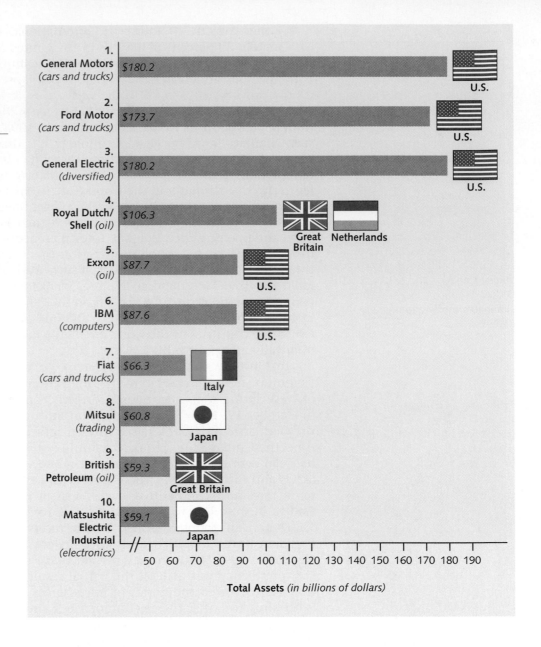

Total Assets *(in billions of dollars)*

(over 50 percent is not uncommon). This applies as well to the distribution of human resources within MNCs. For example, at Matsushita Electric, the large Japan-based MNC, over half of the employees live and work in other countries.[12] People who are citizens of one country, but who are living in another country, are known as **expatriates**. With today's MNCs having over 170,000 foreign affiliates (including branch offices or other companies owned by the parent company), MNCs are greatly responsible for the existence of expatriates throughout the world.

expatriates People who are citizens of one country but who are living in another country.

Economic interdependence. The major result of large investments in foreign countries is a high degree of financial interdependence. That is, the more a given nation's companies make investments in other countries, the more dependent those other countries' economies become on the foreign companies. Today, approximately 9 percent of American companies are foreign-controlled, and in Great Britain and Germany the figures are 14 percent and 17 percent, respectively.[13] In the present economy it is almost impossible for countries to stand alone financially in the world.

Economic interdependence is especially likely among neighboring countries with peaceful political and social relations. American companies, for example, own over half of Canadian manufacturing firms. To the south, Mexico, although traditionally averse to outside intervention, found it necessary to court foreign investment during the 1980s so as to help service its mounting debt. And in 1995, when political unrest in Mexico led to the devaluation of the Mexican peso, U.S. President Bill Clinton put together a package of loans and loan guarantees totaling almost $50 billion to help its southern neighbor. In part, the rationale was that a financially strong Mexico would help stem the tide of illegal migration of Mexican citizens that threatened the U.S. economy. Thus, by helping Mexico, the United States was helping itself, reflecting the financial interdependence between these neighboring nations.

In a move to eliminate trade barriers between the United States, Canada, and Mexico, on new year's day of 1994 these countries ratified the **North American Free Trade Agreement (NAFTA)**. This treaty eliminated tariffs between these three nations, formally acknowledging the highly interdependent nature of their economies. Despite different cultural histories and political systems, the geographic closeness of these three nations encouraged them to cooperate with each other so that they could compete more effectively in the world market. There can be no mistaking the fact that much of the world's business occurs at the international level, and that what happens in one nation can have major impact on what happens elsewhere.

Cultural homogenization. One result of this interdependence is a growing degree of **cultural homogenization**—the tendency for people throughout the world to become culturally similar. To begin thinking about how traditional values might be disappearing, and how people are becoming more alike, consider these facts from the entertainment industry:[14]

- Tokyo's Disneyland draws more visitors each year than either California's Disneyland or Florida's Walt Disney World.
- Japan's most popular film of 1991 was *Terminator 2,* followed by *Home Alone*—both major American motion pictures.
- The popular music network MTV, founded in New York, is seen by hundreds of millions of viewers around the world.

It would appear as if the entertainment world is becoming Americanized, and that some regional cultural forms are fast dissolving—a trend that has many traditionalists understandably upset. Indeed, as pressures toward cultural uniformity increase throughout the world, some loss of cultural uniqueness is bound to result (see Figure 2-3). This trend has led to social movements throughout the world to strengthen local cultures and to protect them from foreign influences (e.g., movements toward the "Asianization of Japan" and the "re-Islamization of the Middle East").[15] Indeed, the economic integration that has strengthened some nation's economies has come at the expense of cultural uniqueness, contributing to ethnic and religious tensions in various places throughout the world.

In conclusion, the trend toward globalization has complex and widespread effects on the lives of people all over the world. As we will see throughout this book, this fact has not escaped the attention of specialists in the field of organizational behavior. In fact, it is widely acknowledged that the management of human resources is an integral aspect of competitiveness in the global arena. As one expert has put it:

> Virtually any type of international problem, in the final analysis, is either created by people or must be solved by people. Hence, having the right people in the right place or the right time emerges as the key to a company's international growth.[16]

North American Free Trade Agreement (NAFTA) An agreement between the United States, Canada, and Mexico, ratified on January 1, 1994, which eliminates tariffs between these nations.

cultural homogenization The tendency for people throughout the world to become culturally similar.

■ **Figure 2-3**

Is the World Becoming Culturally Uniform?

As suggested by this scene, the world is moving in the direction of cultural uniformity. The global nature of today's economy is in large part responsible for this trend.

(**Source:** Cartoon by Ed Fisher. © 1992, Harvard Business Review. Reprinted by permission of Ed Fisher.)

"Make a left at the Coca-Cola bottling plant, then go about two miles past Apple Computer."

Culture and Its Impact

When it comes to the globalization of organizations, the field of OB is primarily interested in the influence of culture on people's attitudes and behaviors at work.[17] The general question of interest is: Do people in various cultures behave similarly or differently with respect to their behavior in organizations?

As with national cultures, organizations are also likely to have various subcultures operating within them, as we note in Chapter 14.

culture The set of values, customs, and beliefs that people have in common with other members of a social unit (e.g., a nation).

multicultural society A society within which there are many racial, ethnic, socioeconomic, and generational groups, each with its own culture.

subculture Smaller cultural groups operating within larger, primary cultural groups, each of which may have its own highly defined culture.

To examine this question we must first clarify what is meant by culture. Most social scientists agree that **culture** may be defined as the set of values, customs, and beliefs that people have in common with other members of a social unit (e.g., a nation).[18] For example, to the extent that the citizens of a specific country share a set of values, customs, and beliefs, they may be said to have a distinct culture. However, it would be erroneous to assume that a country has a single culture shared by everyone. Take the United States as an example. Although there might be a set of widely accepted values shared by most Americans, it would be misleading to claim that there is just one single culture within the U.S. Indeed, it is a **multicultural society**—one within which there are many different racial, ethnic, socioeconomic, and generational groups, each with its own culture. Recognizing this, scientists use the term **subculture** to describe smaller cultural groups operating within larger, primary cultural groups, each of which may have its own well-defined culture.

Culture shock and adjustment. The effects of culture on people often occurs without their awareness. People often have to be confronted with differ-

culture shock The tendency for people to become confused and disoriented as they find it difficult to become adjusted to a new culture.

repatriation The process or readjustment associated with returning to one's native culture after spending time away from it.

ent cultures before they become conscious of their own culture. In fact, when people—such as expatriates working for MNCs—are faced with new cultures, it is not unusual for them to become confused and disoriented—a phenomenon known as **culture shock**.[19] People also experience culture shock when they return to their native cultures after spending time away from it—a process of readjustment known as **repatriation**. In general, the phenomenon of culture shock results from people's recognition of the fact that others may be different from them in ways that they never imagined, and this takes some getting used to.

Specifically, scientists have observed that the process of adjusting to a foreign culture generally follows a U-shaped curve (see Figure 2-4).[20] That is, at first, people are optimistic and excited about learning a new culture. This usually lasts about a month or so. Then, for the next several months, they become frustrated and confused as they struggle to learn the new culture (i.e., culture shock occurs). Finally, after about six months, people adjust to their new cultures and become more accepting of them and satisfied with them. These observations imply that feelings of culture shock are inevitable. Although some degree of frustration may be expected when you first enter a new country, the more time you spend learning its ways, the better you will come to be understanding and accepting of it.[21]

■ **Figure 2-4**
Adjusting to Foreign Culture: The General Stages
People's adjustment to new cultures generally follows the U-shaped curve illustrated here. After an initial period of excitement, culture shock often sets in. Then, after this period of adjustment (about 6 months), the more time spent in the new culture, the better it is accepted.

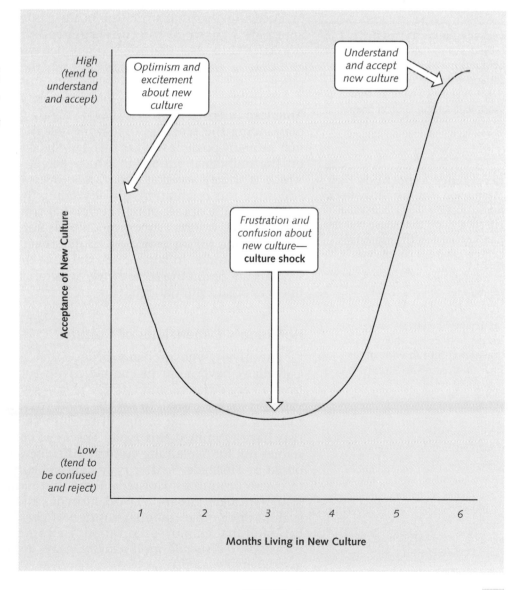

In general, culture shock results from the tendency for people to be highly *parochial* in their assumptions about others, taking a narrow view of the world by believing that there is one best way of doing things. They also tend to be highly *ethnocentric*, believing that their way of doing things is the best way. For example, Americans tend to be highly parochial by speaking only English (whereas most Europeans speak several languages) and ethnocentric by believing that everyone else in the world should learn their language. As we just explained, over time, exposure to other cultures teaches people that there may be many different ways of doing the same thing (making them less parochial), and that these may be equally good, if not better (making them less ethnocentric). Although these biases may have been reasonable for Americans 50 years ago when the United States was the world's dominant economic power (producing three-quarters of its wealth), they would be extremely costly today. Indeed, because the world's economy is global in nature, highly parochial and ethnocentric views cannot be tolerated.

Convergence versus divergence. Analogously, it may be said that highly narrow and biased views about the management of people in organizations may severely limit our understanding of behavior in organizations. During the 1950s and 1960s, management scholars tended to overlook the importance of cultural differences in organizations. They made two key assumptions: (1) the principles of good management are universal, and (2) the best management practices are ones that work well in the United States.[22] This highly inflexible approach is known as the **convergence hypothesis**. Such a biased orientation reflects the fact that the study of behavior in organizations first emerged at a time in which the United States was the world's predominant economic power.

With the ever-growing global economy, it has become clear that an American-oriented approach may be highly misleading when it comes to understanding the practices that work best in various countries. In fact, there may be many possible ways to manage effectively, and these will depend greatly on the individual culture in which people live. This alternative approach, which is widely accepted today, is known as the **divergence hypothesis**. Following this orientation, understanding the behavior of people at work requires carefully appreciating the cultural context within which they operate. For example, whereas American cultural norms suggest that it would not be inappropriate for an employee to question his or her superior, it would be taboo for a worker in Japan to do the same thing. Thus, today's organizational scholars are becoming increasingly sensitive to the ways in which culture influences organizational behavior.

convergence hypothesis The biased assumption that principles of good management are universal and that the best management practices are ones that work well in the United States.

divergence hypothesis The assumption that there may be many possible ways to manage effectively and that these will depend greatly on the individual culture in which people live.

Hofstede's Dimensions of Culture

Intuitively, you probably believe that Americans and English-speaking Canadians have more in common with each other culturally than people from a very different and faraway place—say, Zaire. However, such an observation is highly casual, to say the least. To be more scientific, we would have to know exactly what factors distinguish various cultures. Fortunately, theorists have examined this issue. The most comprehensive and best-accepted framework for explaining cultural differences between nations has been proposed by Hofstede.[23] After systematically surveying 160,000 IBM employees in over 60 countries, Hofstede found that national culture was a much more important determinant of work attitudes and behavior than other variables, such as one's organizational position or personal characteristics. Specifically, he found that employees in various countries differed along four separate dimensions: *individualism/collectivism, power distance, uncertainty avoidance,* and *masculinity/femininity.*

individualism According to Hofstede, a characteristic of culture in which people emphasize taking care of themselves and members of their immediate families.

collectivism According to Hofstede, a characteristic of a culture that orients people toward the good of the group.

power distance According to Hofstede, the degree to which the unequal distribution of power is accepted by people in a culture (high power distance) or rejected by them (low power distance).

Individualism versus collectivism. The distinction between individualism and collectivism is based on the extent to which members of a culture primarily define themselves as individuals as opposed to members of groups. **Individualism** is a characteristic of culture in which people emphasize taking care of themselves and members of their immediate families. By contrast, **collectivism** is a characteristic of a culture that orients people toward the good of the group. In highly collectivist cultures, people take care of others in their groups and expect others to take care of them.

The United States is among the most individualistic countries. Here, people generally believe that they determine their own fates and need to look out for themselves. However, in more collectivist countries such as Colombia and Pakistan, people are generally concerned with fitting in with others. In fact, in Japan—a relatively collectivist nation—there is an old saying that translates as "the nail that sticks out will be pounded down." Clearly, a highly collectivist orientation is expressed by this phrase. (For a summary of some of the countries that score highest and lowest on this dimension, as well as Hofstede's three other dimensions of culture, see Figure 2-5.)

Power distance. It is typically the case throughout the world that some individuals have more wealth and power than others. However, people from various countries are not equally accepting of such inequalities. **Power distance** is the term Hofstede uses to distinguish between countries in terms of the degree to which the unequal distribution of power is accepted or rejected.

People in high power distance countries, such as the Philippines, Mexico, and India, would not think of bypassing their superiors in order to get their jobs done. In these nations employees show a great deal of respect for authority figures and give considerable weight to symbols of rank and status, such as titles. However, people in low power distance countries, such as Austria, Israel, and Denmark, are readily willing to bypass their superiors in the course of doing their jobs. In these nations, although superiors still have authority, they are not held in awe by subordinates. (For your information, the United States ranks below average on power distance.)

Uncertainty avoidance. If there is any one thing for certain it is that the world is full of uncertainty. Whereas this fact is readily accepted by people in some societies, it is highly disquieting to others. This distinction is the basis for

■ **Figure 2-5**
Hofstede's Four Dimensions of Culture: A Summary
In his framework, Hofstede categorized 60 different countries with respect to the four dimensions of culture shown here. Three countries anchoring each end of these dimensions are identified.

(**Source:** Based on information reported by Hofstede, 1980; see Note 23.)

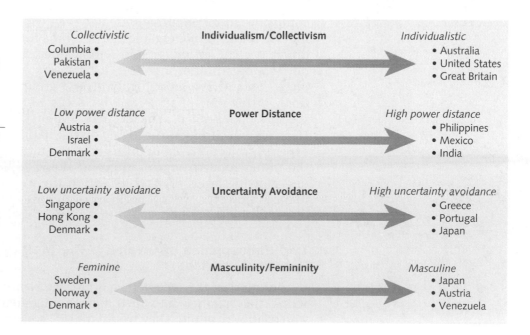

uncertainty avoidance According to Hofstede, the degree to which people in a culture feel threatened by, and attempt to avoid, ambiguous situations.

masculine culture According to Hofstede, cultures in which people are highly materialistic and value assertiveness and the acquisition of money.

feminine culture According to Hofstede, the cultural orientation in which people emphasize concern for others and the relationships among people.

Hofstede's third dimension of culture, **uncertainty avoidance**—the degree to which people feel threatened by, and attempt to avoid, ambiguous situations.

In countries that are high in uncertainty avoidance, such as Greece, Portugal, and Japan, people welcome the stability found in the use of rigid rules and prospects for lifetime employment. By contrast, in the low uncertainty avoidance countries of Singapore, Hong Kong, and Denmark, people tend to be more mobile and change jobs more frequently. As you might imagine, the United States ranks well below average on power distance.

Masculinity/femininity. Hofstede found that people in some countries, such as Japan, Austria, and Venezuela, were highly materialistic. They value assertiveness and the acquisition of money. Such nations are referred to as having a **masculine culture**. By contrast, in other countries, such as the Scandinavian nations, the predominant cultural value emphasizes concern for others and the relationships among people. This orientation Hofstede refers to as a **feminine culture**. (It is important to acknowledge that it was *not* Hofstede's intent to suggest that males and females posses or lack certain characteristics. Although you may feel uneasy with the stereotypical images evoked by Hofstede's terminology, his distinction is an important one and should not be dismissed.)

In "masculine" cultures people tend to define sex roles rigidly and reject the practice of performing jobs outside of one's gender-based stereotype. For example, in Japan there are very few female executives. However, in "feminine" cultures, such as Sweden, women and men may be found doing a wide variety of jobs. Moreover, Swedish businesspeople tend to demonstrate very high degrees of concern for their families. For example, whereas Americans (whose culture is considered relatively "masculine") may work all night on an important project, Swedes would be inclined to stop work at 5:00 P.M. and return to their families. Although Americans may mistake the Swedes' behavior as demonstrating a lack of commitment to their work, the Swedes simply may be demonstrating their cherished cultural value of commitment to the quality of their lives. This is an excellent example of the types of culture clashes that may be expected to arise in a global economy.

The Shifting Demographics of the Workforce: Trends toward Diversity

Thus far, we have been discussing cultural differences between people from companies in different nations. However, widespread cultural differences also may be found *within* organizations. A broad range of people from both sexes, different races, ethnic groups, nationalities, and ages can be found throughout U.S. organizations. In fact, it has been said that today's American workplace contains the most highly diverse group of people ever.[24] The implications of this state of affairs will be discussed throughout this book, including special sections called, **GLOBALIZATION AND DIVERSITY IN TODAY'S ORGANIZATIONS.** Here, we will chronicle the highly diverse nature of today's workforce and share experts' projections about diversity in the future. We will also outline some of the things modern organizations are doing to accommodate—and capitalize on—growing levels of diversity within the workforce. Before getting to these matters, however, we will begin by distinguishing between two approaches to diversity that have been taken in American society.

Two Philosophies of Diversity: The Melting Pot and Cultural Pluralism

For most of the twentieth century, the *melting pot* analogy was used to describe the manner in which new immigrants were assimilated into the American way of life: They would hit U.S. soil and "melt" into a common cul-

melting pot The principle that people from different racial, ethnic, and religious backgrounds are transformed into a common American culture.

cultural pluralism The idea that people's separate cultural identities should be maintained and accepted by others as they work alongside each other.

valuing diversity Encouraging awareness of and respect for different people in the workplace.

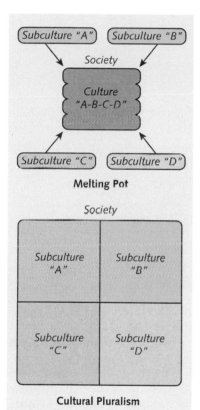

■ **Figure 2-6**
The Melting Pot vs. Cultural Pluralism: A Comparison
The melting pot philosophy asserts that a main culture is created by combining various subcultures (here, shown as "Subculture A," "Subculture B," and so on) that "melt" into a mix representing all the subcultures. By contrast, the cultural pluralism philosophy asserts that people from various subcultures live together in a common society that maintains and recognizes their individual cultural identities.

ture. Formally, the **melting pot** refers to the principle that people from different racial, ethnic, and religious backgrounds are transformed into a common American culture. Although the melting pot analogy implied that American culture would be altered somewhat by the addition of new people to the mix, in reality, it didn't work that way. Instead, because immigration was relatively low in the decades following World War II and over 95 percent of Americans were native born, until the mid-1960s, the stew was primarily white, Anglo-Saxon, and Protestant.[25] Practically speaking, by jumping into the melting pot, it was implied that foreigners would conform to the socio-economic and cultural ways of the American mainstream.

However, things changed in the mid-1960s as the civil rights movement caught on and people began to challenge the dominant hold that the majority had on society. Traditional social ideals were called into question, and respect for differences was nurtured. As this occurred, the melting pot philosophy fell into disrepute. Supplanting it was the notion of **cultural pluralism**—the idea that social harmony does not require people from various cultures to assimilate, or "melt" together into one. Rather, people's separate identities should be maintained and accepted by others. The cultural pluralist would have people from many cultures work alongside each other and not expect them to become the same, but to recognize, accept, and appreciate each other's differences. (For a summary of the distinction between the melting pot and cultural pluralism philosophies, see Figure 2-6.)

The cultural pluralism approach, popular today, is frequently reflected in terms of the movement toward **valuing diversity**—that is, encouraging awareness of and respect for different people in the workplace. In Chapter 6 we will examine the factors affecting the attitudes toward other people and ways to manage diversity in the workforce effectively. Here, however, we will focus on the demographic trends themselves.

Today's—and Tomorrow's—Highly Diverse Workforce

During the late 1950s and early 1960s, several popular TV situation comedies portrayed the typical American family in which a middle-aged white male head of the household worked from 9:00 to 5:00 each day and earned enough money to support several children and a wife who stayed at home and took care of the household. However, this picture is quite far from today's reality in three key respects. First, with huge numbers of women in the workforce, the distinction between the male "bread winner" and the female "care giver" has all but vanished. Second, with shifts in immigration patterns in recent years, the proportion of people of European descent within the American workforce is lower than ever before. Third, large numbers of people in the workforce are growing older and remaining on their jobs longer. We will now examine these three trends.

Women in the workforce: The nontraditional American family. In 1950, 63.9 percent of the U.S. civilian labor force was composed of white males. However, data from the Bureau of Labor Statistics show that this figure consistently dropped in each subsequent decade. By 1990 the comparable figure was 43.1 percent, and by 2005 it is estimated to drop further, to 38.2 percent.[26] The main reason for this decline in the relative proportion of white males is that huge numbers of women have been steadily entering the workforce. As shown in Figure 2-7, over half of all women are employed, and just under half of all people in the workplace are women—and these figures have been rising steadily over the years.[27]

Several social and economic factors contribute to increased participation in the workforce by women.[28] For one, the civil rights movement and the women's movement in the mid-1960s challenged stereotypes that held women back from pursuing careers. And as this occurred, social norms followed suit,

■ **Figure 2-7**

Figure 2-7
Women in the Workplace: Their Numbers Are Rising
Statistics have shown that the percentage of women (relative to men) in the workplace is rising. So too, is the percentage of women who are working outside the home. Both of these trends are expected to continue into the future.

(**Source:** Based on data collected by the U.S. Department of Labor, as reported by Carnevale & Stone, 1995; see Note 24.)

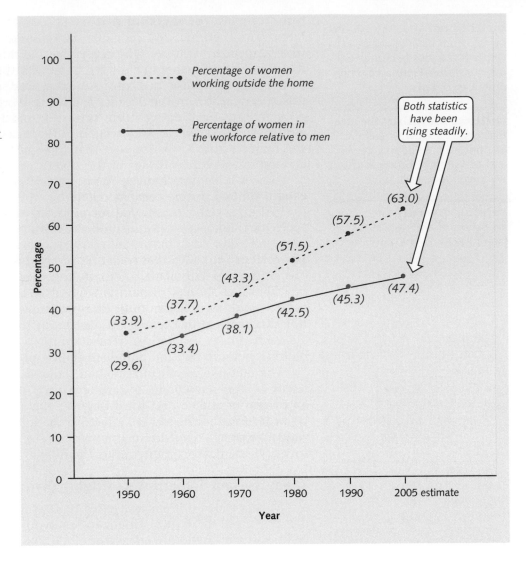

The nature and impact of negative sex-role stereotypes is discussed in Chapters 3 and 6.

making it not only acceptable, but commonplace, for women to combine a career and a family.

Second, economic changes made it both feasible and desirable—if not also necessary—for women to hold jobs outside the home. For example, a proliferation of part-time jobs provided the flexibility needed for women to juggle the demands of both work and family. And, as the real incomes of one-wage-earner families declined in the 1970s, growing numbers of women took jobs to help ease the financial burdens. But, many women also went to work out of necessity. As the divorce rate rose, along with the numbers of unwed mothers, many women became sole heads of households with children and had to work to support themselves and their children.

The trend is clear: In recent years, growing numbers of women began working outside the home even if they had children. Consider just the 15-year period between 1975 and 1990. In 1975 less than a third of women in the workforce had children under 2 years old, whereas in 1990, the figure was over half.[29] The situation-comedy family of the late 1950s and early 1960s is indeed a relic of an earlier time. In 1960 over 60 percent of American families had only a husband in the workforce, but by 1990 it was down to 25 percent—and this figure is expected to drop even further in the years ahead.[30]

Racial and ethnic groups: From minority to majority. Throughout its history, the United States has opened its doors to immigrants, although earlier immigration laws placed strict limits on the numbers of residents permitted from other countries. However, today's immigration laws are less restrictive than those of the past, which favored people from northern Europe.[31] As a result, many people immigrating to the United States today come from the developing nations of the Third World in search of economic security. In addition to legal immigrants seeking more prosperous lives, the U.S. workforce also has swollen with large numbers of illegal migrants (mostly from Mexico), many of whom seek itinerant farm work. It is not only economic relief, but political relief as well, that has brought many foreign people to America's shores. Refugees (most recently from Cuba and Vietnam) seeking relief from political persecution in their homelands also have contributed to the diverse ethnic mix found in today's workplace.

With respect to minority groups, the statistics tell an important story about the future: Today's white majority will become less of a majority. Although white non-Hispanic workers are currently the dominant group, comprising 78.5 percent of the workforce in 1990, this proportion is expected to drop to 73 percent in 2005. At the same time, there will be increases in the numbers of African Americans, Hispanics, and Asians in the workforce (see Figure 2-8). Between 1990 and 2005, minorities will be entering the workforce at a greater rate than the majority, thereby making them even more prevalent. In fact, it

■ **Figure 2-8**
Minorities in the Workplace: Their Numbers Are Rising
Statistics have shown that the relative percentage of whites in the U.S. workforce, although currently highest, is dropping. However, the relative percentage of African Americans, Hispanics, and Asians is rising. As this trend continues, the term "minority" group will lose its meaning.

(**Source:** Based on data collected by the U.S. Department of Labor, as reported by Carnevale & Stone, 1995; see Note 24.)

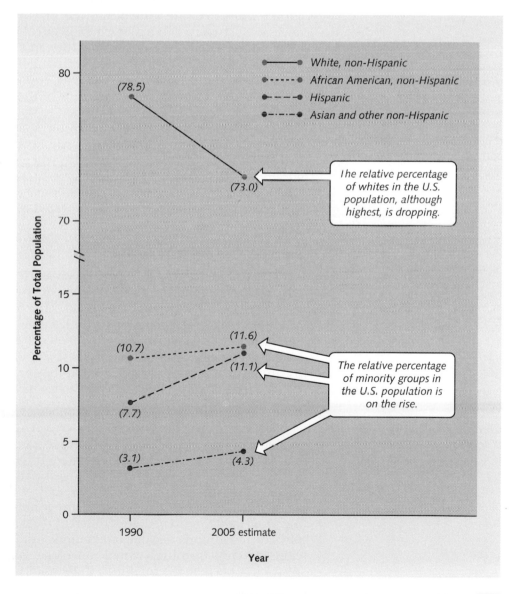

is estimated that by 2050, racial and ethnic minorities will comprise 47 percent of the U.S. population, making obsolete the current term "minority."[32]

Older people: The graying of America. As sociologists tell us, the population grows unevenly over time. It rises and falls with changes in social and economic conditions. For example, in the years after World War II the peacetime economy flourished in the United States. With it, came a large increase in population as soldiers returned from war and began families. The generation of children born during this period is widely referred to as the **baby boom generation**.

With the good lives that these individuals generally lead, they are living longer than the generations before them. By 2001 the first baby boomers will turn 55 and will be counted as "older workers" by labor economists. Only a few years later, the number of older people in the workplace will swell dramatically. Living in a period in which retirement is no longer automatic at age 65, aged baby boomers will comprise a growing part of the population in the years to come. In fact, people over 85 years old are already the fastest-growing segment of the U.S. population.[33]

The fact that people are living and working longer is creating an interesting phenomenon. As people get older, they are likely to suffer from ailments that lead them to require assistance in leading their daily lives. Needing help, the elderly often move into the households of their children, who are likely to be raising their own children, creating a *multigenerational household*. This situation is likely to create a financial strain on the caretakers, who are often forced to choose between such major expenses as college for their children and health care for their elderly parents. Because they are "squeezed" between the demands of the young and old within their households, the middle members of multi-generational households have been referred to as the **sandwich generation**.

Given that there is a large segment of the population about to be getting old, today's young people are expected to become members of the sandwich generation. After all, by 2030, the whole baby boom generation (about one-third of the current U.S. population) will be at least 65 years old. Not surprisingly, experts predict that the sandwich will gain even more layers in the years ahead, and that families with four generations under one roof (great-grandparents, grandparents, parents, and children) will not be uncommon.[34] When this occurs, the sandwich may be squeezed even harder than it is today.

Celebrating Diversity: Accommodating and Capitalizing on Pluralism in the Workplace

Many of today's organizations (such as TI, as described in our PREVIEW CASE) have recognized that the diversity within its workforce can be a source of strategic advantage *if* it is properly managed. After all, a culturally diverse workforce can bring broad perspectives to organizational issues, allowing problems to be approached from a wider variety of angles than might otherwise occur within a more homogeneous workforce. The trick, of course, lies in how to harness the differences between people so that they can be recognized and appreciated rather than subverted. Several approaches have been taken.

Diversity training. A growing number of companies have instituted specific programs, known as **diversity training**, designed to get all employees to not only recognize and accept people who are different from themselves, but to value these differences. These are usually sessions lasting from several hours to several days in which employees participate in exercises typically designed to get them to recognize the prejudices they may have and how to overcome them. Sessions may focus on any number of prejudicial beliefs, including those held toward people of different races and ethnic groups, ages, genders, physical conditions, sexual orientations, and so on. Several companies, including Xerox, Corning, Avon, Fannie Mae, Digital Equipment Corp., and U.S. West have been at the forefront of diversity training efforts.

---

baby boom generation The large group of people born in the United States in the years following World War II.

sandwich generation The generation of people who face economic pressures associated with taking care of their own children and their elderly parents, both of whom who live with them.

diversity training The process of training employees not only to recognize and accept others who are different from themselves, but also to value these differences.

Because we will describe diversity training techniques more fully in Chapter 6, in the context of prejudicial attitudes, we will not elaborate on them here. However, we cannot end this discussion without underscoring a crucial point: Diversity training by itself may be a waste of time unless it is part of a concerted effort to recognize and accept diversity throughout the organization. Lip service alone will not do. For organizations to reap the benefits of diversity in their workforces, the celebration of diversity must be integrated into the core values of the organization (much as with profitability).[35] Formal and informal policies, and actions by everyone from the CEO down, must recognize pluralism in the organization. When this occurs, diversity training programs can be a valuable part of the total effort to manage diversity in an organization.

Two major approaches to diversity training are described in Chapter 6—awareness-based training and skill-based training.

Flexible work arrangements. Four decades ago, when husbands worked outside the home and wives stayed at home with the children, the standard 9-to-5 working hours worked out fine. Today, however, with two-income families, single-parent households, and people taking care of elderly relatives, greater flexibility is needed. The diversity of lifestyles demands a diversity of working arrangements. Fortunately, several practices have gained in popularity in recent years.

flextime programs Policies that give employees some discretion over when they can arrive and leave work, thereby making it easier to adapt their work schedules to the demands of their personal lives.

- **Flextime programs** give employees some discretion over when they can arrive and leave work, thereby making it easier to adapt their work schedules to the demands of their personal lives. Typically, employees must work a common core of hours, such as 9:00 A.M. to 12 noon and 1:00 P.M. to 3:00 P.M. Scheduling of the remaining hours, within certain spans (such as 6:00 to 9:00 A.M. and 3:00 to 6:00 P.M.), is then left up to the employees themselves. Generally, such programs have been well received and have been linked to improvements in performance and job satisfaction, as well as drops in employee turnover and absenteeism.[36] In recent years companies such as Pacific Bell and Duke Power Company have found that flexible work scheduling has helped their employees meet the demands of juggling their work and family lives (see Figure 2-9).[37]

compressed workweeks Scheduling workweeks such that people are permitted to work fewer, but longer days (e.g., four ten-hour days), instead of five days of eight hours each.

- **Compressed workweeks** are programs that allow people to work fewer days but longer hours each day (e.g., four ten-hour days) instead of working five days of eight hours each. The popular practice among firefighters of being on duty for 24 hours, and then off duty for 48 hours is a good example of the compressed workweek. Shell Canada has found that compressed workweek schedules have helped it make more efficient use of its manufacturing plant in Sarnia, Ontario. The Royal Bank of Canada, headquartered in Montreal, has found that compressed-workweek options greatly help its recruitment efforts by offering prospective employees the

■ **Figure 2-9**
Pacific Bell Employees Enjoy Flextime
These employees of Pacific Bell are among a growing number of workers who work under flextime *programs that allow them to determine, within certain limits, their own working hours. This practice helps people balance the demands of their job with their personal lives.*

choice of schedules based on either compressed workweeks (four 9.5-hour days) or standard five-day workweeks.[38]

job sharing A form of regular part-time work in which pairs of employees assume the duties of a single job, splitting its responsibilities, salary, and benefits in proportion to the time worked.

- **Job sharing** is a form of regular part-time work in which pairs of employees assume the duties of a single job, splitting its responsibilities, salary, and benefits in proportion to the time worked. Job sharing is rapidly growing in popularity as people enjoy the kind of work that full-time jobs allow, but require the flexibility of part-time work. Often, job sharing arrangements are temporary. At Xerox, for example, several sets of employees share jobs, including two female employees who once were sales rivals, but who joined forces to share one job when both faced the need to reduce their working hours so they could devote time to their new families.[39] Pella (the Iowa-based manufacturer of windows) has found that job sharing has been successful in reducing absenteeism among its production and clerical employees.[40]

voluntary reduced work time (V-time) programs Programs that allow employees to reduce the amount of time they work by a certain amount (typically 10 or 20 percent), with a proportional reduction in pay.

- **Voluntary reduced work time (V-time) programs** allow employees to reduce the amount of time they work by a certain amount (typically 10 or 20 percent), with a proportional reduction in pay. Over the past few years, these programs have become popular in several state agencies in the United States. For example, various employees of the New York State government have enjoyed having professional careers, but with hours that make it possible for them to also meet their family obligations. Not only does the state benefit from the money saved, but the employees also enjoy the extra time they gain for nonwork pursuits.

flexplace policies Policies that allow employees to spend part of their regular working hours performing their jobs while at home (see *telecommuting*).

- **Flexplace policies** allow employees to spend part of their regular working hours performing their jobs while at home. Flexplace—used at such companies as J.C. Penney and Pacific Bell—makes it possible for employees to avoid the hassle of daily commuting.[41] It also allows companies to comply with governmental regulations (e.g., the Federal Clean Air Act of 1990) requiring them to reduce the number of trips made by their employees. Because flexplace frequently involves the use of computers and telephone lines connecting people to their offices, it is frequently also referred to as *telecommuting* and *telework*. We will describe this innovative work method more fully later in this chapter.

Support facilities. With increasing frequency, companies are taking proactive steps to help employees meet their personal needs and family obligations. In so doing, they make it possible for employees to satisfy the demands imposed by their nonwork lives. And this allows companies to draw on the resources of a diverse group of prospective employees who otherwise might not be able to lend their talents to the organization. Three practices have proven especially useful in this regard.

child-care facilities Sites at or near company locations where parents can leave their children while they are working.

- **Child-care facilities** are sites at or near company locations where parents can leave their children while they are working. America West, for example, believes so strongly in the importance of providing child care that it offers these services 24 hours a day. The company even maintained these benefits while it was going through bankruptcy proceedings in 1991.[42]

elder-care facilities Sites at or near company locations where, while working, employees can leave their elderly relatives (e.g. parents and grandparents) for whom they may serve as caretakers.

- **Elder-care facilities** are provisions made to take care of employees' elderly relatives, such as parents and grandparents, for whom they are responsible.[43] For example, Lancaster Laboratories (in Lancaster, Pennsylvania) provides a place where its employees can bring adult family members who are in need of care during working hours.[44] The *St. Petersburg Times* advises its employees about ways to help meet the problems of elderly family members.[45] Such practices are designed in large part to help avoid some of the problems confronted by the "sandwich generation" described earlier. In fact, given projections that multigenerational families will become increasingly commonplace in the next few decades, we can expect elder-care facilities to grow in popularity.

personal support policies
Widely varied practices (e.g., helping with transportation to and from the job) that assist employees in meeting the demands of their family lives, freeing them to concentrate on their work.

■ **Personal support policies** are widely varied practices that help employees meet the demands of their family lives, freeing them to concentrate on their work. For example, the SAS Institute (Cary, North Carolina) not only offers its employees free, on-site Montessori child care, but also nutritious take-home dinners. Wilton Connor Packaging (Charlotte, North Carolina) provides even more unusual forms of support, such as an on-site laundry, high school equivalency classes, door-to-door transportation, and a children's clothing swap center.[46]

Although these practices may be costly, the organizations that use them are generally convinced that they are in several respects wise investments. First, they help retain highly valued employees—not only keeping them from competitors, but also saving the costs of having to replace them. In fact, officials at AT&T found that the average cost of letting new parents take up to a year of unpaid parental leave was only 32 percent of an employee's annual salary, compared with the 150 percent cost of replacing that person permanently.[47] Second, by alleviating the distractions of having to worry about nonwork issues, employees are freed to concentrate on their jobs and to be their most creative. Research has found that people who use the support systems their employers provide are not only more active in team problem-solving activities, but also almost twice as likely to submit useful suggestions for improvement. Commenting on such findings, Ellen Galinsky, co-president of the Families & Work Institute, said, "There's a cost to *not* providing work and family assistance."[48] A third benefit—and an important one, at that—is that such policies help attract the most qualified human resources, giving companies that use them a competitive edge over those that do not.[49]

Trends in Working Arrangements: New Organizational Forms and Jobs

Ever since the industrial revolution people performed carefully prescribed sets of tasks—known as *jobs*—within large networks of people who answered to those above them—hierarchical arrangements known as *organizations*. This picture, although highly simplistic, does a good job of characterizing the working arrangements that most people had during much of the twentieth century. Now, as this era is drawing to a close, however, we are finding that the essential nature of jobs and organizations as we have known them is changing. Although there are certainly many factors responsible for such change, experts agree that the major catalyst is rapidly advancing computer technology. Currently, the computing power of microprocessors doubles approximately every 18 months. And, as more work is shifted to digital brains, some work that was once performed by human brains becomes obsolete. At the same time, new opportunities arise as people scurry to find their footing amidst the shifting terrain of the high-tech revolution.

As you might imagine, this state of affairs has important implications for the field of OB, many of which will be described throughout this text—and highlighted in special sections called THE ORGANIZATION OF THE FUTURE. In this part of the chapter we will set the stage for these discussions by focusing on some of the most prominent trends in the world of work that have been identified in recent years.

Leaner Organizations: Downsizing and Outsourcing

Technology has made it possible for fewer people to do more work than ever before. *Automation*, the process of replacing people with machines is not new, of course; it has gone on, slowly and steadily, for centuries. Today, however, because it is not large mechanical devices, but the manipulation of dig-

informate The process by which workers manipulate products by "inserting data" between themselves and those objects instead of doing so physically.

We discuss the general topic of workplace technology in Chapters 14 and 15.

downsizing The process of adjusting downward the number of employees required to perform jobs in newly designed organizations.

rightsizing See *downsizing*.

The motivational problems created by losing one's co-workers as a result of downsizing are identified in Chapter 5.

outsourcing The practice of eliminating nonessential aspects of business operations by hiring other companies to perform these tasks.

core competency The main things that an organization does best; those activities most central to its mission.

ital data that is responsible, scientists have referred instead to the *informating* of the workplace. The term **informate** describes the process by which workers manipulate products by "inserting data" between themselves and those objects.[50] When jobs are informated, information technology is used to change a formerly physical task into one that involves manipulating a sequence of digital commands. So, for example, a modern factory worker can move around large sheets of steel by pressing a few buttons on a keypad. Likewise, with the right programming, an order entered into a salesperson's laptop computer can trigger a chain of events involving everything associated with the job: placing an order for supplies, manufacturing the product to exact specifications, delivering the final product, sending out the bill, and even crediting the proper commission to the salesperson's payroll check.

Unlike the gradual process of automation, today's technology—and the process of informating—is occurring so rapidly that the very nature of work is changing as fast as we can keep up. With this, many jobs are disappearing, leaving organizations (at least the most successful ones) smaller than before.[51] For example, whereas Ford employs some 400 people in its accounts payable department, Mazda's highly computerized system does the same work with only 5 people. Although Mazda is considerably smaller, this difference is still quite striking.

In addition to services, product manufacturing also has been informated. At GE's Faunc Automation plant in Charlottesville, Virginia, for example, circuitboards are manufactured by half as many employees as required before informating the facility.[52] It is not only blue-collar, manual-labor jobs that are eliminated, but white-collar, mental-labor jobs as well. In many places, middle managers are no longer needed to make decisions that can now be made by computers. It's little wonder that middle managers, while only 10 percent of the workforce, comprise 20 percent of recent layoffs.

Indeed, organizations have been rapidly reducing the number of employees needed to operate effectively—a process known as **downsizing**.[53] Typically, this process involves more than just laying off people in a move to save money. It is directed at adjusting the number of employees needed to work in newly designed organizations and is therefore also known as **rightsizing**.[54] Whatever you call it, the bottom line is clear: Many organizations need fewer people to operate today than in the past—sometimes, far fewer.

The statistics tell a sobering tale. Since 1979 *Fortune* 500 companies have eliminated a quarter of the jobs they once provided, some 4.4 million positions.[55] One recent survey found that some degree of downsizing has been occurring in about half of all companies—especially in the middle management and supervisory ranks.[56] In fact, figures for the first half of 1993 showed that 2,389 Americans lost their jobs each working day.[57]

Another way organizations are restructuring is by completely eliminating those parts of themselves that focus on non-core sectors of the business (i.e., tasks that are peripheral to the organization), and hiring outside firms to perform these functions instead—a practice known as **outsourcing**.[58] By outsourcing secondary activities, an organization can focus on what it does best, its key capability—what is known as its **core competency**. Companies like ServiceMaster, which provides janitorial services, and ADP, which provides payroll processing services, make it possible for their client organizations to concentrate on the business functions most central to their missions. So, for example, by outsourcing its maintenance work or its payroll processing, a manufacturing company may grow smaller and focus its resources on what it does best, manufacturing.

In some cases, the only way people can tell that their part of the organization no longer exists is that they receive paychecks from someone else. For example, Xerox has taken over all the internal service functions of Bankers Trust (e.g., mailroom, print shop, employee recordkeeping, payroll, telephone switchboard), employing in many cases, the same individuals who used to perform these functions while working for Bankers Trust.[59] Ironically, some businesses providing outsourcing services, such as EDS, a data processing firm with $8.2 billion in annual sales, have become so large that they may outsource some services themselves while providing outsourcing services to their clients.[60]

Some critics fear that outsourcing represents a "hollowing out" of companies—a reduction of functions that weakens organizations by making them more dependent on others.[61] Others counter that outsourcing makes sense when the outsourced work is not highly critical to competitive success (e.g., janitorial services), or when it is so highly critical that it only can succeed by seeking outside assistance.[62] For example, when Apple Computer introduced its first notebook computer, the Macintosh Powerbook 100, it subcontracted its manufacturing to Sony, enabling it to speed entry into the market.[63] Although this practice may sound unusual, it isn't. In fact, one industry analyst has estimated that 30 percent of the largest American industrial firms outsource over half their manufacturing.[64]

The Contingent Workforce: "Permanent Temporary" Employees

Sometimes, instead of eliminating entire organizational functions and buying them back through outside service providers, organizations are eliminating individual jobs and hiring people to perform them on an as-needed basis. Such individuals comprise what has been referred to as the **contingent workforce**—people hired by organizations temporarily, to work as needed for finite periods of time.[65] The contingent workforce includes not only the traditional part-time employees, such as department store Santas, but also freelancers, subcontractors, and independent professionals. As shown in Figure 2-10, the specific jobs contingent workers do are most frequently in clerical fields.[66] Such highly flexible arrangements make it possible for organizations to grow or shrink as needed and to have access to experts with specialized knowledge when these are required.

In view of this trend, it should not be surprising that the greatest growth in jobs in recent years has been seen among temporary and full-time employment agencies (where 899,000 new jobs were created from January 1990 through June 1995).[67] In fact, the contingent workforce is so large that Manpower, the biggest temporary employment agency in the United States, is also the country's largest employer, with 600,000 people on its payroll—some 200,000 more than General Motors.[68]

The trend toward corporate restructuring has caused many companies to keep their staff sizes so small that they must frequently draw on the services of Manpower or another of the U.S.'s 7,000 temporary employment firms for help. In fact, some analysts predict that in just a few years, half of all working Americans—some 60 million people—will be working on a part-time or freelance basis. Specifically, British consultant Charles Handy has described the organization of the future as being more like an apartment than a home for life, "an association of temporary residents gathered together for mutual convenience."[69] Although others believe this prospect is far-fetched, it is clear that a growing number of people are seeking the freedom and variety of temporary employment rather than facing repeated layoffs from ever-downsizing corporations. They are opting for "permanent impermanence" in their jobs, so to speak.

There are, of course, downsides to temporary employment, both for employees and employers.[70] Benefits for temporary employees, which make up about 30 percent of a full-time employee's wages, are typically lacking, and wages are often lower. Moreover, some "unwilling contingent workers" consider their temporary work too stressful and would prefer full-time employment—*if* they could find it. Meanwhile the daily availability of temporary workers is at an all-time high of approximately 2 million, providing a boon to

Contingent Workers: What Kinds of Jobs Do They Do?
Three-quarters of the people in the contingent workforce do clerical work. A smaller percentage of companies use contingent workers to perform jobs in other areas.

(**Source:** Based on data from the Conference Board, as reported by Brotherton, 1995; see Note 66.)

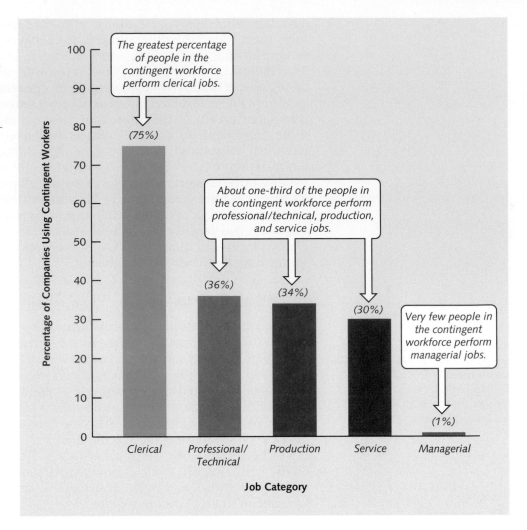

companies seeking their talents. Kolmar Laboratories, a Port Jervis, New York, maker of cosmetics, has filled as many as half of its 600 assembly line jobs with temporary workers. Unfortunately, so much conflict has erupted between the temporary employees (paid $5.60 per hour without benefits) and the permanent employees (paid $9.00 per hour plus benefits) that the expenses of having to rework products and recruit and train new employees have offset the savings in wages.

Many corporate officials strongly adhere to the belief that quality performance depends on the kind of skill and commitment to the organization that temporaries cannot offer. Says Georgia-Pacific CEO, Pete Correll, "Our manufacturing facilities need operators who are well trained and who understand the quality requirements of the job. You can't just drop someone into that. We want workers who will buy into our dream. . . . [71] Indeed, several corporate officials have complained that contingent workers are not as good as permanent ones. One large manufacturing firm that used office temps extensively found that these individuals were disloyal, prone to divulging confidential information. Furthermore, some have complained that because they are unpracticed, temporary workers lack basic job skills and are inclined to perform poorly.[72]

These are important considerations when you take into account the fact that the trend toward hiring contingent workers is fueled by employers' beliefs that temporary workers can help save money. However, as these examples suggest—and as human resource managers have found—there are hidden costs associated with using large numbers of contingent workers.[73] In view of these considerations, it may be said that the flexibility of contingent labor comes at a price. Accordingly, although the size of the permanent workforce may be dwindling, it does not appear that the permanent employee faces any immediate danger of extinction.

However, there is certainly no status quo when it comes to employment these days. Those employees who are finding work are likely to be ones who are highly educated and bring the greatest variety of skills to their employers. With the end of the Cold War, the defense industry, and its boom in manufacturing, has all but come to an end. Add to this the shifting of manufacturing jobs overseas, and it's easy to see how factory work has slowed dramatically. Considerable growth, however, may be seen among **knowledge workers**: professionals, engineers, and scientists—people whose technical skills can contribute to the explosion in high-tech fields.

The individuals who will be most successful at finding work in the years ahead will be those whose training, both academic and technical, makes them most qualified for the kinds of jobs likely to be found in the years ahead. The companies that will predominate in the world market will be those whose workers can contribute the most. And, it will be these individuals who will be the best paid, as opposed to simply those who have hung around the longest. More than ever, the key to success lies in training. But people throughout the world are not equally well trained to face the challenges of doing technical work. In what nations are the most qualified workforces to be found these days? As Figure 2-11 shows, the best-trained employees (with respect to public education, on-the-job training, and computer literacy) may be found in several nations throughout Europe and Asia; the United States ranks sixth overall.[74]

The Virtual Corporation: A Network of Temporary Organizations

As more and more companies are outsourcing various organizational functions and paring down to their core competencies, they might not be able to perform all the tasks required to complete a project. However, they can cer-

knowledge workers Professional people, such as scientists and engineers, whose technical skills can contribute to the explosion in high-tech fields.

A discussion of the basic approaches to job training appears in Chapter 3.

■ **Figure 2-11**
Where in the World Are the Best-Trained Workers?
The most qualified employees in the world (with respect to quality of public education, on-the-job training, and computer literacy) may be found in the countries of western Europe and eastern Asia. The Figure shows rankings of the top 20 countries, in descending order.

(**Source:** Based on data reported by Sasseen, Neff, Hattangadi, & Sasoni, 1994; see Note 74.)

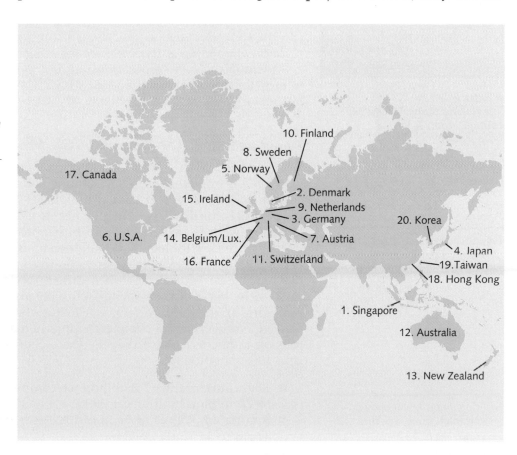

virtual corporation A highly flexible, temporary organization formed by a group of companies that join forces to exploit a specific opportunity.

More permanent organizational alliances are identified as a popular form of organizational design in Chapter 15.

■ **Figure 2-12**
The Rolling Stones' "Voodoo Lounge" Tour: A Virtual Corporation
Michael Cohl directed the group of organizations that worked together temporarily to create the Rolling Stones' 1994–1995 Voodoo Lounge *world tour—a virtual corporation.*

telecommuting The practice of using communications technology so as to enable work to be performed from remote locations, such as the home. (see *flexplace*)

For more information about telecommunicating, see the VIDEO CASE *on p. 579.*

tainly perform their own highly specialized part of it very well. Now, if you put together several organizations whose competencies complement each other and have them work together on a special project, you'd have a very strong group of collaborators. This is the idea behind an organizational arrangement that is growing in popularity—the **virtual corporation**. A virtual corporation is a highly flexible, temporary organization formed by a group of companies that join forces to exploit a specific opportunity.[75]

For example, various companies often come together to work on special projects in the entertainment industry (e.g., to produce a motion picture) and in the field of construction (e.g., to build a shopping center). After all, technologies are changing so rapidly and skills are becoming so specialized these days that no one company can do everything by itself. So, they join forces temporarily to form virtual corporations—not permanent organizations, but temporary ones without their own offices or organization charts. If you think about it, the term makes sense. When you use your personal computer's virtual memory, you are relying on memory that isn't a permanent part of its memory chips, but created temporarily (by allocating a portion of your hard drive to RAM). When the computer is turned off, virtual memory is gone. Likewise, when the project is over, the virtual corporation vanishes as well.

Virtual organizations may be created where you least expect them. For example, the Rolling Stones' 1994–1995 *Voodoo Lounge* world tour may be considered a virtual corporation.[76] Although you may think of it as "only rock 'n' roll," the 65-site international tour was a business—and with worldwide revenues of over $300 million, a very big one at that. Despite its mammoth size, the tour was very much a virtual corporation. Its head was Michael Cohl, who coordinated the tour's operations out of a crate of files, a laptop computer, and a fax machine that he moved from hotel room to hotel room as the tour moved along (see Figure 2-12). One company set up the lighting, another coordinated the stagehands, and another handled the logistics of moving sets that filled 56 trucks from city to city. And after the last date, the Voodoo Lounge virtual corporation disbanded as quickly as it formed. Its various participating organizations joined up with new ones on other projects.

Although virtual corporations are not yet common, experts expect them to grow in popularity in the years ahead.[77] As one consultant has put it, "It's not just a good idea; it's inevitable."[78]

Telecommuting: The Demise of the Office

Question: What current organizational activity simultaneously helps alleviate child-care problems, reduces traffic jams, and cuts air pollution and fuel consumption, while also saving millions of dollars on office space? The answer is **telecommuting**—the practice of using communications technology to enable work to be performed from remote locations, such as the home.

Advanced technology and enlightened attitudes toward work have made it possible for today's employees to be freed from traditional offices. (This is the practice of *flexplace* described earlier.) They can work from their homes, cars, or the decks of their yachts—virtually anywhere they can plug in a computer and phone line. In fact, as wireless communications become more advanced, workers can be completely untethered and hide away with their laptops on a desert island, if they so desire. Statistics reveal that telecommuting is in full swing today:[79]

■ There are currently 7.6 million telecommuters—a figure expected to jump to 25 million by the year 2000.
■ Among employees of *Fortune* 500 firms, 78 percent perform significant amounts of work off-site.

■ Telecommuting is most prevalent among smaller firms: 77 percent of telecommuters work for organizations employing fewer than 100 people.

The computer giant IBM has been one of the first to apply its technology to telecommuting. Although IBM's Midwest division is headquartered in Chicago, few of its 4,000 employees (including salespeople and customer service technicians) show up more than once or twice a week. Instead, they have "gone mobile," using the company's ThinkPad computers, fax-modems, e-mail, and cellular phones to do their work from remote locations. In just a few years, the company has slashed its real estate space by 55 percent, cut the number of fixed computer terminals required, and does a better job of satisfying its customers' needs. And, at the same time, telecommuting has done well for IBM employees themselves: 83 percent report not wanting to return to a traditional office environment. Reports from companies such as Great Plains Software, The Traveler's Insurance Co., U.S. West Communications, and the NPD Group have all reported similar benefits with respect to savings in office expenses, gains in productivity, and satisfaction among employees.[80]

As you might imagine, telecommuting is not for everyone; it also has its limitations.[81] Notably, when employees do not come into contact with each other, it is difficult to build the team spirit that is needed to produce quality goods and services in some organizations. Additionally, telecommuting does not lend itself to all jobs. It works best for jobs that involve information handling, significant amounts of automation, and relatively little face-to-face contact. Sales representatives, computer programmers, word processing technicians, insurance agents, and securities traders are all good candidates for telecommuting.

This is not to say that all individuals performing these jobs should be issued a laptop and sent packing. Good candidates for telecommuting must have the emotional maturity and self-discipline to work without direct supervision. To assist those who have difficulty adjusting to telecommuting, IBM carefully monitors the work of its telecommuters and offers counseling to those who appear to be having trouble.

To function effectively, workers who telecommute must be thoroughly trained in the use of the technologies that are required for them to do their work off-site, as well as the proper conditions for working safely (e.g., avoiding physical problems resulting from staring into video terminals for hours on end and from overusing wrist muscles). They also must be trained in ways to function independently, such as how to manage their time effectively and how to avoid interference from their families while working.

Companies also face the issue of establishing fair wages for telecommuters. For workers who are paid by the amount of work produced, such as the number of insurance claims processed, this is not a problem. Clear criteria for measuring performance (e.g., specific quantity and quality goals) are enormously helpful when paying telecommuters. However, for salaried employees doing jobs for which clear performance criteria are difficult to come by, policies need to be established regarding what telecommuters should do when, for instance, they complete their work in less than the allotted time. At the office, they probably would pitch in and help others, but away from the office they may be tempted to goof off. The key task is to resolve all potentially thorny policy issues regarding pay and performance expectations *before* employees begin telecommuting—and ensuring that they are clearly understood and accepted.

> ## YOU BE THE CONSULTANT
>
> A small manufacturing company has had difficulty attracting and retaining sales associates. To turn things around, it is now considering ways of changing the job to make it more attractive to prospective employees who are highly qualified, but whose personal obligations do not permit them to spend 40 hours a week at the office.
>
> **1.** How can telecommuting be used to help solve this problem? What potential benefits and problems may be expected by using this practice?
>
> **2.** What other types of "flexible working arrangements" or "support facilities" may help? Why?

The Quality Revolution: Total Quality Management and Reengineering

For many years, people complained but could do little when the goods they purchased fell apart, or the service they received was second-rate. After all, if everything in the market is shoddy, there are few alternatives. Then, Japanese companies such as Toyota and Nissan entered the American auto market. Their cars were more reliable, less expensive, and better designed than the offerings from Ford, General Motors, and Chrysler, companies that had become complacent about offering value to their customers. When Japanese automakers began capturing the American auto market in record numbers, American companies were forced to rethink their strategies—and to change their ways.

Today's companies operate quite differently than the American auto companies of decades past. For them, the watchword is not "getting by," but "making things better," what has been referred to as *the quality revolution*. The best organizations are ones that strive to deliver better goods and services at lower prices than ever before. Those that do so flourish, and those that do not tend to fade away. Throughout this text, in special sections called THE QUEST FOR QUALITY, we will be highlighting organizational practices that have been effective at improving quality, either with respect to organizational performance or employees' work lives. Here, however, we will review two approaches to improving quality that have been popularly used in recent years—*total quality management* and *reengineering*.

Total Quality Management: A Commitment to Customers

total quality management (TQM) An organizational strategy of commitment to improving customer satisfaction by developing techniques to carefully manage output quality.

One of the most popular approaches to establishing quality is known as **total quality management (TQM)**—an organizational strategy of commitment to improving customer satisfaction by developing techniques to manage output quality carefully. TQM is not so much a special technique as a well-ingrained set of corporate values—a way of life demonstrating a strong commitment to improving quality in everything that is done.

According to W. Edwards Deming, the best-known advocate of TQM, successful TQM requires that everyone in the organization—from the lowest-level employee to the CEO—must be committed fully to making whatever innovations are necessary to improve quality. This involves both carefully measuring quality (through elaborate statistical procedures) and taking whatever steps are necessary to improve it. Typically, this requires continuously improving the manufacturing process in ways that make it possible for higher quality to result.

For example, in developing its Lexus LS 400, Toyota purchased competing cars from Mercedes and BMW, disassembled them, examined the parts, and developed ways of building an even better car. Spending some $500 million in this process, Toyota was clearly dedicated to creating a superior product. And, given the recognition that Lexus has received among customers for its high quality, it appears as if Toyota's TQM efforts have paid off. The process of comparing one's own products or services with the best from other firms is known as **benchmarking**.

benchmarking The process of seeking to improve quality by comparing one's own products or services with the best products or services of others.

Another key ingredient of TQM is incorporating concern for quality into all aspects of organizational culture (a concept we will discuss more fully in Chapter 14).[82] At Rubbermaid, for example, concern for quality is emphasized not only in the company's manufacturing process but also in its concern for cost, service, speed, and innovation. To ensure that it is meeting quality standards, many companies conduct **quality control audits**—careful examinations of how well they are meeting its standards. For example, companies such as Pepsi Cola and FedEx regularly interview their clients to find out what prob-

quality control audits Careful examinations of how well a company is meeting the standards of quality toward which it is striving.

lems they may be having. These responses are then taken very seriously in making whatever improvements are necessary to avoid problems in the future.

Some companies have been so very successful at achieving high quality in all respects that they have been honored for their accomplishments. In 1988 the U.S. Congress established the Malcolm Baldrige Quality Award (named after President Reagan's late Secretary of Commerce) to recognize American companies that practice effective quality management and make significant improvements in the quality of their goods and services.[83] Up to two companies are given the award each year in each of three categories: manufacturing, service, and small business (any independent company with fewer than 500 full-time employees). For a listing of each year's winners by category, see Table 2-1.

Companies interested in being considered for the award complete a detailed application (running as long as 75 pages) in which they thoroughly document their quality achievements. Winners are determined by a Board of Examiners at the National Institute of Standards and Technology, currently composed of approximately 250 quality experts. The Board reviews each written application, and then visits the sites of companies that have scored high enough to be in contention. Applicants are judged on several criteria, including evidence of customer satisfaction, evidence of improvements in operations, and the extent to which they tap the potential of their employees.

The major goal of the award is to promote quality achievement by recognizing those companies that deliver continually improving value to customers while maximizing their overall productivity and effectiveness. To ensure that all companies can benefit from the winner's experiences, winning companies are expected to share their successful quality strategies with other American firms. This has been done in the form of personal presentations, books, and

■ TABLE 2-1   THE BALDRIGE AWARD: A LIST OF WINNERS

The Malcolm Baldrige Quality Award has been given each year since 1988 to American companies whose practices reflect the highest standards of quality in all aspects of their operations. Here is a listing of the winners in each of the three categories in which an award can be made—manufacturing, small business, and service.

Year	Manufacturing Category	Small Business Category	Service Category
1988	•Motorola, Inc. •Commercial Nuclear Fuel Division of Westinghouse Electric	•Globe Metallurgical, Inc.	[none]
1989	•Miliken & Company •Xerox Business Products and Systems	[none]	[none]
1990	•Cadillac Motor Car Company	•Wallace Co., Inc.	•Federal Express Corporation
1991	•Solectron Corporation •Zytec Corporation	•Marlowe Industries	[none]
1992	•AT&T Network Systems Group •Texas Instruments, Inc.	•Granite Rock Co.	•AT&T Universal Card Services •The Ritz–Carlton Hotel Co.
1993	•Eastman Chemical Company	•Ames Rubber Company	[none]
1994	[none]	•Wainwright Industries	•AT&T Consumer Communication Services •GTE Directories Corp.
1995	•Armstrong World Industries' Building Products Operation •Corning Telecommunications Products Division	[none]	[none]

SOURCE: Information provided by the National Institute of Standards and Technology.

cases presented on videotape.[84] In the case of IBM, preparing its application for the Baldridge Award caused it to examine itself so carefully that benefits came not only from the recognition it received by winning (in 1990), but from the detailed process of preparing the application itself.[85]

Reengineering: Starting All Over

Recent articles in the popular business press have referred to *reengineering* as "the hottest trend in management,"[86] noting that "if this radical idea . . . hasn't landed at your company, it's probably on its way."[87] Pioneered by consultants Michael Hammer and James Champy, **reengineering** is defined as the fundamental rethinking and radical redesign of business processes to achieve drastic improvements in performance.

Reengineering does not involve fixing anything—rather, as the term implies, it means starting over from scratch about the fundamental way things are done. Organizations that use reengineering forget all about how work was performed in the past and start anew with a clean sheet of paper, thinking about how things can be done best right now—hence the term "radical" in the definition.

The main focus of reengineering is the customer. Everything that is done starts with the idea of adding value for the customer: improving service, raising quality, lowering costs. Practices are eradicated simply because they are traditional, or convenient for the company if they don't otherwise help the customer. Doing this involves organizing around process rather than function. That is, work is arranged according to the processes needed to get the job done most effectively (for this reason, reengineering is also known as *process innovation*). For example, in many companies the simple process of order fulfillment is frequently chopped up into single tasks performed by people in many different departments although customers may be better served by assigning it to a single unit responsible for the entire process.

As an example of reengineering in action, consider changes made at IBM Credit Corp., a subsidiary responsible for financing IBM's hardware and software. Before reengineering, the task of processing a credit application was cumbersome and very slow—so slow, in fact, that it frequently cost the company sales. A credit request would come in by phone and would be logged on a

reengineering The fundamental rethinking and radical redesign of business processes to achieve drastic improvements in performance.

We discuss various organizational design strategies more fully in Chapter 15.

■ **Figure 2-13**
A Reengineering Success Story at Hallmark Cards
These employees of Hallmark Cards have seen their company remain the dominant player in the greeting card industry in large part because of reengineering. For example, by bringing together people from various departments, such as writers, artists, and designers (specialists who previously were separated by great distances), to work on developing new greeting cards, Hallmark has been successful in reducing the time needed to bring new products to market. This has helped the company stay ahead of the competition.

piece of paper. The paper then went on a long journey from credit checkers, to "pricers" (who determined what interest rate to charge), to many others who also performed single, specialized functions. Often, applications were bounced back and forth between departments before they were properly completed. Total processing time ranged from six days to two weeks.

Out of curiosity, some IBM senior managers decided one day to walk a financing request through the process, taking it from department to department and asking personnel in each office to put aside whatever they were doing and process this request in the normal fashion, only without the delay. What they found was quite an eye-opener: The actual process took only *90 minutes*; the remaining time was consumed by handing the form off between departments. Enlightened by this demonstration, IBM Credit reengineered its operations by replacing a series of specialists with generalists. Now, one person processes an entire application from beginning to end without handing it off to others.

Did it work? In the newly reengineered jobs, credit approval takes only about 4 hours (much closer to the 90-minute minimum time needed to do the job). Furthermore, the number of applications processed has increased 100-fold—and, using *fewer* employees than before. Other companies, such as Ford, Kodak, Hallmark (see Figure 2-13), Taco Bell, and Bell Atlantic also have used reengineering successfully. Union Carbide claims to have reduced its fixed costs by $400 million in just three years by using reengineering. Don't let all these big names mislead you; small companies also have been using reengineering to achieve success.

Although it is too early to predict the long-term benefits of reengineering, there is good reason to suspect that it will continue to be quite effective—and popular. Because it combines several major principles of OB, we are optimistic that this burgeoning approach will *not* soon become tomorrow's outdated fad.

Corporate Social Responsibility: The Ethical Organization

The history of American business is riddled with sordid tales of magnates who would go to any lengths in their quest for success, destroying in the process, not only the country's natural resources and the public's trust, but also the hopes and dreams of millions of people. For example, Jim Fisk and Jay Gould relied on thugs to remove anyone who got in the way of their development of railroads. Similarly, tales abound of how John D. Rockefeller, founder of Standard Oil, regularly bribed politicians and stepped all over people in his quest to monopolize the oil industry.

By relating these tales we do not mean to imply that unsavory business practices are only a relic of the past. Indeed, they are all too common today. For example, in recent years, incidents of insider trading have brought down one of the world's most powerful brokerage firms, Drexel Burnham Lambert. Accusations of fraudulent practices in its auto repair business have tarnished the reputation of venerable retailing giant Sears.[88] Clearly, human greed has not faded from the business scene. However, something *has* changed—namely, the public's acceptance of unethical behavior on the part of organizations. Consider this statement by a leading expert on business ethics:

> Ethical standards, whether formal or informal, have changed tremendously in the last century. Boldly stated, no one can make the case that ethical standards have fallen in the latter decades of the twentieth century. The reverse is true. Standards are considerably higher. Business-people themselves, as well as the public, expect more sensitive behavior in the conduct of economic enterprise. The issue is not just having the standards, however. It is living up to them.[89]

To the extent that people are increasingly intolerant of unethical business activity, it makes sense for the field of OB to examine the factors that encourage unethical practices. Even more importantly, we need to develop strategies for promoting ethical conduct. Here, we will turn our attention to these matters. But, this is only the beginning. Throughout this book, we will take close-up looks at the ethical aspects of various organizational decisions in special sections named **THE ETHICS ANGLE**.

Why Does Unethical Organizational Behavior Occur?

Unethical organizational practices are embarrassingly commonplace. It is easy to define practices such as dumping chemical wastes into rivers, insider trading on Wall Street, and overcharging the government for Medicaid services as morally wrong. Yet these and many other unethical practices occur almost routinely in many organizations. Why is this so? In other words, what accounts for the unethical actions of people within organizations?

One answer to this question is based on the idea that *organizations often reward behaviors that violate ethical standards*. Consider, for example, how many business executives are expected to deal in bribes and payoffs and how good corporate citizens blowing the whistle on organizational wrongdoings may fear being punished for their actions. Organizations tend to develop *counternorms*—accepted organizational practices that are contrary to prevailing ethical standards.[90] Some of these are summarized in Figure 2-14.

The top of Figure 2-14 identifies being "open and honest" as a prevailing ethical norm. Indeed, governmental regulations requiring full disclosure and freedom of information reinforce society's values toward openness and honesty. Within organizations, however, it is often considered not only acceptable, but desirable, to be much more secretive and deceitful. The practice of *stonewalling*—willingly hiding relevant information—is quite common. One reason for this is that organizations may actually punish those who are too open and honest. Consider, for example, the disclosure that B. F. Goodrich rewarded employees who falsified and withheld data on the quality of aircraft brakes to

For a discussion of the topic of whistle-blowing in organizations, see Chapter 11. For more on norms, see Chapter 8.

■ **Figure 2-14**
Societal Norms vs. Organizational Counternorms
Although societal standards of ethics dictate the appropriateness of certain actions, counternorms that encourage and support opposite practices often develop within organizations.

(**Source:** Based on suggestions by Jansen & Von Glinow, 1985; see Note 90.)

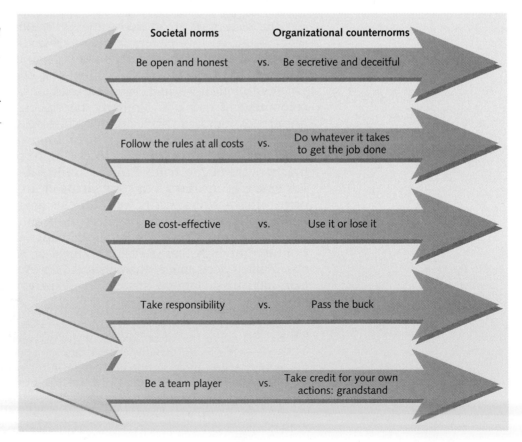

Societal norms | Organizational counternorms

Be open and honest | vs. | Be secretive and deceitful

Follow the rules at all costs | vs. | Do whatever it takes to get the job done

Be cost-effective | vs. | Use it or lose it

Take responsibility | vs. | Pass the buck

Be a team player | vs. | Take credit for your own actions: grandstand win certification. Similarly, it has been reported that executives at Metropolitan Edison encouraged employees to withhold information from the press about the Three Mile Island nuclear accident. In both incidents, the counternorms of secrecy and deceitfulness were accepted and supported by the organization.

As you can see from Figure 2-14, many other organizational counternorms promote ethically questionable practices. That these practices are commonly rewarded and accepted suggests that organizations may be operating within a world that dictates its own set of accepted rules. This reasoning leads to a second explanation as to why organizations act unethically—namely, that certain *managerial values undermine integrity*. In an analysis of executive integrity, Professor Donald M. Wolfe explains that managers have developed some ways of thinking (of which they may be quite unaware) that foster unethical behavior.[91]

One culprit is referred to as the **bottom-line mentality**. This way of thinking supports financial success as the only value to be considered. It promotes short-term solutions that are immediately financially sound even if they cause problems for others within the organization or for the organization as a whole. It promotes the unrealistic belief that everything boils down to a monetary game. As such, rules of morality are merely obstacles, impediments along the way to bottom line financial success.

Wolfe also notes that managers tend to rely on an **exploitative mentality**—the view that encourages "using" people in a way that promotes stereotypes and undermines empathy and compassion. This highly selfish perspective sacrifices concern for others in favor of benefits to one's own immediate interests.

In addition, there is a **Madison Avenue mentality**—a perspective suggesting that anything is right if the public can be convinced that it's right. The idea is that executives may be more concerned about their actions *appearing* to be ethical than about their legitimate morality—a public relations-guided mentality. This kind of thinking leads some companies to hide their unethical actions (e.g., by dumping their toxic wastes under cover of night) or to justify them otherwise by attempting to explain them as completely acceptable.

Recognizing the problems associated with these various orientations is not difficult. Their overemphasis on short-term monetary gain may lead to decisions that not only hurt individuals in the long run, but also threaten the very existence of organizations themselves. Although an organization may make an immediate profit by cutting corners, exploiting people, and convincing others that they have behaved appropriately, it is unlikely that such practices are in the long-term best interest of organizations. Just as people are learning that they cannot continue to exploit their natural environments forever without paying a cost (e.g., depletion of natural resources, hazards allegedly caused by openings in the earth's ozone layer), the same may apply to business environments as well. Indeed, society appears to be increasingly intolerant of organizations that continue to violate moral standards in the name of short-term profit.

It even has been argued that when organizations continue to behave unethically, they may actually find that doing so is unprofitable in the long run. Consumers who find the well-publicized unethical actions of various companies objectionable may cast their votes for greater social responsibility by not patronizing those organizations. In contrast, a growing number of organizations—such as the Body Shop and Tom's of Maine, to name only two—have long engaged in highly ethical practices with respect to the treatment of living beings and the environment and have prospered in great part because of consumers' appreciation of these policies.[92]

What Can Be Done to Promote Ethical Behavior in Organizations?

As you might imagine, getting people to behave ethically isn't a simple matter. Yet, to the extent that "good ethics" may in fact be "good business," as they say, it is worth considering tactics for discouraging unethical behavior.

bottom line mentality The belief that any action is acceptable if it leads to financial gain.

exploitative mentality The view that encourages "using" people in a way that promotes stereotypes and undermines empathy and compassion.

Madison Avenue mentality The belief that any action is acceptable if others can be so convinced.

The first thing that should be done is to *test the ethics of any decision you are contemplating.* In this regard, there are four main questions you should ask yourself:[93]

- *Is it right?* Although it is not always easy to judge whether a certain action is right, there are certain universally accepted principles of right and wrong that should not be violated. For example, it is widely considered wrong to steal.
- *Is it fair?* Fairness demands treating likes as likes. So, for example, two equally qualified people should be paid the same wages for doing the same job.
- *Is it purely selfish?* If the results of your actions benefit only yourself, then they may be unethical. Morally acceptable behaviors are ones that benefit the greatest number and harm the fewest.
- *How would you feel if others found out?* If you think you might be embarrassed by having your actions described on the front page of your local newspaper, then those actions may be ethically dubious.

A second step that can be taken to promote ethical behavior (and one that many organizations have been using) is to develop a **code of ethics**. These are documents describing what the organization stands for and the general rules of conduct expected of employees (e.g., to avoid conflicts of interest, to be honest).[94] Some codes are highly specific, stating, for example, the maximum size of gifts that can be accepted and exactly how people will be punished for violating the rules. Research has shown that codes of ethics are especially effective when they are used in conjunction with training programs that reinforce the company's values.[95] In the absence of such training, too many codes are seen as "window dressing" and are ignored—if they are even read at all.

Third, conduct an **ethics audit**. Just as companies regularly audit their books to check on irregularities in their finances, it is advised that they regularly assess the morality of their employees' behavior so as to identify irregularities in this realm as well. Specifically, an ethics audit involves actively investigating and documenting incidents of dubious ethical value. Then, these unethical practices should be discussed in an open and honest fashion, and a concrete plan should be developed to avoid such actions in the future.

Our fourth recommendation involves something you can do as an individual: *Challenge your rationalizations about ethical behavior.* We all tend to rationalize the things we do so that we can convince ourselves that they are right although they really may be wrong. Some of the most common rationalizations are as follows:

- *Convincing yourself that something is morally acceptable just because it is legally acceptable.* Think of the law as the minimum standard of acceptable behavior, and strive for higher moral standards.
- *Convincing yourself that something is right just because it benefits you.* It may be easy to talk yourself into accepting a bribe because you feel underpaid. Regardless, it is still wrong.
- *Convincing yourself that something is right because you will never get caught.* What's wrong is wrong—even if you don't stand a chance of getting caught.
- *Convincing yourself that something is right because it helps the company.* Don't expect the company to condone your immoral actions, even if doing so gives it an edge. The best companies want to succeed because they have taken the moral high road, not because of the unacceptable practices of its employees.

As you might imagine, it isn't always easy to avoid these rationalizations. Still, do your best to catch yourself in the act of rationalizing your actions. To the extent that you are rationalizing, you may be covering up unethical behavior.

Globalization and Culture

International trade and commerce is becoming increasingly commonplace in the world of business. Companies with operations throughout the world, **multinational corporations (MNCs)** are becomingly increasingly common. As tariffs are eliminated, world markets grow and countries become financially interdependent. One result of this is **cultural homogenization,** the tendency for people throughout the world to become culturally similar.

People living in other countries, or returning home after long visits abroad, often experience feelings of disorientation and confusion known as **culture shock.** However, these feelings tend to disappear as people spend more time in their new surroundings.

In contrast to traditional approaches to management which assume that there is one best way to manage people—the American way—today's scientists recognize that different approaches may operate effectively in different cultures—the **divergence hypothesis.** In fact, Hofstede's framework organizes several important dimensions of culture that distinguish people in various nations with respect to the way they are likely to behave in organizations. These dimensions are **individualism/collectivism, power distance, uncertainty avoidance,** and **masculinity/femininity.**

Diversity in the Workplace

Today's organizations may be characterized not only by cultural differences between them, but within them as well. In fact, a popular philosophy today is **cultural pluralism**—the idea that people's unique identities should be maintained and accepted by others. This is in contrast to the traditional, **melting pot,** philosophy, according to which people blend their cultures, creating a new culture. The cultural pluralism idea is embraced by organizations who make efforts to **value diversity** among their employees.

The American workforce may be characterized as growing in the numbers of women, minorities, and older people. Recognizing these trends, organizations have implemented **diversity training** programs, flexible work arrangements (e.g., **flextime programs, compressed workweeks,** and **job sharing**) and support facilities (e.g., **child-care** and **elder-care**).

Trends in Working Arrangements

Rapid advances in technology have made it possible for organizations to do more work with fewer employees than before. As a result they **downsize,** laying off employees who are no longer needed. They also eliminate non-core functions (e.g., janitorial services, duplication services, payroll processing) by purchasing them from other companies who specialize in these tasks—a popular process known as **outsourcing.** Also adding flexibility in the numbers of employees needed, many companies are simply hiring people on an as-needed basis, creating a **contingent workforce.**

As organizations are growing smaller, they sometimes find it impossible to tackle large projects themselves. Instead, they join forces temporarily with other companies to form temporary companies known as **virtual organizations.** Today, as technology makes it possible for employees to do more work from outside the office, to which they are connected by computers and telephone lines, the practice of **telecommuting** has grown in popularity.

The Quality Revolution

To stay competitive in the world marketplace, today's organizations are more concerned than ever with producing high quality goods and services. An approach known as **total quality management (TQM)** has been popular in recent years. It refers to an organizational strategy of commitment to improving customer satisfaction by developing techniques to manage output quality carefully. Companies that have met rigorous quality standards may be awarded the Malcom Baldridge Quality Award. Companies also attempt to improve the quality of their work by **reengineering.** This involves radically redesigning the way organizational processes are performed, with the ultimate goal of better serving customers.

Ethical and Unethical Behavior in Organizations

Corporate scandals have become commonplace in recent years. These appear to be due, in large part, to the facts that organizations sometimes reward behaviors that violate ethical standards, and some managerial values undermine integrity. For example, the **bottom-line mentality** encourages people to seek short-term profit at all costs.

Ethical behavior in organizations may be fostered by encouraging people to test the morality of the decisions they are contemplating, developing a **code of ethics,** conducting an **ethics audit,** and challenging rationalizations about ethical behavior.

groups, research and prepare a report on what these companies are doing that makes them so quality-minded. Given that Baldrige Award–winning companies are expected to publicize their quality practices so all can learn from them, such information should not be difficult to find. Your school's librarians should be able to help you search through computerized databases to find information about the companies.

4. Your group's report should attempt to answer the following basic questions:
   (a) What are the company's core business activities?
   (b) What has the company done to improve the quality of its goods or services?
   (c) What has the company done to improve relations with its employees?
   (d) What has the company done to promote customer satisfaction?

5. After all the reports have been prepared, members of each group should take turns reporting their findings to the class.

Questions for Discussion

1. Were there any common practices followed by all award winners? Explain.
2. Did the winners in the various categories do things that were very different from each other? Explain.
3. What ideas did you get with respect to how quality may be fostered in the organization within which you work?
4. As this is being written, debates about future federal support for the Baldrige Award are going on. Do you think the Baldrige Award constitutes a wise investment? What general value do you think the Baldrige Award has in promoting quality in organizations?

Take It to the Net

We invite you to visit the Greenberg/Baron page on the Prentice Hall Web site at:

http://www.prenhall.com/~greenob

for this chapter's WorldWide Web exercise.

You can also visit the Web sites for these companies, featured within this chapter:

Avon
http://www.avon.com/

Great Plains Software
http://www.gps.com/

Digital Equipment Corp.
http://www.digital.com/

Manpower
http://www.nauticom.net/www/manpower/

The Body Shop
http://www.the-body-shop.com/

NPD Group
http://www.npd.com/

Fannie Mae
http://www.fanniemae.com/

Pixar
http://www.pixar.com/

PART I:
WHEN EMPLOYEES BECOME OWNERS

On July 12, 1994, thanks to a $4.9 billion buyout deal that put 55 percent of company shares in their hands, United Airlines employees became United Airlines owners. The action was widely hailed as the beginning of a new era in labor-management relations. By the time the buyout was approved by the company's shareholders, United's unions had been involved in a struggle with management for more than a decade. Now United Airlines can boast that it is the largest employee-owned company in the United States.

The buyout resulted in many changes besides those involving company stock. Employees, for instance, gained seats on the board of directors, and Gerald Greenwald, former vice chairman at Chrysler, was named chairman and CEO. Greenwald is in an interesting position: Because he was recruited by United's employees, he works for them, rather than vice versa. One of his highest priorities is thus to improve relations between United's union members and management. He must also reduce feuding among different union groups and boost profitability to keep both public shareholders and employee-owners happy with their new deal. And in fact, he has gotten off to a good start: In 1994, United had net income of $77 million on $14 billion in revenues. Such results helped balance big losses in recent years, including $50 million in 1993, nearly $1 billion in 1992, and $332 million in 1991.

Some of United's new prosperity is the result of cost cutting. The buyout, for example, required United's 80,000 employees to accept pay cuts, and concessions that saved $5 billion. Offsetting those cuts, however, is improved job security: New contracts prevent management both from laying employees off and from selling assets that could cut jobs. Says James Kozar, a United mechanic since 1986: "For me, it all comes down to job security. I got laid off at TWA after nine years, so I know what that's like. Basically, we are making a sacrifice, and that won't be easy. But we've got our jobs, and that means a lot these days." (Admittedly, many employees were concerned that the concessions may have gone too far when they learned that advisors to the buyout negotiations received $45 million in fees.)

Today, employees' attitudes toward United vary. "The nice thing about all this," says reservations agent Melody Sadleir, "is that now I own part of this company. It's like if I own my own house, I want to make sure it looks nice and the grass looks good." By contrast, some airline flight attendants are adding new complaints to resentment that still simmers from perceived mismanagement in the past. The flight attendants union did not support the buyout. Says Kevin Lum, a United flight attendant since 1979: "We've always been treated like angry children who don't deserve what they get. Upper management has been adversarial and confrontational with us for over ten years now." In mid-1995, United's flight attendants handed out leaflets to passengers in major airports. They were protesting management's plan to open flight attendant bases overseas and to hire foreign workers at lower pay levels.

Video source: The changing face of labor on the 100th anniversary of Labor Day. (1994, September 4). *David Brinkley. Additional sources:* Valente, J. (1995, July 12). UAL faces dissension over buyout. *USA Today,* pp. 1B, 2B; Labich, K. (1994, August 22). Will United fly? *Fortune,* pp. 70+; Bryant, A. (1994, July 13). After 7 years, employees win United Airlines. *The New York Times,* pp. A1, D13; Bryant, A. (1994, May 13). Buyout of UAL by its unions looks like winning alternative. *The New York Times,* p. D6; Bernstein, A., & Kelly, K. (1993, December 27). This give-and-take may actually fly. *Business Week,* p. 37.

CHAPTER | **Three**

PERCEPTION AND LEARNING: UNDERSTANDING AND ADAPTING TO THE WORK ENVIRONMENT

LEARNING

■ OBJECTIVES

After reading this chapter you should be able to:

1. Define *social perception* and indicate its relevance to organizational behavior.
2. Explain how the *attribution* process helps us understand the causes of others' behavior.
3. Appreciate the various sources of bias in social perception and how they may be overcome.
4. Understand how the process of social perception operates in the context of performance appraisals, employment interviews, and the cultivation of corporate images.

5. Explain the concept of learning and describe how it operates in organizations.
6. Describe the concepts of *operant conditioning* and *observational learning*.
7. Appreciate how principles of learning are involved in organizational programs involving training, organizational behavior management, and discipline.

Preview

TACO'S TOWER OF KNOWLEDGE PAYS OFF BIG!

The listing of courses at Taco (pronounced TAY-co), over 70 in all, is quite extensive. For the vocationally minded, there's blueprint reading, manufacturing techniques, and employment law. More on the academic side are classes in English as a second language, computing, speech, and algebra. For the hobbyist there are classes in art and gardening. Self-improvement buffs will find classes on weight reduction, smoking cessation, and physical fitness. Relatively standard fare for a community college, you say? Maybe so, but Taco isn't a college. It's a Cranston, Rhode Island, manufacturer of pumps and valves that makes these courses available at no charge to its employees. And when you consider that Taco is a relatively small company (450 employees, with sales in the $80 to $90 million range), this array of course offerings is all the more impressive.

Taco's "learning center," housed in a brick tower that overlooks the factory, cost $250,000 to build in 1992. This is in addition to the $300,000 it takes to run the center each year, including production lost while employees are taking classes. When asked about the rationale behind this considerable expenditure, 82-year-old owner John Hazen White says simply, "I don't have any idea why it happened," adding, "except that I wanted to do it." But White sees the learning center as an investment in the future of his business. Answering his own question "Does it come back to us?" White confidently says, "Of course it does."

Recently, the learning center helped two Taco employees earn high school equivalency degrees and seven others pass the test to become U.S. citizens—outcomes benefiting the company. Likewise, the company profits as employees develop other skills, such as language (many employees have taken conversational Spanish so they can better communicate with their Spanish-speaking colleagues) and basic arithmetic. Even the nonvocational courses are regarded as helping Taco workers develop the broad range of skills they need as human beings, improving the ways they think about themselves.

Taco officials believe that their investment has been paying off. Not only has the company been able to hold the line on the prices it charges for its products, but it also has been able to hang on to its human resources: Taco's rate of turnover is very impressive—less than 1 percent. White's son, 37-year-old Johnny, Taco's executive vice president, is convinced that the learning center has helped the company survive during periods of economic recession, times when its competitors were forced to close.

Despite the extensive nature of Taco's learning center, White is quick to explain that he isn't being completely altruistic. The schooling does much to enhance the image of the company. So highly regarded is the learning center, in fact, that it has attracted such distinguished guest lecturers as the governor of Rhode Island and the chief justice of the state supreme court. Bettering the company by bettering the employees—that's the key to the program's success.

Reading this case, you probably cannot help but consider how these educational experiences have enriched the lives of so many Taco employees. By acquiring new skills, the people who work at Taco enjoy opportunities for advancement and chances to improve their lives. Although they are the same people they were before taking classes, the fact that they have better job skills and life skills is likely to enhance the way others see them. And by making these opportunities available to its employees, Taco has enhanced the way it is viewed as a company in the minds of people in the community, including some of its leaders. What is responsible for the way we come to view other people and the companies in which they work? Clearly, there is an active and complex process going on, a mechanism through which people are able to make sense out of the things they confront in the world around them—the process of *perception*.

Although it may sound mysterious, perception is a fundamental process, and one that explains many different types of situations in organizations. For example, think about what goes on when you apply for a job. Your prospective employer attempts to learn about you—based, most likely, on an interview and your résumé—and makes a judgment about what you'd be like as an employee. Will you be lazy or hard-working? Do you know how to do the job? At the same time, you are attempting to figure out what it would be like to work for that company. Will the boss be pleasant? Will the work be challenging? If hired, you'll be sizing up your new co-workers (who's nice and who's going to stab me in the back?) while they do the same to you (what's the new person like?). Then, as time goes on, you'll be evaluated by your superior (how well is this person doing?). Obviously, there's a lot of perceiving going on here. Understanding the complex nature of perceptual processes, basic as they are to human behavior in organizations, is critical to our understanding of OB, and so it will be one of the key themes of this chapter.

Equally fundamental is another basic psychological process that is highlighted in this case—*learning*. The broad array of classes at Taco provide exceptional opportunities for its employees to add important new capabilities to their repertoires of both job skills and life skills. However, learning may involve much more than formally training people in the classroom. The process of learning is also involved in such everyday activities as attaining information about who holds the power in an organization, how to get things done most effectively, who to talk to in the event of a problem, and even what to eat or avoid at the company cafeteria. Principles of learning are also applied in ways designed to help improve the functioning of organizations by systematically doing things that help maintain desirable employee behaviors and reduce undesirable behaviors. In this chapter, we will not only explain the psychological processes responsible for learning—that is, how it occurs—but also ways in which these processes are used to improve organizational functioning.

Social Perception: The Process of Understanding Others

There can be no doubt about it: The world around us is a very complex place. At any given moment we are flooded with input from our various senses. Yet we do not respond to the world as a random collection of sights, sounds, smells, and tastes. Rather, we notice order and pattern everywhere. This process of making sense out of the vast array of sensory inputs involves the active processing of information, and is known as the process of **perception**. Formally, we may define perception as the process through which people select, organize, and interpret information.[1]

To illustrate this process, let's consider an example. Suppose that you meet your new boss. You know her general reputation as a manager, and you see the way she looks, hear the words she says, and read the memos she writes. In no time at all, you're trying to figure her out. Will she be easy to work with? Will she like me? Will she do a good job for the company? On the basis of whatever information you have available to you (even if it's very little), you will try to understand her and how you will be affected by her. In other words, you will attempt to combine the various things you learn about her into a meaningful picture. Interestingly, this process is so automatic that we are almost never aware of it. Yet it goes on all the time. Clearly, when it comes to understanding the objects and people in our environment, there's a lot more going on than may be obvious.

The process of perception is especially important in the field of OB. Indeed, other people—whether they're bosses, co-workers, subordinates, family, or friends—can have profound effects on us. To understand the people around

perception The process through which we select, organize, and interpret information gathered by our senses in order to understand the world around us.

Meeting New People: An Opportunity for Social Perception
Meeting new people presents many opportunities to combine, integrate, and interpret a great deal of information about them—to implement the process of social perception.

us—to figure out who they are and why they do what they do—may be very helpful to us. After all, you wouldn't want to ask your boss for a raise when you believe he or she is in a bad mood. Clearly, **social perception**—the task of combining, integrating, and interpreting information about others to gain an accurate understanding of them—is very important, especially in organizations (see Figure 3-1).[2]

We will explore various aspects of the social perception process in the sections that follow. To begin, we will summarize the *attribution* process—the way people come to judge the underlying causes of others' behavior. Then, we will note various imperfections of this process—errors and sources of bias that contribute to inaccurate judgments of others—as well as ways of overcoming them. Finally, we will present specific ways in which the attribution process is used in organizations.

social perception The process through which individuals attempt to combine, integrate, and interpret information about others.

The Attribution Process: Judging the Causes of Others' Behavior

A question we often ask about others is "why?" Why did Kim goof up the order? Why did the company president make the policy she did? When we ask such questions, we are attempting to get at two different types of information: (1) what someone is really like (that is, what traits and characteristics does he or she possess?) and (2) what made the person behave as he or she did (that is, what accounted for his or her actions?). People attempt to answer these questions in different ways through the process of **attribution**.[3]

attribution The process through which individuals attempt to determine the causes of others' behavior.

Making Correspondent Inferences: Using Acts to Judge Dispositions

Situations frequently arise in organizations in which we want to know what someone is like. Is your opponent a tough negotiator? Are your co-workers prone to be punctual? The more you know about what people are like, the better equipped you are to know what to expect and how to deal with them. How, precisely, do we go about identifying another's traits? Generally speaking, we do so by observing their behavior and then inferring their traits from this information. The judgments we make about what someone is like based on what we have observed about him or her are known as **correspondent inferences**.[4] Simply put, correspondent inferences are judgments about people's

correspondent inferences Judgments made about what someone is like based on observations of his or her behavior.

dispositions—their traits and characteristics—that correspond to what we have observed of their actions (see Figure 3-2).

At first blush, it would appear to be a simple matter to infer what people are like based on their behavior. A person with a disorganized desk may be thought of as sloppy. Someone who slips on the shop floor may be considered clumsy. Such judgments might be accurate—but not necessarily. After all, the messy desk actually may be the result of a co-worker rummaging through it to find an important report. Similarly, the person who slipped could have encountered oily conditions under which anyone, even the least clumsy individual, would have fallen. In other words, it is important to recognize that the judgments we may make about someone may be inaccurate because there are many possible causes of behavior. Someone's underlying characteristics certainly may play a large role in determining what they do, but as we will explain in the next section, it is also possible for behavior to be shaped by external forces (in our examples, the coworker's actions and the oil on the floor). For this reason, correspondent inferences may not always be accurate.

Another reason why this is so has to do with the tendency for people to conceal some of their traits—especially when they may be viewed as negative. So, for example, a sloppy individual may work hard in public to appear to be organized. Likewise, the unprincipled person may talk a good show about the importance of being ethical. In other words, people often do their best to disguise some of their basic traits. In summary, then, due to two basic facts, the making of correspondent inferences is a risky business: (1) behavior is complex and has many different causes and (2) people sometimes purposely disguise their true characteristics.

Despite such difficulties, we can use several techniques to help make more accurate correspondent inferences. First, we can focus on others' behavior in situations in which they do not *have* to behave in a pleasant or socially acceptable manner. For example, anyone would behave in a courteous manner toward the president of the company, so when people do so, we don't learn too much about them. However, only those who are *really* courteous would be expected to behave politely toward someone of much lower rank—that is, someone toward whom they don't have to behave politely. In other words, someone who is polite toward the company president but condescending toward a secretary is probably really arrogant. The way people behave in situations in which a certain behavior is not clearly expected of them may reveal a great deal about their basic traits and motives.

Similarly, we can learn a great deal about someone by focusing on behavior for which there appears to be only one explanation. For example, imagine finding out that your friend accepts a new job. Upon questioning him, you

■ **Figure 3-2**
Correspondent Inferences: Judging Dispositions Based on Behavior
One of the ways in which we come to judge what others are like is by making inferences about them that follow from what we have observed of their behavior. Such judgments, known as corre- spondent inferences, *are frequently misleading. How might your inferences in this example be inaccurate?*

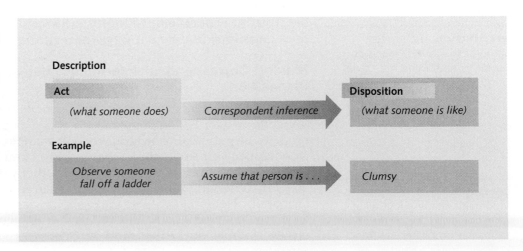

learn that the position is very high-paying, involves interesting work, and is in a desirable location. What have you learned about what's important to your friend? The answer is "not too much." After all, any of these are good reasons to consider taking a position. Now, imagine finding out that the work is very demanding and that the job is in an undesirable location but that it pays very well. In this case, you're more prone to learn something about your friend—namely, that he highly values money. Clearly, the opportunity to make accurate correspondent inferences about people is far greater in situations in which there is only one plausible explanation for their behavior.

Causal Attribution of Responsibility: Answering the Question "Why?"

Imagine finding out that your boss just fired one of your fellow employees. Naturally, you'd ask yourself, "Why did he do that?" Was it because your co-worker violated the company's code of conduct? Or was it because the boss is a cruel and heartless person? These two answers to the question "why?" represent two major classes of explanations for the causes of someone's behavior: *internal* causes, explanations based on actions for which the individual is responsible, and *external* causes, explanations based on situations over which the individual has no control. In this case, the internal cause would be the person's violation of the rules, and the external cause would be the boss's cruel and arbitrary behavior.

Generally speaking, it is very important to be able to determine whether an internal or an external cause was responsible for someone's behavior. Knowing why something happened to someone else might better help you prepare for what might happen to you. For example, in this case, if you believe that your colleague was fired because of something for which she was responsible herself, such as violating a company rule, then you might not feel as vulnerable as you would if you thought she was fired because of the arbitrary, spiteful nature of your boss. In the latter case, you might decide to take some precautionary actions—to do something to protect yourself from your boss, such as staying on his good side or even giving up and finding a new job before you are forced to. The key question of interest to social scientists is: How do people go about judging whether someone's actions were caused by internal or external causes?

An answer to this question is provided by **Kelley's theory of causal attribution**. According to this conceptualization, we base our judgments of internal and external causality on three types of information:[5]

- *Consensus*—the extent to which other people behave in the same manner as the person we're judging. If others do behave similarly, consensus is considered high; if they do not, consensus is considered low.
- *Consistency*—the extent to which the person we're judging acts the same way at other times when he or she is in the same situation. If the person acts the same at other times, consistency is high; if he or she does not, then consistency is low.
- *Distinctiveness*—the extent to which this person behaves in the same manner in other contexts. If he or she behaves the same way in other situations, distinctiveness is low; if he or she behaves differently, distinctiveness is high.

According to the theory, after collecting this information, we combine what we have learned to make our attributions of causality. Here's how. If we learn that other people act like this one (consensus is high), that this person behaves in the same manner at other times (consistency is high), and that this person does not act in the same manner in other situations (distinctiveness is high), we are likely to conclude that this person's behavior stemmed from *external* causes. In contrast, imagine learning that other people do *not* act like

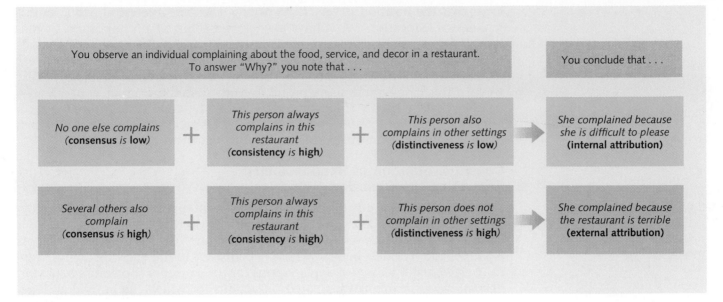

Figure 3-3
Kelley's Theory of Causal Attribution: A Summary
In determining whether others' behavior stems mainly from internal or external causes, we focus on the three types of information illustrated here.

this one (consensus is low), that this person behaves in the same manner at other times (consistency is high), and that this person acts in the same manner in other situations (distinctiveness is low). In this case, we will probably conclude that this person's behavior stemmed from *internal* causes.

Because this explanation is highly abstract, let's consider an example that helps illustrate how the process works. Imagine that you're at a business lunch with several of your company's sales representatives when the sales manager makes some critical remarks about the restaurant's food and service. Further imagine that no one else in your party acts this way (consensus is low), that you have heard her say the same things during other visits to the restaurant (consistency is high), and that you have seen her acting critically in other settings, such as the regional sales meeting (distinctiveness is low). What would you conclude in this situation? Probably that her behavior stems from *internal* causes. In other words, she is a "picky" person, someone who is difficult to please.

Now, imagine the same setting but with different observations. Suppose that several other members of your group also complain about the restaurant (consensus is high), that you have seen this person complain in the same restaurant at other times (consistency is high), but that you have never seen her complain about anything else before (distinctiveness is high). In this case, then you would probably conclude that the sales manager's behavior stems from *external* causes: The restaurant really *is* inferior. For a summary of these contrasting conclusions, see Figure 3-3.

The Imperfect Nature of Social Perception: Bias and How to Overcome It

As you might imagine, people are far from perfect when it comes to making judgments of others. In fact, researchers have noted that there are several important types of biases that interfere with making completely accurate judgments of others. In this section, we will describe some of these errors and ways of overcoming them.

Perceptual Biases: Systematic Errors in Perceiving Others

Some of the errors people make in judging others reflect systematic biases in the ways we think about others in general. These are referred to as **perceptual biases**. We will consider five such biases—the *fundamental at-*

perceptual biases Predispositions that people have to misperceive others in various systematic ways.

tribution error, the *halo effect*, the *similar-to-me-effect*, *first-impression error* and *selective perception*.

The fundamental attribution error. Despite what Kelley's theory says, people are not equally predisposed to reach judgments regarding internal and external causality. Rather, they are more likely to explain others' actions in terms of internal rather than external causes. In other words, we are prone to assume that others' behavior is due to the way they are, their traits and dispositions (e.g., "she's that kind of person"). So, for example, we are more likely to assume that someone who shows up for work late does so because she is lazy rather than because she got caught in traffic. This tendency is so strong that it has been referred to as the **fundamental attribution error**.[6]

This phenomenon stems from the fact that it is far easier to explain someone's actions in terms of his or her traits than to recognize the complex pattern of situational factors that may have affected his or her actions. As you might imagine, this tendency can be quite damaging in organizations. Specifically, it leads us to assume prematurely that people are responsible for the negative things that happen to them (e.g., "he wrecked the company car because he is careless"), without considering external alternatives, ones that may be less damning (e.g., "another driver hit the car"). This tendency can lead to inaccurate judgments about people.

The halo effect: Keeping perceptions consistent. Have you ever heard someone say something like, "She's very smart, so she must also be hardworking"? Or, "He's not too bright, so I guess he's lazy"? If so, then you are already aware of a common perceptual bias known as the **halo effect**.[7] Once we form a positive impression of someone, we tend to view the things that person does in favorable terms—even things about which we have no knowledge. Similarly, a generally negative impression of someone is likely to be associated with negative evaluations of that person's behavior. Both of these tendencies are referred to as halo effects—even the negative case.

In organizations, the halo effect often occurs when superiors rate subordinates using formal performance appraisal forms. In this context (which we will describe more fully later in this chapter), a manager evaluating one of his employees highly on some dimensions may assume that someone so good must also be good at other things and rate that person highly on other dimensions (see Figure 3-4). Put differently, the halo effect may be responsible for finding high correlations between the ratings given to people on various dimensions. When this occurs, the resulting evaluations are inaccurate, and the quality of the resulting evaluations is compromised.

The similar-to-me effect: "If you're like me, you must be pretty good." Another common type of perceptual bias involves the tendency for people to perceive more favorably others who are like themselves than those who are dissimilar. This inclination, known as the **similar-to-me effect**, constitutes a potential source of bias when it comes to judging other people. In fact, research has shown that when superiors rate their subordinates, the more similar the parties are, the higher the rating the superior tends to give.[8] This tendency applies with respect to several different dimensions of similarity—similarity of work values and habits, similarity of beliefs about the way things should be at work, and similarity with respect to demographic variables (such as age, race, gender, and work experience).

This effect appears to be partly the result of the tendency for people to be able to empathize and relate better to similar others and to be more lenient toward them. However, it also appears that subordinates tend to be more trusting and confident in supervisors whom they perceive as similar than those they perceive as dissimilar.[9] As a result, they may have a more positive relationship, and this may lead superiors to judge similar subordinates in a more

fundamental attribution error The tendency to attribute others' actions to internal causes (e.g., their traits) while largely ignoring external factors that also may have influenced their behavior.

halo effect The tendency for our overall impressions of others to affect objective evaluations of their specific traits; perceiving high correlations between characteristics that may be unrelated.

similar-to-me effect The tendency for people to perceive in a positive light others who are believed to be similar to themselves in any of several different ways.

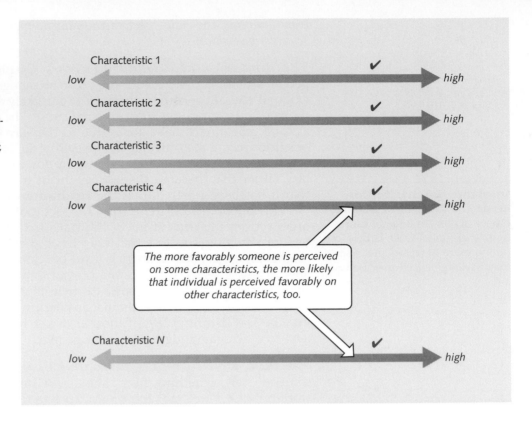

■ **Figure 3-4**
The Halo Effect: A Demonstration
One manifestation of the halo effect is the tendency for people rating others to give either consistently high ratings (if the individual is generally perceived in a positive manner), or low ratings (if the individual is generally perceived in a negative manner). Because each rating dimension is not considered independently, inaccurate evaluations may result.

Characteristic 1
low — high ✔

Characteristic 2
low — high ✔

Characteristic 3
low — high ✔

Characteristic 4
low — high ✔

The more favorably someone is perceived on some characteristics, the more likely that individual is perceived favorably on other characteristics, too.

Characteristic N
low — high ✔

first-impression error The tendency to base our judgments of others on our earlier impressions of them.

favorable light. Regardless of the underlying explanation for the similar-to-me effect, it is important to recognize its important implications: Differences in the way people are perceived are based in large part on the similarities between the perceiver and the individual being perceived.

First-impression error: Confirming one's expectations. Often, the way we judge someone is not based solely on how well that person performs now, but rather on our initial judgments of that individual—that is, our *first impressions.* To the extent that our initial impressions guide our subsequent impressions, we have been victimized by **first-impression error**. As you might imagine, this error can be especially problematic in organizations, where accurately judging others' performance is a crucial managerial task. When a subordinate's performance has improved, that needs to be recognized, but to the extent that current evaluations are based on poor first impressions, recognizing such improvement is impossible. Likewise, inaccurate assessments of performance will result when initially good performers leave positive impressions that linger on even when a manager is confronted with evidence suggesting that one's performance has dropped (for a summary of this process, see Figure 3-5).

Recent evidence by Dougherty, Turban, and Callender suggests that the first-impression error takes very subtle forms.[10] Participants in their study were corporate interviewers who evaluated the application blanks and test scores of prospective employees. These researchers found that the more highly interviewers judged these applicants based on these two criteria alone, the more positively the applicants were treated during the interview process. Analyses made of audiotaped interviews showed that candidates who made initially positive impressions were treated more positively: They were spoken to in a more pleasant interpersonal style and were more likely to be told about the good features of the company. In other words, instead of using the interviews to gather additional unbiased information, the recruiters used them to confirm the first impressions they developed on the basis of the test scores and application blanks. This study provides clear evidence of the first-impression error in action.

■ Figure 3-5

First-Impression Error: A Summary
When a first-impression error *is made,
the way we evaluate someone is more
highly influenced by our initial impressions of that person than by his or
her current performance. In this example, someone who was initially perceived as performing well continues
to be rated highly despite a downturn
in performance.*

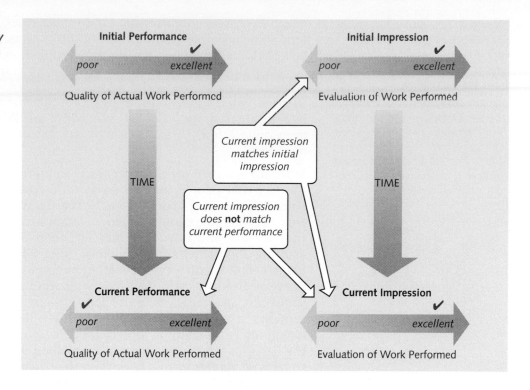

selective perception The tendency to focus on some aspects
of the environment while ignoring others.

Selective perception: Focusing on some things while ignoring others.

A fifth perceptual bias, known as **selective perception** refers to the tendency
for individuals to focus on certain aspects of the environment while ignoring
others.[11] Insofar as people operate in complex environments in which there
are many stimuli that demand our attention, it makes sense that we tend to
be selective, narrowing our perceptual fields. This practice constitutes a bias
insofar as it limits our attention to some stimuli while heightening our attention to other stimuli.

Recent research has shown that this process operates in organizations.
Waller, Huber, and Glick surveyed a large number of top executives from numerous organizations about various aspects of their organizations that contribute to its effectiveness.[12] In general, they found that the executives attended
most to those aspects of the work environments that matched their backgrounds in various functional areas. For example, executives whose backgrounds were in sales and marketing perceived changes in a company's line of
products and services as being most important. Similarly, those who worked
previously in research and development focused more on product designs in
their perceptions of the business environment than on other issues.

In other words, executives tend to be affected by selective perception: They
give greatest attention to those aspects of the business environment that match
their background experiences. This finding underscores our point that the
process of social perception is greatly affected by perceiver variables such as
one's personal history. That is why different people tend to perceive the same
situations very differently.

Stereotypes: Fitting Others into Categories

What comes to mind when you think about people who wear glasses? Are
they studious? Shy? Lackluster? Although there is no evidence of such connections, it is interesting to note that for many people, such images linger in
their minds. Of course, this is only one example. You can probably think of
many other commonly held beliefs about the characteristics of people belonging to specific groups. Such statements usually take the form: "People from

stereotypes Beliefs that all members of specific groups share similar traits and are prone to behave the same way.

The stereotypes we use contribute to the attitudes we hold toward various groups. Thus, the topic of stereotypes will be reintroduced in Chapter 6, where we discuss attitudes toward coworkers.

■ **Figure 3-6**
What Are These People Like?
If you have formed some image of what these individuals are like just from this photograph, you may be relying on stereotypes—judgments of others based on their membership in various groups. Stereotypes may lead to inaccurate judgments, ones that might differ if we took the time to learn about the people we're perceiving.

group *X* possess characteristic *Y*." In most cases, the characteristics described tend to be negative. Assumptions of this type are referred to as **stereotypes**—beliefs that all members of specific groups share similar traits and behaviors.

Deep down inside, many of us know, of course, that not all people from a specific group possess the negative characteristics with which we associate them. In other words, most of us accept that the stereotypes we use are at least partially inaccurate. After all, not *all* *X*s are *Y*; there are exceptions (maybe even quite a few). If so, then why are stereotypes so prevalent? Why do we use them?

Why do we rely on stereotypes? To a great extent, the answer resides in the fact that people tend to do as little cognitive work as possible when it comes to thinking about others.[13] That is, we tend to rely on mental shortcuts. If assigning people to groups allows us to assume that we know what they are like and how they may act, then we can save the tedious work of learning about them as individuals. After all, we come into contact with so many people that it's impractical—if not impossible—to learn everything about them we need to know. So, we rely on readily available information—such as someone's age, race, gender, or job type—as the basis for organizing our perceptions in a coherent way. If you believe that members of group *X* tend to have trait *Y*, then simply observing that someone falls into group *X* becomes the basis for your believing that he or she possesses *Y*. To the extent that the stereotype applies in this case, then the perception will be accurate. However, such mental shorthand often leads us to make inaccurate judgments about people—the price we pay for using stereotypes.

The problem with our tendency to rely on stereotypes, of course, is that it leads us to judge people prematurely, without the benefit of learning more about them than just the categories into which they fit (see Figure 3-6). Still, we all rely on stereotypes at least sometimes; the temptation is far too great to resist.

Using stereotypes in organizations. It is easy to imagine how the use of stereotypes can have powerful effects on the kinds of judgments people make in organizations. For example, if a personnel officer believes that members of certain groups are lazy, then he purposely may avoid hiring or promoting individuals who belong to those groups. The personnel officer may firmly believe that he is using good judgment—gathering all the necessary information

and listening to the candidate carefully. Still, without being aware of it, the stereotypes he holds may influence the way he judges that person. The result, of course, is that the fate of the individual in question is sealed in advance—not necessarily because of anything he or she may have done or said, but by the mere fact that he or she belongs to a certain group. In other words, even people who are not being intentionally bigoted still may be influenced by the stereotypes they hold.

We realize, of course, that the effects of stereotyping others are not always as profound as they are in our example (in which someone was not hired or promoted). Referring to accountants as "bean counters" and professors as "absent minded" are observations that also reflect stereotypes—ones that appear to be only mildly negative. Still, it must be cautioned that holding stereotypes of people in various groups runs the risk of causing miscommunication and conflict between them.

The ways in which stereotypes contribute to problems associated with interpersonal communication and conflict are discussed in Chapters 9 and 11, respectively.

Overcoming Bias in Social Perception: Some Guidelines

For the most part, people's biased perceptions of others are not the result of any malicious intent to inflict harm. Instead, biases in social perception tend to occur because we, as perceivers, are imperfect processors of information. We assume that people are internally responsible for their behavior because we cannot be aware of all the possible situational factors that may be involved. Thus, we make the fundamental attribution error. Further, it is highly impractical to be able to learn everything about someone that may guide our reactions. As a result, we use stereotypes. This does not mean, however, that we cannot minimize the impact of these and other biases. Indeed, there are several steps that can be taken to help promote the accurate perception of others in the workplace:

- *Do not overlook the external causes of others' behavior.* The fundamental attribution error leads us to discount the possibility that people's poor performance may be due to conditions beyond their control. As a result, we may ignore legitimate explanations for poor performance. Ask yourself if anyone else may have performed just as poorly under the same conditions. If the answer is yes, then you should not automatically assume that the poor performer is to blame. Good managers need to make such judgments accurately so that they can decide whether to focus their efforts on developing employees or changing work conditions.
- *Identify and confront your stereotypes.* Let's face it, we all rely on stereotypes—especially when it comes to dealing with new people. Although this tendency is natural, erroneous perceptions are bound to result—and quite possibly, at the expense of someone else. For this reason, it's good to identify the stereotypes you hold. Doing so will help you become more aware of them, taking a giant step toward minimizing their impact on your behavior. After all, unless you are aware of your stereotypes, you may never be able to counter them.
- *Evaluate people based on objective factors.* The more objective the information you use to judge others, the less your judgments will be subjected to perceptual distortion. People tend to bias subjective judgments in ways that are self-serving (such as positively evaluating the work of those we like and negatively evaluating the work of those we dislike). To the extent that evaluations are based on objective information, this error is less likely to occur.
- *Avoid making rash judgments.* It is human nature to jump to conclusions about what people are like, even when we know very little about them. Take the time to get to know people better before convincing yourself that you already know all you need to know about them. What you learn just may make a big difference in your opinion.

We realize that many of these tactics are far easier to extol than to practice. However, to the extent that we conscientiously try to apply these suggestions to our everyday interactions with others in the workplace, we stand a good chance of perceiving people more accurately. And this is a fundamental ingredient in the recipe for managerial success.

Perceiving Others: Organizational Applications

Thus far, we have identified some of the basic processes of social perception and have alluded to ways in which they are involved in organizational behavior. Now, in this section we will make these connections more explicit. Specifically, we will describe the role of perception in three organizational activities: employee performance appraisal, the employment interview, and the organization's development of its corporate image.

Performance Appraisals: Making Formal Judgments about Others

performance appraisal The process of evaluating employees on various work-related dimensions.

One of the most obvious instances in which social perception occurs is when someone formally evaluates the job performance of another. This process, known as **performance appraisal**, occurs in organizations—often on an annual or semiannual basis—for purposes of determining raises, promotions, and training needs.[14] Ideally, this process should be completely rational, leading to unbiased and objective judgments about exactly how well each employee has performed and how he or she should be treated. However, based on what we have said about perception thus far, you're probably not surprised to learn that the performance evaluation process is far from objective. Indeed, people have a limited capacity to process, store, and retrieve information, making them prone to bias when it comes to evaluating others (see Figure 3-7).[15]

Several such biases have been observed by researchers. For example, it has been shown that people's ratings of other's performance depends on the extent to which that performance is consistent with their expectations. Specifically, in one study Hogan asked bank managers to indicate how well they expected their newest tellers to perform their jobs.[16] Four months later, they were asked to rate the tellers' actual job performance. It was found that managers gave higher ratings to those tellers whose performance matched their earlier expectations than to those who did either better or worse than predicted. These effects are unsettling insofar as they suggest that the improved performance of some employees may go unrecognized—or, worse yet, be downgraded. Of course, to the

■ **Figure 3-7**
Performance Appraisals: Subject to Bias
The process of evaluating others' job performance, so vital to making important organizational decisions, such as pay raises, is subject to several sources of error and bias. Acknowledging this, the gentlemen shown here appear to be using quite another basis for determining pay raises.

(Copyright © 1991, 1994 by Andrew Toos. Reprinted by permission.)

"Beats the hell out of performance reviews."

extent that human resource management decisions are made on the basis of several sources of information, not merely judgments by single superiors, it is unlikely that such biased judgments may go uncorrected. Nonetheless, these findings clearly underscore a key point: Perceptions are based not only on the characteristics of the person being perceived, but the perceiver as well.

This conclusion is supported by research showing several different attribution biases in evaluations of job performance. We can illustrate just one of these if we recall our earlier discussion of the similar-to-me effect, showing that people tend to perceive more positively those who are similar to themselves than those who are dissimilar. A recent study by Wayne and Liden has demonstrated this effect in the context of performance appraisals.[17] Studying 111 pairs of superiors who were rating their subordinates in performing a variety of different jobs, they found that the more employees did things to cultivate positive impressions on their superiors (e.g., do favors for them, agree with their opinions), the more their superiors viewed them as being similar to themselves. And the more their superiors judged them to be similar to themselves, the more highly the superiors evaluated their work.

Employees often attempt to make themselves look good to superiors by sharing explanations for their work that focus on the internal reasons underlying good performance and the external reasons underlying poor performance. Indeed, it has been shown that two equally good performers are unlikely to receive the same performance ratings when different attributions are made about the underlying causes of their performance. Managers tend to give higher ratings to individuals whose poor performance is attributed to factors outside the individual's control (e.g., someone who is trying hard but is too inexperienced to succeed) than to those whose poor performance they attribute to internal factors (e.g., those who are believed to be capable but who are just lazy and holding back). In other words, our evaluations of others' performance are qualified by the nature of the attributions we make about that performance.

Findings such as these illustrate our point that organizational performance evaluations are far from the unbiased, rational procedures one would hope to find. Instead, they represent a complex mix of perceptual biases—effects that must be appreciated and well understood if we are to have any chance of ultimately improving the accuracy of the performance evaluation process.

Impression Management in the Employment Interview: Looking Good to Prospective Employers

The desire to make a favorable impression on others is universal. In one way or another, we all do things to control how other people see us, often attempting to get them to think of us in the best light possible. This process is known as **impression management**.[18] Generally, individuals devote considerable attention to the impressions they create in the eyes of others—especially when these others are important, such as prospective employers.

impression management
Efforts by individuals to improve how they appear to others.

The impressions that prospective employers form of us may be based on subtle behaviors, such as how we dress and speak, or more elaborate acts, such as announcing our accomplishments.[19] They may be the result of calculated efforts to get others to think of us in a certain way or be the passive, unintended effects of our actions. When it comes to the employment interview, there are several things job candidates commonly do to enhance the impressions they make. In a recent study Stevens and Kristof audiotaped the interviews between college students looking for jobs and representatives of companies that posted openings at the campus job placement center.[20] The various statements made by the candidates were categorized with respect to the impression management techniques they used. Several tactics were commonly observed. Table 3-1 lists these specific tactics, gives an example of each,

Researchers have system-atically recorded and categorized the things job applicants say to present themselves favorably to the recruiters interviewing them. Here is a listing of techniques used in one sam-ple recently studied, along with the frequencies with which they were used. Descriptions and exam-ples of each technique are also given.

Impression Management Technique	Description (Example)	Frequency of Use
Self-promotion	Directly describing oneself in a positive manner for the situation at hand (e.g., "I am a hard worker").	100%
Personal stories	Describing past events that make oneself look good (e.g., "In my old job, I worked late anytime it was needed").	96%
Opinion conformity	Expressing beliefs that can be assumed to be held by the target (e.g., agreeing with something the interviewer says).	54%
Entitlements	Claiming responsibility for successful past events (e.g., "I was responsible for the 90% sales increase that resulted").	50%
Other enhancement	Making statements that flatter, praise or compliment the target (e.g., "I am very impressed with your company's growth in recent years").	46%
Enhancements	Claiming that a positive event was more positive than it really was (e.g., "Not only did our department improve, but it was the best in the entire company").	42%
Overcoming obstacles	Describing how one succeeded in the face of obstacles that would have lowered performance (e.g., "I managed to get a 3.8 average although I worked two part-time jobs").	33%
Justifications	Accepting responsibility for one's poor performance but denying the negative implications of it (e.g., "Our team didn't win a lot, but it's just how you play the game that really matters").	17%
Excuses	Denying responsibility for one's actions (e.g., "I didn't complete the application form because the placement center ran out of them").	13%

SOURCE: Based on information in Stevens & Kristoff, 1995; see Note 20.

and shows the percentage of candidates who used these techniques. Interestingly, the most common technique was *self-promotion*—flatly asserting that one has desirable characteristics. In this case, candidates commonly described themselves as being hardworking, interpersonally skilled, and goal-oriented, as well as effective leaders.

Importantly, the study also found that candidates used these impression management techniques with great success. The more they relied on these tactics, the more positively they were viewed by the interviewer along several important dimensions (e.g., fit with the organization). This study not only confirms that job candidates do indeed rely on impression management techniques during job interviews, but also that these tend to cultivate the positive impressions desired. With this in mind, the job interview may be seen as an ongoing effort on behalf of candidates to present themselves as favorably as possible and for interviewers to try to see through those attempts, trying to judge candidates accurately. As the evidence suggests, this task may be considered far from simple.

YOU BE THE CONSULTANT

A car dealership has been having problems retaining its new salespeople. The general manager suspects that the problem rests in the selection process: Candidates for sales positions are so convincing that they are selling themselves, making it hard for the company to accurately assess the candidates' shortcomings.

1. What interview questions might be asked that will help "cut through" the smoke created by these expert salespeople?

2. What biases might the dealership face when it comes to accurately assessing these individuals? How might these be overcome?

Corporate Image: Impression Management by Organizations

corporate image The impressions that people have of an organization.

It is not only individuals who desire to cultivate positive impressions of themselves, but entire organizations, too—what has been termed **corporate image**.[21] As you might imagine, the impression an organization makes on people can have a considerable effect on the way these individuals relate to it. Extending our discussion of the job recruitment setting, not only do individual candidates want to make good impressions on prospective employers, but employers want their job offers to be accepted by the best candidates.

The importance of a corporate image in this context has been demonstrated in a study by Gatewood, Gowam, and Lautenschlager.[22] These researchers found that a company's image is strongly related to people's interest in seeking employment with it. Specifically, the more favorably a company's reputation was rated (based on a *Fortune* magazine survey), the more interested a group of college seniors was in working there. (For a list of some of the most admired companies identified in a recent *Fortune* survey, see Table 3-2.[23]) This is important insofar as organizations must effectively recruit prospective employees to function effectively. Given this important point, it seems worthwhile to consider exactly what factors contribute to a corporate image.

Interestingly, Gatewood and his colleagues found that a company's image was positively correlated with the amount of information people had about it (such as from previous work experiences and recruitment ads in college placement guides). In general, longer ads were associated with more positive images. This finding is likely the result of not only what is in the ad, but the mere length of the ad itself. Specifically, because recruitment ads emphasize the benefits of employment with a firm, longer ads describe more benefits than shorter ones, thereby creating even stronger positive images. Moreover, to the extent that people believe that longer ads reflect a company's commitment to obtaining good employees (by their willingness to invest in a large ad), they may be more impressed with a company as a prospective place to work.

Another mechanism that organizations use to promote their corporate images is their *annual reports*—a company's official statement to its stockholders on its activities and financial well-being. Traditionally, these are strikingly beautiful glossy booklets with elaborate photography and glitzy images, trappings of success designed to instill confidence in the minds of investors. In recent years, however, many companies—St. Paul Companies, Avery Dennison, and General Dynamics, among them—have spared such expenses,

■ TABLE 3-2	AMERICA'S MOST ADMIRED COMPANIES	

According to a recent survey by Fortune *magazine, the following companies are the most admired ones in the United States, as based on ratings on eight important characteristics. Positive corporate images are important insofar as they help attract qualified job candidates.*

Rank	Company	Principal Product or Service
1	Rubbermaid	Rubber household products
2	Microsoft	Computer software
3	Coca-Cola	Soft drinks
4	Motorola	Electronic equipment
5	Home Depot	Specialty hardware
6	Intel	Computer chips
7	Procter & Gamble	Soap products
8	3M	Scientific equipment
9	United Parcel Service	Small parcel delivery
10	Hewlett-Packard	Computers and office equipment

SOURCE: Based on Jacob, 1995; see Note 23.

issuing bare-bones annual reports in 1994.[24] They have done so to promote an image of austerity. As today's investors are looking for value, companies are going out of their way to cultivate the impression that they're not wasting money. Looking *too* successful by squandering money on elaborate annual reports may raise questions about where the profits are going. So, whether these publications are elaborate or just plain vanilla, the conclusion is the same: Annual reports are designed to cultivate "the right" corporate image, whatever that may be. Our overall conclusion is clear: Organizations, just like individuals, stand to benefit by making positive impressions on others, and work hard at doing so.

As you might imagine, it is not only in organizations that people seek to make positive impressions, but in other walks of life too. For a look at a fascinating business that has developed recently in Japan from the great concern that the Japanese people have for being perceived positively by others, see the GLOBALIZATION AND DIVERSITY IN TODAY'S ORGANIZATIONS section.

Learning: Adapting to the World around Us

Recall our PREVIEW CASE about Taco, the small company that made a big investment in developing the skills of its employees. Thus far, we have focused on one of the basic human processes involved in this case—perception. Now,

GLOBALIZATION AND DIVERSITY IN TODAY'S ORGANIZATIONS

SAVING FACE IN JAPAN, WHERE RENTING ACQUAINTANCES IS BIG BUSINESS

Generally, we think of the need to make positive impressions on others as a universal phenomenon: We all wish to be highly regarded by others. To be thought of in a negative manner is shameful. However, it appears that people in some nations are more sensitive to shame than others. Among present-day Japanese, the concern over shame is so great that a big business has grown out of the need to avoid shame. Agencies called *benriya* have sprung up to help people avoid the loss of face they would suffer by not having their social events go just right.[25] In general, these agencies provide stand-ins at various functions. These "rented acquaintances" are, in reality, strangers, but no one except the customer ever knows that.

One bride, fearing that a small turnout at her wedding would embarrass her family, paid Kazushi Ookunitani's "All Purpose Company" $10,000 to rent 40 fake friends. To avoid arousing suspicion, the actors were all thoroughly briefed on the bride's background. So convincing was the charade that some even rose to give speeches at the reception. Another bride hired all her guests, except for her parents and one friend, for fear that real friends would get talking and divulge that she was divorced, a status that holds a social stigma in Japan. Men use stand-ins at their weddings too, usually distinguished-

looking gentlemen posing as the grooms' bosses, whose attendance at one's wedding reception is seen as a sign of honor. For one's boss not to attend would be embarrassing, but it must never come to pass—at least if a groom can get an actor to play the part. And during the busy autumn wedding season, such accomplices may be hard to come by.

But these agencies don't limit their business to weddings. *Benriya* employees also have been sent to funerals so that the requisite number of mourners would be present. They've even been hired at welcome-home parties for people just released from prison. Some young men have gone so far as to hire actors posing as thugs to stage unsuccessful muggings just so they could impress their girlfriends with their bravery. Again, these are not the plots of bad situation comedies, but real-life events that have been occurring in Japan.

To understand these activities is to understand the importance of saving face in modern-day Japanese culture. "It has a lot to do with keeping up appearances," says Ookunitani. Indeed, the entire *benriya* industry is designed to help cultivate whatever image one wishes to convey. And, when this task cannot be performed alone, Mr. Ookunitani and his colleagues stand ready to help (for a fee, of course).

we will turn our attention to the other basic psychological process involved in this case—*learning*.

Whether we're talking about how a person develops new job skills, social skills, or general life skills, many of the same basic processes are involved. Clearly, learning is a fundamental process in organizational behavior. In fact, the more a company fosters an environment in which employees are able to learn, the more productive and profitable it is likely to be.[26] Naturally, scientists in the field of OB are extremely interested in understanding the process of learning—both how it occurs, and how it may be applied to the effective functioning of organizations.

Before we turn our attention to these matters, we should first explain exactly what we mean by learning. Specifically, we define **learning** as a relatively permanent change in behavior occurring as a result of experience.[27] Despite its simplicity, several aspects of this definition bear pointing out. First, it's clear that learning requires that some kind of *change* occurs. Second, this change must be more than just temporary. Finally, it must be the result of *experience*—that is, continued contact with the world around us. Given this definition, we cannot say that short-lived performance changes on the job, such as those due to illness or fatigue, are the result of learning. Learning is a difficult concept for scientists to study because it cannot be directly observed. Instead, it must be inferred on the basis of relatively permanent changes in behavior.

We will now consider two of the most prevalent forms of learning that occur in organizations—*operant conditioning* and *observational learning*.

Operant Conditioning: Learning through Rewards and Punishments

Imagine you are a chef working at a catering company where you are planning a special menu for a fussy client. If your dinner menu is accepted and the meal is a hit, the company stands a good chance of adding a huge new account. You work hard at doing the best job possible and present your culinary creations to the skeptical client. Now, how does the story end? If the client loves your meal, your grateful boss gives you a huge raise and a promotion. However, if the client hates it, your boss asks you to turn in your chef's hat. Regardless of which of these outcomes occurs, one thing is certain: Whatever you did in this situation, you will be sure to do it again *if* it was successful and avoid doing it again *if* it failed.

This situation nicely illustrates an important principle of **operant conditioning** (also known as **instrumental conditioning**)—namely, that our behavior produces consequences and the way we behave in the future will depend on what those consequences are. If our actions have pleasant effects, then we will be more likely to repeat them in the future. If, however, our actions have unpleasant effects, we are less likely to repeat them in the future. This phenomenon, known as the **Law of Effect**, is fundamental to operant conditioning. Our knowledge of this phenomenon comes from the work of the famous social scientist B. F. Skinner.[28] Skinner's research has shown us that it is through the connections between our actions and their consequences that we learn to behave in certain ways. We summarize this process in Figure 3-8.

Reinforcement contingencies. Operant conditioning is based on the idea that our behavior is learned because of the positive outcomes that we associate with it. In organizations, for example, people usually find it pleasant and desirable to receive monetary bonuses, paid vacations, and various forms of recognition. The process by which people learn to perform acts leading to such desirable outcomes is known as **positive reinforcement**. The behavior that led to the positive outcomes is likely to occur again, thereby strengthening that behavior. For a reward to serve as a positive reinforcer, it must be made contingent on the specific behavior sought. So, for example, if a sales representative is given a bonus after landing a huge account, that bonus will only

The process of learning is heavily involved in the way newcomers to organizations learn the ropes (known as socialization). We will pay special attention to this process in Chapter 11.

learning A relatively permanent change in behavior occurring as a result of experience.

operant conditioning (or **instrumental conditioning**) The form of learning in which people associate the consequences of their actions with the actions themselves. Behaviors with positive consequences are acquired; behaviors with negative consequences tend to be eliminated.

Law of Effect The tendency for behaviors leading to desirable consequences to be strengthened and those leading to undesirable consequences to be weakened.

positive reinforcement The process by which people learn to perform behaviors that lead to the presentation of desired outcomes.

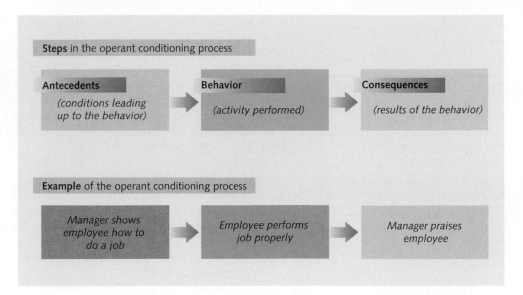

The basic premise of operant conditioning *is that people learn by connecting the consequences of their behavior
with the behavior itself. In this example,
the manager's praise increases the subordinate's tendency to perform the job
properly in the future. Learning occurs
by providing the appropriate antecedents and consequences.*

negative reinforcement (or
avoidance) The process by
which people learn to perform
acts that lead to the removal of
undesired events.

reinforce the person's actions *if* he or she associates it with the landing of the
account. When this occurs, the individual will be more inclined in the future
to do whatever it was that helped get the account.

Sometimes we also learn to perform acts because they permit us to avoid
undesirable consequences. Unpleasant events, such as reprimands, rejection,
probation, and termination are some of the consequences faced for certain
negative actions in the workplace. The process by which people learn to perform acts leading to the avoidance of such undesirable consequences is known
as **negative reinforcement**, or **avoidance**. Whatever response led to the
termination of these undesirable events is likely to occur again, thereby
strengthening that response. For example, you may stay late at the office one
evening to revise a sales presentation because you believe that the boss will
"chew you out" if it's not ready in the morning. You learned how to avoid this
type of aversive situation and behave accordingly.

Thus far, we have identified responses that are strengthened—either because they lead to positive consequences, or the termination of negative consequences. However, the connection between a behavior and its consequences
is not always strengthened; such links also may be weakened. This is what hap-

punishment Decreasing undesirable behavior by following it
with undesirable consequences.

pens in the case of **punishment**. Punishment involves presenting an undesirable or aversive consequence in response to an unwanted behavior. A
behavior accompanied by an undesirable outcome is less likely to recur if the
person associates the negative consequences with the behavior. For example,
if you are chastised by your boss for taking excessively long coffee breaks, you
may be considered punished for this action. As a result, you will be less likely
to take long breaks again in the future.

extinction The process through
which responses that are no
longer reinforced tend to gradually diminish in strength.

The link between a behavior and its consequences also may be weakened
by withholding reward—a process known as **extinction**. When a response that
was once rewarded is no longer rewarded, it tends to weaken and eventually
die out—to be *extinguished*. Let's consider an example. Suppose for many months
you brought boxes of donuts to your weekly staff meetings. Your colleagues always thanked you as they gobbled them down. You were positively reinforced
by their approval, so you continued bringing the donuts. Now, after several
months of eating donuts, your colleagues have begun dieting. So, although
tempting, your donuts go uneaten. After several months of no longer being
praised for your generosity, you will be unlikely to continue bringing donuts.
Your once-rewarded behavior will no doubt cease; it will be extinguished.

The various relationships between a person's behavior and the consequences resulting from it—*positive reinforcement, negative reinforcement, punish-*

contingencies of reinforcement The various relationships between one's behavior and the consequences of that behavior—positive reinforcement, negative reinforcement, punishment, and extinction.

continuous reinforcement A schedule of reinforcement in which all desired behaviors are reinforced.

partial (or **intermittent**) **reinforcement** A schedule of reinforcement in which only some desired behaviors are reinforced. Types include: fixed interval, variable interval, fixed ratio, and variable ratio.

fixed interval schedules Schedules of reinforcement in which a fixed period of time must elapse between the administration of reinforcements.

variable interval schedules Schedules of reinforcement in which a variable period of time (based on some average) must elapse between the administration of reinforcements.

ment, and *extinction*—are known collectively as **contingencies of reinforcement**. They represent the conditions under which rewards and punishments will either be given or taken away. The four contingencies we discussed are summarized in Table 3-3. As we will see later in this chapter, administering these contingencies can be an effective tool for managing behavior in organizations.

Schedules of reinforcement: Patterns of administering rewards. Thus far, our discussion of whether a reward will be presented or withdrawn has assumed that presentation or withdrawal will follow *each* occurrence of behavior. However, it is not always practical (or, as we will see, advisable) to do this. Rewarding *every* desired response made is called **continuous reinforcement**. Unlike animals performing tricks in a circus, however, people on the job are rarely reinforced continuously. Instead, organizational rewards tend to be administered following **partial** (or **intermittent**) **reinforcement** schedules: That is, rewards are administered intermittently, with some desired responses reinforced and others not. Four varieties of partial reinforcement schedules have direct application to organizations.[29]

1. **Fixed interval schedules** are those in which reinforcement is administered the first time the desired behavior occurs after a specific amount of time has passed. For example, the practice of issuing paychecks each Friday at 3:00 P.M. is an example of a fixed interval schedule insofar as the rewards are administered at regular times. Fixed interval schedules are not especially effective in maintaining desired behavior. For example, employees who know that their boss will pass by their desks every day at 11:30 A.M. will make sure they are working hard at that time. However, without the boss around to praise them, they may take an early lunch or otherwise work less hard because they know that they will not be positively reinforced for their efforts or punished for not working.

2. **Variable interval schedules** are those in which a variable amount of time (based on some average amount) must elapse between the administration of reinforcements. For example, consider a bank auditor who pays surprise visits to the branch offices an average of once every six weeks (e.g., visits may be four weeks apart one time and eight weeks apart another time). The auditor may be said to be using a variable interval schedule. Because the bank managers cannot tell exactly when their branch may be audited, they cannot afford to slack off. Not surprisingly, variable interval schedules tend to be more effective than fixed interval schedules.

■ TABLE 3-3	CONTINGENCIES OF REINFORCEMENT: A SUMMARY				
The four reinforcement contingencies may be defined in terms of the presentation or withdrawal of a pleasant or unpleasant stimulus. Positively or negatively reinforced behaviors are strengthened; punished or extinguished behaviors are weakened.	Stimulus Presented or Withdrawn	Desirability of Stimulus	Name of Contingency	Strength of Response	Example
	Presented	Pleasant	Positive reinforcement	Increases	Praise from a supervisor encourages continuing the praised behavior
		Unpleasant	Punishment	Decreases	Criticism from a supervisor discourages enacting the punished behavior
	Withdrawn	Pleasant	Extinction	Decreases	Failing to praise a helpful act reduces the odds of helping in the future
		Unpleasant	Negative reinforcement	Increases	Future criticism is avoided by doing whatever the supervisor wants

fixed ratio schedules
Schedules of reinforcement in which a fixed number of responses must occur between the administration of reinforcements.

variable ratio schedules
Schedules of reinforcement in which a variable number of responses (based on some average) must occur between the administration of reinforcements.

schedules of reinforcement
Rules governing the timing and frequency of the administration of reinforcement.

observational learning (or **modeling**) The form of learning in which people acquire new behaviors by systematically observing the rewards and punishments given to others.

3. **Fixed ratio schedules** are those in which reinforcement is administered the first time the desired behavior occurs after a specified number of such actions have been performed. For example, suppose members of a sales staff know that they will receive a bonus for each $1,000 worth of goods they sell. Immediately after receiving the first reward, performance may slack off. But as their sales begin to approach $2,000, the next level at which reward is expected, performance will once again improve.

4. **Variable ratio schedules** are those in which a variable number of desired responses (based on some average amount) must elapse between the administration of reinforcements. A classic example may be seen in the behavior of people playing slot machines. Most of the time when people put a coin into the slot they lose. But after some unknown number of plays, the machine will pay off. Because gamblers can never tell which pull of the handle will win the jackpot, they are likely to keep on playing for a long time. As you might imagine, variable ratio schedules tend to be more effective than fixed ratio schedules.

The various patterns described are known as **schedules of reinforcement**—rules governing the timing and frequency of the administration of reinforcement. We have summarized these schedules in Figure 3-9. As you review this figure, keep in mind that these schedules represent "pure" forms. Used in practice, several different reinforcement schedules may be combined, making complex new schedules. Still, whether they operate separately or in conjunction with one another, it is important to recognize the strong influences that schedules of reinforcement can have on people's behavior in organizations.

Observational Learning: Learning by Imitating Others

Although operant conditioning is based on the idea that we engage in behaviors for which we are directly reinforced, many of the things we learn on the job are *not* directly reinforced. Suppose, for example, that on your new job you see many of your co-workers complimenting your boss on his attire. Each time someone says something flattering, the boss stops at his or her desk, smiles, and acts friendly. By complimenting the boss, they are reinforced by being granted his social approval. Chances are, after observing this several times, you too will eventually learn to say something nice to the boss. Although you may not have directly experienced the boss's approval, you would expect to receive it based on what you have observed from others. This is an example of a kind of learning known as **observational learning**, or **modeling**.[30] It occurs when someone acquires new knowledge *vicariously*—that is, by observing what happens to others. The person whose behavior is imitated is referred to as the *model*.

For someone to learn by observing a model, several processes must occur.

1. The learner must pay careful *attention* to the model: The greater the attention, the more effective the learning will be. To facilitate learning, models sometimes call attention to themselves. This is what happens when supervisors admonish their subordinates to "pay close attention" to what they're doing.

2. People must have good *retention* of the model's behavior. It helps to be able to develop a verbal description or a mental image of someone's actions in order to remember them. After all, we cannot learn from observing behavior we cannot remember.

3. There must be some *behavioral reproduction* of the model's behavior. Unless people are capable of doing exactly what the models do, they will not be able to learn from observing them. Naturally, this ability may be limited at first but improve with practice.

4. People must have some *motivation* to learn from the model. Of course, we don't emulate every behavior we see but focus on those we have some

■ **Figure 3-9**
Schedules of Reinforcement:
A Summary
The four schedules of reinforcement sum-
marized here represent different ways of
administering reward intermittently.

Fixed Interval

Rewards are given after a constant
amount of time has passed.

Boss gives out pay checks at
the same exact time each week.

Variable Interval

Rewards are given after a
variable amount of time
has passed.

Teacher gives a pop quiz an average
of once a week, but not always on the same day.

Fixed Ratio

Rewards are given after a
constant number of actions
are performed.

A farm hand is paid $1 for every
four boxes of fruit picked and packed.

Variable Ratio

Rewards are given after a
variable number of actions
are performed.

A slot machine pays a large jackpot on
the average of once per million plays.

reason or incentive to match—such as actions for which others are rewarded. For a summary of these processes, see Figure 3-10.

A great deal of what is learned about how to behave in organizations can
be explained as the result of the process of observational learning.[31] On the
job, observational learning is a key part of many formal job-instruction training programs.[32] As we will explain in the next section, trainees given a chance
to observe experts doing their jobs, followed by an opportunity to practice the
desired skills and given feedback on their work, tend to learn new job skills
quite effectively. Observational learning also occurs in a very informal, uncal-
culated manner. For example, people who experience the norms and traditions

The process of observational learning
requires that an observer pay attention
to and remember a model's behavior.
By observing what the model did and
rehearsing those actions, the observer
may learn to imitate the model, but
only if the observer is motivated to do
so (i.e., if the model was rewarded for
behaving as observed).

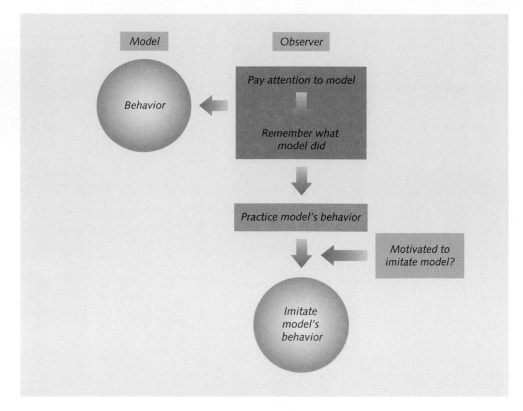

of their organizations and who subsequently incorporate these into their own behavior may be recognized as having learned through observation. It is important to note that people learn not only what to do by observing others, but also what *not* to do. Specifically, research has shown that people observing their co-workers getting punished for behaving inappropriately on the job tend to refrain from engaging in those same actions themselves.[33] As you might imagine, this is a very effective way for people to learn how to behave—and, without ever experiencing any displeasure themselves.

Applications of Learning in Organizations

The principles of learning we have discussed thus far are used in organizations in many different ways. We will now discuss three systematic approaches to incorporating learning in organizations: *training, organizational behavior management*, and *discipline*.

Training: Learning and Developing Job Skills

Probably the most obvious use to which principles of learning may be applied in organizations is **training**—that is, the process through which people systematically acquire and improve the skills and knowledge needed to better job performances. Just as students learn basic educational skills in the classroom, employees must learn job skills. Training is used not only to prepare new employees to meet the challenges of the jobs they will face, but also to upgrade and refine the skills of existing employees. In fact, according to the American Society for Training and Development, American companies spend over $44 billion on training annually.[34]

Training takes many forms. For example, growing in popularity are *apprenticeship programs*, in which classroom training is systematically combined with on-the-job instruction. In view of the importance of such programs in

training The process of systematically teaching employees to acquire and improve job-related skills and knowledge.

THE ETHICS ANGLE

THE TAILHOOK SCANDAL: VICARIOUSLY REINFORCING UNETHICAL BEHAVIOR

In 1992, several hundred men in the U.S. Navy were accused of sexually harassing some 90 U.S. Navy women while attending a meeting at a Las Vegas hotel.[35] The specific accusations are too distasteful to recount, but suffice it to say that the infractions were not only serious but quite widespread. In fact, such incidents of harassment had been going on regularly during these meetings for several years—rituals that the male sailors regarded as fun, rewards associated with attending.

When complaints were issued in the past, Navy brass simply turned a blind eye to the incidents, suggesting that "boys will be boys." In 1992, however, the outcries went public, resulting in the resignation of the Secretary of the Navy. But still, not much else happened. The navy's highest ranking admiral was asked to resign, but he later received a reprieve from the Secretary of Defense. And of the hundreds of men alleged to be involved, only a handful were disciplined at all—and, only very slightly. Two years later, the woman who filed the initial complaint, Lt. Paula Coughlin, was forced to resign from the navy, explaining that the hateful treatment she received following the incident limited her ability to serve. Bottom line: ninety women were assaulted, but not one of the men responsible ever faced a court-martial or any other serious disciplinary action.

Some have questioned whether this response sends the message that at least some degree of sexual harassment is permitted by the navy—unofficially, of course.[36] When undesirable behavior is left unpunished, the message is sent that such behavior is condoned. The message that is learned vicariously by observing such tolerant reactions to unethical behavior must be carefully considered, not only by the U.S. Navy but by any organization desiring to curb such behavior.

---

developing human resources, the U.S. federal government lately has invested hundreds of millions of dollars in apprenticeship programs, encouraging training partnerships between government and private industry.[37]

Also currently popular are *executive training programs*—sessions in which companies systematically attempt to develop the skills of their top managers, such as how to use computer software,[38] or more general skills, such as how to get along with others.[39] This is accomplished either by bringing in outside experts to train personnel in-house, or by sending them to specialized programs conducted by private consulting firms or by colleges and universities.[40]

Many executive training sessions focus on the development of leadership skills. Our discussion of leadership in Chapter 13 highlights some of these approaches.

In fact, some companies (e.g., Apple Computer, the Tennessee Valley Authority, Motorola, and Sprint), are so serious about training that they have developed their own *corporate universities*—centers devoted to handling a company's training needs on a full-time basis. Among the best-known is McDonald's "Hamburger University" in which McDonald's franchisees from all over the world learn and/or polish the skills needed to successfully operate a McDonald's restaurant (see Figure 3-11).

It is important to note that most organizational training is not as formal as the approaches we have been describing. Still, training is involved in everyday job instruction in which employees simply are told about the job, shown how to do it, and allowed to practice as a more experienced co-worker watches and offers suggestions. Informal though it may be, this is also training, and it requires every bit as much attention to the principles of learning for it to be successful as any more formal method.

As you might imagine, no one approach to training is ideal. Some techniques are better suited to learning certain skills because they incorporate more principles of learning. Not surprisingly, the best training programs often use many different approaches, thereby assuring that several different learning principles may be incorporated into training.[41] If you recall some of the ways you learned skills such as how to study, drive, or use a word processor, you probably can appreciate some of the principles that help make training effective. Four major principles are most relevant.

■ **Figure 3-11**
McDonald's "Hamburger University": A Full-Time Training Center
Many of today's companies have opened full-time facilities dedicated to training employees on a wide variety of necessary skills. McDonald's "Hamburger University" is one of the first such centers, and among the most elaborate.

participation Active involvement in the process of learning; more active participation leads to more effective learning.

repetition The process of repeatedly performing a task so that it may be learned.

transfer of training The degree to which the skills learned during training sessions may be applied to performance of one's job.

feedback Knowledge of the results of one's behavior.

1. **Participation**. People not only learn more quickly, but also retain the skills longer when they have actively participated in the learning process. This applies to the learning of both motor tasks as well as cognitive skills. For example, when learning to swim, there's no substitute for actually getting in the water and moving your arms and legs. In the classroom, students who listen attentively to lectures, think about the material, and get involved in discussions tend to learn more effectively than those who just sit passively.

2. **Repetition**. If you know the old adage "Practice makes perfect," you are already aware of the benefits of repetition for learning. Perhaps you learned the multiplication table, or a poem, or a foreign language phrase by going over it repeatedly. Indeed, mentally "rehearsing" such cognitive tasks has been shown to increase our effectiveness at performing them.[42] Scientists have established not only the benefits of repetition on learning, but have shown that these effects are even greater when practice is spread out over time than when it is lumped together. After all, when practice periods are too long, learning can suffer from fatigue, whereas learning a little bit at a time allows the material to sink in.

3. **Transfer of training**. As you might imagine, for training to be most effective, what is learned during training sessions must be applied on the job. In general, the more closely a training program matches the demands and conditions faced on a job, the more effective that training will be. A good example is the elaborate simulation devices used to train pilots and astronauts. More down to earth is the equipment used in many technical schools for people to learn skilled trades such as welding, computer repair, and radiation technology. By closely simulating actual job conditions and equipment, training skills are expected to transfer to the job.

   The same may be said of training on supervisory skills. In this context, research has shown that the benefits of training are best realized when the trainees attempt to apply their newly learned skills in organizations that accept the forms of supervision they learned.[43] However, learning to supervise others in ways that may be resisted back on the job may be not only a waste of time, but potentially disruptive as well.

4. **Feedback**. It is extremely difficult for learning to occur in the absence of feedback—that is, knowledge of the results of one's actions. Feedback provides information about the effectiveness of one's training.[44] Of course, unless you learn what you already are doing well and what be-

haviors you need to correct, you probably will be unable to improve your skills. For example, it is critical for people being trained as word processing operators to know exactly how many words they correctly entered per minute if they are to be able to gauge their improvement.

One type of feedback that has become popular in recent years is known as **360° feedback**—the process of using multiple sources from around the organization to evaluate the work of a single individual. This goes beyond simply collecting feedback from superiors, as is customary, but extends the gathering of feedback from other sources, such as one's peers, direct reports (i.e., immediate subordinates), and customers—even oneself (see Figure 3-12).[45] Many companies—General Electric, AT&T, Digital Equipment Corporation, Nabisco, and Warner-Lambert among them—have used 360° feedback to give more complete performance information to their employees, greatly improving not only their own work but overall corporate productivity as well.

In sum, these four principles—*participation, repetition, transfer of training,* and *feedback*—are key to the effectiveness of any training program. The most effective training programs are those that incorporate as many of these principles as possible. In recent years, large organizations have found it worthwhile not only to train their own employees, as we have been discussing, but also to train the employees of other companies with which they do business. For a closer look at this unusual practice, see the QUEST FOR QUALITY section on page 97.

see the QUEST FOR QUALITY section on page 97.

Organizational Behavior Management: Positively Reinforcing Desirable Organizational Behaviors

Earlier, in describing operant conditioning, we noted that the consequences of our behavior determines whether we repeat it or abandon it. Behaviors that are rewarded tend to be strengthened and repeated in the future. With this in mind, it is possible to administer rewards selectively to help reinforce behaviors that we wish repeated in the future. This is the basic principle behind **organizational behavior management** (also known as **organizational behavior modification**, or more simply, **OB Mod**). Organizational behavior management may be defined as the systematic application of positive reinforcement principles in organizational settings for the purpose of raising the incidence of desirable organizational behaviors.

To be effective in using organizational behavior management programs, managers should follow the steps outlined as follows:[46]

1. *Pinpoint the desired behaviors.* That is, specify exactly what you want done differently (e.g., saying that you want to answer customers' inquiries 50 percent quicker, instead of saying that you want to improve customer service).
2. *Perform a baseline audit.* In other words, determine exactly how well people perform the behavior they wish to change (e.g., how quickly do they currently answer calls?).
3. *Define a criterion standard.* Determine exactly what performance goal is being sought. For example, should all calls be answered within the first 30 seconds?
4. *Choose a reinforcer.* Decide exactly how the desired behavior will be rewarded. Will service agents be given a bonus for answering all calls received in a month within 30 seconds? If so, what form will the bonus take? Many of today's companies have been using nonmonetary incentives, in part because they serve as reminders of one's accomplishments (a $100 check can be gone in no time flat, but the reward value of a trophy on the mantle persists for a long time).[47] Some nonmonetary incentives have been quite exotic, such as the hot air balloon trips over the Napa Valley and mountain climbing expedition to the Swiss Alps offered

---

360° feedback The practice of collecting performance feedback from multiple sources at a variety of organizational levels.

Because 360° feedback also helps assess the performance of an organization as a whole, it is often used in conjunction with organization development efforts. Such practices are presented in Chapter 16.

organizational behavior management (also known as **organizational behavior modification** or **OB Mod**) The practice of altering behavior in organizations by systematically administering rewards.

6. *Periodically reevaluate the program.* Is the goal behavior still performed? Are the rewards still working? Changes in these events over time should be expected. As a result, administrators of behavior management programs must carefully monitor the behaviors they worked so hard to develop.

Organizational behavior management programs have been used successfully to stimulate a variety of behaviors in many different organizations (see summary in Table 3-4).[50] For example, a particularly interesting and effective program has been used in recent years at Diamond International, the Palmer, Massachusetts, company of 325 employees that manufactures Styrofoam egg cartons. In response to sluggish productivity, a simple but elegant reinforcement was put into place. Any employee working for a full year without an industrial accident is given 20 points. Perfect attendance is given 25 points. Once a year, the points are totaled. When employees reach 100 points, they get a blue nylon jacket with the company's logo on it and a patch identifying their membership in the "100 Club." Those earning still more points receive extra awards. For example, at 500 points, employees can select any of a number of small household appliances. These inexpensive prizes go a long way toward symbolizing to employees the company's appreciation for their good work.

This program has helped improve productivity dramatically at Diamond International. After the inauguration of the OB Mod program, output improved 16.5 percent, quality-related errors dropped 40 percent, grievances decreased 72 percent, and time lost due to accidents was lowered by 43.7 percent. The result of all of this has been over $1 million in gross financial benefits from the company—and a much happier workforce. Needless to say, this has been a very simple and effective organizational behavior management program. Although not all such programs are equally successful, evidence suggests that they are generally quite beneficial.

Discipline: Eliminating Undesirable Organizational Behaviors

Just as organizations systematically use rewards to encourage desirable behavior, they also use punishment to discourage undesirable behavior. Problems such as absenteeism, lateness, theft, and substance abuse cost companies vast sums of money, situations many companies attempt to manage by using **discipline**—the systematic administration of punishment.

By administering an unpleasant outcome (e.g., suspension without pay) in response to an undesirable behavior (e.g., excessive tardiness), companies seek

discipline The process of systematically administering punishments.

■ TABLE 3-4	ORGANIZATIONAL BEHAVIOR MANAGEMENT PROGRAMS: SOME SUCCESS STORIES		
Although not all organizational behavior management programs are as successful as the ones summarized here, many have been extremely effective in bringing about improvements in desired behaviors.	**Company**	**Reinforcers Used**	**Results**
	General Electric	Praise and constructive reinforcement	Productivity increased, cost savings resulted
	Weyerhaeuser	Contingent pay, and praise or recognition	Productivity increased in most work groups (by 18–33 percent)
	B. F. Goodrich Chemical	Praise and recognition	Production increased more than 300 percent
	Connecticut General Life Insurance	Time off based on performance	Chronic absenteeism and lateness were drastically reduced
	General Mills	Praise and feedback for meeting objectives	Sales increased

SOURCE: Based on material appearing in Frederiksen, 1982, Note 50.

to minimize that behavior. In one form or another, using discipline is a relatively common practice. Survey research has shown, in fact, that 83 percent of companies use some form of discipline, or at least the threat of discipline, in response to undesirable behaviors.[51] But, as you might imagine, disciplinary actions taken in organizations vary greatly. At one extreme, they may be very formal, such as written warnings that become part of the employee's permanent record. At the other extreme, they may be informal and low-key, such as friendly reminders and off-the-record discussions between supervisors and their problem subordinates. In a recent study, Trahan and Steiner asked a sample of nursing supervisors to list the disciplinary actions they most used.[52] They found that a broad range of disciplinary measures was used, including giving warnings (both oral and written), counseling the employee, putting the employee on probation, and termination. Although these responses come from a limited sample, we suspect that these results are fairly typical of what would be found across a wide variety of jobs.

One very common practice involves using punishment *progressively*—that is, starting mildly and then increasing in severity with each successive infraction. This is the idea behind **progressive discipline**—the practice of basing punishment on the frequency and severity of the infraction.[53] Let's consider an example of how progressive discipline might work for a common problem such as chronic absenteeism or tardiness. First, the supervisor may give the employee an informal oral warning. Then, if the problem persists, there would be an official meeting with the supervisor, during which time a formal warning would be issued. The next offense would result in a formal written warning that becomes part of the employee's personnel record. Subsequent offenses would lead to suspension without pay. And finally, if all this fails, the employee would be terminated. In the case of more serious offenses—such as gambling, for example—some of the preliminary steps would be dropped, and a formal written warning would be given. For the most serious offenses, such as stealing or intentionally damaging company property, officials would move immediately to the most severe step, immediate dismissal.

Companies with the most effective disciplinary programs tend to make the contingencies clear, such as by publicizing punishment rules in the company handbook. When this is done, employees know exactly what kind of behaviors the company will not tolerate, often minimizing the need to actually use discipline at all.

It probably comes as no surprise to you that supervisors do not always punish all inappropriate behaviors they encounter.[54] A key reason for this is that supervisors may feel constrained by limitations imposed by labor unions or by their own lack of formal authority. Also, in the absence of a clear company policy about how to use discipline, individuals may fear strong negative emotional reactions from the punished individual, if not also revenge and retaliation. As a result, many supervisors may turn the other way and simply do nothing when employees behave inappropriately. Although doing nothing may be easy in the short run, ignoring chronic problems is a way of informally approving of them, leading to increasingly serious problems in the future.

With this in mind, companies with the best disciplinary programs make it a practice to take immediate action. At Honda of America, for example, human resource specialist Tim Garrett notes that the company pays very close attention to all infractions of the rules, including ones "that other companies wouldn't think of paying attention to," adding, "if there's a problem, we'll pay attention to it right away."[55]

Obviously, it isn't easy to know exactly when and how to administer punishment, and how it can be done in a way that is considered fair and reasonable. Fortunately, research and theory have pointed to some effective principles that may be followed to maximize the effectiveness of discipline in organizations.[56] We will now consider several of these key principles.

progressive discipline The practice of gradually increasing the severity of punishments for employees who exhibit unacceptable job behavior.

- *Deliver punishment immediately after the undesirable response occurs.* The less time that passes between the occurrence of an undesirable behavior and the administration of a negative consequence, the more strongly people are to make the connection between them. When people make this association, the consequence is likely to serve as a punishment, thereby reducing the probability of the unwanted behavior. With this principle in mind, it is best for managers to talk to their subordinates about their undesirable behaviors immediately after committing them (or, at least as soon thereafter as may be practical). Expressing disapproval after several days or weeks have gone by will be less effective because the passage of time will weaken the association between behavior and its consequences.

- *Give moderate levels of punishment—nothing too high or too low.* If the consequences for performing an undesirable action are not very severe (e.g., rolling one's eyes as a show of disapproval), then it is unlikely to operate as a punishment. After all, it is quite easy to live with such a mild response. In contrast, consequences that are overly severe might be perceived as unfair and inhumane.[57] When this occurs, not only might the individual resign, but a strong signal will also be sent to others about the unreasonableness of the company's actions. In either case, the company risks losing its most valuable assets—its human resources.

- *Punish the undesirable behavior, not the person.* Good punishment is impersonal in nature and focuses on the individual's actions rather than his or her personality. So, for example, when addressing an employee who is repeatedly caught taking excessively long breaks it is unwise to say, "You're lazy and have a bad attitude." Instead, it would be better to say, "By not being at your desk when expected, you're making it more difficult for all of us to get our work done on time." Responding in this manner will be less humiliating for the individual, making the discussion far less unpleasant. Additionally, focusing on exactly what people can do to avoid such disapproval (taking shorter breaks, in this case) increases the likelihood that they will attempt to alter their behavior in the desired fashion. By contrast, the person who feels personally attacked might not only "tune out" the message, but not know exactly how to improve.

- *Use punishment consistently—all the time, for all employees.* Sometimes, managers attempting to be lenient turn a blind eye to infractions of company rules. Doing this may cause more harm than good insofar as it inadvertently reinforces the undesirable behavior (by demonstrating that one can get away with breaking the rules). As a result, it is considered most effective to administer punishment after each occurrence of an undesirable behavior. Similarly, it is important to show consistency in the treatment of all employees. In other words, everyone who commits the same infraction should be punished the same way, regardless of the person administering the punishment. When this occurs, supervisors are unlikely to be accused of showing favoritism. Also, if one supervisor is perceived to be very lenient and another very harsh, subordinates may learn to avoid the harsh supervisor rather than the undesirable behavior.

- *Clearly communicate the reasons for the punishment given.* Making clear exactly what behaviors lead to what disciplinary actions greatly facilitates the effectiveness of punishment. Clearly communicated expectations help strengthen the perceived connection between behavior and its consequences. Wise managers use their opportunities to communicate with subordinates to make clear that the punishment being given does not constitute revenge, but an attempt to eliminate an unwanted behavior (which, of course, it is). Communicating information about poor performance in a personal interview is a good idea, but doing so isn't easy. To make such interviews as effective as possible, managers should conduct them systematically, following the steps outlined in Figure 3-13.[58]

- *Do not follow punishment with noncontingent rewards.* Imagine that you are a supervisor who has just written a formal letter of discipline in reaction to a serious infraction of the rules by a particular subordinate. The disciplined employee is feeling very low, which makes you feel remorseful. Feeling bad, you reduce your guilt by telling the employee that he can take the rest of the day off with pay. Although this may make you feel better, it poses a serious problem: You inadvertently rewarded the person for the unwanted behavior. The serious infraction was punished by the letter but rewarded by the time off. Consequently, the effect of the punishment may be greatly diminished. More seriously, such an action sends the wrong message to the other employees. Soon, they too may learn that you will give them time off if they display the proper degree of dejection. The advice is clear: For punishment to be most effective, supervisors should refrain from inadvertently rewarding undesirable behaviors.

As obvious as this suggestion may be, it is not always followed.[59] In fact, a recent survey has revealed that top executives recognize that today's organizations frequently reward behaviors *opposite* those they really desire.[60] For example, although they tend to hope for teamwork and collaboration, they tend to reward the best individual team member. Similarly, although we tend to hope for high achievement, we tend to reward merely putting in another year of service. Thus, it cannot be said that organizations do a good job of rewarding desirable behaviors. In fact, many times they do just the opposite.

If, after reading all this, you are thinking that it is truly difficult to properly administer rewards and punishments in organizations, you have reached the same conclusion as experts in the field of organizational behavior. Indeed, one of the key skills that makes some managers so effective is their ability to influence others by properly administering rewards and punishments.

■ **Figure 3-13**
Conducting a Disciplinary Interview: Some Key Steps
It is never easy to communicate a performance problem. Following the steps listed here will help ensure that the problem is identified and that the consequences for failing to improve are made clear.

(**Source:** Based on suggestions by Lussier, 1990; see Note 58.)

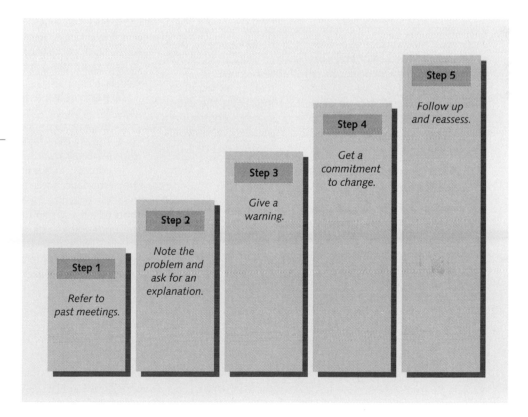

The Processes of Social Perception and Attribution

Perception is the process through which people select, organize, and interpret the information around them. When this process focuses on the interpretation of information about people, it is referred to as **social perception**.

The process of **attribution** involves judging the underlying reasons for people's behavior. Some of our judgments are based on inferences made on the basis of observing others' behavior. These judgments, known as **correspondent inferences**, are often inaccurate. Our search for explanations about the causes of others' behavior leads us to make either judgments of *internal causality* (the individual is responsible for his own actions) or *external causality* (someone or something else is responsible). **Kelley's theory of causal attribution** explains that such judgments will be based on three types of information: *consensus* (whether others act in a similar manner), *consistency* (whether the individual previously acted this way in the same situation), and *distinctiveness* (whether this person acted similarly in different situations).

The Imperfect Nature of Social Perception

Several types of systematic errors, known as **perceptual biases**, limit the accuracy of social perception. These include the **fundamental attribution error** (the tendency to attribute others' actions to internal causes), the **halo effect** (the tendency to perceive others in either consistently positive or negatively terms), the **similar-to-me effect** (the tendency to perceive similar others in a favorable light), **first impression error** (the tendency for initial impressions to guide subsequent ones), and **selective perception** (the tendency for people to focus on only certain aspects of the environment). Perceptual inaccuracies also result from the tendency for people to rely on the use of **stereotypes** (the judgments of others based on the categories to which they belong).

Perceptual biases are not easily overcome, although attempts at doing so can be made by considering the external causes of others' behavior, identifying and confronting one's stereotypes, evaluating others objectively, and avoiding rash judgments.

Applications of Social Perception in Organizations

Biased judgments about others sometimes occur during the process of **performance appraisal**. In this context, research has shown that people judge as superior those individuals whose performance matches their expectations, and those whose good performance is attributed to internal sources and whose poor performance is attributed to external sources.

People are generally interested in getting others to perceive them favorably, and their efforts in this regard are referred to as **impression management**. This process is particularly important in **employment interviews**, although it sometimes interferes with the accuracy of information presented about individuals or companies. An organization's overall impression on people, its **corporate image**, is a determinant of its ability to attract qualified job applicants.

Principles of Learning

Learning refers to relatively permanent changes in behavior occurring as a result of experience. In organizations, two approaches are most common. In the **operant conditioning** approach, individuals learn to behave certain ways based on the consequences of those actions. Stimuli that increase the probability of the behaviors preceding it are known as **reinforcers**. Reinforcement may be either *positive*, if it is based on the presentation of a desirable outcome, or *negative*, if it is based on the withdrawal of an unwanted outcome. The probability of certain responses can be decreased if an unpleasant outcome results (**punishment**), or if a pleasant outcome is withdrawn (**extinction**).

Observational learning involves learning by modeling the behavior of others. By paying attention to and rehearsing the behavior of others, we can learn vicariously, that is, through the model's experiences.

Applications of Learning Principles in Organizations

Learning is directly involved in efforts to teach people to acquire new job skills, the process of **training**. Training is most effective when people can actively participate in the learning process, repeat the desired behaviors, receive feedback on their performance, and learn under conditions closely resembling those found on the job (i.e., *transfer of training*).

Organizational behavior management is a systematic attempt to apply principles of reinforcement to the workplace in order to improve organizational functioning. Studies have shown that reinforcing desired behaviors can greatly improve organizational functioning.

In contrast to applications of reinforcement, **discipline** is the systematic application of punishments to minimize undesirable organizational behaviors. The effects of discipline are most effective when punishment is applied immediately after the undesirable activity, moderately severe, focused on the activity rather than the individual, applied consistently over time, and for all employees, clearly explained and communicated, and not weakened by the use of inadvertent rewards.

1. Describe an organizational situation in which it would be important to judge whether someone's behavior stems primarily from internal or external causes.
2. How do stereotypes influence the way we judge others in organizations? How may stereotypical judgments be overcome?
3. What kinds of things might people do to be able to enhance the impressions they leave on others in organizations?
4. Identify an organizational event in which operant conditioning is used and one in which observational learning is used.
5. Name four different schedules of reinforcement and describe how each may be used in organizations.
6. Describe how principles of reinforcement and punishment are used in organizational behavior management programs and disciplinary programs.

CASE IN POINT

Training on a Shoestring at Connors Communication

One of the dilemmas faced by small businesses is that they have severely limited resources for training their employees. Without training, small businesses do not stand much chance of becoming big ones. Connie Connors, owner of a small but growing public relations firm in New York City, Connors Communication, recognizes this, noting, "To maintain our competitive advantage we have to train." So, she scraped up $40,000 from an already strained budget and developed some very ingenious and effective ways to get the most from her training dollars.

First there's the "TIPS" ("Tips for Improving Performance") program. These are mini training classes developed by the five employees constituting the training committee: half-hour sessions held every two weeks designed to cover whatever topics the employees say they need to learn. According to Connors, "TIPS have ranged from finding your way on-line and perfecting your [sales] pitch, to budget management." These sessions have been run by outside experts as well as more experienced Connors employees. Because the classes are so brief and dedicated to things people want to know, they have been very well attended by the company's 25 employees.

Further in-house training is provided at biannual company meetings, long weekend retreats away from the hustle and bustle of the company's Manhattan office. There, Connors explains the company's pricing structure. She also runs a very practical session on "effective schmoozing" (socializing), complete with opportunities to hone this important public relations skill at a simulated cocktail party. Further tapping existing resources, Connors employees who have been around a while are expected to help train new ones, showing them the ropes in all kinds of informal things (such as office politics)—the "buddy system." Just to make sure that new employees correctly understand the formal workings of the company, they are given a software program that spells it all out. The "Connors Bible," as it is known, identifies the company's clients as well as its official structure and policies.

Acknowledging that training from within is generally not sufficient, Connors employees are also encouraged to attend outside seminars or conferences related to their work. To help, all employees are budgeted funds ranging from $200 to $2,000 to reimburse their expenses. Although this might not go very far, these investments have exposed Connors employees to a wide variety of professional techniques. When you consider that much of what they learn on the outside is passed along inside the company, the investment becomes that much more effective.

Indeed, the head of the TIPS committee, Wendy Handler, has identified several benefits stemming from all these efforts. The company is coming closer to reaching its monthly sales goals, and all employees are now comfortable using the company's e-mail system. Connors Communication's sales have doubled in each of the past three years, and it now does $2 million annual business. With more growth like that, it probably won't be long before Connors Communication increases its training budget. But given the success it has enjoyed on a shoestring budget, we can only wonder whether it will greatly change its training techniques.

Critical Thinking Questions

1. What other inexpensive training methods do you think Connors Communication might introduce to supplement those it is currently using?
2. In what ways is the company's small size both a strength and a weakness when it comes to training?
3. Much of what is done at Connors Communication involves sharing existing knowledge among the employees. What can be done to help bring in new sources of information?
4. Drawing upon the principles of learning discussed in the text, what would you do to enhance the effectiveness of training at Connors Communication?

Experiencing Organizational Behavior

Identifying Occupational Stereotypes

Although we usually reserve our concern over stereotypes for women and members of racial and ethnic minorities, the simple truth is that people can hold stereotypes toward members of just about *any* group. In organizations, people are likely to hold stereotypes about people based on a variable whose importance cannot be overstated—the occupational groups to which they belong. What we expect of people, and the way we treat them, is likely to be affected by stereotypes about their professions. This exercise will help you better understand this phenomenon.

Directions

Using the scale below, rate each of the following occupational groups with respect to how much of the characteristics listed members of these groups tend to show.

1 = not at all
2 = a slight amount
3 = a moderate amount
4 = a great amount
5 = an extreme amount

- Accountants
____ interesting
____ generous
____ intelligent
____ conservative
- Clergy
____ interesting
____ generous
____ intelligent
____ conservative

- Professors
____ interesting
____ generous
____ intelligent
____ conservative
- Physicians
____ interesting
____ generous
____ intelligent
____ conservative

- Lawyers
____ interesting
____ generous
____ intelligent
____ conservative
- Plumbers
____ interesting
____ generous
____ intelligent
____ conservative

Questions for Discussion

1. Did your ratings of the various groups differ? If so, which were perceived most positively and which were perceived most negatively?
2. To what extent did your ratings agree with those of others? In other words, was there general agreement about the stereotypical nature of people in various occupational groups?
3. To what extent were your responses based on specific people you know? How did knowledge, or lack of knowledge, of members of the various occupational groups influence your ratings?
4. Do you believe that by becoming aware of these stereotypes you will perpetuate them in the future or refrain from behaving in accord with them? Explain.

Working in Groups

Role Play: The Disciplinary Interview

Knowing how to discipline employees who behave inappropriately is an important managerial skill. The trick is to change the bad behavior into good behavior permanently, getting people to accept their mistakes and understand how to correct them. As you might imagine, this is often far more difficult than it sounds. After all, people are generally reluctant to admit their errors and may have developed bad work habits that must be overcome. In addition, they tend to resist being chastised and don't like listening to criticism. Thus disciplining others represents quite a challenge for managers, making it a skill worth developing.

Directions

1. Select four students from the class and divide them into two pairs. One person from each pair should read only the role sheet below for Andy F., machine operator, and the other person from each pair should read only the role sheet for Barry B., his supervisor. Send both pairs outside the room until called upon.
2. Members of the class will serve as observers and should read both role sheets.

3. Call in the first pair of role players and ask them to spend about 10–15 minutes playing their roles—that is, acting as they would if they were the characters about whom they just read in the role sheets. They should feel free to assume any additional facts not described in these sheets.
4. Members of the class should observe the role play, taking careful notes. The class should *not* get involved in what the actors are saying, but pay close attention to it.
5. Repeat steps 3 and 4 with the second pair of role players.

Role Sheets

ANDY F., MACHINE OPERATOR:

You have worked at Acme Manufacturing for 6 years now, and have had a good record. Because you do your job so well, you sometimes take liberties and horse around with your buddies. For example, one Friday afternoon you were caught dancing around the shop floor when a good song came on the radio. Barry B., your supervisor, called you on the carpet for leaving your station. You think he has it in for you and is trying to run you off the job. Although you were acting silly, you are convinced that it doesn't matter since you were getting your job done. Now, he has called you in to see him to discuss the situation.

BARRY B., SUPERVISOR:

After several years of experience in other shops, you were hired by Acme Manufacturing to be its new shop supervisor, a job you've had for only 4 months. Things have gone well during that time, but you've been having trouble with one machine operator, Andy F. Andy seems to do an acceptable job, but is not giving it his all. Part of the problem is that he goofs around a lot. You have spoken to him about this informally a few times on the floor, but to no avail. One Friday afternoon you caught him away from his station, dancing around the shop floor. Not only wasn't he doing his own job, but he was distracting the others. You have just called Andy in to see you to discuss the situation.

Questions for Discussion

1. Did the supervisor, Barry B., define the problem in a nonthreatening way?
2. Did each party listen to the other, or did they shut him or her out, merely explaining their own sides of the story?
3. Did Barry B. suggest specific things that Andy F. could do to improve? Were the specific punishments associated with future bad acts spelled out explicitly?
4. Were the discussions impersonal in nature or did the parties focus on each other's personalities?
5. Considering all these questions, which supervisor would you say did a better job of administering discipline? What could be done to improve the way each supervisor conducted the disciplinary meeting?

THE DRIVING FORCE BEHIND DELL COMPUTER

A billionaire by the time he was 30; founder of a fast-growing, high-tech company; an executive whose technical expertise is matched only by his marketing savvy—we must be talking about Bill Gates of Microsoft, right? Wrong! The preceding description also fits Michael Dell, founder and CEO of Dell Computer, Inc.—a company whose sales hit $1.2 billion during one recent quarter, and whose profits have leaped 128 percent during the past year.

Dell sells computers through direct marketing, primarily to high-end users such as corporations and government agencies. By concentrating on such sales, as well as sales to individual consumers, Dell has captured more than 5 percent of the rapidly growing PC market. The man responsible for this growth—and for just about every other major aspect of Dell Computer—is Michael Dell, whose holdings in the company are fast approaching the $1 billion mark.

Michael Dell started early; in fact, he hit on the idea of direct marketing of computers while an undergraduate at the University of Texas. He noticed that sales reps for IBM and other major companies knew less about the PCs they were promoting than did their customers. Recognizing an opportunity when he saw one, Dell formed a company to sell dealers' excess inventory by mail. The results were so encouraging, that Dell soon told his father, Alexander, that he wanted to quit school to run his business full-time. "What do you want to accomplish?" his father asked. Michael's answer: "Compete with IBM." In fact, Michael Dell's entrepreneurial adventures began even earlier than this. At the age of 12, he planned a stamp auction that earned him $1,000 in profits. And during his final year in high school, he earned $18,000 selling papers for local newspapers. How did he convert what most people view as a "pocket change" job into the price of a new BMW—which he bought for cash that summer? By figuring out that the most likely newspaper subscribers were newlyweds and families who had just moved. Dell then tracked them down through innovative techniques such as checking recent marriage licenses, and soon had a thriving business.

Everything hasn't always been "roses" for Michael Dell and his company, though. After a very fast start, Dell Computer ran into several setbacks in the early 1990s. In fact, the company had to scrap an entire new line of notebook computers because of poor production planning. The result? Michael Dell learned from his mistakes and brought experienced, senior managers on board. Dell has also learned to tone down his extraordinary competitiveness. In the past, he rallied members of his management team by telling them that his daughter's first words were "Mommy . . . Daddy . . . Daddy kill Compaq, Daddy kill IBM, Daddy kill Gateway. . . ." Now, as he's matured, he's adopted a more restrained approach. But Dell still retains one characteristic that those who know him best believe he's always had: In contrast to other "high-tech celebrities," he remains a very private person, reluctant to talk about himself or his home life. As he himself put it after one slightly uncomfortable interview in which he tried to avoid questions about the new mansion he was building: "Fame isn't everything it's cracked up to be."

That Michael Dell has had an amazing career is obvious. The question of *why* he has achieved so much so quickly, however, is much more open to debate. Was it favorable market conditions, simple good luck (being a college student at just the right time and in just the right place) or something about Dell himself that put him on the road to such success? The answer certainly involves many different factors, for achievements like Dell's are too complex in nature to stem from one or even a few causes.

Having said that, though, we wish to add that it seems clear that Michael Dell's success has stemmed, to an important extent, from his own *personality*—his unique set of traits and characteristics. In other words, it took a special kind of person with an unusual combination of personal traits to turn the potential opportunities existing in the 1980s into a thriving company. This suggestion, in turn, points to another that is the underlying theme of this chapter: Personal characteristics (sometimes described as *individual differences*) play a key role in many aspects of organizational behavior. To provide you with an overview of what we know about the impact of such factors, we'll proceed as follows.

First, we'll define *personality* more precisely and examine contrasting views concerning its relative importance in human behavior. Next, we'll consider several specific aspects of personality—those that have been found to play an important role in key aspects of organizational behavior. Third, we'll turn briefly to *abilities*—mental and physical capacities to perform various tasks, and the role of such abilities in work-related behavior. Finally, we'll examine various methods used to measure personality and abilities. These measurement techniques are essential if we wish to compare individuals with respect to various traits or abilities and to use this information for making practical decisions, such as whom to hire for a specific job or whom to promote.

Personality: Its Basic Nature and Role in Organizational Behavior

If we learn anything from our experiences with other people it is this: They are all, in some ways, *unique* and all, to a degree, *consistent* in their behavior. That is, all human beings possess a distinct pattern of traits and characteristics not fully duplicated in any other person; furthermore, many of these characteristics are quite stable over time. Thus, if you know someone who is optimistic, confident, and friendly today, the chances are good that he or she also showed the same traits in the past and will continue to show them in the future, too. Moreover, this person will probably also demonstrate such traits in many different situations. The person will be optimistic, friendly, and confident when making a presentation at work and may also show the same style when meeting people for the first time in a local night spot (see Figure 4-1). Together, these two features form the basis for a useful working definition of **personality**, which we'll define as the unique and relatively stable pattern of behavior, thoughts, and emotions shown by individuals.[1] In contrast, *abilities* refer to the capacity to perform various tasks or cognitive activities.[2]

personality The unique and relatively stable patterns of behavior, thoughts, and emotions shown by individuals.

Is Personality Real? The Person-Situation Controversy

Because we often think of behavior as resulting from stable personal traits, you may find it surprising to learn that some social scientists have rejected the notion of personality, arguing instead that how we behave is mainly determined by the external conditions we face.[3] Indeed, several have gone so far as to claim that what we often describe as personality is really an illusion stemming from the fact that we *want* to perceive consistency in others' behavior. Why? Because it makes predicting what they will say or do easier.

On the opposite side of this controversy are social scientists who have argued, just as strongly, that stable traits *do* exist and that these lead people to behave consistently across time and in different settings. In support of their claims, they point to the findings of research in which individuals are studied over extended periods of time. The research does indeed show a fair amount of consistency with respect to many aspects of their behavior.[4] Further support for the reality of personality is provided by research comparing the personalities of identical twins who have been raised together (the usual state of affairs) or, after being separated early in life, in different homes. The findings of such studies indicate that even when raised in sharply different environments, the twins show remarkable similarity in many aspects of their personalities.[5] This evidence, too, supports the view that personality is real—that

■ **Figure 4-1**

Consistency in Individual Behavior
People often show a considerable amount of consistency in their behavior both across situations and over time. Such consistency is a central aspect of personality.

people *do* show a notable degree of consistency in their behavior. Moreover, these studies also indicate that genetic factors may well play a role in certain aspects of personality.

Now for another question: If, as growing evidence indicates, personality is indeed much more than an illusion, to what extent is it responsible for how we behave? In other words, do we behave the way we do in a given situation because of personality, because of situational pressures, or both? The answer suggested by careful research on this topic is both. In other words, behavior in many situations is the result of both an individual's personality and the nature of the situation. For example, consider an individual who is known to all his acquaintances as having a very short fuse; he loses his temper frequently in response to fairly mild provocations.

Now, imagine that one day, this person is stopped for speeding by a state trooper. Will he "blow up" when the officer approaches his car? Perhaps; but it is more likely that he will restrain this tendency and behave in a more polite manner. After all, the costs of losing one's temper in *this* situation are both high and obvious! So, in general, we can say that our behavior is determined by a complex interaction between our personality traits and the external environment; both are important and can affect what we do or say. Almost all social scientists accept this view—known as the **interactionist perspective**—and it is the dominant position in organizational behavior, too.

interactionist perspective
The view that behavior is a result of a complex interplay between personality and situational factors.

An interesting implication of the interactionist perspective—and one with important implications for organizational behavior—is that a given work setting may "fit" with the personalities (and abilities) of specific persons to varying degrees. In other words, some persons may find that their traits and abilities closely match those required by a given job, while others find that their traits and abilities do *not* match these requirements. The degree to which there is a "match" between employees' characteristics and their jobs is known as **person-job fit**, and it has recently been the subject of a considerable amount of research.[6] The basic findings of this work are that people are more productive and satisfied when there is a close match between their personal traits and the demands of the job than when this match is less optimal (see Figure 4-2 for an amusing illustration of this fact).[7]

person-job fit The extent to which individuals possess the traits and competencies required to perform specific jobs.

These findings offer support for the importance of considering individual difference variables in efforts to enhance both productivity and job satisfaction. The closer the fit between individuals' personal traits and the requirements of their jobs, the more positive are the results. In view of this fact, it seems worthwhile to consider potential person-job fit in many orga-

■ Figure 4-2
Person-Job Fit: An Example
As you can readily see, Hagar's personality traits make him especially well-
suited for this particular job. In other
words, the person-job fit is high!

(**Source:** Copyright © 1989. Reprinted with
special permission of King Features
Syndicate.)

nizational contexts—for instance, when individuals are hired or considered for promotion.

Work-Related Aspects of Personality

Now that we have established that personality is indeed real and called attention to its potentially important effects, we'll turn to another task: examining several aspects of personality that appear to influence important aspects of organizational behavior.

The "Big Five" Dimensions of Personality and Organizational Behavior

How many different words can you think of that describe others' personalities? Would you believe *17,953*? That's the number of personality-related words found in a search of an English language dictionary in a study conducted more than 60 years ago.[8] Even after combining words with similar meanings, the list still contained 171 distinct traits. Does this mean that we must consider a huge list of characteristics to understand fully the role of personality in organizational behavior? Fortunately, the answer appears to be no. A growing body of evidence points to the conclusion that, in fact, there may be only five key dimensions to consider.

Because these same five dimensions have emerged in so many different studies conducted in so many different ways, they are often referred to as the **"big five" dimensions of personality**.[9] These dimensions can be described as follows:

"big five" dimensions of personality Five basic dimensions of personality that are assumed to underlie many specific traits.

1. *Conscientiousness*: a dimension ranging from careful, thorough, responsible, organized, self-disciplined, and scrupulous at one end to irresponsible, disorganized, lacking in self-discipline and unscrupulous at the other.
2. *Extraversion-Introversion*: a dimension ranging from sociable, talkative, assertive, and active at one end to retiring, sober, reserved, and cautious at the other.
3. *Agreeableness*: a dimension ranging from good-natured, gentle, cooperative, forgiving, and hopeful at one end to irritable, ruthless, suspicious, uncooperative, and inflexible at the other.
4. *Emotional Stability*: a dimension ranging from anxious, depressed, angry, emotional, insecure, and excitable at one end to calm, enthusiastic, poised, and secure at the other.
5. *Openness to Experience*: a dimension ranging from imaginative, sensitive, intellectual, and polished at one end, to down-to-earth, insensitive, narrow, crude, and simple at the other.

Sample items similar to those used to assess individuals' standing on each of these dimensions are presented in Table 4-1. By completing them, you

than Type B's and, as a result, will perform at higher levels. In fact, however, the situation turns out to be more complex than this. Type A's *do* tend to work faster on many tasks than Type B's, even when no pressure or deadline is involved. Similarly, they are able to get more done in the presence of distractions.[23] In addition, Type A's often seek more challenges in their work than Type B's: Given a choice, they tend to select more difficult or complex tasks.[24]

But Type A's don't *always* perform better than Type B's. For example, Type A's frequently do poorly on tasks requiring patience or careful judgment. They are simply in too much of a hurry to complete such work effectively.[25] Consistent with this idea are surveys revealing that most top executives are Type B's rather than type A's.[26] Several factors probably contribute to this pattern. First, it is possible that type A's simply don't last long enough to rise to the highest management levels; as we'll see in Chapter 7, the health risks of their "always-in-a-hurry" lifestyle are too great! Second, the irritability or hostility often shown by Type A's may have negative effects on their careers, preventing them from rising to the top of their organizations. In fact, Type A's do appear to have very "short fuses"—they often become angry and behave aggressively in situations that other persons tend to ignore.[27] Finally, their impatience is often incompatible with the deliberate, carefully considered decisions required of top-level managers (see Figure 4-3).

Taken together, these findings suggest that neither pattern has an overall edge when it comes to task performance. Although Type A's may excel on tasks

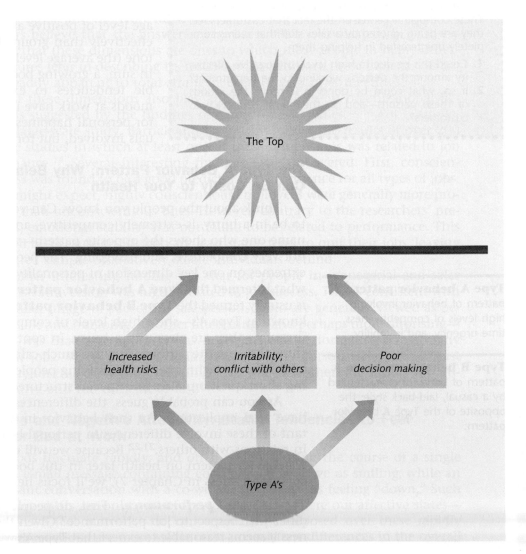

■ **Figure 4-3**
Why Type A's Don't Make It to the Top
Research findings indicate that contrary to what you might guess, most top executives are more Type B than Type A. The factors shown here may provide an explanation for this finding.

involving time pressure or solitary work, Type B's have the advantage when it comes to tasks involving complex judgments and accuracy as opposed to speed. So, the question of whether Type A's or Type B's make more productive employees boils down to the issue of *person-job fit*: The closer the match between job requirements and this aspect of personality, the better performance tends to be. As you'll soon see, the same principle applies to many aspects of personality examined in this chapter.

Type A's and interpersonal relations. What about relations with others? Intuition suggests that here Type B's might well have an edge, and this prediction has been confirmed by research findings. Because of their impatience and irritability, Type A's do tend to annoy their co-workers. Moreover, they are also more likely to lose their tempers and lash out at others. Type A's tend to become involved in more conflicts at work than Type B's.[28] And very recent evidence collected by Baron and Neuman suggests that they may also be more likely to engage in various acts of *workplace aggression* than Type B's.[29] Note that we said *aggression*, not *violence*. As we'll see in Chapter 11, there are many ways in which individuals can seek to harm co-workers other than direct violence against them.

In sum, while Type A's often seem to be cyclones of activity and do tend to move large amounts of work across their desks very quickly, there is definitely a downside to this pattern, both for Type A's themselves and for other members of their organizations. Fortunately, Type A behavior is not set in stone: It can be modified so that such persons retain the "pluses" of being active, committed, and energetic, while eliminating, or at least reducing, the "minuses" associated with impatience, irritability, and hostility.[30]

The Proactive Personality: People Who Shape Their Environments

Earlier, we noted that behavior is often the result of a complex interplay between personal traits on the one hand and situational factors on the other. Put very simply, because they possess various traits, individuals prefer to act in certain ways. Whether they actually behave in these ways, however, depends on the extent to which the situations in which they operate encourage or discourage such behaviors. For example, an individual with a very humorous personality may well make jokes and behave in an amusing or silly manner at parties. In contrast, she or he will probably *not* show such behavior during an interview for an important job.

While situational constraints often exert powerful effects on the expression of personal traits or preferences, it is also clear that the opposite is also true: People do not merely react to situations; sometimes they take active steps to shape them as well. Recently, Bateman and Crant have suggested that individual differences in this respect constitute another important dimension of personality.[31] They note that while some persons react passively to the external environment, adapting to the conditions it imposes, others take a more active approach, seeking to influence their environment and bend it to *their* preferences. They refer to this dimension as the **proactive personality** trait and suggest that it has important implications for organizational behavior. Persons high on this dimension, they suggest, identify opportunities and act on them; they take action, show initiative, and persevere until they manage to bring about meaningful change. In contrast, persons low on this dimension show the opposite pattern: They fail to identify opportunities and make little or no effort to change things; rather, they accept the current state of affairs and try to "make the best of things as they are."

Evidence for the view that this dimension is both measurable and important, is provided by an ingenious study conducted by Crant.[32] In this investigation, real estate agents completed a measure of the proactive personality trait and measures of two of the big five dimensions of personality we discussed

We will examine the role of the Type A behavior pattern in reactions to stress in Chapter 7.

proactive personality A personality trait reflecting the extent to which individuals seek to change the environment to suit their purposes and to capitalize on various opportunities.

earlier—conscientiousness and extraversion. Their scores on these scales were then related to several measures of job performance: The number of houses they sold, the number of listings they generated, and their commission income. Crant predicted that job performance would be related to the proactive personality trait even when the effects of the big five factors were held constant (i.e., removed statistically). Results confirmed this finding. As shown in Figure 4-4, the higher the real estate agents scored in terms of the proactive personality dimension, the more houses they sold, the larger commissions they earned, and the larger the number of listings they obtained.

How could having a proactive personality lead to such effects? As suggested by Crant, it leads the real estate agents to engage in various proactive behaviors—for instance, advertising their services or visiting persons trying to sell their homes themselves and convincing them to list with the agent. Clearly, the tendency to engage in proactive ways—to seek opportunities and develop them, and, more generally, "to make things happen,"—may also be related to performance of many other jobs and to the success of entire organizations.

Growing awareness of this basic fact has led many companies to concentrate on "growing" their *change agents*—people who get results when they are needed most. Such persons seem to combine proactive attitudes—the belief that things *can* get better—with the ability to motivate others. They persuade and cajole the people around them into doing more than they did before, and often, more than they thought they *could* do. Perhaps most of all, these change agents are flexible: If a method or technique works, they'll adopt it.

■ Figure 4-4
The Proactive Personality and Success
The higher real estate agents scored on a measure of the proactive personality dimension, the more successful they were at their jobs.

(**Source:** Based on data from Crant, 1995.)

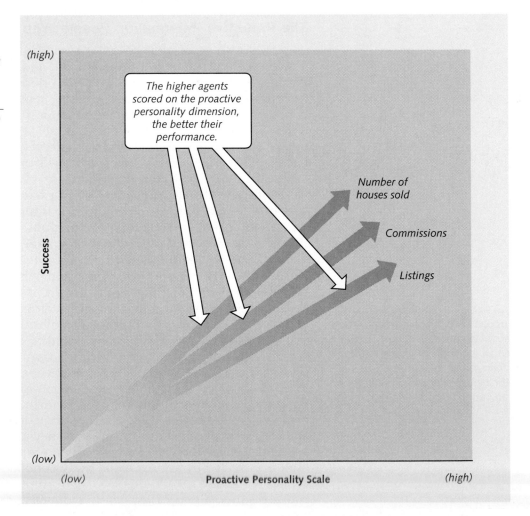

According to John R. Katzenbach, who has studied such persons extensively, change agents are crucial for organizational success. They are the ones who translate new strategies outlined by top management into reality. As Katzenbach notes, it was a shortage of such persons that derailed John Akers's plan to transform IBM in the 1990s. The plan was good, but there were simply not enough change agents in his company to make it happen.[33] To the extent this conclusion is accurate, attracting and retaining such persons is indeed a crucial ingredient in corporate success.

Self-Efficacy: The "Can Do" Facet of Personality

Suppose that two individuals are assigned the same task by their supervisor, and that one is confident of her ability to carry it out successfully, whereas the other has some serious doubts on this score. Which person is more likely to succeed? Assuming that all other factors (for instance, differences in their ability and motivation) are held constant, it is reasonable to predict that the first will do better. Such an individual is higher in **self-efficacy**—the belief in one's own capacity to perform a specific task.[34,35] When considered in the context of a given task, self-efficacy is not, strictly speaking, an aspect of personality. However, people also seem to acquire general expectations about their ability to perform a wide range of tasks in many different contexts. Such generalized beliefs about their task-related capabilities are stable over time, and these can be viewed as an important aspect of personality.

How do beliefs about self-efficacy develop? Existing evidence indicates that there are two major factors involved: *direct experience*—feedback from performing similar tasks in the past—and *vicarious experience*—observations of others' performance on these tasks.[36] On the basis of information from these sources, individuals reach initial conclusions about the skills and abilities required to succeed on the task, whether they possess these, whether there are factors or conditions that may interfere with their performance, and so on. Together, these conclusions shape their current beliefs of self-efficacy. These beliefs, in turn, are then adjusted in the light of new information—for example, further experience with actually performing the task.

Interestingly, recent findings reported by Mitchell and his colleagues suggest that initially, when individuals are acquiring the skills for performing a new task, they devote a great deal of cognitive effort to forming self-efficacy beliefs. They think about many factors that might potentially influence their ability to perform the task—for instance, their alertness, their previous experience, complexity of the task—and exert considerable effort to formulate self-efficacy beliefs. With continued practice, however, they seem to shift to a more *automatic* and less effortful mode of reaching such judgments—one in which they simply consider their previous performance.

Evidence for this kind of shift is provided by an ingenious study conducted by Mitchell and others.[37] In this study, undergraduate students performed a complex air traffic controller task, in which they had to learn a number of different rules in order to perform the task of landing planes safely. The game occurred in discrete trials or sessions and, before several of these trials, participants reported on their self-efficacy and how they reached such judgments. Specifically, they indicated their self-efficacy by reporting their confidence that they could achieve various levels of performance. They also rated the extent to which they considered nine different factors in reaching such judgments: their current alertness, desire to do well, level of effort, current mood, task difficulty, task complexity, task novelty, work disturbances, and past experience with similar tasks. Results indicated that as they gained increasing experience with the tasks, they made such judgments more quickly, and also devoted less attention to many of these factors (see Figure 4-5).

These findings suggest that, as is true with many other tasks we perform, we shift from making self-efficacy judgments in a conscious and careful man-

self-efficacy Individuals' beliefs concerning their ability to perform specific tasks successfully.

self-monitoring A personality trait involving the extent to which individuals adapt their behavior to the demands of specific situations, primarily to make the best possible impression on others.

Self-monitoring also plays an important role in conflict; we'll examine this relationship in Chapter 11.

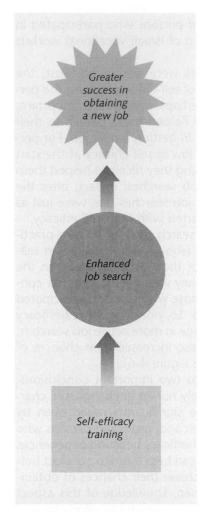

■ **Figure 4-6**
The Benefits of Self-Efficacy Training
Individuals who received training designed to boost their self-efficacy conducted more effective job searches and were more successful in obtaining new jobs than those who did not receive such training.

(**Source:** Based on findings reported by Eden & Aviram, 1993.)

sonality is known as **self-monitoring**, and it, too, has been found to have important implications for organizational behavior.[41]

Self-monitoring and performance. First, and perhaps most important, self-monitoring has been found to be related to several aspects of performance. For instance, high self-monitors tend to do better than low self-monitors in jobs requiring what are known as *boundary spanning* activities. These involve communicating and interacting with different groups of people from contrasting professional or occupational groups.[42] Since they can readily adjust their actions to the normal expectations and styles of each group, high self-monitors are more successful in dealing with them, and this improves their performance. Boundary-spanning roles are very important in most organizations, so it makes good sense to consider assigning people high in self-monitoring to such positions.

Self-monitoring and career success. Second, self-monitoring has important effects upon success in one's career. High self-monitors tend to obtain more promotions than low self-monitors, especially when these involve movement from one company to another.[43] Why are high self-monitors more successful in getting ahead than low self-monitors? Perhaps because their greater willingness to adapt their behavior to each situation they encounter, and to act in ways that please others, helps them to get over the first all-important first round of promotion contests.[44] High self-monitors seem to approach various situation by asking, "What kind of person does this situation require, and how can I best be that person?" In contrast, low self-monitors ask, "How can I best be *me* in this situation?" The result is that high self-monitors make a better impression on others and so get the early promotions. Once they do, they are on the "high road" to success, and their careers prosper.

Another reason behind the success of many high self-monitors may be their ability to empathize with others—to "walk around inside their shoes" or see the world through their eyes. Many observers attribute high self-monitoring to the outstanding success of Orit Gadiesh, head of Bain & Co., a highly successful management consulting firm in Boston.[45] Gadiesh is often noticed first for her flamboyant personal style: Her hair sports several different colors, and her skirts start about eight inches above the knee. It is her ability to look at things from others' perspective, however, that truly impresses her clients. Says James Morgan, CEO of Philip Morris USA, "Orit has that talent for making you feel you're the most important person in the room. She bleeds your blood." It is this high degree of empathy—a characteristic of high self-monitors—that keeps her clients impressed and coming back for more. Interestingly, many studies indicate that women may have an important edge in this respect: They tend to be higher in empathy than men. We'll return to the potential value of empathy in a later discussion of an important form of intelligence.

Self-monitoring and impression management. From our comments so far, you can probably already guess another way in which high and low self-monitors differ: High self-monitors have a distinct edge where the important process of *impression management* is concerned. Since they are willing to change their behavior or style across situations, they are more effective at doing whatever it takes to generate positive reactions from others. And as we saw in Chapter 2, this can yield many important benefits.

Self-monitoring and mentoring. A fourth effect of self-monitoring on organizational behavior involves its role in the *mentoring* process—a topic we'll examine in detail in Chapter 7. In mentoring relationships, younger, less experienced employees receive help and guidance from older, more experienced ones, and often this provides an important boost to their careers.[46] Recent findings reported by Turban and Dougherty indicate that high self-monitors are more likely than low self-monitors to initiate mentoring relationships. Specifically, they are more likely to seek to become acquainted with higher-level managers, to make personal efforts to make their work visible to higher-level managers, and to seek counseling and advice from such persons. The result is that they are more successful in obtaining mentors than low self-monitors, with all the benefits this confers.[47]

The potential downside of self-monitoring. Before you conclude that being high in self-monitoring is an unmixed blessing, we should quickly add that there is a downside to this trait, too. Because they are so changeable—some researchers refer to high self-monitors as "social chameleons"—they run the risk of being viewed as unreliable, inconsistent, or even manipulative by others.[48] Similarly, research findings indicate that self-monitors may tend to form less stable and less deep personal relationships than low self-monitors.[49] Since high self-monitors change their style and behavior across situations, they may seek different friends for each context. In contrast, low self-monitors remain much the same, so they form fewer—but deeper—relationships. In short, self-monitoring, like most other dimensions of personality, has complex effects, and any assessment of the relative costs and benefits of being high or low on this dimension must take careful account of such complexity.

Machiavellianism: Using Others to Get Ahead

In 1513, the Italian philosopher Niccolo Machiavelli published a book entitled *The Prince*. In it, he outlined a ruthless strategy for seizing and holding political power. The essence of his approach was straightforward: Other people can be readily used or manipulated by sticking to a few basic rules. Among the guiding principles he recommended were the following:

> Never show humility; arrogance is far more effective when dealing with others.
> Morality and ethics are for the weak; powerful people feel free to lie, cheat,
> and deceive whenever it suits their purpose.
> It is much better to be feared than loved.

In general, Machiavelli urged those who desired power to adopt a totally pragmatic approach. Let others be swayed by friendship, loyalty, or beliefs about fair play; a truly successful leader, he suggested, should always be above those factors. He or she should be willing to do *whatever it takes to get his or her own way*.

Clearly, most people don't adopt Machiavelli's philosophy. But some, at least, do seem to operate according to these principles. This fact led researchers to propose that acceptance of this ruthless creed involves yet another dimension of personality—one known, appropriately, as **Machiavellianism**. Persons high on this dimension (high Machs, as they are termed) accept Machiavelli's suggestions and seek to manipulate others in a ruthless manner.[50] In contrast, persons low on this dimension (low Machs), reject this approach, and *do* care about fair play, loyalty, and other principles Machiavelli rejected. Machiavellianism is measured by means of a relatively brief questionnaire. Sample items similar to ones on the *Mach Scale* are shown in Table 4-2.

Machiavellianism and success. If high Machs are willing to do whatever it takes to succeed, you might expect that they would tend to be rather successful. The answer seems to be that they are, but primarily in *loosely structured situations*—where there are few established rules.[51] In tightly structured situations, where the rules regarding expected behavior are clearly stated, high Machs do not appear to have an edge.

Dealing with high Machs. Because of their merciless approach to dealing with others, high Machs can be difficult to have around in one's work environment. Because they are attracted to situations in which they can use their

Machiavellianism A personality trait involving willingness to manipulate others for one's own purposes.

Many of the tactics adopted by persons high in Machiavellianism fall under the heading of organizational politics—*a topic we'll examine in detail in Chapter 12.*

The items shown here are similar to those contained on one measure of Machiavellianism. Persons who are high Machs tend to agree strongly with items 1, 3, 4, 5, and 8; persons who are low Machs tend to disagree with these items, and to strongly agree with items 2, 6, and 7.

Instructions: Enter a number next to each item. If you disagree strongly enter 1; if you disagree, enter 2; if you are neutral, enter 3; if you agree enter 4; if you strongly agree, enter 5.

_____ 1. The best way to handle people is to tell them what they want to hear.

_____ 2. When you ask someone to do something for you, it is best to give the real reasons for wanting it rather than giving reasons which might carry more weight.

_____ 3. Anyone who completely trusts anyone else is asking for trouble.

_____ 4. It is hard to get ahead without cutting corners and bending the rules.

_____ 5. It is safest to assume that all people have a vicious streak and that it will come out when they are given a chance.

_____ 6. It is never right to lie to someone else.

_____ 7. Most people are basically good and kind.

_____ 8. Most people will work hard only when they are forced to do so.

devious skills and show little concern for the welfare of others, they can be tough adversaries. Although you cannot always restructure work situations so as to block high Machs, there are several steps you can take to protect yourself from them. Here are a few that may prove effective:

EXPOSE THEM TO OTHERS. One reason high Machs so often get away with breaking promises, lying, and using "dirty tricks" (see Chapter 12) is that in many cases their victims choose to remain silent. This is hardly surprising because few people wish to call attention to the fact that they have been cheated or manipulated. This understandable desire to protect one's ego, however, plays directly into the hands of high Machs, leaving them free to repeat such actions. One means of blocking them is to make their actions public. This warns others and puts them on guard, making it harder for high Machs to get away with their manipulative games.

PAY ATTENTION TO WHAT OTHERS DO, NOT WHAT THEY SAY. High Machs are often masters of deception. They convince other people that they have the others' interests at heart, and they are often at their most persuasive when they are busily cutting the ground out from under their unsuspecting victims. How can you protect yourself against such tactics? In part, by focusing on what others *do* rather than what they say. If their actions suggest that they are cold-bloodedly manipulating the people around them, disregard even fervent claims about commitment to principles of loyalty and fair play: These are just camouflage, designed to mislead you.

AVOID SITUATIONS THAT GIVE HIGH MACHS AN EDGE. To assure their success, high Machs prefer to operate in certain types of situations—ones in which others' emotions run high and in which others are unsure about how to proceed. The reason for this preference is simple: High Machs realize that under such conditions many people will be distracted and less likely to recognize that they are being manipulated. It is usually wise, therefore, to avoid such situations. If this is not possible, you should at least refrain from making important decisions or commitments in them. Such restraint may make it harder for high Machs to use you for their own benefit.

Together, these suggestions may help you to avoid falling under the spell—and into the clutches—of unprincipled high Machs. Given the presence of at least some high Machs in most organizations and the dangers they pose to the unwary, it is worth keeping these suggestions and the existence of this unsettling aspect of personality firmly in mind.

Work-Related Motives: Achievement, Power, and Affiliation

Do you remember the person in your high school class who was named "Most likely to succeed"? If so, you probably recall that this individual was truly competitive: This person wanted to win in every situation—or at least in all the important ones. (Recall Michael Dell from our Preview Case; he certainly seems to fit this description.) Can you remember someone else you've known who was interested not so much in success, but in *power*—in being in charge? And how about the person who was chosen "most popular"; what was his or her central motive? Probably, to be liked by others. In short, if you search your own memory, you'll soon find evidence suggesting that people differ with respect to several basic motives. Not surprisingly, these motives—which focus, respectively, on *achievement*, *power*, and *affiliation*—have been found to exert important effects on organizational behavior. As such, they are certainly worthy of our careful attention here.

Achievement motivation: The quest for excellence. As its name suggests, **achievement motivation** (sometimes termed the *need for achievement*) refers to the strength of an individual's desire to excel—to succeed at difficult tasks and to do them better than other persons. People high in achievement motivation may be characterized as having a highly task-oriented outlook: They are more concerned with getting things done than they are with having good relationships with others. Also, because they are so interested in achieving success, people who have a high amount of achievement motivation tend to seek tasks that are moderately difficult and challenging.[52] Why not tasks that are extremely difficult and challenging? Because the chances of failing on such tasks is too high.

Similarly, such persons reject tasks that are too easy; succeeding on such tasks doesn't constitute "real" achievement. So, for these reasons, persons high in achievement motivation seek and prefer tasks that are moderate in difficulty. In contrast, people low in achievement motivation prefer either extremely difficult or extremely easy tasks. This is because success is almost guaranteed on easy tasks, while failure on extremely difficult ones can be attributed to external causes.

Another characteristic of people high in achievement motivation is a strong desire for feedback on performance: They want to know how well they are doing so they can adjust their goals to make these challenging—but not impossible (we'll consider the topic of goal setting in detail in Chapter 5). Evidence for this preference on the part of persons high in achievement motivation is provided by research conducted by Turban and Keon.[53] They asked management students to read descriptions of companies in which pay and promotions were based entirely on the quality of performance (a *merit-based* pay system) or in which these rewards were based on seniority (a *seniority-based* pay system). Participants—whose achievement motivation had previously been measured—indicated their preferences for working in each company. As shown in Figure 4-7, results indicated that all participants preferred to work for companies with merit-based pay systems. However, this tendency was stronger among people high in achievement motivation. This is not surprising: Such people, after all, are the ones most interested in gaining recognition for their accomplishments.

Given their strong desire to excel, it seems reasonable to expect that people high in achievement motivation will attain greater success in their careers than others. To some extent, this is true. People high in achievement motivation tend to gain promotions more rapidly than those who are low in achievement motivation, at least early in their careers.[54] However, people who are high in achievement motivation are not necessarily superior managers. For example, recent findings indicate that CEOs who are high in achievement motivation are more likely to centralize power—to keep it in the hands of just a

■ **Figure 4-8**
*Achievement Motivation and
Economic Development*
*Some evidence suggests that there is a
strong link between the level of achievement in a given culture and its economic growth.*

**leadership motivation pat-
tern (LMP)** A pattern of personality traits involving high
power motivation, low affiliation
motivation, and a high degree of
self-control.

First, consider the matter of managerial success. What kind of individuals
are most successful as managers? One possibility, suggested by McClelland and
Boyatzis, is that persons most likely to succeed in this role are high in power
motivation but low in affiliation motivation.[61] Such individuals will focus on
gaining influence over others while at the same time avoiding the trap of being unduly concerned about being liked by them. In other words, they will
seek power and influence but won't shy away from the tough decisions and
actions often required by this quest.

Are individuals who possess this combination of traits—known as the **leadership motivation pattern (LMP)**—actually more effective than those who
do not? Some research findings suggest that this is so. However, in addition
to high power motivation and low affiliation motivation, existing evidence indicates that to be successful, managers need another characteristic, too: What
McClelland and Boyatzis term a high degree of *self-control*. This refers to the
ability to keep firm control over one's own behavior—for example, holding
one's temper in check even in the face of provocation. When this trait is coupled with the leadership motivation pattern, a high level of success often results. For instance, persons showing this pattern tend to receive more
promotions than ones who do not.[62]

In sum, it appears that individual differences with respect to several motives are closely linked to important aspects of organizational behavior.
However, the nature of this relationship is far from simple. To understand how
individuals' motives influence their job performance or careers, we must take
careful account not only of the motives themselves, but also of the combinations or patterns in which they occur, the specific jobs being performed, and
the organizational context in which these motives operate. In other words,
once again we come face-to-face with the essential accuracy of the interactionist perspective and the complex interplay between personality and situational factors and constraints.

Morning Persons and Evening Persons

At present, about 20 percent of persons in the United States work at night
or on rotating shifts.[63] This proportion has increased in recent years and seems
likely to continue its upward course, given that more and more businesses are
choosing to operate round the clock.[64] Unfortunately, there appear to be significant costs to this trend: Working at night and especially rotating shifts seem
to adversely affect the health and well-being of persons exposed to them.[65]
Yet, there are some persons who seem to thrive on "the graveyard shift," and
actually prefer it. This fact suggests that there may be large individual differences in what is known as *circadian rhythm*—the times of day at which people
feel most alert and energetic.

In fact, growing evidence suggests that such differences exist and that they are stable over time. In other words, they may constitute yet another important individual difference factor relevant to organizational behavior. More specifically, it appears that most people fall into one of two categories—either they are **morning persons**, who feel most energetic early in the day, or they are **evening persons**, who feel most energetic at night. Presumably, evening persons would find the task of adapting to night work less stressful than morning persons and would, consequently, do better work when exposed to such conditions. Growing evidence indicates that this is indeed the case. For example, in a recent study, Guthrie, Ash, and Bandapudi[66] asked college students to keep diaries in which they reported on the times each day when they slept and the times each day when they studied. In addition, information was obtained from university records concerning the students' class schedules and their academic performance. All participants also completed a brief questionnaire designed to measure the tendency to be a morning or evening person.

Results revealed intriguing differences between participants who were classified as being high in the tendency to be a morning person or high in the tendency to be an evening person. As might be expected, morning persons reported sleeping primarily at night and studying in the morning, while evening persons reported the opposite pattern. Similarly, class schedules for the two groups also indicated interesting differences: Students classified as morning persons tended to schedule their classes earlier in the day than those classified as evening persons. Perhaps most interesting of all, morning persons did better in their early classes than they did in their later ones, while the opposite was true for students who were classified as being evening persons (see Figure 4-9).

These findings, and those of many other studies,[67] suggest that individual differences in circadian rhythms are indeed important from the point of view of job performance. Ideally, only individuals who are at their best late in the day would be assigned to night work. The results of following such a policy might well be better performance, better health, and fewer accidents for employees—outcomes beneficial both to them and their organizations.

Abilities: Having What It Takes

"We hold these truths to be self-evident, that all men are created equal. . . ." This statement, contained in the Declaration of Independence of the United States, is a noble one indeed. (Please read "persons" for "men," of course!) What it means, however, is *not* that all people are born with equal abilities to perform all tasks; rather, it suggests that we are all endowed with equal rights—including the right to test our abilities in a wide range of situations. We all know from our own experience that human beings are definitely *not* equal with respect to various **abilities**—the capacity to perform various tasks. No matter how hard we might have tried, neither one of the authors could ever have become a successful basketball player—we're simply too short! But one of us is an accomplished woodworker while the other is famous among his colleagues for the quickest verbal comebacks in our field. It is clear then that human beings possess a very large number of abilities and that they also differ tremendously with respect to many of these.

While the number of different abilities is very large, it is also clear that most fall into two major categories: *intellectual abilities*, which involve the capacity to perform various cognitive tasks, and *physical abilities*, which refer to the capacity to perform various physical actions. We'll now consider both types briefly.

Students who felt most alert and energetic early in the day (morning persons) did better in early classes than in late classes. In contrast, students who felt most alert and energetic late in the day (evening persons) did better in late classes.

(**Source:** Based on data from Guthrie, Ash, & Bandapudi, 1995.)

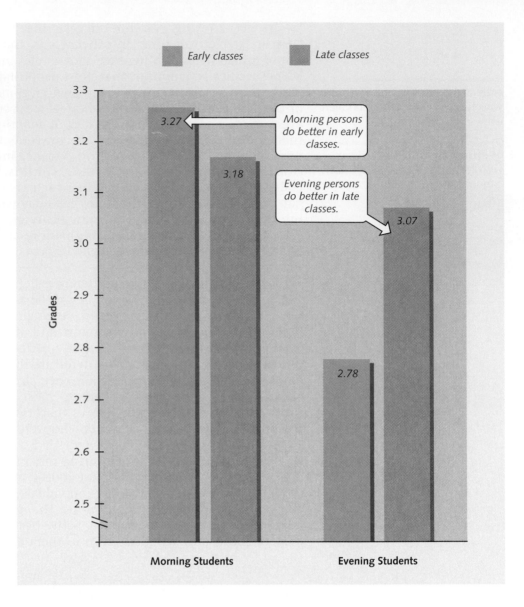

Intellectual Abilities

Different jobs clearly make different intellectual demands on the persons who hold them. Some require high levels of *information processing*—cognitive effort involving the combination, integration, and use of complex information. For example, top-level executives who must plan the long-term strategies of their companies must engage in such activities on a regular basis. Clearly, such persons need considerable cognitive ability to perform their jobs effectively. In contrast, other jobs are far less demanding with respect to such abilities; they are largely routine and do not require careful thought or analysis of information.

The many faces of intelligence. Many tests exist to measure various aspects of human mental abilities. For instance, *IQ tests* are designed to measure *intelligence*—-which is generally defined as the ability to think abstractly and to learn readily from experience.[68] Intelligence, however, is not a single, unitary ability. On the contrary, it is best viewed as a multifaceted process—or jewel, if you will! For example, one recent theory of human intelligence suggests that it actually involves three distinct aspects.[69] The first—known as *componential intelligence*—involves the abilities to think critically and analytically.

A high level of such intelligence is necessary for jobs involving complex decision making and detailed analysis of financial data, to mention just two.

A second type of intelligence is known as *experiential intelligence*. It involves the ability to pull seemingly unrelated information together so as to formulate new ideas. In other words, such intelligence is closely related to *creativity* and is necessary for jobs such as new product development and marketing. Finally, there is *contextual intelligence*. This is the practical side of intelligence; persons high in such intelligence are, in a sense, "streetwise": They can quickly size up a situation and adapt to it. A high level of contextual intelligence might be especially useful in such jobs as direct sales and in serving as a "troubleshooter" with respect to production equipment.

All of these aspects of intelligence relate to what might be termed the *cognitive side* of intelligence—the ability to work with various forms of information. According to Daniel Goleman, however, there is another important kind of intelligence—one he describes as **emotional intelligence** (**EQ** for short).[70] This refers to the ability to both perceive and control emotions—our own and those of other people. Growing evidence indicates that this type of intelligence, too, is important from the point of view of career success.

For example, in one recent study, new life insurance salespersons who scored high in optimism—one aspect of emotional intelligence—sold 37 percent more insurance than their lower-scoring counterparts.[71] Similarly, scientists who are adept at accurately "reading others," and so who tend to be liked by their colleagues, tend to be more productive than scientists who are lower in this aspect of emotional intelligence. Why? Because the highly liked scientists are included in informal e-mail networks and get the latest word on what's happening in the field; their less-liked and less emotionally intelligent associates are cut out of such networks. In short, there's more to intelligence than just being able to mentally manipulate information or mental symbols.

In fact, Goleman argues that there are at least five different components of emotional intelligence and that all can influence our effectiveness on the job: knowing our own emotions, controlling them, recognizing the emotions of others, controlling them, and self-motivation. He views empathy, which we discussed earlier in this chapter, as a key skill in several of these tasks. In short, the emotional side of life, appears to be important in many different ways.

One final point about intelligence: Until recently, the only measures of this central aspect of mental abilities involved paper-and-pencil tests. Recently, however, intelligence has been linked to underlying neural activity in the brain. For example, it has been found that persons who score high on standard tests of intelligence actually show more rapid conduction of neural impulses in certain portions of their brains than other persons.[72] Such findings open up new possibilities for measuring intelligence in relatively direct, biological terms.

Cognitive abilities and memory. While intelligence is important, it is not the entire story where cognitive abilities are concerned. In addition, there are more specific aspects to cognitive functioning that are related to the performance of various kinds of jobs. Among these, the most important appear to be *perceptual speed*—the ability to recognize similarities and differences in visual stimuli quickly—*number aptitude*—the ability to work with numbers in a quick and accurate manner, and *spatial visualization*—the ability to imagine how various objects will look when rotated or moved in space. As you can readily see, persons scoring high or low on each of these abilities may well be especially suited—or unsuited—for specific jobs. For instance, number aptitude is important for such jobs as accounting and financial analysis; perceptual speed is essential for jobs such as air traffic controller or nuclear power plant inspectors, while spatial visualization is important for many kinds of engineering and architecture.

emotional intelligence The ability to perceive and control emotions.

Another cognitive ability—perhaps one of the most important—is memory—the ability to store and later retrieve various forms of information.[73] While we generally think of memory as a single system, careful research actually suggests that there are several different forms of memory. These include (1) *semantic memory*—the capacity to store abstract, general knowledge; (2) *implicit memory*—the ability to retain information that can't be put into words, such as motor skills like riding a bicycle; and (3) *working* or *short-term memory*—the memory system that lets us retain information for very short periods of time, as, for example, when dialing a telephone number. Table 4-3 provides an overview of these and other types of memory.

Memory and aging: Do we really "lose it" as we grow older? Do you ever forget where you have put something down, such as your glasses, a pen, or a book? Do you ever come out of a large shopping mall only to discover that you can't remember where you left your car? Everyone has experiences like these but there is a widespread belief that they become more common as we grow older. In other words, many people believe that memory decreases with age. Is this true? If it is, there is an important implication for organizational behavior: Replace older employees with younger ones in jobs requiring extensive use of memory—that is, most high-level jobs.

Before you jump to this conclusion, however, we should quickly note that research on how memory changes over the course of our lives doesn't actually support such a strategy. Some aspects of memory do seem to decrease with age—especially working memory. In other words, as people grow older, they find it increasingly difficult to hold onto large amounts of information very briefly or to keep several tasks going simultaneously (an action that requires effective working memory).[74] Similarly, *prospective memory*—remembering to perform various actions at specific times—also seems to decline with age.[75] But other kinds of memory—for instance, semantic and implicit memory—remain largely unchanged until well into our 70s and beyond. When the benefits of growing experience are added to this picture, it becomes clear that there are no grounds for assuming that younger employees will always be superior to older ones; on the contrary, the total pattern with respect to memory and other cognitive abilities is quite mixed in nature.

■ TABLE 4-3 MEMORY SYSTEMS: AN OVERVIEW	
As shown here, we actually possess several different kinds of memory, each specialized for performing different tasks.	

Memory System	Function
Semantic memory	Holds general, abstract knowledge—for example, the meaning of words
Implicit memory	Stores information that cannot be expressed verbally—for example, how to ride a bicycle
Working or short-term memory	Holds a small amount of information for very brief periods of time—for example, a telephone number you have just found in the directory as you dial it
Episodic memory	Stores memories for events we have experienced personally
Prospective memory	Holds information about actions we should perform at specific times
Long-term memory	A permanent storage system that holds large amounts of information for very long periods of time—perhaps indefinitely

By the way, you might find it interesting to consider the following examples of exceptional memory abilities:

- History records that Julius Caesar had an exceptional working memory. In fact, he could dictate as many as seven letters at a time to his secretaries.
- Arturo Toscanini, the famous conductor, remembered every note of more than 400 musical scores. Right before one concert, a musician told him, in a panic, that one of the notes on his instrument was broken. Toscanini thought for a moment and then said: "It doesn't matter; that note is not played during this opera."
- Warren Buffet, a highly successful investor, can remember the annual sales, inventory, return on equity, and other financial details of companies whose records he examined decades in the past.

When we consider such feats, it is clear that human memory is indeed an amazingly powerful cognitive ability.

Physical Abilities

While many jobs require a high level of cognitive ability, others do not. Yet, such jobs often require considerable physical ability. Many different physical abilities exist, but from the point of view of job performance, the most important are those involving *strength*—the capacity to exert muscular force against various objects—and *flexibility*—the capacity to engage in bodily movements. The importance of such abilities is obvious with respect to many jobs—for example, construction work, production-line jobs, working on the loading dock, and so on. However, physical abilities are also important for jobs that, at first glance, do not appear to involve large physical component. For instance, secretaries must often sit in specific postures or bend over files for hours at a stretch. Considerable flexibility is needed for such jobs. Similarly, salespersons must often carry samples with them and move quickly from location to location. That's certainly true for the representatives of our publisher, who often have to carry heavy textbooks and climb many flights of stairs each day in order to call on individual professors. So, in sum, physical abilities play a key role in many jobs and should be carefully considered both by individuals seeking to fill these jobs and the organizations that hire them.

Measuring Individual Differences: Some Basic Methods

Physical traits such as height and weight can be measured readily by means of simple tools. Various aspects of personality and intellectual abilities, however, cannot be assessed quite so simply. There are no rulers for measuring self-monitoring and no thermometers for assessing achievement motivation or intelligence. How, then, can we quantify differences between individuals with respect to the various personality characteristics or intellectual abilities we've described? Several methods exist for accomplishing this task. In this section, we'll describe the two that are most important and will then consider some of the essential requirements of all procedures for measuring individual differences.

Objective and Projective Tests

While many different procedures for measuring personality and other individual differences exist, most fall into two major categories, often described by the terms *objective* and *projective*, respectively.

Objective tests such as *inventories* and *questionnaires*, are the most widely used method for measuring personality and many intellectual abilities. In the case of personality, these consist of a series of questions or statements to which individuals respond in various ways. For example, a questionnaire may ask re-

objective tests Questionnaires and inventories designed to measure various aspects of personality

spondents to indicate whether each of a set of statements is true or false about themselves, the extent to which they agree or disagree with various sentences, or to indicate which of a pair of named activities they prefer (see Table 4.1 on p. 112 and the Experiencing Organizational Behavior section at the end of this chapter for some examples). With respect to intellectual abilities, such tests often include problems—both verbal and numerical—that test-takers must complete or solve.

Answers to the questions on objective tests are then scored by means of special keys. The score obtained by a specific person is then compared with those obtained by hundreds or even thousands of other people who have taken the test previously. In this way, an individual's relative standing on the trait or ability being measured can be determined. Because such tests can be scored directly, without requiring any special interpretation of the responses (beyond counting them), they are described as being *objective* in nature.

Projective tests, in contrast, adopt another approach. They are used primarily to measure various aspects of personality and attempt to do so by presenting individuals with ambiguous stimuli such as the drawing in Figure 4-10. Persons taking such tests are then asked to indicate what they see. Since the stimuli are ambiguous in nature, it is assumed that the answers given by respondents reflect various aspects of their personality. In other words, different persons "see" different things in these ambiguous stimuli because they differ from one another in terms of various traits.

The illustration in Figure 4-10 is similar to ones contained in a widely used test designed to measure achievement motivation—the *Thematic Apperception Test.*[76] This test consists of a series of ambiguous drawings, and people completing it are asked to make up a story about each one. These are then carefully analyzed for basic themes, according to highly specific scoring procedures. For instance, if you interpret Figure 4-10 as someone who is saddened by learning that she or he didn't pass a test, this may be an indication that you are worried about failing—a sign that you are relatively high in achievement motivation. It is important to note that the task of scoring and interpreting projective tests is complex and should only be performed by people who have had extensive training in such procedures. Administering such tests and then interpreting them on the basis of intuition or "common sense" would probably lead to false conclusions, and would be unethical, too. However, when projective tests are administered and scored by trained professionals, they can provide valuable information about many different aspects of personality.

Reliability and Validity: Essential Requirements

Regardless of whether they are objective or projective in nature, all measures of personality and intellectual abilities must meet two basic requirements: They must be *reliable* and they must be *valid*. **Reliability** refers to the extent to which a test yields stable, consistent scores over time. For example, consider how useless a tailor's measurements of your waist would be if she or he used an elastic tape measure. Each time a measurement was taken, it would be different from the previous occasion—not because your weight had changed, but because the measuring instrument itself is unreliable. In a similar manner, measures of personality must yield consistent scores if they are to be useful.

How is such reliability established? In several different ways. One that is commonly used in the field of organizational behavior involves statistical procedures that provide an index of *internal consistency*—the extent to which all items on the test are measuring the same thing. Another involves the kind of consistency to which we referred earlier—consistency across time, or *test-retest reliability*. When such reliability is high, individuals obtain highly similar scores each time they complete the test (please see part A of Figure 4-11).

Objective tests are used to measure many other aspects of organizational behavior. As we will see in Chapter 6, such tests are often used to measure work-related attitudes.

projective tests Methods for measuring personality in which individuals respond to ambiguous stimuli. Their responses provide insights into their personality traits.

■ **Figure 4-10**
Projective Tests: An Example
The drawing shown here is similar to those contained in one famous projective test of personality—the Thematic Apperception Test. This test is used to measure individual differences in achievement motivation. Persons taking the test make up a story about each drawing. The contents of these stories is then used to assess the person's achievement motivation and several other motives as well.

(**Source:** From Robert J. Gregory, *Behavior in Organizations*, 2nd ed. Copyright © 1996 by Allyn & Bacon. Reprinted with permission.)

reliability The extent to which a test yields consistent scores on various occasions, and the extent to which all of its items measure the same underlying construct.

Reliability *(top) refers to the extent to
which scores on a test are consistent
over time.* Validity *(bottom) refers to
the extent to which a test actually
measures what it claims to measure.
Both reliability and validity are
measured in several different ways.*

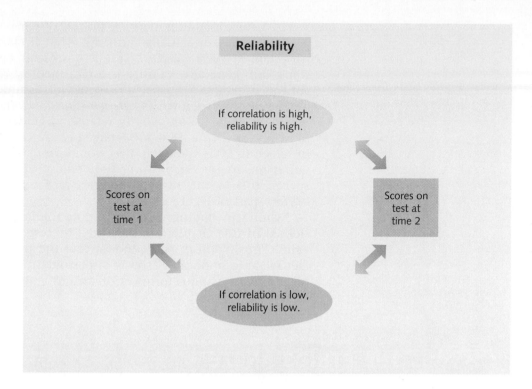

Reliability

If correlation is high,
reliability is high.

Scores on
test at
time 1

Scores on
test at
time 2

If correlation is low,
reliability is low.

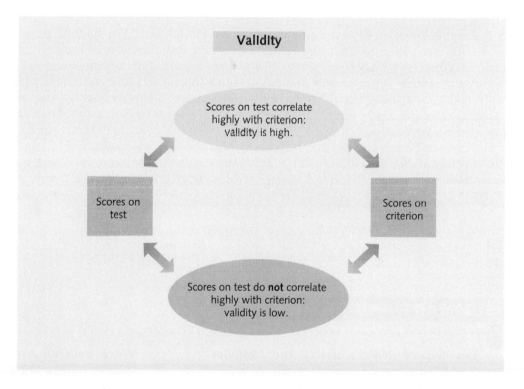

Validity

Scores on test correlate
highly with criterion:
validity is high.

Scores on
test

Scores on
criterion

Scores on test do **not** correlate
highly with criterion:
validity is low.

validity The extent to which a
test actually measures what it
claims to measure.

Another basic requirement for all tests of personality is that they be valid. **Validity** refers to the extent to which a test measures what it actually claims to measure. Interestingly, a test can be high in reliability but low in validity. For example, suppose that to measure intelligence, we recorded the dimensions of your skull and then used this to estimate the size of your brain. Such measurements could be highly reliable—each time we took them, we'd get very much the same physical readings. But would they actually tell us anything about your intelligence? Definitely not; the notion that brain size is directly linked to intelligence has been thoroughly discredited through scientific research.

In a corresponding manner, no test of personality or intellectual abilities is useful unless it actually measures what it claims to measure. But how do we establish such validity? This is a difficult task, requiring many separate steps, but, generally, validity is established by relating scores on the test to various outcomes or aspects of behavior assumed to reflect the trait being measured; this is known as *criterion-related validity*. For example, if scores on a test of intelligence are closely related to grades in school or scores on tests like the GMAT (the General Management Aptitude Test, used by many schools in selecting MBA students), this would provide some evidence for its validity. Other means for establishing the validity of a test exist, but, in several respects, this is the most straightforward and convincing. (Please see the bottom part of Figure 4-11).

Before concluding, we should note that all of the traits and abilities considered in this chapter are measured by tests known to be both reliable and valid. Thus, you can be confident that the findings we have discussed do in fact relate to important aspects of personality—ones that have significant implications for various forms of organizational behavior.

THE ETHICS ANGLE

CAN TESTS HAVE AN ADVERSE IMPACT?

What happens if tests used to measure individual differences—and then for making important decisions concerning specific persons—are *not* valid? Serious problems with important legal ramifications may result. For instance, if scores on a test are not closely related to performance of a specific job, using the test to select job applicants for it is not only on shaky ground from the point of view of ethics: It is simply illegal in the United States and many other countries. For example, if such a test is used for choosing job applicants, and the result is that a smaller proportion of minority applicants than nonminority applicants are hired, the rejected employees can file suit on the basis of *adverse impact*—the fact that use of this test harms the careers of minority applicants to a greater extent than those of nonminority applicants. Clearly, such issues must be carefully considered whenever tests designed to measure individual differences are used as a basis for making hiring or promotion decisions.

SUMMARY AND REVIEW

The Nature of Personality and Abilities

Personality is the unique and relatively stable pattern of behavior, thoughts, and emotions shown by individuals. In contrast, **abilities** refer to the capacity to perform various tasks or cognitive activities. Organizational behavior is often the result of a complex interplay between *individual difference* factors, such as personality and abilities, and situational factors. This fact is recognized in the **interactionist perspective** that is widely accepted in the field of organizational behavior. Because of this interaction between personal and situational factors, work-related outcomes are usually most positive when there is a close match between people's personalities and the requirements of their jobs (known as **person-job fit**).

Work-Related Aspects of Personality

Several aspects of personality are related to important forms of organizational behavior. The **"big five" dimensions of personality**—so named because they appear to be very basic aspects of personality—appear to play a role in successful performance of many jobs. In particular, two of these dimensions, *conscientiousness* and *extraversion*, are good predictors of success in many different jobs. **Positive affectivity** and **negative affectivity**—stable tendencies to experience positive or negative moods at work—are related to the quality of individual decision making and willingness to help others.

Another personality factor related to organizational behavior is the **Type A behavior pattern**. Persons showing this pattern are highly competitive, irritable, and always in a hurry. Such persons tend to perform better than those with the opposite pattern—**Type B**—on tasks requiring speed. However, they may perform less well than Type B's on tasks requiring considered judgment. Type A's experience more conflict with others and may become involved in more instances of workplace aggression. They also experience serious health problems more frequently than Type B's, and this may prevent them from reaching the top in many organizations.

Individuals who believe that they possess the capability to perform many different tasks are high in **self-efficacy**. They often do achieve higher levels of performance than people who lack such confidence in their own abilities.

Persons who seek to change the environment around them and to capitalize on opportunities are described as being high on a trait known as the **proactive personality**. For example, real estate agents high on this dimension sell more houses, earn more commissions, and bring in more new listings than persons low on this dimension. Among the most important aspects of personality from the point of view of organizational behavior is **self-monitoring**. High self-monitors are concerned with making good impressions on others and readily adapt their behavior to match the requirements of a given situation. In contrast, low self-monitors remain much the same person across many different contexts. High self-monitors are more effective *boundary-spanners* than low self-monitors, and are better at *impression management*. High self-monitors also obtain more promotions, and are better at acquiring mentors.

Individuals who adopt a manipulative approach to their relations with others are described as being high in **Machiavellianism**. They are not influenced by considerations of loyalty, friendship, or ethics. Instead, they simply do whatever is needed to get their own way.

People differ with respect to several important *work-related motives*. **Achievement motivation** is the desire to excel. People high in achievement motivation seek situations of moderate difficulty because they are challenging enough to master, but not so difficult as to make failure certain. Such persons prefer jobs in which their accomplishments are recognized on an individual basis—for instance, jobs using merit-based pay. People who are high on **power motivation**—the desire to be in charge, and low on **affiliation motivation**—the desire to have friendly relations with others, and also possess a high degree of self-control, show what is termed

the **leadership motivation pattern (LMP)**. This pattern is related to success in managerial jobs.

Individuals also differ with respect to when they feel most alert and energetic. **Morning persons** are at their best early in the day, while **evening persons** are at their best late in the day. These differences can play an important role in jobs involving shift work.

Abilities

Individuals differ with respect to many abilities. These fall into two major categories: intellectual abilities and physical abilities. Intellectual abilities refer to the capacity to perform cognitive tasks. *Intelligence* is one important intellectual ability and is related to success in many different fields. Recent findings indicate that intelligence is multifaceted rather than unidimensional—several different kinds appear to exist. Each of these forms of intelligence is related to success in various kinds of jobs. Intelligence also involves the ability to perceive and control emotions (**emotional intelligence**). In addition to intelligence, individuals also vary with respect to specific intellectual abilities such as *perceptual speed*, *number aptitude*, and *spatial visualization*. Memory, the ability to store and later retrieve information, is another important aspect of intellectual abilities. Several kinds of memory exist, including semantic memory, implicit memory, and working memory. Contrary to popular belief, most aspects of memory do not decrease sharply as people age.

Physical abilities refer to the capacity to perform various physical actions. Two important components of such abilities are *strength* and *flexibility*.

Measuring Individual Differences

Individual differences in personality and abilities are generally assessed either by objective tests or projective tests. **Objective tests**, used for measuring personality and intellectual abilities, involve questionnaires that are scored using established keys. In contrast, **projective tests** are used exclusively for measuring personality. Such tests expose individuals to ambiguous stimuli and use their interpretations of these stimuli to reach conclusions about important aspects of personality. To be useful, any measure of individual differences must be **reliable**—it must yield consistent measurements over time. In addition, all such tests must be **valid**—they must measure what they claim to measure.

QUESTIONS FOR DISCUSSION

1. Why might two individuals whose personalities are very similar behave differently in a given situation?
2. How does a close *person-job fit* contribute to good performance?
3. What is the difference between being in a good mood and having the characteristic of positive affectivity?
4. Suppose that you were hiring someone to perform a job that required very fast performance. Would you prefer to hire a Type A or Type B person? Why?

5. In what fields do you think individuals high on the *proactive personality* dimension would excel? Why?
6. How does having low self-efficacy interfere with task performance?
7. Why are persons high in self-monitoring so effective in *boundary-spanning positions*? Can you think of jobs that they would *not* do very well?
8. If you suspect that someone with whom you are dealing is high in Machiavellianism, what steps should you

3. Groups are then allowed up to ten minutes to reach a decision. At the end of ten minutes, the instructor announces: "Time is up."

4. Each group is then asked whether they reached a decision, and what it was. In each group, it will probably be found that two persons agreed on how to divide the money and left the third "out in the cold."

Questions for Discussion

1. How did the coalitions of two persons form? Was there a particular person in each group who was largely responsible for the formation of the winning coalition?

2. Why did the third person get left out of the agreement? What did this person say or do—or fail to say or do—that led to his or her being omitted from the two-person coalition that divided the money?

3. Do you think that actions in this situation are related to Machiavellianism? How?

4. How can people low in Machiavellianism protect themselves from being left "out in the cold" in such situations?

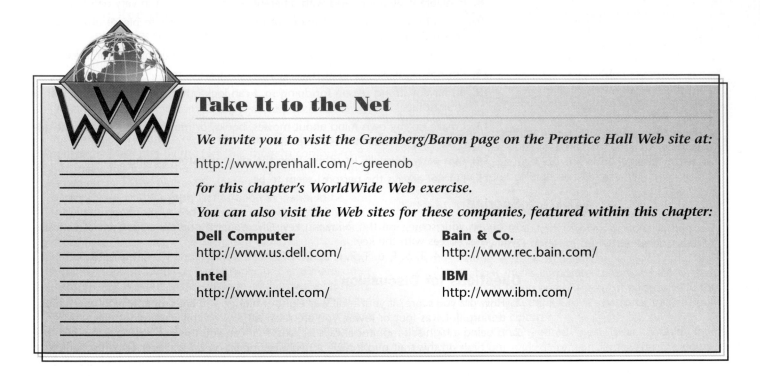

Take It to the Net

We invite you to visit the Greenberg/Baron page on the Prentice Hall Web site at:

http://www.prenhall.com/~greenob

for this chapter's WorldWide Web exercise.

You can also visit the Web sites for these companies, featured within this chapter:

Dell Computer
http://www.us.dell.com/

Bain & Co.
http://www.rec.bain.com/

Intel
http://www.intel.com/

IBM
http://www.ibm.com/

In the fall of 1995, Baltimore Orioles shortstop Cal Ripken, Jr. reached a career milestone that, as the saying goes, was one for the record books. On September 6, as the Orioles beat the California Angels, Ripken played in his 2,131st consecutive baseball game and thus surpassed a record by Lou Gehrig. Commemorating the occasion, President Bill Clinton noted, "Here's a guy with massive talent who loves what he's doing, but he's also shown a kind of dedication and constancy that anybody can identify with and that we need in all walks of life." And how does Cal Ripken explain his achievement? As he told ABC News, "It's just a matter of going out there, feeling passion for something you do, and just do it, not for the sake of the money, not for the sake of anything else but the enjoyment of doing that action."

As the sports world commemorated this historic occasion, stories of other "iron men and women" began to surface. Research has shown, for instance, that the average worker calls in sick 5.6 days each year. However, Grace Chewning, the city clerk in Orlando, Florida, hasn't missed a day of work since 1960; Benny Edens, the head football coach at a Southern California high school, had a perfect attendance record from 1950 until his retirement in 1991. And unlike Mr. Ripken, whose organization required his presence only from April through October, these absence-free performances were logged over the 12-month calendar used by most organizations.

Is there an explanation for such extraordinary performances from ordinary employees? Professor Kenneth P. De Meuse of the University of Wisconsin at Eau Claire thinks that outstanding employee performance records are linked to certain personality characteristics such as tremendous work ethics and a high energy level. In addition, De Meuse believes that good health and good fortune are important factors, as are family support and a love of one's work.

However, De Meuse also sees evidence that the growing number of corporate downsizings and restructurings has created a work environment in which employees do not want to go to work. Indeed, since 1992, absenteeism in the workplace is up 14.1 percent. "The conditions that fostered the Cal Ripkens of the past," contends Professor De Meuse, "are in large measure not present in today's environment."

Video source: The streak: Cal Ripken, Jr. (1995, September 6). *Nightline*. *Additional sources*: Van Gelder, L. (1995, September 17). Baseball's iron men aren't the only ones made of sterner stuff. *The New York Times*, Sec. 3, p. 11; Green, L. (1995, September 1). Chicago worker leaves Cal in the dust. *USA Today*, p. 1A.

CHAPTER | Five

MOTIVATION IN ORGANIZATIONS

■ OBJECTIVES

LEARNING

After reading this chapter you should be able to:

1. Define *motivation* and explain its importance in the field of organizational behavior.

2. Describe *need hierarchy theory* and what it recommends about improving motivation in organizations.

3. Identify and explain the conditions through which *goal setting* can be used to improve job performance.

4. Explain *equity theory* and describe some of the research designed to test its basic tenets.

5. Describe *expectancy theory* and how it may be applied in organizations.

6. Distinguish between *job enlargement* and *job enrichment* as techniques for motivating employees.

7. Describe the *job characteristics model* and its implications for redesigning jobs to enhance motivation.

PHYSICIAN SALES & SERVICE: BIG PROFITS FROM BIG IDEAS

Let's face it, selling medical supplies to doctors' offices isn't exactly glamorous. But, if there's a dollar or two to be made in gauze pads and thermometers, Patrick C. Kelly is going after it. The company he founded 15 years ago, Physician Sales & Service (PSS), has grown an average of 22 percent per year over the past five years, resulting in annual sales of about $500 million.

Company officials credit this phenomenal success to the goal that Kelly set for PSS after its first few struggling years in business: to become the first national physician supply company. Kelly did everything he could to make sure everyone bought into this vision. He articulated the goal in every presentation he made. And, just to make sure it came across, he even printed it on huge banners hung from the warehouse walls. This mission helped reassure the nervous employees of the companies PSS bought out, many of whom came to believe they had a future in a company with such lofty aspirations.

Kelly was intent on having all PSS employees accept his commitment to growth and profitability. To make sure they did, he gave them all a piece of the action—warehouse workers, truck drivers, and office personnel alike. A great portion of their pay is linked to how much they helped the company succeed: The more profitable their branch operations, the higher their semiannual bonuses. So that people can see how they stand, each salesperson's performance figures are posted on the office walls. The branches' overall productivity figures are shared at monthly meetings.

Those employees who really want to share in the company's success can participate in a stock ownership plan in which the company matches any individual stock purchases they make up to 10 percent of their salaries. These incentives have made many PSS employees very wealthy. In fact, about 40 of its 1,800 current employees have become millionaires. Kelly enjoys sharing the company's wealth with those who have worked so hard to bring it about.

But, it's not only the emphasis on profitability that keeps PSS employees going. The company's whole work hard–play hard orientation is key too. Kelly has made having fun a central aspect of life at PSS. Employees have come to enjoy the company's inter-branch volleyball tournaments, its quarterly excursions to Key West for corporate staff, and its monthly P&L meetings held at various recreational sites (e.g., bowling alleys, ballparks, amusement parks). Monthly meetings feature competitions modeled after the old TV show *Family Feud* in which two teams are pitted against each other answering questions about the company (such as its bonus plan, customer service, and the like). Winners are awarded points that can be cashed in for small prizes. Kelly's rationale is straightforward: to reward employees for their knowledge of the business. In fact, each branch has a book of 100 questions to which employees are expected to know the answers. When visiting branches, Kelly has been known to select employees at random and ask them some of these questions. Answer correctly, and he'll press a $20 bill into your hand.

These tactics have helped PSS reach the lofty goal that Kelly set: Today, it is indeed the first physician supply company to operate nationally. Now, Kelly is working on a new goal: to make PSS a billion-dollar company by the end of 2001. Can they make it? "Oh yes," answers Cyndi Aszklar, the New Orleans branch operations manager. "When we say we're going to do something, we do it."

The success enjoyed by PSS is certainly impressive. But, it is by no means accidental. In fact, it can be traced to several important things that Patrick Kelly did to get PSS employees to work as hard as they could. He made sure the employees knew exactly what the company was striving for—and he rewarded them for their efforts toward achieving this mission. He also made it interesting to work at the company. The bottom line: working hard at PSS not only puts cash in your pockets but is an enjoyable activity in and of itself.

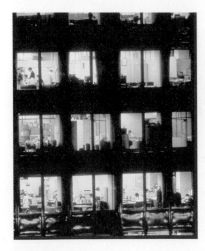

■ Figure 5-1
What Motivates These People?
Peek into the windows of this Tokyo office building and you see people working late into the night. The question of what motivates these and other people to work so hard is one of the most important ones raised in the field of OB.

This case raises some interesting questions. What is it about setting goals that stimulates people to action? How, and under what conditions, do rewards help encourage people to work hard? Why does making the job fun and interesting help so much as well? Combining these into one basic question that reflects the theme of this chapter, we may ask: How do you go about motivating people to work? With an eye toward answering this question we will examine the process of *motivation* in this chapter (see Figure 5-1).

Although people in business may have lots of interesting ideas about how to go about motivating employees, OB's approach is based on science. This is not to say that we are only interested in research and theory—far from it. We are also extremely interested in what these efforts tell us about ways to motivate real people performing real jobs. The point is that our approach, in keeping with the orientation of the field of OB, is based on conducting and applying sound scientific research. Nowhere in the field are these dual interests more clearly realized than in the study of motivation. Indeed, we are interested in asking both theoretical questions, such as "*What* motivates people, and *why*?" and applied questions, such as "*How* can this knowledge be put to practical use?" Hence, our focus in this chapter will be both on theories of motivation and on their practical application.

The theories we will consider represent the major approaches to the topic of motivation as currently studied.[1] Our look at each major approach to motivation will focus on what the theory says, the research bearing on it, and its practical implications. We think this orientation will help you develop a solid understanding of the importance of motivation as a topic of interest to organizational scientists and practitioners. However, before turning to these theories and applications, we will begin by taking a closer look at the concept of motivation itself.

Motivation in Organizations: Its Basic Nature

motivation The set of processes that arouse, direct, and maintain human behavior toward attaining some goal.

Although motivation is a broad and complex concept, organizational scientists have agreed on its basic characteristics.[2] We define **motivation** as the set of processes that arouse, direct, and maintain human behavior toward attaining some goal. The diagram in Figure 5-2 will guide our explanation as we elaborate on this definition.

The first part of our definition deals with *arousal*. This has to do with the drive, or energy behind our actions. For example, people may be guided by their interest in making a good impression on others, doing interesting

■ Figure 5-2
Motivation: Its Basic Components
Motivation involves the arousal, direction, and maintenance of behavior toward a goal. An example of this process is shown here.

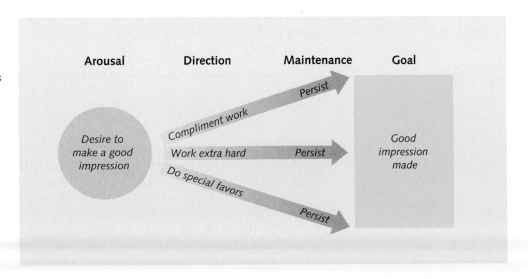

work, being successful at what they do, and so on. Their interest in fulfilling these motives stimulates them to engage in behaviors designed to fulfill them.

But, what will people do to satisfy their motives? Motivation is also concerned with the choices people make, the *direction* their behavior takes. For example, employees interested in cultivating a favorable impression on their supervisors may do many different things: compliment them on their good work, do them special favors, work extra hard on an important project, and the like. Each of these options may be recognized as a path toward meeting the person's goal.

The final part of our definition deals with *maintaining* behavior. How long will people persist at attempting to meet their goal? To give up in advance of goal attainment means not to satisfy the need that stimulated behavior in the first place. Obviously, people who do not persist at meeting their goals (e.g., salespeople who give up before reaching their quotas) cannot be said to be highly motivated.

To summarize, motivation requires all three components: the arousal, direction, and maintenance of goal-directed behavior. An analogy may help tie these components together. Imagine that you are driving down a road on your way home. The arousal part of motivation is like the energy created by the car's engine. The direction component is like the steering wheel, taking you along your chosen path. Finally, the maintenance aspect of the definition is the persistence that keeps you going until you arrive home, reaching your goal.

Now that we have defined motivation, it is time to bring up two important points. First, motivation cannot be seen, but only inferred on the basis of performance. However, *motivation and job performance are not synonymous.* Just because someone performs at a task well does not mean that he or she is highly motivated. This person actually may be very skillful but not putting forth much effort at all. If you're a mathematical genius, for example, you may breeze through your calculus class without hardly trying. By contrast, someone who performs poorly may be putting forth a great deal of effort but still be falling short of a desired goal because he or she lacks the skill needed to succeed. If you've ever tried to learn a new sport but found that you couldn't get the hang of it no matter how hard you tried, you know what we mean.

A second key point is that *motivation is multifaceted.* By this we mean that people may have several different motives operating at once. Sometimes, these may conflict. For example, a word processing operator might be motivated to please his boss by being as productive as possible. However, being too productive may antagonize one's co-workers, who fear that they're being made to look bad. The result is that the two motives may pull the individual in different directions, and the one that wins out is the one that's strongest in that situation.

These examples clearly show that motivation is a complex and important concept in the field of organizational behavior. In fact, many observers of American business trends have attributed problems of sagging production to a general lack of motivation within the workforce.[3] However, to claim that today's employees are poorly motivated would be misleading. After all, surveys show that most Americans would continue to work even if they didn't need the money.[4] Although money is certainly important to people, they are motivated to attain many other goals as well. Because of technological advances that took the drudgery out of many jobs, today's workers are motivated by the prospect of performing jobs that are interesting and challenging—not just jobs that pay well (see Figure 5-3). The field of OB considers a wide variety of factors that motivate people on the job. Our discussion of the various theories that follows will highlight these variables.

■ **Figure 5-3**
*The Quest for Interesting Work:
A Key Motivator*
Surveys showing that people are highly
motivated by interesting work suggest
that this ant may be speaking for all
of us.

(**Source:** Drawing by M. Twohy, © 1994 The
New Yorker Magazine, Inc.)

"I'll quit when it stops being fun."

Need Theories of Motivation

The first approach to motivation we will consider is the most basic: theories that explain motivation in terms of the satisfaction of basic human needs. Indeed, organizational scholars have paid a great deal of attention to the idea that people are motivated to use their jobs as mechanisms for satisfying their needs.

Need Hierarchy Theories

need hierarchy theory

Maslow's theory specifying that there are five human needs (physiological, safety, social, esteem, and self-actualization) and that these are arranged such that lower, more basic needs must be satisfied before higher-level needs become activated.

Probably the best-known concept of human needs in organizations has been proposed by Abraham Maslow.[5] Maslow was a clinical psychologist who introduced a theory of personal adjustment, known as **need hierarchy theory**, based on his observations of patients throughout the years. His premise was that if people grow up in an environment in which their needs are not met, they will be unlikely to function as healthy, well-adjusted individuals. Much of the popularity of Maslow's approach is based on applying the same idea in organizations: That is, unless people get their needs met on the job, they will not function as effectively as possible.

Specifically, Maslow theorized that people have five types of needs and that these are activated in a *hierarchical* manner. This means that the needs are aroused in a specific order from lowest to highest, and that the lowest-order need must be fulfilled before the next highest order need is triggered, and so on. The five major categories of needs are listed on the left side of Figure 5-4. Please refer to this diagram as a summary of the needs as we describe them here.

1. *Physiological needs* are the lowest-order, most basic needs specified by Maslow. These refer to satisfying fundamental biological drives, such as the need for food, air, water, and shelter. To satisfy such needs, organizations must provide employees with a salary that allows them to afford adequate living conditions. Similarly, sufficient opportunities to rest (e.g., coffee breaks) and to engage in physical activity (e.g., fitness and exercise facilities) are also important for people to meet their physiological needs. With increasing frequency, companies are providing exercise and physical fitness programs for their employees to help them stay healthy (see Figure 5-5).[6] The rationale is quite simple: People who are too hungry or too ill to work will hardly be able to make much of a contribution to their companies.

2. *Safety needs*, the second level of need in Maslow's hierarchy, are activated after physiological needs are met. Safety needs refer to the need for a se-

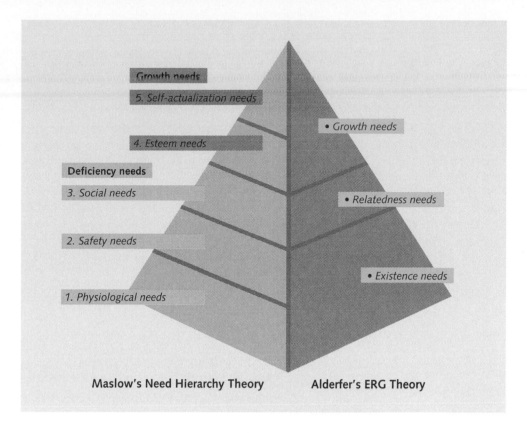

■ **Figure 5-4**
Need Theories: A Comparison
The five needs identified by Maslow's need hierarchy theory (shown at left) correspond to the three needs of Alderfer's ERG theory (shown at right). Whereas Maslow's theory specifies that these needs are activated in order from lowest level to highest level, Alderfer's theory specifies that needs can be activated in any order.

Growth needs

5. Self-actualization needs

• Growth needs

4. Esteem needs

Deficiency needs

3. Social needs

• Relatedness needs

2. Safety needs

1. Physiological needs

• Existence needs

Maslow's Need Hierarchy Theory   **Alderfer's ERG Theory**

cure environment, free from threats of physical or psychological harm. Organizations can do many things to help satisfy safety needs. For example, they may provide employees with safety equipment (e.g., hard hats and goggles), life and health insurance plans, and security forces (e.g., police and fire protection). Similarly, jobs that provide tenure (such as teaching) and no-layoff agreements provide a psychological security blanket that helps satisfy safety needs. All of these practices enable people to do their jobs without fear of harm and in a safe and secure atmosphere.

3. *Social needs*, Maslow's third level of needs, are activated after safety needs have been met. Social needs refer to the need to be affiliative—to have friends, to be loved and accepted by other people. To help meet social needs, organizations may encourage participation in social events, such as office picnics or parties. Company bowling or softball leagues, as well as country club memberships, also provide good opportunities for meeting social needs. Not only do such activities help promote physical fit-

■ **Figure 5-5**
Exercise: One Route to Satisfying People's Physiological Needs
This elevated running track at Nike's 74-acre corporate campus in Beaverton, Oregon, is just one of several fitness amenities the company provides to satisfy its employees' physiological needs by keeping them healthy.

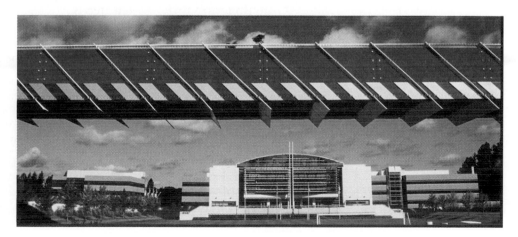

THE ETHICS ANGLE

OPERATION FRONTLINE: FIGHTING THE WAR AGAINST HUNGER

It's a sad fact that millions of low income people today don't get enough nutritious food in their diets. Targeting this problem has been *Operation Frontline*, a recently launched program aimed at teaching people with limited incomes how to budget and plan meals that provide maximum nutritional value with minimum expense.[7] An outgrowth of the *Share Our Strength* program dedicated for over a decade to fighting hunger, *Operation Frontline* brings together volunteer chefs and other culinary professionals who help families at nutritional risk so they can learn to prevent hunger in the long run.

The rationale behind *Operation Frontline* is that hunger can be eliminated by attacking one of its root causes. By learning cooking skills, ways to stretch grocery budgets, and ideas for making inexpensive but nutritious recipes, participants in *Operation Frontline* come away knowing how to improve their diets—and from this, their health. By satisfying this physiological need, people are put on the path to becoming productive, employable members of society.

ness—helping satisfy physiological needs, as we noted above—but they also give employees a chance to socialize and develop friendships.

Taken together as a group, physiological needs, safety needs, and social needs are known as *deficiency needs*. Maslow's idea was that if these needs are not met, an individual will fail to develop into a healthy person—both physically and psychologically. In contrast, the next two highest-order needs, the ones at the top of the hierarchy, are known as *growth needs*. Gratification of these needs is said to help a person grow and to develop to his or her fullest potential.

4. *Esteem needs* are the fourth level of needs. These refer to a person's need to develop self-respect and to gain the approval of others. The desires to achieve success, have prestige, and be recognized by others all fall into this category. Companies do many things to satisfy their employees' esteem needs. They may, for example, have awards banquets to recognize distinguished achievements. Giving monetary bonuses—even small ones—in recognition of employees' suggestions for improvement helps promote their esteem. Nonmonetary awards, such as trophies and plaques, provide reminders of an employee's important contributions, continuously fulfilling esteem needs.[8] Including articles in company newsletters describing an employee's success, giving keys to the executive washroom, assigning private parking spaces, and posting signs identifying the "employee of the month" are also examples of things that can be done to satisfy esteem needs.

5. *Self-actualization needs* are found at the top of Maslow's hierarchy. These are the needs aroused only after all the lower-order needs have been met. **Self-actualization** refers to the need for self-fulfillment—the desire to become all that one is capable of being, developing to one's fullest potential. By working at their maximum creative potential, employees who are self-actualized can be extremely valuable assets to their organizations. Individuals who have self-actualized are working at their peak and represent the most effective use of an organization's human resources.

Research testing Maslow's theory has supported the distinction between deficiency needs and growth needs. Unfortunately the research has shown that not all people are able to satisfy their higher-order needs on the job. For example, Porter found that whereas lower-level managers were able to satisfy only their deficiency needs on the job, managers from the higher echelons of

self-actualization The need to discover who we are and to develop ourselves to the fullest potential.

organizations were able to satisfy both their deficiency and growth needs.[9] In general, Maslow's theory has not received a great deal of support with respect to the specific notions it proposes—namely, the exact needs that exist and the order in which they are activated.[10] Specifically, many researchers have failed to confirm that there are only five basic categories of need and that they are activated in the exact order specified by Maslow.

ERG theory. In response to these criticisms, an alternative formulation has been proposed by Alderfer.[11] His approach, known as **ERG theory**, is much simpler than Maslow's. Alderfer specifies not only that there are only three types of needs instead of five, but also that these are not necessarily activated in any specific order. In fact, Alderfer postulates that any need may be activated at any time. The three needs specified by ERG theory are the needs for *existence, relatedness,* and *growth. Existence* needs correspond to Maslow's physiological needs and safety needs. *Relatedness* needs correspond to Maslow's social needs, the need for meaningful social relationships. Finally, *growth* needs correspond to the esteem needs and self-actualization needs in Maslow's theory—the need for developing one's potential. A summary of Alderfer's ERG theory is shown on the right side of Figure 5-4, along with the corresponding needs proposed by Maslow.

Clearly, ERG theory is much less restrictive than Maslow's need hierarchy theory. Its advantage is that it fits better with research evidence suggesting that although basic needs exist, they are not exactly as specified by Maslow.[12] Despite the fact that need theories are not in complete agreement about the precise number of needs and the relationships between them, they do agree that satisfying human needs is an important part of motivating behavior on the job.

Managerial Applications of Need Theories

Probably the greatest value of need theories lies in the practical implications they have for management. In particular, the theories are important insofar as they suggest specific things that managers can do to help their subordinates become self-actualized. Because self-actualized employees are likely to work at their maximum creative potential, it makes sense to help people attain this state by helping them meet their needs. With this in mind, it is worthwhile to consider what organizations may do to help satisfy their employees' needs.

1. *Promote a healthy workforce.* Some companies are helping satisfy their employees' physiological needs by providing incentives to keep them healthy. For example, Hershey Foods Corporation, and Southern California Edison Company, among others, give insurance rebates to employees with healthy lifestyles, while charging extra premiums to those whose habits (e.g., smoking) put them at greater risk for health problems.[13] To the extent that these incentives encourage employees to adapt healthier lifestyles, the likelihood of satisfying their physiological needs is increased. For a summary of some of the creative ways today's companies are promoting healthy lifestyles—and the resulting benefits—see Table 5-1.[14]

2. *Provide financial security.* Financial security is an important type of safety need. In this regard, some companies are going beyond the more traditional forms of payroll savings and profit-sharing plans. Notably, Com-Corp Industries (an auto parts manufacturer based in Cleveland, Ohio) found that its employees had serious financial difficulties when faced with sending their children to college, leading them to offer very low interest loans (only 3 percent annually for ten years) for this purpose.[15]

   Financial security is a key aspect of job security, particularly in troubled economic times, when layoffs are inevitable. To help soften the blow

ERG theory An alternative to Maslow's need hierarchy theory proposed by Alderfer, which asserts that there are three basic human needs: existence, relatedness, and growth.

The American companies whose wellness programs offer the best range of services and generate the greatest savings are awarded the C. Everett Koop National Health Award. Here are 12 recent winners and a summary of what they've been doing and how both employers and employees benefit.

Company	Program Highlights	Payoff
Aetna	7,600 employees enrolled in five state-of-the-art fitness centers	$282 per year saved for each employee who exercises
L.L. Bean	$200 paid to each employee whose families quit smoking	Annual insurance premiums are half the national average
Champion International	Millworkers pay no deductibles on preventative medical exams and immunizations	Early detection of deadly diseases
Coors	Employees with healthy habits receive awards used to buy extra days off, or financial planning services	Fewer absences
Dow	"Backs in Action" plan encourages exercise and dieting	On-the-job sprains have been reduced by up to 90 percent
DuPont	Provides free medical checkups (e.g., mamographies and flu shots)	Absenteeism due to illness has been reduced
First Chicago	Coaches pregnant women and pays for delivery of babies	Number of underweight babies and C-sections reduced
Johnson & Johnson	Employees' infant children receive free tests and checkups every two months	$13 million per year saved
Quaker	Bonuses of up to $500 for wearing seat belts, not smoking, and exercising	Employees can either keep the money or trade them in for additional benefits
Steelcase	Tests workers for dangerous conditions (e.g., not using seat belts, high cholesterol)	Expects to save about $2 million per year for 10 years
Tenneco	Encouraging healthy eating among pipeline workers	Both waistlines and health-care costs are shrinking
Union Pacific	Workers are encouraged to discuss their unhealthy habits and are taught how to change them	An average of $3 is returned for every $1 invested in this program

(**SOURCE:** Based on information in Tully, 1995; see Note 14.)

outplacement services
Assistance in finding new jobs that companies provide to employees they lay off.

of layoffs, more and more organizations are providing **outplacement services**—assistance in securing new employment. In the most extensive of such programs, AT&T and Wang provided extensive career counseling and job-search assistance to its laid-off employees.[16] Although it is certainly more desirable not to be laid off at all, knowing that such assistance is available, if needed, helps reduce the negative emotional aspects of job insecurity.

3. *Provide opportunities to socialize.* To help satisfy its employees' social needs, IBM each spring holds a "Family Day" picnic near its Armonk, New York headquarters.[17] Some other companies have incorporated social activities deep into the fabric of their cultures. For example, Odetics Inc. (the Anaheim, California, manufacturer of intelligent machine systems) not only has its own repertory theater troupe, but also regular "theme" days (e.g., a "sock hop" in the company's cafeteria), and a standing "fun committee," which organized such events as a lunch-hour employee olympics complete with goofy games.[18]

4. *Recognize employees' accomplishments.* Recognizing employees' accomplishments is an important way to satisfy their esteem needs. In this con-

Mary Kay Recognizes Its Beauty
Consultants' Accomplishments
Jessie Jackson holds a trophy and wears
various pins she received in recognition
of her accomplishments as a Mary Kay
beauty consultant.

nection, GTE Data Services (Temple Terrace, Florida) gives awards to employees who develop ways of improving customer satisfaction or business performance.[19] The big award is a four-day first-class vacation, $500, a plaque, and recognition in the company magazine. Not all such awards are equally extravagant, however. Companies such as American Airlines, Shell Oil, the Campbell Soup Company, AT&T, and each of the big-three automakers (General Motors, Ford, and Chrysler) all offer relatively small nonmonetary gifts (e.g., dinner certificates, VCRs, and computers) to employees in recognition of their accomplishments.[20]

Some companies help recognize their employees' organizational contributions by touting them on the pages of their corporate newsletters. For example, employees of the large pharmaceutical company Merck enjoyed the recognition they received for developing Proscar (a highly successful drug treatment for prostate enlargement) when they saw their pictures in the company newsletter. In fact, it meant more to Merck employees to have their colleagues learn of their success than it did to have their accomplishments touted widely to an anonymous audience on the pages of the *New York Times*.

Few companies have taken the practice of rewarding contributions to the same high art as Mary Kay Cosmetics. Not only are lavish banquets staged to recognize modest contributions to this company's bottom line, but top performers are awarded the most coveted prize of all—a pink Cadillac (see Figure 5-6). As founder Mary Kay Ash puts it, "There are two things people want more than sex and money . . . recognition and praise."[21] Recognition need not be lavish or expensive. It can involve nothing more than a heart-felt "thank you." As Mark Twain once admitted, "I can live for two months on a good compliment."

Whatever form it takes, it is important to caution that awards are only effective at enhancing esteem when they are clearly linked to desired behaviors. Awards that are too general (e.g., a trophy for "best attitude") may not only fail to satisfy esteem needs, but also may minimize the impact of awards that are truly deserved. However, several of today's companies have recognized that one particular reward—time off the job—can be valuable for all employees because it helps satisfy a variety of different needs. For a closer look at this practice, see THE QUEST FOR QUALITY section.

Goal-Setting Theory

Just as people are motivated to satisfy their needs on the job, they are also motivated to strive for and attain goals. In fact, the process of setting goals is one of the most important motivational forces operating on people in orga-

THE QUEST FOR QUALITY

SABBATICALS: TIME OFF SATISFIES MANY NEEDS SIMULTANEOUSLY

*I*n addition to doing things to satisfy employees' needs on the job, many companies have been satisfying their employees' needs by giving them time *off*—leaves known as *sabbaticals*. Once reserved for teachers who were recognized to derive professional benefit by being given time off to update their skills and develop new ones, the concept of sabbaticals has found its way into growing numbers of private companies—among them, such giants as American Express, DuPont, McDonald's, and Xerox.[22] In fact, it has been estimated that various types of corporate leaves are being offered by between 14 and 24 percent of U.S. companies today.

Proponents of such programs have argued that sabbaticals yield several benefits. First, sabbaticals help satisfy employees' basic physiological needs by giving them a chance to earn a well-deserved rest. Officials at Tandem Computers have explicitly recognized this, noting that opportunities for rejuvenation are vital in an industry that changes so rapidly that it often runs people ragged and burns them out. Each of Tandem's 6,500 U.S. employees is given six weeks of paid leave every four years, with which they can do whatever they wish (except work for another company). Similarly, Apple Computer's six-week sabbatical program for all of its 12,000 employees, called Restart, provides chances once every five years for employees to do whatever they want to refresh themselves. Some Apple employees have spent their sabbaticals hiking and windsurfing in exotic places; one even served as a political campaign worker.

Sabbaticals provide yet another important benefit: They reward faithful service, thereby satisfying esteem needs. According to Apple spokesman Frank O'Mahoney, their Restart program "is a symbol that Apple cares for you as a well-balanced person; you're not just a drone."[23] This important source of recognition also is offered by the venerable Wells Fargo Bank. This company's leave program recognizes sabbaticals taken for purposes of personal growth (e.g., one employee trained for the Master's World Swimming Championships) and those taken to perform social service (e.g., one executive went to Lithuania to help its transition from communism to capitalism). A Wells Fargo manager, referred to the sabbatical as "one way we recognize the contributions that long-term employees have made."[24]

Experts caution that sabbaticals can be problematic in organizations in which those who take them are seen as weak and undedicated to the company. To the contrary, organizations with effective sabbatical programs require employees to take leaves without fear of reprisals or damage to their reputations so that both the individual and the company benefit. Indeed, as consultant Joan Kofodimos explains, "growing people is good for the company. Companies have to say, 'Go get a life. That's what we reward around here.'"[25] Indeed, as companies take steps to satisfy their employees' needs, such as by offering sabbaticals, need theories lead us to expect that both employees and their organizations will reap the benefits.

---

goal setting The process of determining specific levels of performance for workers to attain.

A complete description of self-efficacy and a general discussion of the important role it plays in OB appears in Chapter 3.

nizations.[26] We will describe a prominent theory of **goal setting** and then identify some practical suggestions for setting goals effectively.

Locke and Latham's Goal-Setting Theory

Suppose that you are doing a task, such as word processing, when a performance goal is assigned. You are now expected, for example, to type 70 words per minute (wpm) instead of the 60 wpm you've been doing all along. Would you work hard to meet this goal, or would you simply give up? Some insight into the question of how people respond to assigned goals is provided by a model proposed by Locke and Latham.[27] These theorists claim that an assigned goal influences people's beliefs about being able to perform the task in question (i.e., *self-efficacy*) and their personal goals. Both of these factors, in turn, influence performance.

The basic idea behind Locke and Latham's theory is that a goal serves as a motivator because it causes people to compare their present capacity to perform with that required to succeed at the goal. To the extent that people believe they will fall short of a goal, they will feel dissatisfied and work harder to attain it—so long as they believe it is possible for them to do so. When they succeed at meeting a goal, they feel competent and successful.[28] Having a goal enhances performance in large part because the goal makes clear exactly what type and level of performance is expected. Goals also help improve performance because they provide information about how well one is performing a task.

The model also claims that assigned goals will lead to the acceptance of those goals as *personal* goals. In other words, they will be accepted as one's own. This is the idea of **goal commitment**—the extent to which people invest themselves in meeting a goal.[29] Indeed, it has been shown that people will become more committed to a goal to the extent that they desire to attain that goal and believe they have a reasonable chance of doing so.[30] Likewise, the more strongly people believe they are capable of meeting a goal, the more strongly they will accept it as their own. By contrast, workers who perceive themselves as being physically incapable of meeting performance goals, for example, are generally not committed to meeting them, and do not strive to do so.[31]

Finally, the model claims that beliefs about both self-efficacy and personal goals influence task performance. This makes sense insofar as people are willing to exert greater effort when they believe they will succeed than when they believe their efforts will be in vain.[32] Moreover, goals that are not personally accepted will have little capacity to guide behavior. In fact, research has shown that the more strongly people are committed to meeting goals, the better they will perform.[33] In general, Locke and Latham's model of goal setting has been supported by several studies, suggesting that it is a valuable source of insight into how the goal-setting process works.[34]

Managers' Guidelines for Setting Effective Performance Goals

Because researchers have been actively involved in studying the goal-setting process for many years, it is possible to summarize their findings in the form of principles. These represent very practical suggestions that practicing managers can use to enhance motivation.

Assign specific goals. Probably the best-established finding of research on goal setting is that *people perform at higher levels when asked to meet a specific high-performance goal than when simply asked to "do their best" or when no goal at all is assigned.*[35] People tend to find specific goals quite challenging and are motivated to try to meet them—not only to fulfill management's expectations, but also to convince themselves that they have performed well.

A classic study by Latham and Baldes conducted at an Oklahoma lumber camp provides a particularly dramatic demonstration of this principle.[36] The participants in this research were lumber camp crews who hauled logs from forests to their company's nearby sawmill. Over a three-month period before the study began, it was found that the crew loaded trucks to only about 60 percent of their legal capacity, wasting trips that cost the company money. Then, a specific goal was set, challenging the loggers to load the trucks to 94 percent of their capacity before returning to the mill. How effective was this goal in raising performance? The results, summarized in Figure 5-7, show that the goal was extremely effective. In fact, not only was the specific goal effective in raising performance to the goal level in just a few weeks, but the effects were long-lasting as well. In fact, the loggers were found to sustain this level of performance as long as seven years later. The resulting savings for the company was considerable.

This is just one of many studies that clearly demonstrate the effectiveness of setting specific, challenging performance goals. Other research has found that specific goals are also helpful in getting to bring about other desirable organizational goals, such as reducing absenteeism and industrial accidents.[37] Naturally, to reap such beneficial effects, goals must not only be highly specific, but challenging as well.

---

goal commitment The degree to which people accept and strive to attain goals.

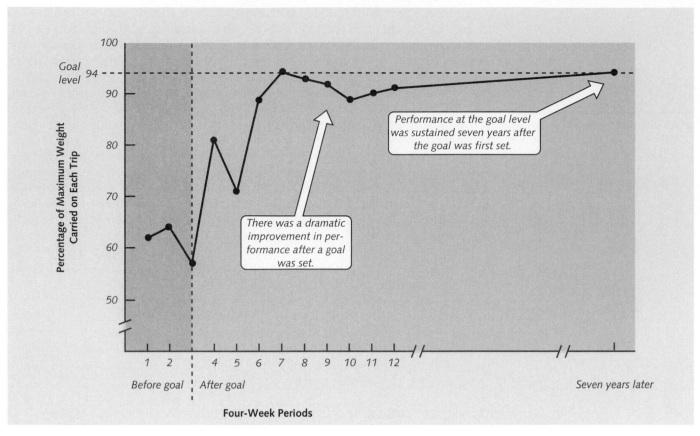

■ **Figure 5-7**

Goal Setting: Some Impressive Effects

The performance of loggers loading timber onto trucks markedly improved after a specific, difficult goal was set. The percentage of the maximum weight of timber loaded onto trucks rose from approximately 60 percent before any goal was set, to approximately 94 percent—the goal level—after the goal was set. Performance remained at this level for as long as seven years later.

(**Source:** Adapted from Latham & Baldes, 1975; see Note 36.)

Assign difficult but acceptable performance goals. The goal set at the logging camp was successful not only because it was specific, but because it pushed crew members to a higher standard. Obviously, a goal that is too easy to attain will *not* bring about the desired increments in performance. For example, if you already type at 70 wpm, a goal of 60 wpm—although specific— would probably *lower* your performance. The key point is that *a goal must be difficult as well as specific for it to raise performance.* At the same time, however, people will work hard to reach challenging goals so long as these are within the limits of their capability. As goals become too difficult, performance suffers because people reject the goals as unrealistic and unattainable.[38]

For example, you may work much harder as a student in a class that challenges your ability than in one that is very easy. At the same time, you would probably give up trying if the only way of passing was to get perfect scores on all exams—a standard you would reject as being unacceptable. In short, specific goals are most effective if they are set neither too low nor too high.

The same phenomenon occurs in organizations. For example, Bell Canada's telephone operators are required to handle calls within 23 seconds, and FedEx's customer service agents are expected to answer customers' questions within 140 seconds.[39] Although both goals were initially considered difficult when they were imposed, the employees of both companies eventually met—or exceeded—these goals, and enjoyed the satisfaction of knowing they succeeded at this task. At a General Electric manufacturing plant, specific goals were set for productivity and cost reduction. Those goals that were perceived as challenging but possible led to improved performance, whereas those thought to be unattainable led to decreased performance.[40] How, then, should goals be set in a manner that strengthens employees' commitment to them?

One obvious way of enhancing goal acceptance is to *involve employees in the goal-setting process.* Research on workers' participation in goal setting has demonstrated that people better accept goals that they have been involved in setting than goals that have been assigned by their supervisors—and they work harder as a result.[41] In other words, participation in the goal-setting process tends to enhance goal commitment. Not only does participation help people better understand and appreciate goals they had a hand in setting, but it also helps ensure that the goals set are not unreasonable.

Provide feedback concerning goal attainment. The final principle of goal setting appears to be glaringly obvious, although in practice it is often not followed: Feedback helps people attain their performance goals. Just as golfers interested in improving their swings need feedback about where their balls are going, so do workers need feedback about how closely they are approaching their performance goals in order to meet them.

The importance of using feedback in conjunction with goal setting has been demonstrated in an ambitious study comparing the performance of work crews in the U.S. Air Force.[42] A standardized index of job performance was used to measure five different groups repeatedly over a two-year period. During the first nine months, a baseline measure of effectiveness was taken that was used to compare the relative impact of feedback and goal setting. Then the groups received feedback for five months (reports detailing how well they performed on various performance measures). After five months of feedback, the goal-setting phase of the study was begun. During this period, the crew members set goals for themselves with respect to their performance on various measures. Then, for the final five months, in addition to the feedback and goal setting, an incentive (time off from work) was made available to crew members who met their goals. The effectiveness of the crews during each phase of the study is summarized in Figure 5-8.

As Figure 5-8 clearly shows, feedback and goal setting dramatically increased group effectiveness. Group feedback improved performance approximately 50 percent over the baseline level. The addition of group goal setting improved it 75 percent over baseline. These findings show that the combination of goal setting and feedback helps raise the effectiveness of group perfor-

Feedback is not only important in gauging one's progress toward meeting goals, but as detailed in Chapter 3, is key to the overall process of learning.

■ **Figure 5-8**
Feedback: An Essential Aspect of Goal Setting
Research on U.S. Air Force crews over a two-year period showed that feedback enhanced performance and that the addition of goal setting enhanced it even more.

(**Source:** Based on data reported by Pritchard, Jones, Roth, Steubing, & Ekberg, 1988; see Note 42.)

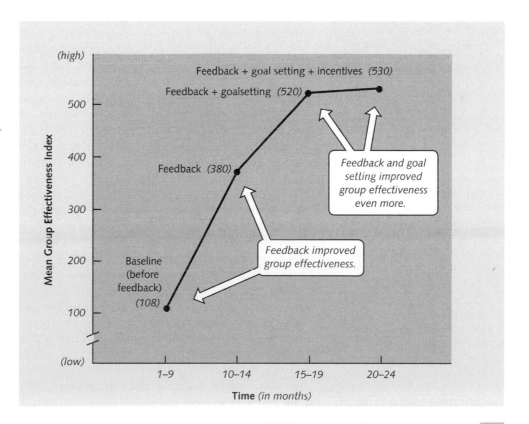

mance. Groups that know how well they're doing and have a target goal to shoot for tend to perform very well. Providing incentives, however, improved performance only negligibly. The real incentive seems to be meeting the challenge of performing up to the level of the goal.

In sum, goal setting is a very effective tool managers can use to motivate people. Setting a specific, acceptably difficult goal and providing feedback about progress toward that goal greatly enhances job performance.

Equity Theory

The theories we've described thus far are based on the operation of completely individual processes—the activation of needs and the responses to goals. The next approach to motivation we will consider, **equity theory**, is also an individual-based theory, but one that adds a social component. Specifically, equity theory views motivation from the perspective of the *social comparisons* people make—that is, what they see when they compare themselves to others.[43] It proposes that individuals are motivated to maintain fair, or *equitable*, relationships among themselves and to avoid those relationships that are unfair, or *inequitable*.[44] The ways in which this is done has been a topic of considerable interest in the field of organizational behavior.

equity theory The theory stating that people strive to maintain ratios of their own outcomes (rewards) to their own inputs (contributions) that are equal to the outcome/input ratios of others with whom they compare themselves.

Adams's Equity Theory

Equity theory, introduced by J. Stacy Adams, proposes that people comparing themselves to others focus on two variables, *outcomes* and *inputs*.[45] **Outcomes** are what we get out of our jobs, including pay, fringe benefits, and prestige. **Inputs** refer to the contributions made, such as the amount of time worked, the amount of effort expended, the number of units produced, and the qualifications brought to the job. Equity theory is concerned with outcomes and inputs as they are *perceived* by the people involved, not necessarily what they might actually be based on any objective standards. Not surprisingly, therefore, people sometimes disagree about what constitutes equitable treatment on the job.

outcomes The rewards employees receive from their jobs, such as salary and recognition.

inputs People's contributions to their jobs, such as their experience, qualifications, or the amount of time worked.

Equity theory states that people compare their outcomes and inputs to those of others and judge the equitableness of these relationships in the form of ratios—that is, relationships of *equal to*, *greater than*, or *less than*. Specifically, they compare the ratios of their own outcomes/inputs to the ratios of other's outcomes/inputs. This "other" that serves as the basis of comparison may be someone else in one's work group, another employee in the organization, an individual working in the same field, or even oneself at an earlier point in time—in short, almost anyone against whom we compare ourselves. As shown in Figure 5-9, these comparisons can result in any of three different states: *overpayment inequity, underpayment inequity*, or *equitable payment*.

overpayment inequity The condition, resulting in feelings of guilt, in which the ratio of one's outcomes to inputs is more than the corresponding ratio of another person with whom that person compares himself or herself.

To illustrate these concepts, let's consider an example. Imagine that Jack and Ray work alongside each other on an assembly line doing the same job. Both men have equal amounts of experience, training and education, and work equally long and hard at their jobs—in other words, their inputs are equivalent. But, suppose Jack is paid a salary of $500 per week while Ray is paid only $350 per week. In this case, Jack's ratio of outcomes/inputs is higher than Ray's, creating a state of **overpayment inequity** for Jack and **underpayment inequity** for Ray (since the ratio of his outcomes/inputs is lower). According to equity theory, Jack, realizing that he is paid more than an equally qualified person doing the same work, will feel *guilty* in response to his overpayment. By contrast, Ray, realizing that he is paid less than an equally qualified person for doing the same work, will feel *angry* in response to his underpayment. Feeling guilty or angry are negative emotional states that peo-

underpayment inequity The condition, resulting in feelings of anger, in which the ratio of one's outcomes to inputs is less than the corresponding ratio of another person with whom that person compares himself or herself.

Equity Theory: An Overview
To judge equity or inequity, people
compare the ratios of their own
outcomes/inputs to the corresponding
ratios of others (or themselves at earlier
points in time). The resulting states—
overpayment inequity, underpayment
inequity, and inequitable payment—and
their associated emotional responses are
summarized here.

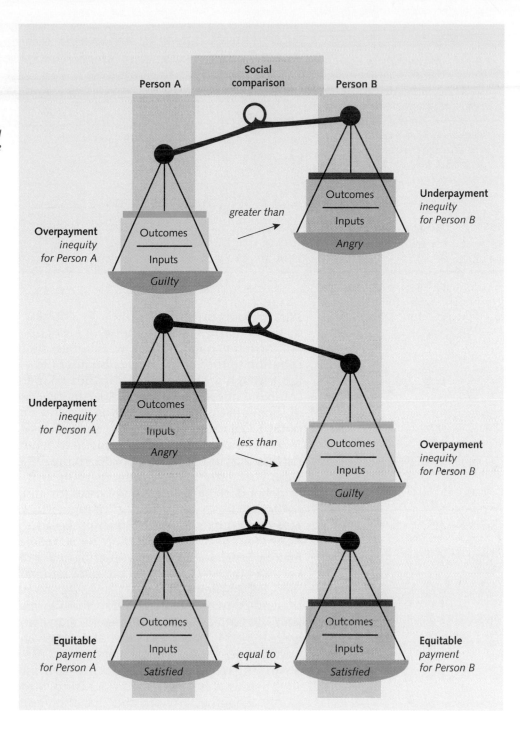

equitable payment The state
in which one person's outcome/
input ratio is equivalent to that of
another person with whom this
individual compares himself or
herself.

ple are motivated to change. Specifically, they will seek to create a state of
equitable payment in which their outcome/input ratios are equal, leading
them to feel *satisfied.*

How can people change inequitable states to equitable ones? Equity theory suggests several possible courses of action (see Table 5-2). In general, people who are underpaid may either lower their inputs or raise their outcomes.
Either action would effectively bring the underpaid individual's outcome/in-
put ratio into line with that of the comparison person. In our example, the
underpaid Ray might lower his inputs—say, by slacking off, arriving at work
late, leaving early, taking longer breaks, doing less work, or lower quality work.
In an extreme case, he may quit his job. He also may attempt to raise his outcomes, such as by asking for a raise, or even taking home company property,

People can respond to over-payment and underpayment inequities in behavioral and/or psychological ways. A few of these are summarized here. These reactions help change the perceived inequities into a state of perceived equity.

Type of Inequity	Type of Reaction	
	Behavioral (What you can do is . . .)	Psychological (What you can think is . . .)
Overpayment inequity	Raise your inputs (e.g., work harder), or lower your outcomes (e.g., work through a paid vacation).	Convince yourself that your outcomes are deserved based on your inputs (e.g., rationalize that you work harder than others and so you deserve more pay).
Underpayment inequity	Lower your inputs (e.g., reduce effort), or raise your outcomes (e.g., get a raise in pay).	Convince yourself that others' inputs are really higher than your own (e.g., rationalize that the comparison worker is really more qualified and so deserves higher outcomes).

such as tools or office supplies. By contrast, the overpaid person, Jack, may do the opposite—raise his inputs or lower his outcomes. For example, he might put forth much more effort, work longer hours, and try to make a greater contribution to the company. He also might lower his outcomes, such as by working through a paid vacation, or not taking advantage of fringe benefits the company offers. These are all specific *behavioral* reactions to inequitable conditions—that is, things people *do* by way of attempting to change inequitable states to equitable ones.

As you might imagine, people may be unwilling to do some of the things necessary to respond behaviorally to inequities. In particular, they may be unwilling to restrict their productivity (in fear of getting caught "goofing off"), or uncomfortable asking their bosses for raises. As a result, they may resort to resolving the inequity not by changing their behavior, but by changing the way they think about the situation. Because equity theory deals with perceptions of fairness or unfairness, it is reasonable to expect that inequitable states may be redressed by merely altering one's thinking about the circumstances. For example, underpaid people may rationalize that others' inputs are really higher than their own (e.g., "I suppose she really *is* more qualified than me"), thereby convincing themselves that the other person's higher outcomes are justified. Similarly, overpaid people may convince themselves that they really *are* better and really do deserve their relatively higher pay. So, by changing the way they see things, people can come to perceive inequitable situations as equitable, thereby effectively reducing their inequity distress.[46]

There is a great deal of evidence to suggest that people are motivated to redress inequities at work and that they respond much as equity theory suggests. For example, research has shown that professional basketball players who are underpaid (i.e., ones who are paid less than others who perform as well or better) score fewer points than those who are equitably paid.[47] That is, they lowered their inputs.

We also know that underpaid workers attempt to raise their outcomes. One way they might do this, although it is unethical, is by stealing from their employers. That this occurs was demonstrated in an organization studied by one of the authors (J.G.). Due to a financial crisis, workers at two manufacturing plants suffered an underpayment inequity created by the introduction of a temporary pay cut of 15 percent.[48] During the ten-week period under which workers received lower pay, company officials noticed that theft of company property increased dramatically. However, in another factory in which comparable work was done by workers paid at their normal rates (the control group), the theft rate remained low (see Figure 5-10). This pattern suggests that

■ **Figure 5-10**
*Employee Theft: A Reaction
to Underpayment*
A study by Greenberg compared theft
rates in factories in which employees
experienced a pay cut and one in which
there was no pay cut. Consistent with
equity theory, the theft rate was highest
among those who experienced the pay
cut.

(**Source:** Based on data reported by
Greenberg, 1990; see Note 48.)

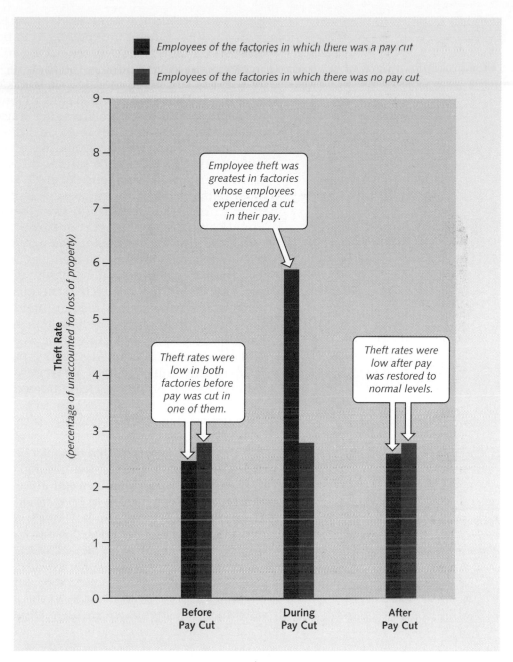

employees may have stolen property in order to compensate for reduced pay. Consistent with this possibility, it was found that when the normal rate of pay was reinstated in the two factories, the theft rate returned to its normal (prepay cut), low level.

Applying Equity Theory: Some Motivational Tips for Managers

Equity theory has some important implications for ways of motivating people. We will highlight several of these here.

1. *Underpayment should be avoided.* Companies that attempt to save money by reducing employees' salaries may find that employees respond in many different ways to even the score. For example, they may steal, shave a few minutes off their work days, or otherwise withhold production.

In recent years, a particularly unsettling form of institutionalizing underpayment has materialized in the form of **two-tier wage structures**—payment systems in which newer employees are paid less than

two-tier wage structures
Payment systems in which newer employees are paid less than employees hired at earlier times to do the same work.

those hired to do the same work at an earlier point in time. Not surprisingly, such systems are considered to be highly unfair, particularly by those in the lower tier.[49] When such a plan was instituted at the Giant Food supermarket chain, two-thirds of the lower-tier employees quit their jobs in the first three months. "It stinks," said one clerk at one Giant store in Los Angeles, "They're paying us lower wages for the same work."[50]

A proposal to institute a two-tier wage system at United Airlines in the mid-1980s led its pilots to go on strike (see Figure 5-11).[51] And, who can blame them? The plan would have virtually cut in half the amount new DC-10 pilots would be earning when they reached the top of their careers—an annual difference of over $64,000 compared to the earlier hired pilots. Clearly, the negative reactions to such forms of inequities should make employers think twice before introducing any plan that would compensate employees unfairly.

2. *Overpayment should be avoided.* You may think that because overpaid employees work hard to deserve their pay, it would be a useful motivational technique to pay people more than they merit. There are several reasons why this would not work. First, the increases in performance shown in response to overpayment inequity tend to be only temporary. As time goes on, people begin to believe that they actually deserve the higher pay they're getting and bring their work level down to normal. A second reason why it is unwise to overpay employees is that when you overpay one employee, you are underpaying all the others. When the majority of the employees feel underpaid, they will lower their performance, resulting in a net *decrease* in productivity—and widespread dissatisfaction. Hence, the conclusion is clear: *Managers should strive to treat all employees equitably.*

We realize, of course, that this may be easier said than done. Part of the difficulty resides in the fact that feelings of equity and inequity are based on perceptions, and these perceptions aren't always easy to control. One approach that may help is to *be open and honest about outcomes and inputs.* People tend to overestimate how much their superiors are paid and therefore tend to feel that their own pay is not as high as it should be.[52] However, if information about pay is shared, inequitable feelings may not result.

3. *Managers should present information about outcomes in a thorough and socially sensitive manner.* This suggestion follows from research showing that people's assessments of fairness on the job go beyond merely what their outcomes and inputs are to their knowledge of *how* these were deter-

For a general discussion of the distortions associated with the process of perception, see Chapter 3.

■ **Figure 5-11**
Striking: A Response to Feelings of Inequity
In the mid-1980s, pilots from United Airlines went on strike to protest a proposed two-tier wage system that would have paid new pilots considerably less than those who were already employed. Their strike was a potent response to their feelings of inequity.

procedural justice Perceptions of the fairness of the procedures used to determine outcomes.

mined—that is, to their sense of **procedural justice**. For example, it has been found that even negative outcomes such as layoffs and pay cuts can be accepted and recognized as fair to the extent that people understand the procedures that brought them about. Such information, particularly when presented in a highly sensitive and caring manner, tends to take some of the sting out of those undesirable outcomes.[53]

To live through a pay freeze is painful, of course, but people are more likely to accept it as fair if a good explanation for it has been provided. Schaubroeck, May, and Brown demonstrated this in their recent study of manufacturing workers' reactions to a pay freeze.[54] Comparisons were made between two groups: one that received a thorough explanation of the procedures necessitating the pay freeze (e.g., information about the organization's economic problems) and one that received no such information. Although all workers were adversely affected by the freeze, those receiving the explanation better accepted it. In particular, it reduced their interest in looking for a new job. These findings suggest that even if managers cannot do anything to eliminate workplace inequities, they may be able to take some of the sting out of them by providing explanations as to why these unfortunate conditions are necessary.

Expectancy Theory

expectancy theory The theory that asserts that motivation is based on people's beliefs about the probability that effort will lead to performance (*expectancy*), multiplied by the probability that performance will lead to reward (*instrumentality*), multiplied by the perceived value of the reward (*valence*).

Instead of focusing on individual needs, goals, or social comparisons, **expectancy theory** takes a broader approach: It looks at the role of motivation in the overall work environment. In essence, the theory asserts that people are motivated to work when they *expect* that they will be able to achieve the things they want from their jobs. Expectancy theory characterizes people as rational beings who think about what they have to do in order to be rewarded and how much the reward means to them before they perform their jobs. But, as we will see, the theory doesn't focus only on what people think. It also recognizes that these thoughts combine with other aspects of the organizational environment to influence job performance.

Basic Elements of Expectancy Theory

Although slightly different versions of expectancy theory have been proposed—including popular ones by Vroom and by Porter and Lawler—expectancy theorists agree that motivation is the result of three different types of beliefs that people have.[55,56] These are as follows:

expectancy The belief that one's efforts will positively influence one's performance.

- **expectancy**—the belief that one's effort will result in performance
- **instrumentality**—the belief that one's performance will be rewarded
- **valence**—the perceived value of the rewards to the recipient.

instrumentality An individual's beliefs regarding the likelihood of being rewarded in accord with his or her own level of performance.

Sometimes people believe that putting forth a great deal of effort means that they will get a lot accomplished. However, in other cases, people do not expect that their efforts will have much effect on how well they do. For example, an employee operating a faulty piece of equipment may have a very low *expectancy* that his or her efforts will lead to high levels of performance. Naturally, someone working under such conditions probably would not continue to exert much effort.

valence The value a person places on the rewards he or she receives from an organization.

Even *if* an employee works hard and performs at a high level, motivation may falter if that performance is not suitably rewarded—that is, if the performance is not perceived as *instrumental* in bringing about the rewards. So, for example, a worker who is extremely productive may be poorly motivated to perform if he or she has already reached the top level of pay given by the company.

Finally, even *if* employees believe that hard work will lead to good performance *and* that they will be rewarded commensurate with their performance, they still may be poorly motivated *if* those so-called rewards have a low *valence* to them. In other words, someone who doesn't value the rewards offered by the organization is not motivated to attain them. As an example, a reward of $100 would not be likely to motivate a multimillionaire, whereas it may be a very desirable reward for someone of more modest means. Only those rewards that have a high positive valence to their recipients will motivate behavior.

Expectancy theory claims that motivation is a multiplicative function of all three components. This means that higher levels of motivation will result when expectancy, instrumentality, and valence are *all* high than when they are all low. The multiplicative assumption also implies that if any one of these three components is zero, the overall level of motivation will be zero. So, for example, even if an employee believes that his or her effort will result in performance, which will result in reward, motivation will be zero if the valance of the reward he or she expects to receive is zero. Figure 5-12 summarizes the definitions of expectancy theory components and shows their relationships.

Figure 5-12 also highlights a point we made in our opening remarks about motivation: that motivation is not equivalent to job performance. Expectancy theory recognizes that motivation is one of several important determinants of job performance. In particular, the theory assumes that *skills and abilities* also contribute to a person's job performance. It's no secret that some people are better suited to performing their jobs than others by virtue of their unique characteristics and special skills and abilities. For example, a tall, strong, well-coordinated person is likely to make a better professional basketball player than a very short, weak, uncoordinated one—even if the shorter person is highly motivated to succeed.

Figure 5-12
Expectancy Theory: An Overview
According to expectancy theory, *motivation is the product of three types of beliefs:* expectancy *(the belief that one's effort will influence performance),* instrumentality *(the belief that one will be rewarded for one's performance), and* valence *(the perceived value of the rewards expected). The theory also recognizes that motivation is only one of several factors responsible for job performance.*

Expectancy theory also recognizes that job performance will be influenced by people's *role perceptions*—in other words, what they believe is expected of them on the job. To the extent that there are disagreements about what one's job duties are, performance may suffer. For example, an assistant manager who believes her primary job duty is to train new employees may find that her performance is downgraded by a supervisor who believes she should be spending more time doing routine paperwork instead. In this case, the person's performance wouldn't suffer as a result of any deficit in motivation, but simply because of misunderstandings about what the job entails.

Finally, expectancy theory also recognizes the role of *opportunities to perform* one's job. Even the best employees may perform at low levels if their opportunities are limited. For example, a highly motivated salesperson may

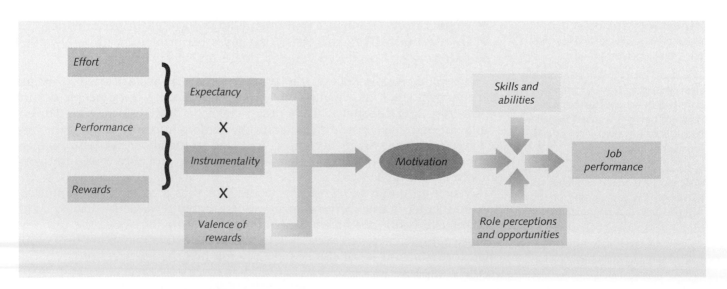

perform poorly if opportunities are restricted (say, the territory is having a financial downturn or available inventory is limited).

It is important to recognize that expectancy theory views motivation as just one of several determinants of job performance. Motivation, combined with a person's skills and abilities, role perceptions, and opportunities, influences job performance.

Expectancy theory has generated a great deal of research and has been successfully applied to understanding behavior in many different organizational settings.[57] Although the theory has received only mixed support about some of its specific aspects (e.g., the multiplicative assumption), it is still one of the dominant approaches to the study of motivation in organizations. Probably the primary reason for expectancy theory's popularity is the many useful suggestions it makes for practicing managers. We will now describe some of the most essential applications of expectancy theory, giving examples from organizations in which they have been implemented.

Managerial Applications of Expectancy Theory

Expectancy theory has several important implications for ways of motivating employees.

1. *Clarify people's expectancies that their effort will lead to performance.* Motivation may be enhanced by training employees to do their jobs more efficiently and so achieve higher levels of performance from their efforts. It also may be possible to enhance effort-performance expectancies by following employees' suggestions about ways to change their jobs. To the extent that employees are aware of problems in their jobs that interfere with their performance, attempting to alleviate these problems may help them perform more effectively. In essence, what we are saying is: *Make the desired performance attainable.* Good supervisors not only make it clear to people what is expected of them, but they also help them attain that level of performance.

2. *Administer rewards that are positively valent to employees.* In other words, the carrot at the end of the stick must be tasty for it to have potential as a motivator. These days, with a highly diverse workforce, it would be misleading to assume that all employees care about having the same rewards. Whereas some might recognize the incentive value of a pay raise, others might prefer additional vacation days, improved insurance benefits, day-care, or elder-care facilities. With this in mind, many companies have introduced **cafeteria-style benefit plans**—incentive systems allowing employees to select their fringe benefits from a menu of available alternatives. Given that fringe benefits represent almost 40 percent of payroll costs, more and more companies are recognizing the value of administering them flexibly.[58] For example, Primerica has had a flexible benefit plan in use since 1978—one that almost 95 percent of the company's 8,000 salaried employees believe is extremely beneficial to them.[59] Today's companies are doing many creative things to help ensure that their employees can achieve rewards that have value to them (see Table 5-3).[60]

3. *Clearly link valued rewards and performance.* In other words, managers should enhance their subordinates' beliefs about instrumentality by specifying exactly what job behaviors will lead to what rewards. To the extent that it is possible for employees to be paid in ways directly linked to their performance—such as through piece-rate incentive systems, sales commission plans, or bonuses—expectancy theory specifies that it would be effective to do so. Indeed, a great deal of research has shown that performance increases can result from carefully implemented merit systems—frequently referred to as **pay-for-performance plans**.[61]

As discussed in Chapter 3, training can be accomplished in many different ways and can serve many different purposes.

cafeteria-style benefit plans
Incentive systems in which employees have an opportunity to select the fringe benefits they want from a menu of available alternatives.

pay-for-performance plan
A payment system in which employees are paid differentially, based on the quantity and quality of their performance. Pay-for-performance plans strengthen *instrumentality* beliefs.

All companies pay their employees, but a few also provide more creative incentives that help ensure that employees receive rewards that have value to them.

Company	Practice
Calvert Group (financial management company, located in Bethesda, MD)	Company reimburses recruiting expenses for all 190 of its employees.
ESP Software Services (computer consultancy firm, located in Minneapolis, MN)	Employees can select either a base salary with no hourly pay, or hourly pay based on time spent on assignment, or a blend of the two.
Rogan (manufacturer of plastic knobs, located in Northbrook, IL)	Employees are not only rewarded for their money-saving contributions, but these also are recognized in the company newsletter.
Ashton Photo (photo-image printer, located in Salem, OR)	Company rewards employees by allowing them to decide on the skills needed to do their jobs best, and lets them grade their own performance.

SOURCE: Based on Ehrenfeld, 1993; see Note 60.

It is important to caution that such systems are usually so highly effective that it is crucial for organizations to consider exactly what employees might do to perform at high levels. For example, in 1992 Sears auto mechanics were paid in proportion to the volume of their repairs. This policy appears to have encouraged the mechanics to make repairs that weren't necessary—or so it was alleged in 1992.[62] (To avoid such problems Sears has since eliminated this method of paying its auto mechanics.) Following from this example, our advice is clear: When you pay people for their performance, be sure you know exactly what performance you're buying.

To further illustrate the importance of selecting only the most desired performance to reward, let's consider IBM's newly instituted pay plan for its 30,000 sales representatives. Previously, most of the pay these reps received was based on flat salary; their compensation was not linked to how well they did. Now, however, their pay is carefully tied to two factors that are essential to the company's success—profitability and customer satisfaction. So, instead of receiving commissions on the amount of the sale, as so many salespeople do, 60 percent of IBMers' commissions are tied to the company's profit on that sale. As a result, the more the company makes, the more the reps make. And to make sure that the reps don't push only high-profit items that customers might not need, the remaining 40 percent of their commissions are based on customer satisfaction. Customers are regularly surveyed about the extent to which their sales representatives helped them meet their business objectives. The better the reps have done in this regard, the greater their commissions. Since introducing this plan in late 1993, IBM has been effective in reversing its unprofitable trend. Although there are certainly many factors responsible for this turnaround, experts are confident that this practice of clearly linking desired performance to individual rewards is a key factor.

Of course, the rewards need not be monetary in nature; even verbal recognition for a job well done can be very effective. In some extreme cases (as at San Diego's Science Applications International Corp.), good performance is rewarded with shares of ownership in the company.[63] Unfortunately, not all incentive plans do as good a job as they should in rewarding desired performance. A recent survey found that only 25 percent of employees see a clear link between good job performance and their pay raises. Obviously many organizations have a long way to go in raising their employees' instrumentality beliefs.[64] However, experts believe that pay–for–performance will constitute a key part of the pay for top managers and executives in the future. For a closer look at the way this practice is expected to operate, see THE ORGANIZATION OF THE FUTURE section.

Job Design: Structuring Tasks for High Motivation

job design An approach to motivation suggesting that jobs can be created so as to enhance people's interest in doing them (see *job enlargement, job enrichment* and the *job characteristics model*).

In Chapter 1 we described the highly influential nature of Taylor's now-rejected "classical" approach to the study of organizations.

---

job enlargement The practice of expanding the content of a job to include more variety and a greater number of tasks at the same level.

The final approach to motivation we will consider is the largest in scope because it is directed at improving the nature of the work performed. The idea behind **job design** is that motivation can be enhanced by making jobs more appealing to people. As you may recall from Chapter 1, Frederick W. Taylor's principle of *scientific management* attempted to stimulate performance by designing jobs in the most efficient fashion. However, treating people like machines often meant having them engage in repetitive movements which they found highly routine and monotonous. Not surprisingly, people became bored with such jobs and frequently quit.[65] Fortunately, today's organizational scientists have found several ways of designing jobs that can not only be performed very efficiently, but also are highly pleasant and enjoyable.

Job Enlargement and Job Enrichment

Imagine that you have a highly routine job, such as tightening the lugs on the left rear wheel of a car as it rolls down the assembly line. Naturally, such a highly repetitive task would be monotonous and not very pleasant. One of the first modern approaches to redesigning jobs suggested that such consequences could be minimized by having people perform an increased number of different tasks all at the same level. This approach is known as **job enlargement.** To enlarge the jobs in our example, workers could be required to tighten the lugs on all four wheels. As a result of such an action, employees have no more responsibility nor use any greater skills, but they perform a wider variety of different tasks at the same level. Adding tasks in this fashion is said to increase the *horizontal job loading* of the position.

A few years ago, American Greetings Corp. enlarged some 400 jobs in its creative division.[66] Now, rather than always working exclusively on Christmas cards, for example, employees will be able to move back and forth between different teams, such as those working on birthday ribbons, humorous mugs, and Valentine's Day gift bags. Employees at American Greetings reportedly enjoy the variety, as do those at RJR Nabisco, Corning, and Eastman Kodak, other companies that have recently allowed employees to make such lateral moves.

Although most reports of the effectiveness of job enlargement have been anecdotal, carefully conducted empirical studies also have examined their impact. For example, Campion and McClelland studied the effects of a job enlargement program instituted at a large financial services company.[67] The unenlarged jobs had different employees perform separate paperwork tasks such as preparing, sorting, coding, and keypunching various forms. The enlarged jobs combined these various functions into larger jobs performed by the same people. Although it was more difficult and expensive to train people to perform the enlarged jobs than the separate jobs, important benefits resulted as well. In particular, employees expressed greater job satisfaction and less boredom. And because one person followed the whole job all the way through, greater opportunities to correct errors existed. Not surprisingly, customers were satisfied with the result.

Unfortunately, in a follow-up investigation of the same company conducted two years later, Campion and McClelland found that not all the beneficial effects continued.[68] Notably, employee satisfaction leveled off and the rate of errors went up, suggesting that as employees got used to their enlarged jobs they found them less interesting and stopped paying attention to all the

We should also note that the model is theorized to be especially effective in describing the behavior of individuals who are high in *growth need strength*—that is, people who have a high need for personal growth and development. People not particularly interested in improving themselves on the job are not expected to experience the theorized psychological reactions to the core job dimensions, nor consequently, to enjoy the beneficial personal and work outcomes predicted by the model.[80] By introducing this variable, the job characteristics model recognizes the important limitation of job enrichment noted earlier—not everyone wants and benefits from enriched jobs.

Based on the proposed relationship between the core job dimensions and their associated psychological reactions, the model claims that job motivation will be highest when the jobs performed rate high on the various dimensions. To assess this relationship, a questionnaire known as the Job Diagnostic Survey (JDS) has been developed to measure the degree to which various job characteristics are present in a particular job.[81] Based on responses to the JDS, we can make predictions about the degree to which a job motivates people who perform it. This is done by using an index known as the **motivating potential score (MPS)**, computed as follows:

motivating potential score (MPS) A mathematical index describing the degree to which a job is designed so as to motivate people, as suggested by the *job characteristics model*. It is computed on the basis of a questionnaire known as the Job Diagnostic Survey (JDS).

$$\text{MPS} = \frac{\text{Skill variety} + \text{Task identity} + \text{Task significance}}{3} \times \text{Autonomy} \times \text{Feedback}$$

The MPS is a summary index of a job's potential for motivating people. The higher the score for a given job, the greater the likelihood of experiencing the personal and work outcomes specified by the model. Knowing a job's MPS helps one identify jobs that might benefit by being redesigned.

The job characteristics model has been the focus of many empirical tests, most of which are supportive of many aspects of the model.[82] One study conducted among a group of South African clerical workers found particularly strong support.[83] The jobs of employees in some of the offices in this company were enriched in accordance with techniques specified by the job characteristics model. Specifically, employees performing the enriched jobs were given opportunities to choose the kinds of tasks they perform (high skill variety), do the entire job (high task identity), receive instructions regarding how their job fit into the organization as a whole (high task significance), freely set their own schedules and inspect their own work (high autonomy), and keep records of their daily productivity (high feedback). Another group of employees, equivalent in all respects except that their jobs were not enriched, served as a control group.

After employees performed the newly designed jobs for six months, comparisons were made between them and their counterparts in the control group. With respect to most of the outcomes specified by the model, individuals performing redesigned jobs showed superior results. Specifically, they reported feeling more internally motivated and more satisfied with their jobs. There were also lower rates of absenteeism and turnover among employees performing the enriched jobs. The only outcome predicted by the model that was not found to differ was actual work performance: People performed equally well in enriched and unenriched jobs. Considering the many factors that are responsible for job performance (as discussed in connection with expectancy theory), this finding should not be too surprising.

Techniques for Designing Jobs That Motivate: Some Managerial Guidelines

The job characteristics model specifies several ways in which jobs can be designed to enhance their motivating potential.[84] In Table 5-4 we present these in the form of general principles.

1. *Combine tasks.* Instead of having several workers each performing a separate part of a whole job, it would be better to have each person perform

The job characteristics model specifies several ways jobs can be designed to incorporate the core job dimensions responsible for enhancing motivation and performance. A few are listed here.

Principles of Job Design	Core Job Dimensions Incorporated
1. Combine jobs, enabling workers to perform the entire job	Skill variety Task identity
2. Establish client relationships, allowing providers of a service to meet the recipients	Skill variety Autonomy Feedback
3. Load jobs vertically, allowing greater responsibility and control over work	Autonomy
4. Open feedback channels, giving workers knowledge of the results of their work	Feedback

SOURCE: Based on information in Hackman, 1976; see Note 85.

the entire job. Doing so helps provide greater skill variety and task identity. For example, Corning Glass Works in Medford, Massachusetts, redesigned jobs so that people who assembled laboratory hot plates put together entire units instead of contributing a single part to the assembly process.[85]

2. *Open feedback channels.* Jobs should be designed to give employees as much feedback as possible. The more people know how well they're doing (be it from customers, supervisors, or co-workers), the better equipped they are to take appropriate corrective action (we already noted the importance of feedback in the learning process in Chapter 3). Sometimes, cues about job performance can be clearly identified as people perform their jobs (as we noted in conjunction with goal setting). In the best cases, open lines of communication between employees and managers are so strongly incorporated into the corporate culture—as has been reported to exist at Boise Cascade's paper products group—that feedback flows without hesitation.[86]

Once again, the topic of feedback, introduced in Chapter 3, is identified as a key determinant of behavior in organizations.

3. *Establish client relationships.* The job characteristic model suggests that jobs should be set up so that the person performing a service (such as an auto mechanic) comes into contact with the recipient of the service. Jobs designed in this manner will not only help the employee by providing feedback, but also provide skill variety (e.g., talking to customers in addition to fixing cars), and enhance autonomy (by giving people the freedom to manage their own relationships with clients) (see Figure 5-15).

This suggestion has been implemented at Sea-Land Service, the large containerized ocean-shipping company.[87] Once this company's mechanics, clerks, and crane operators started meeting with customers, they became much more productive. Having faces to associate with the once-abstract jobs they did clearly helped these employees take their jobs more seriously.

4. *Load jobs vertically.* As we described earlier, loading a job vertically involves giving people greater responsibility for their jobs. Taking responsibility and control over performance away from managers and giving it to their subordinates increases the level of autonomy the jobs offer these lower-level employees. According to a recent poll, autonomy is among the most important things people look for in their jobs—even more important than high pay.[88] In view of this, a growing number of companies are yielding control and giving employees increasing freedom to do their jobs as they wish (within limits, at least).

Consider, for example, Childress Buick Co., a Phoenix, Arizona auto dealership. This company suffered serious customer dissatisfaction and employee

■ **Figure 5-15**
*Establishing Client Relationships:
An Example*
Ernie Garcia spends his mornings delivering shirts for Cadet Uniform Service. In a move to improve customer service, he now spends his afternoons responding to customers' special requests and complaints. Both Ernie and the customers on his route are quite satisfied with the result.

retention problems before owner Rusty Childress began encouraging his employees to use their own judgment and initiative. Sometimes, previously autocratic managers are shocked when they see how hard people work when they are allowed to make their own decisions. Bob Freese, CEO of Alphatronix Inc., in Research Triangle Park, North Carolina, is among the newly converted. "We let employees tell us when they can accomplish a project and what resources they need," he says. "Virtually always they set higher goals than we would ever set for them."[89]

Naturally, autonomy is not a cure-all. If it were *always* effective, all companies would be using it all the time. There are, however, some commonalities between organizations in which it works. For one, companies that have successfully given employees autonomy tend to invest a lot of time and effort in making sure they hire people who can do their jobs properly without close supervision. Second, autonomy works in organizations in which high-quality performance is always expected—and in which it is the performance itself, and not the process, that matters. This is not to say that there are never any boundaries to restrict employees. Indeed, companies that successfully grant autonomy usually provide some guidelines within which employees must operate. But, within these boundaries, it's clear that new levels of motivation—and performance—can be evidenced.

SUMMARY AND REVIEW

The Nature of Motivation

Motivation is concerned with the set of processes that arouse, direct, and maintain behavior toward a goal. It is not equivalent to job performance but is one of several determinants of job performance. Today's work ethic motivates people to seek interesting and challenging jobs, instead of just money.

Need Theories

Maslow's **need hierarchy theory** postulates that people have five types of needs, activated in a specific order from the most basic, lowest-level need (physiological needs) to the highest-level need (need for self-actualization). Although this theory has not been supported by rigorous research studies, it has been quite useful in suggesting several ways of satisfying employees' needs on the job. A less restrictive conceptualization, Alderfer's **ERG theory** proposes that people have only three basic needs: existence, relatedness, and growth.

Following from these theories, companies are encouraged to do several things to motivate their employees. Notably, they should promote a healthy workforce, provide financial security, provide opportunities to socialize, and recognize employees' accomplishments.

Goal-Setting Theory

Locke and Latham's **goal-setting theory** claims that an assigned goal influences a person's beliefs about being able to perform a task (referred to as *self-efficacy*) and his or her personal goals. Both of these factors, in turn, influence performance. Research has shown that people will improve their performance when specific, acceptably difficult goals are set and feedback about task performance is provided. The task of selecting goals that are acceptable to employees is facilitated by allowing employees to participate in the goal-setting process.

Equity Theory

Adams's **equity theory** claims that people desire to attain an equitable balance between the ratios of their work rewards (outcomes) and their job contributions (inputs) and the corresponding ratios of comparison others. Inequitable states of *overpayment* and *underpayment* are undesirable, motivating people to try to attain equitable conditions. Responses to inequity may be either behavioral (e.g., raising or lowering one's performance) or psychological (e.g., thinking differently about work contributions). Research supports equity theory's claim that people lower their inputs in response to perceived underpayment and raise their inputs in response to perceived overpayment. Equity theory suggests that companies should avoid intentionally underpaying or overpaying employees and that managers should thoroughly explain the basis for outcomes in a socially sensitive manner.

Expectancy Theory

Expectancy theory recognizes that motivation is the product of a person's beliefs about **expectancy** (effort will lead to performance), **instrumentality** (performance will result in reward), and **valence** (the perceived value of the rewards). In conjunction with skills, abilities, role perceptions, and opportunities, motivation contributes to job performance. Expectancy theory suggests that motivation may be enhanced by linking rewards to performance (as in **pay-for-performance plans**) and by administering rewards that are highly valued (as may be done using **cafeteria-style benefit plans**).

Job Design

An effective organizational-level technique for motivating people is the designing or redesigning of jobs. **Job design** techniques include **job enlargement** (performing more tasks at the same level) and **job enrichment** (giving people greater responsibility and control over their jobs). The **job characteristics model**, a currently popular approach to enriching jobs, identifies the specific job dimensions that should be enriched (skill variety, task identity, task significance, autonomy, and feedback), and relates these to the critical psychological states influenced by including these dimensions on a job. These psychological states will, in turn, lead to certain beneficial outcomes for both individual employees (e.g., job satisfaction) and the organization (e.g., reduced absenteeism and turnover). Jobs may be designed to enhance motivation by combining tasks, opening feedback channels, establishing client relationships, and loading jobs vertically (i.e., enhancing responsibility for one's work).

QUESTIONS FOR DISCUSSION

1. Based on Maslow's need hierarchy theory, what specific things can be done to enhance an employee's motivation?
2. Why might setting goals be an effective way of motivating people on the job? What steps can be taken to ensure the effectiveness of goal setting in practice?
3. Suppose an employee feels underpaid relative to his or her co-workers. What conditions may have led to these feelings, and how might you expect such an individual to behave on the job?
4. Consider a poor performing employee who explains to his boss that he is trying very hard. According to expectancy theory, what factors would contribute to such effort? What additional factors, besides motivation, contribute to task performance?
5. According to the job characteristics model, what steps might be taken to enhance the motivation of someone performing a sales job?
6. Explain the role that money plays as a motivator in all five of the theories of motivation presented in this chapter.

Keeping Boeing Flying Higher and Higher

Becoming number one in your industry is tough enough, but maintaining that position can be even tougher. Boeing CEO Frank Shrontz was doubtlessly only too aware of this challenge as he mulled over what it took to keep the giant airplane manufacturer flying amidst turbulent skies. Plagued by inefficiencies and mounting competition (primarily from the French company Airbus Industrie), Shrontz knew that the key to Boeing's future success involved convincing the airlines to replace any of their planes that were more than 20 years old. But at a sticker price of $150 million, the 747-400s were not exactly flying out of the showrooms.

The trick, Shrontz was convinced, was to show the airlines how it was less expensive in the long run to replace their old planes with new ones than to pay the high costs of maintaining their old equipment. To lure buyers, Boeing had to keep prices steady and add lots of new features. For these sales to be profitable Boeing was forced to cut manufacturing costs, and Shrontz's plan called for slashing costs by 25 percent. But that's not all. To help the airlines get the equipment they needed at the time they needed it, Shrontz also set out to reduce the time it took to get finished planes out of the Boeing factory and into the airlines' hangars—from 18 months as recently as 1992 to only 8 months today. This goal, too, required vastly improved manufacturing techniques and getting Boeing's technicians to buy into the new operating methods.

These are difficult goals, to be sure, but necessary to keep Boeing aloft. As a first step, Shrontz had Boeing engineers study the manufacturing techniques of some of the world's best companies, including those that made computers and ships. What they learned was that it was necessary to overhaul the highly inefficient way planes were built and to replace them with more standardized methods.

Traditionally, each plane was uniquely configured with respect to such key components as galleys, lavatories, and seats—even engines and landing gears. Parts of old blueprints were reused and customized as needed. Hundreds of thousands of part numbers were copied by hand onto forms. It took over 1,000 engineers working full time one full year just to get all the parts needed to assemble a 767. Then, life-sized mockups were often made out of plastic and wood just to see that the pipes and wiring would run properly throughout the plane. Not surprisingly, once the process of manufacturing planes finally began, errors were common; for example, wrong parts arrived at the factory, halting production.

But this doesn't happen any longer. If you're making a lavatory for a 747, all you do is tap into the Boeing computer and a massive database tells you exactly what parts you need. It even orders them so that they arrive on time. Such tasks as reconfiguring part of one of the company's jumbo jets now takes several weeks less than before—and with greater accuracy. Standardization also has entered into the way various subassemblies are manufactured. Need a door for a 767? No problem. Boeing's "Sheet Metal Center" will provide you the entire unit preassembled. Only a few years ago, it sent bins of parts to the factories, where workers spent hours sorting them before the assembly process could begin. In little more than a year, this approach has cut inventory in half, saving the company millions of dollars.

Bottom line: The newly streamlined Boeing has been flying high. Orders are up and production costs are way down. Down, too, is delivery time for all of the company's products. The new profits help fund the development of new products, keeping Boeing flying high into the twenty-first century.

Critical Thinking Questions

1. The goals that Mr. Shrontz set for Boeing were extremely difficult. What must have been done to make them so highly effective?
2. What do you think would have happened if Mr. Schrontz's goals were even more challenging?
3. In what ways did the new manufacturing methods keep the workers' jobs interesting enough so that they would work hard?
4. How do you think Boeing's computerized database system contributed to the engineers' motivation to do their jobs?

Experiencing Organizational Behavior

Assessing the Work Rewards You Personally Value

According to expectancy theory, one thing companies can do to motivate employees is to give rewards with positive valence. What work-related rewards have the greatest value to you? Completing this questionnaire will help you answer this question.

Directions

Below are ten work-related rewards. For each, circle the number that best describes the value that a particular reward has for you personally. Use the following scale to express your feelings: 1 = no value at all, 2 = slight value, 3 = moderate value, 4 = great value, 5 = extremely great value.

Reward		Personal value			
Good pay	1	2	3	4	5
Prestigious title	1	2	3	4	5
Vacation time	1	2	3	4	5
Job security	1	2	3	4	5
Recognition	1	2	3	4	5
Interesting work	1	2	3	4	5
Pleasant conditions	1	2	3	4	5
Chances to advance	1	2	3	4	5
Flexible schedule	1	2	3	4	5
Friendly coworkers	1	2	3	4	5

Questions for Discussion

1. Based on your answers, which rewards do you value most? Which do you value least? Do you think these preferences will change as you get older and perform different jobs? If so, how?
2. To what extent do you believe that you will be able to attain each of these rewards on your job? Do you expect that the chances of receiving these rewards will improve in the future? Why or why not?
3. Do you believe that the rewards you value most are also the ones valued by other people? Are these reward preferences likely to be the same for all people everywhere, or at least for all workers performing the same job in the same company?
4. Do you ever find yourself thinking about these rewards while on the job? Are you aware of these rewards most of the time, or do they only come to your attention when they are not received?

Working in Groups

Does Goal Setting Really Work? Demonstrate It for Yourself

The tendency for specific, difficult goals to enhance task performance is very well established. The following exercise is designed to help you demonstrate this effect yourself. All you need is a class of students willing to participate and a few simple supplies.

Directions

1. Select a page of text from a book and make several photocopies. Then, carefully count the words, and number each word on one of the copies. This will be your score sheet.
2. Find another class of 30 or more students who don't know anything about goal setting. (We don't want their knowledge of the phenomenon to bias the results.) On a random basis, divide the students into three equal-sized groups.
3. Ask the students in the first group ("baseline" group) to copy as much of the text as they can onto another piece of paper, giving them exactly one minute to do so. Direct them to work at a fast pace. Using the score sheet created in step 1, identify the highest number of words counted by any one of the students. Then, multiply this number by 1.5. This will be the specific, difficult goal level.
4. Ask the students in another group ("specific goal" group) to count the number of words on the same printed page for exactly one minute. Tell them to try to reach the specific goal number identified in step 3.

5. Repeat this process with the third group ("do your best" group) but instead of giving them a specific goal, direct them to "try to do your best at this task."

6. Compute the average number of words copied in the "difficult goal" group and the "do your best" group. Have your instructor compute the appropriate statistical test (a *t*-test, in this case) to determine the statistical significance of the difference between the performance levels of the groups.

Questions for Discussion

1. Was there, in fact, a statistically significant difference between the performance levels of the two groups? If so, did students in the "specific goal" group outperform those in the "do your best" group, as expected? What does this reveal about the effectiveness of goal setting?

2. If the predicted findings were not supported, why do you suppose this happened? What was it about the procedure that may have led to this failure? Was the specific goal (twice the fastest speed in the "baseline" group) too high, making the goal unreachable? Or, was it too low, making the specific goal too easy?

3. What do you think would happen if the goal was lowered, making it easier, or raised, making it more difficult?

4. Do you think it would have helped to provide feedback about goal attainment (e.g., someone counting the number of words copied, and calling this out to the performers as they worked)?

5. For what other kinds of tasks do you believe goal setting may be effective? Specifically, do you believe that you can use goal setting to improve your own performance on something you do? Explain this possibility.

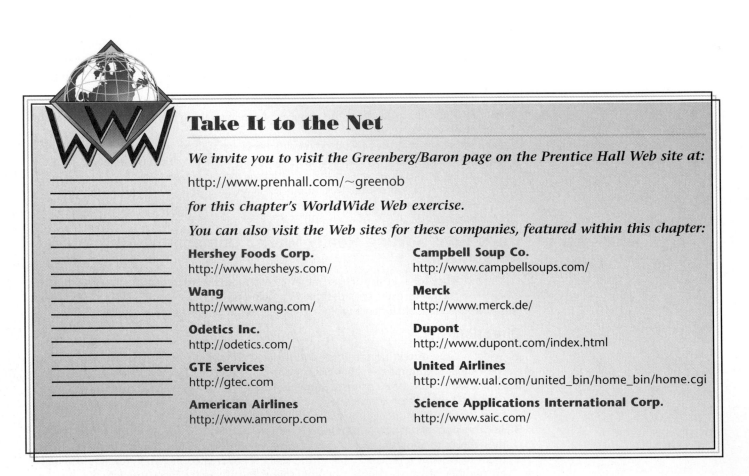

Take It to the Net

We invite you to visit the Greenberg/Baron page on the Prentice Hall Web site at:

http://www.prenhall.com/~greenob

for this chapter's WorldWide Web exercise.

You can also visit the Web sites for these companies, featured within this chapter:

Hershey Foods Corp.
http://www.hersheys.com/

Campbell Soup Co.
http://www.campbellsoups.com/

Wang
http://www.wang.com/

Merck
http://www.merck.de/

Odetics Inc.
http://odetics.com/

Dupont
http://www.dupont.com/index.html

GTE Services
http://gtec.com

United Airlines
http://www.ual.com/united_bin/home_bin/home.cgi

American Airlines
http://www.amrcorp.com

Science Applications International Corp.
http://www.saic.com/

CHAPTER Six

WORK-RELATED ATTITUDES:
FEELINGS ABOUT JOBS, ORGANIZATIONS, AND PEOPLE

■ OBJECTIVES

After reading this chapter you should be able to:

1. Define *attitudes* and understand their basic components.
2. Identify and describe the major theories of *job satisfaction* and the techniques used to measure it.
3. Explain the major causes and consequences of job satisfaction.
4. Describe the major dimensions of *organizational commitment*, including its foci and bases.

5. Describe the major causes and consequences of organizational commitment.
6. Distinguish between *prejudice* and *discrimination*, and describe various types of prejudice in organizations.
7. Describe some of the steps being taken by organizations today to manage *diversity* in the workforce.

LEARNING

WORKPLACE EQUALITY YIELDS HIGH INTEREST AT THE BANK OF MONTREAL

When you're Canada's oldest bank, people probably assume that you're going to be stodgy and conservative. However, Chairman Matthew Barrett and President Tony Comper knew that getting an edge up on the competition (and there's lots of it these days) required incorporating new perspectives into the Bank of Montreal's traditional corporate structure. This meant capitalizing on the rich diversity of its workforce. But opportunities for advancement were far from equal. Although women held 91 percent of the bank's nonmanagerial jobs, they accounted for only 9 percent of executive jobs.

Something had to be done to achieve equality, and Barrett and Comper sprung into action. They formed the Task Force on the Advancement of Women and charged it with the responsibility for identifying barriers to advancement for women and specific plans for breaking them down. The Task Force conducted extensive research and reported that the major barrier to advancement was a series of widely held myths about women executives that held them back. For example, survey findings revealed that women were assumed to be less committed to their companies because they quit their jobs to raise children. However, the reality is that for most jobs at the bank, women actually had *longer* service records than men—a direct contradiction of conventional wisdom.

Johanne M. Totta, vice president of employee programs and workplace equality, reasoned that one of the keys to turning the situation around was to speak the language best understood within the bank—numbers. Typically, managers were used to getting quarterly reports assessing the impact of their work on the bank's financial picture. Now, in addition, managers receive quarterly feedback telling them how well they're doing with respect to meeting equality goals, such as hiring women and helping those already working for the bank learn new skills and advance through the ranks. And, managers' own performance evaluations—and their pay—carefully reflect attainment of these goals.

As a further measure, Advisory Councils have been set up in which a diverse sample of employees at various levels meet quarterly with bank officials to discuss progress and problems with respect to achieving equality. These sessions provide useful feedback to be channeled to Totta's office. More importantly, perhaps, they provide people with helpful ideas for promoting equality that they can take back to their workplaces.

The Bank of Montreal has received several awards for its Workplace Equality Program, including the Distinction Award from the YWCA, and the Mercury Award from the International Communications Academy of Arts and Sciences. For bank officials, however, the highest accolade will come from overcoming the barriers to developing human potential that not only hold back the bank's female employees, but keep it from better serving its customers. As Totta said, "Banks offer about the same rates; it is people who make the difference—the customer service." With 6,000 branches internationally, there are surely a lot of customers to serve. Thus far, it looks as if the Bank of Montreal's Workplace Equality Program promises to be a high-yield investment.

What is behind this systematic effort by the Bank of Montreal to promote equality in the workplace? Primarily, it's the belief that its employees have a great deal to offer and that by giving them equal opportunities, the bank will be able to draw on this human capital to improve its performance. This, in turn, will keep the bank's employees feeling good about working there, keeping them on the job. Obviously, such reactions can have a strong impact on the way we behave in organizations. Indeed, such feelings—*attitudes* as they are called—represent an important part of people's lives, particularly on the job. Our attitudes toward our jobs or organizations—referred to as *work-related attitudes*—may have profound effects not only on the way we perform but also on the quality of life we experience while at work. We will carefully examine these effects in this chapter.

We will begin by describing the general nature of attitudes. With this background behind us, we will take a closer look at several specific types of work-related attitudes. We'll start with *job satisfaction*—essentially, people's positive or negative feelings about their jobs.[1] Specifically, we will describe some of the major factors contributing to feelings of satisfaction and dissatisfaction with one's work, and then consider the consequences of such reactions on organizational behavior.

Building on this, we will turn to another important work-related attitude—*organizational commitment*. This has to do with people's feelings about the organizations for which they work—the degree to which they identify with the organizations that employ them.[2] Finally, we will turn to a special type of attitude with which you are probably already somewhat familiar (unfortunately)—*prejudice*. This involves negative views about others who fall into certain categories, such as women and ethnic minorities, to mention just a few.[3] As we will see, such attitudes can have a seriously disruptive impact on the lives of individuals and the effective functioning of the organizations in which they are employed.

Attitudes: What Are They?

If we asked you how you feel about your job, we'd probably find you to be full of reactions. You might say, for example, that you really like it and think its very interesting. Or perhaps, you may complain about it bitterly and feel bored out of your mind. Maybe, you'd hold views that are more complex, liking some things (e.g., "my boss is great") and disliking others (e.g., "the pay is terrible"). Regardless of exactly how you might feel, the attitudes you express may be recognized as consisting of three major components: an evaluative component, a cognitive component, and a behavioral component.[4] Because these represent the basic building blocks of our definition of attitudes, it will be useful for us to take a closer look at them (see Figure 6-1).

So far, we've been suggesting that attitudes have a great deal to do with how we feel about something. Indeed, this aspect of an attitude, its *evaluative component*, refers to our liking or disliking of any particular person, item, or

■ **Figure 6-1**
Three Basic Components of Attitudes

Attitudes are composed of the three fundamental components shown here: the evaluative *component, the* cognitive *component, and the* behavioral *component.*

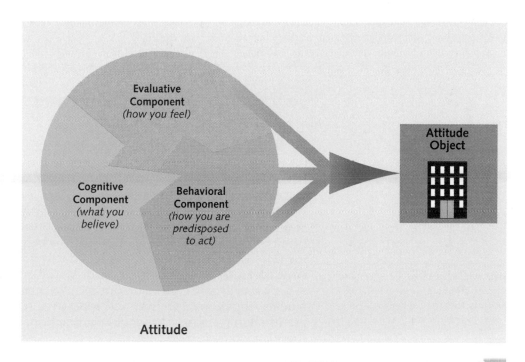

Evaluative Component
(how you feel)

Cognitive Component
(what you believe)

Behavioral Component
(how you are predisposed to act)

Attitude Object

Attitude

event (what might be called the *attitude object*, the focus of our attitude). You may, for example, feel positively or negatively toward your boss, the sculpture in the lobby, or the fact that your company just landed a large contract.

Attitudes involve more than feelings; they also involve knowledge—that is, what you believe to be the case about an attitude object. For example, you might believe that one of your co-workers is paid much more than you, or that your supervisor doesn't know too much about the job. These beliefs, whether they're completely accurate or totally false, comprise the *cognitive component* of attitudes.

As you might imagine, the things you believe about something (e.g., "my boss is embezzling company funds") and the way you feel about it (e.g., "I can't stand working for him") may have some effect on the way you are predisposed to behave (e.g., "I think I'm going to look for a new job"). In other words, attitudes also involve a *behavioral component*—a predisposition to act in a certain way. It is important to note that such a predisposition may not actually be predictive of one's behavior. For example, although you may be interested in taking a new job, you might not actually take one if a better position isn't available, or if there are other aspects of the job you like enough to compensate for the negative feelings. In other words, your intention to behave a certain way may or may not dictate how you will actually behave.

Combining these various components we can define **attitudes** as relatively stable clusters of feelings, beliefs, and behavioral predispositions (i.e., intentions toward some specific object). By including the phrase "relatively stable" in the definition, we are referring to something that is not fleeting and that, once formed, tends to persist. Indeed, as we will explain in the next section, changing attitudes may require considerable effort.

When we speak about **work-related attitudes**, we are talking about those lasting feelings, beliefs, and behavioral tendencies toward various aspects of the job itself, the setting in which the work is conducted, and/or the people involved. As you will discover as you read this chapter, work-related attitudes are associated with many important aspects of organizational behavior, including job performance, absence from work, and voluntary turnover. Such relationships are often very complex, varying across different situations and different people, and are not understandable without a great deal of carefully conducted systematic research.

Now that we have identified the basic nature of attitudes, and the mechanisms by which they are changed, we are prepared to turn our attention to specific work-related attitudes. We will begin by describing a very fundamental work-related attitude—*job satisfaction*, attitudes toward one's job.

Job Satisfaction: Attitudes toward One's Job

If you were to ask people about their jobs, you would likely find that they have strong opinions about how they feel (e.g., "I really dislike what I do"), what they believe (e.g., "we provide important services to the community"), and how they intend to behave (e.g., "I am going to look for a new position"). When you consider that people spend roughly one-third of their lives at work, and that what we do to earn a living represents a central aspect of how we think of ourselves as individuals, such strong feelings should not be surprising. The various attitudes people hold toward their jobs are referred to as **job satisfaction**, one of the most widely studied work-related attitudes, and the topic we will now consider. Formally, we may define job satisfaction as individuals' cognitive, affective, and evaluative reactions toward their jobs.[5]

In taking a closer look at job satisfaction, we will address several major issues. For example, we will consider how job satisfaction is measured, a key is-

attitudes Stable clusters of feelings, beliefs, and behavioral intentions toward specific objects, people, or institutions.

work-related attitudes Attitudes relating to any aspect of work or work settings.

job satisfaction People's cognitive, affective, and evaluative reactions toward their jobs.

sue involved in assessing this concept. We also will describe various theories of job satisfaction, systematic attempts to address how the process of job satisfaction works. Following this, we will review the major factors that are responsible for making people satisfied or dissatisfied with their jobs. Then, finally, we will consider the principal effects of job satisfaction on various aspects of organizational behavior. Before considering these topics, however, we will begin by addressing a very basic question: Are people generally satisfied with their jobs?

Are People Generally Satisfied with Their Jobs?

If you were to make assumptions about people's general levels of job satisfaction from stories you read in the newspaper about disgruntled workers going on strike or even killing their supervisors, you would probably think that people are generally very dissatisfied with their jobs.[6] However, most people are really quite satisfied with their jobs. Demonstrating this, people responding to one recent survey of workers in the United States, Mexico, and Spain, indicated their levels of satisfaction with their work and the behavior of their supervisors.[7] As shown in Figure 6-2, not only were the mean responses to both questions quite high, but uniformly so in all three countries. When considered together with surveys conducted over several decades showing that 80 to 90 percent of people are relatively satisfied with their jobs, a much more optimistic picture emerges than might be suggested by occasional news reports.[8]

As you might imagine, the complete picture is more complex; not everyone doing every type of job is equally satisfied. There exist certain groups for

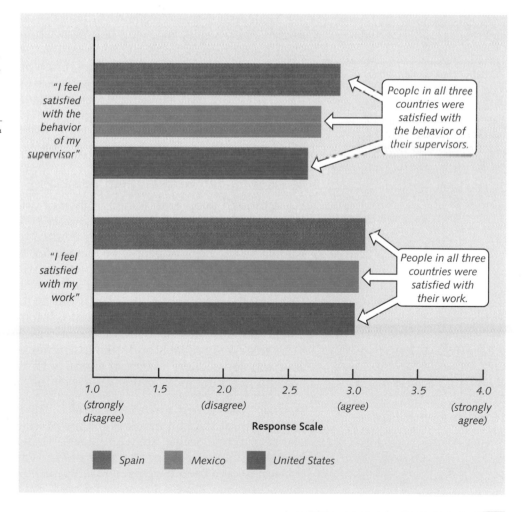

■ Figure 6-2
Are People Satisfied With Their Jobs: A Three-Nation Comparison
When people in Spain, Mexico, and the United States were surveyed about how satisfied they were with their work and the behavior of their supervisors, all responded very positively.

(**Source:** Based on data reported by Page & Wiseman, 1993; see Note 17.)

whom specific patterns of job satisfaction or dissatisfaction have been clearly established. So then, who tends to be most satisfied with their jobs? Here are some key findings:

- White-collar personnel (e.g., managerial and professional people) tend to be more satisfied than blue-collar personnel (e.g., physical laborers, factory workers).[9]
- Older people are generally more satisfied with their jobs than younger people. Interestingly, satisfaction does not increase at an even pace. People become more satisfied with their jobs in their 30s (as they become more successful). Satisfaction levels off in the 40s (as people become disenchanted). Finally, people become more satisfied again in their late 50s (as they resign themselves to their lot in life).[10]
- People who are more experienced on their jobs are more highly satisfied than those who are less experienced.[11] This shouldn't be too surprising since people who are highly dissatisfied with their jobs may be expected to find new jobs when they can.
- Women and members of minority groups, tend to be more dissatisfied with their jobs than men and members of majority groups. This appears to be due to the tendency for victims of employment discrimination to be channeled into lower-level jobs and positions with limited opportunities for advancement.[12]

Not only may certain groups of people be more satisfied with their jobs than others, but in addition some individuals are likely to be either consistently satisfied or dissatisfied with their jobs. The main idea is that job satisfaction is a relatively stable *disposition*, a characteristic of individuals that stays with them across situations.

The idea that some people, by nature, may be predisposed to being either satisfied or dissatisfied with their jobs is in keeping with the concept of positive and negative affect discussed in Chapter 4.

Evidence of this effect was provided in a fascinating study by Staw and Ross.[13] Their survey of over 5,000 men who changed jobs between 1969 and 1971 found that expressions of job satisfaction were relatively stable. In other words, despite the fact that they had different jobs, men who were satisfied or dissatisfied in 1969 were equally satisfied or dissatisfied in 1971. Although some scientists have challenged claims regarding the dispositional stability of job satisfaction, a considerable amount of follow-up research supports Staw and Ross's findings, strengthening the possibility that the tendency to be satisfied or dissatisfied with one's job is a stable disposition.[14]

Measuring Job Satisfaction: Assessing Reactions to Work

Although people have many different attitudes toward various aspects of their jobs, these are not as easy to assess as you might think. Not only can't you directly observe an attitude, but, as we noted, you cannot accurately infer its existence on the basis of people's behavior. So, for the most part, we have to rely on what people tell us to determine their attitudes. However, people are generally not entirely open about their attitudes and keep much of what they feel to themselves. Moreover, sometimes our attitudes are so complex that it's difficult to express them in any coherent fashion—even if we are willing to do so.

In view of these challenges, social scientists have worked hard over the years to develop reliable and valid instruments designed to systematically measure job satisfaction.[15] Several useful techniques have been developed, including *rating scales* or *questionnaires*, *critical incidents*, and *interviews*.

Rating scales and questionnaires. The most common approach to measuring job satisfaction involves the use of questionnaires in which highly specialized rating scales are completed. Using this method, people answer questions allowing them to report their reactions to their jobs. Several different scales have been developed for this purpose, and these vary greatly in form and scope (see Table 6-1).

■ TABLE 6-1   MEASURES OF JOB SATISFACTION: SOME WIDELY USED SCALES

The items shown here are similar to those used in three popular measures of job satisfaction.

Job Descriptive Index (JDI)	Minnesota Satisfaction Questionnaire (MSQ)	Pay Satisfaction Questionnaire (PSQ)
Enter "Yes," "No," or "?" for each description or word below. **Work itself:** ___ Routine ___ Satisfactory ___ Good **Promotions:** ___ Dead-end job ___ Few promotions ___ Good opportunity for promotion	Indicate the extent to which you are satisfied with each aspect of your present job. Enter one number next to each aspect. 1 = Extremely dissatisfied 2 = Not satisfied 3 = Neither satisfied nor dissatisfied 4 = Satisfied 5 = Extremely satisfied ___ Utilization of your abilities ___ Authority ___ Company policies and practices ___ Independence ___ Supervision–human relations	Indicate the extent to which you are satisfied with each aspect of present pay. Enter one number next to each aspect. 1 = Extremely dissatisfied 2 = Not satisfied 3 = Neither satisfied nor dissatisfied 4 = Satisfied 5 = Extremely satisfied **Satisfaction with pay level:** ___ My current pay ___ Size of my salary **Satisfaction with raises:** ___ Typical raises ___ How raises are determined

SOURCE: Based on items from the JDI, MSQ, and PSQ; see Notes 16, 17, and 18.

Job Descriptive Index (JDI) A rating scale for assessing job satisfaction. Individuals respond to this questionnaire by indicating whether or not various adjectives describe aspects of their work.

Minnesota Satisfaction Questionnaire (MSQ) A rating scale for assessing job satisfaction in which people indicate the extent to which they are satisfied with various aspects of their jobs.

Pay Satisfaction Questionnaire (PSQ) A questionnaire designed to assess employees' level of satisfaction with various aspects of their pay (e.g., its overall level, raises, benefits).

One of the most popular instruments is the **Job Descriptive Index (JDI)**, a questionnaire in which people indicate whether or not each of several adjectives describes a particular aspect of their work.[16] Questions on the JDI deal with five distinct aspects of jobs: the work itself, pay, promotional opportunities, supervision, and people (co-workers).

Another widely used measure, the **Minnesota Satisfaction Questionnaire (MSQ)** uses a different approach.[17] People completing this scale rate the extent to which they are satisfied or dissatisfied with various aspects of their jobs (e.g., their pay, chances for advancement). Higher scores reflect higher degrees of job satisfaction.

Although the JDI and the MSQ measure many different aspects of job satisfaction, other scales focus more narrowly on specific facets of satisfaction. For example, as its name suggests, the **Pay Satisfaction Questionnaire (PSQ)** is primarily concerned with attitudes toward various aspects of pay.[18] The PSQ provides valid measures of such critical aspects as satisfaction with pay level, pay raises, fringe benefits, and the structure and administration of the pay system.[19]

An important advantage of rating scales—these and others—is that they can be completed quickly and efficiently by large numbers of people. Another benefit is that when the same questionnaire already has been administered to many thousands of individuals, average scores for people in many kinds of jobs and many types of organizations are available. This makes it possible to compare the scores of people in a given company with these averages and obtain measures of *relative* satisfaction. This may be useful information not only for scientists interested in studying job satisfaction, but also for companies interested in learning about trends in the feelings of its employees. Although most companies that conduct attitude surveys use relatively traditional rating scales such as those noted here, some do things a bit differently. For a look at one company that assesses its employees' attitudes in a rather offbeat way, see THE QUEST FOR QUALITY section.

critical incidents technique A procedure for measuring job satisfaction in which employees describe incidents relating to their work that they have found especially satisfying or dissatisfying.

Critical incidents. A second procedure for assessing job satisfaction is the **critical incident technique**. Here, individuals describe events relating to their work that they have found especially satisfying or dissatisfying. Their replies are then examined to uncover underlying themes. For example, if many employees mentioned on-the-job situations in which they were treated rudely

The "Happiness Index": Assessing Job Satisfaction at Wild Oats Market

*I*n 1984, when Libby Cook, Michael Gilliland, and Randy Clapp opened their tiny grocery store, the Wild Oats Market, in Boulder, Colorado, they always knew how their employees felt. Working with them shoulder to shoulder, they had no difficulty getting feedback. By 1988 their business grew to a dozen stores in three states, and the owners found themselves looking more at spreadsheets than at people. As a result, it became impossible for them to keep in touch with their employees' feelings about their jobs and their suggestions for improvement. To help, Gilliland and his management team developed the company's "Happiness Index," a friendly, unintimidating way of assessing job satisfaction.[20]

In their words, the purpose of the survey is to determine "if morale is giddy or suicidal," so that better working conditions could be created. To keep things from getting boring and to maintain the playful atmosphere that the company promotes, the language is purposely kept unintimidating. None of the other rating instruments you'll come across use labels such as "ecstatic," "awful," "remarkably bad," or "wonderful," but Wild Oats' semi-annual survey does just that. The friendliness of it all keeps 90 percent of employees completing the voluntary, two-page survey (composed of ten rating scales and six open-ended questions).

Besides being fun, one sure reason why employees accept the survey is that they know that the owners pay careful attention to the results, trying to be as responsive as possible. For example, when the employees indicated that they wanted more varied benefits, management responded by giving each employee a $200 annual "wellness allowance" to help cover uninsured expenses such as acupuncture and health club memberships.

In 1994, after employees expressed interest in getting in on the company's success, stock options were added to the list of benefits. For a long time, one of the biggest gripes was that performance reviews were often delayed (because managers were so very busy), causing delays in the raises that stemmed from them. In response to such criticism, the company now makes raises retroactive to the scheduled date of the performance review, regardless of when it actually took place.

Gilliland notes that turnover at Wild Oats stores has steadily decreased since the company started using the survey. Not only does he cite its "therapeutic benefits," but also the useful ways of improving working conditions that have been generated. In fact, he claims that each round of surveys yields some 20 good ideas.

As Wild Oats has grown in the past decade, Cook, Gilliland, and Clapp, no longer stocking shelves with their hourly employees, have found a useful way of keeping in touch with the front lines. Although formal employee surveys are commonly used in large companies, the Wild Oats experience shows us that even small companies—and their employees—stand to benefit from using (and responding to) attitude surveys. The Happiness Index appears to have helped make Wild Oats Market a happy place to work.

by their supervisors, or praised supervisors for sensitivity they showed in a difficult period, this would suggest that supervisory style plays an important role in their job satisfaction.

Interviews and confrontation meetings. A third procedure for assessing job satisfaction involves carefully interviewing employees in face-to-face sessions. By questioning people in person about their attitudes, it is often possible to explore them more deeply than by using highly structured questionnaires. By carefully posing questions to employees and systematically recording their answers, it is possible to learn about the causes of various work-related attitudes. For example, one team of researchers relied on face-to-face meetings with employees to learn their feelings about their company's recent bankruptcy filing.[21] The highly personal approach to data collection was particularly effective in gathering reactions to such a complex and difficult situation.

Sometimes, interviews are designed to have employees "lay it on the line," and discuss their major complaints and concerns. Interviews of this type are known as *confrontation meetings*. If such sessions are conducted skillfully, in an environment in which employees feel free to speak out without retaliation, serious problems that adversely affect job satisfaction but might otherwise remain hidden, can be brought out into the open. This may be a crucial first step toward correcting or eliminating the problems.

As you might imagine, confrontation meetings—or any type of self-report measure, for that matter—are only successful to the extent that people respond honestly and are capable of accurately reporting their feelings. An important key is gaining people's cooperation. With this in mind, it is important for researchers collecting information about job satisfaction to keep all individual's responses completely confidential and to assure them of this clearly. In fact, it is also useful to keep respondents' identities anonymous so that it is impossible to identify anything that any one respondent may have said. In short, it is essential for measures of job satisfaction—or any work-related attitudes, for that matter—to protect respondents' rights to privacy, not only because doing so helps safeguard the validity of the measures, but also because it is unethical to do otherwise.

Theories of Job Satisfaction

What makes some people more satisfied with their jobs than others? What underlying processes account for people's feelings of job satisfaction? Insight into these important questions is provided by various theories of job satisfaction. We will describe two of the most influential approaches—Herzberg's *two-factor theory* and Locke's *value theory*.

Herzberg's two-factor theory. Think about something that may have happened on your job that made you feel especially satisfied or dissatisfied. What were these events? (This is an example of the description of the *critical incident technique* described above.) Over 30 years ago Frederick Herzberg posed this question to more than 200 accountants and engineers and carefully analyzed their responses.[22] What he found was somewhat surprising: Different factors accounted for job satisfaction and dissatisfaction.

Although you might expect that certain factors lead to satisfaction when they are present and dissatisfaction when they are absent, this was *not* the case. Job satisfaction and dissatisfaction were found to stem from different sources (see Figure 6-3). In particular, dissatisfaction was associated with conditions surrounding the jobs (e.g., working conditions, pay, security, quality of supervision, relations with others) rather than the work itself. Because these factors prevent negative reactions, Herzberg referred to them as *hygiene* (or *maintenance*) *factors*. By contrast, satisfaction was associated with factors associated with the work itself or to outcomes directly derived from it, such as the nature of their jobs, achievement in the work, promotion opportunities, and chances for personal growth and recognition. Because such factors were associated with high levels of job satisfaction, Herzberg called them *motivators*.

Concerned, as it is, with both motivators and hygiene factors, Herzberg's theory is referred to as **two-factor theory**. Research testing this theory has yielded mixed results. Some studies have found that job satisfaction and dissatisfaction were based on different factors and that these are in keeping with the distinction made by Herzberg.[23] Other studies, however, have found that factors labeled as hygienes and motivators exerted strong effects on both satisfaction and dissatisfaction, thereby casting doubt on two-factor theory.[24] In view of such equivocal evidence, we must label Herzberg's theory as an intriguing but unverified framework for understanding job satisfaction.

Still, this theory has important implications for managing organizations. Specifically, managers would be well advised to focus their attention on factors known to promote job satisfaction, such as opportunities for personal growth. Indeed, several of today's companies have realized that satisfaction within their workforces is enhanced when they provide opportunities for their employees to develop their repertoire of professional skills on the job. For ex-

two-factor theory (of job satisfaction) A theory, devised by Herzberg, suggesting that satisfaction and dissatisfaction stem from different groups of variables (*motivators* and *hygienes*, respectively).

If you are thinking that this sounds like an example of job enrichment, described in Chapter 5, you are correct. Indeed, two-factor theory was greatly responsible for the development of the job enrichment approach to motivation.

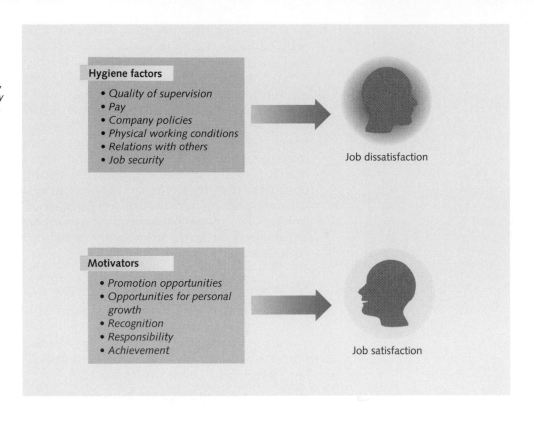

■ **Figure 6-3**
Herzberg's Two-Factor Theory
According to Herzberg's two-factor theory, job satisfaction is caused by a set of factors referred to as motivators, *whereas job dissatisfaction is caused by a different set of factors, known as hygiene factors.*

ample, front-line service workers at Marriott Hotels, known as "guest services associates," are hired to perform a variety of tasks, including checking guests in and out, carrying their bags, and so on.[25] Instead of doing just one job, this approach enables Marriott employees to call upon and develop many of their talents, thereby adding to their level of job satisfaction.

Two-factor theory also implies that steps should be taken to create conditions that help avoid dissatisfaction—and, it specifies the kinds of variables required to do so (i.e., hygiene factors). For example, creating pleasant working conditions may be quite helpful in getting people to avoid being dissatisfied with their jobs. Specifically, research has shown that dissatisfaction is great under conditions that are highly overcrowded, dark, noisy, have extreme temperatures, and poor air quality.[26] These factors, associated with the conditions under which work is performed, but not directly linked to the work itself, contribute much to the levels of job dissatisfaction encountered.

value theory (of job satisfaction) A theory, devised by Locke, suggesting that job satisfaction depends primarily on the match between the outcomes individuals value in their jobs and their perceptions about the availability of such outcomes.

Locke's value theory. A second important theory of job satisfaction is Locke's **value theory**.[27] This conceptualization claims that job satisfaction exists to the extent that the job outcomes (such as rewards) an individual receives matches those outcomes that are desired. The more people receive outcomes they value, the more satisfied they will be; the less they receive outcomes they value, the less satisfied they will be. Locke's approach focuses on *any* outcomes that people value, regardless of what they are. The key to satisfaction in Locke's theory is the *discrepancy* between those aspects of the job one has and those one wants; the greater the discrepancy, the less people are satisfied.

Recent research provides good support for value theory. Using a questionnaire, one team of investigators measured how much of various job facets—such as freedom to work one's own way, learning opportunities, promotion opportunities, and pay level—a diverse group of workers wanted, and how much they felt they already had.[28] They also measured how satisfied the respondents were with each of these facets and how important each facet was to them. As shown in Figure 6-4, an interesting trend emerged: Those aspects of the job about which respondents experienced the greatest discrepancies were

Job Satisfaction: The Result of Getting What We Want
Research has shown that the larger a discrepancy that exists between what people have and what they want with respect to various facets of their jobs (e.g., pay, learning opportunities), the more dissatisfied they are with their jobs. This relationship is greater among those who place a great deal of importance on that facet than among those who consider it less important.

(**Source:** Adapted from McFarlin & Rice, 1992; see Note 28.)

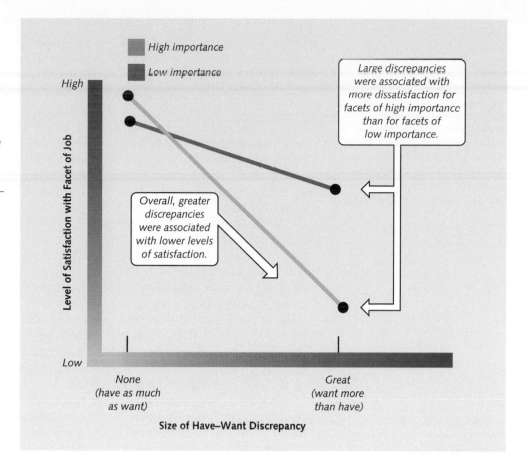

the ones with which they were most dissatisfied, and those with which they experienced the smallest discrepancies were the ones with which they were most satisfied. Interestingly, the researchers also found that this relationship was greater among individuals who placed a high amount of importance on a particular facet of the job. In other words, the more important a particular facet of the job was believed to be, the less satisfied people were when they failed to get as much of this facet as they wanted.

An interesting implication of value theory is that it calls attention to the aspects of the job that need to be changed for job satisfaction to result. Specifically, the theory suggests that these aspects might not be the same ones for all people, but any valued aspects of the job about which people perceive serious discrepancies. By emphasizing values, Locke's theory suggests that job satisfaction may be derived from many factors. Thus, an effective way to satisfy employees would be to find out what they want and, to the extent possible, give it to them.

Believe it or not, this is sometimes easier said than done. In fact, organizations sometimes go through great pains to find out how to satisfy their employees. With this in mind, a growing number of companies, particularly big ones, have been systematically surveying their employees. For example, FedEx has been so interested in tracking the attitudes of its employees that it has started using a fully automated on-line survey. The company relies on information gained from surveys of its 68,000 U.S.-based employees as the key to identifying sources of dissatisfaction among them.

Consequences of Job Dissatisfaction

People talk a great deal about the importance of building employee satisfaction, assuming that morale is critical to the functioning of organizations. As we will see, although job satisfaction does indeed influence organizations, its impact is not always as strong as one might expect. Thus, we might ask: What are the consequences of job dissatisfaction? Our summary will focus on two main variables—employee withdrawal (i.e., absenteeism and turnover) and job performance.

Job satisfaction and employee withdrawal. When employees are dissatisfied with their jobs, they try to find ways of reducing their exposure to them. That is, they stay away from their jobs—behavior known as **employee withdrawal**. Two main forms of employee withdrawal are absenteeism and voluntary turnover.[29] By not showing up to work and/or by quitting to take a new job, people may be expressing their dissatisfaction with their jobs, or attempting to escape from the unpleasant aspects of them they may be experiencing.

With respect to absenteeism, research has shown that the lower individuals' satisfaction with their jobs, the more likely they are to be absent from work.[30] The strength of this relationship, however, is only modest. The reason is that dissatisfaction with one's job is likely to be just one of many factors influencing people's decisions to report or not report to work. For example, even someone who really dislikes her job may not be absent if she believes her presence is necessary to complete an important project. However, another employee might dislike her job so much that she will "play hooky" without showing any concern over how the company will be affected. Thus, although it's not a perfectly reliable reaction to job dissatisfaction, absenteeism is one of its most important consequences.

Another costly form of withdrawal related to job satisfaction is voluntary turnover. The lower people's levels of satisfaction with their jobs, the more likely they are to consider resigning and actually to do so. As in the case of absenteeism, this relationship is modest, for similar reasons.[31] Many factors relating to the individuals, their jobs, and economic conditions shape decisions to move from one job to another. As you might imagine, there are many more variables involved in making turnover decisions. Many of these are described in a model of the voluntary turnover process described by Mobley (see Figure 6-5).[32] According to this conceptualization, job dissatisfaction leads employees to think about the possibility of quitting. This, in turn, leads to the decision to search for another job. Then, if the search is successful, the individual

employee withdrawal
Actions, such as chronic absenteeism and voluntary turnover (i.e., quitting one's job), that enable employees to escape from adverse organizational situations.

■ **Figure 6-5**
Voluntary Turnover: A Model
According to Mobley and his associates, voluntary turnover is a complex process triggered by low levels of job satisfaction. This leads people to think about quitting and then to search for another job. Finally, they form intentions to quit or to remain on their present jobs. At several steps in this process, the probability of finding an acceptable alternative plays a role.

(**Source:** Based on suggestions by Mobley, Horner, & Hollingsworth, 1978; see Note 32.)

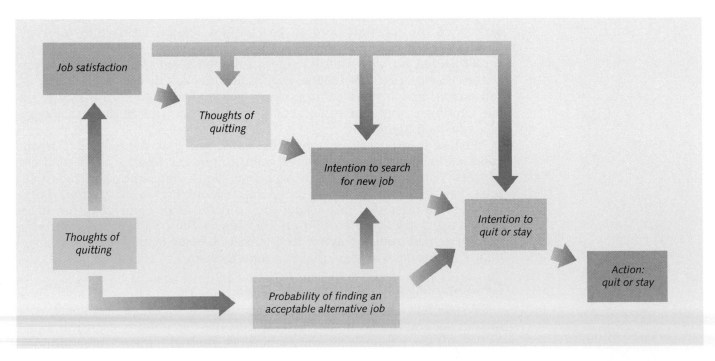

will develop definite intentions either to quit or to remain on the job. Finally, these intentions are reflected in concrete actions.

Mobley's suggestion that economic conditions, and hence the success of an initial search for alternative jobs, exert a strong impact on voluntary turnover is supported by the findings of an interesting study by Carsten and Spector.[33] These researchers examined the results of a large number of previous studies concerned with turnover. For each, they contacted the people who had conducted the study and determined the precise dates during which their data had been collected. Then, Carsten and Spector obtained data on the unemployment rates prevailing at those times. They predicted that the relationship between job satisfaction and turnover would be stronger at times when unemployment was low than when it was high. When unemployment was low, they reasoned, people would recognize that they have many other job opportunities and would be prone to take one when they are highly dissatisfied with their present jobs. By contrast, conditions of high unemployment would limit alternative job options, leading people to stay with their present jobs despite their dissatisfaction with them. This is precisely what they found: The higher the unemployment rates were, the lower was the correlation between job satisfaction and turnover.

Organizations are highly concerned about withdrawal insofar as it is generally very costly. The expenses involved in selecting and training employees to replace those who have resigned can be considerable. Even unscheduled absences can be expensive—averaging between $247 and $534 per employee, by one estimate.[34] Although voluntary turnover is permanent, whereas absenteeism is a short-term reaction, both are effective ways of withdrawing from dissatisfying jobs.

As an example, consider the reactions of the highly dissatisfied bakery workers at the Safeway market in Clackamas, Oregon. So upset with their jobs (particularly the treatment they received from management) were the bakery's 130 employees, that they frequently were absent, quit, and had on-the-job accidents. And these were no minor problems. In one year alone, accidents resulted in 1,740 lost work days—a very expensive problem. Accidents only occurred, of course, when employees showed up. At unpopular times, such as Saturday nights, it was not unusual for as many as 8 percent of the workers to call in sick. Almost no one stayed on the job for more than a year. Clearly, withdrawal was a very disruptive response to dissatisfaction in this organization.

Job satisfaction and task performance. Many people believe that "happy workers are productive workers." But, is this really the case? *Is* job satisfaction, in fact, directly linked to task performance or organizational productivity? Overall, research suggests that the relationship is positive, but not especially strong. In fact, after reviewing hundreds of studies on this topic, researchers found that the mean correlation between job satisfaction and performance is considerably smaller, only .17.[35] Why does job satisfaction have such a limited relationship to performance? There are several explanations.

First, in many work settings, there is little room for large changes in performance. Some jobs are structured so that the people holding them *must* maintain at least some minimum level of performance just to remain at their jobs. For others, there may be very little leeway for exceeding minimum standards. Thus, the range of possible performance in many jobs is highly restricted. Moreover, for many employees, the rate at which they work is closely linked to the work of others or the speed at which various machines operate. As such, their performance may have such little room to fluctuate that it may not be highly responsive to changes in their attitudes.

Second, job satisfaction and performance may actually not be directly linked. Rather, any apparent relationship between them may stem from the fact that both are related to a third factor—receipt of various rewards. As suggested by Porter and Lawler, the relationship may work as follows.[36] Past levels of performance lead to the receipt of both extrinsic rewards (e.g., pay, promotions) and intrinsic rewards (e.g., feelings of accomplishment). If employees judge these to be fair, they may eventually recognize a link between their performance and these outcomes. This, in turn, may have two effects. First, it may encourage high levels of effort, and thus, good performance. Second, it may lead to high levels of job satisfaction. In short, high productivity and high satisfaction may both stem from the same conditions. These two factors, themselves, however, may not be directly linked. For these and other reasons, job satisfaction may not be directly related to performance in many contexts.

Promoting Job Satisfaction: Some Guidelines

In view of the negative consequences of dissatisfaction just discussed, it makes sense to consider ways of raising satisfaction and preventing dissatisfaction on the job. Although an employee's dissatisfaction might not account for all aspects of his or her performance, it is important to try to promote satisfaction if for no other reason than to make people happy. After all, satisfaction is a desirable end in itself. With this in mind, we now turn to an important question: What can be done to promote job satisfaction? Based on what scientists know about this, we offer several suggestions.

1. *Pay people fairly.* People who believe that their organizations' pay systems are inherently unfair tend to be dissatisfied with their jobs. This applies not only to salary and hourly pay, but also to fringe benefits. In fact, when people are given opportunities to select the fringe benefits they most desire, their job satisfaction tends to rise. This idea is consistent with value theory. After all, given the opportunity to receive the fringe benefits they most desire, employees may have little or no discrepancies between those they want and those they actually have.

2. *Improve the quality of supervision.* Satisfaction tends to be highest among those who believe that their supervisors are competent, treat them with respect, and have their best interests in mind. Similarly, job satisfaction is enhanced when employees believe that they have open lines of communication with their superiors.

   For example, in response to the dissatisfaction problems that plagued the Safeway bakery employees described earlier, company officials responded by completely changing their management style. Traditionally, they were highly intimidating and controlling, leaving employees feeling powerless and discouraged. Realizing the problems caused by this iron-fisted style, they began loosening their highly autocratic way, replacing it with a new openness and freedom. Employees were allowed to work together toward solving problems of sanitation and safety and were encouraged to make suggestions about ways to improve things. The results were dramatic: Work days lost due to accidents dropped from 1,740 a year down to 2, absenteeism fell from 8 percent to 0.2 percent, and voluntary turnover was reduced from almost 100 percent annually to less than 10 percent. Clearly, improving the quality of supervision went a long way toward reversing the negative effects of satisfaction at this Safeway bakery.

3. *Decentralize the control of organizational power.* Decentralization is the degree to which the capacity to make decisions resides in several people, as opposed to one or just a handful. When power is decentralized, people are allowed to participate freely in the process of decision making. This arrangement contributes to their feelings of satisfaction because it leads them to believe that they can have some impact on their organizations. By contrast, when the power to make decisions is concentrated in the hands of just a few, employees are likely to feel powerless and ineffective, thereby contributing to their feelings of dissatisfaction.

Beliefs about the perceived relationships between performance and reward are basic to expectancy theory, discussed in Chapter 5.

As we discussed in Chapter 5, equity theory recognizes that people also perceive their pay to be fair to the extent that they recognize that they are rewarded in a manner that recognizes their relative performance contributions.

The concept of centralization and decentralization of power is also discussed in conjunction with the topics of communication (Chapter 9), social influence (Chapter 12) and organizational structure (Chapter 15).

The changes in supervision made at the Safeway bakery provides a good illustration of moving from a highly centralized style to a highly decentralized style. The power to make certain important decisions was shifted into the hands of those who were most affected by them. Because decentralizing power gives people greater opportunities to control aspects of the workplace that affect them, it makes it possible for employees to receive the outcomes they most desire, thereby enhancing their satisfaction.

This dynamic appears to be at work in many of today's organizations. For example, at the Blue Ridge, Georgia, plant of Levi Strauss, the sewing machine operators run the factory themselves (see Figure 6-6). In a less extreme example, a committee of employees meets monthly with the CEO of Palms West Hospital (in Palm Beach County, Florida) to make important decisions concerning the hospital's operation. High satisfaction in these facilities can be traced in large part to the decentralized nature of decision-making power.

4. *Match people to jobs that are congruent with their interests.* People have many interests, and these are only sometimes satisfied on the job. However, the more people find that they are able to fulfill their interests while on the job, the more satisfied they will be with those jobs. For example, a recent study found that college graduates were more satisfied with their jobs when these were consistent with their college majors than when these fell outside their fields of interest.

It is, no doubt, with this in mind that career counselors frequently find it useful to identify people's nonvocational interests. For example, several companies, such as AT&T, IBM, Ford Motor Company, Shell Oil, and Kodak, systematically test and counsel their employees so they can effectively match their skills and interests to those positions to which they are best suited. Some, including Coca Cola, and Disneyland, go so far as to offer individualized counseling to employees so that their personal and professional interests can be identified and matched.

In conclusion, there is good news for managers interested in promoting satisfaction (and avoiding dissatisfaction) among employees. Although it might not always be easy to make a special effort to promote job satisfaction, especially amidst the hectic pace of everyday work, what we know about the benefits of keeping employees satisfied with their jobs suggests that the effort may be extremely worthwhile.

■ **Figure 6-6**
Enhancing Satisfaction by Being the Boss
These sewing machine operators at the Blue Ridge, Georgia, Levi Strauss plant are likely to be highly satisfied with their jobs in great part because they run the factory themselves.

Organizational Commitment: Feelings of Attachment toward Organizations

organizational commitment The extent to which an individual identifies and is involved with his or her organization and/or is unwilling to leave it.

Suppose you really enjoy the work you do and are very satisfied with your job. This doesn't necessarily mean that you will feel positively toward your company as well. In fact, you may even despise it and hope to get out as soon as possible. Similarly, it's possible for you to think your company is a wonderful place to work, although you might be terribly displeased about the job you do. The point we are making is that to understand people's work-related attitudes fully we must go beyond the concept of job satisfaction and also consider people's feelings toward their organizations.[37]

Such attitudes, referred to as **organizational commitment**, reflect the extent to which people identify with and are involved with their organizations and are unwilling to leave them. As you might imagine, many factors are responsible for organizational commitment, and the impact of such attitudes may be quite serious. Before we consider these various consequences of organizational commitment and ways to increase commitment, we will take a closer look at its basic dimensions.

Organizational Commitment: Its Basic Dimensions

To help understand the complex nature of organizational commitment, theorists have broken it down to its basic components. Notably, a distinction has been made between the *foci of commitment*—the particular entity, such as the group or individual to which a person is committed—and the *bases of commitment*—the underlying reasons why the commitment occurs. We will discuss each of these basic dimensions.

Foci of commitment. It is important to note that people can be committed to various entities in their organizations. For example, they may have varying degrees of commitment to their co-workers, subordinates, superiors, customers, the union, or top management—in short, any particular individual or group target. In an attempt to categorize some of these various foci, Becker and Billings distinguished between those whose commitment is concentrated at lower organizational levels, such as one's immediate work group and supervisor, and those who are primarily focused on higher levels, such as top management and the organization as a whole.[38] By combining high and low levels of each of these, they identified the four distinct *commitment profiles* summarized in Table 6-2.

First, individuals who are low in commitment to both their work groups and supervisors as well as low in commitment to top management and the organization are labeled *uncommitted*. By contrast, individuals who are high in commitment to both sets of foci are labeled *committed*. In between are two

■ TABLE 6-2	FOUR DIFFERENT COMMITMENT PROFILES		
Becker and Billings have distinguished between two major foci of commitment: the supervisor and the work group, and top management and the organization. By combining low and high levels of each, the four commitment profiles shown here emerge.		Attachment to Supervisor and Work Group	
	Attachment to Top Management and Organization	Low	High
	Low	Uncommitted	Locally committed
	High	Globally committed	Committed

SOURCE: Based on information in Becker & Billings, 1993; see Note 38.

groups: those who are highly committed to their supervisor and work group but not to top management and the organization—known as *locally committed*; and those who are highly committed to top management and the organization, but not to their supervisor and work group—known as *globally committed*.

In a study conducted at a large military supply organization, Becker and Billings found that employees' attitudes differed in ways consistent with their profiles. For example, individuals falling into the uncommitted category (based on their responses to various questionnaire items) were more interested in quitting their jobs and less interested in helping others than those who were in the committed category. Those who were globally committed and locally committed scored in between these two extremes. In conclusion, although this method of distinguishing between various foci of commitment is still new, it appears to hold a great deal of promise as a tool for understanding a key dimension of organizational commitment.

Bases of commitment.   To fully understand the concept of commitment, we must look at not only various foci, but also its bases—that is, the motives that people have for being committed. Historically, two different approaches to understanding these bases have dominated—the *side-bets orientation* and the individual-organizational *goal congruence orientation*.[39]

side-bets orientation The view of organizational commitment that focuses on the accumulated investments an individual stands to lose if he or she leaves the organization.

Becker's **side-bets orientation** focuses on the accumulated investments an individual stands to lose if he or she leaves the organization.[40] The idea is that over time, leaving an organization becomes more costly because people fear losing what they have invested in the organization and become concerned that they cannot replace these things. For example, people may be unwilling to leave their jobs because they are concerned about being perceived as "job hoppers" and stake their reputation for stability on remaining in their present jobs (i.e., they make a "side bet" on some aspect of themselves on continued organizational membership).

goal-congruence orientation An approach to organizational commitment according to which the degree of agreement between an individual's personal goals and those of the organization is a determinant of organizational commitment.

The individual-organizational **goal-congruence orientation** focuses on the extent to which people identifying with an organization have personal goals that are in keeping with those of the organization. This approach, popularized by Porter and his associates, reflects people's willingness to accept and work toward attaining organizational goals.[41] It views organizational commitment as the result of three factors: (1) acceptance of the organization's goals and values, (2) willingness to help the organization achieve its goals, and (3) the desire to remain within the organization.

As researchers began to study organizational commitment from each of these two perspectives, it became clear that both approaches were useful for understanding organizational commitment—and that a third was necessary.[42] With this in mind, three distinct bases of organizational commitment have been identified—*continuance commitment*, *affective commitment* and *normative commitment*.[43]

continuance commitment The strength of a person's desire to continue working for an organization because he or she needs to do so and cannot afford to do otherwise.

Continuance commitment, related to the side-bets approach, refers to the strength of a person's tendency to need to continue working for an organization because he or she cannot afford to do otherwise. **Affective commitment**, suggested by the goal congruence approach, refers to the strength of a person's desire to continue working for an organization because he or she agrees with it and wants to do so. After researching these two forms of commitment it became apparent that a third type also existed—**normative commitment**.[44] This kind of commitment refers to employees' feelings of obligation to stay with the organization because of pressures from others. For a summary of these three bases of commitment, see Figure 6-7.

affective commitment The strength of a person's desire to work for an organization because he or she agrees with it and wants to do so.

normative commitment The strength of a person's desire to continue working for an organization because he or she feels obligations from others to remain there.

Questionnaires measuring these three bases of commitment have been developed, and research using them has confirmed that the three different forms are, in fact, distinct from each other.[45] By looking at items similar to those used to measure each kind of commitment, shown in the EXPERIENCING ORGA-

■ Figure 6-7
Organizational Commitment:
Three Types
Organizational commitment consists of the three facets shown here: continuance commitment, normative commitment, *and* affective commitment.

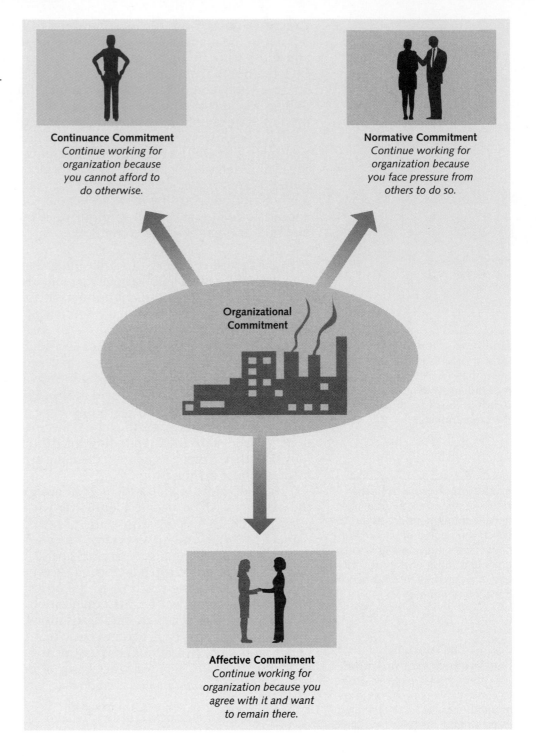

Continuance Commitment
Continue working for organization because you cannot afford to do otherwise.

Normative Commitment
Continue working for organization because you face pressure from others to do so.

Organizational Commitment

Affective Commitment
Continue working for organization because you agree with it and want to remain there.

NIZATIONAL BEHAVIOR exercise on pages 208–209, you will be able to recognize the distinction between the three different forms. By using questionnaires such as this, scientists have been able to identify people's level of commitment to their organizations and link these to various consequences.[46] As you might imagine, the problems associated with low levels of commitment can be quite problematic. We will now summarize these.

Consequences of Low Organizational Commitment

The prediction that people who feel deeply committed to their organizations will behave differently from those who do not seems reasonable. Despite very complex findings, considerable evidence supports this suggestion.[47] Organizational commitment greatly affects several key aspects of work behavior.

First, generally speaking, low levels of organizational commitment tend to be associated with *high levels of absenteeism and voluntary turnover*.[48] In most cases, more committed individuals are less likely to look for new jobs than less committed ones. Interestingly, it appears that people enter jobs with a predisposition toward commitment, and this influences their tendency to stick with their organizations. Lee, Ashford, Walsh, and Mowday demonstrated this in a survey of dropout rates among cadets in the U.S. Air Force Academy.[49] Specifically, they found that the higher the commitment to the Academy cadets had upon entering training, the less likely they were to drop out over the four years it took to receive their degrees.

Second, low organizational commitment is associated with *unwillingness to share and make sacrifices*.[50] It should not be surprising that these types of voluntary acts are related to commitment inasmuch as we can expect those who are most committed to their organizations to be those who give most generously of themselves. People who are uncommitted to their organizations will certainly have little motivation to go out of their way to do any more than they absolutely must on behalf of the organization.[51] In fact, they may be outright selfish and try to get away with doing as little as possible.

Finally, low organizational commitment has *negative personal consequences*. Although one might expect commitment to an organization to detract from one's personal life (based on the idea that it would be costly in terms of time and emotional investment), research suggests otherwise. In a survey of work attitudes among public employees, it was found that those who were most strongly attached to their organizations enjoyed highly successful careers and pleasant nonwork lives.[52] To the extent that work is an important part of people's lives, it makes sense that feeling uncommitted to one's company would contribute to one's feelings of discontent with life in general.

Taking all these findings into account, steps designed to generate high levels of organizational commitment among employees seem worthwhile. A committed work force, it appears, is indeed beneficial to both individuals and organizations.

Suggestions for Enhancing Organizational Commitment

Some determinants of organizational commitment fall outside of managers' spheres of control, giving them few opportunities to enhance these feelings. For example, commitment tends to be lower when the economy is such that employment opportunities are plentiful. An abundance of job options will surely lower continuance commitment, and there's not too much a company can do about it.[53] However, although managers cannot control the economy, they can do several things to make employees want to stay working for the company—that is, to enhance affective commitment.

Chapter 5 presents theories that explain the underlying reasons why enriching jobs may enhance organizational commitment, and describes specific methods for making jobs more enriched.

1. *Enrich jobs*. People tend to be highly committed to their organizations to the extent that they have a good chance to take control over the way they do their jobs and are recognized for making important contributions.[54]

   This approach worked well for the Ford Motor Company (see Figure 6-8). In the early 1980s, Ford confronted a crisis of organizational commitment in the face of budget cuts, layoffs, plant closings, lowered product quality, and other threats. In the words of Ernest J. Savoie, the director of Ford's Employee Development Office:

   > The only solution for Ford, we determined was a total transformation of our company . . to accomplish it, we had to earn the commitment of

■ **Figure 6-8**
*Ford's "Better Idea" for
Enriching Jobs*
*To enhance its employees' feelings
of organizational commitment, the Ford
Motor Company instituted the
Employee Involvement program, a
variety of initiatives designed to get
everyone involved in the decision-mak-
ing process.*

all Ford people. And to acquire that commitment, we had to change the way we managed people.[55]

With this in mind, Ford instituted its *Employee Involvement* program, a systematic way of involving employees in many aspects of corporate decision making. They not only got to perform a wide variety of tasks, but also enjoyed considerable autonomy in doing them (e.g., freedom to schedule work and to stop the assembly line if needed). By 1985, Ford employees were more committed to their jobs—so much so, in fact, that the acrimony that usually resulted at contract renewal time had all but vanished. Although employee involvement may not be the cure for all commitment ills, it was clearly highly effective in this case.

2. *Align the interests of the employees with those of the company.* It only makes sense that employees will remain committed to working in organizations when those employees and the company have the same interests in mind—that is, when what benefits one also benefits the other. This is certainly the case among companies that use *profit-sharing plans*—incentive programs in which employees receive bonuses in proportion to the company's profitability. Such plans are often quite effective in enhancing organizational commitment, especially when they are perceived to be administered fairly.[56]

   For example, the Holland, Michigan, auto parts manufacturer, Prince Corporation, gives its employees yearly bonuses based on several indices: the company's overall profitability, the employee's unit's profitability, and each individual's performance. Similarly, workers at Allied Plywood Corporation (a wholesaler of building materials in Alexandria, Virginia) receive cash bonuses based on company profits, but these are distributed monthly as well as yearly. The monthly bonuses are the same size for all, whereas the annual bonuses are given in proportion to each employee's individual contributions to total profit, days worked, and performance. These plans are good examples of some of the things companies are doing to enhance commitment. Although the plans differ, their underlying rationale is the same: By letting employees share in the company's profits, they are more likely to see their own interests as consistent with those of their company. When these interests are aligned, commitment is high.

3. *Recruit and select newcomers whose values closely match those of the organization.* Just as individuals have certain things they value (e.g., preserving

the natural environment, respect for law and order), so, too, do organizations. In fact, organizations frequently state their values in documents known as **mission statements**—documents in which organizations formally state their basic values and purpose. Some examples of mission statements are shown in Table 6-3.[57] As you might imagine, the more closely the values of an organization match the values of the individuals employed in them, the more strongly those employees will be committed to the organizations.[58] For example, someone who finds environmental pollution unacceptable probably would be unwilling to work in a factory that emits hazardous chemicals into the air. Our advice is clear: Both organizations and prospective new employees should pay close attention to the extent to which their values closely mesh (such as by carefully reviewing the company's mission statement during the interview process). Failure to do so may lead to a very brief—and potentially unsettling—association.

The recruitment process is not only important insofar as it provides opportunities to find people whose values fit those of the organization, but also because of the dynamics of the recruitment process itself. In this connection, the more an organization invests in someone by working hard to lure him or her to the company, the more that individual is likely to return the same investment of energy by expressing commitment toward the organization.[59] In other words, companies that show their employees they care enough to work hard to attract them are likely to find strong commitment among those who are so actively courted.

In conclusion, it is useful to think of organizational commitment as an attitude that may be influenced by managerial actions. Not only might people be selected who are predisposed to be committed to the organization, but also various measures can be taken to enhance commitment in the

■ TABLE 6-3	MISSION STATEMENTS: EXPLICIT STATEMENTS OF CORPORATE VALUES	
In their mission statements organizations state some of their core values. These brief excerpts from actual corporate mission statements will give you a good idea of the range of values expressed in such documents.	**Company**	**Highlight from Mission Statement**
	Avon Products	"We are committed to reaching women more directly and serving them better than any other company in the world. In everything we do, we will endeavor to help women lead more satisfying and fulfilling lives."
	Ben & Jerry's Homemade	"To operate the company in a way that actively recognizes the central role that business plays in the structure of society by initiating innovative ways to improve the quality of life of a broad community: local, national, and international."
	Canadian National Railway	"Safety is critically important and will never be compromised. CN intends to be the safest railway, for the benefit of its employees, customers, and the communities it serves."
	John Hancock Financial Services	"We care about the dignity of each person in this organization. In order to be successful, we treat others with the same respect we seek for ourselves."
	Knight-Ridder	"We are rooted in our founders' conviction that high-quality newspapers—fair, independent, probing, relevant and compassionate—are indispensable to our free society."
	Procter & Gamble	"We will . . . provide an organization and a working environment which attracts the finest people; fully develops and challenges our individual talents, [and] encourages our free and spirited collaboration to drive the business ahead. . . ."
	Southwest Airlines	"Creativity and innovation are encouraged for improving the effectiveness of Southwest Airlines."

SOURCE: Material appearing in Graham & Havlick, 1994; see Note 57.

face of indications that it is suffering. Given the problems associated with having an uncommitted workforce, it would appear wise to consider such efforts carefully.

Prejudice: Negative Attitudes toward Others

"Don't jump to conclusions." That's advice we often hear. But, when it comes to forming attitudes toward others, it is often ignored. Instead, people frequently *do* jump to conclusions about others—and on the basis of very limited information. If you have ever made a judgment about someone else on the basis of his or her ethnic background, age, gender, sexual orientation, or physical condition, then you are well aware of this tendency. As we discussed in conjunction with the topic of *stereotypes* (see Chapter 3), such judgments are frequently negative in nature.

prejudice Negative attitudes toward the members of specific groups, based solely on the fact that they are members of those groups (e.g., age, race, sexual orientation).

A negative attitude we hold toward another based on his or her membership in a particular groups is referred to as **prejudice**.[60] Not only might people holding prejudicial attitudes have negative beliefs and feelings, but these may predispose people to behave in ways consistent with these attitudes. For example, it would not be surprising to find that an employment interviewer who holds negative stereotypes toward members of a certain minority group evaluates negatively a candidate belonging to that group and is disinterested in hiring such an individual. Then, if this prejudicial attitude actually leads the interviewer not to hire the candidate, this may be said to be an act of **discrimination**. That is, the interviewer acted consistently with his or her negative attitude, not giving the candidate a fair chance, treating different people in different ways. The key thing to keep in mind is this: Prejudice is a negative attitude, whereas discrimination is the behavior that follows from it (the behavioral expression of that attitude). For a summary of this idea, see Figure 6-9.

discrimination The behavior consistent with a prejudicial attitude; the act of treating someone negatively because of his or her membership in a specific group.

Diversity versus Prejudice: Competing Organizational Realities

There can be no mistaking the fact that the United States is an ethnically diverse nation—and that it is getting increasingly more so. For example, it has been estimated that by the year 2040, half of the U.S. population will be composed of people of African, Latin, Native American and/or Asian descent. In addition, women—who, for many years only infrequently worked outside the home—are currently filling 65 percent of all new jobs, and in just a few years about half of the civilian workforce will be composed of women.[61] For some companies, diversity is already a reality. For example, at the Solectron Corporation, a computer assembly company in Milpitas, California, 30 nationalities can be found speaking 40 different languages and dialects among the company's 3,200 employees.[62]

Interestingly, as this picture of the highly diverse American workforce unfolds, equally real is the unfortunate fact that prejudice against various groups still exists, and that these prejudices are likely to have serious consequences. Before describing the nature of such prejudicial attitudes, we will first outline some of the general problems that they create.

First, prejudice can be a *source of serious friction or conflict* between people. Although a highly diverse workforce can potentially bring the advantage of differing opinions and perspectives, this may turn into a disadvantage among individuals who hold prejudicial attitudes. Indeed, if one's group membership causes an underlying current of distrust, then the conflict that results may be disruptive to the organization as people fail to cooperate with each other to get their jobs done. In extreme cases, the discriminatory actions that follow from prejudicial attitudes culminate in legal action—be it employees charging their employers with unfair discrimination,[63] or customers charging companies with discriminatory actions.[64]

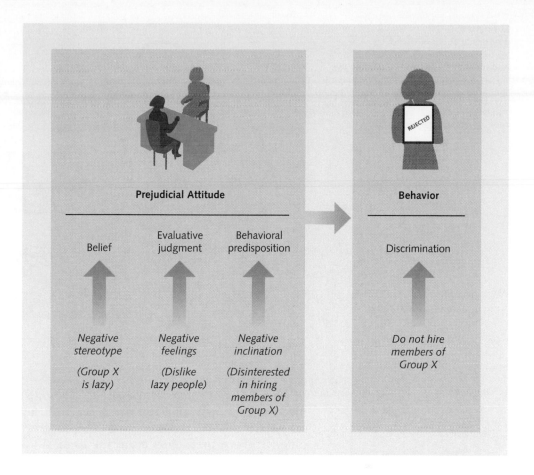

Figure 6-9
Prejudice vs. Discrimination:
A Key Distinction
Prejudice *is an attitude and, as such,*
consists of the three basic components
of attitudes. Discrimination *refers to*
behavior based on that attitude. The
example presented here illustrates this
important distinction.

Prejudicial Attitude

Belief

Evaluative
judgment

Behavioral
predisposition

Negative
stereotype

(Group X
is lazy)

Negative
feelings

(Dislike
lazy people)

Negative
inclination

(Disinterested
in hiring
members of
Group X)

Behavior

Discrimination

Do not hire
members of
Group X

For a discussion of the general na-
ture of organizational conflict, see
Chapter 11.

We will discuss the impact of the
glass ceiling more thoroughly in
Chapter 7.

Second, prejudice may have *adverse effects on the careers of people who are*
the targets of such attitudes. Affected individuals may encounter various forms
of discrimination—some very subtle, but others quite overt—with respect to
hiring, promotion, and pay. For example, although there are more women than
ever in the workforce, they are highly underrepresented in the upper echelons
of organizations—in fact, only 3 percent of senior managers and 5.7 percent
of corporate directors of *Fortune* 500 companies are women.[65] Because the discrimination is quite real, but not openly admitted, it is frequently referred to
as the *glass ceiling* (i.e., a barrier that cannot be seen).

Third, we cannot overlook the devastating psychological impact of prejudice on victims of discrimination. Not only is the victim penalized, but so,
too, are others who share the same background, what has been called *covic-*
timization.[66] To the extent that talented individuals are passed over because of
their membership in certain groups, individuals suffer an affront to their self-
esteem that can be quite harmful. This, of course, is in addition to the loss to
the organization of overlooking talented individuals simply because they are
not white males. In today's highly competitive global economy, this is a mistake that no companies can afford.

Various "Groupisms": Manifestations of Prejudicial Attitudes in the Workplace

If there is any one truly "equal opportunity" for people in today's workplace, it is that we *all* stand a chance of being the victim of prejudice. Indeed,
there are many different forms of *groupism*—prejudices based on membership
in certain groups—and no one is immune (see Figure 6-10).[67]

Prejudice based on age. We're all going to get older (if we're lucky), and,
as people are living longer and the birth rate is holding steady, the median age

"*Well, sir, then I take it you would vote for any cat in preference to a capable dog.*"

of Americans is rising all the time.[68] Despite this trend, it is clear that prejudice based on age is all too common. Although laws in the United States and elsewhere have done much to counter employment discrimination against older workers, prejudices continue to exist.

Part of the problem resides in stereotypes that people have that older workers are too set in their ways to train, and that they will tend to be sick or accident-prone. As in the case of many attitudes, these prejudices are not founded on accurate information. Recent survey findings paint just the opposite picture of older workers. Namely, organizations tend to have extremely positive experiences with older workers: They have good skills, are highly committed to doing their jobs well, and have outstanding safety records.[69]

It is not just older workers who find themselves victims of prejudice but younger ones, too. For them, part of the problem is that as the average age of the workforce advances (from an average of 29 in 1976 to 39 in 2000), there develops a gap in expectations between the more experienced older workers who are in charge and the younger employees just entering the workforce. Specifically, compared to older workers, who grew up in a different time, today's under-30 employees view the world differently. They are more prone to question the way things are done, not to see the government as an ally, and not to expect loyalty. They are likely to consider self-development to be their main interest and are willing to learn whatever skills are necessary to make them marketable. These differing perspectives may lead older employees, who are likely to be their superiors, to feel uncomfortable with their younger colleagues. This is especially problematic as the nature of work shifts so that people with different skills are brought together to work in teams.

We will describe the trend toward relying on teams in Chapter 8.

However, a recent study brings encouraging news. In a survey of employees' attitudes toward older workers, it has been found that even younger workers hold generally positive views of older workers—although these were not quite as positive as older workers hold toward themselves.[70] Interestingly, the same study found that the more time younger people spent working with their older colleagues, the more positive (and less stereotypical) their attitudes were toward them. The implications of this are that simply bringing younger and older workers together may be an effective means of chipping away at age-based stereotypes.

Prejudice based on physical condition. If you think about it, every one of us has one physical feature or another that keeps us from doing a certain kind of work. Some people are not strong enough to load heavy packages onto trucks, others are not athletic enough to play professional sports, and still others might lack the agility and stamina needed to be a firefighter. Thus, although we all may be handicapped in some way, certain physical conditions tend to be the focus of widely held prejudicial attitudes. Such conditions (e.g., blindness, disfigurement, physical paralysis) are said to have *stigmas* attached to them—that is, negative aspects of one's identity.[71]

In the early 1990s, legislation known as the *Americans with Disabilities Act (ADA)* was enacted in the United States for purposes of safeguarding the rights of people with physical and mental disabilities. The rationale behind this law is that just because an employee is limited in some way, it does not mean that accommodations cannot be made to help the individual perform his or her job (see Figure 6-11). Companies that do not comply are subject to legal damages. In fact, the first award under the ADA, $572,000, was presented to an employee fired after missing work while recovering from cancer, and as many as 15,000 discrimination claims were filed in the law's first year alone.[72]

Many companies are finding that it is possible for them to meet the needs of disabled employees quite easily and with little expense. For example, Greiner Engineering, Inc., in Irving, Texas, was able to accommodate its employees in wheelchairs by simply substituting a lighter-weight door on its restrooms, and raising a drafting table by putting bricks under its legs.[73] Although not all accommodations are as easily made, experts are confident that the ADA will be an effective way of minimizing discrimination against employees based on their physical condition.[74]

Prejudice based on sexual orientation. Unlike people with physical disabilities, who are protected from discrimination by federal law, no such protection exists (yet, at least) for another group whose members are frequently victims of prejudice—gay men and lesbian women. Unfortunately, although more people than ever are tolerant of nontraditional sexual orientations, antihomosexual prejudice still exists in the workplace. Indeed, about two-thirds of CEOs from major companies note that they are reluctant to put a homosexual on a top management committee.[75] Not surprisingly, without the law to protect them, and widespread prejudices against them, many gays and lesbians are reluctant to openly make their sexual orientations known.[76]

Fears of being "discovered," exposed as a homosexual, represent a considerable source of stress among such individuals. For example, a gay vice president of a large office equipment manufacturer in Chicago admitted in a magazine interview that he'd like to become the company's CEO, but fears that his chances will be ruined if his sexual orientation became known.[77] Although the pressure of having to go through life (or, at least, an important part of it) with a disguised identity must be extreme, imagine the cumulative effect of such efforts on organizations in which several employees are homosexual. Such misdirection of energy can become quite a serious productivity issue. In the words of consultant Mark Kaplan, "gay and lesbian employees use a lot of time and stress trying to conceal a big part of their identity."[78] To work in an organization with a homophobic culture and to have to endure jokes slurring gays and lesbians can easily distract even the most highly focused employees.

To help avoid these problems—and, out of respect for diverse sexual orientations—many organizations have adopted internal fair employment policies that include sexual orientation. In addition, some companies are actively working to prohibit discrimination on the basis of sexual orientation. Extending this idea, still other companies are now extending fringe benefits, which traditionally have been offered exclusively to opposite-sex partners, to

This idea of designing work so that it may be performed by people with physical disabilities is not new. In fact, as noted in Chapter 1, it dates back to the work of the Gilbreths over 80 years ago.

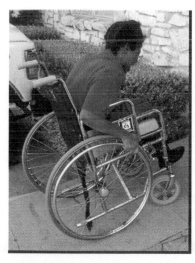

■ **Figure 6-11**
Accommodating People with Physical Handicaps: An Effective Way of Avoiding Discrimination
To comply with the Americans with Disabilities Act, companies are finding simple ways of accommodating employees who have physical handicaps. Doing so not only avoids discrimination, but enables companies to take full advantage of their human resources.

same-sex domestic partners as well. Russ Campanello, vice president of human resources for Lotus Development Corp. (the Cambridge, Massachusetts, developer of software products) notes that his organization's reputation for having such a program has been an important key to its success in attracting highly talented technical personnel.[79] Clearly, although some companies are passively discouraging diversity with respect to sexual orientation, others, by encouraging diversity, are using it to their own—and their employees'—advantage.

Prejudice based on race and national origin. The history of the United States is marked by struggles over acceptance for people of various racial and ethnic groups. Although, as we have documented, the American workplace is more diverse than ever, it is also clear that prejudicial attitudes linger on. The survey results summarized in Figure 6-12, based on data collected from a large sample of American workers in the late 1980s and early 1990s illustrate this point.[80]

Not only do members of various minority groups believe they are the victims of prejudice and discrimination, they are also taking action. As evidence, consider that there was a 30 percent increase in the number of complaints of discrimination based on national origin filed at the Equal Employment Opportunity Commission (EEOC) between 1989 and 1991. Moreover, discrimination victims have been winning such cases. For example, in 1993 the Supreme Court of the state of Washington upheld a $389,000 judgment against a Seattle bank brought by a Cambodian American employee fired because of his accent.[81] Outside the courtroom, companies that discriminate pay in other ways as well—notably, in lost talent and productivity. According to EEOC Commissioner Joy Cherian, employees who feel victimized "may not take the initiative to introduce inventions and other innovations," adding, "every day, American employers are losing millions of dollars because these talents are frozen."[82]

A discussion of the many valuable roles played by mentors, and the nature of the mentorship process, appears in Chapter 7.

To help minimize these problems, some companies are taking concrete steps. For example, AT&T Bell Labs in Murray Hill, New Jersey, is working with managers to find ways of helping the company's many ethnic minority employees get promoted more rapidly. Similarly, Hughes Aircraft Co. of Los Angeles has been assigning mentors to minority group employees to help teach them about the company's culture and the skills needed to succeed.[83] Although both examples are only modest steps, they represent very encouraging trends intended to help reduce a long-standing problem.

Prejudice against women. There can be no mistaking the widespread—and ever-growing—presence of women in today's workforce. In 1991 women composed 46 percent of the American workforce, up from 43 percent in 1981. Also, in 1991, 41 percent of managers were women, compared to only 27 percent only ten years earlier. Still, female senior executives (individuals reporting directly to the CEO) are relatively rare—only 3 percent are women.[84] Is this likely to change in the next ten years? When executives completing a recent *Business Week*/Harris poll were asked how likely it is for their company to have a female CEO in the next ten years, 82 percent said that it was not likely, although they were a bit more optimistic about the longer-term prospects. Thus, it appears that "women populate corporations, but they rarely run them."[85] Equality for women in the workplace is improving, although it is a slow victory, to be sure.

The process of stereotyping is more fully discussed in Chapter 3.

Why is this the case? Although sufficient time may not have passed to allow more women to work their way into the top echelons of organizations, there appear to be more formidable barriers. Most notably, it is clear that powerful *sex role stereotypes* persist, narrow-minded beliefs about the kinds of tasks for which women are most appropriately suited. For example, 8 percent of the respondents to the *Business Week*/Harris survey indicated that women are not aggressive or determined enough to make it to the top. Although this number is small, it provides good evidence of the persistence of a nagging—and highly limiting—stereotype.

Does Racial Discrimination Exist? It Depends on Who You Ask
A survey of American workers (conducted between 1988 and 1992) shows that racial discrimination is believed to be prevalent in many forms. Its main victims, African Americans, tend to be more aware of discrimination than those who are least affected by it, white Americans.

(**Source:** Based on data reported by Fernandez & Barr, 1993; see Note 80.)

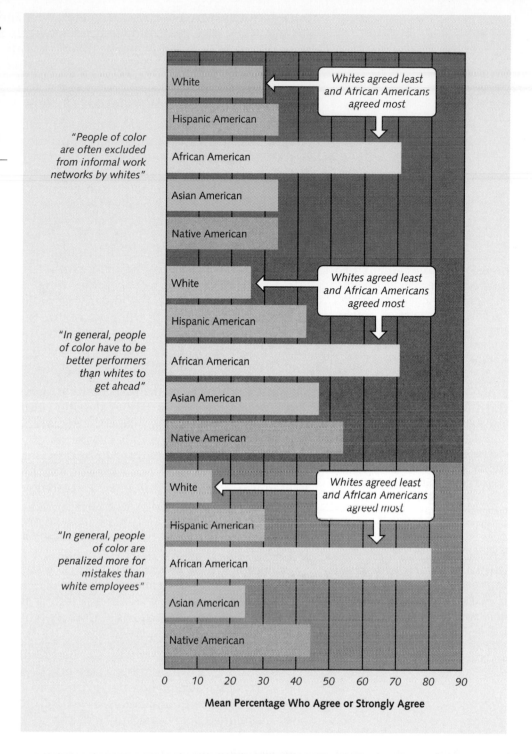

Such stereotypes have kept women from important organizational positions, including that innermost circle of corporate power—boards of directors. Although the numbers of women gaining admission into this special group may be growing, there is evidence that their roles may be limited by the existence of stereotypes. Boards of directors, which provide important direction to organizations, are typically composed of committees dedicated to specific areas of responsibility, such as finance, compensation, and public affairs. However, a recent study found that membership on these committees generally followed gender stereotypes.[86] Specifically, although women were generally equally qualified to hold memberships in all committees, they were typically kept out of committees closely linked to basic corporate governance, such as compensation and finance. They were favored only for membership in committees with more peripheral functions, such as public affairs. Clearly, sex role stereotypes remain alive and well in this one bastion of organizational power.

Managing a Diverse Workforce: Current Practices

There can be little doubt that many organizations have taken steps to bring women and members of minority groups into the workforce. However, many of today's organizations are interested in not just hiring a wider variety of different people, but also creating an atmosphere in which diverse groups can flourish. They are not merely attempting to be socially responsible, but recognize that diversity is a business issue.

As one consultant put it, "A corporation's success will increasingly be determined by its managers' ability to naturally tap the full potential of a diverse workforce."[87] It is with this goal in mind that many organizations are adapting **diversity management programs**—efforts to celebrate diversity by creating supportive, not just neutral, work environments for women and minorities.[88] Simply put, the underlying philosophy of diversity management programs is that cracking the glass ceiling requires that women and minorities are not just tolerated, but valued.[89] In this section of the chapter we will identify various types of diversity management programs and then describe some examples of successful diversity management efforts.

Varieties of diversity management programs.   In general, diversity management programs fall into two categories: *awareness-based diversity training* and *skill-based diversity training*.[90] Specifically, **awareness-based diversity training** is designed to raise people's awareness of diversity issues in the workplace and to get them to recognize the underlying assumptions they make about people. It is a very basic orientation, a starting point—one that takes a cognitive approach. Typically, it involves teaching people about the business necessity of valuing diversity, and makes them sensitive to their own cultural assumptions and biases. This may involve using various experiential exercises that help people view others as individuals as opposed to stereotyped members of groups.

Building on the awareness approach is **skills-based diversity training**. This orientation is designed to develop people's skills with respect to managing diversity. As such, it goes beyond raising awareness to developing the tools needed to interact effectively with others. There are four main tools involved in this process.[91] These include:

- *Cross-cultural understanding*—understanding the cultural differences responsible for why different co-workers behave differently on the job
- *Intercultural communication*—learning to ensure that verbal and nonverbal barriers to communication across cultures are overcome
- *Facilitation skills*—training in how to help others alleviate misunderstanding that may result from cultural differences
- *Flexibility and adaptability*—cultivating the ability to patiently take new and different approaches when dealing with others who are different

Both approaches to diversity training have the same long-term goals. They strive to make interaction between diverse groups of people easier and more effective. Then, once people are paying attention to each other, the road is paved for morale to improve, for productivity to be enhanced, and for people to be able to focus their creative energies. With all of these benefits, organizations are positioned to attain their ultimate goal—to improve their economic position in the marketplace. (For a summary of these approaches, see Figure 6-13.)

Recent evidence paints a very convincing picture of the ultimate effectiveness of diversity management efforts. Wright, Ferris, Hiller, and Kroll rea-

diversity management programs Programs in which employees are taught to celebrate the differences between people and in which organizations create supportive work environments for women and minorities.

awareness-based diversity training A type of diversity management program designed to make people more aware of diversity issues in the workplace and to get them to recognize the underlying assumptions they make about people.

skills-based diversity training An approach to diversity management that goes beyond *awareness-based diversity training* and is designed to develop people's skills with respect to managing diversity.

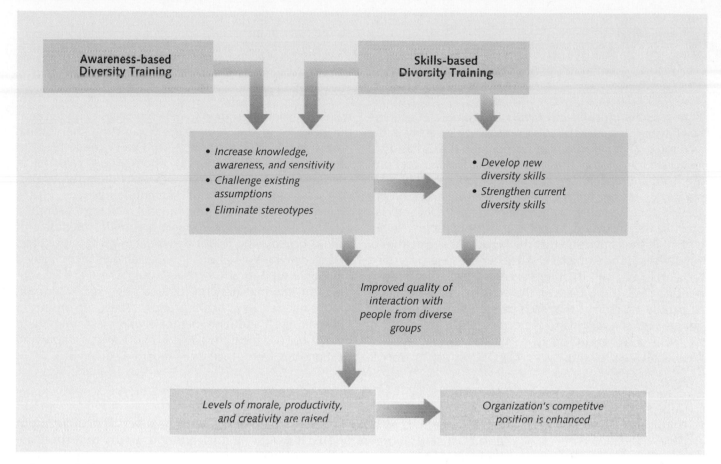

Awareness-based Diversity Training

Skills-based Diversity Training

- Increase knowledge, awareness, and sensitivity
- Challenge existing assumptions
- Eliminate stereotypes

- Develop new diversity skills
- Strengthen current diversity skills

Improved quality of interaction with people from diverse groups

Levels of morale, productivity, and creativity are raised

Organization's competitve position is enhanced

■ **Figure 6-13**
Diversity Management: Two Major Approaches to Training
Skills-based diversity training *builds on the approach taken by* awareness-based diversity training. *However, both approaches strive toward achieving the same goals.*

(**Source:** Adapted from material in Carnevale & Stone, 1995; see Note 90.)

soned that when companies effectively use their human resources they can lower their costs and thereby perform better than their competition.[92] To test this notion they compared two groups of companies from 1986 through 1992. One group was composed of organizations that received awards from the U.S. Department of Labor for their exemplary efforts at managing diversity. The other group was composed of companies that had settled large claims against them for employment discrimination. To compare the performance of these organizations, the researchers relied on a key index of economic success—stock returns. Their findings were striking: Companies that made special efforts to use their diverse human resources were considerably more profitable than those that discriminated against their employees. Wright and his associates explain that the organizations that capitalized on the diversity of their workforces were better able to attract and maintain the talented people needed for organizations to thrive. Clearly, managing diversity makes sense not only because it is the right way to treat people, but also because it is good business.

As shown in the ETHICS ANGLE section (on page 204), DEC is one company that has recognized the benefits of managing diversity. However, it has not been alone. Pepsi Cola, American Express Travel Related Services, and the accounting firm Coopers & Lybrand also have been actively engaged in diversity management efforts.[93] Several companies have gone beyond simply embracing the differences between people, but have created opportunities for diverse groups of people within organizations. For example, Xerox's "Step-Up" program, in existence for some 30 years, has been one of the most thorough and sustained efforts to hire minority group members and train them to succeed.[94] Similarly, Pacific Bell is another company that has made great strides at reaching out to minority group members (e.g., through internship programs), creating jobs for them in positions that have broad opportunities for

VALUING DIFFERENCES AT DEC

One of the most effective ways to promote ethical behavior in organizations is to recognize diversity in the workforce. Digital Equipment Corporation (DEC) has done an outstanding job of this in its "Valuing Differences" program, an approach that focuses on not just accepting people (e.g., giving them opportunities to succeed), but valuing them *because* of their differences.[95] DEC officials provide the following rationale: "The philosophy is anchored in the conviction that the broader the spectrum of differences in the workplace, the richer the synergy among the employees and the more excellent the organization's performance. It is a belief in the constructive potential of all people. It assumes that each person's differences bring unique and special gifts to the organization."[96]

DEC does several things to capitalize on the differences between its employees. (1) DEC invests in special training sessions designed to get employees to understand the diversity in their workplace, examining the cultural norms of the different people who work there. (2) DEC celebrates these differences by sponsoring a calendar of special cultural and educational events designed to provide ways of learning about different people (e.g., "Black History Month," and "International Women's Month"). (3) They help organize support groups for members of various groups who find it beneficial to meet with others of their own race or nationality who can give them needed emotional support and/or career guidance. (4) DEC supports an informal network of small ongoing discussion groups referred to as "core groups." These are groups of between seven and nine members who meet monthly to openly discuss their stereotypes and ways of improving relationships with others they regard as different.

advancement.[97] Although we have been describing the diversity management efforts of several organizations, it would be misleading to imply that these are representative of what most organizations are doing. Accordingly, in the GLOBALIZATION AND DIVERSITY section we ask: How actively involved in diversity management efforts are today's organizations?

A note of caution. Although most companies have been pleased with the ways their diversity management efforts have promoted harmony between employees, some have encountered problems. In the most serious cases, diversity management efforts have backfired, leaving race and gender divisions even greater.[98] The most serious problems have stemmed from the practice of focusing on stereotypes, even positive ones. Thinking of people in stereotypical ways can create barriers that interfere with looking at people as individuals. So, instead of looking at the *average* differences between people (which may reinforce stereotypes), experts recommend that managing diversity demands accepting a *range* of differences between people (a range that promises to become even greater in the years ahead).[99]

With this in mind, managers are advised not to treat someone as special because he or she is a member of a certain group, but because of the unique skills or abilities he or she brings to the job. To the extent that managers are trained to seek, recognize, and develop the talents of their employees regardless of the groups to which they belong, they will help break down the barriers that made diversity training necessary in the first place. In fact, several important notes of caution may be identified, caveats that need to be carefully considered when it comes to conducting diversity training successfully.[100] For a summary of several such concerns, see Table 6-4 (on page 206).

Perhaps the main key to the effectiveness of diversity management is *complete managerial support.*

YOU BE THE CONSULTANT

The president of a large manufacturing company is concerned about racial tension that has been building among employees in the plant. The workforce includes large numbers of people from racial and ethnic minorities. A diversity management program is being considered.

1. Do you think a diversity management program would be useful in this case? If not, why? If so, what steps would you take to initiate such a plan?

2. What potential problems and limitations would you expect to find should a diversity management program be started?

DEALING WITH DIVERSITY:
TAKING THE PULSE OF AMERICAN COMPANIES

A few years ago the American Society for Training and Development surveyed a sample of *Fortune* 1000 companies regarding their stance on diversity issues. The results suggest that diversity management was *not* at the top of their agenda. Only 11 percent reported that it was a high priority, but most—33 percent—indicated they were only beginning to look at it. In fact, a quarter of the companies surveyed indicated that they weren't doing anything at all.[101]

However, an encouraging sign is that the trend is clearly toward more activity, not less. Additional survey findings have reported that 55 percent of employees believe that their company's management has become more strongly supportive of diversity programs over the past two years. Only 4 percent indicated a decrease in attention to diversity management efforts.[102] In fact, 91 percent indicated that their company's senior management considers the treatment of people to be the "make-or-break corporate resource of the 1990s."[103]

Why do companies engage in diversity management efforts? If you're a skeptic, you may believe that the answer lies in attempts to respond to government pressure. However, surveys have shown that this was identified as a contributing factor by only 29 percent of the respondents.[104] By contrast, the same survey found that the two major reasons are:

- Senior managers' awareness of the importance of diversity management programs (identified as a contributing factor by 95 percent of the respondents)
- Recognition of the need to attract and retain a skilled workforce (identified as a contributing factor by 90 percent of the respondents)

What activities do companies engage in to foster diversity in the workforce? A large-scale survey by the Society for Human Resource Management and the Commerce Clearing House have found several activities to be most common.[105] These include:

- Promoting policies that discourage sexual harassment (93 percent of organizations surveyed)
- Providing physical access for employees with physical disabilities (76 percent)
- Offering flexible work schedules (66 percent)
- Allowing days off for religious holidays that may not be officially recognized (58 percent)
- Offering parental leaves (57 percent)

However, this same survey found that organizations did *not* do much in the way of following up on its diversity efforts. Among companies that conduct some type of diversity training, only 30 percent gather any type of formal data to see if it is working. Still fewer, only 20 percent, formally reward managers for their efforts to promote diversity in the workplace.

The bottom line is clear: Although there's a lot of attention paid to diversity in today's organizations, there is generally more talk than action. Still, there are encouraging signs of improvement on the horizon. Given the growing awareness of the importance of diversity management activities, we suspect that more and more companies will be attempting to enhance their competitiveness in the marketplace by capitalizing on the diversity of their workforces.

Indeed, you cannot do something as complex as celebrate diversity with a one-time effort. Successful diversity management requires sustained attention to diversity in all organizational activities. For example, it has been shown that companies that have successful diversity management training programs also tend to require everyone to be trained, define diversity very broadly (i.e., they do not limit it to only one or two groups), and reward managers for their special efforts at increasing diversity.[106] Without "going the extra mile," by completely supporting diversity activities, organizations may find themselves quite disappointed with their efforts.

In conclusion, although mistakes have been made in the way some diversity management programs have been implemented, diversity management programs have, in many cases, greatly helped organizations find ways of tapping the rich pool of talent found in a highly diverse workforce.

For diversity training efforts to be successful they must avoid the potential problems outlined here.

Problem	Description and Solution
Emotional tension is heightened.	Talking about prejudices is likely to make people feel uneasy. Training needs to be conducted in a "safe," comfortable environment.
Possibility of polarization.	Avoid discussions that have yes or no answers (e.g., "should gays be allowed in the military?"). Instead, encourage consideration of a broad range of options.
Some people may have personal "axes to grind."	Training sessions should not provide platforms for people who want to vent about past problems. Facilitators should keep the group on target.
Personal attacks may occur.	Strong opinions on diversity issues may box people into corners. Treat everyone with respect and dignity.
Reactions to training will be varied.	Some may welcome the training whereas others may resent having to go through it. Addressing these feelings should be made a part of training sessions.
White males tend to be blamed.	It is tempting to blame the dominant group, white males, for diversity problems. However, no one group has a monopoly on prejudice and discrimination. White males should discuss their difficulties adjusting to a changing world.
Timing may be problematic.	Avoid adding to stress by not scheduling sessions during periods in which other sensitive events (e.g., layoffs, contract negotiations) are occurring.
Reasons for training may be ingenuine.	Diversity training works best when it is part of a strategic effort on the part of management to change policies so as to make a more "inclusive" organization. However, training conducted because "everyone's doing it" is likely to fail—and maybe even backfire.

SOURCE: Adapted from Gardenswartz & Rowe, 1994; see Note 100.

SUMMARY AND REVIEW

What Are Attitudes?

Attitudes are stable clusters of feelings, beliefs, and behavioral tendencies directed toward some aspect of the external world. **Work-related attitudes** involve such reactions toward various aspects of work settings or the people in them. All attitudes consist of a *cognitive* component (what you believe), an *evaluative* component (how you feel), and a *behavioral* component (the tendency to behave a certain way).

Job Satisfaction

Job satisfaction involves positive or negative attitudes toward one's work. Such attitudes can be measured by completing *rating scales* (such as the JDI or the MSQ), conducting interviews, recounting *critical incidents* (instances found to be especially pleasing or displeasing), and by conducting *interviews* or *confrontation meetings*.

According to Herzberg's **two-factor theory,** job satisfaction and dissatisfaction stem from different factors. Specifically, it claims that factors leading to job satisfaction stem from factors associated with the work itself (known as motivators), and that factors leading to job dissatisfaction

are associated with the conditions surrounding jobs (e.g., the work environment). Evidence for the accuracy of this theory has been mixed. Locke's **value theory** suggests that job satisfaction reflects the apparent match between the outcomes individuals desire from their jobs (what they *value*) and what they believe they are actually receiving.

When people are dissatisfied with their jobs they tend to withdraw. That is, they are frequently absent and are likely to quit their jobs. However, evidence suggests that job performance is only very weakly associated with dissatisfaction. Levels of job satisfaction can be raised by paying people fairly, improving the quality of supervision, decentralizing control of organizational power and matching people to jobs that are congruent with their interests.

Organizational Commitment

Organizational commitment deals with people's attitudes toward their organizations. People can have various targets, or *foci* of commitment, such as top managers, or one's work group. Commitment may be based primarily on three different *bases*. One is **continuance commitment—**

the strength of a person's tendency to continue working for an organization because he or she has to and cannot afford to do otherwise. Another is **affective commitment**—the strength of a person's tendency to continue working for an organization because he or she agrees with its goals and values and desires to stay with it. A third is **normative commitment**—commitment to remain in an organization stemming from social obligations to do so.

Low levels of organizational commitment have been linked to high levels of absenteeism and voluntary turnover, the unwillingness to share and make sacrifices for the company, and negative personal consequences for employees. However, organizational commitment may be enhanced by enriching jobs, aligning the interests of employees with those of the company, and recruiting and selecting newcomers whose values closely match those of the organization.

Prejudice in Work Settings

Prejudice refers to negative attitudes toward members of specific groups, and **discrimination** refers to treating people differently because of these prejudices. Today's workforce is characterized by high levels of diversity, with many groups finding themselves victims of prejudicial attitudes and discriminatory behaviors (based on many different factors, including age, sexual orientation, physical condition, racial or ethnic group membership, and gender) Although people are becoming more tolerant of individuals from diverse groups, prejudicial attitudes persist.

To help tap the rich pool of resources available in today's highly diverse workforce, many companies are using **diversity management programs**—techniques for systematically teaching employees to celebrate the differences between people. Typically, these programs go beyond efforts to recruit and hire women and members of minority groups, to creating supportive work environments for them. Although implementing these programs is potentially difficult, experts acknowledge that the benefits, both organizational and personal, are considerable.

QUESTIONS FOR DISCUSSION

1. Someone tells you that people in general don't like their jobs. Would you agree or disagree with this statement? Why?
2. As a manager, you want to enhance job satisfaction among your subordinates. What steps might you take to accomplish this goal?
3. "Happy workers are productive workers." Do you agree or disagree? Why?
4. Absenteeism and voluntary turnover are costly problems for many companies. What specific steps can be taken to reduce the incidence of these forms of employee withdrawal?
5. Suppose an employee is highly dissatisfied with his or her job and organization but remains on the job and does not look for a new one. How would you explain this person's behavior?
6. "Sexism and racism are a thing of the past." Do you agree or disagree? Why?
7. What steps are today's organizations taking to manage diversity in their workforces? Give an example.

CASE IN POINT

Cultural Diversity at Exxon Chemical

With U.S. headquarters in Houston, Texas, and European regional headquarters in Brussels, Belgium, Exxon Chemical is a huge multinational company. You might think that having employees in many different nations on two continents would lead naturally to acceptance of cultural diversity. But, Exxon Chemical officials did not take this for granted. Recognizing that its highly diverse, international workforce was key to improving the company's performance, as well as its reputation as an international organization, Exxon Chemical recently surveyed its employees to see how well the company was doing.

To this end, a team was put together to "take the temperature of the organization" with respect to the matter of diversity. This involved writing questions, training interviewers to ask them, then visiting 25 European cites, and speaking to 973 different people about the company's acceptance of different people.

Among the many findings were several particularly troublesome observations regarding the way employees saw the company. In their eyes, it was a rather elitist organization and did not encourage people to be themselves—especially if that meant being different in some way. Employees also reported a bias against women and a bias against people who did not speak English. These attitudes, it was feared, would not only demotivate the workforce, but would reduce the competitive advantage that the company would otherwise have if it were able to tap its diverse human resources to their fullest potential.

One of the things Exxon Chemical did to help was to introduce its *Choices* program—a series of courses for European middle managers whose objectives included increasing awareness of the value of diversity within the company. In some of these sessions, managers from Great Britain, Belgium, France, the Netherlands, Germany, Sweden, and the United States were brought together in groups (led by multilingual facilitators) to perform various exercises in which they were required to work cooperatively with each other.

On several occasions these exercises put people in situations in which the dynamics taught a lesson in valuing diversity. For example, some groups were assembled in which a minority of the members spoke a common language that the majority did not speak. As the discussions progressed, an interesting dynamic was observed: Unless conscientious efforts were made to bring the minority group members into the discussions, these individuals tended to talk only to each other and did not make contributions to the group's task. And, on occasions in which these people in the linguistic minority had valuable input to offer, the groups frequently never benefited from hearing from them. As the facilitator later discussed this matter with the group, an important lesson was learned about the importance of tapping the richness of human resources at one's disposal—even if it means going out of one's way to bring someone into the discussion who might otherwise feel left out and unappreciated.

So impressed have Exxon Chemical's managers been with the Choices program that it has been expanded to even more locations throughout the company's huge empire. Although the large numbers make the project quite overwhelming, Exxon Chemical's goal is quite simple: to tap the vast array of diverse resources it already has at its disposal.

Critical Thinking Questions

1. What impediments do you believe Exxon Chemical may face on its way to valuing the diversity of its employee base?
2. What steps can the company take to help overcome these barriers?
3. In addition to the Choices program, what other measures could Exxon Chemical take to help encourage the acceptance of diversity within its workforce? Do you think it is realistic that such measures will actually help encourage diversity in a multinational workplace?
4. Exxon Chemical officials are assuming that there are advantages to having a highly diverse workforce, if these can only be tapped. What, specifically, would you say these advantages are—especially in a large multinational organization, like Exxon Chemical?

SKILLS PORTFOLIO

Experiencing Organizational Behavior

Are You Committed to Your Job?

Questionnaires similar to the one presented here (which is based on established instruments) are used to assess three types of organizational commitment—continuance, affective, and normative. Completing this scale (based on Meyer & Allen, 1991; see Note 44) will give you a good feel for your own level of job commitment and how this important construct is measured.

Directions

In the space to the left of each of the 12 statements below write the one number that reflects the extent to which you agree with it personally. Express your answers using the following scale: 1 = not at all; 2 = slightly; 3 = moderately; 4 = a great deal; 5 = extremely.

____ 1. At this point, I stay on my job more because I have to than because I want to.

____ 2. I feel I strongly belong to my organization.

____ 3. I am reluctant to leave a company once I have been working there.

____ 4. Leaving my job would entail a great deal of personal sacrifice.

____ 5. I feel emotionally connected to the company for which I work.

____ 6. My employer would be very disappointed if I left my job.

____ 7. I don't have any other choice but to stay on my present job.

____ 8. I feel like I am part of the family at the company in which I work.

____ 9. I feel a strong obligation to stay on my job.

____ 10. My life would be greatly disrupted if I left my present job.

_____ **11.** I would be quite pleased to spend the rest of my life working for this organization.

_____ **12.** I stay on my job because people would think poorly of me for leaving.

Scoring

1. Add the scores for items 1, 4, 7, and 10. This reflects your degree of _continuance commitment_.

2. Add the scores for items 2, 5, 8, and 11. This reflects your degree of _affective commitment._

3. Add the scores for items 3, 6, 9, and 12. This reflects your degree of _normative commitment._

Questions for Discussion

1. Which form of commitment does the scale reveal you have most? Which do you have least? Are these differences great, or are they highly similar?

2. Did the scale tell you something you didn't already know about yourself, or did it merely reinforce your intuitive beliefs about your own organizational commitment?

3. To what extent is your organizational commitment, as reflected by this scale, related to your interest in quitting your job and taking a new position?

4. How do your answers to these questions compare to those of your classmates? Are your responses similar to theirs or different from them? Why do you think this is?

Working in Groups

Recognizing Differences in Cultural Values on the Job

One of the major barriers in understanding and appreciating people from other cultures is the fact that they may adopt widely different values—especially when it comes to basic organizational activities, such as hiring. The following exercise (adapted from Gardenswartz & Rowe, 1994; see Note 105) is designed to make you aware of such differences and to sensitize you to their impact on life in organizations.

Directions

1. Divide the class into groups of approximately five to ten students.

2. Review the values differences noted in the chart below.

3. As a group, identify and discuss specific examples of each of the cultural distinctions noted in the chart based on your personal experiences.

4. As a group, discuss the implications of these values differences. Note, for example, specific problems that are likely to arise as a result of such differences.

5. As a class, review the major implications identified by each group in step 4.

In mainstream American culture . . .	But, in many other cultures . . .
■ People's primary obligation is toward their jobs.	■ People's primary obligation is toward their family and friends.
■ Employment is "at will"; an employee may be terminated at the discretion of the organization.	■ Employment is for life.
■ Competition is an accepted way of life.	■ Cooperation is considered better because it promotes harmony between people.
■ People strive for personal achievement	■ Personal ambition is frowned upon; group achievement is highly valued.

Questions for Discussion

1. Was your group, or the class as a whole, generally sensitive to the differences in values noted in this exercise?

2. What were the major organizational implications of the cultural differences in values identified by the class?

3. What do you think could be done to help people recognize and accept these cultural differences in values?

4. Did you come away from this exercise with a better understanding of the way cultural differences between people may impact organizational activities?

Take It to the Net

We invite you to visit the Greenberg/Baron page on the Prentice Hall Web site at:

http://www.prenhall.com~greenob

for this chapter's WorldWide Web exercise.

You can also visit the Web sites for these companies, featured within this chapter:

Bank of Montreal
http://www.bmo.com/

Selectron Inc
http://www.teleport.com/~selectrn/

FedEx
http://www.fedex.com/

Lotus Development Corp
http://www.lotus.com/

Levi Strauss
http://www.levi.com/menu

Coopers & Lybrand
http://www.colybrand.com/

Shell Oil
http://www.shellus.com/

American Express Travel Related Services
http://www.americanexpress.com/

CHAPTER Seven

CAREER DEVELOPMENT AND WORK STRESS

■ OBJECTIVES

After reading this chapter you should be able to:

1. Understand the concept of *socialization* and identify the stages through which it develops.

2. Explain what *mentors* are, what they do, and both the benefits and costs of mentoring to mentors and their protégés.

3. Describe the process through which people choose their careers, and explain how the nature of careers have changed in recent years.

4. Explain how the careers of women and men may differ, including the impact of the *glass ceiling*, and differences in the way men and women react to the *midlife crisis*.

5. Define *stress* and distinguish between stress and strain.

6. Describe some of the major organizational and personal causes of stress, including conflict between work and family responsibilities.

7. Explain the concept of *burnout*, including its major causes and effects.

8. Describe the adverse effects of stress and explain how individual difference factors play a role in such effects.

9. Describe both individual and organizational techniques for managing stress.

BACK FROM THE BRINK—THE FALL AND RISE OF SERGIO ZYMAN

Failure. The very word sends chills up and down the spines of most managers. And not surprisingly; after all, it implies the end to all those dreams of glory, as one's career goes down in flames. Amazing as it may seem, though, many top executives have experienced the bitter pain of failure—sometimes on a colossal scale—only to bounce back. One of the most dramatic examples of this kind of "re-ascent from the ashes" is provided by Sergio Zyman.

In 1990, Zyman was head of U.S. marketing for Coca-Cola, giant of the soft-drink industry. Disturbed by the slow erosion of Coke's market share, most of which had been lost to archrival Pepsi-Cola, Zyman decided on a bold move: Coca-Cola would replace the company's mainstay with a new product—New Coke. The result? One of the biggest marketing fiascoes in history. Consumers soundly rejected New Coke and angrily demanded a return to their old favorite. So large and unsettling was the drop in sales that only 79 days later, "old Coke" was back on the shelves—and Sergio Zyman was out of a job.

Does he now describe his decision to pull old Coke from the market as a mistake? "No," he remarked in a recent interview. "Something between a failure and a bust. The strategy didn't work, but the totality of the action ended up being positive." After his blunder with New Coke, Zyman dropped from sight and worked as a consultant for seven years. "That first year I consulted for 7-Eleven, a reengineering company in France, Continental Airlines, and Jones New York," Zyman reports. Working out of his Atlanta home, he soon built a thriving business. "Marketing is marketing," Zyman states, so his services were certainly very much in demand.

And then, the seemingly impossible happened: His old company wanted him back. For two years the suave CEO of Coca-Cola, Roberto Goizueta, tried to rehire him; he wanted Zyman—who is famous in the soft-drink industry for his abrasive personality—to help shake things up. Ultimately, Zyman agreed, but only after winning promises of almost total freedom. So, like the proverbial Phoenix, he has arisen from the ashes of his previous failure and is now back as head of Coca-Cola's marketing operations. Zyman says he is happy and has no plans to leave again. But even if he did, he indicates, that would be "no problema." "I've always had destinations," he comments. "I know what I'm doing in the morning, how many books I'd read, where I'd ski. The only time I haven't figured out is between 4:30 and six. . . ." In short, he's confident that come what may—even another failure—he'd quickly pick up the pieces and cement them into a new pattern of success.

"**A**mazing," we can almost hear you murmuring. "Someone who made a career-destroying mistake but then bounced back. Must be unique—the only time in history it ever happened." Before you reach that conclusion, take a look at Table 7-1; it lists a number of famous executives who sampled the bitter taste of failure but then built their careers anew. So, Sergio Zyman is definitely *not* alone in this experience. Failure is not a one-way ticket to oblivion where one's career—the sequence of jobs, roles and positions we hold during our working lives—is concerned.[1] On the contrary, for many it is a learning experience which helps them to shape even greater success. As Bill Gates of Microsoft, who likes to hire people who have made mistakes, puts it: "It [failure] shows that they take risks. The way people deal with things that go wrong is an indicator of how they deal with change."

As shown here, many top executives who experience mammoth failure bounce back from these experiences and put their careers back on track.

Executive	Failure	Where They Are Now
Frank Biondi, 50	Fired as CEO of HBO after clashing with his boss, Nick Nicholas	CEO of Viacom, world's largest entertainment company
Michael Carpenter, 48	Fired as CEO of Kidder Peabody after a trade generated $350 million in phony profits	CEO of Traveler's Life Insurance
Steven Jobs, 40	Pushed out of top post at Apple Computer after power struggle with John Sculley	Head of the company that computerized Disney's *Toy Story*—a highly successful venture
Ross Johnson, 63	Lost takeover fight with KKR after losing $400 million on a smokeless cigarette	Chairman of Canadian air-filter company, Bionaire
Key Whitmore, 62	Dumped as CEO of Kodak after lackluster earnings	A devout Mormon, he now supervises 200 young missionaries in London
Michael Miles, 55	As CEO of Philip Morris, his decision to cut Marlboro prices ravaged profits; he quit	Now a special limited partner in buyout firm Forstmann Little; on the Boards of Time Warner and Dell

SOURCE: Based on information in Sellers, 1995.

While failure can be a learning experience, and even a boost to one's later career, it is clear that it also involves very high levels of *stress*—emotional and physiological reactions occurring in response to *stressors,* demands from within and outside an organization.[2] In fact, the stress resulting from failure can be so great that it wreaks havoc with personal health. This fact, in turn, suggests that the two topics on which we'll focus in this chapter—*careers* and *stress* are closely related, and they definitely are: Many of the events and processes that shape our careers influence the level of stress we encounter, and high levels of stress and the effects these produce can strongly affect our careers.

To provide you with basic information on these two important topics, we'll proceed as follows. We'll start with a discussion of two topics relating to careers: *organizational socialization*—the process by which new employees become fully members of their organizations[3] and *mentoring*—a process in which younger and less experienced individuals receive help and guidance from older and more experienced ones.[4] Then, we'll turn to the changing nature of careers themselves. In the past, most persons expected their careers to involve a straightforward climb up the organization's ladder, with each new rung involving increased responsibility and rewards. Now, however, this traditional pattern has been largely replaced by a much more complex picture involving many *lateral moves*, *job rotation*, and similar experiences. We'll consider several of these changes and also examine the effects of *gender* on careers—how the work experiences of women and men differ and the possibility that different factors determine whether they "make it to the top."[5]

After considering the nature of careers, we'll turn to the closely related topic of *stress*. Here, we'll examine the major causes of stress both at work and outside work, and its major effects. Then we'll describe some important techniques for managing stress that can be adopted both by individuals and their organizations. As we'll note repeatedly through our discussion of stress, there are close, two-way links between the experiences individuals have in their careers and the levels of stress they encounter. By considering these two topics in the same chapter, we will be able to emphasize these links and so provide you with a better understanding of both.

Organizational Socialization: The Process of Joining Up

Think back over the jobs you have held in recent years. Can you recall your feelings and reactions during the first few days or weeks on each? If so, you probably remember that these were somewhat uncomfortable periods. As a new employee, you were suddenly confronted with a work environment that was different in many respects from the one you had just left. Most, if not all, of the people around you were strangers, and you had to begin the process of getting to know them—and their personal quirks—from scratch. Unless your job was identical to the one you had before, you also had to learn new procedures, skills, and operations relating to it, as well as policies and practices in force in your new organization. In short, you had to *learn the ropes* so that you could perform your new job effectively.

organizational socialization
The process through which new-comers to an organization become full-fledged members who share its major values and understand its policies and procedures.

The process through which you accomplished this tasks is known as **organizational socialization.** More formally, it can be defined as the process through which individuals are transformed from outsiders to participating, effective members of organizations.[6] In a sense, a career can be viewed as consisting of a series of socialization experiences, as an individual moves into new organizations or new positions. Thus, understanding organizational socialization is important to understanding careers. What happens during organizational socialization? What can organizations do to make this process more efficient? These are the questions on which we'll now focus.

The Nature of Organizational Socialization

Organizational socialization is clearly a continuous process, one that starts before people arrive on the job and continues for weeks or months after they begin working. However, the process can be divided into three basic periods described by one expert on this topic as *getting in, breaking in*, and *settling in* (see Figure 7-1).[7]

Getting in: What happens before people are hired. Can you think of a specific company in which you'd like to work sometime in the future? Why would you like to work there? What is it about this company that makes it such an attractive choice for you? To the extent you can answer these questions, you already recognize that you know quite a bit about an organization even before you start working there. In other words, people often develop expectations about what an organization is like before actually being hired by it. In a sense, then, organizational socialization starts before people accept and fill a new job—a period described in several models of organizational socialization as the *pre-entry period*.[8]

Several sources of information contribute to beliefs about an organization. First, friends or relatives who work there might tell you about their experiences. Second, you might acquire information about an organization from sources such as professional journals, magazine and newspaper articles about it, and corporate annual reports. While these sources of information about an organization are far from perfect—both may paint a rosier picture than is justified by the facts—they are still useful from the point of view of forming preliminary ideas about what it might be like to work for that organization.

Another source of information is that provided by the organization itself—information supplied by recruiters or interviewers. Unfortunately, such information, too, can be biased. Competition for top-notch employees is fierce, so successful recruitment usually involves a skilled combination of salesmanship

Organizational socialization generally
involves the three stages summarized
here: *getting in, breaking in, and* settling in.

(**Source:** Based on suggestions by Feldman,
1981; see Note 7.)

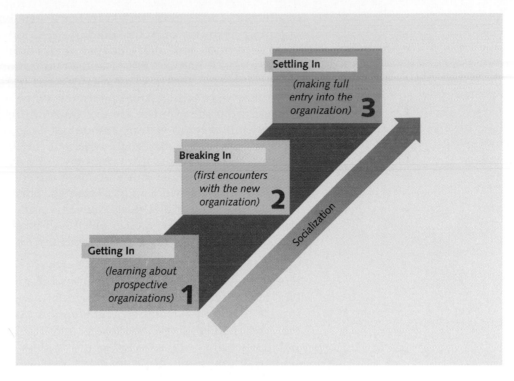

and diplomacy. Recruiters tend to describe their companies in glowing terms, glossing over internal problems and external threats, while emphasizing the positive features. The result is that potential employees often receive unrealistically positive impressions of conditions prevailing in a specific organization. When they arrive on the job and find that their expectations are not met, they experience disappointment, dissatisfaction, and even resentment about being misled. In fact, research findings indicate that the less employees' job expectations are met, the less satisfied and committed they are, and the more likely they are to think about quitting—and to actually do so.[9]

In order to avoid such negative reactions—which are sometimes termed **entry shock**—it is important for organizations to provide job candidates with accurate information about the organization. In other words, prospective employees should be given **realistic job previews**—previews in which they are provided with accurate information about their jobs and the conditions under which they will be performed—so that they can know what to expect if they do enter the organization. Growing evidence indicates that people exposed to realistic job previews later report higher satisfaction and show lower turnover than those who receive glowing, but often misleading, information about their companies.[10] Moreover, as we'll soon see, having realistic expectations helps to smooth the next period in the socialization process, to which we'll now turn.

entry shock The confusion and
disorientation experienced by
many newcomers to an organization.

realistic job previews
Accurate information concerning
the conditions within an organization or job provided to potential employees prior to their
decision to join an organization.

Breaking in: The encounter stage. The second stage in organizational socialization begins when individuals actually assume their new duties. During this stage, they face several key tasks. They must master the skills required by their new jobs.[11] They must become oriented to the practices and procedures of the new organization—the way things are done there. In other words, they must learn the organization's *culture*, the shared attitudes, values, and expectations of existing organization members (see Chapter 14). Third, new members must establish good social relations with others and gain their acceptance.

During the encounter stage—sometimes known as *accommodation*—newcomers learn what the organization expects from them and how to be a participating member of their work group and formal *orientation programs* are conducted. These are designed to teach new employees formally about their organizations—not only day-do-day operations, but also their histories, missions, and traditions. Without such orientation programs, new employees are likely to find it harder to fit in and to understand what the organization is all about. Although much of what is covered in such programs may be learned informally over time, formal programs, when well conducted, are often more efficient from the point of view of transmitting large amounts of information to new employees in a short amount of time. One of the authors experienced such an orientation program when he became a Program Director at the National Science Foundation. All new Program Directors were sent away on a four-day retreat during which many of the complex functions involved in this administrative job were fully explained. Further, several sessions focused on the complex legal and ethical issues involved in awarding and overseeing government grants for research projects. All in all, it was an excellent, firsthand introduction to how orientation programs *should be* run.

Settling in: The metamorphosis stage.   Sometime after an individual enters an organization, she or he attains full member status. Depending on the type and length of orientation program used, this entry may be marked by a formal ceremony—a dinner, a graduation exercise—or it may be quite informal. Alternatively, new employees may receive a concrete sign of their new status when they are accepted as full members—for instance, a pass to the executive dining room. In other cases, especially when training has been short or informal, full acceptance may be signaled through informal actions such as being invited to lunch with "the group."

Whatever form it takes, the settling-in phase of socialization marks important shifts both for individuals and their organizations. Employees make permanent adjustments to their jobs, and organizations now treat them is if they will be long-term members of the work team rather than temporary fill-ins.

Mentoring: One-on-One Socialization

Consider 50 new college graduates hired by a large corporation to do pretty much the same job. All start out on fairly equal footing, but if you returned in one year to see how they were doing, you might already notice substantial differences. Some would be gone, others would be falling behind, and a few would clearly be "leading the pack"—they would already appear to be on the fast track to success. What accounts for these differences? Many factors certainly play a role, but one of the most important of these involves **mentoring**.[12] This is a process in which a more experienced employee—known as a **mentor**—advises, counsels, and otherwise enhances the personal development (and career) of a new employee, known as a **protégé**. If you've ever had an older, more experienced person take you under her or his wing and guide you, then you already know how valuable mentoring can be. In fact, research findings indicate that having a mentor early in one's career is an important predictor of success: The more mentoring people receive, the more promotions they receive and the more highly they are compensated.[13]

Let's now take a closer look at mentoring relationships, examining precisely what mentors do, how mentoring relationships form and change over time, and the role of mentors in career success.

What Do Mentors Do?

Research on the nature of mentor-protégé relationships suggests that mentors do many things for their protégés.[14] For example, they provide much-needed emotional support and confidence for those who are just starting out and are

mentoring The process of serving as a mentor.

mentor A more experienced employee who offers advice, assistance, and protection to a younger and less experienced one (a protégé).

protégé A less experienced (often new) employee whose organizational socialization is facilitated by working with a mentor.

likely to be somewhat insecure. Mentors also help pave the way for their protégés' job success. They nominate them for promotions, provide them with opportunities for them to demonstrate their competence, and generally bring them to the attention of higher management. Mentors also suggest useful strategies for reaching work goals—often, ones protégés might not generate for themselves. Finally, mentors often protect their protégés from the consequences of errors and help them avoid situations that may prove risky for their careers.

In short, mentors do a number of things designed to help their protégés get ahead. Yet, as beneficial as mentor-protégé relationships may be, not all new employees seek out mentors. Individual difference factors, such as the ones we discussed in Chapter 4 seem to play a role in this process. For instance, as we noted in that chapter, persons high in self-monitoring tend to seek out and obtain mentors to a greater extent than persons low in self-monitoring.[15] Perhaps this is because high self-monitors find it easier to adapt their behavior to the requirements of new situations, and this fact includes adapting to the requests and style of potential mentors. Similarly, persons high in need for achievement tend to seek mentors more often than persons low in need for achievement.[16]

Because becoming the protégé of a highly successful person is so potentially valuable to one's career, there is often considerable competition among newcomers for available mentors. As a result, such persons are often quite selective—they choose only those newcomers they view as "the cream of the crop" as their protégés. The winners in this kind of competition are not always the persons with the highest level of talent; sometimes, victory goes to those who are especially skilled at the task of *impression management*—looking good to others. In any case, given the benefits of becoming a protégé, seeking a successful mentor is definitely one strategy newcomers should consider when they enter a new organization. The career they boost may well be their own.

Mentors also act as models *for their protégés, helping them to learn through the process of observational learning* we described in Chapter 3.

How Mentoring Relationships Form and Change

As we have just noted, mentor-protégé relationships do not form at random. Rather, they are often the results of a complex selection process in which both mentors and potential protégés play an active role. Mentors, of course, don't want to waste their time and effort on just anybody. Rather, they seek to choose only the best and most promising newcomers for their protégés. The process by which they do so is not always explicit, but given that potential protégés outnumber potential mentors in most organizations, careful selection of potential protégés does tend to occur.

Protégés, of course, engage in selection, too. They generally seek mentors who are older and more experienced than themselves, and ones who are known to be successful in the organization. Once they identify potential mentors, they may take active steps to establish a relationship with this person.

How, precisely, do they go about initiating mentor-protégé bonds? Research findings suggest that they tend to rely on certain tactics for building such a relationship.[17] Specifically, would-be protégés seem to focus on such activities as seeking *personal* interactions with their boss, negotiating the terms of their relationships directly (known as *direct* tactics), and expressing willingness to exceed their boss's expectations (*noncontractual* tactics). Persons who do not enter into mentor-protégé relationships, in contrast, tend to use other tactics, such as trying to put themselves in a favorable light (*regulative* tactics) and demonstrating conformity to formal role requirements and the boss's expectations (*contractual* tactics).

But what happens to mentoring relationships once they are established? Do they remain unchanged for long periods of time? Research on this issue indicates that, in fact, most mentor-protégé relationships pass through several distinct phases.[18] The first, known as *initiation*, lasts from six months to a year and represents the period during which the relationships gets started and takes on importance for both parties. The second phase, known as *cultivation,* may last from two to five years. During this time, the bond between mentor and protégé deepens, and the young individual may make rapid career progress because of the skilled assistance she or he is receiving.

The third stage, *separation,* begins when the protégé feels it is time to assert independence and strike out on his or her own, or when there is some externally produced change in their roles—for instance, the protégé is promoted or the mentor is transferred. Separation also can occur if the mentor feels unable to continue providing support and guidance to the protégé (e.g., if the mentor becomes ill). This stage can be quite stressful if the mentor resents the protégé's growing independence, or if the protégé feels that the mentor has withdrawn support prematurely.

If this separation is successful, the relationship may enter a final stage, termed *redefinition.* Here, both persons perceive their bond primarily as one of friendship. They come to treat one another as equals, and the roles of mentor and protégé fade away. However, the mentor may continue to take pride in the accomplishments of her or his former protégé. Likewise, the protégé may continue to feel gratitude toward the former mentor. Although there is bound to be variation in the way mentor-protégé relationships actually develop, it seems safe to conclude that these phases represent a relatively accurate picture of the way in which many of these relationships unfold.

At this point, we should note that many companies do not leave the formation of mentor-protégé relationships to chance. Rather, they have formal programs in which newcomers are assigned to more experienced persons who are expected to serve as their mentors. For a summary of what some companies are doing in this respect, see Table 7-2.

Gender, Race, and Mentoring

It is a basic fact of social relationships that in general, people tend to prefer, like, and feel more comfortable around persons who are similar to themselves than persons who are different.[19] Thus, they tend to form friendships and other personal relationships not with persons who are opposite to themselves in traits, attitudes, or background, but with persons who are generally similar. Does this principle apply to mentoring relationships? Growing evidence suggests that it does. In general, women and minorities (e.g., African Americans) seem to find it more difficult to obtain mentors in their organizations than white males.[20] There are exceptions to this overall pattern, but it appears that women and minorities are at a distinct disadvantage where obtaining a mentor is concerned.[21] One reason for this state of affairs seems to involve the principle we stated earlier: Even today, most managers in the United States and many other countries are white males, and such persons feel most comfortable around persons of similar background.

However, other factors, too, play a role. In recent surveys, women have reported less willingness to serve as mentors than men.[22] Apparently, this is because they have greater concern than men about the potential negative consequences that may follow if they adopt a protégé and this person fails.

On the other side of the coin, many male managers express concerns about serving as a mentor for female employees: They fear that the close relationships that develop may be misperceived as romantic entanglements.[23] Given the fact that having a mentor early in one's career is often highly beneficial,

■ TABLE 7-2   MENTORSHIP PROGRAMS: WHAT SOME COMPANIES ARE DOING

Because the mentoring process is so important, many companies have been unwilling to leave it to chance. Thus, they have developed formal mechanisms for encouraging the formation of mentoring relationships.

SOURCE: Based on information in Granfield, M., (1992, November). "'90s mentoring: Circles and quads." *Working Woman*, p. 15.

Company	Description
Colgate Palmolive	All new white-collar employees are assigned individual higher-ranking employees to serve as mentors.
NYNEX	Mentoring circles, consisting of six lower-ranking and two higher-ranking female employees, meet monthly to discuss work-related issues.
Dow Jones	Groups of four are formed consisting of a high-level mentor and three others: a white male, a woman of any race, and a minority group member of either gender.
Chubb & Son Insurance	In its Sponsorship Program, three protégés are assigned to each of ten different mentors.

it seems important for organizations to take active steps to reduce these barriers and to increase mentoring opportunities for women and minorities. Failing to do so may deny persons in these groups access to one vital ingredient in career success.

Careers: New Forms, New Strategies

"Where do you want to work when you complete your studies?" When we were in college, the answer given by most persons was simple: "For a big, Fortune 500 company." At the time, this answer made sense. Big companies offered what seemed to be the surest route to the top: a series of steps up the corporate ladder leading to ever-greater responsibilities—and rewards. Now, however, most students, especially those completing their MBAs, have a different answer. A few statistics may be of interest:

■ In 1989, 70 percent of Stanford University's graduating class of MBAs joined big companies; in 1994, less than 50 percent did so.

■ At Northwestern's Kellogg School, fully 43 percent of recent graduates have spurned large companies to take jobs with consulting firms instead.

■ At Harvard, some manufacturing companies have stopped coming to campus because so few students turned out for the recruitment sessions and most of the persons to whom they made job offers rejected them.[24]

Facts like these suggest that there is something major in the wind where ideas about the nature of careers are concerned. Common conceptions of what careers will—or should be—like have altered greatly in recent years, partly as a result of equally sweeping changes in the business world. In other words, if people currently hold different conceptions of what their careers will be like than was true in the past, it is because they are increasingly aware of the tremendous shifts that have occurred in the way many companies do business, including how they hire, train, promote, and retain their employees.

career The evolving sequence of a person's work experience over time.

In this section, we'll focus on several important aspects of a **career**—the evolving sequence of a person's work experience over time—and their changing nature. First, we'll consider the question of how individuals make vocational choices—why they choose specific jobs. Next, we'll examine some of the major ways in which careers have changed in recent years and how individuals can best react to such changes in planning their own careers. Finally, we'll consider the role of gender in careers, addressing the question of whether women and men have different career experiences and if so, why this may be so.

Choosing a Job: Making Vocational Choices

How do people end up in specific jobs? For instance, how did the people shown in Figure 7-2 choose these unusual positions? Many different factors play a role in this process, but here, we'll focus on several that appear to be most important.

■ **Figure 7-2**
Vocational Choice: Why Do People Choose Jobs like These?
Many factors play a role in vocational choice. Two of the most important involve person-job fit *and people's ideas of how similar they are to the persons who perform these jobs (i.e., their prototypes).*

To understand the first of these factors, ask yourself this question: What kind of person becomes an attorney? A professional soldier? An elementary school teacher? Do your descriptions of these persons differ? If so, they reflect your understanding of a basic fact: Persons possessing specific characteristics are attracted to certain kinds of jobs. This is the idea of person-job fit that we discussed in Chapter 4—the suggestion that because of their personal characteristics (traits or abilities), individuals are better suited for performing some jobs than others.

Some researchers who have studied this relationship believe that people generally tend to select jobs that match their personalities, abilities, and values, and findings tend to confirm this idea.[25,26] The closer the person-job fit, the greater individuals' job satisfaction.[27] In fact, many people tend to assign greater importance to this kind of "fit" than to pay or promotional opportunities when choosing a job.[28,29]

Another factor that strongly influences job choices is people's beliefs about the future of these jobs. In other words, we tend to be quite rational in our choice of jobs, focusing on ones we believe will offer growing opportunities, while avoiding ones that seem to be declining in these respects. Most people know that there isn't much call for blacksmiths or train conductors today, so they tend to drop these jobs from consideration, even if they find them personally appealing. In contrast, there are many jobs that can be expected to grow in numbers—and opportunities—in the future. These are the ones that tend to capture individuals' attention when they are considering which jobs to enter. For a closer look at jobs and careers that promise to be "hot" in the future, please see the ORGANIZATION OF THE FUTURE section.

Career Planning: Charting Your Future

Have you ever seen the comedy *How to Succeed in Business Without Really Trying*? It offers a tongue-in-cheek look at how someone lacking in special talent or skills can rise quickly to the top through a combination of remarkable impression management, good luck, and ruthless (if humorous) manipulation. As the story unfolds, the hero (or "antihero") moves through a series of jobs, each one higher in pay and status than the last—and also on a higher floor in the company's huge building.

While single-track career paths like this one still exist, they are becoming the exception rather than the rule. In the closing years of the twentieth century, careers do *not* generally involve a straightforward climb through a successive series of clearly defined steps. On the contrary, they more frequently include lateral moves, rotation through several different jobs, geographic relocations, and—increasingly—periods of time spent as an independent contractor or subcontractor rather than as a regular, full-time employee.

Why have these shifts in the nature of careers occurred? Mainly because organizations themselves have altered. First, many have adopted a much flatter internal structure. The number of managers—especially middle-level managers—has decreased sharply, and companies have sought to respond to increased global competition by becoming "lean and mean."[30] At the same time, organizations have redrawn their boundaries to focus more directly on their core business and core competencies, while at the same time, relying more and more on specialists from outside the company. Instead of maintaining large internal staffs of experts, organizations are, increasingly, turning to external contractors to meet specific needs as they arise. The result of these trends, when coupled with major efforts to restructure or engage in "reengineering," are clear: Traditional career paths, in which someone is hired and then remains with the same company, and even the same unit for years or decades, are vanishing.[31] Given this radically altered set of conditions, what kind of career goals and career paths should individuals seek?

Person-job fit *plays an important role in many aspects of organizational behavior, including job satisfaction (see Chapter 6) and job performance (see Chapter 4).*

We will examine several aspects of organizational change in Chapter 15.

Figure 7-3
Career Tracks in Today's Organizations
Among the major types of careers open to individuals in modern organizations are these four: (1) corporate strategists, (2) project managers, (3) resource providers, and (4) talents.

job rotation Lateral transfers of employees between jobs in an organization.

ate as freelance consultants. Even if they are full-time, regular employees, persons filling the role of *talent* should view themselves as self-employed: They are there not only to do a job for an employer, but also to add to their own skills and experience. Remember: In today's organizations, insiders must compete, more and more, with each other and with outside consultants offering similar skills and expertise. For this reason alone, it's best for all individuals to focus on improving their own skills—thus making themselves better able to compete and more marketable should they leave the organization. An overview of the four career tracks we have discussed is presented in Figure 7-3.

Job rotation: A key ingredient in career development. It is one thing to recommend that employees view their jobs as learning experiences, and quite another to translate this general principle into concrete steps they can take to reach this goal. How, precisely, can individuals use their jobs as a base for acquiring marketable skills? Fortunately, recent research on this issue offers a clear-cut answer. One important way in which they can accomplish these goals is through judicious use of **job rotation**—lateral transfers of employees between jobs in an organization.[35] Recent findings indicate that job rotation is experienced primarily by high-performing employees relatively early in their careers, and that it is correlated with such positive outcomes as promotion rate and salary growth.[36] In addition, the persons who experience it perceive that job rotation has added to their skills and knowledge (see Figure 7-4). The career implications of these findings are obvious: If you are offered job rotation, don't hesitate to accept it. The benefits of doing so can be substantial.

Figure 7-4
Job Rotation: A Plus for Many Careers
As shown here, job rotation tended to occur early in individuals' careers and to be more common for high-performing than low-performing persons. In addition, it was related to both promotion rate and salary growth.

(**Source:** Based on findings reported by Campion, Cheraskin, & Stevens, 1994; see Note 34.)

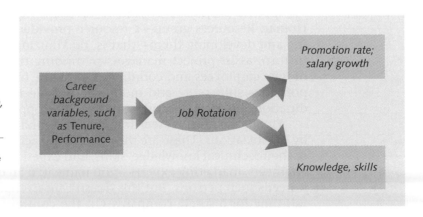

Current Practice: Signs of Trouble in Your Career

How can you tell if your career is *not* on track—not proceeding along the lines described above? Here are some tips. Everyone—even Ziggy—wants to have a successful career (see Figure 7-5). In the past, it was relatively easy to judge whether a person was on track in this respect. Individuals knew that if their careers were going well, they would move through a regular series of promotions, occurring at fairly predictable times. Now, as we've already noted, such linear career tracks are increasingly rare. Given this fact, how can you determine whether your career is going well—or poorly? Experts on careers suggest paying careful attention to the following points:

- Ask yourself whether you are learning: If you can't state clearly what you've learned during the past six months or what you expect to learn in the next six months, your career may be at a standstill—and in trouble.
- Ask yourself: "If my job were open, would I get it?" If you have doubts on this score, it means that you are falling behind in terms of acquiring new skills.
- Do you know what you are contributing? Today, employees' value is being judged increasingly in terms of what they provide to their organizations, not their seniority or experience. If you can't state clearly what you are contributing, your career may be dead in the water.
- Ask yourself: "What would I do if my job disappeared tomorrow?" If you have done a good job of increasing your skills and knowledge base, you should be able to answer: "I'd be able to get another job at least as good as this one." If you can't answer that way, you are probably not making good personal progress.
- Are you being exploited? If you suspect that you are—that you are being asked to sacrifice your own welfare or personal growth for the good of the company, you should begin to wonder about the value of this particular job for your career.
- Are you worried about your job? If you are, experts agree, you probably should be. People who know what they are contributing and how valuable (invaluable?) they are to their companies, have few concerns in this regard. If you have such concerns, watch out: They may well be justified.

■ **Figure 7-5**
*How **NOT** to Achieve Success!*
Almost everyone wants success, but in today's highly competitive and rapidly changing world, it seems harder to obtain than ever before. Few persons want to find themselves in the situation faced by Ziggy.

We examined the potential role of prejudice toward females in Chapter 6.

here. However, recent studies seem to point to these conclusions: Yes, there is a glass ceiling in terms of the share of top jobs that go to females—this number is much lower than would be predicted on the basis of the proportion of females in the workplace. But no, the glass ceiling does not appear to result from a conscious effort on the part of male executives to keep women out of their domain.[43] Rather, more subtle factors seem to produce this effect. We have already considered one of these: women may receive fewer developmental opportunities than men[44]—fewer experiences that help prepare them for top-level jobs.

Another factor producing such effects is belief in the glass ceiling itself: believing in the existence of this barrier may prevent many women from applying for top management positions.[45] In a sense, then, the glass ceiling may operate in a self-fulfilling manner: Women believe it is there, so they don't try for the top jobs—thus confirming the glass ceiling.

Because of such factors, and others as well—for instance, the tendency to assign lower performance ratings to females than males (described in Chapter 6)—there may indeed be a glass ceiling that affects women's careers. However, attributing this to male prejudice—even subtle forms of prejudice—does not appear to be justified by existing evidence.

Women executives and the "midlife crisis": Why some choose to opt out of the system. Prior to 1970, large numbers of women did not move into management jobs after graduating from college. After 1970, however, this situation changed radically so that, as we noted above, more than 40 percent of all management-level jobs in the United States are now held by women. What has been the career experience of the women who helped to break this barrier in the early 1970s? Many have clearly obtained a great deal of success. They are vice presidents, senior partners, and CEOs. Despite such achievement, however, an increasing number of such successful women are now choosing to opt out—they are leaving highly paid, high-pressure jobs for ones they find more personally rewarding. For example, consider the results of a recent survey conducted by Yankelovich Partners with 300 career women ages 35 to 49. These women were highly successful: 94 percent were managers or executives, and more than half had salaries above $60,000 per year. But consider these disturbing results:[46]

- More than 40 percent said they felt "trapped" in their current jobs.
- A majority said that they did not have enough time for their personal lives.
- More than a third said that they were bored with their lives.
- An amazing 87 percent said that they were currently contemplating a major change in their lives—leaving their current jobs to start their own business, going back to school, or seeking another career.
- Fifty-six percent reported that one of their friends was seeking therapy for personal problems.

Interestingly, these complaints and many others seemed to rise to a peak between ages 40–44—the traditional center of what has been termed the **midlife crisis**—a period in life when many people experience grave doubts and increasing dissatisfaction with the past and future course of their lives (see Figure 7-7).[47]

Why are so many successful women experiencing these reactions? Many report feeling that because of their success, they have proved themselves—shown what they can do. Now, they are increasingly unhappy about having to play the game by what they view as "the old male rules." Consider the experience of one female professional, Denise Kuhlman, a 37-year-old attorney. Her specialty was bankruptcy, and many of her days were spent in negotiations and deal making. The confrontational style of these discussions left her cold. As she puts it: "It's a guy kind of thing. You're working by their rules."

midlife crisis A period of great emotional turmoil and uncertainty, supposedly experienced by many individuals during middle age.

Many successful women in their mid-40s report negative feelings about their jobs and personal lives. As shown here, such reactions seem to peak when people are between the ages of 40 and 45.

(**Source:** Based on data reported in *Fortune*, September 18, 1995; see Note 45.)

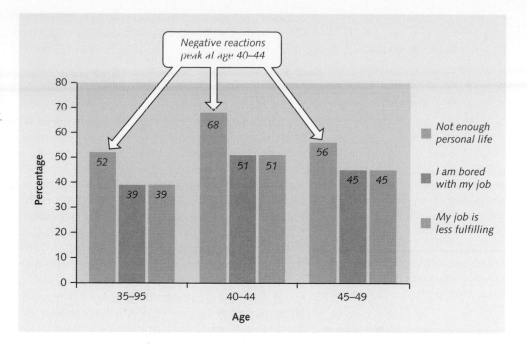

So dissatisfied with this situation did she become, that she saved her money for more than two years and then quit to return to graduate school in psychology. "I have no intention of practicing law in the future," she says. "In my heart of hearts, I want to do things that are good for people."

Ms. Kuhlman is not alone; thousands of other successful women holding high-paying executive and professional jobs have concluded that the personal costs of such a lifestyle are more than they are willing to pay. Will this trend continue in the future? It is difficult to say. Women now in the their 40s—the first generation to invade previously all-male bastions in the business world—were raised in the 1950s and 1960s, a time when traditional roles for women and men were still the norm. Perhaps younger women, raised with greater exposure to models of female achievement, will react differently at midlife; indeed, perhaps they will not experience a midlife crisis at all.

Judging from increased entrepreneurial activity among young women, another possibility is that many will avoid the issue entirely by starting their own businesses. In fact, in the United States, fully 70 percent of teenagers—females and males alike—currently say they would like to start their own business someday.[48] Consider, for example, Lizzie Denis and Louise Kramer, who became unhappy with the slow pace of baking cookies on traditional racks. Their solution: the Double-Decker Baking Rack. With the financial help of their families, they founded a company—L&L Products—and began marketing the rack. To date, thousands have been sold, at large chains such as Macy's and Marshall Field's, as well as through catalogs. The company has already become profitable, and customers seem to like the no-nonsense copy placed on the package by the teenaged inventors: "We hope you'll agree that the Double Decker Baking Rack does make sense and buy it. Then we can go to college or the mall."

What about men; are they, too, opting out at midlife? Apparently not.[49] Trapped by still-rigid sex roles, many feel that such behavior would be unacceptable for a man. As one puts it, "Men have responsibilities, and women have choices." When asked how their spouses would react if they announced that they were having a midlife crisis, most indicated that they would probably say something like this: "Are you out of your mind? Get back to work!" Of course, these are only perceptions; what would actually happen if men chose to opt out is uncertain. What does seem clear, however, is that for complex reasons, many men feel less able to change their lives—and careers—in the same manner that increasing numbers of successful women are choosing.

Stress: Its Basic Nature

Have you ever experienced situations in which you felt that you were about to be overwhelmed by your job and pressures relating to it? If so, then you are already familiar with *stress*.[50] Indeed, in one recent survey, fully 46 percent of American workers felt that their jobs are highly stressful.[51] What, precisely, is stress? Many definitions exist, but in general, **stress** refers to a complex pattern of emotional states, physiological reactions, and related thoughts occurring in response to external demands (**stressors**). A related term—**strain**—refers to the effects of stress, primarily to deviations from normal states or performance resulting from exposure to stressful events. As we'll soon see, these can involve physical symptoms, reduced performance, and many other changes in behavior.

A key point to keep in mind with respect to stress is that whether, and to what extent it occurs in a given situation, depends heavily on people's interpretation of what is happening to them—their *cognitive appraisal* of the stressors they confront.[52] Stress occurs only to the extent that people perceive that (1) the situation they face is somehow threatening to them, and (2) they will be unable to cope with these potential dangers or demands—that the situation is, in some sense, beyond their control.[53]

stress The pattern of emotional states, cognitions, and physiological reactions occurring in response to *stressors*.

stressors Various factors in the external environment that induce stress among people exposed to them.

strain Deviations from normal states or functioning resulting from stress.

Stress: Its Major Causes

What factors contribute to stress in work settings? We called attention to one at the start of this chapter: failure in one's career. Many other factors, too, influence the level of stress individuals experience at work. For purposes of clarity, we'll divide these into two major categories: factors relating to organizations or jobs, and factors relating to other aspects of individuals' lives.

Work-Related Causes of Stress

As anyone who has ever held a job well knows, work settings are often highly stressful environments. Yet, they vary greatly in this respect. Some jobs and organizations expose individuals to high levels of stress while others involve much lower levels of stress. What factors account for these differences?

Occupational demands: Some jobs are more stressful than others. Consider the following jobs: production manager, librarian, emergency room physician, janitor, firefighter, college professor, airline pilot. Do they differ in stressfulness? Obviously, they do. Some jobs, such as emergency room physician, firefighter, and airline pilot, expose the people who hold them to high levels of stress. Others, such as college professor or librarian, do not. This basic fact—that some jobs are much more stressful than others—has been confirmed by the results of a survey involving more than 130 different occupations.[54] The results indicated that several jobs —for example, physician, office manager, foreman, wait person—are quite high in stress. In contrast, others, such as maid, craft worker, farm laborer, are much lower.

What, precisely, makes some jobs more stressful than others? Apparently, several factors.[55] Jobs become increasingly stressful to the extent that they require (1) making decisions, (2) constant monitoring of devices or materials, (3) repeated exchange of information with others, (4) unpleasant physical conditions, and (5) performing unstructured rather than structured tasks.

Conflict between work and nonwork: Stress from competing demands.

When we were children, our mothers did not work outside the home, and neither did those of our friends. Today, of course, the situation is totally different. In a majority of families with children, both spouses work full-time. The result is a constant juggling of work and family responsibilities (known as *work juggling*). Further, incompatibilities between their work and family obligations expose them to what is widely recognized as another important cause of stress: **role conflict**, which is usually defined as incompatibility between the expectations of parties or between aspects of a single role. In this case, the expectations of spouses and children conflict, in many cases, with the expectations of bosses and co-workers.

How stressful is such family–work role conflict? Recent research findings indicate that it is stressful indeed. For example, in recent studies, Williams, Alliger, and their colleagues have employed a novel technique known as *experience sampling* to study this issue.[56,57] In this procedure, individuals wear a watch or other small device that signals them, at either random or prearranged times during the day, to record their current activities, levels of stress, current moods, and other reactions on a special form. Research using such experience-sampling procedures indicates that juggling work and family tasks often causes individuals to experience feelings of distress and other negative mood states.

Fortunately, additional findings indicate that such effects can be lessened by high levels of social support in work settings.[58] And as we'll see in a later section, the level of stress produced by such factors can also be lessened by certain employment policies—for instance, flexible work scheduling and supportive supervisors.[59]

Role ambiguity: Stress from uncertainty.

Even if individuals are able to avoid the stress associated with role conflict, they may still encounter another source of job-related stress: **role ambiguity**. This occurs when individuals experience uncertainty about what actions to take to fulfill a job. Most people dislike uncertainty and find it quite stressful, but it is difficult to avoid. In fact, role ambiguity is quite common: 35 to 60 percent of employees surveyed report experiencing it to some degree.[60]

Interestingly, the amount of role ambiguity experienced by employees seems to differ sharply from culture to culture. In a recent study involving participants from 21 different countries, Peterson and his colleagues found that in countries where large differences in status or power between managers and subordinates are the norm (high power distance countries) role ambiguity is relatively low.[61] Similarly, such ambiguity was also found to be relatively low in countries where people prefer to act as members of groups rather than as individuals (low individualism). These are considered to be basic dimensions along which many cultures vary.[62] As shown in Figure 7-8 (on page 232), role ambiguity was relatively low in Asian and African countries known to be high in power distance but low in individualism; in contrast, role ambiguity was higher in Western countries which are low in power distance and high in individualism.

Overload and underload: Doing too much or too little.

When the phrase "work-related stress" is mentioned, most people think of scenes in which employees are working frantically, doing more than they can handle. Such images relate to overload, which, in fact, can take two different forms. **Quantitative overload** occurs in situations where individuals are asked to do more work than they can complete in a specific period of time. In contrast, **qualitative overload** refers to employees' beliefs that they lack the required skills or abilities to perform a given job. Both types of overload are unpleasant and can lead to high levels of stress.[63]

Overload is only part of the total picture, however. While being asked to do too much can be stressful, so can being asked to do too little. Here again,

role conflict Incompatible demands made on an individual by different groups or persons.

role ambiguity Uncertainty among employees about the key requirements of their jobs.

Ambiguity concerning one's job responsibilities is also an important cause of job dissatisfaction (see Chapter 6).

quantitative overload A situation in which individuals are required to do more work than they can actually accomplish in a given period of time.

qualitative overload The belief among employees that they lack the skills or abilities needed to perform their jobs.

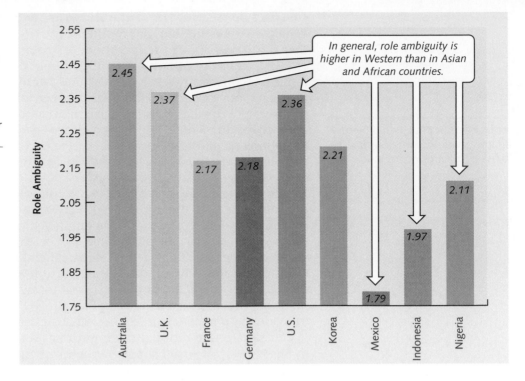

■ **Figure 7-8**
Culture and Role Ambiguity
In a recent study conducted in 21 different countries, it was found that role ambiguity was lower in Asian and African countries than in many Western countries. Apparently, this is due to the fact that Western countries are lower in power distance and higher in individualism.

(**Source:** Based on data reported by Peterson et al., 1995; see Note 59.)

---

quantitative underload A situation in which individuals have so little to do that they spend much of their time doing nothing.

qualitative underload The lack of mental stimulation that accompanies many routine, repetitive jobs.

sexual harassment Unwanted contact or communication of a sexual nature.

there are two types of *under*load: **quantitative underload**, which refers to the boredom that results from having too little to do, and **qualitative underload**, which refers to the lack of mental stimulation that accompanies many routine, repetitive jobs.

Responsibility for others: A heavy burden. Research findings indicate that in general, people who are responsible for others—who must motivate them, reward or punish them, communicate with them—experience higher levels of stress than those who handle other organizational functions.[64] Such people are more likely to report feelings of tension and anxiety, and are actually more likely to show overt symptoms of stress such as ulcers or hypertension.

There are two major reasons for this difference. First, it is managers who must, ultimately, confront the human costs of organizational policies and decisions. For example, they must deliver negative feedback and then witness the distress it generates. Second, it is their task to deal with the many frictions that are a normal part of human relations at work. This involves listening to endless complaints, mediating disputes, promoting cooperation, and exercising leadership. All these tasks are demanding and can contribute to the total burden of stress experienced by managers.

Lack of social support: The costs of isolation. One old saying suggests that "Misery loves company," and existing evidence indicates that it is definitely true where stress is concerned. When confronted with stressful situations, we fare much better when we have a network of friends and associates to whom we can turn for support and counsel. In fact, several studies indicate that managers who believe they have the friendship and support of their immediate supervisors and co-workers report fewer physical symptoms when exposed to high levels of stress than those who do not feel that they enjoy such support. Indeed, in one recent study, Doby and Caplan found that employees were particularly likely to experience adverse effects from exposure to stressors that threatened their relationships or reputation with their supervisor.[65]

Sexual harassment: A pervasive problem in work settings. Teresa Harris was a manager at Forklift Systems, Inc., in Nashville, Tennessee, when she encountered **sexual harassment**—defined in the United States as unwelcome sexual advances, requests for sexual favors, and other verbal or physical conduct of a sexual nature—from her boss, Charles Hardy. During her two and a half years with the company, he often made remarks such as "You're a woman, what do you know." and "We need a man as the rental manager." He suggested to her in front of other employees that they go to a nearby motel to "negotiate her raise." Occasionally, he asked Ms. Harris to remove coins from his pants pocket and would drop items on the floor and ask her to pick them up. The last straw came when, after Harris had negotiated a deal with a customer, he remarked, in front of other employees: "What did you promise the guy . . . some sex Saturday night?" At this point, Harris quit her job and filed suit against Hardy and her former company. It took several years, but she took her case to the Supreme Court and, in 1993, finally won.

While this is certainly an extreme case, various forms of sexual harassment are far from rare in today's work settings, and they are certainly an important source of stress for many individuals. Indeed, in one recent poll fully 31 percent of employed women indicated that they had been the object of such harassment on at least one occasion. In contrast, only 7 percent of male respondents to the same survey indicated that they had been the victim of such actions. It's important to note, by the way, that sexual harassment is not restricted to the kind of extreme and unpleasant actions encountered by Ms. Harris; in the United States it can involve any actions of a sexual nature that create a hostile work environment for employees—actions such as posting offensive pinups, staring at portions of co-workers' anatomy, or making repeated remarks about their appearance. In short, a boss or fellow employee doesn't have to request sexual favors or make these a term of employment to commit sexual harassment: Many other forms of behavior meet the legal definition.

Is such harassment more common today than it was in the past? Statistics suggests that this may be so: The number of complaints filed by employees rose from 4,272 in 1981 to almost 6,000 by 1990, and have doubled again since then.[66] Whether this is due to an actual increase in the incidence of sexual harassment or merely to greater reporting of its occurrence is impossible to say. Certainly, media attention to this problem has increased tremendously in recent years. Regardless of any effects of the media, however, it is clear that for every case of sexual harassment reported, many more go unrecorded. In fact, only 10 percent of women who report having experienced sexual harassment indicate that they actually reported the incident.[67] Findings such as these suggest that organizations must take concerted action to protect their employees from this devastating cause of stress.

Unpleasant physical working conditions. Because of legislation aimed at protecting the health and well-being of employees, most work settings today are relatively safe and comfortable. The word *relatively* should be emphasized, however, because even within the limits imposed by law, there is room for a wide range of variation. In fact, many individuals report that the physical conditions under which they work cause them considerable stress. In particular, many employees identify such factors as excessive variations in temperature, inadequate or glaring lighting, dusty or polluted air, and noise as major causes of stress at work.[68] With respect to noise, the sound of human voices, in particular, appears to be stressful and distracting, and interferes greatly with effective performance on many tasks.[69,70]

Causes of Stress Outside Work

Although work is clearly one of the most important activities in many people's lives, it is not the only activity. For this reason, events occurring outside work settings often generate stress that persists and, as we noted earlier, is carried back to work.[71] While many different factors contribute to

for example, an audience watching your performance—can interfere with effective performance.[80]

Having said all this, we must note that there are exceptions to the general rule that stress interferes with task performance. Some individuals do seem to "rise to the occasion" and turn in exceptional performance at times of high stress. This may result from the fact that they are truly expert in the tasks being performed. Alternatively, the individuals involved may view stress as a *challenge* rather than as a *threat*. As we noted earlier, such cognitive appraisal plays a key role in determining the level of stress we experience.

Second, large individual differences exist with respect to the impact of stress on task performance. As your own experience may suggest, some individuals—the Type A's we described in Chapter 4, for instance—seem to thrive on stress. They actively seek arousal and high levels of sensation or stimulation. For such people, stress is exhilarating and may improve their performance. In contrast, other people react in an opposite manner. They seek to avoid arousal and high levels of sensation. Such persons find stress upsetting, and it may interfere with their performance on many tasks.

In sum, taking available evidence into account, the most reasonable conclusion seems to be: In many situations, stress interferes with task performance. However, its precise effects depend on the nature of the tasks being performed, the expertise of the persons performing them, and several personality traits. For this reason, generalizations about the impact of stress on task performance should be made with considerable caution.

Stress and Psychological Well-being: Burnout

Most jobs involve some degree of stress. Yet somehow, the people holding them manage to cope. Some individuals, however, are not so fortunate. Over time, they seem to be worn down psychologically by repeated exposure to stress. Such people are often described as suffering from **burnout**—a syndrome involving several kinds of exhaustion coupled with several kinds of negative attitudes.

burnout A syndrome resulting from prolonged exposure to stress, consisting of physical, emotional, and mental exhaustion plus feelings of a lack of personal accomplishment.

With respect to exhaustion, victims of burnout often suffer from *physical exhaustion, emotional exhaustion,* and *attitudinal exhaustion.* Physical exhaustion is just what you might expect: reduced energy coupled with symptoms of physical strain such as frequent headaches, nausea, poor sleep, and loss of appetite. Emotional exhaustion involves feelings of depression, helplessness, and being trapped in one's job. Finally, attitudinal exhaustion (often known as *depersonalization*) involves cynical beliefs about others—for instance, the view that they are all incompetent and callous—coupled with negative beliefs about oneself, one's job, one's organization, or even one's entire life. To put it simply, persons experiencing such exhaustion come to view the world around them through dark gray rather than rose-colored glasses. Finally, victims of burnout often report feelings of *low personal accomplishment*; they feel that they haven't accomplished much in the past and won't succeed in the future, either. Figure 7-9 gives an overview of the major components of burnout.

Burnout: Some major causes. What are the causes of burnout? As we have already noted, the primary factor seems to be prolonged exposure to stress. However, other variables also play a role. A number of conditions within an organization plus several personal characteristics seem to determine whether and to what degree individuals experience burnout.[81] For example, job conditions suggesting that one's efforts are useless, ineffective, or unappreciated seem to contribute to burnout.[82] Under such conditions, individuals develop the feelings of low personal accomplishment that are an important part of burnout. Similarly, poor opportunities for promotion and the presence of inflexible rules and procedures lead employees to feel that they are trapped in an unfair system and contribute to the development of

■ Figure 7-9
■ Figure 7-9
Burnout: Its Major Components
When people are exposed to high levels of stress over prolonged periods of time, they may experience burnout. This syndrome involves physical, mental, and attitudinal exhaustion, plus feelings of low personal accomplishment.

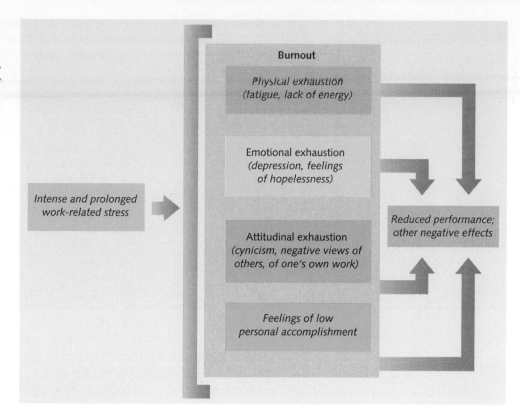

negative views about their jobs.[83] Another important factor is the *leadership style* used by employees' supervisors. The lower the amount of consideration demonstrated by their supervisors (i.e., the less they are concerned with employees' welfare or with maintaining good relations with them), the higher employees' reported levels of burnout.[84] (We'll discuss various styles of leadership in Chapter 13.)

Burnout: Can it be reversed? Before concluding, we should comment briefly on one final question: Can burnout be reversed? Fortunately, growing evidence suggests that it can. With appropriate help, victims of burnout can recover from their physical and psychological exhaustion. If ongoing stress is reduced, if burnout victims gain added support from friends and co-workers, and if they cultivate hobbies and other outside interests, at least some people can escape form the dead-end trap of burnout. Such results can be attained, however, only through active efforts designed to overcome burnout and to change the conditions that produce it.

Stress and Health: The Silent Killer

How strong is the link between stress and personal health? According to medical experts, very strong indeed. In fact, some authorities estimate that stress plays a role in anywhere from 50 to 70 percent of all forms of physical illness.[85] Moreover, included in these figures are some of the most serious and life-threatening ailments known to medical science: heart disease and stroke, ulcers, headaches, diabetes, cancer.

In addition to its role in such *degenerative diseases*, growing evidence indicates that stress may also play a key role in *infectious diseases*—diseases that are caused by infectious agents such as bacteria or viruses. Many studies indicate that exposure to high levels of stress increase susceptibility to diseases such as upper respiratory infections, herpes virus infections, and various bacterial infections.[86] So, in sum, it often exerts powerful, adverse effects on personal health.

The traits described here have been found to influence the extent to which individuals are susceptible to the harmful effects of stress.

Personal Characteristic	Description; Effects
Type A Behavior Pattern	Always in a hurry; highly competitive, irritable. Highly susceptible to the adverse effects of stress.
Optimism	Hopeful outlook on life; see situations in a positive light; expect favorable outcomes. These traits lead to problem-focused coping which helps such people deal with stress.
Hardiness	High levels of commitment to their jobs; believe they can control their outcomes; see stress as challenge. Together these traits make them resistant to the adverse effects of stress.
Tension Discharge Rate	Persons high in this trait dissipate job-related tension quickly at the end of the day. This reduces the harmful effects of such stress on them.

SOURCE: Based on a review of pertinent literature by R. A. Baron.

We examined the nature of the Type A behavior patterns, and its effects on several forms of organizational behavior, in Chapter 4.

Individual differences in resistance to stress. Earlier, we noted that while most people are adversely affected by stress, some seem to thrive on such conditions. Here, we want to expand on that point by noting that several personal characteristics seem to play a role in such differences. In other words, to the extent individuals possess certain traits, they may be more—or less—susceptible to the potentially harmful effects of stress. We've already mentioned one of these: the Type A behavior pattern. While Type A people seem to seek out high levels of stress—for instance, by taking on several jobs at once—this behavior is somewhat self-destructive: Many studies indicate that Type A persons are more susceptible to the harmful effects of stress than Type B persons.[87,88]

Other personal characteristics, too, have been found to influence the impact of stress on personal health; several of these are summarized in Table 7-5. As you can see, to the extent individuals possess these traits, they appear to be "buffered" or protected against the harmful effects of stress. Thus, these traits appear to be adaptive from this important perspective.

Managing Stress: Some Effective Techniques

Stress itself may be unavoidable, but this doesn't mean that its harmful effects, too, are inescapable. In fact, there are many steps both individuals and organizations can take to minimize the adverse impact of stress. Let's take a closer look at several of these.

Personal Approaches to Stress Management

What can you do as an individual to protect yourself from the serious consequences of stress? Four major strategies appear to be most useful.

Lifestyle management: The effect of diet and exercise. More than sixteen years ago, one of us encountered the harmful effects of stress in a dramatic way. He was serving as a Program Director at the National Science Foundation at a time when large budget cuts were being implemented (Ronald Reagan had just become president). The result: He had to tell many scientists whose research had been funded by grants for many years that this was the end of the line. The stress induced by this repeated experience soon showed up in physical symptoms: fatigue and increased blood pressure. The solution?

Baron took up running and, soon, was feeling better than ever. This personal experience underscores the value of exercise as a powerful defense against stress—a conclusion that is supported by many research studies. Getting into good physical shape is one of the best things you can do to increase your resistance to stress.[89]

Good diet, too, is an integral part of such efforts. As the old saying goes "We are what we eat," and if you eat wisely—and avoid gaining weight—the benefits where stress resistance is concerned are obvious.

Physiological techniques: Relaxation and meditation. When you think of successful executives at work, what picture comes to mind? Someone trying to speak on three phones at once while reading a report and speaking to a visitor? That's close to the common conception of how such people live. Definitely *not* part of this image is someone resting calmly in a serene setting. Yet, for a growing number of today's employees, this picture is quite common. At Symmetric (a Lexington, Massachusetts software developer), for example, many of the company's 125 employees spend as long as 20 minutes a day behind closed office doors quietly meditating.[90] Their company doesn't merely tolerate this practice: It encourages it and has even paid consultants to teach employees how to relax in this manner. Many other organizations, too, have adopted this practice: Marriott, Polaroid, the The Boston Co. (an investment firm), to name a few.

What's going on in these companies is an effort to help become more productive by providing them with techniques for coping more effectively with stress. One such technique is known as **meditation**, a process in which people learn to clear their minds of external thoughts, often by repeating a single syllable over and over again. Meditation requires sitting quietly in a comfortable position, closing your eyes, relaxing your muscles, and breathing slowly. The trick is to keep other thoughts that would break your restful state from entering your mind. Doing this once or twice a day for 10–20 minutes per session is believed to be an effective way of reducing stress and increasing one's capacity to work and to enjoy life generally.[91]

A related technique is **relaxation training.** In this method, people learn how first to tense and then to relax their muscles.[92] By becoming familiar with the differences between these states, people become able to induce relaxation whenever they feel themselves becoming too tense. (An exercise explaining how to apply this techniques is included at the end of this chapter.)

Cognitive techniques: Thinking yourself out of stress. Do you worry too much? Surveys indicate that almost 90 percent of all people answer "Yes."[93] Moreover, many realize that they worry about issues that are either unimportant, outside their control, or both. Clearly, worrying about such matters is a waste of cognitive effort and can contribute to increased stress. By reducing such worrying, many persons can help reduce the stress they experience.

Excessive worrying is not the only thing we do that contributes to our own stress, however. Often, we engage in what have been termed *awfulizing* or *castastrophizing*—patterns of thought in which we magnify the effects of failure, not being perfect, or being rejected by others. Such thinking, too, often adds to our level of stress. Reducing such irrational and self-defeating cognitions, therefore, can be another useful step in combating stress. Clearly, Sergio Zyman, the top executive discussed in our chapter PREVIEW CASE did not fall prey to such thinking; on the contrary, he took crushing failure in stride—and so bounced back without experiencing the devastating effects that such stress could potentially produce.

Perhaps the guiding principle in all cognitive techniques for managing stress is this: We must realize that we can't always change the world around us, but we can change our reactions to it. In other words, we don't have to permit ourselves to worry excessively about things we can't change, strive for

meditation A technique for inducing relaxation in which individuals clear disturbing thoughts from their minds by repeating a single syllable.

relaxation training Procedures through which individuals learn to relax in order to reduce anxiety or stress.

absolute perfection, or allow irritating but minor situations to drive us up the wall. Instead, we can actively decide to avoid such reactions and in this manner, reduce our own stress.

Organization-Based Strategies for Managing Stress

Can organizations, too, take steps to reduce the level of stress experienced by their employees? Absolutely. (See the ETHICS ANGLE section for a concrete example.) Several organization-based or organization-initiated tactics can be highly effective in this regard.

Family-supportive practices: Helping to reduce the stress of work-family conflicts. As we noted earlier, the task of juggling work and family obligations is an important source of stress for many persons at the present time. Given this basic fact, it seems reasonable to suggest that organizational policies designed to help lessen such role conflict might also be effective in reducing stress and *strain*—the negative effects resulting from it. Growing evidence indicates that this is, indeed, the case. For example, in a recent study on this issue, Thomas and Ganster asked nurses and nursing supervisors to complete a questionnaire designed to measure the extent to which their organizations had adopted policies designed to reduce work-family conflict (*family-supportive policies*), the amount of work-family conflict they experienced, and psychological, physiological, and behavioral signs of strain.[94] The questionnaire also included a measure of perceived control over work and family life because Thomas and Ganster hypothesized that family-supportive practices would reduce work-family conflict directly, and also through increased feelings of personal control (see Figure 7-10). Among the **family-supportive policies** investigated were information and referral services (e.g., referrals for child care, written materials on parenting), dependent services (e.g. on-site day care, on-site care for sick children), flexible work schedules, and supervisor support (e.g., switching schedules to accommodate family responsibilities).

Results indicated that several family-supportive policies did indeed have beneficial effects. Specifically, policies such as flexible scheduling and supportive supervisor behaviors increased feelings of personal control, reduced work-family conflict, and so reduced several aspects of strain—for example, depression, health complaints, and even blood cholesterol levels. In short, it appeared that when organizations adopted policies designed to reduce the degree of work-family conflict their employees experienced, the stress they experi-

family-supportive policies
Policies adopted by an organization that help reduce the conflict between family and work obligations.

THE ETHICS ANGLE

FEAR AS A MANAGEMENT TOOL

When Ricardo Semler took over his family's manufacturing business in Brazil, *fear* was the dominant management system in place. Armed guards patrolled the factory floor, frisked workers as they left the plant, and timed their trips to the bathroom.[95] If an employee broke a piece of equipment, they had to replace it out of their wages. At first Semler went along with this philosophy of "management-through-intimidation," but when he collapsed in exhaustion, and was told by the physician that he was the most "stressed-out" 25-year-old the doctor had ever seen, he decided on major change. Fear was replaced by freedom, as employees were given the right to run their own jobs—and the company. They could wear what they wanted, come and go as they chose, and even set their own salaries. The only hitch: They had to reapply for their jobs every six months. Results have been favorable: Sales and earnings are up. But not everyone agrees with this new approach. Decision making tends to be chaotic, and it's not clear how long-term strategy will be set. But many employees certainly think that their new freedom is far better than their old fear.

Family-Supportive Policies: An Effective Means of Reducing Stress
Several family-supportive policies (e.g., flexible scheduling, supportive supervisor behaviors) increase feelings of personal control among employees and serve to reduce work-family conflict. These effects, in turn, tend to reduce several aspects of strain—for example, depression, health complaints, and even blood cholesterol levels.

(**Source:** Based on data reported by Thomas & Ganster, 1995; see Note 58.)

enced was decreased. Since the adverse effects of stress (i.e., strain) have been found to exert negative effects on employee performance, such policies appear to benefit organizations as well as individual employees.

stress management programs Systematic efforts by organizations designed to help employees reduce and/or prevent stress.

Stress management programs. Another step organizations can take to help their employees manage stress is **stress management programs**.[96] These involve extensive in-house training that concentrates on many of the techniques described earlier (e.g., meditation, relaxation, lifestyle management), as well as others. For example, the Equitable Life Insurance company's "Emotional Health Program" offers a program in stress management to its employees that relies mostly on the physiological techniques described above. Company officials estimate that each $33 it spends on employees helps relieve symptoms that would have cost the company $100 in lost productivity.[97] Because many companies cannot afford to create their own stress management programs, they often rely on prepackaged programs provided by outside consultants, or on off-the-shelf audiovisual programs on videocassettes.

employee assistance programs (EAPs) Plans that provide employees with assistance in meeting various problems (e.g., substance abuse, career planning, financial and legal problems).

Companies that do not use stress management programs have other systematic ways of helping their employees. Many provide help through their **employee assistant programs (EAPs)**—plans that provide employees with assistance in meeting various problems (e.g., substance abuse, career planning, financial and legal problems). The Metropolitan Life Insurance Company (MetLife) is one company whose EAP has been actively involved in helping its employees reduce stress.[98] It reaches out to its 42,000 U.S. employees by providing toll-free telephone consultation for those in need of help, as well as access to on-site and external medical and psychological professionals. Although few EAPs are as extensive as MetLife's, the cost-effective nature of such programs is making them an increasingly common form of worker benefit in today's organizations.

SUMMARY AND REVIEW

Organizational Socialization

The process through which newcomers learn the ropes in their organizations and become full-fledged members is known as **organizational socialization**. This process involves three distinct stages: *getting in, breaking in,* and *settling in.* **Realistic job previews** during the recruitment of newcomers help them avoid unrealistically optimistic or pessimistic expectations, and so **entry shock**. Organizations often expose newcomers to formal *socialization programs;* however, newcomers themselves play an active role in the socialization process through their *information-search* activities.

Mentoring

A one-on-one form of socialization known as **mentoring** occurs when an experienced employee (a **mentor**) advises, counsels, and aids the personal development of a new employee (a **protégé**). Mentors not only pave the way for their protégé's job success; they also provide a source of emotional support to them. Mentoring relationships benefit both parties. Typically, the mentoring relationships move through four phases: *initiation, cultivation, separation,* and *redefinition.* Because of their personal characteristics—for example, being high in self-monitoring or need for achievement—some persons are more successful in obtaining mentors than others.

Research has shown that because individuals are generally more comfortable interacting with persons who are similar to themselves, females and members of various minorities often have less opportunities to obtain a mentor than other persons. For this reason, it is important for organizations to take active steps to reduce such barriers and increase mentoring for women and minorities.

Careers

A **career** is the evolving sequence of a person's work experiences over time. Common conceptions of what careers will—or should be—like have altered greatly in recent years, partly as a result of equally sweeping changes in the business world. When people make vocational decisions, they often consider the extent to which their values and attitudes match those of a perspective organization—*person-job fit.* Careers now rarely involve movement through a series of steps up the corporate ladder. On the contrary, they more frequently include lateral moves, rotation through several different jobs, geographic relocations, and—increasingly—periods of time spent as an independent contractor or subcontractor rather than as a regular, full-time employee.

Because individuals can no longer count on job security, most experts on careers agree that they should focus on using each job or assignment as a means for acquiring valuable skills. In short, they should view their careers as a series of opportunities for gaining new proficiencies that will increase their value on the job market. Individuals can fill four distinct roles in today's organizations: planners of *corporate strategy, project managers, resource providers,* who provide the financial and human resources needed by project managers, and *talents,* persons who offer specific technical skills and knowledge. **Job rotation**, lateral transfers of employees between jobs in an organizations, is often beneficial for those who experience it. Individuals can tell their careers are in trouble when they feel that they are not acquiring new skills, would not be able to get their job if it were open, are uncertain about what they are contributing, and are worried about their job.

Large Japanese companies often offer their employees *lifetime employment.* These organizations have adopted this policy because it offers important benefits—for example, rapid acceptance of new technology by employees and retention of employees who have been trained by the company. However, employees who become "free riders" are not retained; rather, they are shunted into dead-end assignments, or asked to retire early.

Although the careers of women and men appear to be affected by many of the same factors, some of these operate differently for the two genders. For example, while men's careers are often facilitated by marriage and children, women's careers are sometimes impaired by these factors—apparently, because women still take most of the responsibility for household management and child rearing. Women often receive fewer developmental experiences at work, and this can adversely affect their careers. The **glass ceiling** appears to be real—few women are promoted to very high level jobs. However, it does not to stem from conscious efforts to block females' advancement; rather, it may derive from more subtle factors such as belief in the glass ceiling, which keeps many women from applying for high-level jobs. Recently, many women who entered the job market in the early 1970s have reported experiencing **midlife crises**, which cause them to give up their successful careers and seek other, often less hectic, lifestyles.

The Basic Nature of Stress

Stress refers to a complex pattern of emotional states, physiological reactions, and related thoughts occurring in response to external demands (**stressors**). In contrast, **strain** refers to the effects of stress, primarily to deviations from normal states or performance resulting from exposure to stressful events.

Major Causes of Stress

Stress stems from both *work-related* causes and factors outside work. One of the most important work-related causes of stress involves **role conflict** resulting from the competing demands of work and family obligations. Other important work-related causes of stress include occupational demands, **role ambiguity, overload** and **underload**, responsibility for others, lack of social support, and **sexual harassment**. Causes of stress outside work include traumatic life events and the **daily hassles** of everyday life.

Effects of Stress

Stress adversely influences task performance, even at relatively low levels. In addition, it exerts harmful effects on psychological well-being. Prolonged exposure to stress can lead to **burnout**, a syndrome consisting of physical, emotional, and mental exhaustion, plus intense feelings of low personal accomplishment.

Stress also exerts harmful effects on health. It has been linked to various *degenerative diseases* such as heart disease, high blood pressure, ulcers, and diabetes, and to *infectious diseases* as well. Some persons are more resistant to the adverse effects than others. Type B's, for instance, are more resistant to stress than Type A's.

Managing Stress

Techniques for managing stress exist at both the personal and organizational level. Personal techniques include *lifestyle management,* such as good diet and exercise, *physiological techniques,* such as meditation and relaxation, and *cognitive techniques,* which involve changes in the way individuals think about stress and the situations that produce it.

Organization-based tactics for managing stress include the adoption of **family-supportive policies**, such as flexible work schedules and provision of day care for children, and **stress-management programs**, designed to teach employees various techniques for managing stress. **Employee assistance programs**, which assist employees in dealing with important problems (e.g., substance abuse, career planning, financial and legal problems), are yet another organization-based strategy for managing stress.

QUESTIONS FOR DISCUSSION

1. What concrete steps can organizations take with respect to new hires to assure that they do not experience *entry shock* upon joining the company?
2. How could you go about increasing the availability of mentors to women and minorities?
3. What are the potential benefits of job rotation? Are there any potential drawbacks to such experience?
4. Do you think it's true that women have more choice with respect to changing their careers at midlife than men? If so, why? If not, why?
5. Why are fewer and fewer graduates of MBA programs choosing to work for large corporations? Do you think their reluctance to accept such jobs is justified?
6. Why are the cognitive appraisals that individuals have about a given situation so important in determining the level of stress they experience in it?
7. Suppose that a female manager made several comments about the physique of a male subordinate: Would this constitute sexual harassment? Why?
8. Suppose you were faced with the task of choosing employees for a high-stress job. What personal characteristics would you seek in these individuals? What characteristics would you try to avoid?
9. What policies can organizations adopt to reduce stress among their employees resulting from family-work conflicts?
10. What steps can individuals take to effectively manage the stress to which they are exposed?

CASE IN POINT

Toyota, The Child Care Expert?

Conflict between family and work responsibilities is a major cause of stress in today's workplace. When such conflict is magnified by round-the-clock production schedules, however, the problem can quickly get out of hand. How would you like to have a couple of young children at home and find it necessary to work the "graveyard shift?" This is the situation faced by many employees in today's world of 24-hour manufacturing. One company, Toyota Motors, recognizes this problem for what it is: a major cause of employee stress that can strongly interfere with their performance.

To help employees cope with such problems, Toyota Motors runs a child-care center in its Georgetown, Kentucky, assembly plant. There, parents of employees working on night shifts, can deposit their children and know that they'll be safe—and busy. To help get the youngsters on the same biological clock as their parents, employees of the child-care center help their charges fight sleep by helping them to bake cookies, play musical instruments, and engage in vigorous physical play. The goal is keeping the kids up until midnight, when they bed-down for a two-hour nap. When their parents end their shift, at 2:00 A.M., they can pick up their children and spend some time with them. If, instead, the children remained at home and went to sleep early in the evening, they'd never even see their parents, who will be soundly sleeping themselves the next morning. As one parent puts it: "I don't get to read him bedtime stories, and that's hard. But we do get to spend some of the day together now, and that's a big help."

Critical Thinking Questions

1. Do you think that running this subsidized child-care center is "good business" for Toyota? In other words, do the savings in terms of increased employee productivity justify the costs?
2. What about the children's health: Are the benefits of spending some time with their parents great enough to offset the costs of putting young children on a late-night schedule?
3. How else could Toyota help employees to handle this problem?
4. Should Toyota consider the possibility of hiring for its night shifts, only employees without young children? Would this be legal? Ethical?

Experiencing Organizational Behavior

Developing a Personal Career Plan

One of the most important things people can do to fulfill their career goals is to develop a career plan. Overall, there are five steps in this process, the first three of which you can do right now. The final two will have to wait until you're already on the job.

Directions

To complete each of the first three steps in the career-planning process, ask yourself the questions listed below and record your answers. To come up with the most accurate assessment, try to answer the questions as honestly as possible.

Step 1: Personal Assessment
    a. What special skills and aptitudes can you bring to your job?
    b. What are your most serious weaknesses and limitations? (Really try to be honest on this one.
    c. What types of jobs do you like to do?
    d. To what extent do the jobs you've identified in step *c* require the skills identified in step *a*? And to what extent might they suffer from the limitations identified in step 2?

Step 2: Opportunities Analysis
    a. How has the economy affected various job prospects?
    b. Is there an overabundance or a shortage of people to fill various jobs you might consider?

Step 3: Career Objectives
    a. What are your long-term goals? (5–10 years)?
    b. What are your intermediate goals (3–5 years)?
    c. What are your short-term goals (1–3 years)?

Step 4: Implement Plan

Step 5: Revise Plan as Necessary

(Select a position. Then, after working on it, monitor your progress, solicit feedback, compare the results to your objectives, and revise your plan as needed. Remember: The key to successful career management is *not* necessarily obtaining promotions. Rather it is building your skills base so that you will be a desirable employee for many different companies.)

Working in Groups

The Worry Exercise

Everyone worries, but the trick is to worry *constructively*, not *destructively*. This exercise will help you to move toward this goal, while gaining insight into what other people aside from yourself worry about.

Directions

1. First, all members of the class list the things they worry about. This list of current worries should include as many issues and problems as possible—everything that each person is worrying about at the present time.
2. Next, the class is divided into groups, and each group does the following:
    (a) First, each person, in turn, presents one of her/his worries.
    (b) The group then decides where each of these worries fits in the chart below.

	Important	**Unimportant**
Can Be Controlled		
Can't Be Controlled		

3. After this activity is completed, each group reports on its findings.

Questions for Discussion

1. Did members of the class admit to worrying about issues and problems they could not control and which were unimportant?
2. Why do people worry about such matters?
3. Does worrying about them make any sense? Can it produce harmful effects?
4. How can people who worry about things they can't control and that are unimportant stop doing so?

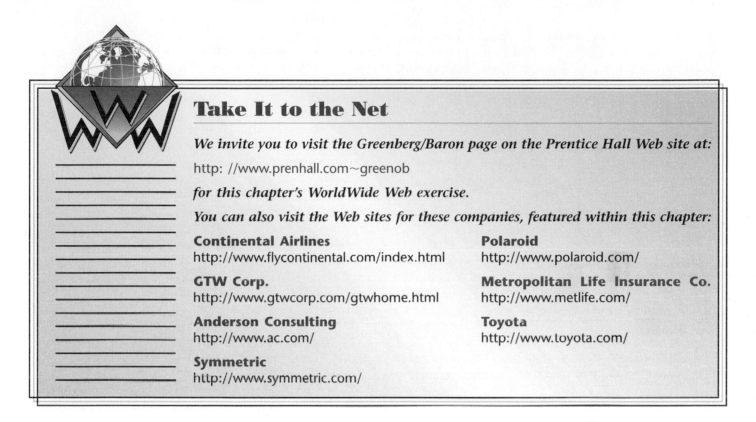

Take It to the Net

We invite you to visit the Greenberg/Baron page on the Prentice Hall Web site at:

http: //www.prenhall.com~greenob

for this chapter's WorldWide Web exercise.

You can also visit the Web sites for these companies, featured within this chapter:

Continental Airlines
http://www.flycontinental.com/index.html

Polaroid
http://www.polaroid.com/

GTW Corp.
http://www.gtwcorp.com/gtwhome.html

Metropolitan Life Insurance Co.
http://www.metlife.com/

Anderson Consulting
http://www.ac.com/

Toyota
http://www.toyota.com/

Symmetric
http://www.symmetric.com/

A recent study by the Families and Work Institute found that 87 percent of the American work-force has some family responsibility which could interfere with a job. For many working men, the traditional attitude of "the job comes first" is giving way to "my family comes first." While working women have struggled for years to balance the demands of career and family, some men who find themselves on the so-called "daddy track" are demanding—and receiving—shorter work weeks, more time off to spend with sick children, and less time on the road. Such assertiveness by men in the 1990s is one reason why the American workplace is becoming more family-friendly.

Still, for some men, the "daddy track" can slow down career advancement. According to one study of working men and women with MBAs, men in dual-career families earned $23,000 less annually than men whose wives were homemakers. The researchers believe that lower salaries are correlated to the extent to which the men shared such household responsibilities as picking up kids after school. Another study found that men whose wives worked received raises 20 percent below those of colleagues. One possible explanation was upper management's perception—conscious or unconscious—that men who are the sole breadwinners for their families deserve bigger raises. Another interesting statistic released by the Pacific Research Institute for Public Policy shows that among childless women and men between the ages of 27 and 33, women earn close to 98 percent of men's salaries.

Besides finding themselves on a slower advancement track, some family-oriented men may even find that their careers are in jeopardy. Consider the case of Jeff Coulter, who worked 50 hour weeks as a member of Microsoft's sales staff, often coming in early but generally leaving by 5:00 or 5:30 P.M. At one point, he was told that "it's a disadvantage to have any priority other than work." Coulter was eventually fired; and has since sued Microsoft on the grounds that he was discriminated against for his marital status.

Conversely, employees without obligations to young families often resent the liberties or special treatment now enjoyed by some male colleagues. In some instances, the grumbling is from employees whose children were born before organizations offered paternity leaves. Co-workers without families often resent putting in 12-hour days: while others leave at 5:00 P.M. Some women also complain of a double standard: When women take time away from work because of family obligations, they often feel that they have to make up excuses or else run the risk of co-worker disapproval. Family-oriented men, on the other hand, are viewed as being "90s-style dads." Complains one female lawyer with two young sons: "When a man brings a child to work or shows up late because he has to take a kid to the doctor, it is totally acceptable." As one marketing executive explained, "It's *au courant* and fashionable for a guy to walk into a meeting late and say, 'I'm sorry, I had a problem with my kid.'"

Video Source: The joys and risks of the "Daddy track." (1991, August 14). *Nightline*. *Additional Sources*: Lublin, J. S. (1995, July 13). Yea to that '90s Dad, devoted to the kids . . . but he's out again? *Wall Street Journal*, pp. A1, A11; Platz, D. (1995, March). Supporting employees who are parents: A worksite child-rearing program. *Business Horizons*, *38*(2), 81–82; Working life: Work versus family. (1995, July). *Training & Development*, pp. 71–72; Michaels, B. (1995, April). *Personnel Journal*, pp. 85–93.

CHAPTER | **Eight**

GROUP DYNAMICS AND TEAMWORK

■ OBJECTIVES

LEARNING

After reading this chapter you should be able to:

1. Define what is meant by a *group*, and explain why it is not just a collection of people.
2. Identify different types of groups operating within organizations and understand how they develop.
3. Describe the importance of *norms*, *roles*, *status*, and *cohesiveness* within organizations.
4. Explain how individual performance in groups is affected by the presence of others (*social facilitation*), the cultural diversity of group membership, and the number of others with whom one is working (*social loafing*).

5. Define what *teams* are and how they may be distinguished from groups in general.
6. Describe the various types of teams that exist in organizations and the steps that should be followed in creating them.
7. Understand the evidence regarding the effectiveness of teams in organizations.
8. Explain the factors responsible for the failure of some teams to operate as effectively as possible.
9. Identify things that can be done to build high-performance teams.

TEAMING UP FOR A TURNAROUND AT PUBLISHED IMAGE

None of the neighboring businesses felt anything that August day in 1993 when Eric Gershman "blew up" Published Image, the company he founded only five years earlier. Although no blast occurred, tremors rippled throughout this small but growing Boston concern of which Gershman was president. The impact was felt by all 26 of its employees and its clients, mutual fund companies for which it publishes newsletters to shareholders. The only casualty was the company's old way of operating—a very rigid, bureaucratic approach that led it to the brink of failure in 1991.

What was destroyed that day was a company that suffered from a 50 percent annual turnover rate and that was making so many factual errors in its publications that it was losing a third of its clients each year. Clearly, something had to change while there was anything left to salvage. So, on that fateful summer day, called "The United Day" within the company, Gershman completely reorganized the way employees of Published Image went about doing their jobs.

Out was a highly departmentalized approach in which employees did only those narrow tasks defined as their jobs, and sought only to please their bosses. In was a team approach in which sales, editorial, and production specialists worked together to do whatever was needed to satisfy clients. Although employees of Published Image still specialize in their own areas of expertise, they now approach their jobs more broadly, pitching in wherever needed to meet schedules. On any given day, for example, account executive Shelley Danse may be found doing research for writers, proofreading copy, and even helping lay out art. In short, she does whatever it takes to get the project done well and out on time. Under the old system she would have spent all her time bringing in new business, even if the company couldn't handle it all. Today, however, her teammates are involved in the sales processes from the very beginning, and work is much less likely to get backed up. The result is a much more efficient operation.

Things turned around at Published Image almost immediately after the 1993 overhaul. Annual revenue doubled to $4 million, and profit margins jumped from 3 percent to 20 percent. Turnover has been almost eliminated, and the client base is no longer eroding. Clients, like Fleet Financial Group, which used to complain about the factual errors in its four newsletters, now find little to gripe about. Fleet's vice president, Peter Herhily, welcomes the fact that he now can call on any of the team members who prepare the newsletters for his company to discuss anything he has on his mind. And, they are only too glad to oblige. Not only are they spurred by pride but financial reward as well. Teams scoring high on measures of timeliness and accuracy are rewarded with bonuses that can run as high as 15 percent of an employee's base pay.

Now that Published Image is run by autonomous teams, Gershman spends most of his time giving advice and none of his time giving orders. The better those teams have become, the less he is called upon for help. In fact, he hopes to soon be so successful that the company will run without him. And, if things continue to progress as they have, Mr. Gershman just might fulfill the wish of unemployment that he has worked so hard to achieve.

The turnaround at Published Image is certainly quite impressive, and the practice of relying on teams of people working in concert seems to be the key. Its employees share a strong concern for the company, and everyone wants to help satisfy its customers. The team members also appear to have a strong camaraderie, doing whatever it takes to get the job done well. What is it that makes groups of employees like those at Published Image so successful? Are all such work teams effective, or is this case unusual? How should such groups be formed? What problems might be expected and how can they be overcome? These questions are all basic to the topics of *group dynamics* and *teamwork*, the two major foci of this chapter.

Group dynamics focuses on the nature of groups—the variables governing their formation and development, their structure, and their interrelationships with individuals, other groups, and the organizations within which they exist.[1] **Teamwork** refers to the practice of using teams, special kinds of groups in which members are mutually committed to some goal, and share the leadership toward attaining it. Given the prevalence of groups in organizations, and the growing popularity of teams, the importance of these topics in the field of organizational behavior is easy to appreciate.

Because groups exist in all types of social settings, the study of group dynamics has a long history in the social sciences—including OB.[2] In this chapter we will draw upon this work. Specifically, we will describe the nature of groups by defining what groups are, identifying various types of groups and why they form, explaining the various stages through which groups develop, and describing the dynamics of the way groups are structured. Following this, we will shift our attention to how effectively groups operate. Specifically, we will describe how people are affected by the presence of others, how the cultural makeup of a group affects performance, and the tendency for people to withhold their individual performance under certain conditions. Then, in the second half of the chapter we will describe special kinds of groups known as *teams*. Specifically, we will define teams and distinguish them from groups, describe various types of teams that exist, and identify some basic steps in creating teams. Finally, we will describe the performance of teams, examining the evidence regarding team effectiveness, the obstacles that sometimes lead teams to fail, and tips for making teams reach high levels of performance.

Groups at Work: Their Basic Nature

To understand the dynamics of groups and their influence on individual and organizational functioning, we must begin by raising some basic questions—namely, what is a group, what types of groups exist, why do people join groups, how do groups come into being, and how are groups structured? We will now address these questions.

What Is a Group? A Working Definition

Imagine three people waiting in line at the cashier's stand at a supermarket. Now compare them to the board of directors of a large corporation. Which collection would you consider to be a "group"? Although in our everyday language we may refer to the people waiting in line as a group, they are not a group in the same sense as the members of the board. Obviously, a group is more than simply a collection of people. But, what exactly is it that makes a group a group? Social scientists have formally defined a **group** as a collection of two or more interacting individuals with a stable pattern of relationships between them who share common goals and who perceive themselves as being a group.[3] To help us examine this definition more closely, we summarize the four key characteristics of groups in Figure 8-1.

One of the most obvious characteristics of groups is that they are composed of *two or more people in social interaction*. In other words, the members of a group must have some influence on each other. The interaction between the parties may be either verbal (such as sharing strategies for a corporate takeover) or nonverbal (such as exchanging smiles in the hallway), but the parties must have some impact on each other to be considered a group.

Groups also must possess a *stable structure*. Although groups can change, and often do, there must be some stable relationships that keep group members together and functioning as a unit. A collection of individuals that will

*To be a group, four different criteria
must be met: there must be two or
more people in social interaction, they
must also share common goals, have a
stable group structure, and perceive
themselves as being a group.*

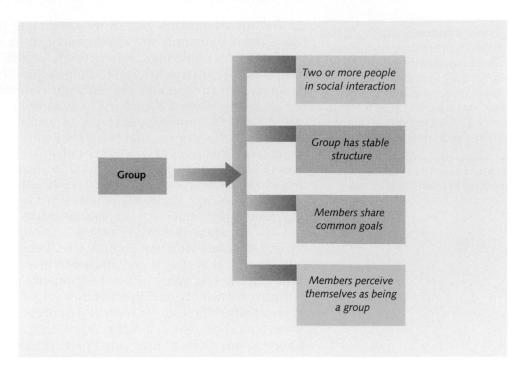

stantly changes (e.g., the people inside an office waiting room at any given time) cannot be thought of as a group. To be a group, a greater level of stability would be required.

A third characteristic of groups is that their *members share common interests or goals*. For example, members of a stamp collecting club constitute a group that is sustained by the mutual interest of members. Some groups form because members with common interests help each other achieve a mutual goal. For example, the owners and employees of a sewing shop constitute a group formed around a common interest in sewing, and the common goal of making money.

Finally, to be a group, the individuals involved must *perceive themselves as a group*. Groups are composed of people who recognize each other as a member of their group and can distinguish these individuals from nonmembers. The members of a corporate finance committee or a chess club, for example, know who is in their group and who is not. In contrast, shoppers in a checkout line probably don't think of each other as being members of a group. Although they stand physically close to each other and may have passing conversations, they have little in common (except, perhaps, a shared interest in reaching the end of the line) and fail to identify themselves with the others in the line.

By defining groups in terms of these four characteristics, we have identified a group as a very special collection of individuals. As we shall see, these characteristics are responsible for the important effects groups have on organizational behavior. To better understand these effects, we will now review the wide variety of groups that operate within organizations.

Types of Groups

What do the following have in common: a military combat unit, three couples getting together for dinner, the board of directors of a large corporation, and the three-person cockpit crew of a commercial airliner? As you probably guessed, the answer is that they are all groups. But, of course, they are very different kinds of groups, ones people join for different reasons.

Formal and Informal groups. The most basic way of identifying types of groups is to distinguish between *formal groups* and *informal groups* (see Figure

formal groups Groups that are created by the organization, intentionally designed to direct its members toward some organizational goal.

8-2). **Formal groups** are created by the organization and are intentionally designed to direct members toward some important organizational goal. One type of formal group is referred to as a *command group*—a group determined by the connections between individuals who are a formal part of the organization (i.e., those who can legitimately give orders to others). For example, a command group may be formed by the vice president of marketing who gathers together her regional marketing directors from around the country to hear their ideas about a new national advertising campaign. The point is that command groups are determined by the organization's rules regarding who reports to whom, and usually consist of a supervisor and his or her subordinates.

A formal organizational group also may be formed around some specific task. Such a group is referred to as a *task group*. Unlike command groups, a task group may be composed of individuals with some special interest or expertise in a specific area regardless of their positions in the organizational hierarchy. For example, a company may have a committee on equal employment opportunities whose members monitor the fair hiring practices of the organization. It may be composed of personnel specialists, corporate vice presidents, and workers from the shop floor. Whether they are permanent committees, known as *standing committees*, or temporary ones formed for special purposes (such as a committee formed to recommend solutions to a parking problem), known as *ad hoc committees* or *task forces*, task groups are common in organizations.

informal groups Groups that develop naturally among people, without any direction from the organization within which they operate.

As you know, not all groups found in organizations are as formal as those we've identified. Many groups are informal in nature. **Informal groups** develop naturally among an organization's personnel without any direction from the management of the organization within which they operate. One key factor in the formation of informal groups is a common interest shared by its members. For example, a group of employees who band together to seek union representation, or who march together to protest their company's pollution of the environment, may be called an *interest group*. The common goal sought by members of an interest group may unite workers at many different organizational levels. The key factor is that membership in an interest group is voluntary—it is not created by the organization, but encouraged by an expression of common interests.

Of course, sometimes the interests that bind individuals together are far more diffuse. Groups may develop out of a common interest in participating in sports, or going to the movies, or just getting together to talk. These kinds of informal groups are known as *friendship groups*. A group of co-workers who hang out together during lunch may also bowl or play cards together after work. Friendship groups extend beyond the workplace because they provide

■ **Figure 8-2**
Varieties of Groups in Organizations
Within organizations one may find formal groups (such as command groups *and* task groups*) and informal groups (such as* interest groups *and* friendship groups*).*

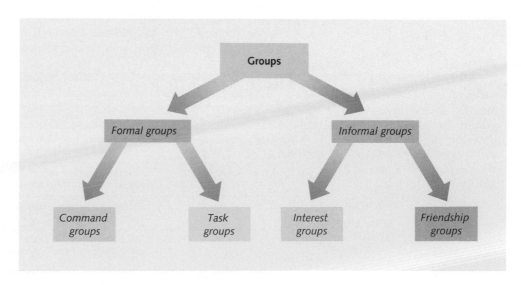

opportunities for satisfying the social needs of workers that are so important to their well-being.

Informal work groups are an important part of life in organizations. Although they develop without direct encouragement from management, friendships often originate out of formal organizational contact. For example, three employees working alongside each other on an assembly line may get to talking and discover their mutual interest in basketball and decide to get together to shoot hoops after work. As we will see, such friendships can bind people together, helping them cooperate with each other, having beneficial effects on organizational functioning.

Why Do People Join Groups?

We have already noted that people often join groups to satisfy their mutual interests and goals. To the extent that getting together with others allows us to achieve ends that would not be possible alone, forming groups makes a great deal of sense. In fact, organizations can be thought of as collections of groups that are focused toward achieving the mutual goal of achieving success for the company. But, this is not the only motivation that people have for joining groups. There are also several additional reasons (see the summary in Table 8-1).

Not only do groups form for purposes of mutually achieving goals, they also frequently form for purposes of seeking protection from other groups. If you've ever heard the phrase, "there's safety in numbers," you are probably already aware that people join groups because they seek the security of group membership. Historically, for example, trade unions, such as the AFL/CIO, the UAW, and the Teamsters, have been formed by labor for purposes of seeking protection against abuses by management. Similarly, professional associations, such as the American Medical Association and the American Bar Association were created, in large part, for purposes of protecting their constituents against undesirable governmental legislation.

This is not to say that groups are always designed to promote some instrumental good; indeed, they also exist because they appeal to a basic psychological need to be social. As we already discussed in the context of Maslow's need hierarchy theory (in Chapter 5), people are social animals; they have a basic need to interact with others. Groups provide good opportunities for friendships to develop—hence, for social needs to be fulfilled.

We discussed the importance of social needs and esteem needs in conjunction with our description of Maslow's need hierarchy theory in Chapter 5.

Also as suggested by Maslow, people have a basic desire for their self-esteem to be fulfilled. Group memberships can be a very effective way of nurturing self-esteem. For example, if a group to which one belongs is successful (such as a sales group that meets its quota), the self-esteem of all members (and supporters) may be boosted. Similarly, election to membership in an exclusive group (e.g., a national honor society) will surely raise one's self-esteem.

As we have shown, people are attracted to groups for many different reasons. Despite the fact that people may have different motives for forming

■ TABLE 8-1	WHY DO PEOPLE JOIN GROUPS? SOME MAJOR REASONS	
People become members of groups for a variety of different reasons. Any one or more of the following may explain why people join groups.	**Reason**	**Explanation**
	■ To satisfy mutual interests and goals	By banding together, people can share their interests (e.g., hobbies) and help meet their mutual goals.
	■ To achieve security	Groups provide safety in numbers, protection against a common enemy.
	■ To fill social needs	Being in groups helps satisfy people's basic need to be with others.
	■ To fill need for self-esteem	Membership in certain groups provides people with opportunities to feel good about their accomplishments.

groups, it is interesting to note that once formed, groups develop in remarkably similar ways. We will now turn our attention to this issue.

Stages in the Development of Groups

Just as infants develop in certain ways during their first months of life, groups also show relatively stable signs of maturation and development.[4] One popular theory identifies five distinct stages through which groups develop.[5] As we describe these below, you may want to review our summary of the five stages shown in Figure 8-3.

The first stage of group development is known as *forming*. During this stage, the members get acquainted with each other. They establish the ground rules by trying to find out what behaviors are acceptable, with respect to both the job (how productive they are expected to be) and interpersonal relations (who's really in charge). During the *forming* stage, people tend to be a bit confused and uncertain about how to act in the group and how beneficial it will be to become a member of the group. Once the individuals come to think of themselves as members of a group, the forming stage is complete.

The second stage of group development is referred to as *storming*. As the name implies, this stage is characterized by a high degree of conflict within the group. Members often resist the control of the group's leaders and show hostility toward each other. If these conflicts are not resolved and group members withdraw, the group may disband. However, as conflicts are resolved and the group's leadership is accepted, the storming stage is complete.

The third stage of group development is known as *norming*. During this stage, the group becomes more cohesive, and identification as a member of the group becomes greater. Close relationships develop, shared feelings become common, and a keen interest in finding mutually agreeable solutions develops. Feelings of camaraderie and shared responsibility for the group's activities are heightened. The norming stage is complete when the members of the group accept a common set of expectations that constitutes an acceptable way of doing things.

The fourth stage is known as *performing*. By this stage, questions about group relationships and leadership have been resolved and the group is ready

■ Figure 8-3
The Five Stages of Group Development
In general, groups develop according to the five stages summarized here.

(**Source:** Based on information in Tuckman & Jensen, 1977; see Note 5.)

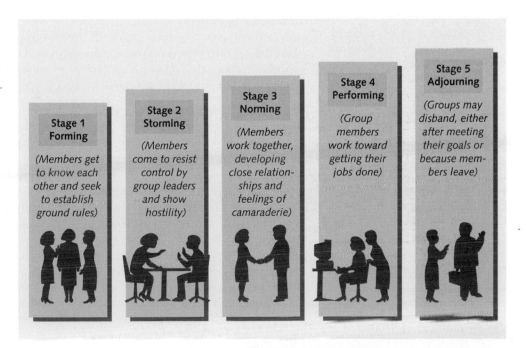

Stage 1
Forming

(Members get to know each other and seek to establish ground rules)

Stage 2
Storming

(Members come to resist control by group leaders and show hostility)

Stage 3
Norming

(Members work together, developing close relationships and feelings of camaraderie)

Stage 4
Performing

(Group members work toward getting their jobs done)

Stage 5
Adjourning

(Groups may disband, either after meeting their goals or because members leave)

to work. Having fully developed, the group may now devote its energy to getting the job done—the group's good relations and acceptance of the leadership helps the group perform well.

Recognizing that not all groups last forever, the final stage is known as *adjourning*. Groups may cease to exist because they have met their goals and are no longer needed (such as an ad hoc group created to raise money for a charity project), in which case the end is abrupt. Other groups may adjourn gradually, as the group disintegrates, either because members leave or because the norms that have developed are no longer effective for the group.

To illustrate these various stages, imagine that you have just joined several of your colleagues on your company's newly created budget committee. At first, you and your associates feel each other out: You watch to see who comes up with the best ideas, whose suggestions are most widely accepted, who seems to take charge, and the like (the forming stage). Then, as members struggle to gain influence over others, you may see a battle over control of the committee (the storming stage). Soon, this will be resolved, and an accepted leader will emerge. At this stage, the group members will become highly cooperative, working together in harmony, and doing things together, such as going out to lunch as a group (the norming stage). Now, it becomes possible for committee members to work together at doing their best, giving it their all (the performing stage). Then, once the budget is created and approved, the group's task is over, and it is disbanded (the adjourning stage).

It is important to keep in mind that groups can be in any one stage of development at any given time. Moreover, the amount of time a group may spend in any given stage is highly variable. In fact, research has revealed that the boundaries between the various stages may not be clearly distinct and that several stages may be combined—especially as deadline pressures force groups to take action.[6] It is best, then, to think of this five-stage model as a general framework of group formation. Although many of the stages may be followed, the dynamic nature of groups makes it unlikely that they will progress through the various stages in a completely predictable order.

The Structure of Work Groups

As noted earlier, one of the key characteristics of a group is its stable structure. When social scientists use the term **group structure**, they are referring to the interrelationships between the individuals constituting a group, the characteristics that make group functioning orderly and predictable. In this section, we will describe four different aspects of group structure: the various parts played by group members (*roles*), the rules and expectations that develop within groups (*norms*), the prestige of group membership (*status*), and the members' sense of belonging (*cohesiveness*).

Roles: The many hats we wear. One of the primary structural elements of groups is members' tendencies to play specific roles in group interaction, often more than one (see Figure 8-4). Social scientists use the term "role" in much the same way as a director of a play would refer to the character who plays a part. Indeed, the part one plays in the overall group structure is what we mean by a role. More formally, we may define a **role** as the typical behaviors that characterize a person in a social context.[7]

In organizations, many roles are assigned by virtue of an individual's position within an organization. For example, a boss may be expected to give orders, and a teacher may be expected to lecture and to give exams. These are behaviors expected of the individual in that role. The person holding the role is known as a **role incumbent**, and the behaviors expected of that person are known as **role expectations**. The person holding the office of the president of the United States (the role incumbent) has certain role expectations simply because he or she currently has that post. When a new president takes

The topics of power and leadership in organizations will be discussed in Chapters 12 and 13, respectively.

group structure The pattern of interrelationships between the individuals constituting a group; the guidelines of group behavior that make group functioning orderly and predictable.

role The typical behavior that characterizes a person in a specific social context.

role incumbent A person holding a particular role.

role expectations The behaviors expected of someone in a particular role.

■ **Figure 8-4**
Playing Roles: Wearing Several Different Hats
The roles people play in organizations represent specific sets of behaviors that characterize their positions. It is not unusual for people to have to play more than one role at a time.

(**Source:** Copyright © 1992 by Henry R. Martin. Reprinted by permission.)

OFFICE CLOWN
RECEPTIONIST
FILE CLERK
ACCOUNTANT
SECRETARY
SECURITY
JANITOR
PRESIDENT

WHEN YOU'RE SELF EMPLOYED YOU WEAR MANY HATS

We will discuss the topic of formal power more extensively in Chapter 12.

role ambiguity Confusion arising from not knowing what one is expected to do as the holder of a role.

role differentiation The tendency for various specialized roles to emerge as groups develop.

office, that person assumes the same role and has the same formal powers as the previous president.

The role incumbent's recognition of the expectations of his or her role helps avoid the social disorganization that surely would result if clear role expectations did not exist. Sometimes, however, workers may be confused about the things that are expected of them on the job, such as their level of authority or their responsibility. Such **role ambiguity**, as it is called, is typically experienced by new members of organizations who have not had much of a chance to "learn the ropes," and often results in job dissatisfaction, a lack of commitment to the organization, and an interest in leaving the job.[8]

As work groups and social groups develop, the various group members come to play different roles in the social structure—a process referred to as **role differentiation**. The emergence of different roles in groups is a naturally occurring process. Think of committees to which you have belonged. Was there someone who joked and made people feel better, and another member who worked hard to get the group to focus on the issue at hand? These examples of differentiated roles are typical of role behaviors that emerge in groups. Organizations, for example, often have their "office comedian" who makes everyone laugh, or the "company gossip" who shares others' secrets, or the "grand old man" who tells newcomers the stories about the company's "good old days."

Group researchers long ago found that one person may emerge who, more than anyone else, helps the group reach its goal.[9] Such a person is said to play the *task-oriented role*. In addition, another group member may emerge who is quite supportive and nurturant, someone who makes everyone else feel good. Such a person is said to *play a socioemotional (or relations-oriented) role*. Still others may be recognized for the things they do for themselves, often at the expense of the group—individuals recognized for playing a *self-oriented role*. Many specific role behaviors can fall into one or another of these categories. Some of these more specific subroles are listed in Table 8-2. Although this simple dis-

Organizational roles may be differentiated into task-oriented, relations-oriented (or socioemotional), and self-oriented roles—each of which has several subroles. A number of these are shown here.

Task-oriented roles	Relations-oriented roles	Self-oriented roles
Initiator-contributors	**Harmonizers**	**Blockers**
Recommend new solutions to group problems	*Mediate group conflicts*	*Act stubborn and resistant to the group*
Information seekers	**Compromisers**	**Recognition seekers**
Attempt to obtain the necessary facts	*Shift own opinions to create group harmony*	*Call attention to their own achievements*
Opinion givers	**Encouragers**	**Dominators**
Share own opinions with others	*Praise and encourage others*	*Assert authority by manipulating the group*
Energizers	**Expediters**	**Avoiders**
Stimulate the group into action whenever interest drops	*Suggest ways the groups can operate more smoothly*	*Maintain distance, isolate themselves from fellow group members*

SOURCE: Based on Benne & Sheats, 1948; see Note 9.

tinction will help us understand some of the roles found in work groups, we should note that more complex conceptualizations have been proposed, including one that identifies as many as 26 different roles.[10] These efforts at understanding role differentiation, regardless of how simple or complex the distinctions may be, help make the point that similarities between groups may be recognized by the common roles members play.

Norms: A group's unspoken rules.   One feature of groups that enhances their orderly functioning is the existence of group norms. **Norms** may be defined as generally agreed upon informal rules that guide group members' behavior.[11] They represent shared ways of viewing the world. Norms differ from organizational rules in that they are not formal and written. In fact, group members may not even be aware of the subtle group norms that exist and regulate their behavior. Yet, they have profound effects on behavior. Norms regulate the behavior of groups in important ways, such as by fostering workers' honesty and loyalty to the company, establishing appropriate ways to dress, and dictating when it is acceptable to be late for or absent from work.

norms Generally agreed on informal rules that guide group members' behavior.

If you recall the pressures placed on you by your peers as you grew up to dress or wear your hair in certain styles, you are well aware of the profound normative pressures exerted by groups. Norms can be either *prescriptive*—dictating the behaviors that should be performed—or *proscriptive*—dictating the behaviors that should be avoided. For example, groups may develop prescriptive norms to follow their leader or to help a group member who needs assistance. They also may develop proscriptive norms to avoid absences or to refrain from telling each other's secrets to the boss. Sometimes the pressure to conform to norms is subtle, as in the dirty looks given a manager by his peers for dressing too casually for the job. Other times, normative pressures may be quite severe, such as when one production worker sabotages another's work because he is performing at too high a level, making his co-workers look bad.

The question of how group norms develop has been of considerable interest to organizational researchers.[12] An insightful analysis of this process has been presented by Feldman (see summary in Table 8-3).[13] First, norms develop because of *precedents set over time*. Whatever behaviors emerge at a first group meeting will usually set the standard for how that group is to operate. Initial group patterns of behavior frequently become normative, such as where people sit and how formal or informal the meeting will be. Such routines help establish a predictable, orderly interaction pattern.

This table summarizes four ways in which group norms can develop.

Basis of Norm Development	Example
1. Precedents set over time	Seating location of each group member around a table
2. Carryovers from other situations	Professional standards of conduct
3. Explicit statements from others	Working a certain way because you are told "that's how we do it around here"
4. Critical events in group history	After the organization suffers a loss due to one person's divulging company secrets, a norm develops to maintain secrecy

SOURCE: Based on Feldman, 1984; see Note 13.

Second, norms develop because of *carryovers from other situations.* Group members usually draw from their previous experiences to guide their behaviors in new situations. The norms governing professional behavior apply here. For example, the norm for a physician to behave ethically and to exercise a pleasant bedside manner is generalizable from one hospital to another. Such carryover norms can assist in making interaction easier in new social situations.

Third, sometimes norms also develop in *response to an explicit statement by a superior or co-worker.* Newcomers to groups quickly "learn the ropes" when someone tells them, "That's the way we do it around here." This explanation is an explicit statement of the norms; it describes what one should do or avoid doing to be accepted by the group. Often, the explicit statement of group norms represents the accepted desires of more powerful or experienced group members.[14]

Fourth and finally, group norms may develop out of *critical events in the group's history.* If an employee releases an important organizational secret to a

The process of organizational socialization, discussed in Chapter 7, examines how people "learn the ropes" in a new organization.

THE ETHICS ANGLE

THE NORM FOR PUNISHING UNETHICAL BEHAVIOR AT IBM

If you're an employee of IBM, even a high-level manager, chances are good that if you get caught violating ethical principles you will not be demoted or transferred, but fired. The norm to take swift and decisive action toward those who break moral rules developed years ago when then-President Thomas J. Watson Jr. learned a hard lesson about the consequences of turning a blind eye to unethical behavior.[15]

On one occasion, some IBM plant managers started a chain letter—a "pyramid" scam in which they sent U.S. savings bonds to five other employees, who would write to five others, who would send bonds back to the sender, and so on. Such schemes generally only benefit the people at the beginning of the chain. One day, after a recipient of one of the letters complained to Watson, he brought it to the attention of the division head. This individual admitted that the managers' actions were improper and ordered them to stop. But, he chose not to

fire the offenders. Watson didn't agree with that decision but decided to let the matter rest.

Unfortunately, this came back to haunt him. Years later in the same division, a low-level employee was fired after he was caught selling engineering diagrams to a competitor. The employee was outraged and did his best to publicly humiliate Watson. Among the things that angered the fired employee was that years earlier the company failed to fire the higher-ranking managers for their improper acts. Although two wrongs might not make a right, the employee was indignant about the apparent dual standard.

After this incident occurred, Watson was quick to overrule division heads who failed to fire those who violated ethical standards. Following Watson's lead, and the lesson he learned from this critical incident, the norm developed at IBM to fire employees at any level who violate ethical standards—a norm that is said to exist to this day.

competitor, causing a loss to the company, a norm to maintain secrecy may develop out of this incident.

Status: The prestige of group membership. Have you ever been attracted to a group because of the prestige accorded its members? You may have wanted to join a certain fraternity or sorority because it is highly regarded by the students. Students hoping to attend a certain university may look forward to wearing that school's insignia on their clothing. No doubt, members of Super Bowl–winning football teams proudly sport their Super Bowl rings to identify themselves as members of a championship team. Clearly, one potential reward of group membership is the status associated with being in that group. Even within social groups, different members are accorded different levels of prestige. Fraternity and sorority officers, and committee chairpersons, for example, may be recognized as more important members of their respective groups. This is the idea behind **status**—the relative social position or rank given to groups or group members by others.[16]

Within most organizations, status may be recognized as both formal and informal in nature. *Formal status* refers to attempts to differentiate between the degrees of formal authority given employees by an organization. This is typically accomplished through the use of **status symbols**—objects reflecting the position of an individual within an organization's hierarchy. Some examples of status symbols include job titles (e.g., Director); perquisites, or perks, (e.g., a reserved parking space); the opportunity to do desirable and highly regarded work (e.g., serving on important committees); and luxurious working conditions (e.g., a large, private office that is lavishly decorated) (see Figure 8-5).[17]

Status symbols help groups in many ways.[18] For one, such symbols remind organizational members of their relative roles, thereby reducing uncertainty and providing stability to the social order (e.g., your small desk reminds you of your lower organizational rank). In addition, they provide assurance of the various rewards available to those who perform at a superior level (e.g., "maybe one day I'll have a reserved parking spot"). They also provide a sense of identification by reminding members of the group's values (e.g., a gang's jacket may remind its wearer of his expected loyalty and boldness). It is, therefore, not surprising that organizations do much to reinforce formal status through the use of status symbols.

Symbols of *informal status* within organizations are also widespread. These refer to the prestige accorded individuals with certain characteristics that are not formally dictated by the organization. For example, employees who are older and more experienced may be perceived as higher in status by their co-

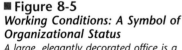

status The relative prestige, social position, or rank given to groups or individuals by others.

status symbols Objects reflecting the position of any individual within an organization's hierarchy of power.

■ **Figure 8-5**
Working Conditions: A Symbol of Organizational Status
A large, elegantly decorated office is a sure symbol of the occupant's high status within the organization.

workers. Those who have special skills (such as the home run hitters on a baseball team) also may be regarded as having higher status than others. In some organizations, the lower value placed on the work of women and members of minority groups by some individuals also can be considered an example of informal status in operation.[19]

One of the best-established findings in the study of group dynamics is that higher-status people tend to be more influential than lower-status people. This phenomenon may be seen in a classic study of decision making in three-man bomber crews.[20] After the crews had difficulty solving a problem, the experimenter planted clues to the solution with either a low-status group member (the tail gunner) or a high-status group member (the pilot). It was found that the solutions offered by the pilots were far more likely to be adopted than the same solutions presented by the tail gunners. Apparently, the greater status accorded the pilots (because they tended to be more experienced and hold higher military ranks) was responsible for the greater influence they wielded. Similar findings have been obtained in analyses of jury deliberations. Research in this area has shown that members of juries having high-status jobs (such as professional people) tend to exert greater influence over their fellow jurors than others holding lower occupational status.[21]

Cohesiveness: Getting the team spirit.

cohesiveness The strength of group members' desires to remain part of their groups.

Cohesiveness: Getting the team spirit. One obvious determinant of any group's structure is its **cohesiveness**—the strength of group members' desires to remain part of their groups. Highly cohesive work groups are ones in which the members are attracted to each other, accept the group's goals, and help work toward meeting them. In very uncohesive groups, the members dislike each other and may even work at cross-purposes.[22] In essence, cohesiveness refers to a "we" feeling, an "esprit de corps," a sense of belonging to a group.

Several important factors have been shown to influence the extent to which group members tend to "stick together." One such factor involves the severity of initiation into the group. Research has shown that the greater the difficulty people overcome to become a member of a group, the more cohesive the group will be.[23] To understand this, consider how highly cohesive certain groups may be that you have worked hard to join. Was it particularly difficult to "make the cut" on your sports team? The rigorous requirements for gaining entry into elite groups, such as the most prestigious medical schools and military training schools, may well be responsible for the high degree of camaraderie found in such groups. Having "passed the test" tends to keep individuals together and separates them from those who are unwilling or unable to "pay the price" of admission.

Group cohesion also tends to be strengthened under conditions of high external threat or competition. When workers face a "common enemy," they tend to draw together. Such cohesion not only makes workers feel safer and better protected, but also aids them by encouraging them to work closely together and to coordinate their efforts toward the common enemy. Under such conditions, petty disagreements that may have caused dissension within groups tend to be put aside so that a coordinated attack on the enemy can be mobilized.

Research also has shown that the cohesiveness of groups is established by several additional factors.[24] For one, cohesiveness generally tends to be greater the more time group members spend together. Obviously, limited interaction cannot help but interfere with opportunities to develop bonds between group members. Similarly, cohesiveness tends to be greater in smaller groups. Generally speaking, groups that are too large make it difficult for members to interact and, therefore, for cohesiveness to reach a high level. Finally, because "nothing succeeds like success," groups with a history of success tend to be highly cohesive. It is often said that "everyone loves a winner," and the success of a group tends to help unite its members as they rally around their success. For this reason, employees tend to be loyal to successful companies.

Although we often hear about the benefits of highly cohesive groups, the consequences of cohesiveness are not always positive. In fact, research has shown both positive and negative effects of cohesiveness (see Figure 8-6). On the positive side, people are known to enjoy belonging to highly cohesive groups. Members of closely knit work groups participate more fully in their group's activities, more readily accept their group's goals, and are absent from their jobs less often than members of less cohesive groups.[25] Not surprisingly, cohesive groups tend to work together quite well and are sometimes exceptionally productive. In fact, research has shown that high levels of group cohesiveness tend to be associated with low levels of voluntary turnover.[26] People's willingness to work together quite well and to conform to the group's norms is often responsible for their success, and their willingness to stay with the group.[27]

However, the tendency for members of highly cohesive groups to go along with their fellow members' wishes sometimes has negative consequences for the ultimate group product. Consider, for example, the actions of the highly cohesive Committee to Re-elect President Nixon preceding the 1972 presidential election. The Watergate conspirators were a highly cohesive group—so cohesive that they were blinded to the possibility that they were committing illegal and unethical acts. Strong pressures within the group to "not rock the boat" may have discouraged members from challenging others' actions that appeared to be wrong. Poor decisions resulting from too high a level of cohesiveness reflect a phenomenon known as *groupthink*.[28] Groupthink occurs when a group is so cohesive that its members potentially lose sight of its ultimate goals for fear of disrupting the group itself.

Group cohesion can influence productivity in many additional ways. It makes sense that after a group experiences success, its members will feel more committed to each other. Similarly, we might expect a cohesive group to work well together and to achieve a high level of success. However, a work group whose members are strongly committed to each other does not necessarily perform well within an organization.[29] For example, if a group's goals are contrary to the organization's goals, a highly cohesive group may actually do a great deal of harm to an organization, working against its interests. Highly cohesive group members who conspire to sabotage their employers are a good example. Apparently, group cohesiveness can have either positive *or* negative effects on performance.

Because of the negative impact of groupthink on the quality of group decisions, we will discuss this phenomenon in greater detail in the context of decision making in Chapter 10.

■ **Figure 8-6**
Group Cohesiveness: Its Causes and Consequences
As summarized here, several factors contribute to a group's cohesiveness. High levels of cohesiveness may have both positive and negative consequences.

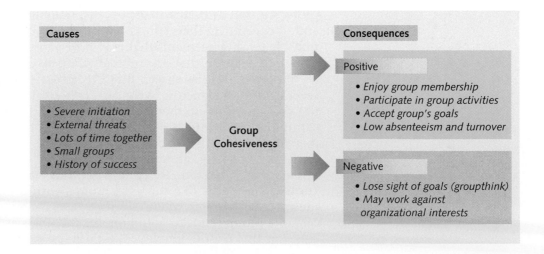

The Dynamics of Individual Performance in Groups

Now that we have reviewed the basic nature of groups and teams, we will turn to an aspect of group dynamics most relevant to the field of organizational behavior—the effects of groups on individual performance. Specifically, we will take a look at three different issues in this connection. First, we will consider how people's work performance is affected by the presence of others. Second, we will examine how the composition of groups—in particular, their racial and ethnic diversity—affects performance. Third, we will describe how performance is affected by group size.

Social Facilitation: Individual Performance in the Presence of Others

Imagine that you have been studying drama for five years and you are now ready for your first acting audition in front of some Hollywood producers. You have been rehearsing diligently for several months, getting ready for the part. Now you are no longer alone at home with your script in front of you. Your name is announced and silence fills the auditorium as you walk to the front of the stage. How will you perform now that you are in front of an audience? Will you freeze, forgetting the lines you studied so intensely when you practiced alone? Or will the audience spur you on to your best performance yet? In other words, what impact will the presence of the audience have on your behavior?

After studying this question for a century, using a wide variety of tasks and situations, social scientists found that the answer is not straightforward.[30] Sometimes people were found to perform better in the presence of others than when alone, and sometimes they were found to perform better alone than in the presence of others. This tendency for the presence of others to enhance an individual's performance at times and to impair it at other times is known as **social facilitation**. (Although the word "facilitation" implies improvements in task performance, scientists use the term "social facilitation" to refer to both performance improvements and decrements stemming from the presence of others.) What accounts for these seemingly contradictory findings?

Explaining social facilitation. According to Robert Zajonc, the matter boils down to several basic psychological processes.[31] First, Zajonc explained that social facilitation was the result of the heightened emotional arousal (e.g., feelings of tension and excitement) people experience when in the presence of others. (Wouldn't you feel more tension playing the piano in front of an audience than alone?) Second, when people are aroused, they tend to perform the most dominant response—their most likely behavior in that setting. (Returning the smile of a smiling co-worker may be considered an example of a dominant act; it is a very well learned act to smile at another who smiles at you.) If someone is performing a very well learned act, the dominant response would be a correct one (such as speaking the right lines during your fiftieth performance). However, if the behavior in question is relatively novel, newly learned, the dominant response would likely be incorrect (such as speaking incorrect lines during an audition). Together, these ideas are known as Zajonc's **drive theory of social facilitation**.[32] According to this theory, the presence of others increases arousal, which increases the tendency to perform the most dominant responses. If these responses are correct, the resulting performance will he enhanced; if they are incorrect, the performance will be impaired. Based on these processes, performance either may be helped (if the task is well learned) or hindered (if the task is not well learned). (For a summary of this process see Figure 8-7.)

A considerable amount of research has shown support for this theory: People perform better on tasks in the presence of others if that task is very well learned, but poorer if it is not well learned. However, it is still unclear exactly *why* this effect occurs. Three positions receive a considerable amount of support. First, according to Zajonc, people become aroused simply because the

---

social facilitation The tendency for the presence of others sometimes to enhance an individual's performance and at other times to impair it.

drive theory of social facilitation The theory according to which the presence of others increases arousal, which increases people's tendencies to perform the dominant response. If that response is well learned, performance will improve. But, if it is novel, performance will be impaired.

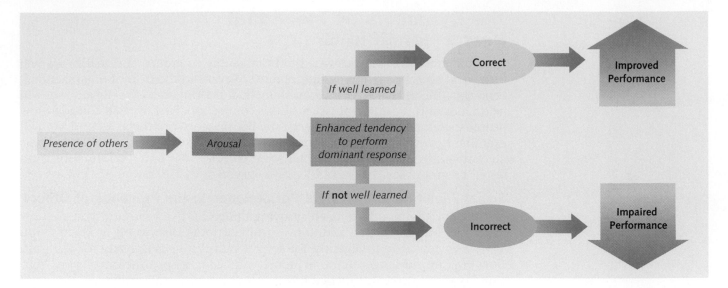

■ Figure 8-7
Social Facilitation: A Drive Theory Approach
Zajonc's drive theory of social facilitation states that the presence of others is arousing. This, in turn, enhances the tendency to perform the most dominant (i.e., strongest) responses. If these are correct (such as if the task is well learned), performance will be improved, but if these are incorrect (such as if the task is novel), performance will suffer.

evaluation apprehension
The fear of being evaluated or judged by another person.

distraction-conflict model
A conceptualization explaining social facilitation in terms of the tendency for others' presence to cause a conflict between directing attention to others versus the task at hand.

computerized performance monitoring The process of using computers to monitor job performance.

others are there, what he calls their "mere presence." However, other scientists have modified Zajonc's approach, claiming that the arousal resulting from others is not due to the fact that others are simply there, but that these others can potentially evaluate the person. Their major idea, our second explanation, is that social facilitation results from **evaluation apprehension**—the fear of being evaluated or judged by another person.[33] Indeed, people may be aroused by performing a task in the presence of others because of their concern over what those others might think of them. For example, lower-level employees may suffer evaluation apprehension when they are worried about what their supervisor thinks of their work. Finally, a third explanation, known as the **distraction-conflict model** recognizes that the presence of others creates a conflict between paying attention to others and paying attention to the task at hand.[34] The conflict created by these tendencies leads to increased arousal, which, in turn, leads to social facilitation. If you've ever tried doing a homework assignment while your friends or family watch TV nearby, you're probably already aware of the conflict that competing demands for your attention can create.

Although many researchers currently favor the distraction-conflict explanation of social facilitation, all three explanations provide some important insights into social facilitation. In other words, while the processes underlying social facilitation are somewhat unclear, the effect itself may have a profound influence on organizational behavior.

Computerized performance monitoring: Social facilitation via an "electronic presence." If you read George Orwell's classic book *1984*, you will recall "Big Brother," the all-knowing power that monitored people's every moves. As often occurs, the science fiction of one era eventually becomes scientific fact in another. In the case of "Big Brother," in the workplace, at least, Orwell wasn't many years off in his predictions. The use of computers to monitor work performance today is becoming increasingly common. **Computerized performance monitoring** is already widely used in the insurance, banking, communications, and transportation industries, and it promises to become even more prevalent in tomorrow's organizations.[35] In view of this, it is important to learn about the effects of monitoring on people's job performance.

One way of understanding how computerized monitoring may influence performance is by extending our thinking about social facilitation. After all, instead of having an individual who is physically present to watch, this technique is akin to doing the same thing indirectly, by computer—an "electronic presence." Imagine, for example, that you are entering data into a computer terminal. You can be monitored in a direct physical way by an individual looking over your shoulder or indirectly by someone checking a computerized record of the speed and accuracy of your every keystroke. If the task being performed is a complex one, social facilitation research suggests that the physical presence of an observer would lead to reduced performance. But would the same thing occur when there is only an electronic presence?

A study by Aiello and Svec provides an answer to this question.[36] Participants in this research were college students who performed complex anagram tasks (unscrambling letters to form words) by entering their responses into a computer terminal. The conditions under which they performed this task were systematically varied by the researchers in several different ways, three of which are relevant here. One group of participants (the "control" condition) performed the task without anyone observing them work in any form. A second group (the "person monitored" condition) was monitored by stationing two female observers immediately behind them as they performed their task in front of the computer. Finally, a third group of subjects (the "computer monitoring" condition) was told that their performance would be monitored by people who could see their work on another computer to which theirs was connected on a network. (To make this convincing, participants were shown the other computer equipment.) Participants performed the task for 10 minutes, after which the researchers counted the number of anagrams solved correctly by people in each condition. A summary of these findings is shown in Figure 8-8.

As these data show, people performed worse when others were physically observing them (person monitored group) than when they performed the task alone (control group). This finding is in keeping with research and theory on social facilitation, according to which performance on complex tasks is expected to suffer when in the presence of others. Even more interesting is the finding that performance also suffered when it was monitored by computer—that is, even when people were not distracted by having others looking over their shoulders. Apparently, performance can suffer even when the presence of another is known to exist, although imperceptible.

■ Figure 8-8
Computer Monitoring: Evidence of Its Counterproductive Effects
Participants in a recent study performed complex tasks either alone, or while being monitored by a computer or by two other people who were physically present. Consistent with other research on social facilitation, people performed the complex task worse in the presence of others than alone. They also performed more poorly when they were monitored by the "electronic presence" of a computer.

(**Source:** Based on data reported by Aiello & Svec, 1993; see Note 36.)

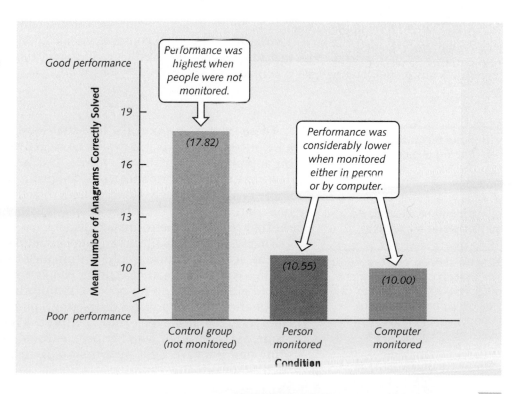

THE ORGANIZATION OF THE FUTURE

Videoconferencing: Groups in Cyberspace

If you've ever attempted to schedule a group meeting, then you surely know how difficult it can be to find a mutually acceptable time when several busy people can get together. This problem is compounded when the meeting involves people in distant locations. In such cases, we must consider not only the time spent meeting, but also the considerable downtime and expense associated with travel. With an eye toward reducing these obstacles, we are now beginning to see a technological advance that brings people together electronically, in "virtual" space, as opposed to physical space. It's called **videoconferencing**—the practice of using technology to provide audio and video links (either limited or full motion) between work sites, allowing visual communication between people who are not physically present.

Although videoconferencing is still quite expensive and in limited use today, experts predict that it is likely to become more common in the future. If for no other reason, the savings in travel costs alone may make it cost effective. One company that has made this investment is BASF's Fibers Division. This firm, which spent $1 million on videoconferencing equipment at 24 worldwide sites now enjoys an annual savings of $10.4 million on travel expenses.[37] In addition to the considerable money saved, company officials now find it easier to schedule meetings. Although it is no easy task to find a common time when a group of busy professionals can step into their nearest videoconferencing facility, it is certainly much simpler to do this than to arrange to bring them together physically. Given the increased ease of coordination gained through videoconferencing, it is no surprise that some companies have used this technology to gain a competitive advantage. For example, Bata Shoes, with operations in 60 countries has used videoconferencing to reduce its product-development time by some 90 percent.[38]

A more limited form of multimedia conferencing is **shared-screen conferencing**—connecting computer workstations so as to provide concurrent displays of information and interaction between several individuals.[39] Group members using this technology can call up a common document on their desktop computers and work on it at the same time. This might involve something simple such as drafting a memo, or a more complex process, such as drawing a new design on a blackboard program. It's even possible for some members of the group to send completely private side-messages to each other, without the others knowing it—the high-tech equivalent of whispering something into another's ear.[40]

These emerging technologies are clearly still in their infancy, but they are becoming increasingly popular in many organizations. Although only large businesses may be able to afford the huge investment in videoconferencing equipment, even small companies can rent public videoconferencing facilities for as long as they need them. Several private businesses, such as many Kinko's locations, offer this service. And given how satisfied companies have been with these services, we may expect to see more videoconferencing in the future. As one management consultant put it, "Although the next decade does not promise the total replacement of face-to-face meetings with electronic togetherness, new varieties of computer-mediated interactions among people will nevertheless increase."[41]

videoconferencing The practice of using technology to provide audio and video links (either limited or full-motion) between work sites, allowing visual communication between people who are not physically present.

shared-screen conferencing The process of connecting computer workstations so as to provide concurrent displays of information and interaction between several individuals.

These findings support the idea that social facilitation may be due to people's concerns about being evaluated negatively by another—that is, evaluation apprehension. In the case of the task at hand, participants in the study knew that their performance could be just as easily evaluated by watching a remote computer as by watching them directly. Accordingly, opportunities for evaluation existed in both conditions, possibly accounting for the apprehension that led to the performance decrements found.

There is also a very important applied implication of these results—namely, that the act of monitoring job performance to keep levels high may actually backfire. That is, instead of causing people to improve their performance (for fear of being caught doing poorly), monitoring might actually interfere with performance (by providing a distracting source of evaluation). Because participants in Aiello and Svec's study performed their tasks for only brief periods of time, we cannot tell whether people would eventually get used to the monitoring and improve their performance over time. However, until further research addresses this question, we must issue the following caution: Using computers to monitor work performance might impair the very performance monitoring is intended to improve. "Big Brother" just might be defeating his own purposes. (A growing trend in today's organizations involves using computers not only for monitoring performance, but also for bringing groups together electronically when they cannot be together physically. For a closer look at this practice, see the ORGANIZATION OF THE FUTURE section.)

Performance in Culturally Diverse Groups

For many years, the task of composing work groups involved finding individuals with the right blend of skills and getting them to work together—a task that was challenging enough. Today, however, as the workplace grows increasingly diverse with respect to the racial and ethnic group composition of its members, there's a new consideration. How does a group's cultural diversity affect its task performance? Although attempts to answer this question do not have the long history of research on social facilitation, recent research has provided some good insight.

For example, considering this question, Watson, Kumar, and Michaelsen reasoned that when a culturally diverse group first forms, its members will need time to be able to adjust to the racial and ethnic differences between them.[42] To the extent that people's differing perspectives and styles may interfere with their ability to work together, then task performance may be expected to suffer. As time goes on, however, and group members learn to interact with each other despite their different backgrounds, performance differences should disappear. The researchers tested these hypotheses by assigning college students enrolled in a management class to two kinds of four-person groups. *Homogeneous groups* were composed of members from the same racial and ethnic background. *Diverse groups* were created by assembling groups consisting of one white American, one African American, one Hispanic American, and one foreign national. After being formed, the groups were asked to analyze business cases (a task with which management students were familiar). The groups worked on four occasions scheduled one month apart. Their analyses were then scored (using several different predetermined criteria) by experts who did not know which groups were diverse and which were homogeneous. How did following these two different recipes for group composition influence task performance? The data summarized in Figure 8-9 bear on this question.

■ **Figure 8-9**
Task Performance in Culturally Diverse Groups: An Experimental Demonstration
An experiment found that although culturally diverse groups performed worse than homogeneous groups at first, these differences disappeared over time.

(**Source:** Based on data reported by Watson, Kumar, & Michaelsen, 1993; see Note 42.)

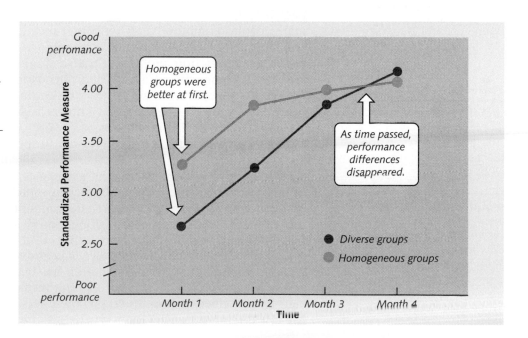

As shown in Figure 8-9, the answer depends on the length of time the group had worked together. At first, the homogeneous group did considerably better than the diverse group. Then, during the second session these differences grew smaller. By the third session, the differences almost completely disappeared, and by the fourth session they did (in fact, the diverse group even did slightly better than the homogeneous group). Although all groups improved their performance over time, as you would expect, the initial advantage of homogeneous groups was found to be only a temporary condition found in newly created groups. As group members had more experiences working with each other, the differences between them became less of a source of interference.

Because research on the effects of racial and ethnic group composition on task performance is just beginning, we do not yet know if these same results would hold for different kinds of tasks. We also don't know whether diverse groups would eventually perform even better than homogeneous ones. In fact, on tasks in which differing perspectives might help a group do its job, diverse groups may be expected to have an edge over heterogeneous ones. Although several key questions about the effects of diversity on group performance remain unanswered, the importance of this factor as a variable in group performance is clearly established.

Social Loafing: "Free Riding" When Working with Others

Have you ever worked with several others helping a friend move into a new apartment, each carrying and transporting part of the load from the old place to the new one? Or, how about sitting around a table with others stuffing political campaign letters into envelopes and addressing them to potential donors? Although these tasks may seem quite different, they actually share an important common characteristic: performing each requires only a single individual, but several people's work can be pooled to yield greater outcomes. Insofar as each person's contributions can be added together with another's, such tasks have been referred to as **additive tasks**.[43]

If you've ever performed additive tasks, such as the ones described here, there's a good chance that you found yourself working not quite as hard as you would have if you did them alone. Does this sound familiar to you? Indeed, a considerable amount of research has found that when several people combine their efforts on additive tasks, each individual contributes less than he or she would when performing the same task alone.[44] As suggested by the old saying "many hands make light the work," a group of people would be expected to be more productive than any one individual. However, when several people combine their efforts on additive tasks, each individual's contribution tends to be less. Five people working together raking leaves will *not* be five times more productive than a single individual working alone; there are always some who go along for a "free ride." In fact, the more individuals who are contributing to an additive task, the less each individual's contribution tends to be—a phenomenon known as **social loafing**.[45]

This effect was first noted almost 70 years ago by a German scientist named Max Ringelmann, who compared the amount of force exerted by different-sized groups of people pulling on a rope.[46] Specifically, he found that one person pulling on a rope alone exerted an average of 63 kilograms of force. However, in groups of three, the per person force dropped to 53 kilograms, and in groups of eight it was reduced to only 31 kilograms per person—less than half the effort exerted by people working alone. Social loafing effects of this type have been observed in many different studies conducted in recent years.[47] The general form of the social loafing effect is portrayed in Figure 8-10.

The phenomenon of social loafing has been explained by **social impact theory**.[48] According to this theory, the impact of any social force acting on a group is divided equally among its members. The larger the size of the group, the less the impact of the force on any one member. As a result, the more peo-

additive tasks Types of group tasks in which the individual efforts of several people are added together to form the group's product.

social loafing The tendency for group members to exert less individual effort on an additive task as the size of the group increases.

social impact theory The theory that explains social loafing in terms of the diffused responsibility for doing what is expected of each member of a group. The larger the size of a group, the less each member is influenced by the social forces acting on the group.

■ **Figure 8-10**
Social Loafing: Its General Form
According to the social loafing effect, when individuals work together on an additive task, the more people contributing to the group's task, the less effort each individual exerts.

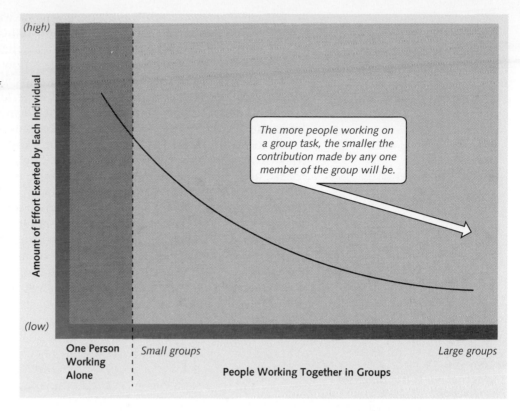

The more people working on a group task, the smaller the contribution made by any one member of the group will be.

ple who might contribute to a group's product, the less pressure each person faces to perform well—that is, the responsibility for doing the job is diffused over more people. As a result, each group member feels less responsible for behaving appropriately, and social loafing occurs.

Although feeling less responsible for an outcome is clearly one possible explanation for the social loafing phenomenon, the effect also may result from other experiences likely to arise among people performing their jobs. For example, people may engage in social loafing because they feel that the presence of others makes their contributions less needed—that is, more dispensable. Demonstrating this phenomenon, Weldon and Mustari had college students perform a judgment task (e.g., assessing the desirability of a job as the basis of describing it to potential applicants) and told them either that they were the only ones performing the task or that their judgments would be one of two or one of sixteen judgments used to make a final assessment.[49] The experimenters reasoned that people who believed their judgments would be one of many would take their jobs less seriously, spending less time on the task and making less complex judgments. In fact, this is exactly what they found. The larger the size of the group, the more dispensable people believed their judgments were, and the less complex these judgments were found to be. These data strongly support the idea that social loafing occurs because people believe that in larger groups their contributions are less necessary than when working alone.

Is social loafing a universal phenomenon? A simple way of understanding social loafing is that it occurs because people are more interested in themselves (getting the most for themselves while doing the least) than their fellow group members (who are forced to do their work for them). That this phenomenon occurs in the United States should not be particularly surprising in view of the tendency for American culture to be highly individualistic (i.e., individual accomplishments and personal success are highly valued). However, people in collectivistic nations, such as Israel and the People's Republic of China, place a high value on shared responsibility and the collective good of all. In collectivistic cultures, people working in groups would not be expected to engage in social loafing because doing so would have them fail in their social responsibility to the group (a responsibility that does not prevail in individualistic cultures). In fact, to the extent that people in collectivistic cultures are strongly motivated to help their fellow group members, they would be expected to be *more* productive in groups than alone. That is, not only wouldn't they loaf, but they would work especially hard.

An experiment by Earley tested these ideas.[50] In this research managers from the United States, Israel, and the People's Republic of China were each asked to complete an "in-basket" exercise. This task simulated the daily activities of managers in all three countries, such as writing memos, filling out forms, and rating job applicants. They were all asked to perform this task as well as they could for a period of one hour, but under one of two different conditions: either *alone*, or as part of a *group* of ten. Research participants who worked alone were simply asked to write their names on each item they completed and to turn it in. In the group condition participants were told that their group's overall performance would be assessed at the end of the performance period. Fellow group members were not physically present but were described as being highly similar to themselves with respect to their family and religious backgrounds as well as their interests. (Earley reasoned that groups of this type would be ones whose members people would be especially reluctant

■ **Figure 8-11**
Social Loafing: Is It a Universal Phenomenon?

Research compared the group and individual performance of people performing a managerial task in three countries: the People's Republic of China, Israel, and the United States. Although individual performance alone was lower than performance as part of a group in the United States (i.e., social loafing occurred), the opposite was found in China and Israel. The more collectivistic *nature of these cultures discouraged people from letting down their fellow group members.*

(**Source:** Based on data reported by Earley, 1993; see Note 50.)

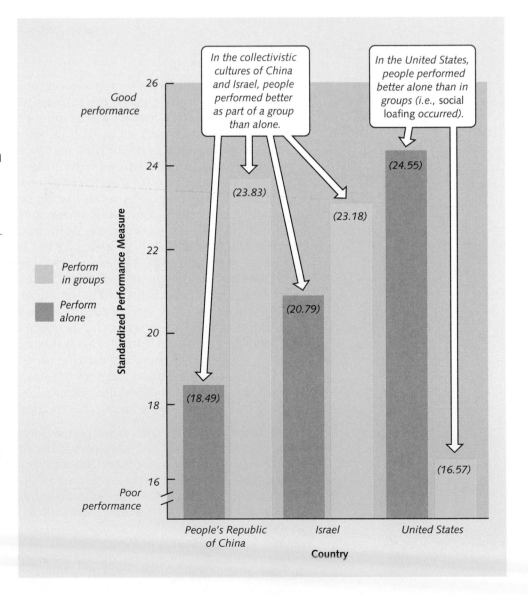

The distinction between individualistic and collectivistic cultures is discussed in Chapter 2, in conjunction with Hofstede's cultural framework.

to let down by loafing.) To compare the various groups, Earley scored each participant's in-basket exercises by converting the responses to standardized performance scores. Did social loafing occur, and in which countries? The results are summarized in Figure 8-11.

These data clearly show that social loafing occurred in the United States. That is, individual performance was significantly lower among people working in groups than those working alone. However, the opposite was found in each of the two highly collectivistic cultures, the People's Republic of China and Israel. In both these countries, individuals performed at higher levels when working in groups than when working alone. In these nations, people not only failed to loaf in groups, but they worked *harder* than they did when alone. Because they strongly identified with their groups and were concerned about the welfare of its members, members of collectivistic cultures placed their group's interests ahead of their own. (It is important to note that these findings only occurred when people believed that they had strong ties to the members of their groups.)

Earley's research suggests that culture plays an important part in determining people's tendencies to engage in social loafing. Although it is tempting to think of social loafing as an inevitable aspect of human nature, it appears that the phenomenon is not as universal as you might think. Instead, loafing appears to be a manifestation of cultural values: Among cultural groups in which individualism is stressed, individual interests guide performance, but among groups in which collectivism is stressed, group interests guide performance.

Tips for eliminating social loafing. Obviously, the tendency for people to reduce their effort when working with others could be a serious problem in organizations. Fortunately, research has shown that there are several ways in which social loafing can be overcome. One possible antidote to social loafing is to *make each performer identifiable*. Social loafing may occur when people feel they can get away with "taking it easy"—namely, under conditions in which each individual's contributions cannot be determined. A variety of studies on the practice of "public posting" support this idea.[51] This research has found that when each individual's contribution to a task is displayed where it can be seen by others (e.g., weekly sales figures posted on a chart), people are less likely to slack off than when only overall group (or companywide) performance is made available. In other words, the more one's individual contribution to a group effort is highlighted, the more pressure each person feels to make a group contribution. Thus, social loafing can be overcome if one's contributions to an additive task are identified: Potential loafers are not likely to loaf if they fear getting caught.

Another way to overcome social loafing is to *make work tasks more important and interesting*. Research has revealed that people are unlikely to go along for a free ride when the task they are performing is believed to be vital to the organization.[52] For example, George found that the less meaningful salespeople believed their jobs were, the more they engaged in social loafing—especially when they thought their supervisors knew little about how well they were working.[53] To help in this regard, corporate officials should deliberately attempt to make jobs more intrinsically interesting to employees. To the extent that jobs are interesting, people may be less likely to loaf. It also has been suggested that managers should *reward individuals for contributing to their group's performance*—that is, encourage their interest in their group's performance.[54] Doing this (e.g., giving all salespeople in a territory a bonus if they jointly exceed their sales goal) may help employees focus more on collective concerns and less on individualistic concerns, increasing their obligations to their fellow group members. This is important, of course, in that the success of an organization is more likely to be influenced by the collective efforts of groups than by the individual contributions of any one member.

As we discussed in Chapter 5, designing jobs so as to make them seem more important and interesting is also an effective way of enhancing motivation.

Another mechanism for overcoming social loafing is to *use punishment threats*. To the extent that performance decrements may be controlled by threatening to punish the individuals slacking off, loafing may be reduced. This effect was demonstrated in an experiment by Miles and Greenberg.[55] The participants in this study were members of high school swim teams who swam either alone or in relay races during practice sessions. In some conditions, the coach threatened the team by telling them that everyone would have to swim "penalty laps" if anyone on the team failed to meet a specified difficult time for swimming 100 yards freestyle. In a control group, no punishment threats were issued. How did the punishment threats influence task performance? The researchers found that people swam faster alone than as part of relay teams when no punishment was threatened, thereby confirming the social loafing effect. However, when punishment threats were made, group performance increased, thereby eliminating the social loafing effect.

Together, these findings suggest that social loafing is a potent force—and one that can be a serious threat to organizational performance. But, it can be controlled in several ways that counteract the desire to loaf, such as by making loafing socially embarrassing or harmful to other individual interests.

Teams: Special Kinds of Groups

Now that you have a clear understanding of groups and how they operate, we can compare them to another type of collection of individuals known as *teams*. In this section we will define what is meant by teams and how they are different from groups. We will then describe various types of teams that may be found in organizations. Finally, we will present guidelines for creating teams in organizations

Defining Teams and Distinguishing Them from Groups

If you think about some of the groups we've described thus far in this chapter, such as the ones in use at Published Image (in our PREVIEW CASE) and the hypothetical corporate budget committee described earlier, you'll probably realize that they are somehow different. Although they are each composed of several individuals working together toward common goals, the connections between the employees at Published Image appear to be much deeper in scope. Although the budget committee members may be interested in what they're doing, the group members at Published Image seem more highly committed to their work and are more highly involved in the way their jobs are done. This is not to say that there is necessarily anything wrong with the corporate budget committee; in fact, it would appear to be a rather typical group. The groups at Published Image, however, are examples of special kinds of groups known as *teams*. A **team** may be defined as a group whose members have complementary skills and are committed to a common purpose or set of performance goals for which they hold themselves mutually accountable.[56]

At this point, it is probably not entirely clear to you exactly how a team is different from an ordinary group. This confusion probably stems in part from the fact that people often refer to their groups as teams, although they are really not teams.[57] Yet, there are several important distinctions between them (see Figure 8-12).

First, in groups, performance typically depends on the work of individual members. The performance of a team, however, depends on both individual contributions and *collective work products*—the joint outcome of team members working in concert.

A second difference has to do with where accountability for the job lies. Typically, members of groups pool their resources to attain a goal, although it

team A group whose members have complementary skills and are committed to a common purpose or set of performance goals for which they hold themselves mutually accountable.

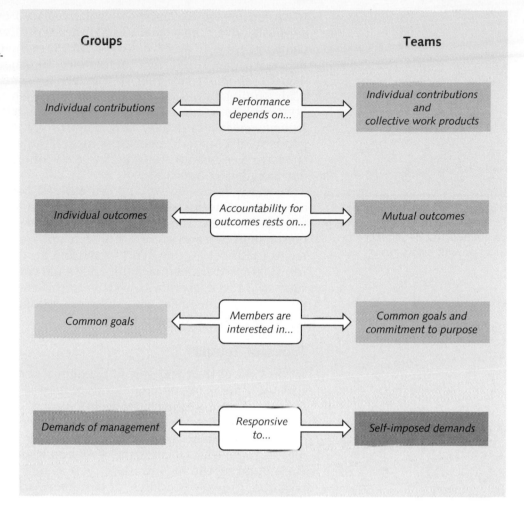

Groups		Teams
Individual contributions	← Performance depends on... →	Individual contributions and collective work products
Individual outcomes	← Accountability for outcomes rests on... →	Mutual outcomes
Common goals	← Members are interested in... →	Common goals and commitment to purpose
Demands of management	← Responsive to... →	Self-imposed demands

is individual performance that is taken into consideration when it comes to issuing rewards. Members of groups usually do not take responsibility for any results other than their own. By contrast, teams focus on both individual and *mutual accountability*. That is, they work together to produce an outcome (e.g., a product, service, or decision) that represents their joint contributions, and each team member shares responsibility for that outcome. The key difference is this: In groups, the supervisor holds individual members accountable for their work, whereas in teams, members hold themselves accountable.

Third, whereas group members may share a common interest goal, team members also share a *common commitment to purpose*. Moreover, these purposes typically are concerned with winning in some way, such as being first or best at something. For example, a work team in a manufacturing plant of a financially troubled company may be highly committed to making the company the top one in its industry. Another team, one in a public high school, may be committed to preparing all its graduates for the challenges of the world better than any other school in the district. Team members focusing jointly on such lofty purposes, in conjunction with specific performance goals, become heavily invested in its activities. In fact, teams are said to establish "ownership" of their purposes, and usually spend a great deal of time establishing their purposes. Like groups, teams use goals to monitor their progress. Teams, however, also have a broader purpose which supplies a source of meaning and emotional energy to the activities performed.

Fourth, in organizations, teams differ from groups with respect to the nature of their connections to management. Work groups are typically required to be responsive to demands regularly placed on them by management. By contrast, once management establishes the mission for a team, and sets the challenge for it to achieve, it typically gives the team enough flexibility to do its job without any further interference. In other words, teams are to varying degrees *self-managing*—that is, they are to some extent free to set their own goals, timing, and the approach that they wish to take, usually without management interference. Thus, many teams are described as being *autonomous* or *semiautonomous* in nature. This is not to say that teams are completely independent of corporate management and supervision. They still must be responsive to demands from higher-levels (often, higher-level teams, known as *top management teams*).

Clearly, teams are very special entities. Some teams go beyond the characteristics of teams described here and are known as **high-performance teams**. These are teams whose members are deeply committed to one another's personal growth and success.[58] Such teams are referred to as high-performance teams inasmuch as they tend to perform at much higher levels than ordinary teams (whose members lack this additional commitment to others' growth and success). Indeed, as we will see later in this chapter, the best-performing teams tend to have members who show exceptionally high levels of mutual care, trust, and respect for each other.

Types of Teams

In view of their widespread popularity, it should not be surprising to learn that there are many different kinds of teams. To help make sense out of these, scientists have categorized teams into several different commonly found types which vary along four major dimensions (see Figure 8-13).[59]

The first dimension has to do with their major *purpose or mission*. In this regard, some teams—known as *work teams*—are primarily concerned with the work done by the organization, such as developing and manufacturing new products, providing services for customers, and so on. Their principle focus is on using the organization's resources to effectively create its results (be they goods or services). (The teams at Published Image, described in our PREVIEW CASE, appear to be of this type.) Other teams—known as *improvement teams*—are primarily oriented toward the mission of increasing the effectiveness of the processes that are used by the organization. For example, Texas Instruments

---

high-performance teams
Teams whose members are deeply committed to one another's personal growth and success.

■ **Figure 8-13**
Types of Teams
The teams found in organizations may be distinguished from each other with respect to the four major dimensions identified here.

(**Source:** Based on suggestions by Mohrman, 1993; see Note 59.)

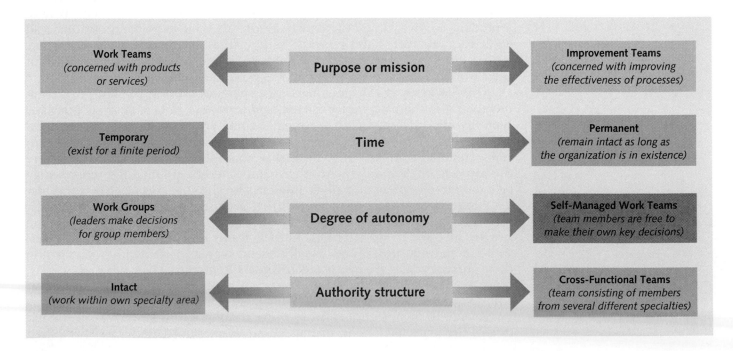

has relied on teams to help improve the quality of operations at its plant in Malaysia.[60]

A second dimension has to do with *time*. Specifically, some teams are only *temporary* and are established for a specific project with a finite life. For example, a team set up to develop a new product would be considered temporary. As soon as its job is done, it disbands. However, other kinds of teams are *permanent* and stay intact as long as the organization is operating. For instance, teams focusing on providing effective customer service tend to be permanent parts of many organizations.

A third distinction has to do with the degree to which teams operate autonomously.[61] At one end of the scale we may have *work groups*, in which leaders make decisions on behalf of group members, whose job it is to follow the leader's orders. This traditional kind of group is becoming less popular as more organizations are turning to the opposite end of the scale, where employees are free to make their own key decisions. Such groups are commonly referred to as **self-managed work teams**.

Typically, self-managed work teams consist of small numbers of employees, often around ten, who take on duties that used to be performed by their supervisors. This is likely to include making work assignments, deciding on the pace of work, determining how quality is to be assessed, and even who gets to join the team. In fact, the more self-managed teams do, the less they have to be supervised at all. (It is with this in mind that Eric Gershman, the founder of Published Image, described in our PREVIEW CASE, hopes to eliminate his own job.)

Consider these examples of some of the ways members of self-managed work teams are assuming supervisory duties:[62]

- Team members at a Colgate-Palmolive factory in Ohio write their own technical training manuals.
- Work teams at Lake Superior Paper Industries schedule their own work assignments and vacations.
- At Weirton Steel, a work team recommended a $5 million capital improvement in renovating an aging mill.
- The Brazilian baking equipment manufacturer, Semco S/A, had team members decide where to locate the company's new plant.

As these examples illustrate, self-managed work teams are given wide latitude over a broad range of important areas of organizational decision making. Self-managed work teams are not only in widespread use today, but they are growing in popularity. In fact, it has been estimated that 20 percent of American companies use them, and that this figure is well on the way to 50 percent.[63] The list of companies using teams includes many large corporations, such as Xerox, Hewlett-Packard, Honeywell, and PepsiCo. In fact, Procter & Gamble, Cummins Engine, and General Motors have used self-managed work teams for over 30 years.[64]

The fourth dimension reflects the team's connection to the organization's overall *authority structure*—that is, the connection between various formal job responsibilities. In some organizations teams remain *intact* with respect to their organizational functions. For example, at Ralston-Purina projects are structured such that people work together on certain products all the time and do not apply their specialty to a wide range of products. Within such organizations, teams can operate without the ambiguities created by straying from one's area of expertise.

However, with growing frequency, we are seeing teams that cross over various functional units (e.g., marketing, finance, human resources, and so on). Such teams are commonly referred to as **cross-functional teams**. These are teams composed of employees at identical organizational levels, but from different specialty areas, to work together on a task. (The teams at Published Image

---

self-managed work teams
Teams whose members are permitted to make key decisions about how their work is done.

A complete discussion of the structure of authority relations in organizations appears in Chapter 15.

---

cross-functional teams
Teams represented by people from different specialty areas within organizations.

are cross-functional.) Cross-functional teams represent an effective way of bringing people together from throughout the organization to cooperate with each other on the diverse tasks needed to complete large projects. In organizations using cross-functional teams, the boundaries between all teams must be considered permeable. Indeed, people are frequently members of more than one team—a situation often required for organizations to function effectively. For example, members of an organization's manufacturing team must carefully coordinate their activities with members of its marketing team. To the extent that people are involved in several different kinds of teams, they may gain broader perspectives and make more important contributions to their various teams.

For over a decade, many automobile manufacturers—including the major American and Japanese companies—have relied on cross-functional teams to create and manufacture new models. As a case in point, the successful Dodge Neon was completely created by cross-functional teams of experts from throughout Chrysler. Similarly, in the aircraft industry, Boeing created cross-functional teams that designed and manufactured its latest aircraft, the 777 (see Figure 8-14). In both cases, the use of teams has been credited with both the record speed with which the products came to market and their exceptional quality. As you might imagine, cross-functional teams are difficult to manage. It takes time for specialists in different areas to learn to communicate with each other and to coordinate their efforts. It also takes time to develop the mutual trust and acceptance that is required for people to work closely with each other. However, in view of the great successes of cross-functional teams, the effort required to make them work out appears to be worthwhile.

Managers' Guidelines for Creating Teams

As you might imagine, assembling a team is no easy task. Doing so requires not only having the right combination of skilled people, but also individuals who are willing to work together with others as a team. A model proposed by Hackman provides some useful guidance on how to design work teams effectively, suggesting that the process proceeds in four distinct stages.[65] As we present this model, you may find it useful to refer to the summary in Table 8-4.

The first stage of creating an effective team is known as *prework*. One of the most important objectives of this phase is to determine whether a team should be created. A manager may decide to have several individuals working alone answer to him, or a team may be created if it is believed that it may de-

■ **Figure 8-14**
The Boeing 777: A Product of Cross-Functional Teams
Large projects, such as the design and production of commercial aircraft, are often aided by the use of cross-functional teams. Such teams of Boeing employees helped produce the company's latest product, the model 777 airliner.

For teams to function effectively, they must be created properly. The four stages outlined here summarize how this may be accomplished.

Stage 1: Do Prework	Stage 2: Create Performance Conditions	Stage 3: Form and Build the Team	Stage 4: Provide Ongoing Assistance
■ Decide what work needs to be done. ■ Determine if a team is necessary to accomplish the task. ■ Determine what authority the team should have. ■ Decide on the team's goals.	■ Provide all the needed materials and equipment to do the job. ■ Ensure that the team consists of all personnel necessary to do the job.	■ Establish boundaries—that is, who is and is not in the team. ■ Arrive at an agreement regarding the tasks to be performed. ■ Clarify the behaviors expected of each team member.	■ Intervene to eliminate team problems (e.g., members not doing their share). ■ Replenish or upgrade material resources. ■ Replace members who leave the team.

SOURCE: Based on information in Hackman, 1987; see Note 65.

velop the most creative and insightful ways to get things done. In considering this, it is important to note exactly what work needs to be done. The team's objectives must be established, and an inventory of the skills needed to do the job should be made. In addition, decisions should be made in advance about what authority the team should have. They may just be advisory to the manager, or they may be given full responsibility and authority for executing their task (i.e., they may be *self-regulating*).

Building on this, stage two involves *creating performance conditions*. In this stage, organizational officials are to ensure that the team has the proper conditions under which to carry out its work. Resources necessary for the team's success should be provided. This involves both material resources (e.g., tools, equipment, and money), human resources (e.g., the appropriate blend of skilled professionals), and support from the organization (e.g., willingness to let the team do its own work as it sees fit). Unless managers help create the proper conditions for team success, they are contributing to its failure.

Stage three involves *forming and building the team*. Three things can be done to help a team get off to a good start. First, managers should form boundaries—clearly establish who is and who is not a member of the team. Some teams fail simply because membership in it is left unclear. Reducing such ambiguity can help avoid confusion and frustration. Second, members must accept the team's overall mission and purpose. Unless they do, failure is inevitable. Third, organizational officials should clarify the team's mission and responsibilities—make perfectly clear exactly what it is expected to do (but not necessarily *how* to do it). Will team members be responsible for monitoring and planning their own work? If so, such expectations should be spelled out explicitly.

Finally, once a team is functioning, supervisors should *provide ongoing assistance*. Although once teams start operating they often guide themselves, managers may be able to help by providing opportunities for the team to eliminate problems and perform even better. For example, disruptive team members may be either counseled or replaced. Similarly, material resources may have to be replenished or upgraded. Although it may be unwise for a manager to intervene in the successful affairs of a team that has taken on its own life, it also may be unwise to neglect opportunities to help a team do even better.

As you ponder these suggestions, you will doubtlessly recognize the considerable managerial skill and hard work it takes to create and manage teams effectively. However, as managers learn these skills, and as individuals gain successful experiences as members of effective work teams, the deliberate steps outlined above may become second nature to all concerned. As Hackman concludes, "When that stage is reached, the considerable investment required to learn how to use work teams well can pay substantial dividends—in work effectiveness and in the quality of the experience of both managers and [team] members."[66] As we will describe later in this chapter, both the potential pitfalls and benefits of work teams can be considerable.

Effective Team Performance

In recent years, the popular press has been filled with impressive claims about the success of teams in improving quality, customer service, productivity, and the bottom line. Here is just a sampling of the findings cited:

- Teams at Corning lowered defect rates from 1,800 parts per million to 9 parts per million at its specialty cellular ceramics plant.[67]
- At General Electric's plant in Salisbury, North Carolina, productivity was two and a half times higher than at other plants where people made the same products.[68]
- After introducing teams at the *Orange County Register*, customer service operators answered phone calls in half the time.[69]
- After switching to teams, Westinghouse Furniture Systems saw a 74 percent productivity increase in three years.[70]
- Turnaround time at the Georgia facility of the Carrier Division of United Technologies Corp. went from two weeks to two days after teams were introduced.[71]

Such reports lead us to believe that teams in general can produce very impressive results. However, it is important to consider whether or not these findings are typical. In this section we will examine evidence bearing on this question. Then, we will focus on some of the obstacles to team success and some of the things that can be done to help promote highly successful teams.

How Successful Are Teams? A Look at the Evidence

Questions regarding the effectiveness of teams in the workplace are not easy to answer. Not only are there many different kinds of teams doing different kinds of jobs operating in organizations, but their effectiveness is influenced by a wide variety of factors that go well beyond any possible benefits of teams, such as managerial support, the economy, available resources, and the like. As a result, understanding the true effectiveness of teams is a tricky business, at best. This difficulty has been fueled in recent years by cover stories in the top business periodicals touting the success of teams.[72,73] How much of this is hype stemming from the latest management fad, and how much should be accepted as valid evidence for the effectiveness of teams? Fortunately, several types of research investigations have examined this issue.[74]

One of the most direct ways of learning about companies' experiences with work teams is to survey the officials of organizations that use them. In a large-scale study, Lawler, Mohrman, and Ledford did just that.[75] Their sample consisted of several hundred of the 1,000 largest companies in the United States. About 47 percent used some work teams, although these were typically in place in only a few selected sites, not throughout the entire organizations. Where they were used, however, they were generally highly regarded. Survey results collected in 1987 and again in 1990 revealed that whereas 53 percent characterized the teams as "successful" or "very successful" in 1987, this figure grew to 60 percent only three years later. For both years, almost all the other responses fell into the "undecided" category; "unsuccessful" or "very unsuccessful" responses occurred in only 1 percent of the cases each year.

These optimistic results are further supported by in-depth case studies of numerous teams in many different organizations.[76] Research of this type, although difficult to quantify and to compare across organizations, provides some interesting insight into what makes teams successful and why. For example, Manz and Sims studied the work teams used in General Motors' battery plant in Fitzgerald, Georgia.[77] The 320 employees at this facility operate in various teams, including managers working together in *support teams*, middle-level teams of *coordinators* (similar to foremen and technicians), and *employee teams*, natural work units of three to nineteen members performing specific tasks. Although the teams work closely together, coordinating their activities, they function almost as separate businesses. Because plant employees must perform many different tasks in their teams, they are not paid based on their positions, but for their knowledge and competence. In fact, the highest-paid employees are individuals who have demonstrated their competence (usually by highly demanding tests) on all the jobs performed in at least two different teams. This is GM's way of rewarding people for broadening their perspectives, appreciating "the other guy's problems." By many measures, the Fitzgerald plant has been very effective. Its production costs are lower than comparable units in traditionally run plants. Furthermore, employee turnover is also much lower than average. Employee satisfaction surveys also reveal that job satisfaction at this plant is among the highest found at any General Motors facility.

Teams also have been successful in service businesses. For example, consider IDS, the financial services subsidiary of American Express.[78] In response to rapid growth in the mid-1980s, IDS officials realized that their operations were becoming highly inefficient and created several teams to work on reorganizing the company's operations. Like many companies, the move to teams wasn't readily accepted by all employees. Particularly resistant were individuals who before the teams were established had high-status jobs, with high pay to match. Naturally, they resented becoming co-equals with others when teams were formed. Still, these employees—and all others, for that matter—soon benefited from the company's improved operations. Accuracy in the processing of paperwork (e.g., orders to buy or sell stock) rose from 70 percent before teams were created to over 99 percent afterwards. With the help of employee teams, IDS's operations become so efficient that response time improved by 96 percent: from several minutes to only a few seconds. During the stock market crash of October 1987, this quick response capability is credited for saving lots of money for IDS's customers.

These cases are two examples of very different companies that used teams in different ways, but with something in common—high levels of success (albeit not without some difficulties). And, there are many more.[79] Although there are far too many cases to review here (in fact, entire books have been devoted to summarizing such cases), we think you'll find it fascinating to review the summary of company experiences with teams in Table 8-5.[80,81]

As Table 8-5 makes clear, many companies have reported having successful experiences with teams. Case studies paint a consistent picture of the effectiveness of teams, making the use of teams one of today's most popular management trends. The problem with such reports, of course, is that they may not be entirely objective. After all, companies may be unwilling to broadcast their failures to the world. This is not to say that case studies cannot be trusted. Indeed, when the information is gathered by outside researchers (such as those reported here), the stories they tell about how teams are used and the results of using them can be quite revealing.[82] Still, there is a need for completely objective, empirical studies of team effectiveness.

Research of this type is now just beginning to be done. In one such investigation Pearson compared various aspects of work performance and attitudes of two groups of employees at a railroad car repair facility in Australia: Those who were assembled into teams that could freely decide how to do their jobs, and those whose work was structured in the more traditional, nonautonomous fashion.[83] After the work teams had been in place for several

Case studies have reported many remarkable outcomes stemming from teams. Here is just a sampling of the impressive results.

Company	Result
Federal Express	Reduced errors (e.g., incorrect bills, lost packages) by 13 percent in 1989
Corning	Defects dropped from 1,800 parts per million to only 9 parts per million in its cellular ceramics plant
Shenandoah Life Insurance Co.	Saved $200,000 per year in reduced staffing while increasing volume of work handled by 33 percent
Xerox	Increased productivity by 30 percent
Tektronix	One team produces as many products in 3 days as an entire assembly line used to produce in 14 days
Carrier (division of United Technologies Corporation)	Reduced unit turnaround time from two weeks to 2 days
Westinghouse Furniture Systems	Productivity increased by 74 percent within three years
Sealed Air	Waste reduced by 50 percent, and downtime cut from 20 percent to 5 percent
Eli Lilly	Fastest-ever rollout time for a new medical product
Citibank	Substantially improved customer satisfaction ratings in 11 key areas
Exxon	$10 million saving in 6 months

SOURCES: Based on information in Wellins et al., 1991, see Note 71; Katzenbach & Smith, 1993, see Note 79; and Osburn et al., 1990, see Note 81.

months, it was found that they had significantly fewer accidents, as well as lower rates of absenteeism and turnover. Unfortunately, not all empirical studies paint such an optimistic picture of the benefits of work teams. For example, Wall, Kemp, Jackson, and Clegg examined the long-term effects of using work teams in an English manufacturing plant.[84] Although they found that employees were more satisfied with their jobs in teams compared to those in conventional work arrangements (in which individuals take orders from a supervisor), they were individually no more productive. However, because the use of teams made it possible for the organization to eliminate several supervisory positions, the company became more profitable.

These two studies do not paint a clear and convincing case for the overall effectiveness of teams. While teams are generally well received—that is, people enjoy working in them—it is not yet apparent that they are responsible for making individuals any more productive. From an organizational perspective, teams appear to be an effective way of eliminating layers of management. When people are highly committed toward achieving excellence, it is not surprising that their companies may reap the results. In fact, it is precisely these types of beneficial outcomes that are being reported by the case studies we summarized above. (Researchers are just beginning to understand that team effectiveness is closely related to national culture. For a look at one aspect of this relationship, see the GLOBALIZATION AND DIVERSITY section.)

Potential Obstacles to Success: Why Do Some Teams Fail?

Although we have reported many success stories about teams, we also have hinted at several possible problems and difficulties in implementing them. After all, working in a team demands a great deal, and not everyone may be ready for them. Fortunately, we can learn from these experiences. Analyses of failed attempts at introducing teams into the workplace suggest several obstacles to team success, pitfalls that can be avoided if you know about them.

COMPARING TEAM EFFECTIVENESS IN JAPAN, THE UNITED STATES, AND GREAT BRITAIN

When your team confronts a problem that requires it to seek advice, where would it be most likely to turn: a company policy manual, informal policies, advice from superiors, advice from fellow teammates, or your own experience? And, how effective are these various alternatives? Research has shown that the answer to both questions depends on the national culture of the teams in question.

If you recall from Chapter 2 the distinction between highly individualistic cultures (such as the United States and Great Britain) and highly collectivistic cultures (such as Japan), it should not be difficult to envision differences between the ways teams from each culture operate. After all, in individualistic cultures people tend to be self-reliant whereas in collectivistic cultures people tend to be group-oriented. As such, we would expect people from collectivistic cultures to consult their teammates, whereas people from individualistic cultures would rely on their own experiences. A recent study by Smith, Peterson and Misumi found just this.[85] Specifically, they surveyed team members in the United States, Great Britain, and Japan about how likely they would be to take certain actions in response to problems confronted in their teams. Their findings were clear: In Japan, people were most likely to consult their fellow team members, whereas in the United States and Great Britain, people were most likely to rely on their own previous experience and training. These results suggest that national culture is likely to influence the way team members operate when they face problems.

However, a question remains as to which of the various strategies is most effective? To answer this question the researchers examined the association between the various strategies the teams preferred and how productive supervisors rated the teams as being. The results were quite interesting. In general, Japanese teams were regarded as more productive to the extent that they relied on company manuals for help. However, teams from the United States and Great Britain were rated as being more productive to the extent that they relied on their own previous experiences. These findings are in keeping with the tendency for Japanese people to rely closely on formal procedures insofar as they represent the collective wisdom of the past, and the tendency for the more individualistic Americans and British people to put their faith in their individual experiences.[86]

It is important to note that the findings of Smith and his associates need to be interpreted with caution insofar as they relied on supervisors' ratings of team productivity instead of objective measures. The problem is that the results could stem from either of two possibilities: (1) supervisors gave higher ratings to teams because they adhered to culturally endorsed practices, or (2) supervisors gave higher ratings because these practices were, in reality, most effective. Unfortunately, this research does not rule out the first possibility. However, the study does provide very good evidence that the effectiveness of team performance is likely to be closely linked to cultural differences in the way teams operate. For this reason, researchers interested in the matter of team effectiveness would be well advised to consider the influence of national culture in their future studies.

First, some teams fail because their members are *unwilling to cooperate with each other*. This is what happened a few years ago at Dow Chemical Company's plastics group in Midland, Michigan, where a team was put into place to create a new plastic resin.[87] Some members (those in the research field) wanted to spend several months developing and testing new options, while others (those on the manufacturing end) wanted to slightly alter existing products and start up production right away. Neither side budged, and the project eventually stalled. By contrast, when team members share a common vision and are committed to attaining it, they are generally very cooperative with each other, leading to success (see Figure 8-15).

A second reason why some teams are not effective is that they *fail to receive support from management*. Consider, for example, the experience at the Lenexa, Kansas, plant of the Puritan-Bennett Corporation, a manufacturer of respiratory equipment.[88] After seven years of working to develop improved software for its respirators, product development teams did not get the job done, despite the fact that the industry average for such tasks is only three years. According to Roger J. Dolida, the company's director of research and de-

Lack of Cooperation: An
Important Barrier to Team Success
The development of a new plastic resin
at Dow Chemical Company was im-
peded by lack of cooperation between
those on the research and the manufacturing ends of the process.

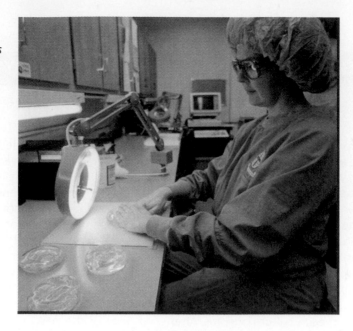

velopment, the problem is that management never made the project a priority, and refused to free up another key person needed to do the job. As he put
it, "If top management doesn't buy into the idea . . . teams can go nowhere."[89]

A third obstacle to group success, and a relatively common one, is that *some*
managers are unwilling to relinquish control. Good supervisors work their way up
from the plant floor by giving orders and having them followed. However, team
leaders have to build consensus and must allow team members to make decisions together. As you might expect, letting go of control isn't always easy for
some to do. This problem emerged at Bausch & Lomb's sunglasses plant in
Rochester, New York.[90] In 1989 some 1,400 employees were put into 38 teams.
By 1992 about half the supervisors had not adjusted to the change, despite receiving thorough training in how to work as part of a team. They argued bitterly with team members whenever their ideas were not accepted by the team,
and eventually they were reassigned. An even tougher approach was taken at
the Shelby Die Casting Company, a metal-casting firm in Shelby, Mississippi.[91]
When its former supervisors refused to cooperate as co-equals in their teams,
the company eliminated their jobs, and let the workers run their own teams.
The result: The company saved $250,000 in annual wages, productivity jumped
50 percent, and company profits almost doubled. The message sent by both
companies is clear: Those who cannot adjust to teamwork are unwelcome.

Fourth, teams might fail not only because their members do not cooperate with each other, but also because they *fail to cooperate with other teams*. This
problem occurred in General Electric's medical systems division when it assigned two teams of engineers, one in Waukesha, Wisconsin, and another in
Hino, Japan, the task of creating software for two new ultrasound devices.[92]
Shortly, teams pushed features that made their products popular only in their
own countries and duplicated each other's efforts. When the teams met, language and cultural barriers separated them, further distancing the teams from
each other. Without close cooperation between teams (as well as within them),
organizations are not likely to reap the benefits they hoped for when creating
teams in the first place.[93]

Building High-Performance Teams: Some Tips

As we just described, making teams work effectively is no easy task. Success
is not automatic. Rather, teams need to be carefully cared for and maintained
in order for them to accomplish their missions. As one expert expressed it,

Recall our discussion of training techniques in Chapter 3.

"Teams are the Ferraris of work design. They're high performance but high maintenance and expensive."[94] What, then, could be done to help make teams as effective as possible? Based on analyses of successful teams, several keys to success may be identified.[95] Here are several such tips:

1. *Diversify team membership.* Teams function most effectively when they are composed of highly skilled individuals who can bring a variety of different skills and experiences to the task at hand.[96]

2. *Keep teams small in size.* Effective teams consist of the smallest number of people needed to do the work. Coordination is difficult when teams are too large, and overload is likely when teams are too small. Generally, about 10–12 members is ideal.[97]

3. *Select the right team members.* There are some individuals who enjoy working in teams and others who prefer to work alone. To the extent that it is possible to do so, problems can be eliminated by not forcing loners onto teams. Similarly, it is important to select team members based on their skills or potential skills. Insofar as the success of teams demands that they work together closely on a wide variety of tasks, it is essential for them to have a complementary set of skills. This includes not only job skills but also interpersonal skills (especially since getting along with one's teammates is so very important).

4. *Train, train, train.* For teams to function effectively, members must have all the technical skills needed to do their jobs. This may well involve cross-training on the key aspects of others' specialty areas. It is also essential for them to be well trained in the interpersonal process skills needed for team members to get along with each other. Given the great responsibilities team members have, it also is advised that they be trained in the most effective ways to make decisions. With these considerations in mind, work teams at Colgate-Palmolive Company's liquid detergents plant in Cambridge, Ohio, initially receive 120 hours of training in such skills as quality management, problem solving, and team interaction, and subsequently receive advanced training in all these areas.

5. *Clarify goals.* When team members have a well-defined mission, they are likely to all pull in the same direction and attempt to reach the same team goals. It is therefore important that team goals be clearly articulated.

6. *Link individual rewards to team performance.* To the extent that team members are rewarded for their groups' successes by getting to share in the financial rewards, they are likely to be highly committed to striving for success.

7. *Use appropriate performance measures.* Teams work best when they develop their own measures of success. Furthermore, these measures should be based on the processes involved instead of the outcomes. For example, instead of measuring profitability, a traditional measure of success, a manufacturing team may concentrate on measures that have some diagnostic value, such as the average time per service call or the number of late service calls. After all, team members who are aware of these indices may be able to do something in response to them.

8. *Encourage participation.* To the extent that team members are allowed to participate in making decisions, the more likely they are to feel committed to those decisions. Thus, for teams to be committed to their work, it is essential for all team members to be involved.

9. *Cultivate team spirit and social support.* Teams work most effectively when they have a "can-do" attitude, believing that they can succeed. This is

often encouraged when team members lend interpersonal and task support to their teammates. Just as importantly, if not more so, support must come from top management. To the extent that team members suspect that management is not fully behind them, they will be unlikely to dedicate themselves to the task at hand.

10. *Foster communication and cooperation.* Naturally, team members must carefully communicate and cooperate with each other so that they can coordinate their efforts toward their common goal. At the same time, they must communicate and cooperate with other teams. In so doing, the overall success of the organization is fostered.

11. *Emphasize the urgency of the team's task.* Team members are prone to rally around challenges that compel them to meet high performance standards. For example, a few years ago, employees at Ampex Corporation worked hard to make their teams successful when they recognized the changes necessitated by the shift from analog to digital technology. Unless the company met these challenges, the plug surely would be pulled. Realizing that the company's future was at stake, work teams fast-forwarded Ampex into a position of prominence in its industry.

12. *Clarify the rules of behavior.* Effective teams have clear rules about what behaviors are and are not expected. For example, at Texas Instruments' Defense System and Electronics Group, rules about good attendance, giving only constructive criticism, and maintaining confidentiality are carefully followed.

13. *Regularly confront teams with new facts.* Fresh approaches are likely to be prompted by fresh information, and introducing new facts may present the kind of challenges that teams need to stay innovative. For example, when information about pending cutbacks in defense spending was introduced to teams at Florida's Harris Corporation (an electronics manufacturer), new technologies were developed that positioned the company to land large contracts in nonmilitary government organizations—including a $1.7 billion contract to upgrade the FAA's air traffic control system.

14. *Acknowledge and reward vital contributions to the team.* As indicated in Chapter 3, rewarding desired behavior is a key way of ensuring that the behavior will be repeated in the future. Rewards don't have to be large to work. For example, members of Kodak's Team Zebra, its black-and-white film manufacturing group, are given dinner certificates when they are singled out for making special contributions.[98]

If after reading this list you are thinking that it is no easy matter to get teams to work effectively, you have reached the same conclusion as countless practicing managers. Indeed, you don't just form teams and then sit back and watch the amazing results pour in. Teams can be very useful tools, but using them effectively requires a great deal of work. It is important to caution that although these suggestions are important, they alone do not ensure the success of work teams. Many other factors, such as the economy, the existence of competitors, and the company's financial picture are also important determinants of organizational success. However, in view of the considerable gains that have been found to occur, the effort would appear to be well worthwhile.

SUMMARY AND REVIEW

• •

The Nature of Groups

A **group** is defined as a collection of two or more interacting individuals with a stable pattern of relationships between them who share common goals and who perceive themselves as being a group. Within organizations, there are two major classes of groups—*formal groups* and *informal groups*. Groups often develop by going through five principal stages—*forming, storming, norming, performing,* and *adjourning*.

The structure of groups is determined by four key factors: *roles,* the typical pattern of behavior in a social context; *norms,* generally agreed upon informal rules; *status,* the prestige accorded group members; and *cohesiveness,* the pressures faced by group members to remain in their groups.

Individual Performance In Groups

Individual productivity is influenced by the presence of other group members. Sometimes, a person's performance improves in the presence of others (when the job they are doing is well learned), and sometimes performance declines in the presence of others (when the job is novel). This phenomenon is known as **social facilitation**. Not only is performance influenced by the presence of others, but by the group's racial/ethnic diversity. Performance in diverse groups is initially worse than performance in homogeneous groups, although these differences disappear with repeated involvement with the group.

On *additive tasks,* in which each member's individual contributions are combined, **social loafing** occurs. According to this phenomenon, the more people who work on a task, the less each group member contributes to it. Loafing can be reduced by making workers identifiable, making the work important and interesting, rewarding people for their group contributions, and threatening punishment.

The Nature of Teams

Teams are special kinds of groups, ones whose members focus on collective, rather than individual, work products, are mutually accountable to each other, share a common commitment to purpose, and are usually self-managing. Teams differ with respect to four dimensions: their *purpose or mission* (work or improvement), *time* (temporary or permanent), *degree of autonomy* (none or self-managed) and *authority structure* (overlaid or intact). Creating teams involves four steps: prework, creating performance conditions, forming and building a team, and providing ongoing assistance.

Team Performance

In surveys, organizational officials report that teams operating in their organizations have mostly been successful. Comprehensive case studies also have found organizational productivity gains (e.g., increased outcome, improved quality, lowered costs) resulting from the use of teams. However, more objective field research has found that while employees are generally more satisfied in teams than working under traditional management, they tend to be no more productive at the individual level. Many of the organizational benefits resulting from teams appear to come from the elimination of middle management positions.

Despite some evidence of the team successes, some teams fail. This is often because team members are unwilling to cooperate with each other, they fail to receive support from management, some managers are unwilling to relinquish control, and some teams fail to coordinate their efforts effectively with other teams. However, with some effort, teams can bring exceptionally high levels of performance. Among the many key factors contributing to team success are diversity in team membership, small size, effective training, using clear goals, and encouraging participation.

QUESTIONS FOR DISCUSSION

• •

1. What is the difference between a collection of individuals and a *group*? Why is a "group" of people waiting in line to see a movie not really a group?

2. Identify the stages of *group development* described in the text and apply them to any group to which you belong. Do all the stages apply?

3. Give examples demonstrating how *norms, roles,* and *status* operate within any groups to which you may belong.

4. Imagine that you are about to go on stage to give a solo piano recital. How would the phenomenon of *social facilitation* account for your performance.

5. Describe an incident of *social loafing* in which you may have been involved (e.g., a class project). What might be done to overcome this effect?

6. What makes a team a special form of group? Is a baseball team really a team or is it just a group?

7. Based on the evidence regarding the effectiveness of teams, would you say that the popularity of teams today is well founded?

8. Suppose you were to compose a work team in your organization. What potential pitfalls would you expect? What might you be able to do to help make that team perform at high levels?

XEL: The Little Telecommunications Company That Could

The telecommunications industry is populated by giants, like AT&T and Northern Telecom. So, when you're a David in an ocean of Goliaths, you have to do something different than the competition—and much better—just to stay afloat. This was the situation Bill Sanko and his partners faced in the mid-1980s when they broke off from GTE and started their own 180-employee telecommunications equipment company, XEL Communications, Inc. Sanko knew that the success of his fledgling operation depended on providing speedy responses to customers' needs at reasonable prices. The custom circuit boards XEL was selling (mostly to its former parent, GTE) were taking about eight weeks to produce. This was much too long, and the company began to struggle. Customers became disgruntled, and too much money was tied up in inventory.

The problem, Sanko realized, was that it took too many individuals to get anything done, and jobs were poorly coordinated. So Sanko and his colleagues decided that the solution to their problem would be to eliminate the many layers of management that were slowing down the process. In its place they would substitute small teams of people responsible for getting their jobs done.

XEL's teams typically are composed of about a dozen members, people with individual responsibilities that are clearly identified and agreed to mutually by all team members. Teams track their own attendance, on-time deliveries, and other aspects of job performance. Regularly each day, team members meet to plan their parts in meeting the company's weekly schedule. All of this goes on without management intervention. In fact, only once each quarter does management get involved—during a meeting in which each team makes a presentation describing what it has accomplished

By 1993, only five years after the teams began, things dramatically turned around at XEL. Since introducing teams, the cost of assembly dropped 25 percent, and inventory has been reduced 50 percent, all while increasing quality levels 30 percent. And, that eight-week production time? It dropped to only four days—and is still falling. Importantly, sales figures reflect these dramatic improvements: Between 1992 and 1993 sales jumped from $17 million to $25 million.

This success hasn't been exactly easy for XEL. Because team members work so closely together, adding new members has been a challenge. Teams are so concerned about getting their jobs done that they are often impatient with newcomers, fearing that their output will suffer. Another problem has been that in some groups, the freedom has proven to be too much. In XEL's stockroom, for example, some employees were abusing the system by cheating on their time cards. At first, problem employees were replaced, but eventually stockroom teams had to be disbanded and replaced by full-time supervisors with disciplinary authority.

As far as Bill Sanko and his colleagues at XEL are concerned, these adjustments are a small price to pay for an approach that has worked so effectively. XEL has been so successful, in fact, that it was chosen to be featured on a video about team-based management produced by the Association for Manufacturing Excellence.

Critical Thinking Questions

1. What measures could XEL take to help make its teams as effective as possible?
2. What problems are XEL's teams likely to face and how can they be overcome?

SKILLS PORTFOLIO

Experiencing Organizational Behavior

Why Do You Join Groups?

Groups are important in people's lives, and we join them for several different reasons. However, chances are good that you haven't given too much thought to the matter of why you may have joined certain groups in the first place. So, to identify these reasons, you may find it enlightening to complete the following questionnaire.

Directions

Think of a group you recently joined (e.g., a sports league, a campus club, a fraternity or sorority, a committee in your company). Then, indicate the importance of each of the following reasons for joining by using the following scale: 1 = not at all important; 2 = slightly important; 3 = moderately important; 4 = greatly important; 5 = extremely important.

I joined this group because . . . .

____ **1.** I had something important in common with the other members.
____ **2.** By joining the group, I had greater clout.
____ **3.** People in the group shared my interests.
____ **4.** The group helped me feel safe and secure.
____ **5.** I enjoy being with other people.
____ **6.** I thought the people in the group would make me feel good about myself.
____ **7.** I wanted to feel less lonely.
____ **8.** I expected the group members to recognize my accomplishments.

Scoring

1. Add your responses to numbers 1 and 3. This score reflects your interest in joining the group *to seek the satisfaction of mutual interests and goals.*
2. Add your responses to numbers 2 and 4. This score reflects your interest in joining the group *to achieve security.*
3. Add your responses to numbers 5 and 7. This score reflects your interest in joining the group *to fill social needs.*
4. Add your responses to numbers 6 and 8. This score reflects your interest in joining the group *to seek the fulfillment of self-esteem (feeling good about yourself) that others can provide.*

Questions for Discussion

1. What were your strongest (highest score) and weakest (lowest score) reasons for joining this group?
2. Besides the four reasons identified here, what other reasons did you have for joining this group?
3. Would your scores be different if you thought about another group you may have joined? Repeat the questionnaire to find out.

Working in Groups

Demonstrating the Social Loafing Effect

The social loafing effect is quite strong and is likely to occur in many different situations in which people make individual contributions to an additive group task. This exercise is designed to demonstrate the effect firsthand in your own class.

Directions

1. Divide the class into groups of different sizes. Between five and ten people should work alone. In addition, there should be a group of two, a group of three, a group of four, and so on, until all members of the class have been assigned to a group. If the class is small, assign students to groups of vastly different sizes, such as two, seven, and fifteen. Form the groups by putting together at tables people from the same group.
2. Each person should be given a page or two from a telephone directory and a stack of index cards. Then have the individuals and the members of each group perform the same additive task—copying entries from the telephone directory onto index cards. Allow exactly 10 minutes for the task to be performed, and encourage everyone to work as hard as they can.
3. After the time is up, count the number of entries copied.
4. For each group, and for all the individuals, compute the average per person performance by dividing the total number of entries copied by the number of people in the group.
5. At the board, the instructor should graph the results. Along the vertical axis show the average number of entries copied per person. Along the horizontal axis show the size of the work groups—one, two, three, four, and so on. The graph should look like the one in Figure 8-10.

Questions for Discussion

1. Was the social loafing effect demonstrated? What is the basis for this conclusion?
2. If the social loafing effect was not found, why do you think this occurred? Do you think it might have been due to the possibility that your familiarity with the effect led you to avoid it? Test this possibility by replicating the exercise using people who do not know about the phenomenon (e.g., another class), then compare the results.

3. Did members of smaller groups feel more responsible for their group's performance than members of larger groups?
4. What could have been done to counteract any "free riding" that may have occurred in this demonstration?

Take It to the Net

We invite you to visit the Greenberg/Baron page on the Prentice Hall Web site at:

http://www.prenhall.com/~greenob

for this chapter's WorldWide Web exercise.

You can also visit the Web sites for these companies, featured within this chapter:

BASF Fibers Division
http://www.basf.com/fibers/

Texas Instruments
http://www.ti.com/

Colgate-Palmolive
http://www.colgate.com/

Hewlett-Packard
http://www.hp.com/

Honeywell
http://www.iac.honeywell.com/

Cummins Engine
http://www.cummins.com/chome.html

Puritan Bennett Corp
http://www.nellcorpb.com/

Dow Chemical
http://www.dow.com/

CHAPTER Nine

INTERPERSONAL COMMUNICATION IN ORGANIZATIONS

■ OBJECTIVES

LEARNING

After reading this chapter you should be able to:

1. Describe the process of *communication* and its role in organizations.

2. Identify various forms of verbal media used in organizations and explain which ones are most appropriate for communicating messages of different types.

3. Explain how style of dress and the use of time and space are used to communicate nonverbally in organizations.

4. Describe various types of individual differences with respect to how people communicate with each other.

5. Distinguish between formal and informal *communication networks*, and explain the influence of each on organizational communication.

6. Describe how the formal structure of an organization influences the nature of the communication that occurs within it.

7. Identify and describe measures that can be taken by both individuals and organizations to improve the effectiveness of organizational communication.

CHILDRESS BUICK/KIA: KEEPING CUSTOMERS SATISFIED BY KEEPING EMPLOYEES INFORMED

George Russel ("Rusty") Childress knew that the business of selling cars was challenging, at best. With dealers' profit margins hovering around a razor-thin 1 percent, and with 10 percent of dealers losing money in recent years, Rusty knew from his dad, "Mr. C.," the founder of the business, that making it—indeed, even staying afloat—demanded something special. This was especially true in fast-growing Phoenix, where competing auto dealerships were springing up like desert cactus. Yet, Childress Buick/Kia has beaten the odds. With profits and customer satisfaction over twice the national average and employee turnover far less than average, it's clear that Childress is doing something right. As far as Childress is concerned, the key lies not in any one big thing, but a lot of little things—all boiling down to communication.

At Childress, the employee manual doesn't address such mundane issues as sick leave, but focuses on such topics as active listening and interpersonal communication—the very skills that are emphasized in the company's seven-week orientation program, "Childress College." The company goes out of its way to keep its 122 employees informed about everything that goes on. A monthly newsletter, *Squeaks and Rattles* not only announces birthdays and other personal milestones, but devotes considerable space to announcing employees' accomplishments (affectionately called "attaboys") and their suggestions for improvement. Supplementing this, Rusty himself sends out a weekly e-mail newsletter, *Dealer Direct*, to all employees with access to a computer. It might contain solicitations to join various teams or the latest sales information from Buick or Kia (a Korean auto company that began exporting to the United States in 1993).

About a year after Childress introduced these newsletters, he polled the employees to see how effectively the company was communicating internally. He expected to receive high grades, but to his surprise, the employees still didn't feel fully aware of what was going on at the dealership. Digging in his heels, Childress opened up several new channels of communication. One innovation is the "Suggestion Connection," a variation on the old suggestion box. Employees write their suggestions on any of several chalk boards posted throughout the dealership. A committee then reviews each idea and gets feedback to the employees who came up with it. There are also quarterly town-hall meetings in which Childress delivers his "state-of-the-dealership" address in the showroom. But it is not only Childress who can acknowledge his employees' accomplishments. Anyone who spots one of his or her co-workers doing something special can describe it on a yellow paper disk, called a "round of applause," and pin it onto a special bulletin board.

The channels of communication at Childress run both up and down the corporate ladder. Any employee who wants to reach Rusty can do so via a "hotline" that rings right on his desk. Even technicians who, at most dealerships, are generally not kept up-to-date on sales issues are brought into the loop. They regularly receive summaries of management meetings in mailboxes installed for this very purpose.

Childress is convinced that internal communication has been key to the company's success. The more employees know about what each other is doing, the more effectively they can pull together to improve customer service. And this appears to be exactly what is going on. That's one big "attaboy" and a "round of applause" for Rusty.

Very few owners of auto dealerships—or any business, for that matter—go to the same lengths as Rusty Childress to promote communication within their companies. By going out of his way to make sure that everyone in the company knows what's going on, Childress has put into action his belief that open communications is vital to organizational success. Given the company's record, it's clear he has been on the right track.

■ Figure 9-1
Communication: An Important Process in Organizations
This gentleman appears to be realizing something that both scientists and practicing managers have appreciated for some time—that the process of communication is central to organizational functioning.

(**Source:** Copyright © 1992, 1994 Leo Cullum.)

Rusty Childress is not alone in his beliefs about the importance of communication in organizations. Indeed, experts consider communication to be a key process underlying all aspects of organizational operations.[1] In fact, employees' overall performance is strongly related to their competence as communicators.[2] Contemporary scholars have variously referred to organizational communication as "the social glue . . . that continues to keep the organization tied together,"[3] and "the essence of organization."[4] Writing many years earlier, well-known management theorist and former New Jersey Bell Telephone President Chester Barnard said, "The structure, extensiveness and scope of the organization are almost entirely determined by communication techniques."[5] This strong statement makes sense if you consider that supervisors spend as much as 80 percent of their time engaging in some form of communication, such as speaking or listening to others, or writing to and reading material from others (see Figure 9-1).[6]

Given the importance of communication in organizations, we will closely examine this process in this chapter. To begin, we will define the process of communication and characterize its role in organizations. Following this, we will describe the two basic forms of communication: verbal and nonverbal. Then, we will examine several of the major influences on communication at the individual, group and organizational levels. These include individual differences, formal and informal communication networks, and organizational structure—aspects of the social and work environments that shape the nature and direction of the flow of information. Finally, we will turn to several barriers to effective communication—both individual and organizational in nature—and examine techniques for overcoming them.

Communication: Its Basic Nature

Before we can fully appreciate the process of organizational communication, we need to address some basic issues. To begin, we will formally define what we mean by *communication* and then elaborate on the process by which it occurs. Following this, we will describe the important role that communication plays in organizations.

Communication: A Working Definition and Description of the Process

What do the following situations have in common?

■ The district manager posts a notice stating that smoking is prohibited on company property.

- An executive prepares a report about the financial status of a potential corporate takeover prospect.
- A taxi dispatcher directs Cab 54 to pick up a fare at 1065 Cherry Drive.
- A foreman smiles at one of his subordinates and pats him on the back in recognition of a job well done.

The answer, if you haven't already guessed it, is that each of these incidents involves some form of *communication*. Although you probably already have a good idea of what communication entails, we can better understand communication in organizations by defining it precisely and describing the nature of the communication process.

With this in mind, we define **communication** as the process by which a person, group, or organization (the *sender*) transmits some type of information (the *message*) to another person, group, or organization (the *receiver*). To clarify this definition, and to further elaborate on how the process works, we have summarized it in Figure 9-2. You may find it helpful to follow along with this diagram as we describe the various steps.

Encoding. The communication process begins when one party has an idea that it wishes to transmit to another (either party may be an individual, a group, or an entire organization). It is the sender's mission to transform the idea into a form that can be sent to and understood by the receiver. This is what happens in the process of **encoding**—translating an idea into a form, such as written or spoken language, that can be recognized by a receiver. We encode information when we select the words we use to write a letter or speak to someone in person. This process is critical if we are to clearly communicate our ideas. Unfortunately, people are far from perfect when it comes to encoding their ideas (although, as we will note later, this skill can be improved).

Channel of communication. After a message is encoded, it is ready to be transmitted over one or more *channels of communication*, the pathways along which information travels, to reach the desired receiver. Telephone lines, radio and television signals, fiber-optic cables, mail routes, and even the air waves that carry the vibrations of our voices all represent potential channels of communication. Of course, the form of encoding largely determines the way information may be transmitted. Visual information—such as pictures and written words—may be mailed, delivered in person by a courier, shipped by an express delivery service, or sent electronically, such as via modems, fax machines and satellite dishes. Oral information may be transmitted over the telephone, via radio and television waves, and, of course, the old-fashioned way,

communication The process by which a person, group, or organization (the sender) transmits some type of information (the message) to another person, group, or organization (the receiver).

encoding The process by which an idea is transformed so that it can be transmitted to, and recognized by, a receiver (e.g., a written or spoken message).

■ **Figure 9-2**
The Communication Process
Communication generally follows the steps outlined here. Senders encode messages and transmit them via one or more communication channels to receivers, who then decode them. The process continues as the original receiver sends feedback to the original sender. Factors distorting or limiting the flow of information, known as noise, may enter into the process at any point.

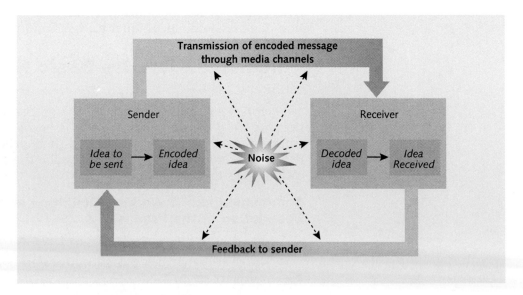

in person. Whatever channel is used, the goal is the same: to send the encoded message accurately to a desired receiver.

Decoding.   Once a message is received, the recipient must begin the process of **decoding**—converting the message back into the sender's original ideas. This can involve many different subprocesses, such as comprehending spoken and written words, interpreting facial expressions, and the like. To the extent that the sender's message is accurately decoded by the receiver, the ideas understood will be the ones intended. Of course, our ability to comprehend and interpret information received from others may be imperfect (e.g., restricted by unclear messages or by our own language skills). Thus, as in the case of encoding, limitations in our ability to decode information represent another potential weakness in the communication process—but, as we will describe later in this chapter, one that can be overcome.

Feedback.   Finally, once a message has been decoded, the process can continue with the receiver transmitting a new message back to the original sender. This part of the process is known as **feedback**—knowledge about the impact of messages on receivers. Receiving feedback allows senders to determine whether their messages have been understood properly. At the same time, giving feedback can help convince receivers that the sender really cares about what he or she has to say. Once received, feedback can trigger another idea from the sender, and another cycle of transferring information may begin. For this reason, we have characterized the process of communication summarized in Figure 9-2 as continuous.

Noise.   Despite the apparent simplicity of the communication process, it rarely operates as flawlessly as we have described it here. As we will see, there are many potential barriers to effective communication. The name given to factors that distort the clarity of a message is **noise**. As we have shown in Figure 9-2, noise can occur at any point along the communication process. For example, messages that are poorly encoded (e.g., written in an unclear way) or poorly decoded (e.g., not comprehended), or channels of communication that are too full of static (e.g., receivers' attentions are diverted from the message) may reduce communication's effectiveness. These factors, and others (e.g., time pressure, organizational politics), may contribute to the distortion of information transmitted from one party to another and to the complexity of the communication process. As you continue reading this chapter, you will come to appreciate many of the factors that make the process of organizational communication so very complex and important.

The Fundamental Role of Communication in Organizations

When you think about people in organizations communicating with each other, what image comes to mind? A typical picture might involve one person telling another what to do. Indeed, one key purpose of organizational communication is to *direct action*, that is, to get others to behave in a desired fashion. However, communication in organizations often involves not only single efforts, but also concerted action. Thus, for an organization to function, individuals and groups must carefully coordinate their efforts and activities.[7] The waiter must take the customer's order and pass it along to the chef. The market researcher must collect information about consumers' needs and share it with the people in charge of manufacturing and advertising. Communication is the key to these attempts at coordination. Without it, people would not know what to do, and organizations would not be able to function effectively— if at all. In other words, it may be said that another key function of communication in organizations is to *achieve coordinated action*.

This function is served by the systematic sharing of information. Indeed, *information*—whether it's data about a product's sales performance, directions

---

decoding The process by which a receiver of messages transforms them back into the sender's ideas.

feedback Knowledge about the impact of messages on receivers.

noise Factors capable of distorting the clarity of messages at any point during the communication process.

In Chapter 12 we will explain when and why political motives lead to the distortion of information communicated within organizations.

to a customer's residence, or instructions on how to perform a task—is the core of all organizational activities. It would be misleading, however, to imply that communication involves only the sharing of facts and data. There is also an *interpersonal* facet of organizational communication, a focus on the social relations between people.[8] For example, communication is also highly involved in such important purposes as *developing friendships* and *building trust and acceptance*. As you know, what you say and how you say it can have profound effects on the extent to which others like you. To the extent that people are interested in creating a pleasant interpersonal atmosphere in the workplace, they must be highly concerned about communication.

Verbal Communication: The Written and Spoken Word

verbal communication The transmission of messages using words, either written or spoken.

Because you are reading this book, we know you are familiar with **verbal communication**—transmitting and receiving ideas using words. Verbal communication can be either *oral*, using spoken language in forms such as face-to-face talks, telephone conversations, tape recordings, and the like, or *written*, in forms such as memos, letters, order blanks, and electronic mail, to name just a few. Because both oral and written communications involve the use of words, they fall under the heading of verbal communication.

Varieties of Verbal Media in Organizations

Verbal media can be distinguished with respect to their capacity to convey information (see Figure 9-3).[9] Some verbal media, such as *face-to-face discussions* are considered especially *rich* insofar as they not only provide vast amounts of information, but are also highly personal in nature and provide opportunities for immediate feedback. A bit less rich are non-face-to-face interactive media, such as the *telephone*. However, not all business communication requires a two-way flow of information. For example, further toward the *lean* end of the continuum are personal, but static media, such as *memos* (written messages used for communication within an organization) and *letters* (written messages used for external communication).[10] This includes one-way communications sent either physically (e.g., by letter), or electronically (e.g., via fax or e-mail). Finally, at the most lean end of the continuum are highly impersonal, static media, such as *flyers* and *bulletins*, written information that is targeted broadly, and not aimed at any one specific individual.

Two types of written media deserve special mention because of the important role they play in organizations—*newsletters* and *employee handbooks*.

■ **Figure 9-3**
A Continuum of Verbal Communication Media
Verbal communication media may be characterized along a continuum ranging from highly rich, interactive media, such as face-to-face discussions, to lean, static media, such as flyers and bulletins.

(**Source:** Adapted from Lengel & Daft, 1988; see Note 9.)

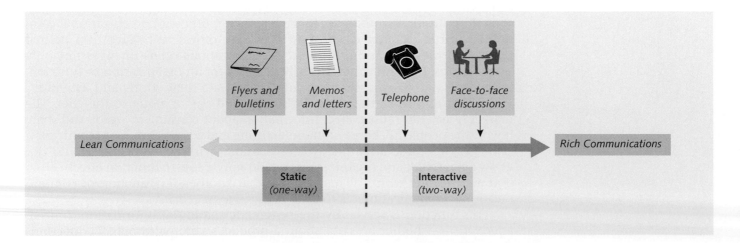

Newsletters. Although they are impersonal and aimed at a general audience, **newsletters** serve important functions in organizations, a point illustrated clearly by Childress in our PREVIEW CASE. Newsletters are regularly published internal documents describing information of interest to employees regarding an array of business and nonbusiness issues affecting them.[11] Approximately one-third of companies rely on newsletters, typically as a means of supplementing other means of communicating important information, such as group meetings.[12]

McDonnell Aircraft Company, for example, relies on its newsletter as a means of communicating information about its merit pay system, a medium that has been very well received (see Figure 9-4).[13] In fact, research at McDonnell Aircraft has shown that the more time its employees spend examining their company's newsletter, the more satisfied they are with their company's pay policy, and the fairer they believe it to be.[14] Newsletters appear to be effective devices in improving employees' attitudes and morale not only because of the information they provide about matters of interest to them, but also because the mere act of publishing a newsletter sends a message that the company cares enough about its employees to communicate with them. As Bob Sturgeon, owner of Granger, Iowa's Barr-Nunn Transportation explains it, his company's newsletter is designed "to show them [drivers] that someone back here is concerned about their welfare."[15]

Employee handbooks. Another important internal publication used in organizations is the **employee handbook**—a document describing to employees basic information about the company. It is a general reference regarding the company's background, the nature of its business, and its rules.[16] Specifically, the major purposes of employee handbooks are (1) to explain key aspects of the company's policies, (2) to clarify the expectations of the company and employees toward each other, and (3) to express the company's philosophy.[17]

Handbooks are more popular today than ever before. This is not only because clarifying company policies may help prevent lawsuits, but also because corporate officials are recognizing that explicit statements about what their company stands for is a useful means of effectively socializing new employees and

■ **Figure 9-4**
The Corporate Newsletter: An Effective Communications Tool
McDonnell Aircraft employees rely on their company's newsletter, Team Talk, as a means of keeping abreast of corporate policies and events.

We discussed the process of socializing new employees, and its importance, in Chapter 7.

promoting the company's values. As the major formal means of communicating pertinent company information to employees, employee handbooks are, in the opinion of one expert, "the most important document a company can have."[18]

Uses of Oral and Written Communication: Matching the Medium to the Message

Now that we have reviewed various types of verbal communication, it makes sense to consider what types are most effective, and when. In this regard, research has shown that *communication is most effective when it uses multiple channels, such as both oral and written messages*.[19] Apparently, oral messages are useful in getting others' immediate attention, and the follow-up written portion helps make the message more permanent, something that can be referred to in the future. Oral messages also have the benefit of allowing for immediate two-way communication between parties, whereas written communiqués are frequently only one-way or take too long for a response.

Not surprisingly, researchers have found that two-way communications (e.g., face-to-face discussions, telephone conversations) are more commonly used in organizations than one-way communications (e.g., memos). For example, Klauss and Bass found that approximately 83 percent of the communications taking place among civilian employees of a U.S. Navy agency used two-way media.[20] In fact, 55 percent of all communications were individual face-to-face interactions. One-way, written communications tended to be reserved for more formal, official messages that needed to be referred to in the future at the receiver's convenience (e.g., official announcements about position openings). Apparently, both written and spoken communications have their place in organizational communication.

Additional research has shown that a medium's effectiveness depends on how appropriate it is for the kind of message being sent. Specifically, Daft, Lengel, and Treviño reasoned that oral media (e.g., telephone conversations, face-to-face meetings) are preferable to written media (e.g., notes, memos) when messages are ambiguous (requiring a great deal of assistance in interpreting them), whereas written media are preferable when messages are clear.[21] The researchers surveyed a sample of managers about the medium they preferred using to communicate messages that differed with respect to their clarity or ambiguity. (For example, "giving a subordinate a set of cost figures" was prejudged to be a very unambiguous type of message, whereas "getting an explanation about a complicated technical matter" was prejudged to be a very ambiguous message.) The results, summarized in Figure 9-5, show that the choice of medium was related to the clarity or ambiguity of the messages.

The data reveal that the more ambiguous the message, the more managers preferred using oral media (such as telephones or face-to-face contact), and also that the clearer the message, the more managers preferred using written media (such as letters or memos). Apparently, most managers were sensitive to the need to use communications media that allowed them to take advantage of the rich avenues for two-way oral communications when necessary, and to use the more efficient one-way, written communications when these were adequate. Note, however, that although many managers selected media based on the pattern described here (people identified as "media-sensitive"), others did not. They made their media choices almost randomly (this group was referred to as "media-insensitive").

Further analysis of the data revealed that these differences were related to the managers' job performance. Those who were media-sensitive were expected to be more effective than those who were media-insensitive. After all, effective communication is an important part of managers' activities, and using the appropriate medium could enhance their effectiveness. Comparisons of the performance ratings of managers in the media-sensitive and media-insensitive

Oral vs. Written Communication: Preference for Media Depends on the Message

Research has shown that managers' preferences for a communications medium depends on the degree of clarity or ambiguity of the message being sent. Oral media (e.g., telephones or face-to-face contact) are preferred for ambiguous messages. Written media (letters or memos) are preferred for clear messages.

(**Source:** Based on data reported by Daft, Lengel, & Treviño, 1987; see Note 21.)

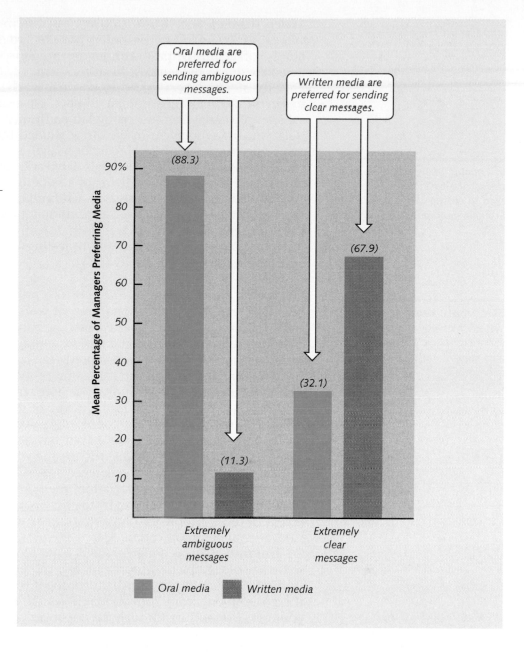

groups supported this hypothesis. Specifically, whereas most of the media-sensitive managers (87 percent) received their company's highest performance ratings, only about half of the media-insensitive managers (47 percent) received equally high evaluations. Apparently, the skill of selecting the appropriate communications medium is an important aspect of a manager's success. Unfortunately, it is difficult to say whether the managers' choices of communications media were directly responsible for their success, or whether their media sensitivity was part of an overall set of managerial skills that together led to their success. Still, these findings highlight the importance of making appropriate media choices in successful managerial communication.

When Words Go High-Tech: Special Issues of Electronic Media

In the past decade or two, advances in technology have transformed the way people engage in verbal communication while on the job. In particular, three forms of technology have revolutionized organizational communication—*video display terminals*, *electronic mail*, and *voice messaging*.

Video display terminals (VDTs). In the modern office *video display terminals (VDTs)* linked to computers have replaced the paper-cluttered desks of office workers in the past. Although computers vastly improve office productivity, there is a hidden cost in using them.

Clerical employees forced to do their work in the shadow of a computer screen all day may miss human contact, especially when they are encased in cubicles separated from others by tall partitions. In an attempt to escape such isolation, the employees in an office studied by Zuboff mischievously pried open the seam of a metal partition that separated them from their co-workers.[22] People reported feeling isolated and solitary, and longed for the kind of informal contact denied them by the design of their surroundings. When contact between managers and their subordinates is restricted, critical opportunities to identify and solve organizational problems may be lost. Ironically, the same technology that makes people so efficient often makes interpersonal collaboration unnecessary, adding to feelings of isolation, which may undermine some of the productivity gains.

Electronic mail (e-mail). One of the primary technological advances in organizational communication in recent years has been the use of **electronic mail** (popularly referred to as **e-mail**), a system whereby people use personal computer terminals to send and receive messages between each other. The electronic transmission of messages represents a communication revolution in that it allows for the very rapid transmission of information and the simultaneous sharing of identical information by people regardless of how widely dispersed they may be. What may be lost in terms of depth and richness of communication is more than made up for by high levels of efficiency.[23] As you probably know, communication via e-mail has become quite routine, as various online services make it possible for anyone with even modest computer hardware and software to send and receive e-mail. Indeed, based on projections from the Electronic Mail Association, the number of people using e-mail is estimated to be over 100 million by the time you read this.[24] This unprecedented access to other people and organizations is revolutionizing the nature of organizational communication.

Unfortunately, as e-mail systems have proliferated, with them have come some age-old problems—most notably, the potential for invasion of privacy. Ironically, although the fourth amendment to the U.S. Constitution prohibits the government from "unreasonable search and seizure," it does *not* restrict your boss from rifling through the papers in your office—or, tapping into your computer. Employers have argued that the practice is justified because they need to keep tabs on their employees to ensure that they are doing what they are supposed to do. Because companies own the computer systems, corporate officials feel justified accessing them whenever they wish. Indeed, a recent survey revealed that one out of five supervisors has on at least one occasion examined employees' computer files, e-mail, or voice mail, allegedly for purposes of investigating larceny or measuring performance.[25] Somehow, the remoteness of electronic snooping makes people feel less uncomfortable than they would about breaking into an employee's file drawer.

In recent years, laws have been enacted, such as the Electronic Communications Privacy Act, that safeguard the privacy of electronic messages sent over telephone lines. However, such laws apply only to public networks, such as CompuServe, not to private facilities, such as corporate computer systems. In the United States, attempts to enact legislation that would restrict employer's rights to eavesdrop on their employees (e.g., the proposed Privacy for Consumers and Workers Act) have been unsuccessful. The bottom line (today, at least) is clear: Employers *can*, and *do*, examine their employees' communications. So, if as an employee you are concerned about potential invasions of privacy, you may wish to follow the advice of Bill Moroney, executive direc-

In Chapter 14 we will more fully discuss the feelings of isolation that tend to emerge when people work in highly automated environments.

electronic mail (e-mail) A system whereby people use personal computer terminals to send and receive messages between each other.

Because many organizations do not have explicit policies about communication, employees do not know what levels of privacy they can expect. The following points represent what many experts consider the basic features of a good electronic privacy communication policy.

■ Employees are entitled to reasonable expectations of personal privacy on the job.

■ Employees know what electronic surveillance tools are used, and how management uses the collected data.

■ Management uses electronic monitoring or searches of data files, network communications, or electronic mail to the minimum extent possible. Continuous monitoring is not permitted.

■ Employees participate in decisions about how and when electronic monitoring or searches take place.

■ Data are gathered and used only for clearly defined work-related purposes.

■ Management will not engage in secret monitoring or searches, except when credible evidence of criminal activity or other serious wrongdoing comes to light.

■ Monitoring data will not be the sole factor in evaluating employee performance.

■ Employees can inspect, challenge, and correct electronic records kept on their activities or files captured through electronic means.

■ Records no longer relevant to the purposes for which they were collected will be destroyed.

■ Monitoring data that identify individual employees will not be released to any third party, except to comply with legal requirements.

■ Employees or prospective employees cannot waive privacy rights.

■ Managers who violate these privacy principles are subject to discipline or termination.

SOURCE: From "Bosses with X-ray Eyes" by Charles Piller in *MACWORLD*, July 1993, p. 121. Reprinted courtesy of Macworld Communications, 501 Second St., San Francisco, CA 94107.

tor of the Electronic Messaging Association: "Don't put anything in writing that you wouldn't want other people to read."[26] Meanwhile, it is widely recommended that companies develop clear policies about the privacy of employee communication.[27] For a summary of points that should be included in such a policy, see Table 9-1.

Voice messaging.   Although e-mail can be very quick and efficient, it lacks the capacity to send a personal message using one's own voice. However, another technology known as **voice messaging** (or **voice mail**) allows for just that. Voice messaging systems use computers to convert human speech into digital information saved on a hard disk for playback any time from any touch-tone telephone.

voice messaging (voice mail) A system that uses a computer to convert human speech into digital information saved on a hard disk for playback later by the receiver at any time from any touch-tone telephone.

Because 76 percent of all business calls are nonimmediate in nature (i.e., they do not require instantaneous action), and 56 percent of all calls completed involve one-way communication (i.e., they either give or receive information, but not both), voice messaging is frequently very useful.[28] Voice messaging allows people to avoid wasting time playing "telephone tag" and permits the highly efficient use of voice as an information tool because it precludes the need to translate messages into written characters or keystrokes. Voice messaging systems are so efficient, in fact, that they have been credited with saving an average of $2,000 per employee annually.[29] Given its ease of use, it is not surprising that researchers have found voice mail to be generally well accepted.[30]

Nonverbal Communication: Speaking without Words

nonverbal communication The transmission of messages without the use of words (e.g., by gestures, the use of space).

As we noted in Chapter 3, nonverbal cues such as smiles and glances are important sources of information influencing our impressions of people. Here we will describe other vehicles of **nonverbal communication**, the transmission of messages without the use of words. Specifically, some of the most prevalent nonverbal communication cues in organizations have to do with people's manner of dress and their use of time and space.

Style of Dress: Communicating by Appearance

If you have ever heard the expression "clothes make the man (or woman)," you are probably already aware of the importance of mode of dress as a communication vehicle. This is especially the case in organizations where, as self-styled "wardrobe engineer" John T. Malloy reminds us, what we wear communicates a great deal about our competence as employees.[31] In fact, research has shown that compared to people dressing inappropriately for job interviews (e.g., T-shirts and jeans), those dressing appropriately (e.g., business suits) feel more confident about themselves and, as a result, ask for higher starting salaries—on average, $4,000 higher.[32]

Despite what fashion consultants might advise, there does not exist a simple formula for exactly how to "dress for success." As you might imagine, what we communicate about ourselves by the clothing we wear is not a simple matter. Importantly, we cannot make up for the absence of critical job skills simply by putting on the right clothes. People who are qualified for jobs, however, may communicate certain things about themselves by the way they dress. Clearly, one of the key messages sent by the clothes people wear is their understanding of the *appropriate* way of presenting themselves for the job.

Of course, what is appropriate dress for one kind of job may not be appropriate for another. For example, people working at a small software development firm may be out of place wearing a coat and tie, just as bankers would be inappropriately attired in T-shirts and jeans. As Bing Gordon, co-founder of the video game company Electronic Arts, put it, "If somebody wears a suit to work around here, it's a sure sign that he is interviewing."[33] Although the interviewee may feel obligated to dress up for an interview, even in an organization with an informal style, you can be sure that shortly after starting the job he or she will quickly adapt to its customary, informal style of dress.

Time: The Waiting Game

Another important mechanism of nonverbal communication in organizations is the use of time. Have you ever waited in the outer office of a doctor or dentist? Surely you have—after all, they have special "waiting rooms" just for this purpose. Why do you have to wait for such people? Mainly, because they have special skills that create high demands for their services. As a result, their time is organized in a manner that is most efficient *for them*—by keeping others lined up to see them at their convenience.[34]

Medical professionals are not the only ones who make people wait to see them. In fact, individuals in high-status positions often communicate the idea that their time is more valuable than others' (and therefore that they hold higher-status positions) by making others wait to see them. This is a very subtle, but important, form of nonverbal communication. Typically, the longer you have to wait to see someone, the higher the organizational status that person has attained. This has been shown in a study by Greenberg.[35] Participants in this investigation were applicants for a job as office manager at various companies who waited to be interviewed with people of higher status (vice presidents), lower status (assistant office managers), or equal status (another office manager). Greenberg found that the higher the status of the person job candidates waited to see, the longer they had to wait. The vice president interviewers communicated their higher status to the candidates by making them wait longest to see them. In contrast, assistant office manager interviewers communicated their lower status to candidates by being prompt—an act conveying deference and respect.

The Use of Space: What Does It Say about You?

Like time, space is another important communication vehicle. Research has shown that one's organizational status is communicated by the amount of space at one's disposal. Generally speaking, the more space one commands, the more powerful one is likely to be in an organization. For example, higher-status life insurance underwriters in one organization were found to have larger desks and larger offices than lower-status underwriter trainees.[36] Not only does the amount of space communicate organizational status, but also the way that space is arranged. For example, among faculty members at a small college, senior professors were more likely to arrange their offices so as to separate themselves from visitors with their desks, whereas junior professors were less likely to impose such physical barriers.[37] These various office arrangements systematically communicated different things about the occupants. Specifically, professors who did not distance themselves from their students by use of their desks were seen as more open and unbiased in their dealing with students than those who used their desks as a physical barrier.

The use of space appears to have symbolic value in communicating something about group interaction. Consider, for example, who usually sits at the head of a rectangular table. In most cases, it is the group leader. It is, in fact, traditional for leaders to do so. But at the same time, studies have shown that people emerging as the leaders of groups tend to be ones who just happened to be sitting at the table heads.[38] Apparently, *where* a person sits influences the available communication possibilities. Sitting at the head of a rectangular table enables a person to see everyone else and to be seen by them. That leaders tend to emerge from such positions is, therefore, not surprising (see Figure 9-6).

It is not only individuals who communicate something about themselves by the use of space, but organizations as well.[39] For example, according to John Sculley, former president of PepsiCo, his company's world headquarters were designed to communicate to visitors that they were seeing "the most important company in the world."[40] Similarly, by adding a second office tower to its company headquarters in Cincinnati, Procter & Gamble was said to be attempting to create a gateway-like complex that communicated the company's connection to the community.[41] As these examples suggest, organizations, as well as individuals, use space to communicate symbolically certain aspects of their identities.

In concluding this section, we note that the nonverbal mechanisms we have presented here, as important as they are, represent only a single channel of communication. Both verbal and nonverbal channels are important sources of information used in conjunction with each other in the process of

■ **Figure 9-6**
The Head of the Table: A Good Location for Communication
In part because of the ease with which they can see others and be seen by them, people who sit at the heads of rectangular tables enjoy effective communication with others seated at the sides.

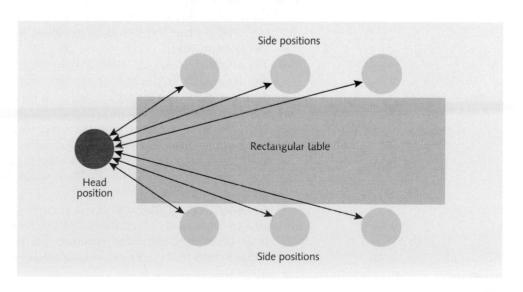

Side positions

Rectangular table

Head position

Side positions

communication. Thus, although we separated the various forms of communication for purposes of presenting them to you, it is important to realize that they operate together, complementing each other in complex ways in actual practice.

Individual Differences in Communication

As you know from experience, different people tend to communicate in different ways. Two people saying the same thing might do so very differently and communicate their messages in ways that may have different effects on you. In other words, there seem to be individual differences in the way people communicate. Researchers have verified that such differences are indeed real. We now will examine key individual differences in communication—differences based on personal style, gender, and nationality.

Personal Communication Style

Steve and Charlie are two supervisors who are approached by a subordinate, Greg, to discuss the possibility of receiving a salary increase. They both think that Greg is not deserving of the raise he requests. However, Steve and Charlie each go about communicating their feelings quite differently. Steve couldn't have been more direct. "I'll be frank," he said, "a raise is out of the question." Charlie's approach was far more analytical: "Well, Greg, let's look at the big picture. I see here in your file that we just gave you a raise two months ago, and that you're not scheduled for another salary review for four months. Let me share with you some of the numbers and thoroughly explain why the company will have to stick with that schedule . . . ."

Although the message was the same in both cases, Steve and Charlie presented it quite differently. In other words, they appear to differ with respect to their **personal communication style**—the consistent ways people go about communicating with others. As you might imagine, some personal communication styles may be more effective than others—particularly, depending on the other person involved and the situation they are in. Communication style is learned, and so it can change. But, before we can consider changing how we communicate, we must first recognize the style we use. With this in mind, Linda McCallister has identified six major communication styles, one of which is likely to describe most people (for a summary, see Figure 9-7).[42]

- *The Noble*: Such individuals tend not to filter what they are thinking but come right out and say what's on their minds (like Steve, in our example). Nobles use few words to get their messages across. They cut right to the bottom line.
- *The Socratic*: These are people who believe in carefully discussing things before making decisions. Socratics enjoy the process of arguing their points and are not afraid to engage in long-winded discussions. They have a penchant for details and often "talk in footnotes."
- *The Reflective*: These individuals are concerned with the interpersonal aspects of communication. They do not wish to offend others, and they are great listeners. Reflectives would sooner say nothing, or tell you what you want to hear (even if it's a "little white lie"), than say something that might cause conflict.
- *The Magistrate*: A magistrate is a person whose style is a mix of part Noble and part Socratic. Magistrates tell you exactly what they think and make their cases in great detail (such as Charlie, in our example). These individuals tend to have an air of superiority about them as they tend to dominate the discussion.

personal communication style The consistent ways people go about communicating with others (e.g., the *Noble*, the *Socratic*, the *Reflective*, the *Magistrate*, the *Candidate*, and the *Senator*).

Personal communication style is not the same as personality, but it is most likely related to several of the personality variables discussed in Chapter 4.

■ Figure 9-7
*Personal Communication Styles:
A Summary*
*People tend to communicate using one
of six different personal communication styles. These styles, and their interrelationships, are summarized here.*

(**Source:** Based on suggestions by
McCallister, 1994; see Note 42.)

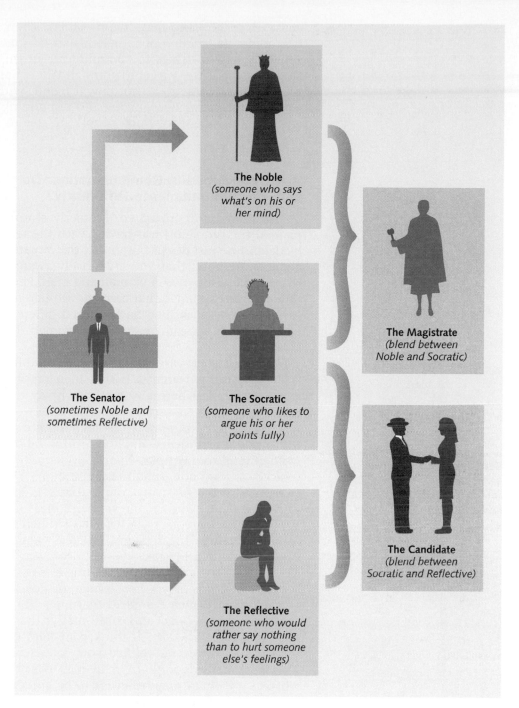

- *The Candidate*: Such individuals have a style that is a mix between Socratics and Reflectives. As such, they tend to be warm and supportive, while also being analytical and chatty. They base their interactions on a great deal of information, and do so in a very likable manner.
- *The Senator*: A Senator is an individual who has developed both the Noble style *and* the Reflective style. They do not mix the two styles. Rather, they move back and forth between the two of them as needed.

It is important to keep in mind that we all have the potential to use any of these styles.[43] However, we generally tend to rely on one style more than any other. Each has its strengths and weaknesses, and no one style is better than another. They are simply different. Effective communication begins with understanding your own style (see the EXPERIENCING ORGANIZATIONAL BEHAVIOR ex ercise on p. 326) and that used by others. Then, when you first meet another, it is advisable to attempt to match that person's style. This is because people generally expect others to communicate in the same manner as themselves. However, the better we get to know and accept another's communication style, the better we come to accept how it blends with our own. In either case, the advice is the same: Recognizing and responding to communication styles can enhance the extent to which people are able to communicate effectively with one another.

Sex Differences in Communication: Do Women and Men Communicate Differently?

Infuriated and frustrated, Kimberly stormed out of Mike's office. "I explained the problem I was having with the temporary employees," she grumbled, "but he just doesn't listen!" If this situation sounds at all familiar to you, chances are good that you are already aware of the communication barriers that often exist between women and men. Recently, Deborah Tannen, a sociolinguist, has explained that men and women frequently miscommunicate with each other because they have learned different ways of using language.[44] In general, what appears "natural" to women doesn't come easily to men, and vice versa.

When it comes to communication, the basic difference between women and men, Tannen argues, is that men emphasize and reinforce their status when they talk, whereas women downplay their status. Rather, women focus on creating positive social connections between themselves and others. Thus, whereas men tend to say "I," women tend to say "we." Similarly, whereas men try to exude confidence and boast, thinking of questions as signs of weakness, women tend to downplay their confidence (even when they are sure they are correct) and are not afraid to ask questions. (What comes to mind here is the stereotypical image of the couple that gets lost on some dusty back road because the man overrules the woman's pleas to ask for directions.)

This difference in style between women and men explains why they respond differently to problems. Whereas women tend to listen and lend social support, men tend to take control by offering advice. When men do this, they are asserting their power, contributing to a communication barrier between the sexes. Not surprisingly, whereas men may complain that women are "too emotional," women may complain that men "do not listen." Similarly, men tend to be much more direct and confrontative than women. Although a man might come right out and say, "I think your sales figures are inaccurate," a woman might ask, "Have you verified your sales figures by comparing them to this morning's daily report?" A man may consider this approach to be sneaky, whereas a woman may believe it to be kinder and gentler than a more direct statement. Likewise, women may interpret a man's directness as unsympathetic.

The implications of this set of differences come to the surface once we point out another of Tannen's findings: People in powerful positions tend to reward people whose linguistic styles match their own.[45] As a result, in most organizations, where men tend to be in charge, the contributions of women are often downplayed because the things they say tend to be misinterpreted. The woman who politely defers to a dominant male speaker at a meeting may come across (to men, at least) as being passive. As a result, her contributions may never come to the table. However, the woman who breaks from this pattern and interjects her ideas may come across (again, to men) as being pushy and aggressive. And here too, her contributions may be discounted. In both cases, the communication barrier has caused a situation in which organizations are not only breeding conflict, but they are not taking advantage of the skills and abilities of their female employees. The solution, although not easy, lies in appreciating and accepting the different styles that people have. As

Sex differences in communication styles may well be related to sex role stereotypes. These are described in Chapter 6.

Tannen put it: "Talk is the lifeblood of managerial work, and understanding that different people have different ways of saying what they mean will make it possible to take advantage of the talents of people with a broad range of linguistic styles."[46]

Cross-Cultural Differences in Communication

In Chapter 2 we noted that the phenomenon of globalization presents many challenges. Clearly, one of the most immediate challenges has to do with communication. When people speak different languages, it makes sense that communication between them may be imperfect.

Part of the problem is that different words may mean different things to different people.[47] For example, as hard as it might be for people from countries with long-standing capitalist economies to realize, Russians have difficulty understanding words such as "efficiency" and "free market," which have no direct translation in their own language. People who have never known a free-market economy while they were growing up certainly may find it difficult to grasp the concept. It is therefore not surprising to find that communication barriers have been found to exist when American executives attempt to conduct business in Russia (see Figure 9-8).[48]

In addition to different vocabularies, cross-cultural communication is made difficult by the fact that in different languages even the same word can mean different things. Just imagine, for example, how confused an American executive might become when she speaks to her counterpart in Israel, where the same Hebrew word, *shalom*, means both "hello" and "goodbye" (as well as "peace"). Confusion is bound to arise. The same may be said for cultural differences in the tone of speech used in different settings. Whereas Americans might feel free to say the word "you" in both formal and informal situations, the French have different words in each (*tu* for informal speech, and *vous* for formal speech). To confuse these may be tantamount to misinterpreting the nature of the social setting, a potentially costly blunder—and all because of a failure to recognize the subtleties of cross-cultural communication. What can be done to eliminate blunders likely to be caused by the barriers inherent in cross-cultural communication? In the GLOBALIZATION AND DIVERSITY section we outline several key suggestions.

Communication difficulties are but one manifestation of the growing trend toward globalization of organizations discussed in Chapter 2.

YOU BE THE CONSULTANT

A produce distribution company located in a large city has a highly diverse workforce: There are lots of men and women working there who are new immigrants to this country. Unfortunately, the company is experiencing a serious problem with key jobs either not getting done at all or getting done incorrectly.

1. Explain why this situation might be linked to communication problems within the workforce.
2. What could be done at an individual level to help solve the problem?
3. What advice would you give with respect to changing the nature of the organization so as to help solve the problem?

■ **Figure 9-8**
Russian-American Communication Barriers
Although Russian citizens, such as industrialist Giorgi Kovalenko (general director of the Poliplast plastics factory in Rybinsk), are quickly learning capitalist ways, their exposure to many years of communism has left them lacking a basic business vocabulary that often hinders communication with capitalist nations.

Communication Networks: Formal Channels of Information in Groups

Imagine two different work groups in the Sales and Marketing Division of a large corporation. One consists of a team of creative writers, artists, and market researchers sitting around a table working together on developing the company's new advertising campaign. Another includes field representatives in various territories who report to regional sales managers throughout the country about consumers' preferences for various products. These people, in turn, analyze this information and report it to the vice president of sales and marketing. If you think about how these two groups differ, one key variable becomes obvious: The pattern of communication within them is not the same. Members of the creative team working on the advertising campaign can all communicate with each other at once, whereas people in the sales force speak only to those who are immediately above or below them. The patterns determining which organizational units (either people

GLOBALIZATION AND DIVERSITY IN TODAY'S ORGANIZATIONS

BREAKING DOWN THE BARRIERS TO CROSS-CULTURAL COMMUNICATION

As we have noted, the potential for miscommunication between people from different cultures is considerable. However, short of becoming expert in foreign languages and cultures, there are several steps that can be taken to promote cross-cultural communication.[49]

1. *Observe, but do not evaluate.* Suppose while touring a factory in a foreign country you observe several assembly-line workers sitting down and talking instead of working. Based on your own country's culture, this would be inappropriate, a sure sign of laziness. Fearing what this means about the plant's productivity, you develop second thoughts about doing business with that company. However, the more you learn about these workers' national culture, you discover that they were engaging in a traditional work break ritual: resting while remaining on the work site. The people in question were merely doing what was expected of them culturally and may not be lazy after all. The point is that you evaluated the situation by applying your own cultural values, and were misled by them. To avoid such problems, it is advisable in cross-cultural communications to describe what you observe (i.e., the workers are resting) rather than to use these observations as the basis for making evaluations (i.e., the workers are lazy). Doing so can help you avoid serious misinterpretation.

2. *Do not jump to conclusions.* When we perceive various situations, we tend to assume that our judgments are correct. However, experts caution that when it comes to cross-national settings, we should consider our judgments more as educated guesses than as certain conclusions. If you think that something is correct (such as your interpretation of the lazy workers in the above example), it is best to compare these to the judgments of experts in the local culture than to assume you are correct. By confirming the accuracy of your judgments, misinterpretation is less likely.

3. *Assume that people are different from yourself.* Most of us tend to assume that others are similar to ourselves until we learn otherwise. However, such an assumption is likely to lead us down the wrong track. Seasoned international managers know this. They take the opposite stance, assuming that others are different until proven otherwise. Because they "know that they don't know," they are less likely to be surprised by differences they don't expect—but which are inevitable.

4. *Take the other person's perspective.* Try to see the situation through the eyes of your foreign colleague. Consider this individual's values and experiences and ask yourself how he or she might view things differently. To the extent that you can effectively switch roles, you will be able to avoid the narrow-mindedness ("cultural myopia") with which we all tend to make decisions.

Although these measures may be easier said than done, with a little practice they can be mastered. Given that such practices are key to the success of international managers, the effort involved in following them would appear to be well worthwhile.

---

communication networks
Pre-established patterns dictating who may communicate with whom.

or groups) communicate to which other units are referred to as **communication networks**.

Varieties of Formal Communication Networks

As you might imagine, there are many different possible communication networks within organizations. Do such arrangements matter? Do they make any difference in how well groups do their jobs and how satisfied group members feel? A considerable amount of research has shown that the nature of the communication linkages between group members can greatly influence group functioning.[50] So that we can appreciate these research findings, let's first consider some of the possible configurations of connections between people. Some of the most commonly studied possibilities are shown in Figure 9-9. (These various diagrams depict communication networks that have five members, although they can have any number of members from three or more.) In each diagram, the circles represent individual

■ **Figure 9-9**
Communication Networks: Some Basic Types
Some examples of five-person communication networks are shown here. Decentralized networks, such as the circle and the comcon, give all members equal opportunities to communicate with each other. Centralized networks, such as the Y, wheel, and chain contain members (marked by a purple circle) through whom messages must pass to reach others.

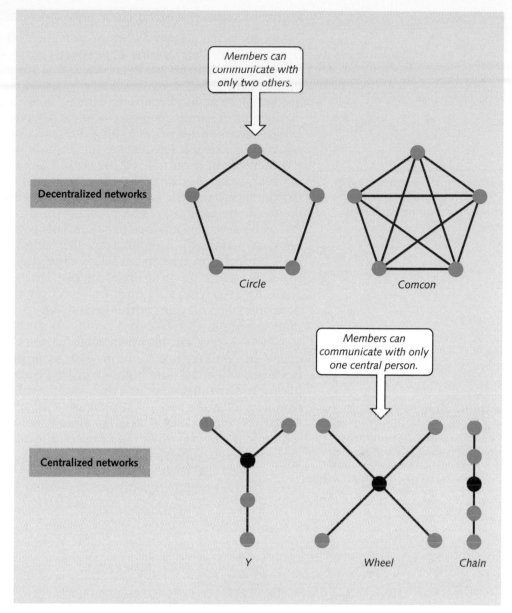

Members can communicate with only two others.

Decentralized networks

Circle

Comcon

Members can communicate with only one central person.

Centralized networks

Y   Wheel   Chain

centralization The degree to which information must flow through a specific central member of a communication network.

centralized networks Communication networks that have central members through which all information must pass to reach other members (e.g., the *Y*, the *wheel*, and the *chain*).

decentralized networks Communication networks in which all members play an equal role in the transmittal of information (e.g., the *circle* and the *comcon*).

The concepts of centralization and decentralization apply not only to groups, but as we will describe in Chapter 16, to the design of organizations as well.

people and the lines connecting them represent two-way lines of communication between them. (Some communication flows only in one direction, but for simplicity's sake only two-way, mutual communication flows will be used in our examples.)

As Figure 9-9 highlights, communication networks may differ with respect to a key feature: their degree of **centralization.** Briefly, this refers to the degree to which information must flow through a specific member of the network. As you can see in Figure 9-9, communication networks such as the *Y*, *wheel*, and *chain* are identified as **centralized networks**. For members of centralized networks to communicate with each other, they must go through a central person who is at the "crossroads" of the information flow. In contrast, the *circle* and *comcon* are referred to as **decentralized networks** because information can freely flow between members without going through a central person. People in decentralized networks have equal access to information, whereas those in centralized networks are unequal because the individuals at the centers have access to more information than those at the periphery.

Formal Communication Networks and Task Performance

Research has shown that these differences in communication networks are responsible for determining how effectively groups will perform various jobs. Generally speaking, it has been found that when the tasks being performed are simple, centralized networks perform better, but when the tasks are complex, decentralized networks perform better.[51] Specifically, comparing these two types of network: *Centralized networks are faster and more accurate on simple tasks, whereas decentralized networks are faster and more accurate on complex tasks.*

Why is this so? The answer has to do with the pressures put on the central member of a centralized network. The more information any one member of a group has to deal with, the greater the degree of **saturation** that person experiences. If you've ever tried working on several homework assignments at the same time, you probably already know how information saturation can cause performance to suffer. This is what happens when a centralized network performs a complex task. The central person becomes so overloaded with information that the group is slowed down and many errors are made. However, when the problem is simple, the central person can easily solve it alone after receiving all the information from the other members. Decentralized networks have no one central person, so information and work demands are more evenly distributed. As a result, on simple tasks the information needed to solve the problem may be spread out over all the group members, causing delays in coming to a solution. This same feature represents an advantage, however, when tasks are highly complex because it prevents any single member from becoming saturated and lowering the group's performance. (See our summary of these processes in Figure 9-10.) In short, centralization is a double-edged sword. When tasks are simple, centralization facilitates getting the job done. However, when tasks are complex, it may cause saturation, bringing performance to a halt.

Research also shows that centralized and decentralized networks differ in terms of their members' satisfaction. Would you be more satisfied as a mem-

saturation The amount of information a single member of a communication network must handle.

■ **Figure 9-10**
Comparing the Performance of Centralized and Decentralized Communication Networks
As shown here, centralized *networks are superior on simple tasks (top), and* decentralized *networks are superior on complex tasks (bottom).*

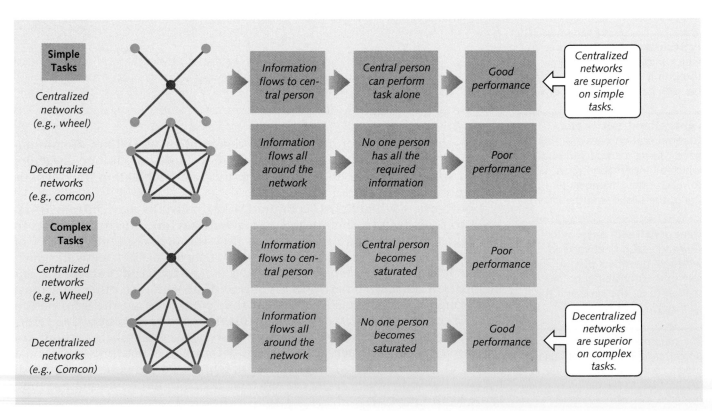

ber of a centralized or decentralized network? Most people enjoy the greater equality in decision making that occurs in decentralized networks. Such groups give everyone involved an equal status. In contrast, as a peripheral member of a centralized network, you would be less powerful than the central member and left out of the decision-making process. The central member controls more of the flow of information and is clearly more important, leading many peripheral members to feel that their contributions are not fully appreciated. Together, these factors combine to cause lower overall levels of satisfaction among members of centralized networks compared with those in decentralized networks.

Although formal communication networks clearly play an important role in organizations, they represent only one of several factors responsible for organizational communication. One important consideration is that although the lines of communication between people can greatly influence their job performance and satisfaction, the various advantages and limitations of different communication networks tend to disappear the longer the groups are in operation.[52] As group members gain more experience interacting with each other, they may learn to overcome the limitations imposed by their communication networks. (For example, they may learn to send messages to specific individuals who have proven themselves in the past to be particularly competent at solving certain kinds of problems.) In other words, although the differences between various communication networks may be quite significant, they may be only temporary, accounting for the behavior of newly formed groups more than the behavior of highly experienced groups.

Another important point is that any formal lines of communication operate in organizations in conjunction with widespread informal networks that also may help groups accomplish their goals. Even if formal channels impede the communication of information, informal connections between people—such as friendships or contacts in other departments—may help the communication process. As we will describe next, the informal connections between people are extremely important in organizational communications.

Informal Communication Networks: Behind the Organizational Chart

For a moment, think about the people with whom you communicate during the course of an average day. Friends, family members, classmates, and colleagues at work are among those with whom you may have *informal communication*—information shared without any formally imposed obligations or restrictions. When you think about it carefully, you may be surprised to realize how widespread our informal networks can be. You know someone who knows someone else who knows your best friend—and before long, your informal networks become very far-reaching. Informal communication networks, in part because they are so widespread, constitute an important avenue by which information flows in organizations. In fact, in a recent survey middle managers ranked informal networks as better sources of organizational information than formal networks.[53] Therefore, if an organization's formal communication represents its skeleton, its informal communication constitutes its central nervous system.[54]

Organizations' Hidden Pathways

It is easy to imagine how important the flow of informal information may be within organizations. People transmit information to those with whom they come into contact, thereby providing conduits through which messages can travel. We also tend to communicate most with those who are similar to ourselves on such key variables as age and time working on the job.[55] Because we are more comfortable with similar people than with dissimilar ones, we tend to spend more time with them and, of course, communicate with them more. As a result, many informal gender-segregated networks tend to form in organizations (what among men has been referred to as the *old-boys network*).

To the extent that these associations may isolate people from others in power who may be different from themselves, this practice is limiting.[56] At the same time, however, exposure to similar others with whom people feel comfortable provides valuable sources of information. For example, many African American business leaders have formed informal networks with others of their same race so as to help them share ways of succeeding in a business world in which they constitute an ethnic minority—alliances that have been helpful to the careers of many.[57] This informal observation is in keeping with scientific evidence showing that the more involved people are in their organizations' communication networks, the more powerful and influential they become.[58]

For more on this topic, see the discussion of mentoring appearing in Chapter 7.

The idea that people are connected informally also has been used to explain a very important organizational phenomenon—turnover. Do people resign from their jobs in ways that are random and unrelated to each other? A study by Krackhardt and Porter suggests that they do not, but that turnover is related to the informal communication patterns between people.[59] These investigators theorized that voluntary turnover (employees freely electing to resign their jobs) occurs as a result of a *snowball effect*. A snowball does not accumulate snowflakes randomly, but collects those that are in its path. Analogously, it was reasoned, patterns of voluntary turnover may not be independently distributed within a work group, but may be the result of people's influences on each other. Thus, predicting which people will resign from their jobs may be based, in large part, on knowledge of the communication patterns within groups. Someone who leaves her job for a better one in another organization may know someone who has already done so. Krackhardt and Porter found support for this snowball effect among teenagers working in fast-food restaurants. Specifically, turnover tended to be concentrated among groups of people who communicated informally with each other a great deal before they resigned. (For a suggestion regarding how this may operate, see Figure 9-11). This study provides an excellent example of the importance of informal patterns of communication in organizations.

Informal communication networks are characterized by the fact that they often are composed of individuals at different organizational levels. People can tell anyone in the network whatever informal information they wish. For example, one investigator found that jokes and funny stories tended to cross organizational boundaries, and were freely shared by those in both the managerial and nonmanagerial ranks of organizations.[60] On the other hand, it would be quite unlikely—and considered "out of line"—for a lower-level employee to communicate something to an upper-level employee about how to do the job. What flows within the pathways of informal communication is informal information, messages not necessarily related to individuals' work.

The Grapevine and the Rumor Mill

When anyone can tell something informal to anyone else, it results in a very rapid flow of information along what is commonly referred to as the **grapevine**—the pathways along which unofficial, informal information travels. In contrast to a formal organizational message, which might take several days to reach its desired audience, information traveling along the organizational grapevine tends to flow very rapidly, often within hours. This is not only because informal communication can cross formal organizational boundaries (e.g., you might be able to tell a good joke to almost anyone, not just your boss or subordinates with whom you are required to communicate), but also because informal information tends to be communicated orally.

grapevine An organization's informal channels of communication, based mainly on friendship or acquaintance.

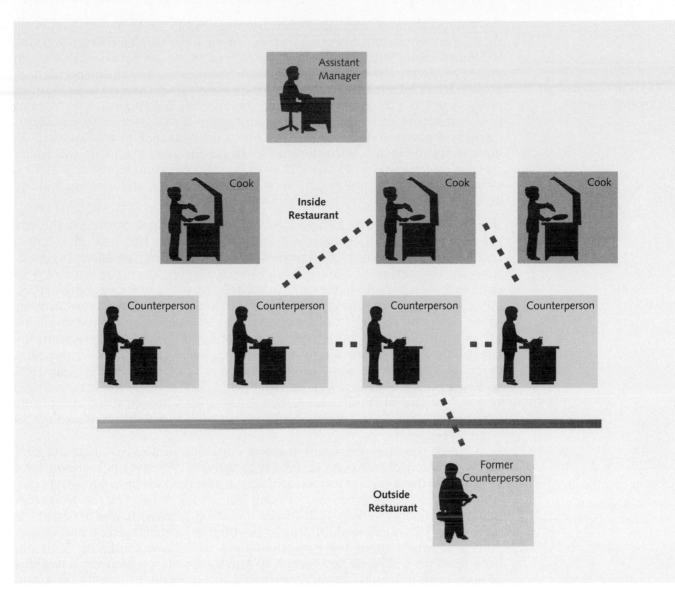

■ **Figure 9-11**
*Informal Communication
Networks: A Predictor of Turnover
Patterns*
The informal networks of communication between people (shown in dotted lines) provide channels through which messages about better job opportunities may be communicated. Patterns of voluntary turnover have been linked to the existence of such informal networks.

(**Source:** Based on suggestions by Krackhardt & Porter, 1986; see Note 59.)

The problem of inaccuracy. As we noted earlier, oral messages are communicated faster than written ones but may become increasingly inaccurate as they flow from person to person. Because of the confusion grapevines may cause, some people have sought to eliminate them, but they are not necessarily bad. Informally socializing with our co-workers can help make work groups more cohesive, and also may provide excellent opportunities for desired human contact, keeping the work environment stimulating. Grapevines must be considered an inevitable fact of life in organizations.[61]

It is interesting to note that most of the information communicated along the grapevine is accurate. In fact, one study found that 82 percent of the information communicated along a particular company's organizational grapevine on a single occasion was accurate.[62] The problem with interpreting this figure is that the inaccurate portions of some messages may alter their overall meaning. If, for example, a story is going around that someone got passed by for promotion over a lower-ranking employee, it may cause quite a bit of dissension in the workplace. However, suppose everything is true except that the person turned down the promotion because it involved relocating. This important fact completely alters the situation. Only one fact needs to be inaccurate for the accuracy of communication to suffer

This problem of inaccuracy is clearly responsible for giving the grapevine such a bad reputation. In extreme cases, information may be transmitted that is almost totally without any basis in fact and is usually unverifiable. Such messages are known as **rumors**. Typically, rumors are based on speculation, an overactive imagination, and wishful thinking, rather than on facts. Rumors race like wildfire through organizations because the information they present is so interesting and ambiguous. The ambiguity leaves it open to embellishment as it passes orally from one person to the next. Before you know it, almost everyone in the organization has heard the rumor, and its inaccurate message becomes taken as fact ("It must be true, everyone knows it"). Hence, even if there was, at one point, some truth to a rumor, the message quickly becomes untrue.

Organizations can be injured by rumors. If you've ever been the victim of a personal rumor, then you know how difficult they can be to crush and how profound their effects can be. This is especially so when organizations are the victims of rumors. For example, rumors about the possibility of corporate takeovers may not only influence the value of a company's stock, but also threaten its employees' feelings of job security. Sometimes, rumors about company products can be very costly. For example, a rumor about the use of worms in McDonald's hamburgers circulated in the Chicago area in the late 1970s. Even though the rumor was completely untrue, sales dropped as much as 30 percent in some restaurants.[63] You may recall that in June 1993 stories appeared in the press stating that people across the United States found syringes in cans of Pepsi-Cola. Although the stories proved to be completely without fact, the hoax cost Pepsi plenty in terms of investigative and advertising expenses.[64]

One of the most persistent nagging corporate rumors has tied the consumer-products giant Procter & Gamble to satanism.[65] Since 1980, rumors have swirled that the company's moon-and-stars trademark was linked to witchcraft. Although the company has emphatically denied the rumor and has won court judgments against various individuals spreading rumors, it has persisted. As recently as 1995 P&G sued an Amway distributor for making false and defamatory statements about the company's links to devil worshipping. This has been the sixth suit P&G filed against an Amway distributor (Amway sells a line of competing products through a network of independent distributors), and its fifteenth suit overall.

Combating rumors: Some suggestions. What can be done to counter the effects of rumors? Although this is a difficult question to answer, evidence suggests that directly refuting a rumor may not always counter its effects. Although Pepsi officials denied the reports about their tainted product, the rumor was not only implausible, but was also quickly disproven by independent investigators from the Food and Drug Administration.

Sometimes, however, as the P&G rumor illustrates, rumors are more difficult to disprove and do not die quickly. In such cases, directly refuting the rumors only fuels the fire. When you directly refute a rumor (e.g., "I didn't do it"), you actually may help spread it among those who have not already heard about it ("Oh, I didn't know people thought that") and strengthen it among those who have already heard it ("If it weren't true, they wouldn't be protesting so much"). In the case of P&G, the problem is compounded by the allegation that some parties may be making a concerted effort to keep the rumor alive. In such cases, directing the public's attention away from the rumor may help minimize its adverse impact. For instance, the company can focus its advertising on other positive things the public knows about it. In research studying the McDonald's rumor, for example, it was found that reminding people of other things they thought about McDonald's (e.g., that it is a clean, family-oriented place) helped counter the negative effects of the rumor.[66]

If you should ever become the victim of a rumor, try immediately to refute it with indisputable facts if you can. But, if it lingers on, try directing people's attention to other positive things they already believe about you. Although rumors may be impossible to stop, with some effort their effects can be effectively managed.

Organizational Structure: Directing the Flow of Messages

Although the basic process of communication described thus far is similar in many different contexts, a unique feature of organizations has a profound impact on the communication process—namely, their structure. Organizations are often designed in ways that dictate who may and may not communicate with whom. Given this, we may ask: How is the communication process affected by the structure of an organization? **Organizational structure** refers to the formally prescribed pattern of interrelationships existing between the various units of an organization. Although we will have a great deal more to say about organizational structure in Chapter 15, here we describe the many important ways in which organizational structure influences communication.

Organizational Structure: Its Impact on Communication

An organization's structure may be described using a diagram known as an **organizational chart**. Such a diagram provides a graphic representation of an organization's structure. It may be likened to an X ray showing the organization's skeleton, an outline of the planned, formal connections between its various units.[67] An organizational chart showing the structure of part of a fictitious organization is shown in Figure 9-12. (Keep in mind that this diagram represents only *one* possible way of structuring an organization. Several other possibilities are described in detail in Chapter 15.)

Note the various boxes in the diagram and the lines connecting them. Each box represents a person performing a specific job. The diagram shows the titles of the individuals performing the various jobs and the formally prescribed pattern of communication between them. These are relatively fixed and de-

organizational structure
The formally prescribed pattern of interrelationships existing between the various units of an organization.

organizational chart A diagram showing the formal structure of an organization, indicating who is to communicate with whom.

■ **Figure 9-12**
The Organization Chart: An Organization's Formal Communication Network
An organization chart, such as this simple one, shows the formally prescribed patterns of communication in an organization. Different types of messages typically flow upward, downward, and horizontally throughout organizations.

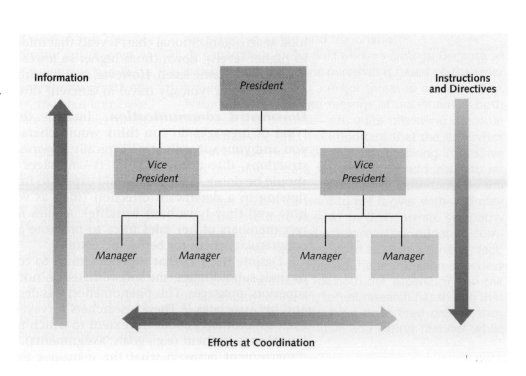

Information

President

Vice President

Vice President

Manager

Manager

Manager

Manager

Instructions and Directives

Efforts at Coordination

■ TABLE 9-2

A MEMO THAT LEAVES YOU SCRATCHING YOUR HEAD: "WHAT DID HE SAY"?

Too frequently, business communication suffers from being needlessly dense and difficult to interpret. Here is an example of text from an offending memo, a translation, and a suggestion for how it may be improved.

SOURCE: From *Corporate Dandelions: How the Weed of Bureaucracy Is Choking America's Companies—And What You Can Do to Uproot It.* © 1993, Craig J. Cantoni, Published by AMACOM, a division of the American Management Association. All rights reserved. Reprinted with permission.

ORIGINAL MESSAGE:

"As per your subject memo, we are researching the history of Price Promotion #18B to establish why the new price sheets were not received by the sales force in advance of the effective date of the promotion. It is unclear from your memo how widespread the problem was or if it was just isolated in certain geographies. Therefore, we will need additional facts on where you think the problem occurred. As you know, we have gotten complaints from sales people in the past that they did not receive the promotions, only to find out later that they had lost them due to their own disorganization."

TRANSLATION:

"We screwed up but are not going to admit it."

IMPROVED MESSAGE:

"Thanks for bringing the problem with this promotion to my attention. It looks like we screwed up at this end in getting the proofs to the printer on schedule. My staff and I feel badly about this and will take steps to provide better service."

---

tention to and comprehend only a small percentage of the information directed at them.[92] Most of us usually think of listening as a passive process of taking in information sent by others, but when done correctly the process of listening is much more active.[93] For example, good listeners ask questions if they don't understand something, and they nod or otherwise signal when they understand. Such cues provide critical feedback to communicators about the extent to which they are coming across. As a listener, you can help the communication process by letting the sender know if and how his or her messages are coming across to you. *Asking questions* and *putting the speaker's ideas into your own words* are helpful ways of ensuring you are taking in all the information presented.

It is also very useful to avoid distractions in the environment and to concentrate on what the other person is saying. When listening to others *avoid jumping to conclusions or evaluating their remarks*. It is important to take in completely what is being said before you respond. Simply dismissing someone because you don't like what is being said is much too easy. Doing so, of course, poses a formidable barrier to effective communication.

Being a good listener also involves making sure you are aware of others' main points. What is the speaker trying to say? *Make sure you understand another's ideas before you formulate your reply*. Too many of us interrupt speakers with our own ideas before we have fully heard theirs. If this sounds like something you do, rest assured that it is not only quite common, but also correctable.

Although it requires some effort, incorporating these suggestions into your own listening habits cannot help but make you a better listener. Indeed, many organizations have sought to help their employees in this way. For example, the corporate giant Unisys has for some time systematically trained thousands of its employees in effective listening skills (using seminars and self-training cassettes). Clearly, Unisys is among those companies acknowledging the importance of good listening skills in promoting effective organizational communication.

The development of listening skills requires identifying the individual elements of listening, the separate skills that contribute to listening effectiveness. Brownell has proposed that listening effectiveness may be understood in terms of the behavioral indicators that individuals perceive as related to effective listening, skills clustered into six groups known as the **HURIER model**.[94] The term *HURIER* is an acronym composed of the initials of the words reflecting the component skills of effective listening: *h*earing, *u*nderstanding, *r*emembering, *i*nterpreting, *e*valuating, and *r*esponding. For a sum-

HURIER model The conceptualization that describes effective listening as made up of the following six components: *h*earing, *u*nderstanding, *r*emembering, *i*nterpreting, *e*valuating, and *r*esponding.

mary of these individual skills, see Figure 9-14. Although it might seem easy to do the six things needed to be a good listener, we are not all as good as we think we are in this capacity, suggesting that listening might not be as easy as it seems.

Management consultant Nancy K. Austin would agree, and explains that when you invite people to talk to you about their problems on the job, you're implicitly making a promise to listen to them.[95] Of course, when you do, you may feel hostile and defensive toward the speaker and become more interested in speaking up and setting the record straight if you don't like what you hear. This is the challenge of listening. Good listeners should resist this temptation and pay careful attention to the speaker. When they cannot do so, they should admit the problem and reschedule another opportunity to get together. Austin also advises people to "be an equal opportunity listener," that is, to pay attention not only to those whose high status commands our attention, but also to anyone at any level, and to make time to hear them all in a democratic fashion. The idea is not only that people at any job level might have something to say, but also that they may feel good about you as a manager for having shown consideration to them. Austin notes that by listening to an employee, you are saying, "You are smart and have important things to say; you are worth my time."[96] Such a message is critical to establishing the kind of open, two-way communication essential for top management.

Research has confirmed the importance of listening as a management skill. In fact, it has shown that the better a person is as a listener, the more likely he or she is to rapidly rise up the organizational hierarchy[97] and to perform well as a manager.[98] Apparently, good listening skills are an important aspect of one's ability to succeed as a manager. Yet, people tend to be insensitive to how others perceive their listening skills. In a survey of employees in the hospitality industry, Brownell found that almost all the managers indicated that they felt their listening skills were either "good" or "very good," although most of their subordinates did not agree.[99] Such overconfidence in one's own listening ability can be a barrier to seeking training in listening skills inasmuch as people who believe they are already good listeners may have little motivation to seek training in that area. This is unfortunate, because Brownell also found that among those who were rated as better listeners by their subordinates was a significant number of managers who had earlier been trained in listening skills. Such evidence suggests that this type of training may indeed pay off.

■ **Figure 9-14**
The HURIER Model: Components of Effective Listening
Research has shown that the six skills identified here—hearing, understanding, remembering, interpreting, evaluating, and responding—contribute greatly to the effectiveness of listening.

(**Source:** Based on suggestions by Brownell, 1985; see Note 94.)

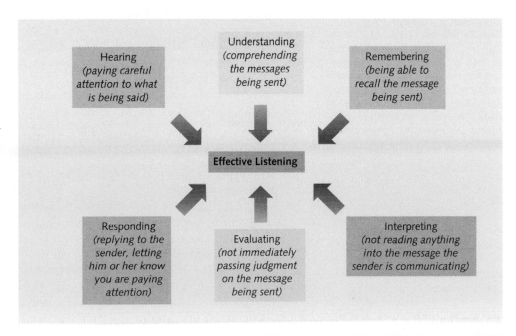

Gauge the Flow of Information: Avoiding Overload

Imagine a busy manager surrounded by a tall stack of papers, with a telephone receiver in each ear and a crowd of people gathered around, waiting to talk to her. Obviously, the many demands put on this person can slow down the system and make its operation less effective. When any part of a communication network becomes bogged down with more information than it can handle effectively, a condition of **overload** is said to exist. Consider, for example, the bottleneck in the flow of routine financial information that might result when the members of the accounting department of an organization are tied up preparing corporate tax returns. (Such an overloaded condition is analogous to the experience of saturation encountered by central members of a centralized communication network described earlier in this chapter.) Naturally, such a state poses a serious threat to effective organizational communication. Fortunately, however, several steps can be taken to manage information more effectively.

For one, organizations may employ *gatekeepers*, people whose jobs require them to control the flow of information to potentially overloaded units. For example, administrative assistants are responsible for making sure that busy executives are not overloaded by the demands of other people or groups. Newspaper editors and television news directors also may be thought of as gatekeepers, since such individuals decide what news will and will not be shared with the public. It is an essential part of these individuals' jobs to avoid overloading others by gauging the flow of information to them.

Overload also can be avoided through *queuing*. This term refers to lining up incoming information so that it can be managed in an orderly fashion. The practices of "stacking" jets as they approach a busy airport and making customers take a number (i.e., defining their position in the line) at a busy deli counter are both designed to avoid the chaos that may otherwise result when too many demands are made on the system at once. For a summary of these techniques, see Figure 9-15.

When systems are overloaded, *distortion* and *omission* are likely to result. That is, messages may be either changed or left out when they are passed from one organizational unit to the next. If you've ever played the parlor game "telephone" (in which one person whispers a message to another, who passes it on

overload The condition in which a unit of an organization becomes overburdened with too much incoming information.

■ Figure 9-15
Overload: A Problem That Can Be Solved
Overload, *receiving too many messages at once, can seriously interfere with organizational functioning. This problem can be minimized by using* gatekeepers *(individuals who control the flow of information) and* queuing *(lining up incoming information so that it arrives in an orderly fashion).*

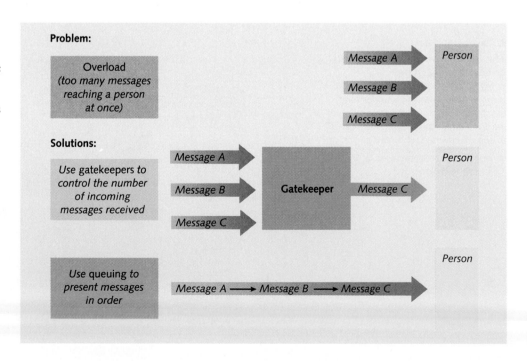

to another, and so on until it reaches the last person), you have likely experienced—or contributed to—the ways messages get distorted and omitted. When you consider the important messages that are often communicated in organizations, these problems can be very serious. They also tend to be quite extreme. A dramatic demonstration of this was reported in a study tracing the flow of downward communication in more than 100 organizations. The researchers found that messages communicated downward over five levels lost approximately 80 percent of their original information by the time they reached their destination at the lowest level of the organizational hierarchy.[100] Obviously, something needs to be done.

One strategy that has proven effective in avoiding the problems of distortion and omission is *redundancy*. Making messages redundant involves transmitting them again, often in another form or via another channel. For example, in attempting to communicate an important message to her subordinates, a manager may tell them the message and then follow it up with a written memo. In fact, managers frequently encourage this practice.[101] Another practice that can help avoid distortion and omission is *verification*. This refers to making sure messages have been received accurately. Pilots use verification when they repeat the messages given them by air traffic controllers. Doing so assures both parties that the messages the pilots heard were the actual messages the controllers sent. Given how busy pilots may be during takeoffs and landings and the interference inherent in radio transmissions, coupled with the vital importance of the messages themselves, the practice of verifying messages is a wise safety measure. The practice not only is used in airline communication systems, but may be used by individual communicators as well. Active listeners may wish to verify that they correctly understood a speaker and do so by paraphrasing the speaker's remarks within a question, asking "If I understood, you were saying. . . ."

Obtain Feedback: Opening Upward Channels of Communication

We have already discussed the role of feedback in conjunction with learning, in Chapter 3, and motivation, in Chapter 5.

To operate effectively, organizations must be able to communicate accurately with those who keep them running—their employees. Unfortunately, the vast majority of employees believe that the feedback between themselves and their organizations is not as good as it should be.[102] For various reasons, people are often unwilling or unable to communicate their ideas to top management. Part of the problem is the lack of available channels for upward communication and people's reluctance to use whatever ones exist. How, then, can organizations obtain information from their employees, improving the upward flow of communication? Several techniques exist for effectively soliciting feedback (see Table 9-3).

Suggestion systems. One means of facilitating upward communication in organizations is *suggestion systems*. Too often, employees' good ideas about how to improve organizational functioning fail to work their way up the organizational chart because the people with the ideas do not know how to reach the people who can implement them. Even worse, they may feel they will not be listened to even if they can reach the right person. Suggestion boxes are designed to help avoid these problems, to help provide a conduit for employees' ideas. (Recall the "suggestion connection" used at Childress Buick/Kia in our PREVIEW CASE.) Research has found that about 15 percent of employees use their companies' suggestion boxes, and that about 25 percent of the suggestions made are implemented.[103] Employees are usually rewarded for their successful suggestions, either with a flat monetary reward or some percentage of the money saved by implementing the suggestion.

Corporate hotlines. A second method of providing important information is through *corporate hotlines*—telephone lines staffed by corporate personnel ready to answer employees' questions, listen to their comments, and

The techniques summarized here are designed to improve organizational functioning by providing top management with information about the attitudes and ideas of the workforce. They are used to promote the upward flow of information.

Technique	Description
Employee surveys	Questionnaires assessing workers' attitudes and opinions about key areas of organizational functioning, especially when results are shared with the workforce.
Suggestion systems	Formal mechanisms through which employees can submit ideas for improving things in organizations (often by putting a note in a suggestion box); good ideas are implemented and the people who submitted them are rewarded.
Corporate hotlines	Telephone numbers employees may call to ask questions about important organizational matters; useful in addressing workers' concerns before they become too serious.
Brown bag meetings	Sessions in which subordinates and superiors meet informally over breakfast or lunch to discuss organizational matters.
Skip-level meetings	Meetings between subordinates and superiors two or more levels above them in the organizational hierarchy.

the like.[104] A good example of this is the "Let's Talk" program that AT&T developed to answer its employees' questions during its 1980s antitrust divestiture. By providing personnel with easy access to information, companies benefit in several ways. Doing so not only shows employees that the company cares about them, but it also encourages them to address their concerns before the issues become more serious. In addition, by keeping track of the kinds of questions and concerns voiced, top management is given invaluable insight into ways of improving organizational conditions. These days, inasmuch as 40 percent of calls to hotlines are made after regular working hours or on weekends, companies are finding it difficult to staff their own hotlines. As a result, some organizations have begun to outsource their hotline services. In fact, several companies—such as Pinkerton Services Group, the largest supplier of outsources hotlines—have emerged in response to this need.[105]

Brown bag and skip-level meetings. A third set of techniques known as *"brown bag" meetings* and *"skip-level" meetings* are designed to facilitate communication between people who don't usually get together because they work at different organizational levels.[106] Brown bag meetings are informal get-togethers over breakfast or lunch (brought in from home, hence the term "brown bag") at which people discuss what's going on in the company. The informal nature of the meetings is designed to encourage the open sharing of ideas (eating a sandwich out of a bag is an equalizer).

Skip-level meetings do essentially the same thing. These are gatherings of employees with corporate superiors who are more than one level higher than themselves in the organizational hierarchy. The idea is that new lines of communication can be established by bringing together people who are two or more levels apart, individuals who usually don't come into contact with each other.

Employee surveys. Finally, *employee surveys* can be used to gather information about employees' attitudes and opinions about key areas of organizational operations. Questionnaires administered at regular intervals may be useful for spotting changes in attitudes as they occur. Such surveys tend to be quite effective when their results are shared with employees, especially when the feedback is used as the basis for changing the way things are done.

SEARS INSTALLS THE "ETHICS ASSIST" LINE

Although Sears, Roebuck and Co. has been around for over 100 years, company officials have not taken its success for granted. To help ensure at least another century of retailing leadership, in 1994 Sears introduced several initiatives to guide employees in making ethical decisions, including an ethics hotline known as the "Ethics Assist" line.[107] Officials stress that it is not designed to catch wrongdoers by being a line for snitchers, 1-800-RAT-FINK. Rather, this toll-free phone line is designed to be a user-friendly resource that helps give Sears employees direction in distinguishing between right and wrong.

According to William E. Griffin, Sears' vice president of ethics and business policy, the hotline works because it is not a stand-alone effort. Rather, it is part of a highly focused effort to get Sears employees to follow high moral standards in everything they do. There are supporting documents, including a 20-page code of conduct, and a brochure called "Doing the Right Things for the Right Reasons."

But it is not only literature that drives the ethics efforts at Sears; issuing brochures and establishing hotlines alone doesn't make for an ethical company. These initiatives are supplemented by having store managers meet with their employees to emphasize the company's ethical values. The idea was to make it clear that ethics was not the concern of a few high-and-mighty moralists at the corporate office, but rather, a vital concern of their own immediate managers. Any Sears employee who has any doubts can simply phone the Ethics Assist line to be reminded.

SUMMARY AND REVIEW

The Basic Nature of Communication

The process of **communication** occurs when a sender of information *encodes* a message and transmits it over communication channels to a receiver, who *decodes* it and then sends *feedback*. Factors interfering with these processes are known as *noise*.

Communication is used in organizations not only to direct individual action, but also to achieve coordinated action. Although the heart of communication is information, communication is also used to develop friendships and to build interpersonal trust and acceptance in organizations.

Verbal Communication

Communication in both oral and written forms is commonly used in organizations. Verbal media range from those that are highly personal and provide opportunities for immediate feedback, such as face-to-face discussions, to those that are impersonal and one-way, such as flyers and bulletins. *Newsletters* are important written documents used to communicate relevant news of value to employees. *Employee handbooks* are used to provide important information about a company's background, business, and rules.

Research has shown that communication is most effective when it relies on both oral and written messages. People prefer oral media to written media when messages are ambiguous, and written media to oral media when messages are clear. Furthermore, individuals who match in this manner the media they use to the ambiguity of the situations they confront tend to be more successful managers than those who do not. Communicators in modern organizations have a new array of media available to them, including *video display terminals, electronic mail,* and *voice messaging systems*.

Nonverbal Communication

People tend to have greater self-confidence when they dress appropriately for the jobs they perform, although there are widespread differences in what constitutes appropriate dress. Research has shown that people communicate their higher organizational status by requiring lower-ranking individuals to spend more time waiting for them. Status is also communicated nonverbally by the use of space: Higher-status people tend to sit at the heads of rectangular tables.

Individual Differences in Communication

People tend to have different **personal communication styles**. Six such styles have been identified: the *Noble*, the *Socratic*, the *Reflective*, the *Magistrate*, the *Candidate*, and the *Senator*. Interpersonal communication is enhanced when people's styles match, or when one person anticipates another's style.

There are also sex differences in communication. Whereas men tend to communicate with the intent of emphasizing their status, women tend to focus on making positive social connections. Such differences frequently lead to miscommunication between men and women.

Cross-cultural communication is hampered by the fact that people from different cultures frequently misunderstand each other's intentions. This may stem from different vocabularies and subtle differences in the meanings of words that may not be understood outside the culture.

Formal Communication Networks

Formally imposed patterns of communication, called **communication networks**, influence job performance and satisfaction over brief periods of time. **Centralized networks** have certain members through whom messages must travel. In **decentralized networks**, however, all members play an equal role in transmitting information. On simple tasks, centralized networks perform faster and more accurately; on complex tasks, decentralized networks do better. Members of decentralized networks tend to be more satisfied than members of centralized networks.

Informal Communication Networks

Information also flows along *informal communication networks*. These informal connections between people are responsible for spreading information very rapidly because they transcend formal organizational boundaries. Informal pathways known as the **grapevine** are often responsible for the rapid transmission of partially inaccurate information known as **rumors**. Rumors may be costly to organizations as well as individuals. Fortunately, there are several ways they can be combated.

The Influence of Organizational Structure on Communication

Communication also is influenced by **organizational structure**, the formally prescribed pattern of interrelationships between people in organizations. Structure dictates who must communicate with whom (as reflected in an **organizational chart**, a diagram outlining these reporting relationships) and the form that communication takes. Orders flow down an organizational hierarchy, and information flows upward. However, the upward flow of information is often distorted insofar as people are reluctant to share bad news with their superiors. Attempts at coordination characterize horizontal communication, messages between organizational members at the same level.

Executives tend to communicate differently when sending messages inside and outside their organizations. Internal communications tend to focus on threats more than opportunities, whereas external communications tend to focus on opportunities more than threats.

Overcoming Communication Barriers

People can become better communicators by keeping their messages brief, clear, and avoiding the use of **jargon** when communicating with those who may not be familiar with such specialized terms. They also may improve their *listening* skills, learning to listen actively (thinking about and questioning the speaker) and attentively (without distraction).

The problem of **overload** can be reduced by using *gatekeepers* (individuals who control the flow of information to others) or by *queuing* (the orderly lining up of incoming information). The *distortion* and *omission* of messages can be minimized by making messages *redundant* and by encouraging their *verification*. At the organizational level, communication may be improved by using techniques that open upward channels of communication to employee feedback (e.g., *suggestion systems*, *corporate hotlines*, and *employee surveys*).

QUESTIONS FOR DISCUSSION

1. Using an example of an everyday communication in an organization (e.g., a supervisor asking her assistant for the month's production schedule), describe how the communication process operates (e.g., how information is encoded, etc.).
2. Imagine that you are a district manager attempting to explain a new corporate policy to a group of plant managers. Should this be accomplished using written or spoken communication, or both? Explain your decision.
3. Suppose you're interviewing for a job. Describe how the way you dress and the interviewer's use of time and space can influence what you each communicate to each other.
4. You have a new co-worker with whom you find yourself having difficulty communicating. Explain the kinds of individual differences that might be responsible for this and what can be done to overcome them.
5. Your company is being victimized by a totally untrue rumor about a pending merger. What steps would you recommend taking to put the story to an end? Explain.
6. In Shakespeare's *Hamlet*, Polonius said, "Give every man thine ear, but few thy voice." Discuss the implications of this advice for being an active listener. What other suggestions should be followed for enhancing the effectiveness of listening?

Communicating All the Right Messages at General Motors

Something was wrong at the Saginaw Division of General Motors. Ron Actis, the facility's director of public affairs, sensed "a lack of trust between management and labor, [and] poor communications throughout the division. . . ." An employee survey confirmed his suspicions, and the problem was taking its toll on both productivity and morale.

Actis knew he had to get "the right message to the right audience at the right time with the right medium." He took a multipronged approach to opening a two-way dialogue between management and labor. Realizing that success depended on management support, he started at the top. He inundated GM's highest-ranking managers with reports from technical journals and popular magazines that demonstrated his point: Effective communication can improve productivity.

But, convincing management was only the beginning. An effective communication system had to be designed. With this in mind, Actis changed the content of the *Daily Newsletter*, a one-page publication distributed throughout the plant. General stories about the auto industry were replaced by stories with greater local interest, the division in particular. Readership increased dramatically; the plant's 20,000 employees became hooked on learning about what was going on under their roof.

This was just one of several publications Actis relied on to keep people informed. He also started a monthly tabloid, the *Steering Column*, mailed to employees' homes and distributed within the Saginaw community. Actis also targeted publications to specific groups. For example, a bimonthly newsletter, *Report to Supervisors*, contained tips for improving communication and advance information about key issues. To improve relations between management and the unions, *Joint Activities*, contained features describing ways of reducing costs, improving quality, and staying competitive. A quarterly video magazine, *Perspective*, containing interviews with managers, customers, employees, suppliers, and union officials, did a good job of getting people at all levels talking to each other.

Appreciating that such conversations were too important to leave to chance, Actis also initiated a series of face-to-face meetings between labor and management. These turned into candid, no-holds-barred sessions in which various business issues were intensely discussed. Responses to such meetings have been so positive that as many as 17 different labor-management sessions are regularly held at the plant, some meeting as often as weekly.

Biannual communication audits (surveys assessing communication practices) have revealed that these various efforts have been successful. Before Actis's plan, fewer than half of the Saginaw Division's employees believed anything management said. Four years after the plan, the level of trust grew dramatically: More than 80 percent of the employees not only believed management, but also were pleased with the effectiveness of the company's various mechanisms in getting information to them.

Although it is difficult to link any single program to a company's bottom-line performance, the Saginaw Division's financial picture dramatically improved during the first seven years in which Mr. Actis's communication plan was in effect. Not only did annual operating costs decrease in the neighborhood of 5 percent, but sales per employee doubled, and the level of on-time deliveries improved to 100 percent. Many GM officials are convinced that these figures are due in large part to the fact that management and labor now see each other as sharing an interest in doing the best possible job for the company.

Critical Thinking Questions

1. In what ways did the things that Mr. Actis did at General Motors help overcome the company's communication problems? What made his actions so effective?
2. To what extent do you think that the success enjoyed by General Motors might be generalized to other types of organizations? Would these same actions work just as well in a service business, for example?
3. What additional steps could be taken to enhance communication in this General Motors plant?

Experiencing Organizational Behavior

Assessing Your Personal Communication Style

When you read about the six different personal communication styles on pp. 300–302, did you have some idea of which one you tend to use? The following test, based on questions similar to those used by scientists to test communication style (McCallister, 1994; see Note 42), will give you a good idea of your own personal communication style.

Directions

Read all 18 of the following statements. For each one, think of how you *actually* communicate (and not what you think you should do). If you believe that the statement describes how you usually communicate, mark a "Y" for "yes." If you believe the statement does not describe how you usually communicate, mark an "N" for "no."

_____ **1.** When I talk to others I tend to be direct and straightforward.
_____ **2.** I am a "tell it like it is" kind of person.
_____ **3.** I freely share my opinions with others.
_____ **4.** I usually say the first thing that comes to my mind.
_____ **5.** I tend to get impatient when others speak.
_____ **6.** I tend to avoid long, detailed discussions.
_____ **7.** I very much enjoy chatting with other people.
_____ **8.** I tend to give very long, exact directions to others.
_____ **9.** I am sometimes accused of being redundant.
_____ **10.** I am prone to explain things by using anecdotes and examples.
_____ **11.** I enjoy arguing and debating things with others.
_____ **12.** I have seen people "tune me out" when I speak.
_____ **13.** People tend to tell me their problems.
_____ **14.** I tend to ignore people who seem angry.
_____ **15.** I tend to be soft-spoken.
_____ **16.** I may tell another person that I agree with him or her, even if I do not.
_____ **17.** People tend to interrupt me when I am speaking to them.
_____ **18.** I tend to be polite and supportive when I talk to people.

Scoring

1. Add the number of Y's in response to items 1 through 6. This is your Noble score.
2. Add the number of Y's in response to items 7 through 12. This is your Socratic score.
3. Add the number of Y's in response to items 13 through 18. This is your Reflective score.
4. To determine your style, compare your scores to each other.
   (a) If your Noble score is higher than the other two, you are a Noble. If your Socratic score is higher than the other two, you are a Socratic. If your Reflective score is much higher than the other two, you are a Reflective. These are the three dominant styles.
   (b) If your Noble and Socratic scores are close to each other, but far from your Reflective score, you are a Magistrate. If your Socratic and Reflective scores are close to each other, but far from your Noble score, you are a Candidate. If your Noble and Reflective scores are close to each other, but far from your Socratic score, you are a Senator.
   (c) If all three of your scores are very close to each other, you might not be aware of how you communicate. Retake the test, concentrating on what you actually do, instead of what you think you should do.

Questions for Discussion

1. What style did the test reveal that you have? How did this compare to the style you thought you had before you took the test?
2. Based on the descriptions of the personal communication styles in the text, were you able to guess in advance which test items were indicative of which styles? What additional items may be added to the test to assess each style?
3. How effective do you think you would be in altering your communication style to match another's?

Working in Groups

Sharpening Your Listening Skills

Are you a good listener, a *really* good listener—one who understands exactly what someone else is saying to you? Most of us tend to think that we are much better than we really are when it comes to this important skill. After all, we've been listening to others our whole lives. And, with that much practice, we must certainly be okay. To gain some insight into your own listening skills, try the following group exercise.

Directions

1. Divide the class into pairs of people who do not already know each other. Arrange the chairs so that the people within each pair are facing one another, but separated from the other pairs.
2. Within each pair, one person should be selected as the speaker, and the other, the listener. The speaker should tell the listener about a specific incident on the job or at school in which he or she was somehow harmed (e.g., disappointed by not getting a raise, being embarrassed by a teacher or boss, losing a battle with a co-worker, getting fired, etc.), and how he or she felt about it. The total discussion should last about 10–15 minutes.
3. Listeners should carefully attempt to follow the suggestions for good listening summarized in Figure 9-15. To help, the instructor should discuss these with the class.
4. After the conversations are over, review the suggestions with your partner. Discuss which ones the listener followed and which ones were ignored. Try to be as open and honest as possible about assessing your own, and the other's strengths and weaknesses. Speakers should consider the extent to which they felt the listeners were really paying attention to them.
5. Repeat steps 2 through 4, but change roles. Speakers now become listeners, and listeners now become speakers.
6. As a class, share your experiences as speakers and listeners.

Questions for Discussion

1. What did this exercise teach you about your own skills as a listener? Are you as good as you thought? Do you think you can improve?
2. Was there general agreement or disagreement about each listener's strengths and weaknesses? Explain.
3. After the discussion about the first listener's effectiveness, you might expect the second listener to do a better job. Was this the case in your own group or throughout the class?
4. Which particular listening skills were easiest and most difficult to put into practice? Are there certain conditions under which good listening skills may be difficult to implement?
5. Do you think you will learn something from this exercise that will get you to improve your listening skills in other situations? If so, what? If not, why not?

Take It to the Net

We invite you to visit the Greenberg/Baron page on the Prentice Hall Web site at:

http://www.prenhall.com/~greenob

for this chapter's WorldWide Web exercise.

You can also visit the Web sites for these companies, featured within this chapter:

McDonnell Aircraft
http://www.mdc.com/

Kia
http://www.soback.kornet.nm.kr/~kiarnd/main.html

Electronic Arts
http://www.ea.com/

PepsiCo
http://www.pepsi.com/

Tandem Computers
http://www.tandem.com/

Unisys
http://www.unisys.com/

General Motors
http://www.gm.com/index.htm

Ten

DECISION MAKING IN ORGANIZATIONS

■ OBJECTIVES

LEARNING

After reading this chapter you should be able to:

1. Identify the steps in the *analytical model of decision making*.
2. Describe reliable individual and cultural differences with respect to *decision styles*.
3. Distinguish between *programmed* vs. *nonprogrammed* decisions, *certain* vs. *uncertain* decisions, and *top-down* vs. *empowered* decisions.
4. Understand the *rational-economic model*, the *administrative model*, and *image theory* as approaches to decision making.
5. Describe how *framing* effects, the reliance on *heuristics*, a bias toward *implicit favorites*, and the *escalation of commitment* phenomenon dictate against high-quality decisions in organizations.

6. Compare the advantages and disadvantages of using groups and individuals to make decisions in organizations.
7. Describe the conditions under which groups make better decisions than individuals and the conditions under which individuals make better decisions than groups.
8. Explain *groupthink* and how it may be a barrier to effective group decisions.
9. Describe techniques that can be used to improve the quality of group decisions (e.g., *individual decision training*, the *Delphi technique*, the *nominal group technique*, and the *stepladder technique*).

BABY SUPERSTORE: ALL GROWN-UP

If there was any one thing that Jack Tate learned upon graduating from Harvard Law School, it was that he didn't want to be a lawyer. Although he hung his shingle in front of an office in Greenville, South Carolina, where he practiced law for a few years, his heart was never really in it. His consuming passion was a brainstorm he had one day while shopping for his 9-month-old daughter: Instead of having to go to many different stores to buy items for newborns, why not sell everything under one roof, supermarket-style? If you offered diapers, toys, cribs, clothes, and infant formula in a single store, you'd make life so convenient for new parents with hectic schedules that they'd surely beat a path to your door. Tate's optimism convinced bankers to loan him $200,000 in March 1971, and Carolina Baby was born. A month later, he gave up the law practice. Jack Tate was now a retailing entrepreneur.

Joining Tate in the venture was Linda Robertson, his former part-time legal secretary, who caught Tate's infectious enthusiasm for Carolina Baby. Business was so good that only two years later Tate and Robertson opened up a second store, this one in Easley, South Carolina. As their business grew, they narrowed its scope. No longer did they carry lines for all children through the pre-teen years; infants and toddlers were its new focus. Their rationale was clear: First-time parents need to buy a lot of things for their newborns (e.g., strollers, changing tables, car seats), making a huge market.

While narrowing their product lines, Tate and Robertson also enlarged their retail spaces. Realizing that they were paying premium rent in shopping malls, they moved to less expensive spots in strip cen-

ters throughout the Carolinas. By 1987, with 26 stores averaging 6,000 square feet each, their sales hit $14.5 million. That same year, they opened up one much larger location—a 20,000 square foot warehouse store in Marietta, Georgia. When sales jumped 50 percent per square foot, Tate and Robertson knew they were onto something big. They changed the name to match, and Baby Superstore was launched. Shortly thereafter, all stores were moved to large warehouse locations. Down came the interior walls and ceilings, and up came stacks of merchandise piled high into the rafters. Modeling Baby Superstore after successful building-supply chain Home Depot, Tate and Robertson now offered not only convenience but also huge selection and low prices.

The formula worked. By 1992, sales had reached $63 million at 26 Baby Superstores. Two years later, the company went public, and its stock price rose quickly. This took Robertson from being a $55 per week secretary to a company president with a $50 million stake in the company. The company itself now has plenty of cash to fuel growth. More stores are being added all the time and not only in the South. In fact, if Tate's projections are correct, by the time you read this there should be some 145 Baby Superstores throughout the United States, with annual revenues of $1 billion.

To look at Jack Tate today in his small A-frame house outside remote Pumpkintown, South Carolina, you'd never guess that he's a very wealthy man—that is, unless you spot him in his personal Learjet or Bell LongRanger IV helicopter. Extravagant? Maybe, but a man does have to commute to and from work.

You may consider Jack Tate's tale a success story, and it surely is. But, it's more than that. It's a tale of a string of decisions: leaving a law practice, creating a new business, hiring a former secretary, opening new stores, narrowing the line of merchandise, opening larger warehouse stores, taking the company public, and even selecting which aircraft to buy for the flight to work. Although you might not be making these kinds of decisions (at least yet), you are probably no stranger to *decision making*. If you've ever wrestled over decisions about what college to attend or what job to take, you probably already have a good idea about how difficult it can be to make the right decision. If you think about the difficulties involved in making decisions in your own life,

■ Figure 10-1
Decision Making: A Basic
Organizational Process
The making of decisions by both indi-
viduals and groups is a fundamental
aspect of life in organizations. This par-
ticular group, however, appears not to
be taking the task as seriously as it
might.

(**Source:** Drawing by Bernard Schoenbaum;
© 1988 The New Yorker, Inc.)

"No decision. They're still sleeping on it"

decision making The process
of making choices from among
several alternatives.

you can surely appreciate how complicated—and important—the process of
decision making can be in organizations, where the stakes are often considerable and the impact is widespread. Although we will provide much more detail
throughout this chapter, **decision making** may be defined as the process of
making choices from among several alternatives.

It is safe to say that decision making is one of the most important—if not
the most important—of all managerial activities.[1] Management theorists and
researchers agree that decision making represents one of the most common
and most crucial work roles of executives. Everyday, people in organizations
make decisions about a wide variety of topics ranging from the mundane to
the monumental (see Figure 10-1).[2] Understanding how these decisions are
made, and how they can be improved, is an important goal of the field of organizational behavior.

This chapter will examine theories, research, and practical managerial techniques concerned with decision making in organizations both by individuals
and groups. Beginning with individuals, we will review various perspectives
on how people go about making decisions. We then will identify factors that
may adversely affect the quality of individual decisions and ways of combating them—that is, techniques for improving the quality of decisions. Then, we
will shift our focus to group decisions, focusing on the conditions under which
individuals and groups are each better suited to making decisions. Finally, we
will describe some of the factors that make group decisions imperfect and various techniques that can be used to improve the quality of group decisions.
But first, we will begin by examining the general nature of the decision-making process and the wide variety of decisions made in organizations.

Decision Making: Its Basic Nature

We begin by examining the basic nature of the decision-making process
itself. With this in mind, we will present a model describing the general steps
by which decisions are made. We will then consider the idea that all people
don't make decisions in exactly the same manner. Specifically, we will discuss
individual differences and cultural differences in the ways people go about
making decisions.

A General, Analytical Model of Decision Making

Traditionally, scientists have found it useful to conceptualize the process of decision making as a series of analytical steps that groups or individuals take to solve problems.[3] A general model of the decision-making process can help us understand the complex nature of organizational decision making (see Figure 10-2).[4] This approach highlights two important aspects of decision making: *formulation*, the process of understanding a problem and making a decision about it, and *implementation*, the process of carrying out the decision made.[5] As we present this model, keep in mind that all decisions might not fully conform to the neat, eight-step pattern described (e.g., steps may be skipped and/or combined).[6] However, for the purpose of pointing out the general way the decision-making process operates, the model is quite useful.

1. The first step is *problem identification*. To decide how to solve a problem, one must first recognize and identify the problem. For example, an executive may identify as a problem the fact that the company cannot meet its payroll obligations. This step isn't always as easy as it sounds. In fact, research has shown that people often distort, omit, ignore, and/or discount information around them that provides important cues regarding the existence of problems.[7] You may recall from our discussion of the social perception process (see Chapter 3) that people do not always accurately perceive social situations. It is easy to imagine that someone may fail to recognize a problem if doing so makes him or her uncomfortable. Denying a problem may be the first impediment on the road to solving it.

2. After a problem is identified, the next step is to *define the objectives to be met in solving the problem*. It is important to conceive of problems in such a way that possible solutions can be identified. The problem identified in our example may be defined as not having enough money, or in busi-

■ Figure 10-2

The Traditional, Analytical Model of Decision Making

In general, the process of decision making follows the eight steps outlined here. Note how each step may be applied to a hypothetical organizational problem: having insufficient funds to meet payroll obligations.

(**Source:** Based on information in Wedley & Field, 1983; see Note 4.)

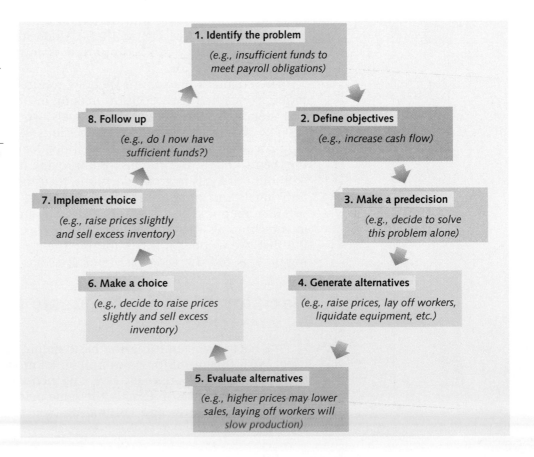

ness terms "inadequate cash flow." By looking at the problem in this way, the objective is clear: Increase available cash reserves. Any possible solution to the problem should be evaluated relative to this objective. A good solution is one that meets it.

3. The third step in the decision-making process is to *make a predecision*. A **predecision** is a decision about how to make a decision. By assessing the type of problem in question and other aspects of the situation, managers may opt to make a decision themselves, delegate the decision to another, or have a group make the decision. Decisions about how to make a decision should be based on research that tells us about the nature of the decisions made under different circumstances, many of which we will review later in this chapter.

For many years, managers have been relying on their own intuition or empirically based information about organizational behavior (contained in books like this) for the guidance needed to make predecisions. Recently, however, computer programs have been developed summarizing much of this information in a form that gives managers ready access to a wealth of social science information that may help them decide how to make decisions.[8] Such **decision support systems (DSS)**, as they are called, can only be as good as the social science information that goes into developing them. Research has shown that DSS techniques are effective in helping people make decisions about solving problems.[9] The use of decision-making technology leads to outcomes believed to be better than those made in the absence of such techniques. Moreover, computer-based DSS techniques have been found to be especially helpful in getting people to generate a higher number of alternative solutions.[10]

4. The fourth step in the process is *alternative generation*, the stage in which possible solutions to the problem are identified. In attempting to come up with solutions, people tend to rely on previously used approaches that might provide ready-made answers for them.[11] In our example, some possible ways of solving the revenue shortage problem would be to reduce the workforce, sell unnecessary equipment and material, or increase sales.

5. Because all these possibilities may not be equally feasible, the fifth step calls for *evaluating alternative solutions*. Which solution is best? What would be the most effective way of raising the revenue needed to meet the payroll? The various alternatives need to be identified. Some may be more effective than others, and some may be more difficult to implement than others. For example, although increasing sales would help solve the problem, that is much easier said than done. It is a solution, but not an immediately practical one.

6. Next, in the sixth step, *a choice is made*. After several alternatives are evaluated, one that is considered acceptable is chosen. As we will describe shortly, different approaches to decision making offer different views of how thoroughly people consider alternatives and how optimal their chosen alternatives are. Choosing which course of action to take is the step that most often comes to mind when we think about the decision-making process.

7. The seventh step calls for *implementation of the chosen alternative*. That is, the chosen alternative is carried out.

8. The eighth and final step is *follow-up*. Monitoring the effectiveness of the decisions they put into action is important to the success of organizations. Does the problem still exist? Have any new problems been caused by implementing the solution? In other words, it is important to seek feedback about the effectiveness of any attempted solution. For this reason, the decision-making process is presented as circular in Figure 10-2. If the solution works, the problem may be considered solved. If not, a new solution will have to be attempted.

predecision A decision about what process to follow in making a decision.

decision support systems (DSS) Computer programs in which information about organizational behavior is presented to decision makers in a manner that helps them structure their responses to decisions.

It is important to reiterate that this is a very general model of the decision-making process. Although it may not be followed exactly as specified in all circumstances, it paints a good picture of the general nature of a complex set of operations.

Decision Style: Individual Differences in Decision Making

Do all individuals go about making decisions the same way, or are there differences in the general approaches people take? In general, research has shown that there are meaningful differences between people with respect to their orientation toward decisions—that is, their **decision style**.

Whereas some people are primarily concerned with achieving success at any cost, others are more concerned about the effects of their decisions on others. Furthermore, some individuals tend to be more logical and analytical in their approach to problems whereas others are more intuitive and creative. Clearly, important differences exist in the approaches decision-makers take to problems. The **decision-style model** classifies four major decision styles (see summary in Figure 10-3).[12]

1. The *directive style* is characterized by people who prefer simple, clear solutions to problems. Individuals with this style tend to make decisions rapidly because they use little information and do not consider many alternatives. They tend to rely on existing rules to make their decisions and aggressively use their status to achieve results.

2. By contrast, individuals with the *analytical style* tend to be more willing to consider complex solutions based on ambiguous information. People with this style tend to analyze their decisions carefully using as much data as possible. Such individuals tend to enjoy solving problems. They want the best possible answers and are willing to use innovative methods to achieve them.

3. Compared to the directive and analytical styles, people with the *conceptual style* tend to be more socially oriented in their approach to problems. Their approach is humanistic and artistic. Such individuals tend to consider many broad alternatives when dealing with problems and to solve them creatively. They have a strong future orientation and enjoy initiating new ideas.

4. Individuals with the *behavioral style* may be characterized as having a deep concern for the organizations in which they work and the personal development of their co-workers. They are highly supportive of others

decision style Differences between people with respect to their orientations toward decisions.

Compare decision styles to various personality differences between people described in Chapter 4.

decision-style model The conceptualization according to which people use one of four predominant decision styles: *directive, analytical, conceptual,* and *behavioral.*

■ **Figure 10-3**
Decision-Style Model: A Summary
Research has shown that people tend to adhere to one of the four decision *styles summarized here.*

(**Source:** Based on information in Rowe, Boulgaides, & McGrath, 1984; see Note 12.)

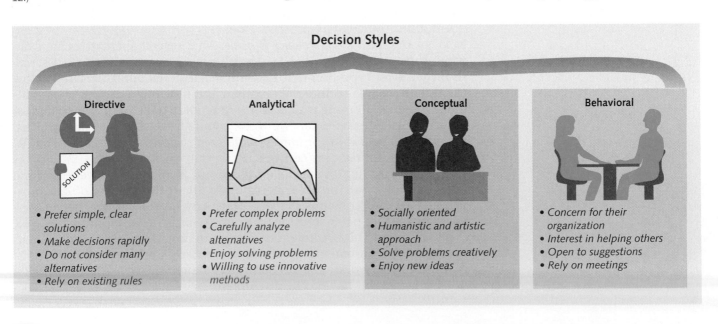

Decision Styles

Directive
- *Prefer simple, clear solutions*
- *Make decisions rapidly*
- *Do not consider many alternatives*
- *Rely on existing rules*

Analytical
- *Prefer complex problems*
- *Carefully analyze alternatives*
- *Enjoy solving problems*
- *Willing to use innovative methods*

Conceptual
- *Socially oriented*
- *Humanistic and artistic approach*
- *Solve problems creatively*
- *Enjoy new ideas*

Behavioral
- *Concern for their organization*
- *Interest in helping others*
- *Open to suggestions*
- *Rely on meetings*

and very concerned about others' achievements, frequently helping them meet their goals. Such individuals tend to be open to suggestions from others and, therefore, tend to rely on meetings for making decisions.

It is important to point out that although most managers may have one dominant style, they use many different styles. In fact, those who can shift between styles—that is, those who are most flexible in their approach to decision making—have highly complex, individualistic styles of their own. Despite this, people's dominant styles reveal a great deal about the way they tend to make decisions. Not surprisingly, conflicts often occur between individuals with different styles. For example, a manager with a highly directive style may have a hard time accepting the slow, deliberate actions of a subordinate with an analytical style.

Researchers have argued that being aware of people's decision styles is a potentially useful way of understanding social interactions in organizations. With this in mind, Rowe and his associates have developed an instrument known as the *decision-style inventory*, a questionnaire designed to reveal the relative strength of people's decision styles.[13] The higher an individual scores with respect to a given decision style, the more likely that style is to dominate his or her decision making. (To give you a feel for how the various decision styles are measured, and your own personal decision style, see the EXPERIENCING ORGANIZATIONAL BEHAVIOR section on pp. 364–365.)

Research using the decision-style inventory has revealed some interesting findings. For example, when the inventory was given to a sample of corporate presidents, their scores on each of the four categories were found to be approximately equal. Apparently, they had no one dominant style but were able to switch back and forth between categories with ease. Further research has shown that different groups tend to have, on average, different styles that dominate their decision making. For example, military leaders tend to have high conceptual style scores. They were not the highly domineering individuals that stereotypes suggest. Rather, they were highly conceptual and people-oriented in their approach. Such findings paint a far more humanistic and less authoritarian picture of military officers than many would guess.

In conclusion, research on decision styles suggests that people tend to take very different approaches to the decisions they make. Their personalities, coupled with their interpersonal skills, lead them to approach decisions in consistently different ways—that is, using different decision styles. Although research on decision styles is relatively new, it is already clear that understanding such stylistic differences is a key factor in appreciating potential conflicts likely to arise between decision makers.

Cultural Differences in Decision Making

People are people, and the process of decision making is essentially the same all over the world—right? Not exactly. Even if people were to follow the same basic steps when making decisions, there exist widespread differences in the *way* people from various cultures may go about doing so.[14] Because we tend to take for granted the way we do things in our own countries, especially such basic tasks as making decisions, some of these differences may seem quite surprising.

For example, suppose you are managing a large construction project when you discover that one of your most important suppliers will be several months late in delivering the necessary materials. What would you do? You're probably thinking, "This is a silly question; I'd simply try to get another supplier." If you're from the United States, this is probably just what you'd do. But, if you're from Thailand, Indonesia, or Malaysia, chances are good that you'd simply accept the situation as fate and allow the project to be delayed. In other words, to the American, Canadian, or Western European manager, the situa tion may be perceived as a problem in need of a decision, whereas no such problem would be recognized by Thai, Indonesian, or Malaysian managers. Thus, as basic as it seems that decision making begins with recognizing that a problem exists, it is important to note that not all people are likely to perceive the same situations as problems.

Cultures also differ with respect to the nature of the decision-making unit they typically employ. In the United States, for example, where people tend to be highly individualistic, individual decisions are commonly made. However, in more collectivist cultures, such as Japan, it would be considered inconceivable for someone to make a decision without first gaining the acceptance of his or her immediate colleagues.

Similarly, there exist cultural differences with respect to *who* is expected to make decisions. In Sweden, for example, it is traditional for employees at all levels to be involved in the decisions affecting them. However, in India, where autocratic decision making is expected, it would be considered a sign of weakness for a manager to consult a subordinate about a decision.

Another cultural difference in decision making has to do with the amount of time taken to make a decision. For example, in the United States, one mark of a good decision maker is that he or she is "decisive," willing to take on an important decision and make it without delay. However, in some other cultures, time urgency is downplayed. In Egypt, for example, the more important the matter, the more time the decision maker is expected to take in reaching a decision. Throughout the Middle East reaching a decision quickly would be perceived as overly hasty.

As these examples illustrate, there exist some interesting differences in the ways people from various countries go about formulating and implementing decisions. Understanding such differences is an important first step toward developing appropriate strategies for conducting business at a global level.[15]

The Broad Spectrum of Decisions in Organizations

As you might imagine, because decision making is so fundamental to organizations, decisions themselves tend to be of many different kinds. Understanding the wide variety of decisions that are made in organizations is an important first step toward understanding the nature of the decision-making process. With this in mind, we will distinguish between decisions in three important ways: how routine they are, how much risk is involved, and who in the organization gets to make them.

Programmed versus Nonprogrammed Decisions

Think of a decision that is made repeatedly, according to a preestablished set of alternatives. For example, a word processing operator may decide to make a backup copy of the day's work on disk, or a manager of a fast-food restaurant may decide to order hamburger buns as the supply starts to get low. Decisions such as these are known as **programmed decisions**—routine decisions, made by lower-level personnel, that rely on predetermined courses of action.

By contrast, we may identify **nonprogrammed decisions**—ones for which there are no ready-made solutions. The decision maker confronts a unique situation in which the solutions are novel. A research scientist attempting to find a cure for a rare disease faces a problem that is poorly structured. Unlike the order clerk, whose course of action is clear when the supply of paper clips runs low, the scientist in this example must rely on creativity rather than preexisting answers to solve the problem at hand.

Certain types of nonprogrammed decisions are known as **strategic decisions**.[16] These decisions are typically made by coalitions of high-level execu-

Recall the distinction between individualistic and collectivist cultures described in Chapter 2.

For insight into cultural differences in decision making, see the description of cross-cultural differences appearing in Chapter 2.

programmed decisions
Highly routine decisions made according to preestablished organizational routines and procedures.

nonprogrammed decisions
Decisions made about a highly novel problem for which there is no prespecified course of action.

strategic decisions
Nonprogrammed decisions typically made by high-level executives regarding the direction their organization should take to achieve its mission.

tives and have important long-term implications for the organization. Strategic decisions reflect a consistent pattern for directing the organization in some specified fashion—that is, according to an underlying organizational philosophy or mission. For example, an organization may make a strategic decision to grow at a specified yearly rate, or to be guided by a certain code of corporate ethics. Both of these decisions are likely to be considered "strategic" because they guide the future direction of the organization.

Table 10-1 summarizes the differences between programmed and nonprogrammed decisions with respect to three important questions. First, *what type of tasks are involved*? Programmed decisions are made on tasks that are common and routine, whereas nonprogrammed decisions are made on unique and novel tasks. Second, *how much reliance is there on organizational policies*? In making programmed decisions, the decision maker can count on guidance from statements of organizational policy and procedure. However, nonprogrammed decisions require the use of creative solutions that are implemented for the first time; past solutions may provide little guidance. Finally, *who makes the decisions*? Not surprisingly, nonprogrammed decisions typically are made by upper-level organizational personnel, whereas the more routine, well-structured decisions are usually relegated to lower-level personnel.[17]

Certain versus Uncertain Decisions

Just think of how easy it would be to make decisions if we knew what the future had in store. Making the best investments in the stock market would simply be a matter of looking up the changes in tomorrow's newspaper. Of course, we never know exactly what the future holds, but we can be more certain at some times than others. Certainty about the factors on which decisions are made is highly desired in organizational decision making.

Degrees of certainty and uncertainty are expressed as statements of *risk*. All organizational decisions involve some degree of risk—ranging from complete certainty (no risk) to complete uncertainty, "a stab in the dark" (high risk). To make the best possible decisions in organizations, people seek to "manage" the risks they take—that is, minimizing the riskiness of a decision by gaining access to information relevant to the decision.[18]

What makes an outcome risky or not is the *probability* of obtaining the desired outcome. Decision makers attempt to obtain information about the probabilities, or odds, of certain events occurring given that other events have occurred. For example, a financial analyst may report that a certain stock has risen 80 percent of the time that the prime rate has dropped, or a meteorologist may report that the precipitation probability is 50 percent (i.e., in the past it rained or showed half the time certain atmospheric conditions existed). These data may be considered reports of *objective probabilities* because they are based

■ TABLE 10-1	PROGRAMMED AND NONPROGRAMMED DECISIONS: A COMPARISON		
The two major types of organizational decisions— programmed decisions and nonprogrammed decisions— differ with respect to the types of task on which they are made, the degree to which solutions may be found in existing organizational policies, and the typical decision-making unit.		Type of Decision	
	Variable	Programmed Decisions	Nonprogrammed Decisions
	Type of task	Simple, routine	Complex, creative
	Reliance on organizational policies	Considerable guidance from past decisions	No guidance from past decisions
	Typical decision maker	Lower-level workers (usually alone)	Upper-level supervisors (usually in groups)

on concrete, verifiable data. Many decisions are also based on *subjective probabilities*—personal beliefs or hunches about what will happen (see Figure 10-4). For example, a gambler who bets on a horse because it has a name similar to one of his children's or a person who suspects it's going to rain because he just washed his car is basing these judgments on subjective probabilities.

Obviously, uncertainty is an undesirable characteristic in decision making. We may view much of what decision makers do in organizations as attempting to reduce uncertainty (i.e., putting the odds in their favor) so they can make better decisions. How do organizations respond when faced with highly uncertain conditions when they don't know what the future holds for them? Studies have shown that decision uncertainty can be reduced by *establishing linkages with other organizations*. The more an organization knows about what another organization will do, the greater certainty it will have in making decisions.[19] This is part of a general tendency for organizational decision makers to respond to uncertainty by reducing the unpredictability of other organizations in their business environments. Those outside organizations with which managers have the greatest contact are most likely to be the ones whose actions are copied.[20]

In general, what reduces uncertainty in decision-making situations? The answer is *information*. Knowledge about the past and the present can be used to help make projections about the future. A modern executive's access to data needed to make important decisions may be as close as the nearest computer terminal. Indeed, computer technology has greatly aided managers' ability to make decisions quickly, using the most accurate and thorough information available.[21] A variety of on-line information services are designed to provide organizational decision makers with the latest information relevant to the decisions they are making.

Of course, not all information needed to make decisions comes from computers. Many managerial decisions are also based on the decision maker's past experiences and intuition.[22] This is not to say that top managers rely on subjective information in making decisions (although they might), but that their history of past decisions—both successes and failures—is often given great weight in the decision-making process. In other words, when it comes to making decisions, people often rely on what has worked for them in the past. Part of the reason this strategy is often successful is because experienced decision makers tend to make better use of information relevant to the decisions they are making.[23] Individuals who have expertise in certain subjects know what

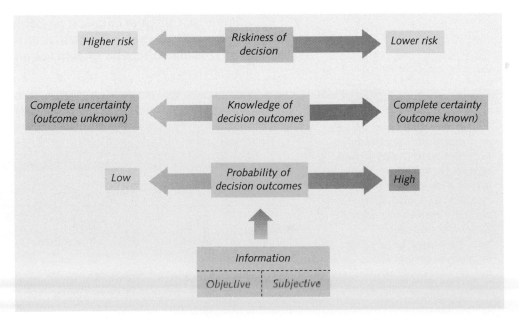

■ **Figure 10-4**
The Riskiness of a Decision:
A Summary
Decisions differ with respect to their degree of riskiness, based on how certain (high probability) or uncertain (low probability) various outcomes may be. Information—both objective and subjective—is used as the basis for estimating the probability of a decision outcome.

information is most relevant and also how to interpret it to make the best decisions. It is therefore not surprising that people seek experienced professionals, such as doctors and lawyers who are seasoned veterans in their fields, when it comes to making important decisions. With high levels of expertise comes information relevant to assessing the riskiness of decision alternatives, and how to reduce it.

Top-Down versus Empowered Decisions

Traditionally, in organizations the job of making all but the most trivial decisions belonged to managers. In fact, organizational scientist Herbert Simon, who won a Nobel prize for his work on the economics of decision making, has gone so far as to describe decision making as synonymous with managing.[24] Subordinates collected information and gave it to superiors, who used it to make decisions. This approach, known as **top-down decision making** puts decision-making power in the hands of managers, leaving lower-level workers little or no opportunities to make decisions. If this sounds familiar to you, it is because it has been the way most organizations have operated.

Today, however, a new approach has come into vogue which is in many ways exactly the opposite. The idea of **empowered decision making** allows employees to make the decisions required to do their jobs without first seeking supervisory approval. As the name implies, it gives them the power to decide what they need to do in order to do their jobs effectively. The rationale for this philosophy of decision making is that the people who do the jobs know what's best, so having someone else make the decision may not make the most sense. In addition, when people are empowered to make their own decisions they are more likely to accept the consequences of those decisions. If the decision was a good one, they can feel good about it. If not, then they have learned a valuable lesson for the next time. In either case, people are more committed to courses of action based on decisions they have made themselves than ones based on decisions that others have made. And, such commitment can be important to keeping the organization functioning effectively.

Many different companies today are empowering their employees to make a wide variety of decisions. As an example, the Ritz-Carlton hotel chain has empowered each of its employees to spend up to $2,000 of the company's money per day to fix whatever they find that needs to be repaired. No longer would a chambermaid who finds a broken lamp in one of the guest rooms need to fill out a form which gets passed from one person to the next. He or she is empowered to get the right person to get the job done right away. Similarly, employees at Volvo's assembly plant in Kalmar, Sweden, are empowered to make decisions about how to do their work (see Figure 10-5). In fact, this practice has been going on in Sweden for many years.

It is not only individual employees who might be empowered, but work teams as well. For example, employees at the Chesapeake Packaging Company's box plant in Baltimore, Maryland, are organized into eight separate internal companies.[25] Each such unit is empowered to make its own decisions about key issues, be it ordering, purchasing new equipment, or measuring their own work. Indeed, the concept of self-managed work teams discussed in Chapter 8 involves systematically empowering several individuals working together with the tools needed to make the most effective decisions possible.

Individual Decisions: How Are They Made?

Now that we have identified the types of decisions people make in organizations, we are prepared to consider the matter of how people go about making them. Perhaps you are thinking, "What do you mean, don't you just think

top-down decision making The practice of vesting decision-making power in the hands of superiors as opposed to lower-level employees.

empowered decision making The practice of vesting power for making decisions in the hands of employees themselves.

The concept of empowerment is also discussed in the context of teams in Chapter 8 and power in Chapter 12.

■ **Figure 10-5**
Volvo Employees Make Empowered Decisions
People working at Volvo's assembly plant in Kalmar, Sweden, are empowered to make a wide variety of decisions about how to do their jobs. Work teams themselves, not top management, takes responsibility for scheduling tasks and distributing rewards.

THE ETHICS ANGLE

MAGUIRE GROUP EMPOWERS EMPLOYEES TO DECIDE OWN ETHICS POLICY

How do you create a corporate ethics policy that employees really accept? This was the question that officials asked themselves at Maguire Group, a professional architecture and engineering firm in Foxborough, Massachusetts. After the company president was forced to resign for having bribed local government officials from whom they sought contracts, all employees would have to buy into a strong set of ethical standards if the company was to reestablish its leadership in the industry. As Maguire's retired senior vice president of human resources, Mary Rendini tells the story that the decision was made to have the document created by the very individuals whose ethical behavior was on the line every day—not just the lawyers and top managers, but all employees throughout the 350-person company.[26]

A task force of 27 employees from throughout the company was broken into five working teams, each charged with the responsibility for drafting various sections of a code of ethics (e.g., policies regarding gifts, political contributions, entertaining prospective clients, and the like). For over eight months these individuals carefully researched and debated their work, drafting and redrafting documents, coordinating their efforts to compose a corporate ethics policy. Instead of coming from the top down (e.g., high-ranking managers and attorneys), the words and ideas are their own.

Maguire's *Code of Ethics and Business Conduct Guidelines* has been effective at reducing the number of ethics violations in the company. This employee-authored document has received wide recognition in the industry for the innovative manner in which it was created—and, most importantly, for the high standards of integrity it has reinforced in the company.

---

things over and do what you think is best?" Although this sometimes may be true, you will see that there's a lot more to decision making than meets the eye. In fact, scientists have considered several different approaches to how individuals make decisions. Here, we will review three of the most important ones.

The Rational-Economic Model: In Search of the Ideal Decision

We all like to think that we are "rational" people who make the best possible decisions. But what exactly does it mean to make a *rational* decision? Organizational scientists view **rational decisions** as ones that maximize the attainment of goals, whether they are the goals of a person, a group, or an entire organization.[27] What would be the most rational way for an individual to go about making a decision? Economists interested in predicting market conditions and prices have relied on a **rational-economic model** of decision making, which assumes that decisions are optimal in every way. An economically rational decision maker will attempt to maximize his or her profits by systematically searching for the *optimum* solution to a problem. For this to occur, the decision maker must have complete and perfect information, and be able to process all this information in an accurate and unbiased fashion.[28]

In many respects, rational-economic decisions follow the same steps outlined in our analytical model of decision making (see Figure 10-2). However, what makes the rational-economic approach special is that it calls for the decision maker to recognize *all* alternative courses of action (step 4) and to evaluate accurately and completely each one (step 5). It views decision makers as attempting to make *optimal* decisions.

Of course, the rational-economic approach to decision making does not fully appreciate the fallibility of the human decision maker. Based on the assumption that people have access to complete and perfect information and use it to make perfect decisions, the model can be considered a *normative* (also called *prescriptive*) approach—one that describes how decision makers ideally

rational decisions Decisions that maximize the chance of attaining an individual's, group's, or organization's goals.

rational-economic model The model of decision making according to which decision makers consider all possible alternatives to problems before selecting the optimal solution.

ought to behave so as to make the best possible decisions. It does not describe how decision makers actually behave in most circumstances. This task is undertaken by the next major approach to individual decision making, the *administrative model*.

The Administrative Model: Exploring the Limits of Human Rationality

As you know from your own experience, people generally do not act in a completely rational-economic manner. To illustrate this point, consider how a personnel department might select a new receptionist. After several applicants are interviewed, the personnel manager might choose the best candidate seen so far and stop interviewing. Had the manager been following a rational-economic model, he or she would have had to interview all possible candidates before deciding on the best one. However, by ending the search after finding a candidate who was just good enough, the manager is using a much simpler approach.

The process used in this example characterizes an approach to decision making known as the **administrative model**.[29] This conceptualization recognizes that decision makers may have a limited view of the problems confronting them. The number of solutions that can be recognized or implemented is limited by the capabilities of the decision maker and the available resources of the organization. Also, decision makers do not have perfect information about the consequences of their decisions, so they cannot tell which one is best.

How are decisions made according to the administrative model? Instead of considering all possible solutions, decision makers consider solutions as they become available. Then they decide on the first alternative that meets their criteria for acceptability. Thus, the decision maker selects a solution that may be just good enough, although not optimal. Such decisions are referred to as **satisficing decisions**. Of course, a satisficing decision is much easier to make than an optimal decision. In most decision-making situations, satisficing decisions are acceptable and are more likely to be made than optimal ones.[30] The following analogy is used to compare the two types of decisions: making an optimal decision is like searching a haystack for the sharpest needle, but making a satisficing decision is like searching a haystack for a needle just sharp enough with which to sew.

As we have noted, it is often impractical for people to make completely optimal, rational decisions. The administrative model recognizes the **bounded rationality** under which most organizational decision makers must operate. The idea is that people lack the cognitive skills required to formulate and solve highly complex business problems in a completely objective, rational way.[31] It should not be surprising that the administrative model does a better job than the rational-economic model of describing how decision makers actually behave. The approach is said to be *descriptive* (also called *proscriptive*) in nature. This interest in examining the actual, imperfect behavior of decision makers, rather than specifying the ideal, economically rational behaviors that decision makers ought to engage in, lies at the heart of the distinction between the administrative and rational-economic models. Our point is not that decision makers do not want to behave rationally, but that restrictions posed by the innate capabilities of the decision makers preclude "perfect" decisions.

Image Theory: An Intuitive Approach to Decision Making

If you think about it, you'll probably realize that some, but certainly not all, decisions are made following the logical steps of our general model of decision making. Consider Elizabeth Barrett Browning's poetic question "How do I love thee? Let me count the ways."[32] It's unlikely that anyone would ultimately answer the question by carefully counting what one loves about another (although many such characteristics can be enumerated). Instead, a more

---

administrative model A model of decision making that recognizes the *bounded rationality* that limits the making of optimally rational-economic decisions.

satisficing decisions Decisions made by selecting the first minimally acceptable alternative as it becomes available.

bounded rationality The major assumption of the administrative model—that organizational, social, and human limitations lead to the making of *satisficing* rather than optimal decisions.

intuitive-based decision making is likely, not only for matters of the heart, but for a variety of important organizational decisions as well.[33]

The point is that selecting the best alternative by weighing all the options is not always a major concern when making a decision. People also consider how various decision alternatives fit with their personal standards as well as their personal goals and plans. The best decision for someone might not be the best for someone else. In other words, people may make decisions in a more automatic, *intuitive* fashion than is traditionally recognized. Representative of this approach is Beach and Mitchell's **image theory**.[34] This approach to decision making is summarized in Figure 10-6.

Image theory deals primarily with decisions about adopting a certain course of action (e.g., should the company develop a new product line?) or changing a current course of action (e.g., should the company drop a present product line?). According to the theory, people make adoption decisions on the basis of a simple two-step process. The first step is the *compatibility test*, a comparison of the degree to which a particular course of action is consistent with various images—particularly individual principles, current goals, and plans for the future. If any lack of compatibility exists with respect to these considerations, a rejection decision is made. If the compatibility test is passed, then the *profitability test* is carried out. That is, people consider the extent to which using various alternatives best fits their values, goals, and plans. The decision is then made to accept the best candidate. These tests are used within a certain *decision frame*—that is, with consideration of meaningful information about the decision context (such as past experiences). The basic idea is that we learn from the past and are guided by it when making decisions. The example shown in Figure 10-6 highlights this contemporary approach to decision making.

According to image theory, the decision-making process is very rapid and simple. The theory suggests that people do not ponder and reflect over decisions but make them using a smooth, intuitive process with minimal cognitive processing. If you've ever found yourself saying that something "seemed like the right thing to do," or "something doesn't feel right," you're probably well aware of the kind of intuitive thinking that goes on in a great deal of decision making. Recent research suggests that when it comes to making rela-

image theory A theory of decision making that recognizes that decisions are made in an automatic, intuitive fashion. According to the theory, people will adopt a course of action that best fits their individual principles, current goals, and plans for the future.

■ **Figure 10-6**
Image Theory: A Summary and Example
According to image theory, *decisions are made in a relatively automatic, intuitive fashion following the two steps outlined here.*

(**Source:** Adapted from Mitchell & Beach, 1990; see Note 34.)

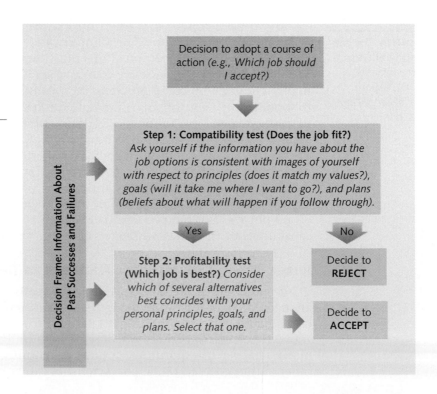

tively simple decisions, people tend to behave as suggested by image theory.[35] For example, it has been found that people decide against various options when past evidence suggests that these decisions may be incompatible with their images of the future.[36]

To summarize, in contrast with the rational-economic approach, the administrative model and image theory represent ways that people actually go about making decisions. Both of these approaches have received support, and neither should be seen as a replacement for the other. Instead, several different processes may be involved in decision making. Not all decision making is carried out the same way: Sometimes decision making might be analytical, and sometimes it might be more intuitive. Modern organizational behavior scholars recognize the value of both approaches. Something both approaches have in common is that they recognize the fallibility of the human decision maker. With this in mind, we will now turn our attention to the imperfect nature of individual decisions.

Individual Decisions: What Makes Them Imperfect?

Let's face it, as a whole, people are less than perfect when it comes to making decisions. Mistakes are made all the time. Obviously, people have limited capacities to process information accurately and thoroughly, like a computer. For example, we often focus on irrelevant information in making decisions.[37] We also fail to use all the information made available to us, in part because we may forget some of it.[38] Beyond these general limitations in human information-processing capacity, we may note several systematic determinants of imperfect decisions, factors that contribute to the imperfect nature of people's decisions. These variables reside not only within individuals themselves (e.g., biases in the way people make decisions) but also the organizations within which we operate. We will now examine five major factors contributing to the imperfect nature of individual decisions.

Framing Effects

framing The presentation of a problem to an individual, either in negative terms (leading to risk-seeking) or positive terms (leading to risk-aversion).

One well-established decision-making bias has to do with the tendency for people to make different decisions based on how the problem is presented to them—that is, the **framing** of a problem. Specifically, Kahneman and Tversky have noted that when problems are framed in a manner that emphasizes the positive gains to be received, people tend to shy away from taking risks and go for the sure thing (i.e., decision makers are said to be *risk-averse*). However, when problems are framed in a manner that emphasizes the potential losses to be suffered, people are more willing to take risks so as to avoid those losses (i.e., decision makers are said to make *risk-seeking* decisions).[39] To illustrate this phenomenon consider the following example:

> The government is preparing to combat a rare disease expected to take 600 lives. Two alternative programs to combat the disease have been proposed, each of which, scientists believe, will have certain consequences. *Program A* will save 200 people, if adopted. *Program B* has a one-third chance of saving all 600 people, but a two-thirds chance of saving no one. Which program do you prefer?

When Kahneman and Tversky presented such a problem to people, 72 percent expressed a preference for Program A, and 28 percent for Program B. In other words, they preferred the "sure thing" of saving 200 people over the one-third possibility of saving them all. However, a curious thing happened when the description of the programs was framed in negative terms. Specifically:

> *Program C* was described as allowing 400 people to die, if adopted. *Program D* was described as allowing a one-third probability that no one would die, and

a two-thirds probability that all 600 would die. Now which program would you prefer?

Compare these four programs. Program C is just another way of stating the outcomes of Program A, and Program D is just another way of stating the outcomes of Program B. However, Programs C and D are framed in negative terms, which led to opposite preferences: 22 percent favored Program C and 78 percent favored Program D (for a summary, see Figure 10-7). In other words, people tended to avoid risk when the problem was framed in terms of "lives saved" (i.e., in positive terms) but to seek risk when the problem was framed in terms of "lives lost" (i.e., in negative terms). This classic effect has been replicated in several studies.[40]

Scientists believe that such effects are due to the tendency for people to perceive equivalent situations framed differently as not really equivalent.[41] In other words, focusing on the glass as "half full" leads people to think about it differently than when it is presented as being "half empty," although they might recognize intellectually that the two are really the same. Such findings illustrate our point that people are not completely rational decision makers but are systematically biased by the cognitive distortions created by simple differences in the way situations are framed.

Reliance on Heuristics

Framing effects are not the only cognitive biases to which decision makers are subjected. It also has been established that people often attempt to simplify the complex decisions they face by using **heuristics**—simple rules of thumb that guide them through a complex array of decision alternatives.[42] Although heuristics are potentially useful to decision makers, they represent potential impediments to decision making. Two very common types of heuristics may be identified.

First, the **availability heuristic** refers to the tendency for people to base their judgments on information that is readily available to them—even though

heuristics Simple decision rules (rules of thumb) used to make quick decisions about complex problems.

availability heuristic The tendency for people to base their judgments on information that is readily available to them although it may be potentially inaccurate, thereby adversely affecting decision quality.

■ **Figure 10-7**
Framing Effects: An Empirical Demonstration
Research has found that differences in the framing of a problem have profound effects on the decisions individuals make. As shown here, when a problem is framed in positive terms (e.g., lives saved by a medical decision), people prefer a certain outcome, a sure thing (i.e., they avoid risk). However, when the same problem is framed in negative terms (e.g., lives lost by a medical decision), people prefer a less certain outcome (i.e., they seek risk).

(**Source:** Based on data reported by Kahneman & Tversky, 1984; see Note 40.)

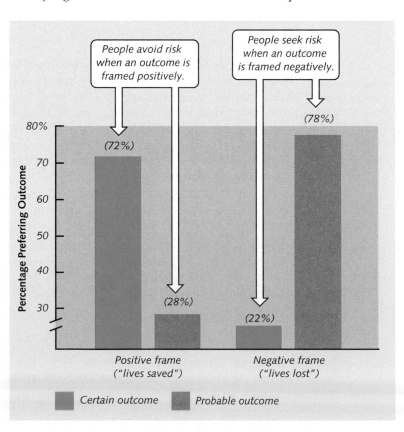

it might not be accurate. Suppose, for example, that an executive needs to know the percentage of entering college freshmen who go on to graduate. There is not enough time to gather the appropriate statistics, so she bases her judgments on her own recollections of when she was a college student. If the percentage she recalls graduating, based on her own experiences, is higher or lower than the usual number, her estimate will be off accordingly. In other words, basing judgments solely on information that is conveniently available increases the possibility of making inaccurate decisions. Yet, the availability heuristic is often used when making decisions.[43]

Second, the **representativeness heuristic** refers to the tendency to perceive others in stereotypical ways if they appear to be typical representatives of the category to which they belong. For example, suppose you believe that accountants are bright, mild-mannered individuals, whereas salespeople are less intelligent but much more extroverted. Further, imagine that there are twice as many salespeople as accountants at a party. You meet someone at the party who is bright and mild-mannered. Although mathematically the odds are two to one that this person is a salesperson rather than an accountant, chances are you will guess that the individual is an accountant because she possesses the traits you associate with accountants. In other words, you believe this person to be representative of accountants in general—so much so that you would knowingly go against the mathematical odds in making your judgment. Research has consistently found that people tend to make this type of error in judgment, thereby providing good support for the existence of the representativeness heuristic.[44]

It is important to note that heuristics do not *always* interfere with the quality of decisions made. In fact, they can be quite helpful. People often use rules of thumb to help simplify the complex decisions they face. For example, management scientists employ many useful heuristics to aid decisions regarding such matters as where to locate warehouses or how to compose an investment portfolio.[45] We also use heuristics in our everyday lives, such as when we play chess ("control the center of the board") or blackjack ("hit on 16, stick on 17"). However, the representativeness heuristic and the availability heuristic may be recognized as impediments to superior decisions because they discourage people from collecting and processing as much information as they should. Making judgments on the basis of only readily available information, or on stereotypical beliefs, although making things simple for the decision maker, does so at a potentially high cost—poor decisions. Thus, these systematic biases represent potentially serious impediments to individual decision making.

Bias toward Implicit Favorites

Don was about to receive his MBA. This was going to be his big chance to move to San Francisco, the city by the bay. Don had long dreamed of living there, and his first "real" job, he hoped, was going to be his ticket. As the corporate recruiters made their annual migration to campus, Don eagerly signed up for several interviews. One of the first was Baxter, Marsh, and Hidalgo, a medium-sized consulting firm in San Francisco. The salary was right and the people seemed pleasant, a combination that excited Don very much. Apparently the interest was mutual; soon Don was offered a position.

Does the story end here? Not quite. It was only March, and Don felt he shouldn't jump at the first job to come along, even though he really wanted it. So, to do "the sensible thing," he signed up for more interviews. Shortly thereafter, Dixon, Timpkin, and Dinglethorpe, a local firm, made Don a more attractive offer. Not only was the salary higher, but, there was every indication that the job promised a much brighter future than the one in San Francisco.

What would he do? Actually, Don didn't consider it much of a dilemma. After thinking it over, he came to the conclusion that the work at Dixon, Timpkin, and Dinglethorpe was much too low level—not enough exciting

representativeness heuristic
The tendency to perceive others in stereotypical ways if they appear to be typical representatives of the category to which they belong.

The powerful effects of stereotypes in organizations are discussed more fully in Chapters 3 and 6.

clients to challenge him. And the starting salary wasn't really all *that* much better than it was at Baxter, Marsh, and Hidalgo. The day after graduation Don was packing for his new office overlooking the Golden Gate Bridge.

Do you think the way Don made his decision was atypical? He seemed to have his mind made up in advance about the job in San Francisco, and didn't really give the other one a chance. Research suggests that people make decisions in this way all the time. That is, people tend to pick an **implicit favorite** option (i.e., a preferred alternative) very early in the decision-making process.[46] Then, the other options they consider subsequently are not given serious consideration. Rather, they are merely used to convince oneself that the implicit favorite is indeed the best choice. An alternative considered for this purpose is known as a **confirmation candidate**. It is not unusual to find that people psychologically distort their beliefs about confirmation candidates so as to justify selecting their implicit favorites. Don did this when he convinced himself that the job offered by the local firm really wasn't as good as it seemed.

Research has shown that people make decisions very early in the decision process. For example, in one study of the job recruitment process investigators found that they could predict 87 percent of the jobs that students would take as early as two months before the students acknowledged that they actually had made a decision.[47] Apparently, people's decisions are biased by the tendency for them not to consider all the relevant information available to them. In fact, they tend to bias their judgments of the strengths and weaknesses of various alternatives so as to make them fit their already-made decision, their implicit favorite.[48] This phenomenon clearly suggests that people not only fail to consider all possible alternatives when making decisions, but that they even fail to consider all readily available alternatives. Instead, they tend to make up their minds very early and convince themselves that they are right. As you might imagine, this bias toward implicit favorites is likely to limit severely the quality of decisions that are made.

Escalation of Commitment: Throwing Good Money after Bad

Because decisions are made all the time in organizations, some of these inevitably will be unsuccessful. What would you say is the rational thing to do when a poor decision has been made? Obviously, the ineffective action should be stopped or reversed. In other words, it would make sense to "cut your losses and run." However, people don't always respond in this manner. In fact, it is not unusual to find that ineffective decisions are sometimes followed up with still further ineffective decisions.

Imagine, for example, that you have invested money in a company, but the company appears to be failing. Rather than lose your initial investment, you may invest still more money in the hope of salvaging your first investment. The more you invest, the more you may be tempted to save those earlier investments by making later investments. That is to say, people sometimes may be found "throwing good money after bad" because they have "too much invested to quit." This is known as the **escalation of commitment phenomenon**—the tendency for people to continue to support previously unsuccessful courses of action because they have sunk costs invested in them.[49]

Although this might not seem like a rational thing to do, this strategy is frequently followed. Consider, for example, how large banks and governments may invest money in foreign governments in the hope of turning them around even though such a result becomes increasingly unlikely. Similarly, the organizers of Expo '86 in British Columbia continued pouring money into the fair long after it became apparent that it would be a big money-losing proposition.[50]

Why do people do this? If you think about it, you may realize that the failure to back your own previous courses of action in an organization would be taken as an admission of failure—a politically difficult act to face in an or-

---

implicit favorite One's preferred decision alternative, selected even before all options have been considered.

confirmation candidate A decision alternative considered only for purposes of convincing oneself of the wisdom of selecting the *implicit favorite*.

escalation of commitment phenomenon The tendency for individuals to continue to support previously unsuccessful courses of action.

ganization. In other words, people may be very concerned about "saving face"—looking good in the eyes of others and oneself.[51] Staw and his associates have recognized that this tendency for *self-justification* is primarily responsible for people's inclination to protect their beliefs about themselves as rational, competent decision makers by convincing themselves and others that they made the right decision all along, and are willing to back it up.[52] Although there are other possible reasons for the escalation of commitment phenomenon, research supports the self-justification explanation.[53] For a summary of the escalation of commitment phenomenon, see Figure 10-8.

Researchers have noted several conditions under which people will refrain from escalating their commitment to a failing course of action.[54] Notably, it has been found that people will stop making failing investments under conditions in which the *available funds for making further investments are limited* and the *threat of failure is overwhelmingly obvious.*[55] For example, when the Long Island Lighting Company decided in 1989 to abandon plans to operate a nuclear power plant in Shoreham, New York, it was in the face of 23 year's worth of intense political and financial pressure (a strong antinuclear movement and billions of dollars of cost overruns).[56]

It also has been found that people will refrain from escalating commitment when they can *diffuse their responsibility for the earlier failing actions.* That is, the more people feel they are just one of several people responsible for a failing course of action, the less likely they are to commit to further failing actions.[57] In other words, the less one is responsible for an earlier failure, the less one may be motivated to justify those earlier failures by making further investments in them.

Finally, it has been found that people are unwilling to escalate commitment to a course of action when it is made clear that the *total amount invested exceeds the amount expected to be gained.*[58] Although people may wish to invest in projects that enable them to recoup their initial investments, there is little reason for them to do so when it is obvious that doing so will be a losing proposition. Under such conditions, it is difficult to justify doing so, even if one "hopes against hope" that it will work out. Indeed, research has shown that decision makers do indeed refrain from escalating commitment to decisions when it is made clear that the overall benefit to be gained is less than the overall costs to be borne.[59] This finding was more apparent among students with accounting backgrounds than those without such backgrounds, presumably because their training predisposed them to be more sensitive to these issues.

■ **Figure 10-8**
Escalation of Commitment: An Overview
According to the escalation of commitment phenomenon, *people who have repeatedly made poor decisions will continue to support those failing courses of action in order to justify their decisions. Under some conditions, summarized here, the effect will not occur.*

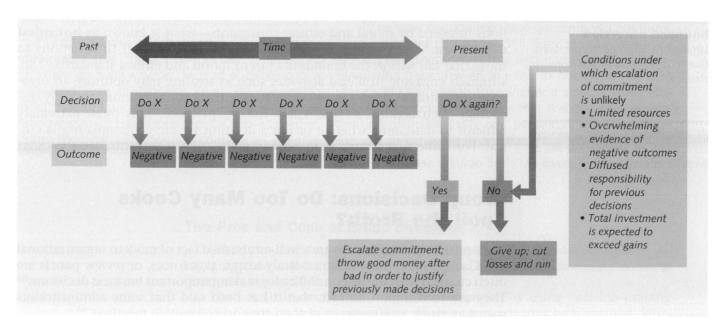

■ **Figure 10-9**
*Group Decision Making:
Advantages and Disadvantages*
*Should groups be used to make deci-
sions, as opposed to individuals? The
answer depends largely on the trade-
offs summarized here.*

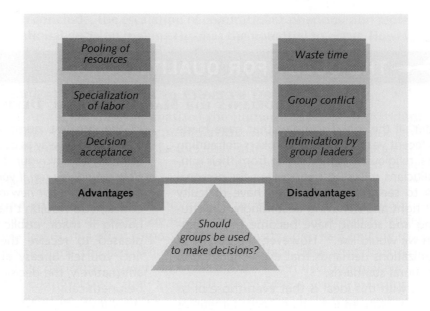

bringing people together may increase the amount of knowledge and information available for making good decisions. In other words, there may be a
pooling of resources. A related benefit is that in decision-making groups there
can be a *specialization of labor*. With enough people around to share the work
load, individuals can perform only those tasks at which they are best, thereby
potentially improving the quality of the group's efforts. Another benefit is that
group decisions are likely to enjoy *greater acceptance* than individual decisions.
People involved in making decisions may be expected to understand those decisions better and be more committed to carrying them out than decisions
made by someone else.[69]

Of course, there are also some problems associated with using decision-
making groups. One obvious drawback is that groups are likely to *waste time*.
The time spent socializing before getting down to business may be a drain on
the group and be very costly to organizations. Another possible problem is
that potential disagreement over important matters may breed ill will and *group
conflict*. Although constructive disagreement can actually lead to better group
outcomes, highly disruptive conflict may interfere with group decisions.
Indeed, with corporate power and personal pride at stake, it is not at all surprising to find that lack of agreement can cause bad feelings to develop between group members. Finally, we may expect groups to be ineffective
sometimes because of members' *intimidation by group leaders*. A group composed of several "yes" men or women trying to please a dominant leader tends
to discourage open and honest discussion of solutions. In view of these problems, it is easy to understand the old adage "a camel is a horse put together
by a committee."

Given the several pros and cons of using groups to make decisions, we
must conclude that neither groups nor individuals are always superior.
Obviously, there are important trade-offs involved in using either one to make
decisions. Since there are advantages associated with both group and individual decision makers, a question arises as to *when* each should be used. That is,
under what conditions might individuals or groups be expected to make superior decisions? Fortunately, research has addressed this important question.[70]

When Are Groups Superior to Individuals?

Imagine a situation in which an important decision has to be made about
a complex problem—such as whether one company should merge with another. This is not the kind of problem about which any one individual work-

*For a discussion of other causes of
conflict and the impact of conflict
in organizations, see Chapter 11.*

ing alone would be able to make a good decision. Its highly complex nature may overwhelm even an expert, thereby setting the stage for a group to do a better job.

Whether a group actually will do better than an individual depends on several important considerations. For one, we must consider who is in the group. Successful groups tend to be composed of *heterogeneous group members with complementary skills*. So, for example, a group composed of lawyers, accountants, real estate agents, and other experts may make much better decisions on the merger problem than would a group composed of specialists in only one field. Indeed, research has shown that the diversity of opinions offered by group members is one of the major advantages of using groups to make decisions.[71]

As you might imagine, it is not enough simply to have skills. For a group to be successful, its members also must be able to communicate their ideas freely to each other in an open, nonhostile manner. Conditions under which one individual (or group) intimidates another from contributing his or her expertise can easily negate any potential gain associated with composing groups of heterogeneous experts. After all, *having* expertise and being able to make a contribution by *using* that expertise are two different things. Indeed, research has shown that only when the contributions of the most qualified group members are given the greatest weight does the group derive any benefit from that member's presence.[72] Thus, for groups to be superior to individuals, they must be composed of a heterogeneous collection of experts with complementary skills who can freely and openly contribute to their group's product.

As an example of this, Michaelsen, Watson, and Black studied the performance of 222 groups of approximately six students who worked together extensively on class projects (team learning exercises) over the course of a semester.[73] Assignments to groups were made so as to create units that were as broadly diversified as possible. The teams had to work together on answering exam questions about the material they studied. The questions were generally difficult, some requiring the ability to analyze and synthesize complex concepts. The researchers were interested in comparing the performance of the groups as a whole with that of individual members. Their findings are summarized in Figure 10-10.

As shown in Figure 10-10, the average score on the exams completed jointly by group members was not only higher than that of the average group member, but also higher than that of the best group member. In fact, of the 222 groups studied, 215 (97 percent) outperformed their best member, 4 groups tied their best member, and only 3 groups scored lower than their best member. Clearly, these findings support the idea that *on complex tasks, a benefit is derived from combining individuals into groups that goes beyond the contribution of what the best group member can do.* People can help each other solve complex problems not only by pooling their resources, but also by correcting each other's answers and assisting each other to come up with ideas. There is also likely to be the intangible *synergy* created when a group of people help each other and create a climate for success.

In contrast to complex decision tasks, imagine a situation in which a judgment is required on a simple problem with a readily verifiable answer. For example, imagine that you are asked to translate a phrase from a relatively obscure language into English. Groups might do better than individuals on such a task, but probably because the odds are increased that someone in the group knows the language and can perform the translation for the group. However, there is no reason to expect that even a large group will be able to perform such a task better than a single individual who has the required expertise. In fact, an expert working alone may do even better than a group. This is because an expert individual performing a simple task may be distracted by others and suffer from having to convince them of the correctness of his or her solution. For

The success of heterogeneous groups is related to one reason why racially and ethnically diverse groups are considered desirable in organizations, as discussed in Chapter 2.

■ Figure 10-10

Group vs. Individual Performance on a Complex Task: Empirical Evidence

Research comparing the performance of groups and individuals on a complex learning task has shown that groups as a whole performed better than either the average individual or even the best individual in the group. Such findings support the idea that the benefit of working in groups goes beyond the simple combination of individual skills.

(**Source:** Based on data reported by Michaelsen, Watson, & Black, 1989; see Note 73.)

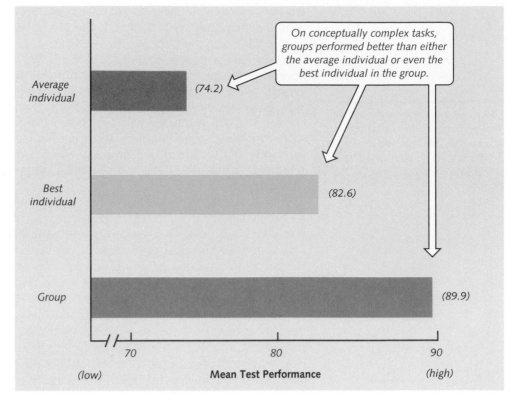

On conceptually complex tasks, groups performed better than either the average individual or even the best individual in the group.

■ Figure 10-11

Group Decisions: When Are They Superior to Individual Decisions?

When performing complex problems, groups are superior to individuals if certain conditions prevail (e.g., members have heterogeneous, complementary skills, they can freely share ideas, and good ideas are accepted). However, when performing simple problems, groups perform only as well as the best individual in the group, and then only if that person has the correct answer and that response is accepted by the group.

this reason, exceptional individuals tend to outperform entire committees on simple tasks.[74] In such cases, for groups to benefit from a pooling of resources, there must be some resources to pool. The pooling of ignorance does not help. In other words, the question "Are two heads better than one?" can be answered this way: *on simple tasks, two heads may be better than one if at least one of those heads has enough of what it takes to succeed.*

In summary, whether groups perform better than individuals depends on the nature of the task performed and the expertise of the people involved. We have summarized some of these key considerations in Figure 10-11.

When Are Individuals Superior to Groups?

As we have described thus far, groups may be expected to perform better than the average or even the exceptional individual under certain conditions. However, there are also conditions under which individuals are superior to

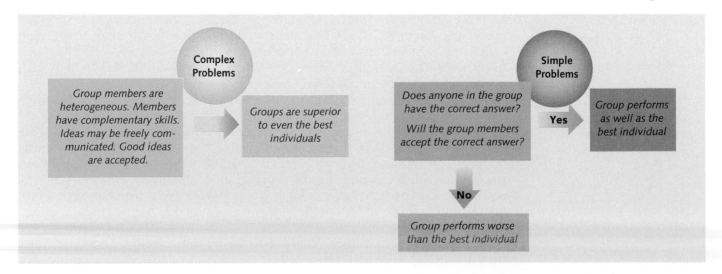

groups. Most of the problems faced by organizations require a great deal of creative thinking. For example, a company deciding how to use a newly developed adhesive in its consumer products is facing decisions on a poorly structured task. Although you would expect that the complexity of such creative problems would give groups a natural advantage, this is not the case. In fact, research has shown that *on poorly structured, creative tasks, individuals perform better than groups.*[75]

An approach to solving creative problems commonly used by groups is **brainstorming**. This technique was developed by advertising executive Alex Osborn as a tool for coming up with creative, new ideas.[76] The members of brainstorming groups are encouraged to present their ideas in an uncritical way and to discuss freely and openly all ideas on the floor. Specifically, members of brainstorming groups are required to follow four main rules:

1. Avoid criticizing others' ideas.
2. Share even far-out suggestions.
3. Offer as many comments as possible.
4. Build on others' ideas to create your own.

Does brainstorming improve the quality of creative decisions? To answer this question, Bouchard and his associates conducted a study in which they compared the effectiveness of individuals and brainstorming groups working on creative problems.[77] Specifically, participants were given 35 minutes to consider the consequences of situations such as "What if everybody went blind?" or "What if everybody grew an extra thumb on each hand?" Clearly, the novel nature of such problems requires a great deal of creativity. Comparisons were made of the number of solutions generated by groups of four or seven people and a like number of individuals working on the same problems alone. The results were clear: Individuals were significantly more productive than groups.

In summary, groups perform worse than individuals when working on creative tasks. A great part of the problem is that some individuals feel inhibited by the presence of others even though one rule of brainstorming is that even far-out ideas may be shared. To the extent that people wish to avoid feeling foolish as a result of saying silly things, their creativity may be inhibited when in groups. Similarly, groups may inhibit creativity by slowing down the process of bringing ideas to fruition.

Groupthink: Too Much Cohesiveness Can Be a Dangerous Thing

One reason groups may fare so poorly on complex tasks lies in the dynamics of group interaction. As we noted in Chapter 8, when members of a group develop a very strong group spirit—or a high level of *cohesiveness*—they sometimes become so concerned about not disrupting the like-mindedness of the group that they may be reluctant to challenge the group's decisions. When this happens, group members tend to isolate themselves from outside information, and the process of critical thinking deteriorates. This phenomenon is referred to as **groupthink**.[78]

The Nature of Groupthink

The concept of groupthink was proposed initially as an attempt to explain ineffective decisions made by U.S. government officials that led to fiascoes such as the Bay of Pigs invasion in Cuba and the Vietnam War.[79] Analyses of each of these cases have revealed that the president's advisers actually *discouraged* more effective decision making. An examination of the conditions under which the decision was made to launch the ill-fated space shuttle *Challenger* in January 1986 revealed that it too resulted from groupthink.[80] Post

brainstorming A technique designed to foster group productivity by encouraging interacting group members to express their ideas in a noncritical fashion.

groupthink The tendency for members of highly cohesive groups to conform to group pressures regarding a certain decision so strongly that they fail to think critically, rejecting the potentially correcting influences of outsiders.

hoc analyses of conversations between key personnel suggested that the team that made the decision to launch the shuttle under freezing conditions did so while insulating itself from the engineers who knew how the equipment should function. Given that NASA had such a successful history, the decision makers operated with a sense of invulnerability. They also worked so closely together and were under such intense pressure to launch the shuttle without further delay that they all collectively went along with the launch decision, creating the illusion of unanimous agreement. For a summary of the groupthink phenomenon, including some of its symptoms, see Figure 10-12.

Groupthink doesn't occur only in governmental decision making, of course, but also in the private sector (although the failures may be less well publicized). For example, analyses of the business policies of large corporations such as Lockheed and Chrysler have suggested that it was the failure of top management teams to respond to changing market conditions that at one time led them to the brink of disaster.[81] The problem is that members of very cohesive groups may have considerable confidence in their group's decisions, making them unlikely to raise doubts about these actions (i.e., "the group seems to know what it's doing"). As a result, they may suspend their own critical thinking in favor of conforming to the group. When group members become fiercely loyal to each other, they may ignore potentially useful information from other sources that challenges the group's decisions. The result of this process is that the group's decisions may be completely uninformed, irrational, or even immoral.[82]

Strategies for Avoiding Groupthink

So as not to conclude on an entirely pessimistic note, we point out that several strategies can effectively combat groupthink. Here are a few proven techniques:

1. *Promote open inquiry*. Remember: Groupthink arises in response to group members' reluctance to "rock the boat." Group leaders should encourage members to be skeptical of all solutions and to avoid reaching premature

■ **Figure 10-12**
Groupthink: An Overview
Groupthink occurs when highly cohesive conditions discourage group members from challenging the group's actions. Poor quality decisions result.

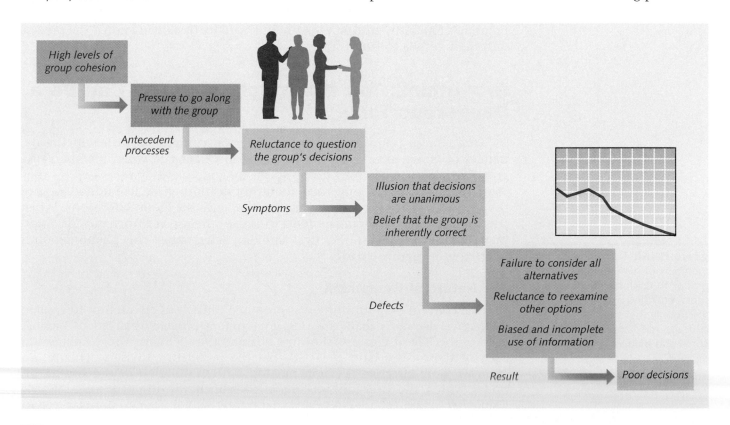

High levels of group cohesion

Pressure to go along with the group

Antecedent processes

Reluctance to question the group's decisions

Symptoms

Illusion that decisions are unanimous

Belief that the group is inherently correct

Failure to consider all alternatives

Reluctance to reexamine other options

Defects

Biased and incomplete use of information

Result

Poor decisions

agreements. It sometimes helps to play the role of *devil's advocate*, that is, to find fault intentionally with a proposed solution.[83] Research has shown that when this is done, groups make higher-quality decisions.[84] In fact, some corporate executives use exercises in which conflict is intentionally generated just so the negative aspects of a decision can be identified before it's too late.[85] This is not to say that leaders should be argumentative. Rather, raising a nonthreatening question to force both sides of an issue can be very helpful in improving the quality of decisions.

2. *Use subgroups.* Because the decisions made by any one group may be the result of groupthink, basing decisions on the recommendations of two groups is a useful check. If the two groups disagree, a discussion of their differences is likely to raise important issues. However, if the two groups agree, you can be relatively confident that their conclusions are not *both* the result of groupthink.

3. *Admit shortcomings.* When groupthink occurs, group members feel very confident that they are doing the right thing. Such feelings of perfection discourage people from considering opposing information. However, if group members acknowledge some of the flaws and limitations of their decisions, they may be more open to corrective influences. Keep in mind that no decision is perfect. Asking others to point out their misgivings about a group's decisions may help avoid the illusion of perfection that contributes to groupthink.

4. *Hold second-chance meetings.* Before implementing a decision, it is a good idea to hold a *second-chance meeting* during which group members are asked to express any doubts and propose any new ideas they may have. Alfred P. Sloan, former head of General Motors, is known to have postponed acting on important matters until any group disagreement was resolved.[86] As people get tired of working on problems, they may hastily reach agreement on a solution. Second-chance meetings can be useful devices for seeing if a solution still seems good even after "sleeping on it."

Given the extremely adverse effects groupthink can have on organizations, practicing managers would be wise to put these simple suggestions into action. The alternative—facing the consequences of groupthink—clearly suggests the need for serious consideration of this issue.

Improving the Effectiveness of Group Decisions: Some Techniques

As we have made clear in this chapter, certain advantages can be gained from sometimes using individuals and sometimes using groups to make decisions. A decision-making technique that combines the best features of groups and individuals, while minimizing the disadvantages, would be ideal. Several techniques designed to realize the "best of both worlds" have been widely used in organizations. These include techniques that involve the structuring of group discussions in special ways. An even more basic approach to improving the effectiveness of group decisions involves training decision makers in ways of avoiding some of the pitfalls of group decision making. We will begin this section of the chapter with a discussion of this training approach to improving group decisions and then go on to consider various ways of creating specially structured groups.

Training Individuals to Improve Group Performance

As we noted earlier in this chapter, how well groups solve problems depends in part on the composition of those groups. If at least one group member is capable of coming up with a solution, groups may benefit by that individual's expertise. Based on this reasoning, it follows that the more qualified individual group members are to solve problems, the better their groups as a whole will perform.

This is but one of the many possible uses of training in organizations described more fully in Chapter 3.

Researchers Bottger and Yetton found that individuals trained to avoid four common types of errors significantly reduced the number of mistakes made by their groups when attempting to solve a creative problem.[87] Specifically, participants in the study were asked to be aware of and to try to avoid four common problems:

1. *Hypervigilance*: This state involves frantically searching for quick solutions to problems, going from one idea to another out of a sense of desperation that one idea isn't working and that another needs to be considered before time runs out. A poor, "last chance" solution may be adopted to relieve anxiety. This problem may be avoided by keeping in mind that it is best to stick with one suggestion and work it out thoroughly, and reassuring the person solving the problem that his or her level of skill and education is adequate to perform the task at hand. In other words, a little reassurance may go a long way toward keeping individuals on the right track and avoiding the problem of hypervigilance.

2. *Unconflicted adherence*: Many decision makers make the mistake of sticking to the first idea that comes into their heads without more deeply evaluating the consequences. As a result, such people are unlikely to become aware of any problems associated with their ideas or to consider other possibilities. To avoid *unconflicted adherence*, decision makers are urged to (1) think about the difficulties associated with their ideas, (2) force themselves to consider different ideas, and (3) consider the special and unique characteristics of the problem they are facing and avoid carrying over assumptions from previous problems.

3. *Unconflicted change*: Sometimes people are too quick to change their minds and adopt the first new idea to come along. To avoid such unconflicted change, decision makers are encouraged to ask themselves about (1) the risks and problems of adopting that solution, (2) the good points of the first idea, and (3) the relative strengths and weaknesses of both ideas.

4. *Defensive avoidance*: Too often decision makers fail to solve problems effectively because they avoid working on the task at hand. To minimize this problem, they should do three things. First, they should attempt to *avoid procrastination*. Don't put off the problem indefinitely just because you cannot come up with a solution right away. Continue to budget some of your time on even the most frustrating problems. Second, *avoid disowning responsibility*. It is easy to minimize the importance of a problem by saying "It doesn't matter, so who cares?" Avoid giving up so soon. Finally, *don't ignore potentially corrective information*. It is tempting to put your nagging doubts about the quality of a solution to rest in order to be finished with it. Good decision makers would not do so. Rather, they use their doubts to test and potentially improve the quality of their ideas.

The encouraging aspect of Bottger and Yetton's findings is that merely having members of problem-solving groups consider these four potential pitfalls was an effective way of improving the quality of their groups' solutions. Apparently, how well groups perform depends to a great extent on the problem-solving skills of the individual group members. Attempting to avoid the four major pitfalls described here appears to be an effective method of improving individual decision-making skills—and hence the quality of group decisions. Obviously, this is only one approach that can improve organizational decision making. For a close-up description of how training in decision-making techniques can also be adapted to one highly specialized situation, see the ORGANIZATION OF THE FUTURE section.

DECISIONS AT 30,000 FEET: TECHNOLOGY HELPS PILOTS AVOID FATAL ERRORS

A poor decision by an executive may lead a company down the road to ruin. A poor decision by a physician may lead to the death of a patient. But a poor decision by a commercial airline pilot may take hundreds of lives at once, including his or her own. Indeed, "pilot error" has been cited as the cause of a growing number of commercial airline crashes.[88] To avoid such tragedies, the airline industry has focused on things that can be done to improve the quality of the decisions made by pilots. As you might imagine, such improvements usually involve the use of high-tech instruments—especially devices that warn pilots of unforeseen weather hazards. But, technology itself can be ineffective unless pilots are carefully trained to make decisions about when and how to take appropriate precautionary maneuvers. Fortunately for the flying public, efforts are presently underway to improve the decision making of tomorrow's commercial aviators.

One of the most vexing problems pilots encounter results from *wind shear*, a condition created when a microburst (a small area of very turbulent wind) causes a sudden downdraft leading to a loss of lift. Reports by investigators from the National Transportation and Safety Board have shown that wind shear has been a factor in many accidents or near accidents in the past few decades.[89] Wind shear is not a condition that can be avoided by completely mechanical means; it requires quick action on the part of pilots in response to proper warnings. For example, on July 11, 1988, several pilots flew into an area over Denver reported to have microburst activity because they were not adequately warned in advance. To the extent that pilots can accurately interpret the signals they receive, they are better able to take the correct, timely actions needed to guide their aircraft safely.

What can be done to help in such situations? Specifically, what type of information should be presented to pilots, when, and in what form? This question was considered by Lee in an intensive investigation of 18 experienced commercial air crews (i.e., a captain and a first officer) who were studied in an elaborate flight simulator.[90] After being familiarized with the training apparatus, crews were required to fly a simulated round-trip between Salt Lake City and Denver. The flight conditions were made to match closely those over Denver on July 11, 1988. Crews were assigned to one of two groups differing with respect to the nature of the weather-related information they received. In the *control group*, crews received only the standard oral weather briefings given by air traffic control transmissions. In the *experimental* group, this information was supplemented by visual displays (simulated ground-based Doppler radar) that warned pilots of wind shear as they approached the runway. How did these differences influence air crews' decision-making behavior?

The results revealed some critical differences. Whereas 17 percent of the discussion in the experimental group dealt with wind shear, attention to the topic was virtually nonexistent in the control group. The investigators also analyzed the results with respect to decision time—that is, the average time that elapsed from the alert to the captain's decision about what approach to take in landing. Crews assigned to experimental group made decisions more quickly than those assigned to the control group. These data reveal that the visual presentation of redundant data allowed airline cockpit crews to make critical decisions about avoiding microbursts much faster. In fact, a mean difference of approximately one minute (and 700–800 feet of additional altitude) was found—margins that may be critical to avoiding potentially dangerous conditions.

Although additional factors may be involved in potentially dangerous air travel situations, these results strongly suggest the need to use redundant visual information to supplement oral information. Given that good information is the key to good decision making, such knowledge about the most effective ways to present critical information may be exceptionally useful. Although such redundant visual displays may be costly to introduce, one must consider these costs relative to the loss of life that might occur when the appropriate visual display technology is not put into place. Findings such as these strongly suggest that although human decision making is highly imperfect, the use of technology is helping to improve it.

The Delphi Technique: Decisions by Expert Consensus

According to Greek mythology, people interested in seeing what fate the future held for them could seek the counsel of the Delphic oracle. Today's organizational decision makers sometimes consult experts to help them make the best decisions as well. A technique developed by the Rand Corporation, known as the **Delphi technique**, represents a systematic way of collecting and organizing the opinions of several experts into a single decision.[91] The steps in the process are summarized in Figure 10-13.

The Delphi process starts by enlisting the cooperation of experts and presenting the problem to them, usually in a letter. Each expert then proposes what he or she believes is the most appropriate solution. The group leader compiles all of these individual responses and reproduces them so they can be shared with all the other experts in a second mailing. At this point, each expert comments on the others' ideas and proposes another solution. These individual solutions are returned to the leader, who compiles them and looks for a consensus of opinions. If a consensus is reached, the decision is made. If not, the process of sharing reactions with others is repeated until a consensus is eventually obtained.

The obvious advantage of using the Delphi technique to make decisions is that it allows for the collection of expert judgments without the great costs and logistical difficulties of bringing many experts together for a face-to-face meeting. However, the technique is not without limitations. As you might imagine, the Delphi process can be very time-consuming. Sending out letters, waiting for everyone to respond, transcribing and disseminating the responses, and repeating the process until a consensus is reached can take quite a long time. Experts have estimated that the minimum time required to use the Delphi technique would be more than 44 days. In one case, the process took five months to complete.[92] Obviously, the Delphi approach would not be appropriate for making decisions in crisis situations or whenever else time is of the essence. However, the approach has been successfully employed to make de-

Delphi technique A method of improving group decisions using the opinions of experts, which are solicited by mail and then compiled. The expert consensus of opinions is used to make a decision.

■ **Figure 10-13**
The Delphi Group: A Summary
The Delphi technique allows decisions to be made by several experts without encountering many of the disadvantages of face-to-face group interaction.

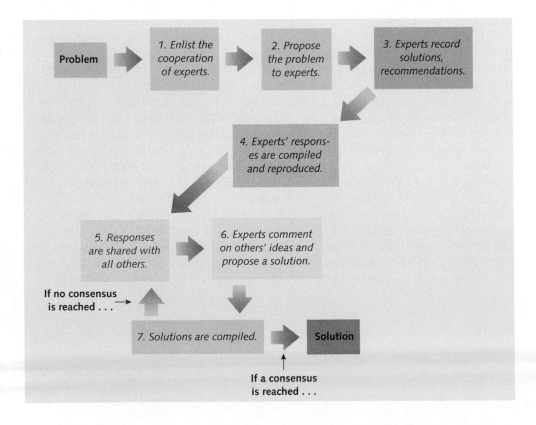

cisions such as what items to put on a conference agenda and what the potential impact of implementing new land-use policies would be.[93]

The Nominal Group Technique: A Structured Group Meeting

When there are only a few hours available to make a decision, group discussion sessions can be held in which members interact with each other in an orderly, focused fashion aimed at solving problems. The **nominal group technique (NGT)** brings together a small number of individuals (usually about seven to ten) who systematically offer their individual solutions to a problem and share their personal reactions to others' solutions.[94] The technique is referred to as "nominal" because the individuals involved form a group in name only. The participants do not attempt to agree as a group on any solution, but rather vote on all the solutions proposed. For an outline of the steps in the process, see Figure 10-14.

As shown in Figure 10-14, the nominal group process begins by gathering the group members together around a table and identifying the problem at hand. Then each member writes down his or her solutions. Next, one at a time, each member presents his or her solutions to the group and the leader writes these down on a chart. This process continues until all the ideas have been expressed. Following this, each solution is discussed, clarified, and evaluated by the group members. Each member is given a chance to voice his or her reactions to each idea. After all the ideas have been evaluated, the group members privately rank-order their preferred solutions. The idea that receives the highest rank is taken as the group's decision.

The NGT has several advantages and disadvantages.[95] We have already noted that this approach can be used to arrive at group decisions in only a few hours. The benefit of the technique is that it discourages any pressure to

■ Figure 10-14
The Nominal Group Technique: An Overview
The nominal group technique structures face-to-face meetings in a way that allows for the open expression and evaluation of ideas.

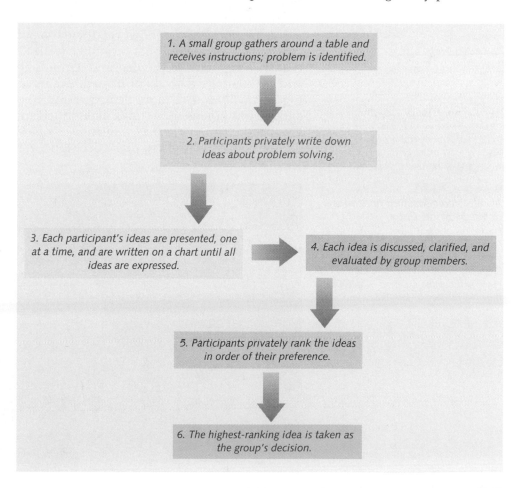

1. A small group gathers around a table and receives instructions; problem is identified.

2. Participants privately write down ideas about problem solving.

3. Each participant's ideas are presented, one at a time, and are written on a chart until all ideas are expressed.

4. Each idea is discussed, clarified, and evaluated by group members.

5. Participants privately rank the ideas in order of their preference.

6. The highest-ranking idea is taken as the group's decision.

conform to the wishes of a high-status group member because all ideas are evaluated and the preferences are expressed in private balloting. The technique must be considered limited, however, in that it requires the use of a trained group leader. In addition, using NGT successfully requires that only one narrowly defined problem be considered at a time. So, for very complex problems, many NGT sessions would have to be run—and only *if* the problem under consideration can be broken down into smaller parts.

Although nominal groups traditionally meet in face-to-face settings, advances in modern technology enable nominal groups to meet even when its members are far away from each other. Specifically, **electronic meeting systems** have been used, in which individuals in different locations participate in group conferences by means of telephone lines or direct satellite transmissions.[96] The messages may be sent either via characters on a computer monitor or images viewed during a teleconference. Despite their high-tech look, automated decision conferences are really just nominal groups meeting in a manner that approximates face-to-face contact. Insofar as electronic meetings allow for groups to assemble more conveniently than face-to-face meetings, they are growing in popularity. Presently, such companies as GE Appliances, U.S. West, and Marriott Corp. (see Figure 10-15) have relied on electronic meetings.

It is important to consider the relative effectiveness of nominal groups and Delphi groups over face-to-face interacting groups. In general, research has shown the superiority of these special approaches to decision making in many ways on a variety of decision problems.[97] For example, the effectiveness of both techniques has been demonstrated in a study by Van de Ven and Delbecq in which seven-member groups (nominal, Delphi, and interacting) worked on the task of defining the job of a dormitory counselor.[98] Nominal groups tended to be the most satisfied with their work and made the best-quality judgments. In addition, both nominal groups and Delphi groups were much more productive than interacting groups.

As we noted earlier, however, there is a potential benefit to be derived from face-to-face interaction that cannot be realized in nominal and Delphi groups—that is, acceptance of the decision. Groups are likely to accept their decisions and be committed to them if members have been actively involved in making them. Thus, the more detached and impersonal atmosphere of nominal and Delphi groups sometimes makes their members less likely to accept their groups' decisions. We may conclude, then, that there is no one best type of group that can be used to make decisions. Which type is most appropriate de-

electronic meeting systems
The practice of bringing individuals from different locations together for a meeting via telephone or satellite transmissions, either on television monitors or via shared space on a computer screen.

■ **Figure 10-15**
An Electronic Meeting in Progress at the Marriott Corp.
Employees of the Marriott Corp. rely on electronic meetings to bring together individuals in distant locations so that they may confer on topics of mutual interest without the expenses of getting together for face-to-face meetings.

pends on the trade-offs decision makers are willing to make in terms of speed, quality, and commitment.[99]

The Stepladder Technique: Systematically Incorporating New Members

stepladder technique A technique for improving the quality of group decisions that minimizes the tendency for group members to be unwilling to present their ideas by adding new members to a group one at a time and requiring each to present his or her ideas independently to a group that already has discussed the problem at hand.

Another way of structuring group interaction known as the **stepladder technique** has been introduced by Rogelberg, Barnes-Farrell and Lowe.[100] This approach minimizes the tendency for group members to be unwilling to present their ideas by adding new members to a group one at a time and requiring each to present his or her ideas independently to a group that already has discussed the problem at hand. To begin, each of two people works on a problem independently and then come together to present their ideas and discuss solutions jointly. While the two-person group is working, a third person working alone also considers the problem. Then, this individual presents his or her ideas to the group and joins in a three-person discussion of a possible solution. During this period a fourth person works on the problem alone and then presents his or her ideas to the group and joins in a four-person group discussion. After each new person has been added to the group, the entire group works together at finding a solution. (For a summary of the steps in this technique, see Figure 10-16.)

In following this procedure, it is important for each individual to be given enough time to work on the problem before he or she joins the group. Then, each person must be given enough time to present thoroughly his or her ideas to the group. Groups then must have sufficient time to discuss the problem at hand and reach a preliminary decision before the next person is added. The final decision is then made only after all individuals have been added to the group.

The rationale underlying this procedure is that by forcing each person to present independent ideas

YOU BE THE CONSULTANT

A large product-distribution company is having a problem during its group meetings: One department manager is constantly disrupting the meetings while trying to get his ideas across. He has so consistently intimidated his co-workers that they are reluctant to speak up. As a result, their ideas are not coming across.

1. Explain what steps might be taken to avoid this problem.
2. What are the advantages and disadvantages of the tactic you identify?

■ **Figure 10-16**
The Stepladder Technique: A Summary
By systematically adding new individuals into decision-making groups, the stepladder technique *helps increase the quality of the decisions made.*

(**Source:** Adapted from Rogelberg, Barnes-Farrell, & Lowe, 1992; see Note 100.)

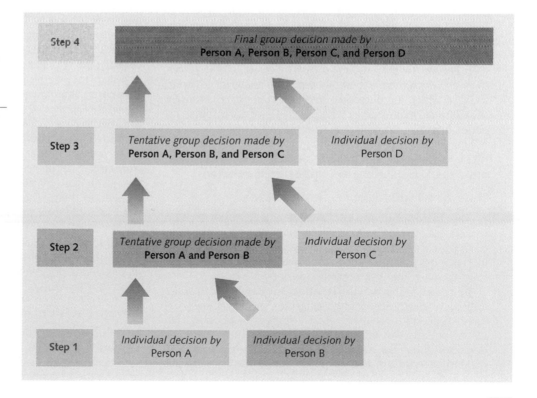

without knowing how the rest of the group has decided, the new person will not be influenced by the group, and the group is required to consider a constant infusion of new ideas. If this is so, then groups solving problems using the stepladder technique would be expected to make better decisions than conventional groups meeting all at once to discuss the same problem.

In an experiment comparing both types of groups, this is exactly what Rogelberg and his associates found. Moreover, members of stepladder groups reported feeling generally more positive about their group experiences. Although the stepladder technique is new, this evidence suggests that it holds a great deal of promise as a way of enhancing the decision-making capacity of groups.

SUMMARY AND REVIEW

The Nature of Decision Making

Traditionally, theorists have looked at **decision making** as the multistep process through which a problem is identified, solution objectives are defined, a **predecision** is made (i.e., a decision about how to make a decision), alternatives are generated and evaluated, and an alternative is chosen, implemented, and then followed up.

There are individual differences in the way people make decisions. Generally, individuals have one dominant decision style, either *directive*, *analytical*, *conceptual*, or *behavioral*. Research also has shown that people in different cultures tend to make decisions in different ways.

The Broad Spectrum of Organizational Decisions

Decisions made in organizations can be characterized as being either **programmed**, routine decisions made according to preexisting guidelines, or **nonprogrammed**, decisions requiring novel and creative solutions. Decisions also differ with respect to the amount of risk involved, ranging from those in which the decision outcomes are relatively *certain* to those in which the outcomes are highly *uncertain*. Uncertain situations are expressed as statements of probability based on either objective or subjective information. Finally, decisions may be differentiated with respect to whether they are made by high-level organizational officials (**top-down decisions**) or by employees themselves (**empowered decisions**).

How Are Individual Decisions Made?

The **rational-economic model** characterizes decision makers as thoroughly searching through perfect information to make an optimal decision. This is a *normative* approach, in that it describes how decision makers ideally ought to behave to make the best possible decisions.

In contrast, the **administrative model** is a *descriptive* approach, which describes how decision makers actually behave. It recognizes that limitations imposed by people's ability to process the information needed to make complex decisions (*bounded rationality*) restrict decision makers to making **satisficing decisions**—solutions that are not optimal, but good enough.

An alternative approach, **image theory**, recognizes that decisions are made in an automatic, intuitive fashion. It claims that people will adopt a course of action that best fits their individual principles, current goals, and plans for the future.

Impediments to Optimal Individual Decisions

People make imperfect decisions due to cognitive biases. One such bias, **framing**, refers to the tendency for people to make different decisions based on how a problem is presented. For example, when a problem is presented in a way that emphasizes positive gains to be received, people tend to make conservative, risk-averse, decisions, whereas when the same problem is presented in a way that emphasizes potential losses to be suffered, people tend to make riskier decisions.

Simple rules of thumb, known as **heuristics**, also may bias decisions. For example, according to the **availability heuristic**, people base their judgments on information readily available to them, and according to the **representativeness heuristic**, people are perceived in stereotypical ways if they appear to be representatives of the categories to which they belong. People are biased toward **implicit favorites**, alternatives they prefer in advance of considering all the options. Other alternatives, **confirmation candidates**, are considered for purposes of convincing oneself that one's implicit favorite is the best alternative.

According to the **escalation of commitment phenomenon**, people continue to support previously unsuccessful courses of action because they have sunk costs invested in them. This occurs in large part because people need to justify their previous actions and wish to avoid having to admit that their initial decision was a mistake. Individual decisions are also limited by organizational factors, such as time constraints, political "facesaving" pressure, and *bounded discretion* (moral and ethical restrictions imposed on decisions).

Group Decision Making

Groups are superior to individual members when they are composed of a heterogeneous mix of experts who possess complementary skills. However, groups may not be any better than the best member of the group when performing a task that has a simple, verifiable answer. Compared with individuals, face-to-face **brainstorming** groups tend to make inferior decisions on creative problems. However, when brainstorming is done electronically—that is, by using computer terminals to send messages—the quality of decisions tends to improve.

Groupthink is a major obstacle to effective group decisions. It refers to the tendency for strong conformity pressures within groups to lead to the breakdown of critical thinking and to encourage premature acceptance of potentially questionable solutions. Groupthink appears to have been responsible for major decision fiascoes, such as the U.S. invasion of the Bay of Pigs in Cuba and the decision to launch the ill-fated space shuttle *Challenger*.

Techniques for Improving Group Decisions

The quality of group decisions can be enhanced in several different ways. First, the quality of group decisions has been shown to improve following individual training in problem-solving skills. Second, using the **Delphi technique**, the judgments of experts are systematically gathered and used to form a single joint decision. Third, the **nominal group technique** is a method of structuring group meetings so as to elicit and evaluate the opinions of all members. Finally, the **stepladder technique** systematically adds new individuals to decision-making groups one at a time, requiring the presentation and discussion of new ideas.

QUESTIONS FOR DISCUSSION

1. Argue pro or con: "All people make decisions in the same manner."
2. Think of any decision you recently made. Would you characterize it as programmed or nonprogrammed? Highly certain or highly uncertain? Top-down or empowered? Explain your answers.
3. Describe a decision that you are likely to make following the administrative model and one that you are likely to make using the intuitive approach of image theory.
4. Identify ways in which decisions you have made may have been biased by framing, heuristics, the use of implicit favorites, and the escalation of commitment.
5. Imagine that you are a manager facing the problem of not attracting enough high-quality personnel to your organization. Would you attempt to solve this problem alone or by committee? Explain your reasoning.
6. Groupthink is a potentially serious impediment to group decision making. Describe this phenomenon and review some things that can be done to avoid it.
7. Suppose you find out that a certain important organizational decision has to be made by a group, but you suspect that a better decision might be made by an individual. Describe three different ways you could use groups to make a decision while at the same time avoiding many of the problems associated with groups.

CASE IN POINT

The Classic Case of Coke Classic: Fizzled Decision Making

"Don't mess with success," the saying goes. But, on April 23, 1985, Coca-Cola's CEO Roberto Goizueta did just that. In a surprise announcement he declared that the highly successful 99-year-old formula was going to be replaced by a sweeter, "new Coke."

As you might imagine, this decision was not made readily. After spending some $4 million on market research over four and a half years, it seemed like the new formula would be a hit. After all, 200,000 people were involved in the taste tests. Further, a poll of consumers, ad agency officials, and outside consultants agreed that the new Coke would be a hit.

Soon after the new Coke was introduced, however, complaints started pouring in from the American public, and sales nose-dived. As time went on, people never accepted the new formula, and cries from soda drinkers got louder. Cases of the original formula Coke were imported from foreign countries and sold on the black market for ten times the normal price. Protest groups formed, and a class action lawsuit was planned to bring back the beloved original formula Coca-Cola.

Needless to say, company officials were caught off guard by the way their decision backfired. In retrospect, they blame the way the market research was done. Consumers who said they liked the new formula never dreamed that they would be endorsing the elimination of the classic formula Coke. Other company officials said that the poor decision resulted from the fact that a number of top company officials came to their posts from foreign operations and were not completely familiar with the way Americans in general viewed Coca-Cola—a cherished icon undeserving of change. According to one bottler, had "good ol' boys" from the South been running the company, the whole mess never would have occurred.

On July 11, 1995, less than three months after Goizueta's announcement, he made another announcement: Original Coke would return under the name "Coca-Cola Classic," and the new product would remain on the market as simply "Coca-Cola." In short order, the newly returned original formula outsold the revised one by at least a two-to-one margin, and as much as nine-to-one in some cities. Together, the overall market share of both "Coca-Cola" and "Coca-Cola Classic" rose to the pre-April 25 level.

Critical Thinking Questions

1. Using the analytical model of decision making, how do you think the process unfolded to decide to change Coca-Cola's formula?
2. What did Coca-Cola Co. do to reduce the uncertainty that surrounded its decision to change the formula?
3. Do you agree with the one bottler's observation that executives more familiar with American culture may have made a different decision? Explain your answer.
4. Do you think groupthink may have been involved in the decision? Explain how it may have operated in this context.

SKILLS PORTFOLIO

Experiencing Organizational Behavior

What Is Your Personal Decision Style?

As you read about the various personal decision styles, did you put yourself into any one of the categories? To get a feel for what the *Decision-Style Inventory* reveals about your personal decision style, complete this exercise. It is based on questions similar to those appearing in the actual instrument (Rowe, Boulgaides, & McGrath, 1984; see Note 12).

Directions

For each of the following questions, select the one alternative that best describes how you see yourself in your typical work situation.

1. When performing my job, I usually look for
   a. practical results
   b. the best solutions to problems
   c. new ideas or approaches
   d. pleasant working conditions
2. When faced with a problem, I usually
   a. use approaches that have worked in the past
   b. analyze it carefully
   c. try to find a creative approach
   d. rely on my feelings
3. When making plans, I usually emphasize
   a. the problems I currently face
   b. attaining objectives
   c. future goals
   d. developing my career
4. The kind of information I usually prefer to use is
   a. specific facts
   b. complete and accurate data
   c. broad information covering many options
   d. data that is limited and simple to understand
5. Whenever I am uncertain about what to do, I
   a. rely on my intuition
   b. look for facts
   c. try to find a compromise
   d. wait, and decide later
6. The people with whom I work best are usually
   a. ambitious and full of energy
   b. self-confident

    c. open-minded
    d. trusting and polite
7. The decisions I make are usually
    a. direct and realistic
    b. abstract or systematic
    c. broad and flexible
    d. sensitive to others' needs

Scoring

1. For each *a* you select, give yourself a point in the *directive* category.
2. For each *b* you select, give yourself a point in the *analytical* category.
3. For each *c* you select, give yourself a point in the *conceptual* category.
4. For each *d* you select, give yourself a point in the *behavioral* category.

The points reflect the relative strength of your preferences for each decision style.

Questions for Discussion

1. What style did the test reveal that you have? How did this compare to the style you thought you had before you took the test?
2. Based on the descriptions of the personal decision styles in the text, were you able to guess in advance which test items were indicative of which styles? What additional items may be added to the test to assess each style?

Working in Groups

Running a Nominal Group: Try It Yourself

A great deal can be learned about nominal groups by running one—or, at least, participating in one—yourself. Doing so will not only help illustrate the procedure, but demonstrate how effectively it works.

Directions

1. Select a topic suitable for discussion in a nominal group composed of students in your class. It should be a topic that is narrowly defined and on which people have many different opinions (these work best in nominal groups). Some possible examples include:

■ What should your school's student leaders be doing for you?
■ What can be done to improve the quality of instruction in your institution?
■ What can be done to improve the quality of jobs your school's students receive when graduating?

2. Divide the class into groups of approximately ten. Arrange each group in a circle, or around a table, if possible. In each group, select one person to serve as the group facilitator.
3. Following the steps outlined in Figure 10-14, facilitators should guide their groups in discussions regarding the focal question identified in step 1, above. Allow approximately 45 minutes to 1 hour to complete this process.
4. If time allows, select a different focal question and a different group leader, and repeat the procedure.

Questions for Discussion

1. Collectively, how did the group answer the question? Do you believe that this answer accurately reflected the feelings of the group?
2. How did the various groups' answers compare? Were they similar or different? Why?
3. What were the major problems, if any, associated with the nominal group experience? For example, were there any group members who were reluctant to wait their turns before speaking up?
4. If you conducted more than one nominal group discussion with different leaders, was the process smoother the second time around, as everyone learned how it works?
5. How do you think your group experiences would have differed had you used a totally unstructured, traditional face-to-face group instead of a nominal group?

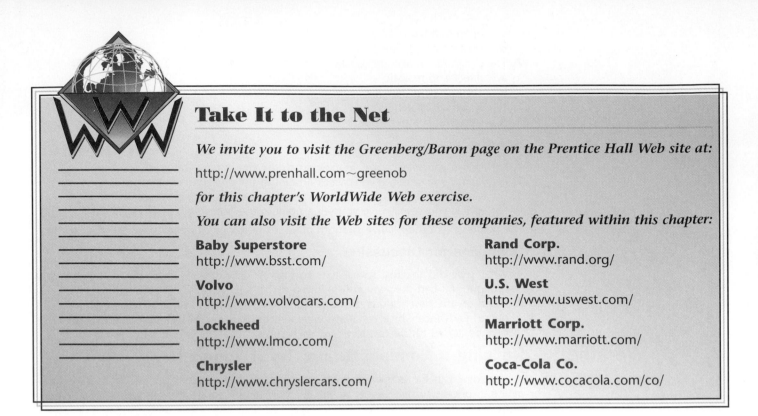

Take It to the Net

We invite you to visit the Greenberg/Baron page on the Prentice Hall Web site at:

http://www.prenhall.com~greenob

for this chapter's WorldWide Web exercise.

You can also visit the Web sites for these companies, featured within this chapter:

Baby Superstore
http://www.bsst.com/

Volvo
http://www.volvocars.com/

Lockheed
http://www.lmco.com/

Chrysler
http://www.chryslercars.com/

Rand Corp.
http://www.rand.org/

U.S. West
http://www.uswest.com/

Marriott Corp.
http://www.marriott.com/

Coca-Cola Co.
http://www.cocacola.com/co/

CHAPTER Eleven

HELPING, COOPERATION, AND CONFLICT IN ORGANIZATIONS

LEARNING ■ OBJECTIVES

After reading this chapter you should be able to:

1. Define *prosocial behavior* and distinguish it from altruism.

2. Describe *organizational citizenship behavior* and the major forms it often takes.

3. Explain the nature of *whistle-blowing* and describe some of the ethical issues it raises.

4. Explain the basic nature of *cooperation* and describe both individual and organizational factors that influence its occurrence.

5. Define *trust* and explain its relationship to both organizational citizenship behavior and cooperation.

6. Define *conflict* and indicate how it can produce positive as well as negative effects.

7. Describe various styles of managing conflict and the basic dimensions that underlie them.

8. List several organizational and interpersonal causes of conflict.

9. Describe several effective means for managing conflict.

10. Distinguish between *workplace violence* and *workplace aggression*.

11. Describe causes of workplace aggression and techniques for reducing this harmful form of organizational behavior.

Preview

RUBBERMAID HITS THE SKIDS

Rubbermaid, the name has long been synonymous with "quality" in the eyes of many consumers. So strong is this link, in fact, that the company's line of plastic (not rubber) products, ranging from food storage containers and garbage cans to plastic storage sheds, has held a dominant position in the marketplace for decades. In the past few years, however, Rubbermaid has hit a very large bump on the road to success. Sales slowed sharply in the first half of 1995, and both earnings and the company's stock quickly followed suit.

Problems began in 1993 when, for the first time since its founding in the 1950s, Rubbermaid failed to attain its self-set goal of a 15 percent annual gain in sales. This figure was only 8 percent in 1993 and 10 percent in 1994, results may be even worse in 1995. As John Mariotti, a former top executive at Rubbermaid who quit in 1994; puts it, "Rubbermaid is a company that has strained so hard it has pulled a muscle." He attributes part of the company's current problems to unwillingness to lower that 15 percent annual growth figure—one he, and many others, feels is no longer feasible for a company of Rubbermaid's size. But other factors, too, seem important.

In recent years, the price of resin, the raw material for many of Rubbermaid's products, soared, virtually doubling in only 18 months. How did Rubbermaid react to this sudden rise in its costs? By raising its prices to customers, including giant Wal-Mart, it's largest single account. When customers protested, Rubbermaid adopted a confrontational stance, insisting on its price increases and refusing to help retailers in any major way. The result was that large customers balked and reduced the amount of shelf space they devoted to Rubbermaid's products.

When a leader stumbles, there are always competitors waiting in the wings, and this is what quickly happened. Several of its competitors—small companies Rubbermaid executives refer to as "ankle-biters"—passed less of their increased costs along to customers, thus gaining a price advantage with retailers. As Rubbermaid President Chuck Carrol puts it, "We should have been helping customers increase their sales rather than fighting with them so long over prices." Consumers, too, are angry and deserting Rubbermaid's products. The *premium gap*—the extra amount shoppers are willing to pay for Rubbermaid's legendary quality—has, in the opinion of many, simply gotten too large. Now long-term customers are turning to less expensive, competing brands. Can Rubbermaid regain its former momentum and marketplace dominance? Perhaps. Its CEO, Wolfgang Schmitt, believes that the company will benefit from the increased competition and from the lessons it has learned. But one thing is certain: It will probably adopt a more cooperative stance vis-à-vis its large customers in the years ahead.

What would you have done if you were running Rubbermaid a few years ago? Would you have passed the increased costs you experienced along to your best customers in the form of price increases? Would you have done so in the same way Rubbermaid did, adopting a "take it or leave it" stance? From one perspective, such an approach seems reasonable: The buyer-seller relationship is, traditionally, one involving a large element of competition—efforts by each side to maximize its own outcomes, often at the expense of others. But in this case, and in many others, competition can prove very costly.

cooperation A process in which individuals or groups work together to attain shared goals.

Another, and sharply different, approach involves **cooperation**—a process in which individuals or organizations seek to coordinate their efforts in order to maximize joint outcomes or reach shared goals.[1] Such an approach was possible in this situation and would have involved efforts by Rubbermaid to consider customers' outcomes as well as its own, plus working cooperatively with them to help them deal with the higher prices.

In many situations, a choice between these contrasting strategies exists. The fact that it does raises an intriguing question: What factors lead individuals, groups, or organizations to choose one approach over the other? This will be one of the key questions on which we will focus in this chapter. In more general terms, we will examine three basic processes relating to the extent to which individuals, groups, or organizations, work with—or against—one another. The first of these processes is known as **prosocial behavior** and involves actions that benefit others within an organization, usually without requiring anything obvious or immediate in return. Growing evidence indicates that prosocial behavior plays an important role in organizational effectiveness, so it is clearly a topic worthy of careful attention.[2] The second process, *cooperation*, involves mutual, two-way assistance in which individuals, groups, or organizations provide benefits to each other in a reciprocal, joint manner. Many factors influence cooperation, and as we'll soon see, it can occur between as well as within organizations.[3]

The third major topic we'll consider is *conflict*, which is often defined as a process which develops when individuals or groups perceive that actions by others have, or will soon, exert negative effects on their important interests.[4] Such perceptions often trigger a costly spiral that produces negative outcomes for both parties. Indeed, long-standing, bitter conflicts may proceed to the point at which both sides become more concerned with harming their opponents than with maximizing their own outcomes (see Figure 11-1).

Closely related to conflict in several respects, but also distinct from it, is the topic of workplace violence or, more generally, *workplace aggression*—actions through which individuals seek to harm one or more target persons in their organizations.[5] What forms does workplace aggression take? Are these increasing in frequency, and if so, why? These are the questions we'll address with respect to this disturbing form of organizational behavior.

Prosocial Behavior: Helping Others at Work

Is there such a thing as pure *altruism*—actions by one person that benefit one or more others under conditions in which the donor expects nothing in return? Philosophers have long puzzled over this question, and more recently, social scientists have entered the debate.[6] Disappointingly, their research casts

prosocial behavior Actions that benefit others within an organization.

■ Figure 11-1
The Escalation of Conflict
Intense, prolonged conflicts often escalate to the point at which both sides are more concerned with harming the other than in protecting or maximizing their own interests.

considerable doubt on the existence of totally selfless helping. It is true: Individuals do sometimes offer help to others—or even risk their lives for them—without expecting anything tangible in return. (Parents who sacrifice their own lives for those of their children provide a dramatic example.) But such actions appear to be quite rare, and, in most instances where individuals help others, they do seem to anticipate *some* form of compensation. This return on their investment can be quite subtle—for example, the warm glow of feeling that one has "done the right thing" or the pleasure of seeing another person's joy or relief. Yet, such gains are certainly real and seem to provide at least a portion of the motivation behind seemingly altruistic acts.

While pure altruism seems to be relatively rare, it is clear that people do frequently engage in prosocial behavior—actions that help others in various ways. Moreover, such behavior is quite common in work settings, and may contribute, in important ways, to the success and effectiveness of organizations. While many forms of prosocial behavior exist in organizations,[7] several of the most important are included within the concept of **organizational citizenship behavior (OCB)**—actions by organization members that exceed the formal requirements of their job and are, therefore, "above and beyond the call of duty."[8] We'll now examine such behavior more closely, considering the various forms it takes, factors that influence its occurrence, and the effects it can exert on both individuals and organizations.

Organizational Citizenship Behavior: Some Basic Forms

According to widely accepted definitions of *organizational citizenship behavior* (or *OCB* for short), such actions involve three major components. First, they exceed the role requirements (or formal descriptions) of employees' jobs. Second, they are discretionary in nature—individuals decide to perform them in a voluntary manner. Third, they are not generally recognized by the formal reward structure of the organization. While there is general agreement about the first two of these requirements, we should note that experts don't agree about the third: Some believe that certain forms of prosocial behavior are, indeed, recognized by formal reward structures. Such behaviors are described by the term **organizational spontaneity** to distinguish them from OCB.[9]

Putting such complexities aside, there *is* general agreement on what kinds of behavior OCB involves. Briefly, these fall into five basic categories:

- *Altruism*: Have you ever offered to aid a co-worker with a difficult project? If so, you have engaged in this type of OCB.
- *Conscientiousness*: Going well beyond the minimum requirements in such areas as attendance, obeying rules, taking breaks, and so on. If you pride yourself on never missing a day at work, you are engaging in this type of OCB.
- *Civic virtue*: Participation in and concern about the life of the organization. This behavior involves such actions as attending voluntary meetings and reading announcements, rather than tossing them into the "circular file."
- *Sportsmanship*: Willingness to tolerate less than ideal circumstances without complaining. If you've followed the dictum "Grin and bear it" at work, then you have engaged in such behavior.
- *Courtesy*: Behaviors aimed at preventing interpersonal problems with others. Examples of each of these five types of organizational citizenship behavior are shown in Table 11-1.[10]

Organizational Citizenship Behavior: Factors Affecting Its Occurrence

What factors lead individuals to engage in various forms of OCB? Why, in short, do employees sometimes go well "beyond the call of duty" in performing their jobs? Recent findings indicate that a number of different factors prob-

organizational citizenship behavior (OCB) Actions by organization members that exceed the formal requirements of their job and are, therefore, "above and beyond the call of duty."

organizational spontaneity Prosocial behavior within an organization that may or may not be recognized by the formal reward system.

While organizational citizenship behavior *(OCB) can take many different forms, most seem to fall into the major categories shown here.*

Form of OCB	Examples
Altruism	Helping a co-worker with a project; switching vacation dates with another person; volunteering
Conscientiousness	Never missing a day of work; coming to work early if needed; not spending time on personal calls
Civic virtue	Attending voluntary meetings and functions; reading memos; keeping up with new information
Sportsmanship	"Grin and bear it"; making do without complaint; Not finding fault with the organization
Courtesy	"Turning the other cheek" to avoid problems; not "blowing up" when provoked

Perceptions of procedural and distributive justice also play an important role in motivation, as we saw in Chapter 5.

The nature of punishment, and its effects upon employees' behavior, were discussed in detail in Chapter 3.

ably play a role. One of the most important of these appears to be *trust*—the belief among employees that they will be treated fairly by their organization and, more specifically, by their immediate supervisor. Briefly, recent findings indicate that to the extent employees believe that their supervisors' decisions follow principles of distributive and procedural fairness, the greater their trust in these persons. And the greater such trust, the greater is employees' willingness to engage in prosocial behavior (see Figure 11-2).[11]

Trust in one's supervisor is not the only determinant of OCB, however. Additional findings indicate that it is influenced by several other factors, too. One of the most important of these is simply employees' perceptions of the breadth of their jobs—what behaviors are "in-role" and what behaviors are "extra-role" in nature.[12] In other words, the more broadly employees define their jobs, the more likely they are to engage in actions often viewed as involving OCB. In fact, from the employees' point of view, they may simply be doing things that are actually part of their jobs.[13]

Finally, employees' willingness to engage in OCB seems to be strongly influenced by their perceptions of any *punishment* they receive. Employees who perceive punishment as fair, and under their control—a process to which they can have input and which they can influence—the greater their tendency to engage in OCB.[14] Overall, then, it appears that many different factors influence employees' tendencies to engage in OCB and "go the extra mile" for their organizations.

YOU BE THE CONSULTANT

An organization is having difficulties in recruiting top-notch employees. The Director of Human Resources believes that this may be due to the fact that disgruntled former employees—and even some current employees—are saying negative things about the company, thus harming its reputation.

1. How could the Human Resources Director find out if this is so?
2. If it is the case that the company's reputation is being damaged by disgruntled employees, what steps could be taken to reverse this state of affairs—to increase the likelihood that former and current employees say positive things about the company and boost its reputation?

■ Figure 11-2
Procedural Justice, Trust, and OCB
The greater the extent to which employees' perceive that their supervisor's decisions follow principles of distributive and procedural justice, the greater their trust in the supervisors, and the greater their tendency to engage in prosocial behavior.

(**Source:** Based on findings reported by Konovsky & Pugh, 1994; see Note 11.)

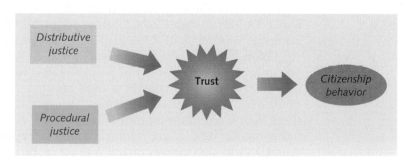

Effects of OCB: Does It Really Matter?

More than 30 years ago, one leading organizational theorist suggested that there are three major ingredients in organizational effectiveness: (1) the organization must recruit and retain excellent employees, (2) these employees must carry out the requirements of their jobs, and (3) they must also engage in innovative, spontaneous activity that goes beyond formal job descriptions or role requirements.[15] Despite the tremendous changes that have occurred in the intervening years, these observations still impress us as a sound prescription for organizational excellence. And as you can readily see, the third point relates to organizational citizenship behavior. We have already described some of the conditions that seem to encourage such behavior by employees; clearly, organizations wishing to increase the incidence of OCB should pay careful attention to these points. But a basic question remains: Does OCB really enhance organizational performance?

This question is more difficult to answer than it might at first appear, because many aspects of OCB are *not* included in standard measures of individual or group performance. Moreover, organizational citizenship behaviors are, by definition, not generally part of formal reward systems: Individuals perform them for reasons other than the external rewards they hope to receive. Yet, despite these complexities, a growing body of evidence suggests that OCB does indeed contribute to organizational excellence. For instance, willingness to engage in OCB has been found to be related to such factors as organizational commitment and job satisfaction—variables that *do* impinge on the bottom line.[16] In addition, OCB often involves tendencies by employees to make positive statements about their organizations—to praise them to others. This can enhance an organization's reputation and a positive reputation, in turn, has been shown to have many beneficial effects on an organization—for example, increased ease of hiring first-rate employees.[17] For these and other reasons, it seems clear that OCB does indeed contribute to an organization's overall effectiveness. Such contributions may not always be easy to measure, but this in no way implies that they are not real, or are unimportant.

Whistle-Blowing: Helping an Organization by Dissenting with It

whistle-blowing Calling attention to actions or practices that are inconsistent with established organizational norms or policies.

Before concluding our discussion of *prosocial behavior* in work settings, we should call attention to a very different way in which employees sometimes seek to help their organizations. This is known as **whistle-blowing**, which involves disclosure by employees of illegal, immoral, or illegitimate practices by employers to people or organizations able to do something about it.[18] Is whistle-blowing a prosocial action? From the point of view of society, it usually is. In many instances, the actions of whistle-blowers can protect the health, safety, or economic welfare of the general public.

For example, consider the case of Bill Bush, who in 1974 blew the whistle on the National Aeronautics and Space Administration for circulating an internal memo ordering supervisors such as Bush not to consider employees older than 54 for promotion. Bush felt that this was a violation of both law and ethical principles and exposed the memo. Or consider A. Ernest Fitzgerald, who reported what he considered to be wasteful practices in the United States Air Force; he testified before Congress about $7.00 hammers for which the government was charged $356 and $.25 washers that were purchased for $693!

What happens when someone blows the whistle in this manner? Not what you might expect. Instead of being treated like heroes and heroines, whistle-blowers are often punished for their actions. As Thomas Devine, legal director of the Government Accountability Project in Washington, D.C., puts it: "If there is one common denominator among whistle blowers, it is that they face harassment, retaliation, and professional apocalypse."[19] Such persons frequently find themselves facing a long, uphill battle as they attempt to prove the wrongdoing they have reported. They often lose their jobs—their companies are all too quick to find "other" grounds for dismissing them; and then they discover that they have been "blackballed" in their industry or profession and can't find another.

Indeed, the list of punishments for whistle-blowers seems endless. For example, when Charles D. Varnadore complained about lax conditions under which many employees at the Oak Ridge National Laboratory were exposed to high levels of radiation, he was promptly transferred by his supervisor to a room full of toxic and radioactive substances.[20] Quite a reward for attempting to safeguard the health of his fellow workers. Clearly, then, whistle-blowers sacrifice a lot in their efforts to protect innocent victims.

Does whistle-blowing really qualify as prosocial behavior? Or are whistle-blowers merely disgruntled employees, looking for a way to "get even" with their organizations? The latter conclusion can be ruled out in most cases. Careful study of whistle-blowing incidents indicates that most whistle-blowers are motivated to correct what they perceive as wrong doing. Moreover, most have tried to work inside their companies before informing the public or legal authorities about the situation. They "go public" only when these efforts fail.[21]

Yet, despite this fact, the situation remains complex. Whether such actions are or are not prosocial in nature depends on the motivation underlying them. If, in contrast to the conditions described above, a whistle-blower benefits from his or her actions while the organization suffers, or if the whistle-blower's actions are part of personal quest for vengeance, the actions cannot be viewed as prosocial with respect to the organization.

So, before a whistle-blower's actions can be regarded as prosocial in nature, they must be motivated by an underlying desire to help the organization and/or its employees—an assurance it may be difficult to obtain. See the ETHICS ANGLE section for more information on the ethical complexities involved in whistle-blowing.

THE ETHICS ANGLE

THE COSTS OF WHISTLE-BLOWING

The proverbial "stuff" truly hit the fan when Mark Whitacre, a top executive at Archer Midlands Daniel, blew the whistle on his employer. He accused the company of fixing prices on important corn-based products—citric acid (used in many fruit juices) and high fructose corn syrup (the sweetener used in many soft drinks)—thus reaping huge, illegal profits. In fact, Whitacre worked closely with the FBI, helping to train agents so that they could infiltrate the company and gather evidence. He even provided tape recordings in which top management at ADM made statements indicating that they were, indeed, implicated in the price fixing.

The result: Whitacre was fired from his executive-level job by ADM, which accused him of stealing at least $2.5 million from the company while acting as an undercover agent for the FBI. Whitacre furiously denies these charges and seems genuinely surprised by his dismissal from ADM. Was he right to blow the whistle on a company that had treated him very well? Should he have agreed to act for the FBI in order to uncover a price-fixing scheme? Whitacre is convinced that he did the right thing, but many of his former co-workers feel he acted not out of an altruistic desire to help the public, but out of complex motives of his own. And it does seem clear that he would have remained silent if the FBI hadn't begun its own investigations of ADM.

Situations like this one serve to underscore the ethical enigmas posed by whistle-blowing, and underscore the importance of establishing conditions within organizations under which (1) employees are encouraged to come forward, internally, with ethical concerns, and (2) their charges and complaints are given full and careful attention. Only to the extent these conditions are met can the situations that lead to whistle-blowing be corrected while minimizing danger to the persons brave enough to call them to others' attention.

Cooperation: Mutual Assistance in Work Settings

cooperation A process in which individuals or groups work together to attain shared goals.

Although prosocial behavior is quite common in work settings, another pattern known as **cooperation** is even more widespread.[22] In cooperation, assistance is mutual, and two or more individuals, groups, or organizations work together toward shared goals and for their mutual benefit.[23] Cooperation is a very common form of coordination in work settings, partly because, by cooperating, the persons or groups involved can often accomplish more than they can by working alone.

Given the obvious benefits that can result from cooperation, a basic question arises: Why, if it is so useful, does cooperation often fail to develop? Why don't people seeking the same (or at least similar) goals always join forces? Although there are many factors involved, the most important reason is that cooperation simply *cannot* develop in some situations, because the goals sought by the individuals or groups involved cannot be shared. Two people seeking the same job or promotion, for instance, cannot join forces to attain it: The reward can go to only one. Similarly, two companies courting the same potential merger candidate cannot cooperate to reach their goal: Only one can conclude the merger.

competition A process in which individuals or groups seek to attain desired goals at the expense of others seeking the same goals.

In cases such as these, an alternative form of behavior known as **competition** often develops. As we noted previously, this is a pattern in which each person, group, or organization seeks to maximize its own gains, often at the expense of others.[24] In some contexts, competition is both natural and understandable. People and groups do have to compete for scarce resources and rewards. And organizations themselves must compete in the marketplace for supplies, government contracts, customers, and market share. In many instances, however, competition is not dictated by current conditions, and cooperation might well develop. What factors serve to tip the balance toward or away from cooperation in such instances? As we'll soon see, both individual and organization-level factors play a role.

Individual Factors and Cooperation

Several factors affecting the tendency to cooperate function primarily through their impact on individuals. They influence the perceptions and reactions of specific persons and in this manner shape decisions about whether to cooperate or compete with others. Among the most important of these are the principle of *reciprocity*, and several *personal characteristics*.

reciprocity The tendency to treat others as they have treated us.

Reciprocity: The matching game. Throughout life, we are urged to follow the "Golden Rule"—to do unto others as we would have them do unto us. Despite such appeals, however, we usually behave in a different manner. Most people tend to react to others not as they would prefer to be treated, but rather as they have actually been treated by these persons (or others) in the past. In short, people follow the principle of **reciprocity** much of the time: They return the kind of treatment they have previously received.[25] The choice between cooperation and competition is no exception to this powerful rule. When others act in a competitive manner, we usually respond in the same way. If, in contrast, they behave cooperatively, we usually match *this* pattern.[26]

So, in short, reciprocity appears to be the guiding principle of cooperation. The key task in establishing cooperation in organizations, then, seems to be that of getting it started. Once individuals, groups, or units have begun to cooperate, the process may be largely self-sustaining. To encourage cooperation, therefore, managers should do everything possible to get the process under way. After it begins, the obvious benefits of cooperation, plus powerful tendencies toward reciprocity, may tend to maintain it at high levels.

Trust: A powerful antecedent of cooperation. Earlier, we noted that *trust* is an important determinant of organizational citizenship behavior: The greater employees' trust in their supervisors, the greater their tendency to engage in OCB.[27] It should not be surprising to learn, therefore, that **trust**—which can be defined, more broadly, as an individual's confidence in the good will of others, and the belief that they will make efforts consistent with the group's goals—also plays an important role in cooperation.[28] Specifically, recent findings indicate that the greater the degree of trust individuals have in their co-workers, the more likely they are to cooperate with them.[29] Moreover, it appears that there are two distinct kinds of trust, and that these may be related in distinct ways to increased cooperation.[30]

The first type of trust is known as *cognition-based trust*, which refers to our beliefs about others' reliability and trustworthiness. It is measured by the extent of agreement with such items as "Given this person's track record, I see no reason to doubt his/her competence and preparation for the job." The second type of trust is known as *affect-based trust*, which refers to the emotional bond between individuals—bonds involving genuine care and concern for the welfare of others. It is measured by items such as: "I should say that we have both made considerable emotional investments in our working relationship."

To study the impact of these two kinds of trust on various forms of cooperation, McAllister recently conducted an investigation in which managers completed measures designed to assess both their affect- and cognition-based trust in peers, the antecedents of such trust, and the extent to which they cooperated with these persons. As shown in Figure 11-3, results indicated that affect-based trust was influenced by the frequency with which the managers interacted with their peers and prior helping from these persons. Such trust influenced several forms of helping and cooperation, and, indirectly, both managers' and peers' performance. In contrast, cognition-based trust exerted its effects through affect-based trust. The higher such trust, the higher affect-based trust; however, cognition-based trust did not influence cooperation directly.

Additional findings indicate that trust derives, in part, from perceptions that one's boss or leader has reached decisions through the use of fair procedures (procedural justice).[31] Further, the higher such trust, the greater employees' commitment to their bosses' or leaders decisions.

In sum, trust is an important determinant of cooperation. Since cooperation, in turn, yields many beneficial effects—increased performance, coordination, and reduced costs (through, for example, reduced cycle time), it appears that efforts to build high levels of trust among persons who work together is an activity well worth the effort involved. Does the tendency to trust vary around the world, in different cultures? For information on this intriguing possibility—and its effects—see the GLOBALIZATION AND DIVERSITY section on the following page.

■ **Figure 11-3**
Trust, Cooperation, and Job Performance

Managers' affect-based trust in peers is influenced by several different factors, including frequency of interaction between managers and subordinates and prior helping by the manager. Such trust, in turn, influences several forms of cooperation and helping, and also job performance.

(**Source:** Based on findings reported by McAllister, 1995; see Note 27.)

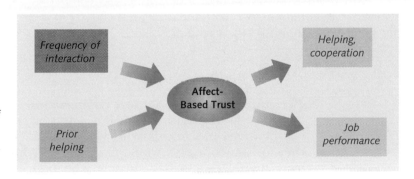

TRUST: DOES IT DIFFER AROUND THE WORLD?

Trust, we've noted, has important effects on both citizenship behavior and cooperation: The higher the level of trust individuals have in their bosses or peers, the more willing they are to engage in OCB and various forms of cooperation. We've also seen that trust is influenced by several factors that may be present in organizations to varying degrees. Thus, assuring that these factors are present to a great extent can increase helping and coordination.

But putting such factors aside, we can now ask another question: Does the tendency to trust others differ across various cultures? If it does, this has important implications for management practices in various countries. In fact, a growing body of evidence indicates that cultural differences with respect to trust do exist. This, in itself, is not very surprising, but the nature of these differences is another matter. For instance, in which culture do you think individuals tend to show higher levels of trust in others—Japan or the United States? Given the emphasis in Japanese culture on stable, long-term relationships (in business as well as personal life), your first reply may be "Japan, of course." Actually, however, several studies designed to measure levels of trust in Japan and the United States have reported precisely the opposite result: Americans turn out to be more trusting than Japanese.[32]

How can this be so? Recent studies by two Japanese researchers, Yamagishi and Yamagishi, suggests that the answer lies in the definition of *trust* and in the distinction between *trust* and *assurance*.[33] Trust can be viewed as a tendency to infer more benign intentions on the part of others than is actually justified by existing information. In contrast, *assurance* refers to the belief that others will continue to act in a predictable manner *because of incentives that make it worth their while to do so*. There is no assumption that their intentions are good—or that they should be trusted.

Going further, Yamagishi and Yamagishi propose that what is often mistaken for a high level of trust in Japanese society is really a high level of assurance: Since long-term relationships are a central part of Japanese culture, and acting in accordance with them is highly valued, individuals know that others will continue to honor these relationships. At the same time, though, Japanese individuals do *not* attribute such predictability to others' good intentions or positive traits. On the contrary, they recognize that these outcomes stem mainly from the structure of the relationships rather than personal characteristics such as being honest or trustworthy. In the United States, in contrast, long-term relationships are less prevalent, so faith that others will treat us fairly, or at least predictably, tends to stem, instead, from personal trust. The conclusion: Americans will actually be more trusting than Japanese.

In fact, when Japanese and Americans complete measures designed to assess both trust and assurance, this prediction is confirmed. Americans are indeed higher in general trust than Japanese—they more strongly agreed with such statements as "Most people are basically honest" and "Most people are basically good and kind." Moreover, this is true whether the other persons involved were strangers or personal acquaintances. In contrast, Japanese score higher in terms of assurance; for example, they perceive greater value in dealing with others through personal relations than do Americans. Finally, and perhaps most surprising of all, Americans rated themselves as more honest and fair than did the Japanese participants.

In sum, research findings offer support for the view that what is often mistaken for high levels of *trust* in Japanese society are really high levels of mutual assurance—the certainty that others will act in predictable ways because they are involved with the perceiver in long-term, stable relationships. Outside the context of such relationships, Americans are actually more trusting than Japanese—they assume that other persons, strangers as well as friends, are more likely to behave in an honest manner and out of good intentions. What do these findings suggest with respect to management practice? Since high levels of assurance may generate the same kinds of beneficial outcomes of high levels of trust, they imply that perhaps American organizations would benefit from establishing the kind of long-term relationships that appear to be more common in Japan. We'll have more to say about some of the steps American companies are taking to achieve this goal later in this chapter in a QUEST FOR QUALITY section.

Personal orientations and cooperation. Think about the many people you have known during your life. Can you remember ones who were highly competitive—individuals who viewed most situations as contests in which they, or someone else, would triumph? In contrast, can you recall others who were highly cooperative—people who preferred to minimize differences between their own outcomes and those of others? You probably have little difficulty in bringing examples of both types to mind, for large individual differences in the tendencies to prefer cooperation or competition exist. Such differences, in turn, seem to reflect contrasting perspectives toward working with others—perspectives that individuals carry with them from situation to situation and over relatively long periods of time.[34]

Research on such differences suggests, in fact, that on the basis of their relative preferences for cooperation or competition, individuals can be divided into four distinct groups. A sizable proportion are **competitors**—their primary motive is doing better than others. In fact, extreme competitors prefer negative outcomes that are better than those obtained by other persons than positive ones that are worse than those obtained by their opponents. A second group can be described as **individualists**. These are people who have little interest in the outcomes of others and don't really care whether these persons do better or worse than they do. Their major focus is simply on gaining as much as possible in every situation.

A third group can be classified as **cooperators**. They are primarily concerned with maximizing joint outcomes—the total received by themselves and others. They want everyone they work with to be satisfied with their rewards and do not wish to defeat them. Finally, a few people can be described as **equalizers**. Their major goal is minimizing differences between their own performance or outcomes and those of others. In short, they wish to assure that everyone they work with receives the same basic results. Figure 11-4 presents an overview of the motives of these four types of people.[35]

Another, and closely related dimension along which individuals differ, and which is also closely related to cooperation, is one referred to as **individualism-collectivism**.[36] Persons high in individualism attach greater importance to their personal interests than to those of groups to which they belong, and will "take care of #1" if their personal interests and those of the group conflict in any way. In contrast, persons high on collectivism attach more importance to group interests than to their own interests and put those of the group above their own if these conflict. Cultures differ greatly with respect to these dimensions; some—for example, many Asian and African cultures—are high on collectivism, while others—European and North American cultures—are high on individualism. Such differences, in turn, can strongly influence the behavior of individuals. In fact, it appears that while persons high in collectivitism cooperate with others under a wide range of conditions, persons high in individualism are much more selective in terms of such cooperation:

competitors Individuals who are primarily concerned with exceeding the outcomes of others.

individualists People primarily concerned with maximizing their own outcomes.

cooperators Individuals who are primarily concerned with maximizing joint outcomes.

equalizers Individuals primarily concerned with assuring equality of outcomes among all people who work together on joint projects.

individualism-collectivism A dimension of cultures relating to the extent to which individuals in these cultures attach primary importance to their own interests or to those of groups to which they belong.

Recall the distinction between individualistic and collectivistic cultures discussed in Chapter 2.

■ **Figure 11-4**
Personal Orientations Toward Working with Others
As shown here, individuals with different orientations toward working with others demonstrate sharply contrasting patterns of motives. These differences, in turn, influence their behavior in a wide range of situations.

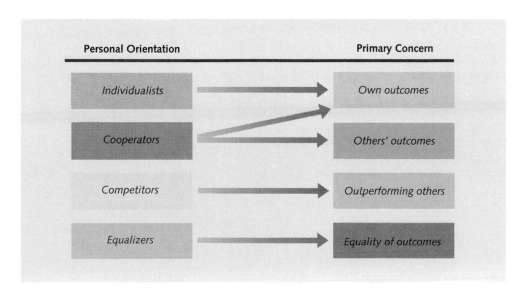

They cooperate only when their individual contributions to a team project are readily apparent, and when in small groups (see Figure 11-5).[37]

In sum, individual differences do seem to matter to an important degree where cooperation is concerned. Managers should recognize this fact and consider its relevance to several key personnel decisions—hiring, promotion, and work assignments.

Organizational Factors and Cooperation

The fact that organizations differ greatly in their internal levels of cooperation is obvious. Some—typically those that are quite successful—demonstrate a high degree of coordination between their various departments.[38] What accounts for these differences? Individual factors provide only a partial answer. Several factors relating to an organization's internal structure and function also play a role.

Reward systems and organizational structure. Consider the following situation. A large insurance company has two major divisions: Consumer Underwriting (which issues policies for individuals) and Commercial Underwriting (which issues policies for businesses). The company has a bonus system in which annual bonuses are distributed to individuals in the more profitable division. This results in a high degree of competition between the units. At first glance, this might seem beneficial. However, it may lead to situations in which sales personnel from one division actively interfere with efforts of sales personnel from the other division. For example, while working hard to win a multimillion-dollar policy with a large manufacturing concern, agents from the Commercial Underwriting division actually may discourage top managers within this company from seeking individual life and property policies from their own company; after all, this will contribute to the sales of their rival, Consumer Underwriting. And the opposite pattern is true as well. Agents for the consumer division may discourage large clients from seeking policies for their businesses from the commercial division.

Although this might seem to be an extreme case, it reflects conditions that are all too common in many organizations. Reward systems are often "winner-take-all" in form. This fact, coupled with internal differentiation, tends to reduce coordination between units or divisions, as each seeks to maximize its own rewards. This is not to imply that such internal competition is necessarily bad or counterproductive—far from it. Still, managers should assure that it does not reach a level where it hinders the functioning and success of the entire organization.

■ Figure 11-5
Collectivism, Individualism, and Cooperation
Persons high in collectivism show a high level of cooperation under a wide range of conditions. In contrast, persons high on individualism show cooperation only under certain conditions.

(**Source:** Based on findings reported by Wagner, 1995; see Note 37.)

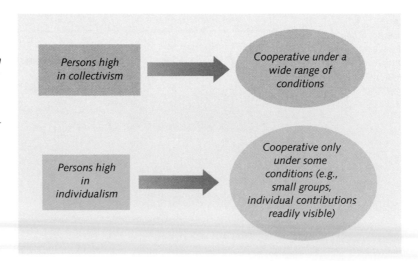

Interdependence among employees: The nature of specific jobs.
Imagine two organizations. In the first, the major tasks performed by employees can be completed alone; there is no need for individuals to work closely with others. In the second, the tasks performed by employees cannot be completed alone; they must work together closely to do their jobs. In which organization will higher levels of cooperation develop? Obviously, the second. The reason for this difference, too, is apparent. The level of cooperation attained is determined by the nature of the work performed: The greater the degree of interdependence among employees, the higher cooperation among them tends to be. This relationship has been verified in many studies, so it appears to be a strong and general one.[39]

Cooperation across Organizations

When we think about relations between different organizations in the same industry, the first word that comes to mind is *competition*. We tend to concentrate on the ways in which such organizations compete with one another and the strategies they adopt to improve their competitive advantage in the marketplace. Yet, there are also situations in which independent organizations choose to coordinate their actions or efforts to attain mutual gains. In short, there are important instances of what might be termed **interorganizational coordination**. Why would organizations in the same industry ever agree to cooperate with one another? Primarily under three sets of conditions.

First, such coordination may occur when independent companies conclude that by joining forces, they can greatly increase their potential gains. A dramatic example of the benefits that can result from "joining forces" in such situations is provided by OPEC, which, during the 1970s and early 1980s, seized worldwide control of the petroleum market.

Second, interorganizational coordination often occurs when one or more new competitors enter a mature and previously stable market. This occurred in the United States in the late 1970s and early 1980s, when the sales of Japanese automobiles rose to very high levels. In response to this external threat, major U.S. manufacturers joined forces to lobby for government protection. They succeeded and legislation restricting the import of Japanese cars gave them the breathing room they needed to improve their own products.

Third, such coordination sometimes develops as a response to rapidly changing environmental conditions. New patterns of trade, advances in technology, shifts in government policies, and other trends combine to create an environment in which independent organizations find it difficult to continue "business as usual." One response to such conditions is *merger*—becoming part of a larger company. Another is the formation of a **consortium**—a confederation in which organizations maintain their formal independence but agree to coordinate their activities through a central management. In the United States, the growing complexity and expense of medical technology has put increasing pressure on independent hospitals, with the result that many have joined *multihospital consortia*.[40] By doing so, they have been able to control rising costs, provide a better mix of medical services, and avoid duplication of personnel and equipment.

One of the most dramatic recent examples of interorganizational cooperation is provided by SEMATECH, a consortium of semiconductor companies in the United States.[41] SEMATECH was formed in response to a dramatic drop in the market share of United States companies—from a high of 85 percent in the mid-1980s, down to a projected 20 percent by 1993. (The consortium was formed in 1987, so this projection was made at that time.) The 14 companies that founded SEMATECH (see Figure 11-6) were accustomed to competing fiercely with one another, so this was a wrenching change from their usual way of doing business. However, all recognized that they were facing a major emer-

---

interorganizational coordination Instances or situations in which independent organizations choose to coordinate their actions or efforts to attain mutual gains.

---

consortium A confederation in which organizations maintain their formal independence but agree to coordinate their activities through a central management.

**SEMATECH: An Important
Consortium in the United States**
SEMATECH was founded by 14 independent semiconductor companies in
the United States to help them survive
intense foreign competition. Shown here
are representatives of the founding
companies in an early meeting.

gency and that only by working together could they develop the technology
and manufacturing clout needed to fend off strong, external competition.[42]

Once formed, SEMATECH moved rapidly toward its major goals—increasing the number of usable chips that could be manufactured from each wafer
of silicon and making each chip capable of doing more. Ultimately, these technological advances did save the United States industry from what seemed to
be a rapid ride to oblivion. But stay tuned: In today's business environment,
change is indeed the only constant, so the story is far from over, and new sur-
prises undoubtedly lie in store for both SEMATECH, its member companies,
and its overseas competitors.

Conflict: Its Nature, Causes, and Effects

If prosocial behavior and cooperation constitute one end of a continuum
describing how individuals and groups work together in organizations, then
conflict certainly lies at or near the other end. This term has many meanings,
but in the context of organizational behavior, it refers primarily to instances
in which units or individuals within an organization work *against* rather than
with one another.[43] More formally, according to one widely accepted definition, **conflict** is a process in which one party perceives that another party has
taken some action that will exert negative effects on its major interest, or is
about to take such actions. The key elements in conflict, then, seem to include
(1) opposing interests between individuals or groups, (2) recognition of such
opposition, (3) the belief by each side that the other will thwart (or has already
thwarted) these interests, and (4) actions that actually produce such thwarting.

Unfortunately, conflict, defined in this manner, is all too common in modern organizations. Moreover, its effects are far too costly to ignore. Practicing
managers report that they spend approximately 20 percent of their time dealing with conflict and its effects.[44] And the smoldering resentment and broken relationships that are the aftermath of many conflicts can persist for
months or even years, continuing to exact a major toll in precious human resources long after the situation that initiated the conflict is merely a memory.
For these reasons, organizational conflict is an important topic for the field of
OB, one deserving of our careful attention. In this section, we will provide an
overview of current knowledge about this costly process. First, we will exam-

conflict A process that begins
when individuals or groups perceive that others have taken or
will soon take actions incompatible with their own major interests.

ine two basic dimensions that underlie many forms of conflict. Second, we will consider various causes of conflict. Finally, we'll examine major effects of conflict which, you may be surprised to learn, are sometimes positive as well as negative in nature.

Integration and Distribution: Basic Dimensions of Conflict

Consider this actual incident: Mark, a marketing expert for a telephone company, persuaded two of his friends to start a company of their own together. They were good friends, so he was certain they would succeed. Soon, though, it became apparent that his partners had goals that contrasted strikingly with his. "They wanted the company to pay for their cars and to conduct meetings in the Bahamas," the disillusioned founder notes, "I wanted to plow our money back into the business." Over and over they outvoted him, until, finally, drained of all resources, the company collapsed. Now, Mark doesn't even nod to his former partners when he passes them in the street. "I never thought a business relationship could overpower friendship," he notes, "but this one did. Where money's involved, people change."[45]

This incident provides a textbook illustration of two basic dimensions that seem to play a role in many conflicts: **distribution**—concern with one's own outcomes, and **integration**—concern with the outcomes of others. Mark was clearly concerned with integration—he wanted the company, and therefore both he and his partners, to thrive. His friends, however, had different ideas: All they wanted to do was "take care of #1"—themselves. So they outvoted their more conservative partner and stripped the company of all its assets for their own gain.

A large body of research evidence indicates that these two dimensions are important and that, moreover, they are largely independent. Thus, in a given situation, it is possible to pursue actions that are high in both distribution and integration, low in both, or high in one and low in the other.[46] In fact, various combinations of these motives underlie five distinct styles of handling conflict with others when it occurs: *competing, collaborating, avoiding, accommodating,* and *compromising*.[47] The relative positions of each of these styles or approaches in terms of the key dimensions of distribution and integration are shown in Figure 11-7. As you can see, *competition* is high on distribution but low on integration; *compromise* is in the middle on both dimensions; and *avoidance* is low on both. *Accommodation*—giving others what they want—is high on integration but low on distribution. Finally, *collaboration* is high on both dimensions.

In view of our earlier discussion of individual differences with respect to preferences for cooperation and competition, you will not find it surprising to learn that individuals differ greatly in their tendencies to prefer these various conflict-handling styles.[48] What you may find more unexpected, however, is the fact that cultures differ in this respect, too. In many Western cultures, which, as we saw earlier, are *individualistic* in orientation, there is a strong preference for competition (sometimes known as *dominating*). In contrast, in many African and Asian cultures, which are *collectivistic* in orientation, preferences for accommodating and avoiding are relatively strong.[49] Such differences are worth noting, because they have important implications for conflict management—a topic we'll consider in detail later in this chapter.

Major Causes of Conflict

As we noted before, conflict involves the presence or perceptions of opposing interests. Yet, this condition, by itself, is neither necessary nor sufficient for the occurrence of actual conflict. Open confrontations sometimes fail to develop despite the existence of incompatible interests. Conflict sometimes emerges even when opposing interests are not present. Clearly, then, many

distribution A basic dimension of conflict situations, referring to the extent to which individuals show concern for their own outcomes.

integration A basic dimension of conflict situations, referring to the extent to which individuals show concern for others' outcomes.

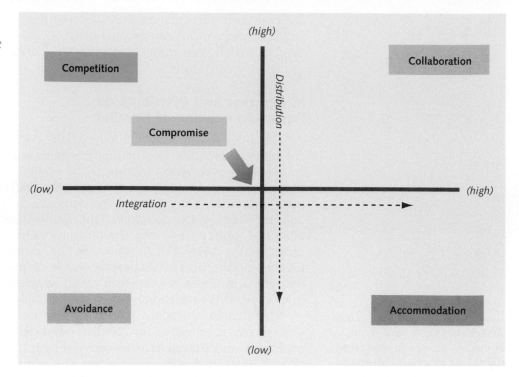

As we saw in Chapter 7, uncertainty is also a major cause of stress; in fact, high levels of stress often seem to intensify ongoing conflicts or contribute to the initiation of new ones.

factors and conditions contribute to the occurrence of conflict. These can be divided in two major groups: factors relating to organizational structure or functioning, and factors relating to interpersonal relations.

Organizational causes of conflict. Perhaps the most obvious organization-based cause of conflict is *competition over scarce resources.* No organization has unlimited resources, and conflicts often arise over the division or distribution of space, money, equipment, or personnel. Each side tends to overestimate its contribution to the organization and therefore its fair share of available resources. The result can be intense, prolonged conflict.

Two additional, and closely related causes of conflict, are *ambiguity over responsibility* and *ambiguity over jurisdiction.* Groups of individuals within an organization are sometimes uncertain as to who is responsible for performing various tasks or duties. When this occurs, each involved party disclaims responsibility, and conflict can develop over this issue. Similarly, uncertainty frequently exists over who has jurisdiction or authority. Figure 11-8 provides a summary of these and other organization-based causes of conflict.

Interpersonal causes of organizational conflict. Take a look at the cartoon in Figure 11-9. Do you think the person who is saying "It's always nice besting you again" is setting the stage for future conflict with the other character? It seems likely that he is, because no one likes to "lose face," and seeing one's opponent gloat after a victory is one sure way to set strong desire for revenge in operation.[50] This cartoon suggests that conflict often stems from *interpersonal factors*—aspects of relations between individuals, as well as from organizational structure or underlying conflicts of interest, and this conclusion is supported by a growing body of research findings. What are these interpersonal factors? Here is an overview of several of the most important.

The cartoon in Figure 11.9 calls attention to the potential conflict-enhancing effects of *grudges.* People who have lost face while dealing with others often spend a lot of time and energy planning revenge against them. In fact, such grudges can persist for years, with obvious negative effects for organizations or work groups.[51]

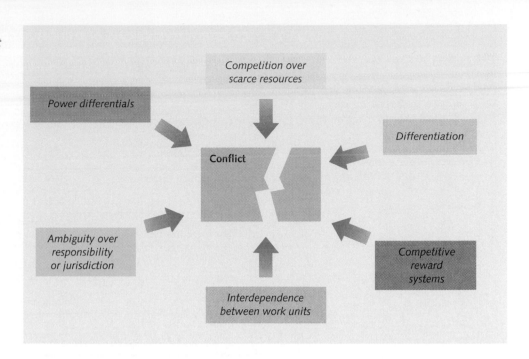

Second, conflict often stems from (or is intensified by) *faulty attributions*—errors concerning the causes behind others' behavior. When individuals find that their interests have been thwarted by another person, they generally try to determine why this person acted the way he or she did. Was it malevolence, a desire to harm them? Or did the provoker's actions stem from factors beyond his or her control? A growing body of evidence suggests that when people reach the former conclusion, anger and subsequent conflict are more likely and more intense than when they reach the latter conclusion.[52]

A third interpersonal factor of considerable importance in generating organizational conflict might be termed *faulty communication*. This refers to the fact that individuals often communicate with others in a way that angers or annoys them, even though it is not their intention to do so. In other cases, conflict involves *inappropriate criticism*—negative feedback delivered in a manner that angers the recipient rather than helping this person to do a better job. What makes criticism *constructive* rather than *destructive*? Research findings points to the factors shown in Table 11-2.[53,54]

■ Figure 11-9
Interpersonal Factors Often Play an Important Role in Conflict
Do you think that the person shown gloating here is setting himself up for further conflict with his defeated opponent?

(**Source:** Drawing by Lorenz; © 1980 The New Yorker Magazine, Inc.)

"Drop back soon, Benzinger. It's always nice besting you again."

The factors listed here distinguish constructive criticism (negative feedback that may be accepted by the recipient and improve her or his performance) from destructive criticism (negative feedback likely to be rejected by the recipient and unlikely to improve his or her performance).

Constructive Criticism	Destructive Criticism
Considerate—protected self-esteem of recipient	Inconsiderate—harsh, sarcastic, biting
Does not contain threats	Contains threats
Timely—occurs as soon as possible after the substandard performance	Not timely—occurs after an inappropriate delay
Does not attribute poor performance to internal causes	Attributes poor performance to internal causes (e.g., lack of effort, motivation, ability)
Specific—focuses on aspects of performance that were inadequate	General—a sweeping condemnation of performance
Focuses on performance, not on the recipient	Focuses on the recipient—his or her personal characteristics
Motivated by desire to help the recipient improve	Motivated by anger, desire to assert dominance over recipient, desire for revenge
Offers concrete suggestions for improvement	Offers no concrete suggestions for improvement

A fourth interpersonal source of conflict is *distrust*.[55] The more strongly people suspect that someone or some group is out to get them, the more likely they are to have a relationship with that person or group that is riddled with conflict. In general, companies that are considered great places in which to work are characterized by high levels of trust between people at all levels; and as we saw earlier in this chapter, trust is conducive to both cooperation and citizenship behavior.[56]

Finally, several *personal characteristics*, too seem to play a role in organizational conflict (see Chapter 3). For example, *Type A* individuals report becoming involved in conflict with others more often than *Type B* persons (see our discussion of this characteristic in Chapter 6). Conversely, people who are high in *self-monitoring*—those who are highly aware of how others are reacting to them—report resolving conflict in relatively productive ways (e.g., through collaboration or compromise) to a greater extent than persons who are low in self-monitoring.[57]

In sum considerable evidence suggests that conflict in work settings often stems from relations between individuals and from their personal traits as well as from underlying structural (organization-based) factors.

The Effects of Conflict: Definitely a Mixed Bag

In everyday speech, the term *conflict* has strong negative connotations. It seems to impiy anger, direct confrontations, and harsh, damaging behavior. In fact, however, conflict in work settings operates like the proverbial "double-edged sword." Depending on why it occurs and how it develops, conflict can yield beneficial as well as harmful effects.

The negative effects of conflict.   Some of the negative effects produced by conflict are too obvious to require much comment. For example, it often yields strong negative emotions and this can be quite stressful. Conflict frequently interferes with communication between individuals, groups, or divisions. In this way, it can all but eliminate coordination between them. Third, it diverts attention and needed energies away from major tasks and efforts to attain key organizational goals. In all these ways, conflict can seriously interfere with organizational effectiveness.

For example, consider recent events concerning the famed Rockefeller Center in New York City (see Figure 11-10). In 1989, Mitsubishi Estate, a subsidiary of the giant Japanese company Mitsubishi, bought an 80 percent interest in the property from Rockefeller Trusts—a trust run for the benefit of more than 100 descendants of the legendary John D. Rockefeller. Within a few years, the New York real estate market tumbled, and losses on the property mounted. At this point, Mitsubishi sought help from the Rockefeller Trust, only to be rejected. Top executives at Mitsubishi felt that they had already been humiliated by the Rockefellers because they paid far too much for the property. Thus, they wanted the Rockefellers to make a "face-saving" gesture—a relatively modest cash contribution that would allow Mitsubishi to regain its image as a savvy investor. The refusal caused so much bad feeling—and conflict—that Mitsubishi decided to push the property into bankruptcy rather than give in. As one observer put it, "Above all else, it seems, Mitsubishi's executives are determined to prevent the Rockefellers from regaining control of the property. To that end, they are likely to pour out large sums to cut deals with creditors."[58] In this case, as in many others, conflict has proven costly for both parties involved.

Other effects of conflict are more subtle and are, therefore, sometimes overlooked. First, it has been found that conflict between groups often encourages their leaders to shift from participative to authoritarian styles.[59] The reason for this is that groups experiencing stress require firm direction. Recognizing this fact, their leaders adopt more controlling tactics when conflict develops. As a result of such changes, the group experiencing conflict tends to provide less pleasant work environments than ones not faced with this type of stress.

Second, conflict increases the tendency of both sides to engage in negative stereotyping. As we noted earlier, the members of opposing groups or units tend to emphasize the differences between them. These differences are interpreted in a negative light, so that each side views the other in increasingly unfavorable terms.

Finally, conflict leads each side to close ranks and emphasize loyalty to their own department or group. Anyone who suggests, even tentatively, that the other side's position has some merit is viewed as a traitor and is strongly censured. As a result, it becomes increasingly difficult for opponents to take each other's perspectives—a development that sharply reduces the likelihood of an effective resolution of their differences, and increases the likelihood of *groupthink* (see Chapter 10).

The positive effects of conflict. The picture is not entirely bleak, however. Although conflict often has a disruptive impact on organizations, it can sometimes yield benefits as well. The most important of these are:

As we will see in Chapter 16, change is frequently required for organizational survival.

- Conflict serves to bring problems that have previously been ignored out into the open.
- Conflict motivates people on both sides of an issue to know and understand each others' positions more fully.[60]
- Conflict often encourages the consideration of new ideas and approaches, facilitating innovation and change.[61]
- Conflict can lead to better decisions: When decision makers receive information incompatible with their views—which is often the case when conflict exists—they tend to make better decisions than when controversy does not exist.[62] This only occurs, of course, when the conflict forces people to challenge their assumptions, confront new ideas, and consider new positions. If, however, people resent having to engage in such activities, results may be far more disruptive.[63]
- Conflict enhances group loyalty, increasing motivation and performance within the groups or units involved.

- Conflict, especially *cognitive conflict,* in which opposing views are brought out into the open and fully discussed, can enhance organizational commitment.[64,65]

In sum, conflict can actually contribute to organizational effectiveness. Note, however, that benefits occur only when conflict is carefully managed and does not get out of control. If conflict is permitted to become extreme, rationality—and the potential benefits described above—may vanish in a haze of intense negative emotions.

Conflict Management: Increasing the Benefits and Minimizing the Costs

If conflict can yield benefits as well as costs, the key task organizations face with respect to this process is *managing* its occurrence. In short, the overall goal should not be the elimination of conflict, but rather that of maximizing its potential benefits, while minimizing its potential costs. A number of techniques for reaching this goal exist, and in this section, we will examine several of the most useful.

Bargaining: The Universal Process

bargaining (or **negotiation**) A process in which two or more parties in a dispute exchange offers, counteroffers, and concessions in an effort to attain a mutually acceptable agreement.

By far the most common strategy for resolving organizational conflicts, and therefore for managing them effectively, is **bargaining** (or **negotiation**).[66] In this process, opposing sides exchange offers, counteroffers, and concessions, either directly or through representatives. If the process is successful, a solution acceptable to both parties is attained and the conflict is resolved, perhaps with some "extras," such as enhanced understanding and improved relations between the two sides thrown in as well. If, instead, bargaining is unsuccessful, costly deadlock may result and the conflict may intensify. What factors determine which of these outcomes occurs? Given the importance of bargaining and its occurrence in virtually all spheres of life, this question has been the subject of intensive study for decades.[67] Here, briefly, are some of the key findings of this research.

Specific tactics. One group of factors that strongly affects the outcomes of negotiations involves the specific tactics adopted by bargainers. Many of these are designed to reduce opponents' aspirations—to convince them that they have little chance of reaching their goals and should, instead, accept offers that are actually quite favorable to the sides proposing them. Many strategies can be used for this purpose. For example, one side can suggest that it has other potential partners and will withdraw from the current negotiations if its proposals are not accepted.

Similarly, one party to a dispute can claim that its break-even point is much lower than it really is—a procedure known as the "big lie" technique.[68] If the other side accepts this information, it may make sizable concessions. Third, the course of negotiations and final settlements are often strongly affected by the nature of initial offers. Relatively extreme offers seem to put strong pressure on opponents to make concessions, resulting in settlements favorable to the side adopting such positions.[69] On the other hand, if initial offers are too extreme, opponents may be angered and decide to seek other negotiating partners.

Framing: Cognitive lenses for viewing conflict. A second group of factors that strongly determines the nature and outcomes of bargaining involves what has been termed **framing**—the cognitive set or focus adopted by bargainers.[70] In other words, framing refers to the ways in which bargainers perceive or define the situation. What are such frames like? One important study of this topic indicated that cognitive frames for perceiving conflict situations

framing In the context of bargaining, refers to the cognitive set or focus adopted by bargainers

may vary along three key dimensions.[71] One, the *relationship/task* dimension, refers to whether bargainers are focused on their relationship with opponents or on the task—the material aspects of the dispute (money, property, etc.).

The second dimension, *emotional/intellectual*, reflects the degree to which bargainers direct their attention to affective or emotional components of the dispute (jealousy, hatred, frustration, anger), or to the actions and behaviors that occur quite apart from these emotions. Finally, the third, *cooperate/win*, refers to the extent to which disputants focus on maximizing the benefits to both parties, or, alternatively, on winning—defeating their opponent and maximizing their own gain, even at this person's expense. These three dimensions, which are largely independent, are summarized in Figure 11-11.

A growing body of evidence indicates that framing exerts powerful effects on bargaining.[72,73] Specifically, disputants who adopt task or cooperation-focused frames attain higher personal and joint outcomes in the negotiation than those who adopt a win-focused frame. Similarly, those with intellectual and relationship-focused frames are often more satisfied with the negotiation than those with task or emotion-focused frames.

Perceptions of the situation. A third aspect of negotiations that plays an important role in this process is the perceptions of the persons involved.[74] Studies by Thompson and her colleagues reveal that negotiators often enter bargaining situations with important misperceptions. In particular, they seem to begin with the view that their own interests and those of the other side are entirely incompatible—the **incompatibility error**. This, of course, causes them to overlook interests that are actually compatible. In addition, they tend to begin with the view, often false, that the other party places the same importance or priority that they do on each issue, a tendency known as the **fixed-sum error**. Both of these assumptions are false and often prevent bargainers from obtaining an agreement that is maximally beneficial to both sides.

Fortunately, these misperceptions concerning interests and priorities often change during the course of negotiations, fading over time, often within the first few minutes of negotiations.[75] However, many negotiators retain these false perceptions even over prolonged periods of bargaining, with the result that both parties experience lower payoffs than would otherwise be true. As might be expected, the smaller such errors in perception (i.e., the more accurate the bargainers' perceptions of each others' outcomes are), the higher the

incompatibility error The perception on the part of bargainers that their own interests and that of the other side are completely incompatible.

fixed-sum error The perception on the part of bargainers that the other party places the same importance or priority as they do on each issue.

■ **Figure 11-11**
Cognitive Frames in Bargaining
Bargainers often frame the situation in which they are involved along the three dimensions shown here: relationship/task, emotional/intellectual, cooperative/win. Such framing exerts strong effects on their behavior during negotiations.

(**Source:** Based on suggestions by Pinkley, 1990; see Note 71.)

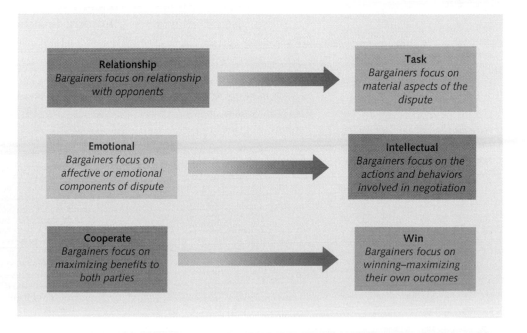

joint payoffs obtained by both sides.[76] Clearly, then, steps designed to improve the accuracy of negotiators' perceptions of the situations they face and each others' interests and priorities can go a long way toward enhancing the outcomes of this process.

Win-win versus win-lose orientations. Perhaps the single most important factor determining the success of negotiations in producing settlements satisfactory to both sides, however, involves participants' overall orientation toward this process. Three decades ago, Walton and McKersie pointed out that people taking part in negotiations can approach such discussions from either of two distinct perspectives.[77] On the one hand, they can view negotiations as "win-lose" situations in which gains by one side are necessarily linked with losses for the other. On the other hand, people can approach negotiations as potential "win-win" situations—ones in which the interests of the two sides are not necessarily incompatible and in which the potential gains of both can be maximized.[78]

Not all situations offer the potential for such agreements, but many that at first glance seem to involve simple head-on clashes between the two sides do, in fact, provide such possibilities. If participants are willing to explore all options carefully, and exert the effort required to identify creative potential solutions, they can attain integrative agreements—ones that offer greater joint benefits than simple compromise (splitting all differences down the middle.)

Table 11-3 summarizes some of the ways in which such *integrative agreements* can be attained. Examine this table carefully because we are certain that you will find many situations in your own career when the approaches it describes will come in handy.

Third-Party Intervention: Mediation and Arbitration

Despite the best efforts of both sides, negotiations sometimes deadlock. When they do, the aid of a third party, someone not directly involved in the dispute, is often sought. Such third-party intervention can take many forms, but the most common are known as *mediation* and *arbitration*.[79]

In **mediation**, the third party attempts, through various tactics, to facilitate voluntary agreements between the disputants. Mediators have no formal power and cannot impose an agreement on the two sides. Instead, they seek to clarify the issues involved and enhance the communication between the opponents. Mediators sometimes offer specific recommendations for compromise or integrative solutions; in other cases, they merely guide dis-

mediation A form of third-party intervention in disputes in which the intervener does not have the authority to dictate an agreement.

■ TABLE 11-3	TECHNIQUES FOR REACHING INTEGRATIVE AGREEMENTS

Several strategies can be useful in attaining integrative agreements in bargaining. A few of the major ones are summarized here.

Type of Agreement	Description
Broadening the pie	Available resources are broadened so that both sides can obtain their major goals.
Nonspecific compensation	One side gets what it wants; the other is compensated on an unrelated issue.
Logrolling	Each party makes concessions on low-priority issues in exchange for concessions on issues that it values more highly.
Cost cutting	One party gets what it desires, and the costs to the other party are reduced or eliminated.
Bridging	Neither party gets its initial demands, but a new option that satisfies the major interests of both sides is developed.

arbitration A form of third-party intervention in disputes in which the intervening person has the power to determine the terms of an agreement.

putants toward developing such solutions themselves. Their role is primarily that of *facilitator*—helping the two sides toward agreements they both find acceptable.[80]

In contrast, third parties are more powerful during **arbitration**. Specifically, arbitrators do have the power to impose (or at least strongly recommend) the terms of an agreement. In *binding arbitration*, the two sides agree in advance to accept these terms. In *voluntary arbitration*, though, the two sides retain the freedom to reject the recommended agreement (although the personal stature and expertise of the arbitrator may make it difficult for them to do so.). In *conventional arbitration*, the arbitrator can offer any package of terms he or she wishes. However, in *final-offer arbitration*, the arbitrator merely chooses between final offers made by the disputants.

Both mediation and arbitration can be helpful in resolving organizational conflicts. However, both suffer from certain drawbacks. Because it requires voluntary compliance by the disputing parties, mediation often proves ineffective. Indeed, it may simply serve to underscore the depth of the differences between the two sides. Arbitration also suffers from several potential problems. First, it may exert a *chilling effect* on negotiations, bringing voluntary progress to a halt. Since both sides know the arbitrator will resolve the dispute for them, they see little point in engaging in serious bargaining, which, after all, is hard work. Second, one or both sides may come to suspect that the arbitrator is biased. The result: disputants become increasingly reluctant to agree to arbitration. Third, arbitration tends to cost more and take longer than mediation.[81] Finally, there is some indication that commitment to arbitrated settlements is weaker than that to directly negotiated ones.

The Induction of Superordinate Goals

superordinate goals Goals shared by the parties in a conflict or dispute.

At several points in this chapter, we have noted that individuals often divide the world into two opposing camps: "us" and "them." They perceive members of their own group as quite different from, and usually better than, people belonging to other groups. These dual tendencies to magnify the differences between one's own group and others and to disparage outsiders are very powerful and are as common in organizations as in other settings.[82] Further, they seem to play a central role in many conflicts between various departments, divisions, and work groups. How can they be countered? One answer, suggested by research findings, is through the induction of **superordinate goals**—ones that tie the interests of the two sides together.[83] The basic idea behind this approach is simple: By inducing conflicting parties to focus on and work toward common objectives, the barriers between them—ones that interfere with communication, coordination, and agreement—can be weakened. When this occurs, the chances for cooperation rather than conflict are enhanced. To see how organizations are using both bargaining and superordinate goals to improve their bottom line, see the QUEST FOR QUALITY section.

Workplace Violence and Workplace Aggression

Dearborn, Mich.—A Ford worker opened fire with a handgun as a union meeting was breaking up Saturday, killing two fellow workers and wounding two others, police said. . . . French [the attacker] left the room during the meeting, returned about 20 minutes later with a .357-caliber Magnum and started shooting. . . . French, 47, refused to give a motive. . . . (Associated Press, September 11, 1994).

workplace violence Direct physical assaults by present or former employees against other persons in their organizations.

Newspapers and magazines have been filled in recent years with accounts of such **workplace violence**—direct physical assaults by present or former employees against other persons in their organizations. Disturbing statistics

WHEN SUPPLIERS BECOME PARTNERS—NOT ADVERSARIES

*I*n order to improve the "bottom line," many organizations have adopted stringent cost-cutting measures. They have downsized, replaced full-time employees with contract labor, invested heavily in new, efficient equipment, and even cut travel and other executive perks. The gains from such steps have been significant, but as many organizations have learned, they do have limits. On average, manufacturing companies spend only about 6 percent of sales on labor, and 3 percent on overhead. In contrast, they spend fully 55 percent on raw materials and other supplies. Why not seek to enhance profitability by focusing on these costs? The answer, a growing number of companies is discovering, is "Why not?!"

One approach to meeting this goal would be to hammer away at suppliers, beating them down on price as much as possible. But this can backfire. Suppliers can be pushed only so far; and when large companies reduce the profit margins of their suppliers, they reduce the ability of these companies to invest in equipment that would make them more efficient—and so enable them to reduce prices still more.

As we noted in Chapter 3, growing realization of this fact has led some companies to seek a partnership with their suppliers.[84] Rather than treating them as adversaries across the bargaining table, they view them as partners whose outcomes are intimately linked to their own. Thus, not only do they offer them training and assistance, they adopt a win-win approach in which superordinate goals shared by both organizations—greater efficiency and reduced prices—are established. For example, consider the case of Allied Signal, an $11.8 billion per year maker of auto parts and aerospace electronics. To reduce the costs of the components it uses in its operations, it has worked out win-win arrangements with many of its suppliers. For example, in 1993, Allied Signal offered to double its orders from Mech-Tronics, but only if Mech-Tronics would cut its prices 10 percent. These terms initially eliminated Mech-Tronics' profits, but with help from Allied Signal in improving its efficiency, the higher volume soon paid off. The result? Both companies gained.

In another case, Allied Signal demanded a 6 percent a year reduction in costs for aluminum castings it bought from Baja Oriente of Ensenada, Mexico. To help Baja meet this goal, Allied Signal increased its orders from $500,000 in 1991 to more than $6 million in 1994. This allowed Baja to spread its fixed costs over more units. In addition, the larger orders have allowed Baja to swing into longer production runs, which reduces time spent on changeovers. This has helped it to cut costs—and to meet Allied Signal's demands. Again, both companies benefited from a cooperative arrangement.

Here are a few other steps companies are taking in their efforts to reduce the costs of materials and supplies:

- *Leveraging their buying power*: Companies are centralizing purchasing so that all operations place their orders at once. Larger orders often qualify for lower prices, so the savings can be large.
- *Committing to a handful of suppliers*: Instead of seeking competitive bids from dozens of suppliers, large companies are working with a few tried-and-trusted suppliers. This helps the suppliers improve their efficiency and, ultimately, to offer lower prices.
- *Developing internal sources of goods and services*: Some companies—especially very large ones—find that they can supply some of their own needs. For example, Tenneco set up a purchasing subsidiary, TennEcon Services, that provides the company with phone service and overnight mail delivery—at rates lower than outside sources such as AT&T, MCI and Sprint can meet.

In short, many companies are finding that purchasing—long ignored as being a dull, necessary evil—can be a major contributor to the quest for quality. Yes, it's mundane, but as it is used more effectively, it is beginning to change the way many organizations do business.

seem to suggest that media attention to such events is fully justified: Each week, an average of *15 people* are murdered at work in the United States alone, a total of more than 7,600 during the past ten years.[85] Clearly, workplace violence represents an end point on the continuum of working with or against others we have addressed in this chapter. In this section, we will examine the nature of workplace violence and its relation to other forms of antisocial behavior at work. Then we'll turn to the causes of such behavior. Finally, we'll examine several techniques for reducing its occurrence.

Workplace Violence: The Tip of the Iceberg?

Instances of workplace violence are dramatic, to say the least. And given the numbers listed above, many persons have concluded that work settings are dangerous places indeed. Closer examination of existing evidence, however, reveals a somewhat different picture. Yes, thousands of persons are killed by others at work every year. However, it turns out that a large majority of such violence occurs in connection with robberies and related crimes (see Figure 11-12).

In other words, contrary to popular belief, most workplace violence does not involve instances in which angry employees suddenly explode into open violence. Rather, it occurs when individuals are attacked by persons from outside their workplace who have entered it for criminal purposes. Moreover, growing evidence suggests that workplace violence is really only the dramatic and unsettling tip of a broader problem: **workplace aggression**—efforts by individuals to harm others with whom they work, or have worked, or the organizations in which they are presently, or were previously, employed.

Workplace aggression, like aggression in any context, can take many different forms. It can be verbal as well as physical—for example, spreading false, damaging rumors about another person. It can be *passive* as well as active—failing to return phone calls, withholding action on some issue of importance to the target person. It can be *indirect* as well as direct—damaging property belonging to the target person, or failing to speak in defense of the target person when this is necessary. In fact, considerable evidence suggests that in many situations, persons seeking to harm others with whom they work prefer to do this in relatively *covert* ways—they prefer actions that make it difficult for the intended target to identify them as the source of such harm, or even to know whether they are the victim of intentional harm-doing or merely negative circumstances.[86]

Consistent with this pattern, a recent study by Neuman and Baron found that verbal and passive forms of workplace aggression were more frequent in many organizations than physical and active.[87] This in no way implies that instances of workplace violence are unimportant; on the contrary, they are often devastating in their effects. However, it appears that they are relatively rare occurrences in work settings and that other, less dramatic forms of aggression are more prevalent. Since these forms may also cause considerable harm to the

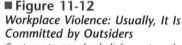

workplace aggression Efforts by individuals to harm other members of their organization, persons with whom they previously worked, or their organization itself.

■ **Figure 11-12**
Workplace Violence: Usually, It Is Committed by Outsiders
Contrary to popular belief, most workplace violence does not involve physical assaults by one organization member on another. Rather, most violence in workplaces occurs during robberies and other crimes, and is performed by outsiders to an organization.

(**Source:** Based on data from the Bureau of Labor Statistics, 1992.)

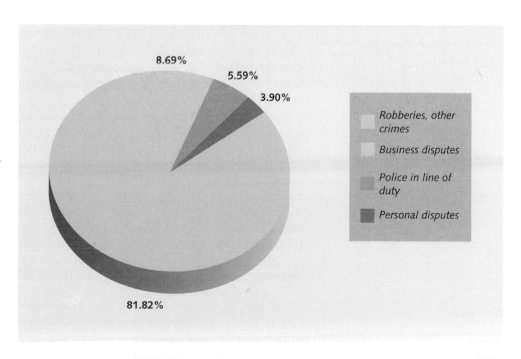

intended victims, however, they pose a serious problem for organizations and their employees alike.

The Causes of Workplace Aggression

Is workplace aggression increasing? Some statistics suggest that it is. For example, during one recent year, the Bureau of Labor Statistics reports that 1,004 employees were murdered on the job—a rate more than one-third higher than the annual average during the 1980s.[88] Such statistics have led some experts to conclude that workplace aggression is indeed increasing in frequency.[89] However, existing evidence is too limited in scope to permit firm conclusion in this respect.

What are the causes of workplace aggression? In one sense, the same as the causes of aggression in any other context. Modern theories of human aggression suggest that behavior directed toward the goal of harming others stems from many factors.[90] Most of these, however, fall into four major categories.

First, aggression sometimes stems from the characteristics of individuals. Some people have "shorter fuses," unstable personalities, and specific traits that predispose them toward aggression in any context, including organizations. Such factors include the *Type A behavior pattern*, which we discussed in Chapter 6, and a trait known as the **hostile attributional bias**.[91] Persons high on this latter characteristic tend to perceive others' actions as stemming from hostile intentions, even when this is not the case. In other words, such persons are very low on trust; and while high levels of trust lead to citizenship and cooperation, low levels seem to promote hostility and aggression.

Second, aggression, like conflict, often stems from interpersonal sources. People who work together do often "rub each other the wrong way"—they annoy, frustrate, and anger each other. Moreover, they often perceive others as having treated them unfairly in some manner. When they do, anger and the desire for revenge may come into play, with the result that workplace aggression, too, increases. This pattern is clearly evident with respect to employee thefts and vandalism. In the past, it was assumed that thefts, at least, stemmed primarily from economic motives—the gains that would result from stealing valuable items. Recent findings, however, indicate that employees often steal from their companies as a way of "evening the scales"—paying them back for perceived injustice.[92]

Third, aggression can stem from environmental conditions that, seemingly, have little or nothing to do with harming others. Unpleasant environmental conditions—uncomfortable temperatures, high levels of noise, polluted air, glaring lights—can induce negative feelings among the persons exposed to them. Such *negative affect*, in turn, has been found to increase aggression in many situations.[93]

Finally, and perhaps most important of all, growing evidence indicates that some of the changes that have occurred recently in many organizations—changes such as increased workforce diversity, downsizing, wage freezes, restructuring—may be contributing to increased aggression among employees.[94] How can such changes produce an increase in workplace aggression? Again, by inducing psychological states among employees that have been found to increase the likelihood of overt aggression. Downsizing and layoffs, for example, have been found to induce anger, anxiety, and frustration among both the persons who are fired and survivors—those who remain.[95]

Similarly, increased workforce diversity sometimes leads to increased interpersonal friction between persons from different cultural backgrounds who, quite literally, don't speak each other's language.[96] We could continue, but the main point should be clear: The wrenching changes that have occurred recently in many organizations may be yet another factor contributing to what appears to be a rising spiral of workplace aggression.

hostile attributional bias A tendency to perceive others' actions as stemming from malevolent intentions, even when this is not the case

We noted in Chapter 6 that unpleasant physical (environmental) conditions are an important cause of work-related stress.

The Prevention and Control of Workplace Aggression

Can anything be done to reduce the incidence of workplace aggression? In other words, can this process be managed effectively? Research on this issue is just beginning, but some steps and techniques do seem useful in this regard. First, efforts can be made to *screen* prospective employees. Those with a history of aggressive behavior, or those who evidence high levels of traits associated with aggression, may be more prone than other persons to become involved in workplace aggression. Thus, efforts should be made to avoid hiring them whenever possible. As noted recently by Folger and Skarlicki, some persons are more likely to "explode" aggressively than others when faced with difficult, unpleasant conditions.[97] Thus, developing techniques for accurately identifying such persons have the potential to yield handsome dividends with respect to reducing workplace aggression.

A second approach to reducing workplace aggression involves the establishment of clear disciplinary procedures for such behavior. Aggression cannot thrive in an environment where it is made clear that such behavior is viewed as inappropriate and that instances of workplace aggression will be met with swift and certain punishment. Programs of *progressive punishment* have been found to be effective in deterring other forms of behavior considered inappropriate in work settings, and there is every reason to assume that such procedures can be effective—if used with care—in deterring at least some forms of workplace aggression.[98]

Third, since workplace aggression often stems from anger and feelings of having been treated unfairly, such behavior may be reduced by assuring high levels of *organizational justice*. In particular, two aspects of such justice—interpersonal justice and informational justice—are especially important.[99] Interpersonal justice refers to demonstrating sensitivity for others, especially in the context of the distribution of outcomes they receive. In contrast, informational justice refers to providing individuals with adequate explanations of, and reasons for, the procedures used to determine those outcomes. To the extent these types of justice are present in a work setting, instances of workplace aggression may be held to a minimum.

Finally, training of employees, too, may be helpful. Although instances of physical violence are relatively rare, they do occur. Thus, employees should be trained in techniques for responding to threats posed by present and previous employees as well as customers. Efforts to develop systematic programs for equipping managers with the skills needed to recognize potentially dangerous situations and, perhaps, to defuse them, are currently underway.[100]

Through these and other steps, the incidence of workplace aggression may be reduced. It is our view that workplace aggression poses a threat not only to the safety and well-being of individual employees, but also to the effectiveness of their organizations as well. Quests for vengeance and personal vendettas tend to drain time and energy away from more productive activities. Thus, we believe that efforts to manage workplace aggression are worthwhile not simply from the standpoint of ethics, but from the perspective of enhanced organizational effectiveness as well.

The effects of punishment or discipline on employee behavior were examined in detail in Chapter 3.

Prosocial Behavior: Helping Others At Work

People often engage in **prosocial behavior** in work settings, performing actions that benefit others. One important form of prosocial behavior is **organizational citizenship behavior (OCB)**, which involves actions by organization members that exceed the formal requirements of their jobs. The incidence of OCB is increased by several factors, including employees' trust in their supervisors, their perceptions of the breadth of their jobs, and their perceptions concerning the fairness of any punishments they have received. **Whistle-blowing**—disclosure by employees of illegal, immoral, or illegitimate practices to others who can right the wrong—may be considered prosocial actions, but they often prove costly to both organizations and the individuals involved.

Cooperation: Mutual Assistance in Organizations

Cooperation involves mutual assistance or coordination between two or more persons or groups. Its occurrence in work settings is affected by factors relating to individuals (e.g., strong tendencies toward reciprocity, personality orientations concerning cooperation), and by several organizational factors (e.g., reward systems, interdependence among employees). **Competition,** a sharply contrasting pattern, develops when individuals, groups, or organizations seek to achieve gains at others' expense. Cooperation sometimes develops between organizations—a process known as **interorganizational coordination**. One important form of such coordination involves the formation of a **consortium**—a confederation in which organizations maintain their formal independence, but agree to coordinate their activities through a central management.

Conflict: Its Nature, Causes, and Effects

Conflict is a process that begins when one person or group perceives that another person or group has taken or is about to take some action inconsistent with the perceiver's major interests. Conflict situations involve two basic dimensions; **distribution**, concern with one's own outcomes, and **integration**, concern with others' outcomes. Contrasting styles or approaches to resolving conflict, such as *competing, collaborating, avoiding, accommodation,* and *compromising,* reflect specific points along these dimensions. Conflict in work settings often stems from organizational factors, such as competition over scarce resources and ambiguity over jurisdiction or responsibility. However, it also stems from interpersonal factors such as *attributional errors, faulty commu-*

nication, and personal characteristics such as the Type A behavior pattern and the **hostile attributional bias**.

Conflict often exerts negative effects on organizations, interfering with communication and coordination. However, it sometimes produces positive results. These include bringing problems out into the open, increased consideration of new ideas, and enhanced organizational commitment.

Conflict Management

A key task with respect to conflict is managing its occurrence—maximizing its benefits while reducing its potential costs. **Bargaining** (or **negotiation**) is the most common procedure for resolving organizational conflicts. Many factors influence the course and outcomes of bargaining, including specific tactics used by participants, their cognitive **frames** with respect to the bargaining situation, their perceptions of each others' interests and priorities, and the overall approach to bargaining—"win-lose" or "win-win."

Third-party interventions such as **mediation** and **arbitration** can also prove helpful in resolving conflicts. Another approach involves the induction of **superordinate goals**—ones shared by both sides. This technique has recently been used by many manufacturing companies in dealings with their suppliers.

Workplace Violence and Workplace Aggression

Dramatic incidents of **workplace violence** have been much in the news recently. While large numbers of persons are killed at work, however, most of these deaths result from robberies and other crimes, not assaults by organization members. Efforts by individuals to harm others with whom they work—**workplace aggression**—can take many forms other than direct physical attacks. Such behavior may be passive as well as active, and indirect as well as direct. Many factors influence the occurrence of workplace aggression, including personal characteristics, friction in interpersonal relations, and unpleasant physical conditions. In addition, changes that have occurred recently in many workplaces—downsizing, increased workforce diversity, increased use of part-time employees—may contribute to such behavior.

Efforts to reduce workplace aggression include screening for "high-risk" employees, clear disapproval of such behavior coupled with appropriate disciplinary procedures, assuring high levels of organizational justice, and training employees on how to deal with such behavior.

1. What kinds of organizational citizenship behaviors have you observed in your own work experience? Why, if individuals receive no direct benefit for engaging in such actions, do they ever perform them?

2. What factors in an organization might lead to high levels of trust between employees? Would it be worthwhile to assure that these factors are present?

3. What are the ethical issues one must consider when deciding whether or not to blow the whistle on an organization suspected of some wrongdoing?

4. What role do cultural factors play in cooperation? In other words, would you expect to observe different levels of cooperation in different cultures? Why?

5. Do you think that individuals differ with respect to their preferred modes of resolving conflicts (e.g., compromise, collaboration, competition)? Would these differences show up in all situations or only under certain circumstances?

6. "Conflict doesn't exist until it is recognized by the parties involved." Do you agree with this statement? Why or why not?

7. Growing evidence indicates that conflict can sometimes produce positive results. Have you ever experienced positive results from a conflict? If so, why do you think such effects occurred?

8. If people in your organization are frequently in conflict with each other, what techniques could you use to reduce the number or intensity of these conflicts?

9. Do you think that workplace violence and workplace aggression are increasing? If so, why? If not, why?

CASE IN POINT

When Rivals Become Mortal Enemies: How Sony Used the "Ultimate Weapon" in Thailand

Price wars, most experts agree, are a mistake. The outcome is often a blood-letting for both sides, with customers being (temporarily) the only winners. But in today's international business, which is becoming ever more competitive, some companies are using this *ultimate weapon* and getting away with it. Consider how Sony assaulted its arch rival Matsushita in Thailand.

When Sony first entered this market, Matsushita already had more than one-third of the market for consumer electronics. Kazunori Somaya, Sony's head of operations in Thailand sized up the situation and decided that a price should be part of his basic strategy. So he cut the price of Sony's 21-inch television to that of Matsushita's 20-inch set. That forced Matsushita to lower the price of its product, but Sony kept up the pressure, lowering the price still further. The result? When the price difference between Matsushita's 20-inch set and its top-selling 14-inch set decreased to only $40, sales of this key product were threatened. Matsushita gave up and dropped the 20-inch set, thus giving Sony the opening it needed.

That was not the only strategy Somaya used to wrest market share from his arch rival, however. In addition, as he put it, he borrowed a strategy from Chairman Mao, the famed Chinese leader, and "surrounded" Matsushita. As Somaya puts it: "Mao didn't attack Shanghai directly. First he captured the rice fields, and then he attacked the city." Somaya followed a similar strategy, introducing his products in stores outside the center of Bangkok—areas where Sony was not dominant. Then, once he had seized these markets, he launched the price war described above. Of course, while the battle is won for Sony, the war is far from over. Matsushita is certain to strike back. In the battle between rival companies, it is clear that only those who can continue to surprise their opponents again will manage to remain on top.

Critical Thinking Questions

1. Do you think the price-cutting tactics used by Sony are ethical? If so, why? If not, why?

2. How could Matsushita have fought back when it discovered what Sony was doing? Or was it already too late once Sony had launched its strategy?

3. What counterattack do you think Matsushita should adopt now, given that it has lost an important market segment to Sony?

Experiencing Organizational Behavior

Personal Styles of Conflict Management

Conflict among people is a common and inescapable part of life. Given this fact, it is important for all of us to *manage* conflict effectively when it arises. How do *you* deal with such situations? What is your preferred mode of handling disagreements and conflicts with others? The following exercise is designed to give you some insights into this important issue.

Directions

First, recall three events in which you have experienced conflict with others. On a sheet of paper, describe each briefly, and then answer each of the five following questions with respect to each. (It may help to make three copies of the questionnaire.)

1. To what extent did you try to resolve this conflict through *avoidance*—sidestepping the issue, withdrawing from the situation?

Did not do this						Did do this
1	2	3	4	5	6	7

2. To what extent did you try to resolve this conflict through *accommodation*—giving into the other person.

Did not do this						Did do this
1	2	3	4	5	6	7

3. To what extent did you try to resolve this conflict through *competition*—trying to win, standing up for your rights or views?

Did not do this						Did do this
1	2	3	4	5	6	7

4. To what extent did you try to resolve this conflict through *compromise*—finding the middle ground between your position and the other person's?

Did not do this						Did do this
1	2	3	4	5	6	7

5. To what extent did you try to resolve this conflict through *collaboration*—working with the other person to find some solution that would satisfy both of your basic needs or concerns?

Did not do this						Did do this
1	2	3	4	5	6	7

Questions for Discussion

1. Do you notice any consistencies in your responses? Did you prefer one basic mode of resolving conflict over the others?

2. If you did, what effects do you think this will have on your success in handling a wide range of conflicts?

3. Do you think that you would prefer different modes of handling conflicts in different situations—for example, depending on the person with whom you are having the conflict?

4. Do you think you could alter your preferred mode or modes for handling conflicts? If so, how?

Working in Groups

The Good Mood–Helping Effect: One Reason Why "Wining and Dining" Others Often Works

What do you do when you want a favor from another person? One strategy is just to come out and ask for what you want. But most people know that asking for help "cold" is not always the best approach. Sometimes, it is useful either to wait until others are in a good mood, or, if you don't care to bide your time, to take steps to put them into such a mood. This can be accomplished in several different ways—through praise, through giving them a small gift, through exposing them to something amusing or funny. As long as their mood is improved, the chances that they will say "yes" are increased. This exercise demonstrates the power of such effects.

Directions

The class is divided into two parts. One half, who will serve as JOB APPLICANTS, reads the following information:

Your task is to play the role of a job candidate during a brief job interview. The job is a general entry-level management position, and you are to do everything you can to come across well and increase the chances that you'll be selected.

The other half, who will play the role of INTERVIEWERS, is divided into two parts. One receives the following information:

Your task is to play the role of an interviewer during a brief job interview. You will ask the following questions of the candidate. Supposedly, you will then evaluate this person's performance. HOWEVER, YOU WILL ACTUALLY PROVIDE A VERY FAVORABLE EVALUATION NO MATTER WHAT THE OTHER PERSON SAYS OR DOES (see attached form). Then, after the demonstration is over, you will ask this person, in a matter-of-fact manner, for a small favor—the loan of their notes from today's class.

The other group receives the same instructions with this exception:

HOWEVER, YOU WILL ACTUALLY PROVIDE AN UNFAVORABLE EVALUATION NO MATTER WHAT THE OTHER PERSON SAYS OR DOES . . .

Questions to be asked by Interviewers:

1. What is your major?
2. What is your grade point average?
3. What would you say is your best trait?
4. What would you say is your worst trait or failing?
5. How would you describe your work habits?
6. How well do you get along with other people?

Evaluation Form (to be given to job applicants after the interview):

1. Qualifications (check one):
   ____Very Poor   ____Poor   ____Average   ____Good   ____Excellent
2. Motivation (check one):
   ____Very Poor   ____Poor   ____Average   ____Good   ____Excellent
3. Interpersonal skills:
   ____Very Poor   ____Poor   ____Average   ____Good   ____Excellent
4. Probability of being a successful employee:
   ____Very Poor   ____Poor   ____Average   ____Good   ____Excellent
5. Overall rating:
   ____Very Poor   ____Poor   ____Average   ____Good   ____Excellent

Group One (Favorable Evaluation): Check items as follows: Good, Excellent, Excellent, Excellent, Excellent

Group Two (Unfavorable Evaluation): Check items as follows: Poor, Poor, Average, Poor, Average

After students in both groups make their request, a tabulation is made of how many Job Applicants agreed to the request in each condition (Favorable Evaluation, Unfavorable Evaluation).

Questions for Discussion

1. Did the favorable evaluation improve the mood of persons who received it?
2. Did the unfavorable evaluation decrease the mood of persons who received it?
3. What other techniques could be used to put people in a good mood?
4. Have you ever used this technique yourself or had someone use it on you?

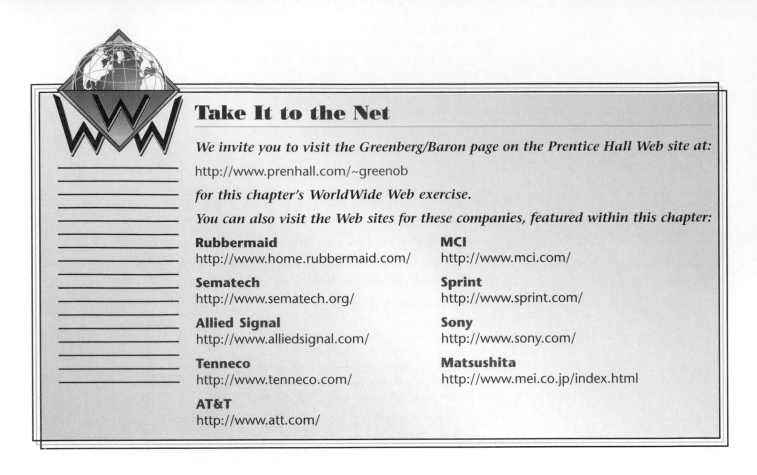

Take It to the Net

We invite you to visit the Greenberg/Baron page on the Prentice Hall Web site at:

http://www.prenhall.com/~greenob

for this chapter's WorldWide Web exercise.

You can also visit the Web sites for these companies, featured within this chapter:

Rubbermaid
http://www.home.rubbermaid.com/

MCI
http://www.mci.com/

Sematech
http://www.sematech.org/

Sprint
http://www.sprint.com/

Allied Signal
http://www.alliedsignal.com/

Sony
http://www.sony.com/

Tenneco
http://www.tenneco.com/

Matsushita
http://www.mei.co.jp/index.html

AT&T
http://www.att.com/

PART IV:
DO COMMUNICATION RITUALS HOLD
BACK WOMEN IN THE WORKPLACE?

Women in the workplace often have to deal with discrimination and stereotypes, sometimes even on the part of other women. But are women themselves responsible for how they are treated at work? Perhaps so, according to Deborah Tannen, author of *Talking from 9 to 5*. Tannen, who also authored *You Just Don't Understand*, asserts that women are passed over for promotions, raises, and credit for good work because their communication style or "rituals" differ markedly from those of men. "These conversational rituals," Tannen says, "can be the basis for underestimating a woman's capabilities. She can be seen as incompetent, whereas she thinks she is being considerate. She could be seen as lacking in confidence, whereas she simply feels she's being a good person, not flaunting her authority."

Tannen contends that conversational differences between men and women helped to create the so-called "glass ceiling" that keeps women from entering the ranks of top management in proportionate numbers. While writing her new book, Tannen observed formal and informal conversations between women and men and bosses and subordinates in a number of companies. "In all the companies I observed," she writes, "I met women who did not seem to be getting full credit for the jobs they were doing." She cites the example of a woman who, as head of a major division of a company, had the title "director" while six men in charge of other divisions in the same company were "vice presidents" even though all seven did the same work.

Tannen argues that while women are more likely to do excellent jobs and expect corresponding rewards, men are more likely to let others—especially superiors—know about the work they are doing. She advises women that "in addition to doing excellent work, you must make sure that your work is recognized. . . . Doing brilliantly at a project that no one knows about will do little good in terms of personal advancement; doing well at a high-profile project, or one that puts you into contact with someone in power who will thereby gain firsthand knowledge of your skill, may make the big difference when that person speaks up at a meeting at which promotions are decided."

Tannen counters her critics by arguing that "talking, like walking, is something we do without stopping to question how we are doing it. Just as we cheerfully take a walk without thinking about which foot to move forward, we simply open our mouths and say what seems self-evidently appropriate, given the situation and the person we are talking to. In other words, ordinary conversation has a ritual character, and the conversational rituals typical of women and men, though they obviously have a lot in common—otherwise we couldn't talk to each other—can also be different. And even subtle differences can lead to gross misinterpretation. In a situation in which one person is judging another and holds the key to a gate the other wants to pass through, the consequences of style differences can be dire indeed."

Video source: He says she says—women's business style is a handicap. (1994, October 21). *20/20*, no. 1442. *Additional sources:* Tannen, D. (1994). *Talking from 9 to 5*, New York: William Morrow; Noble, B. P. (1994, October 23). Sex differences, or something else? *The New York Times*, Sec. 3, p. 23.

CHAPTER | **Twelve**

INFLUENCE, POWER, AND POLITICS IN ORGANIZATIONS

■ OBJECTIVES

LEARNING

After reading this chapter you should be able to:

1. Distinguish among *social influence*, *power*, and *politics* in organizations.

2. Characterize the major varieties of social influence that exist.

3. Describe the conditions under which social influence is used.

4. Identify the major types of individual power in organizations and the conditions under which each is used.

5. Explain the two major approaches to the development of subunit power in organizations (the *resource-dependency model* and the *strategic contingencies model*).

6. Describe when and where *organizational politics* is likely to occur and the forms it is likely to take.

7. Explain the major ethical issues surrounding the use of political behavior in organizations.

CASE Preview

BILL GATES: HE DOESN'T RUN THE WORLD—YET

Few people command as much respect—even from their enemies—as Bill Gates, founder and chairman of software giant Microsoft. After all, the operating systems his company created, everything from DOS through the latest version of Windows, are required to run 80 percent of the world's personal computers. By making the operating systems, Microsoft has been able to get a critical head start on its competitors in launching mainstay software applications such as word processing programs (Microsoft Word), electronic spreadsheets (Excel), and even games (Microsoft Flight Simulator). Indeed, Microsoft's revenues have, in recent years, been greater than that of all its competitors combined—nearly $5 billion in 1994. Not surprisingly, the company has been hugely profitable, and it has made Gates a multibillionaire (his net worth has been estimated at some $10 billion).

Having won the desktop computer wars, you'd think Gates would be content with the incredible amount of power (let alone money) he has amassed. But as far as Gates is concerned, this is only the beginning. He is planning for the day that everyone has a computer and the market is flat. Microsoft is involved in many new ventures, including the Microsoft Network (an on-line service) launched concurrently with the August 1995 release of Windows 95, and the new interactive-cable TV news network MSNBC. All this is in addition to various electronic banking services, wireless data transmission services, and various multimedia entertainment projects (including Dreamworks SKG, with media moguls Steven Spielberg, Jeffrey Katzenbach, and David Geffen).

Because Microsoft has its hands in so many different pots, both competitors and the federal government have become concerned that Gates has developed a choke hold on a vital industry. Reflecting this alarm, in 1995 the U.S. Justice Department blocked Microsoft's $2 billion bid to buy Intuit, the maker of Quicken, the popular electronic checkbook program. This move was seen as a blow to Gates's intention to control every commercial transaction in cyberspace.

There appears to be good reason to suspect that Gates's intentions are serious. After all, he has a long history of using strong-arm business tactics. Years ago, for example, Microsoft programmers were accused of adding lines of code to early versions of DOS so that a competing product, the popular spreadsheet Lotus 1-2-3, would not work properly. "DOS ain't done 'til Lotus won't run" is alleged to have been the battle-cry at Microsoft headquarters outside Seattle. Today's Microsoft is no less ruthless. For example, legal papers accuse Gates of personally threatening to stop developing Macintosh applications if Apple failed to cease work on a programming tool that would compete with Microsoft. And the would-be deal with Intuit? It came about as Microsoft strongly hinted that it could do a lot to derail Quicken with the billions of dollars it planned on spending to buy the company. "Sell it or lose it" appeared to be the message. Such bullying tactics have led to a growing list of Microsoft detractors. Among them is Robert Frankenberg, Novell's CEO, who has referred to Microsoft's practices as "blatantly illegal." Although Gates admits no wrongdoing, he notes that Microsoft is usually involved in as many as 60 different lawsuits at a time.

Despite the questionable nature of some of Microsoft's practices, one thing is for certain: Bill Gates has become one of the most powerful people in the world, a world that has been revolutionized by his visions and actions. And, whatever twists and turns tomorrow's technology may take, you can be sure that Microsoft will be leading the way, with Bill Gates heading the charge.

Although few individuals control as many valuable resources as Bill Gates, his saga illustrates a basic fact of life in organizations: People attempt to influence the actions of other individuals and companies. This occurs whether we're talking about a dispatcher asking a newspaper delivery person to complete the route more quickly or the board of directors pressuring a CEO to make the company more profitable. Efforts to get others to behave as desired, known as *social influence*, are commonplace in all social settings, especially organizations. A large part of this process involves the use of *power*—the formal capacity to exert influence over others. Not only does Bill Gates have a great deal of power, but he appears to seek even more. In fact, he has taken great strides to protect his own interests and those of his company, even at the expense of being ruthless with his competitors, efforts known as *organizational politics*.

Because the processes of influence, power, and politics play key roles in organizational functioning, we will devote this chapter to examining them. Specifically, we will describe the tactics used to influence others in organizations. Then we will examine how power is attained—both by individuals and by organizational subunits—and how that power is used. Following this, we will examine the political mechanisms used to gain power—what they are and when they occur. As part of this discussion, we will also pay special attention to the ethical aspects of organizational politics insofar as activities of this nature may be of questionable morality due to their potentially adverse effects on others. Before turning to these topics, however, we will begin by carefully distinguishing between the concepts of influence, power, and politics.

Organizational Influence Power and Politics: Some Key Distinctions

Imagine that you are a supervisor heading a group of a dozen staff members working on an important new project for your company. Tomorrow is the day you're supposed to make a big presentation to company officials, but the report isn't quite ready. If only several staff members will work a few hours extra, the job will be done on time. Unfortunately, a company party is scheduled for tonight and nobody wants to work late. Question: What can you do to persuade some of your staff to work late and complete the job? In other words, how will you attempt to influence their behavior?

social influence Attempts to affect another in a desired fashion.

The concept of **social influence** refers to attempts (whether successful or unsuccessful) to affect another in a desired fashion (see Figure 12–1). It may be said that we have influenced someone to the extent that our behavior has had an effect—even if unintended—on that person. Although we may attempt to affect another's behavior in a certain fashion, our attempts may be unsuccessful. This would not mean, however, that we did not influence the person, just that we did not influence him or her successfully.

To illustrate this point, let's return to our example of a boss needing people to work overtime on party night. Imagine that you see the boss coming out of her office, and you expect her to ask you to work overtime. Uninterested in doing so, you walk away from your desk, hoping that the boss has not seen you and will ask someone else instead. In this case, can we say that the boss influenced you? Although she was unsuccessful, she clearly *did* have an effect on you. After all, you ran away from her. Thus, we *can* say that the boss influenced you. However, we *cannot* say that the boss influenced your behavior as desired. For that to be true, the boss would have to have been successful in bringing about the intended effects—in this case, getting you to stay and work overtime.

power The capacity to change the behavior or attitudes of others in a desired manner.

Where do power and politics fit in? As illustrated in Figure 12-1, **power** refers to the potential to influence another successfully. More formally, it is the capacity to change the behavior or attitudes of another in a desired fashion.[1] In contrast with social influence (actions that affect others), the related concept of power refers to the *capacity* to have a desired effect on others. As we will detail in the next section, there are several different sources of such power. For now, however, assume that the boss has power over you by virtue of her access to considerable resources that enable her to reward you with raises (in exchange for being cooperative) or punish you by not supporting your promotion (if you refrain from pitching in). These represent the formal actions the supervisor can take to attempt to influence you successfully. That is, they are the sources of power.

*When someone attempts to get another
to act in a desired fashion, that person
is seeking to influence the other. The capacity to exert influence over another is
known as power. Unofficial uses of
power to enhance or protect one's self-in-
terest is known as organizational politics.*

organizational politics (or
politics) Unauthorized uses of
power that enhance or protect
one's own or one's group's personal interests.

Often, when people exercise their power, they take into account their own individual interests. For example, the supervisor in our story may be motivated by an interest in promoting—or at least saving—her own career by making sure that the report gets done on time. This is not to say that she might not also recognize the value of the report to the company. It's just that her actions are motivated primarily by her own selfish concerns. The actions taken to satisfy these concerns reflect **organizational politics**. This term refers to unauthorized uses of power that enhance or protect one's own or one's group's personal interests.[2] If this kind of behavior sounds quite negative, you are correct. In fact, it is technically illegitimate in both its means and ends and, not surprisingly, typically a source of conflict. Later in this chapter we will describe many types of political actions that exist, ways in which people can use their power to promote their personal interests in organizations.

Now that we have clarified the distinctions between social influence, power, and politics, we will focus on each of these concepts separately in the remainder of this chapter. We will begin with the process of social influence.

Social Influence: Having an Impact on Others

By what means do you persuade others to fulfill your wishes? Are you straightforward and tell people what you want them to do, or are you more inclined to emphasize why they should do what you say and what will happen to them if they do not do so (see Figure 12-2)? Is it your style to pressure people, or to convince them to do what you want by getting them to like you? Regardless of your answers, you are confronting the challenge of *social influence*—getting others to do what you want.

It is widely acknowledged that successful managers are those who are adept at influencing others.[3] We will summarize the social influence techniques used, and then review when and how people use their influence over others.

Tactics of Social Influence

In recent years, researchers have examined several major techniques that people use to influence each other in organizations.[4] These are as follows.[5]

■ *Rational persuasion*—Using logical arguments and facts to persuade another that a desired result will occur.
■ *Inspirational appeal*—Arousing enthusiasm by appealing to one's values and ideals.
■ *Consultation*—Asking for participation in decision making or planning a change.

■ Figure 12-2
Social Influence: An Everyday Organizational Phenomenon
Social influence takes many forms in organizations, one of which involves directly telling someone else what you want him or her to do.

(**Source:** Copyright © 1992, 1994 by Charles Barsotti.)

"Terrific, but you're still expected to wear a tie to work like everyone else."

- *Ingratiation*—Getting someone to do what you want by putting her in a good mood or getting her to like you.
- *Exchange*—Promising some benefits in exchange for complying with a request.
- *Personal appeal*—Appealing to feelings of loyalty and friendship before making a request.
- *Coalition building*—Persuading by seeking the assistance of others, or by noting the support of others.
- *Legitimating*—Pointing out one's authority to make a request, or verifying that it is consistent with prevailing organizational policies and practices.
- *Pressure*—Seeking compliance by using demands, threats, or intimidation.

Research has shown that these various tactics are used differently based on whether one is attempting to influence another who is at a higher, lower, or equivalent organizational level.[6] In general, the most popularly used techniques to influence people at all levels were consultation, inspirational appeal, and rational persuasion.[7] Each one of these techniques involves getting someone else to accept a request as being highly desirable, and each is socially acceptable for influencing people at all levels. It is therefore not surprising that people who use these techniques are believed to be highly effective in carrying out their responsibilities.

By contrast. the more socially undesirable forms of influence, pressure and legitimating, were much less frequently used. In fact, pressure, when it was used, was more likely to be relied on as a follow-up technique than as a tool for one's initial influence attempt—and then, only for subordinates. It is important to note that some techniques such as ingratiation, coalition, personal appeal, and exchange, are more likely to be used in combination with other techniques than used alone. Clearly, people attempt to influence others using a wide variety of different combinations of techniques. However, as a general rule, more open, consultative techniques are believed to be more appropriate than more coercive techniques.[8]

Putting Influence Tactics to Work

As you might imagine, when people decide to use a certain influence tactic, they take into account the reaction they anticipate from the person being influenced. Specifically, research findings indicate that people attempting to influence their bosses used upward appeals and ingratiation when they believed their bosses were inclined to be highly authoritarian, but used rational persuasion when they believed their bosses were highly participative.[9] This makes sense if you imagine that influence requires a highly coercive action (such as appealing to one's superior) to influence an authoritarian boss, whereas a participative boss might be more amenable to learning about a rational argument. These findings are important because they suggest that people's use of power is a function of not simply their own characteristics, but also their beliefs about the likely effects of their actions.

The social influence tactics we've been discussing can be effective in changing people's behavior. Typically, we think of such techniques as helpful in bringing about behavior that is adaptive to oneself and helpful to the organization. Returning to our "overtime" example, it certainly would be helpful to your boss and the organization as a whole for you to work overtime. Doing so also would benefit you to the extent that you are credited for your last-minute contribution; indeed, a good manager would remember and reward you for your good organizational citizenship. However, because people are typically part of many different social groups, they may confront several conflicting sources of social power—including some that may be quite negative. For a look at one particular set of negative influences and evidence bearing on its culture-specific nature, see the GLOBALIZATION AND DIVERSITY section.

Recall the discussion of organizational citizenship behavior appearing in Chapter 11.

Individual Power: A Basis For Influence

As defined earlier, *power* involves the potential to influence others—both the things they do and the ways they feel about something. In this section, we will focus on the individual bases of power—that is, factors that give people the capacity to control others successfully. It is an inevitable fact of organizational life that some individuals can boast a greater capacity to influence people successfully than others. Within organizations, the distribution of power is typically unequal. Why is this so? What sources of power do people have at their disposal? We will consider several specific bases of power falling into two major categories—that which comes with one's office and that which comes from oneself as an individual.

Position Power: Influence That Comes with the Office

A great deal of the power people have in organizations comes from the posts they hold. In other words, they are able to influence others because of the formal power associated with their jobs. This is known as **position power**. For example, there are certain powers that the president of the United States has simply because he or she holds office (e.g., signing bills into law, making treaties, etc.). These formal powers remain vested in the position and are available to anyone who holds that position. When the president's term is up, these powers transfer to the new officeholder. There are four bases of position power: *legitimate power*, *reward power*, *coercive power*, and *information power*.

position power Power based on one's formal position in an organization.

legitimate power Power based on the recognition and acceptance of one's authority.

Legitimate power. The power that people have because others recognize and accept their authority is known as **legitimate power**. As an example, students recognize that their instructors have the authority to make class policies and to determine grades, giving them legitimate power over the class. If someone were to challenge the teacher's decision, saying, "Who are you to do that?" the answer might be, "I'm the instructor, that's who." This exchange would clarify the legitimacy of the officeholder's behavior. However, it is important to note that legitimate power covers a relatively narrow range of influence and that it may be inappropriate to overstep these bounds. For example, whereas a boss may require her secretary to type and fax a company document using her legitimate power to do so, it would be an abuse of power to ask that

How Strong Is Peer Influence?
Comparing the United States and Denmark

What percentage of your peers smoke? What percentage drink alcohol? The way you will answer these questions is likely to depend on whether you smoke or drink yourself. That is, when it comes to estimating the prevalence of others' behavior, our judgments tend to be self-enhancing. In fact, research has shown that smokers and drinkers tend to overestimate the percentage of their peers who smoke and drink by greater margins than nonsmokers and nondrinkers. By so doing, smokers and drinkers appear to be convincing themselves that these seemingly unwise activities are not really as inappropriate as they are made out to be. This general tendency for people to believe that certain actions are more common than they really are is known as the **false-consensus effect**. The idea is simple: To the extent that we believe that "everybody's doing it," it becomes easier to justify doing that same thing ourselves, if we are inclined to do so, even if we can articulate why we should not be engaging in these behaviors.

This phenomenon has been applied to understanding the intense peer pressure that adolescents face to drink and smoke. Although young people frequently are taught that it is injurious to their health to use alcohol and tobacco, they often do so anyway in large part because they believe that the majority of their friends are doing so.[10] As a result, they feel pressured socially into drinking and smoking to go along with their peers. If this is in fact the mechanism through which young people experience peer pressure, then it follows that the false-consensus effect would be stronger in those cultures, such as the United States, in which people are highly competitive and have strong orientations toward achieving individual success than in cultures, such as Denmark, in which people are less competitive and have weaker orientations toward achieving individual success (recall our discussion of Hofstede's typology in Chapter 2). After all, to the extent that people strive for success, they find it necessary to compare themselves to others so they can gauge how well they are

doing. And, the more they consider others' behaviors, the more likely they will be to use these comparisons as the basis for judging their own behavior. Thus, whereas Americans may be inclined to make self-enhancing comparisons to their peers, making them prone to the false-consensus effect, Danes would be less inclined to compare themselves to others and would therefore be less likely to be subjected to the false-consensus effect.

This reasoning was tested in a recent study by Gibbons and his associates.[11] These researchers administered a large questionnaire to a group of American adolescents (ages 13–15) and a like group of Danish adolescents. They were asked questions about their interest in social comparison and achieving success, and also, to estimate the percentages of adolescents who smoke and drink alcohol. The findings supported this logic. American youngsters expressed greater interest in social comparison and greater interest in achieving success than their Danish counterparts. Americans also exhibited stronger false-consensus effects. That is, the American sample overestimated the percentage of others their same age who smoked more so than the Danish sample. The same pattern also was found for drinking alcohol.

These findings suggest that the false-consensus effect is not a universal phenomenon. Instead, it is stronger in cultures, such as the United States, in which people are more attuned to others' evaluations. Thus, although peer pressure may exert powerful effects on behavior, it is important to caution that these effects may not be equally strong throughout the world. As such, it is a likely possibility that the use of various social influence tactics are not as universal in nature as they are assumed to be. Unfortunately, very little is known about the generalizability of our understanding of the way people use social influence. If we are to learn any one lesson from the Gibbons study, it is surely that to understand social influence processes fully we must take into account the cultural contexts within which they operate.

---

false-consensus effect The general tendency for people to believe that certain actions are more common than they really are.

reward power The individual power base derived from an individual's capacity to administer valued rewards to others.

secretary to type her son's homework assignment. This is not to say that the secretary might not take on the task as a favor, but doing so would not be the direct result of the boss's formal authority. Legitimate power applies only to the range of behaviors that are recognized and accepted as appropriate by the parties and institution involved.

Reward power. Associated with holding certain jobs comes the power to control the rewards others receive—that is, **reward power**. Extending our teacher-student example, instructors have reward power over students insofar as they may reward them with high grades and glowing letters of recommendation. In the case of managers, the rewards available may be either tangible, such as raises and promotions, or intangible, such as praise and recognition. In both cases, access to these desired outcomes gives power to the individuals who control them.

Coercive power. By contrast, power also results from the capacity to control punishments—that is, **coercive power**. Although most managers do not like using the threat of punishments, it is a fact of organizational life that many people rely on coercive power. If any boss has ever directly told you, "Do what I say, or else," or even implied it, you are probably all too familiar with coercive power. Often, people have power simply because others know that they have the opportunity to punish them, even if the threat of doing so is not made explicit. For example, in the military, when your commanding officer asks you to do something, you may comply since that request can turn into an order, with severe consequences for not going along. In private organizations, threats of demotions, suspensions without pay, and assignments to undesirable duties may enhance the coercive power of many managers.

Information power. The fourth source of power available to people by virtue of their positions is based on the data and other knowledge—known as **information power**. Traditionally, people in top positions have available to them unique sources of information that are not available to others (e.g., knowledge of company performance, market trends, and so on). As they say, "Knowledge is power," and such information greatly contributes to the power of people in many jobs. Although information power still exists, it is becoming a less potent source of influence in many of today's organizations. The reason is that technology has made it possible for more information to be available to more people than ever before. As a result, information need no longer be the unique property of a few people holding special positions.

Personal Power: Influence That Comes from the Individual

Thus far, all the sources of influence we've discussed have been based on an individual's position in an organization. However, this is not the only way people are able to influence others (for a review, see Figure 12-3). There's also power derived from an individual's own unique qualities or characteristics. This is known as **personal power**. There are four sources of personal power: *rational persuasion, expert power, referent power,* and *charisma.*

Rational persuasion. In the early 1990s Apple Computer's former chairman John Scully didn't like what he saw when he looked into the future. Apple was doing well, but computer sales threatened to flatten out in the years ahead. The future of the company, he envisioned, involved applying Apple's user-friendly digital technology in new areas. Integrating telephones, computers, televisions, and entertainment systems was the key. So, Scully's first task was to get Apple's then-Chief Operating Officer Michael H. Spindler and the board of directors to share his dream. After drawing on all his knowledge of the computer business and carefully studying what needed to be done to make the dream a reality, Scully thoroughly explained his plan for changing Apple from a single-product company with a straightforward distribution system to a multiproduct, multibusiness conglomerate. Spindler and the board were convinced, and Apple's new strategy was launched.

Scully used a very popular technique of social influence known as **rational persuasion**. This approach relies on logical arguments and factual evidence to convince others that a certain idea is acceptable. Rational persuasion is highly effective when the parties involved are intelligent enough to make their cases strongly and to understand them clearly. Given that it is based on clear logic, good evidence, and the desire to help the company, rational per

---

Keep in mind (based on our discussion of the concepts of reinforcement in Chapter 2 and valence in Chapter 5) that rewards may enhance one's power only to the extent that they are actually desired by the recipients.

coercive power The individual power base derived from the capacity to administer punishment to others.

As cautioned in Chapter 3, punishments may have undesirable side effects if they are overly harsh or inconsistently administered.

information power The extent to which one has access to information that makes him or her especially influential.

personal power The power that one derives because of his or her individual qualities or characteristics.

rational persuasion Using logical arguments and factual evidence to convince others that an idea is acceptable.

Individual power consists of two major types—position power *(stemming from one's formal organizational role)* and personal power *(stemming from one's personal characteristics)*. Four specific types of power may be identified in each category.

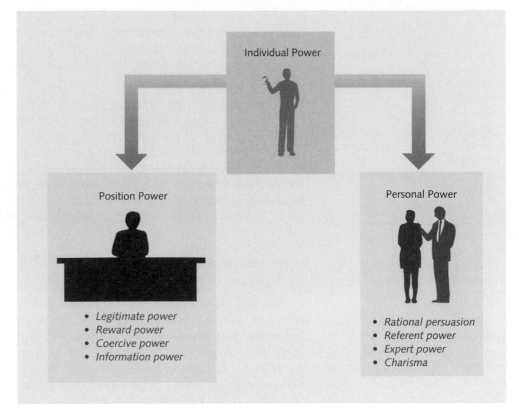

Individual Power

Position Power
- *Legitimate power*
- *Reward power*
- *Coercive power*
- *Information power*

Personal Power
- *Rational persuasion*
- *Referent power*
- *Expert power*
- *Charisma*

suasion tends to be highly effective. (Although, in retrospect, some critics have blamed Apple's recent financial problems on poor decisions by Apple executives, these same officials certainly cannot be faulted for presenting their ideas in the rational manner they did.[12]) Not surprisingly, rational persuasion is among the most popular types of influence used in organizations.

Expert power. In addition to rational persuasion, it's clear that Scully's ideas were accepted because of the considerable expertise he had in the business. Thus, it can be said that he had **expert power**—that is, power based on superior knowledge of a certain field. Likewise, a coach has power over athletes to the extent that he or she is recognized by them as knowing what is best. Once experts have proven themselves, their power over others can be considerable. After all, people will respect and want to follow those in the know.

Should a supervisor's expertise be shown to be lacking, any power he or she may have based on that expertise is threatened. Insofar as no one is expected to be an expert on everything, this is not necessarily problematic. The less-than-expert person can simply admit his or her shortcomings and seek guidance from others. Where problems develop, however, is if someone in a position of power has not yet developed a level of expertise that is acknowledged and respected by lower-ranking persons (especially when these individuals believe they are more expert). Those who have not demonstrated their expertise clearly lack this important source of power. However, people whose expertise is highly regarded are among the most powerful people in organizations.

Referent power. As you surely know, it is not only expertise but personal qualities that form the basis of our admiration for others in organizations. Individuals who are liked and respected by others can get them to alter their actions, a type of influence known as **referent power**. Senior managers who possess desirable qualities and good reputations may find that they have referent power over younger managers who identify with them and wish to emulate them.

expert power The individual power base derived from an individual's recognized superior skills and abilities in a certain area.

referent power The individual power base derived from the degree to which one is liked and admired by others.

Charisma. Some people are liked so much by others that they are said to
have the quality of **charisma**—an engaging and magnetic personality. There's
no ignoring the fact that some people become highly influential because of
their highly charismatic ways. What makes such individuals so influential?
There appear to be several factors involved. First, highly charismatic people
have definite visions of the future of their organizations and how to get there.
Mary Kay Ash, the founder of Mary Kay Cosmetics, is widely regarded to be
such a visionary. Second, people with charisma tend to be excellent communicators. They tend to rely on colorful language and exciting metaphors to ex-
cite the crowd. They also supplement their words with emotionally expressive
and animated gestures. The president of Coca-Cola has been known to do this.
Third, charismatic individuals inspire trust. Their integrity is never challenged,
and is a source of their strength. Former U.S. president John F. Kennedy has
been so described by many historians. Fourth, people with charisma make others feel good about themselves. They are receptive to others' feelings and acknowledge them readily. "Congratulations on a job well done" is a phrase that
may flow freely from a charismatic individual.

This use of the term charisma *is
similar to the way it will be used to
refer to a characteristic of a leader
in Chapter 13.*

To summarize, people may influence others by virtue of both the jobs they
have, and their individual characteristics. For a summary of the factors within
each category, refer to Figure 12-3. To see how scientists measure different types
of social influence, and to make some preliminary judgments about the types
of influence your own supervisor uses, see the EXPERIENCING ORGANIZATIONAL BE-
HAVIOR section on p. 429.

Power: How Is It Used?

As you might imagine, there is widespread overlap in the ways people use
power. Only sometimes is a single source of power used; indeed, it is recognized that the various power bases are closely related to each other.[13] For example, the more someone uses coercive power, the less that person is liked,
and hence, the lower his or her referent power tends to be. Similarly, managers who have expert power are also likely to have legitimate power because
their directing others within the field of expertise is accepted. In addition, the
higher someone's organizational position, the more legitimate power that person has, which in turn is usually accompanied by greater opportunities to use
reward and coercion.[14] Clearly, then, the various bases of power should not
be thought of as completely separate and distinct from each other. They are
often used together in varying combinations (see Figure 12-4).

What bases of power do people prefer to use? Although the answer to this
question is quite complex, research has shown that people prefer using expert
power most and coercive power least often.[15] These findings are limited to the
power bases we've identified thus far. However, when we broaden the question and ask people to report exactly sources of power they have on their jobs,

■ Figure 12-4
*What Bases of Power Are Being
Used Here?*
*People frequently rely on several bases
of social power. This military instructor
is likely to have legitimate power (by
virtue of his rank) and expert power
(by virtue of his specialized knowledge),
as well as several other sources of
power at his disposal.*

a fascinating picture emerges. Figure 12-5 depicts the results of a survey in which 216 CEOs of American corporations were asked to rank order the importance of a series of specific sources of power.[16] The figures indicate the percentage of executives who included that source of power among their top three choices. These findings indicate not only that top executives rely on a broad range of powers, but also that they base these powers on support from people located in a host of other places throughout their organizations. Interestingly, when asked about how much power they currently had compared to ten years ago, only 19 percent said they now had more power. Thirty-six percent indicated that they had the same amount of power, and the largest group, 42 percent, indicated that they had less power.

Although many different forms of power tend to be used to influence subordinates, research has shown that expert power is the preferred form used to influence peers and superiors.[17] After all, it is almost always appropriate to try to get others to go along with you if you justify your attempt on the basis of your expertise. In contrast, coercive tactics tend to be frowned on in general and are especially inappropriate when one is attempting to influence a higher-ranking person.[18] Influencing superiors is tricky because of the *counterpower* they have. When attempting to influence another who is believed to have no power at his or her disposal, one doesn't have to worry about fear of retaliation. When dealing with an individual with considerably greater power, however, one can do little other than simply comply with that more powerful person.

However, the situation is complicated by the fact that one party may have higher power on one dimension, and another party may have higher power on another dimension. Consider, for example, the case of some secretaries who have acquired power because they have been with their companies for many years. They know the ropes and can get things done for you if they want, or they can get you hopelessly bogged down in red tape. Their expert knowledge

■ **Figure 12-5**
American CEOs: What Are Their Power Bases
A survey of more than 200 American CEOs revealed that they obtained their power primarily by cultivating the support of others at different levels throughout the organization.

(**Source:** Based on data appearing in Stewart, 1989; see Note 16.)

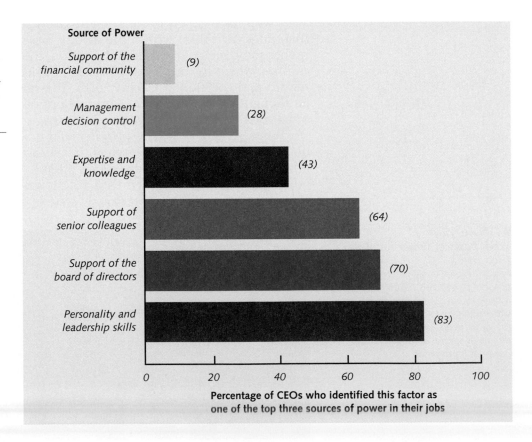

THE PRESCRIPTION FOR A CHRONIC POWER ABUSER

The problem with power is that it sometimes goes to one's head, leading to ethically dubious behavior. And when it does, the impact on an organization can be devastating. This was the case with Robert Schoellhorn, the former CEO of Abbott Labs.[19] After guiding the large pharmaceutical company through some of its best years in the early 1980s, Schoellhorn enjoyed the recognition he received.

By the mid-1980s, however, Schoellhorn became "drunk with power." He surrounded himself with subordinates who would do whatever he wanted and would never challenge him. Anyone who dared not go along with Schoellhorn was out—including three company presidents in eight years. Schoellhorn spent millions of dollars in company funds on not one, but two corporate

jets—one each to usher around himself and his new wife (and former secretary). All that was on his mind was to maintain his image as a leader, even if it meant making short-sighted decisions. When he cut research and development funds to boost short-term corporate earnings, the company went into a tailspin.

By March 1990 the board of directors had had enough and fired Schoellhorn, just months before he was due to retire. However, flexing his muscles to the end, Schoellhorn did not take the ouster lying down. In a rare move for a top executive, he sued his former employer. Eventually he received a $5.2 million settlement—a lot of money, but an amount the board of directors considered a small price to pay to rid itself of its power-hungry chief executive.[20]

gives them a great sense of power over others. Although they may lack the legitimate power of their executive bosses, secretaries' expertise can be a valuable source of counterpower over those with more formal powers.

Empowerment: The Shifting Bases of Power in Today's Organizations

A phenomenon is occurring in a growing number of today's organizations: Power is shifting out of the offices of managers and into the hands of employees themselves. Many of today's workers are not being "managed" in the traditional, authoritarian styles that have been used by managers of generations past. Instead, power is often shifted down the ladder to a team of workers allowed to make decisions themselves. This is the idea of **empowerment**—the passing of responsibility and authority from managers to employees. For many years workers have used the excuse, "I did it because my manager told me to." However, as employees become empowered in the workplace, this explanation is no longer likely to be heard. It is important to note that empowerment involves more than simply giving employees leeway in determining how to carry out a leader's stated mission. Beyond autonomy, it also involves sharing the appropriate information and knowledge that allows employees to do what is needed to help the organization meet its goals.

To underscore this point: The key to empowering people successfully is the sharing of expert information (as opposed to the hoarding of information that has been popular in the past). Today's managers are likely to be more open than their predecessors. As such, they are likely to empower employees by widely disseminating information, allowing better decisions to be made. For example, at Next Computer, CEO Steven Jobs (best known as one of the co-founders of Apple Computer) strongly believes that employees must be privy to vital information about sales and profits and such for them to appreciate the work they do. In fact, Jobs goes so far as to make available a list of each employee's pay. When questions arise as to why someone else may be getting paid more, Jobs uses that occasion to explain what he sees as the differences

empowerment The passing of responsibility and authority from managers to employees.

Naturally, empowerment involves the use of empowered decision making described in Chapter 9.

between their contributions. Such information, he believes, helps cultivate the impression that company management is being straight with them and has nothing to hide—in other words, that they're not abusing their power.

As you might imagine, empowerment may be seen as not just a simple yes-or-no option, but a matter of degree.[21] At one end of the scale are companies, such as the traditional assembly lines, in which workers have virtually no power to determine how to do their jobs. At the opposite end are jobs in which employees have complete control over what they do and how they do it. We see this at companies using self-managed work teams, as described in Chapter 8 (see Figure 12-6). For example, at Chapparel Steel, managers are free to hire, train, and use new employees however they think best.[22] At W. L. Gore & Associates (manufacturer of Gore-tex, a synthetic material used in camping equipment), the empowerment philosophy is so strongly entrenched that employees work without any fixed, assigned sets of responsibilities.[23] Between these two extremes are companies whose employees have some degree of responsibility for their work and have a voice in important decisions, but are not completely free to work however they see fit. A growing number of companies fall into this category, including the General Motors Saturn plant in Spring Hill, Tennessee.[24]

When employees are empowered, their supervisors are less likely to be "bosses" who push people around (using coercive power) and more likely to serve as teachers, or "facilitators" who guide their teams by using their knowledge and experience (i.e., their expert power). In the words of John Ring, the director of Okidata (the Tokyo-based maker of printers and other office tools), "To influence people you have to prove you're right."[25]

Whereas traditional managers usually told people what to do and how and when to do it, supervisors of empowered workers are more inclined to ask questions to get people to solve problems and make decisions on their own. Consider, for example, the job of Dee Zalentatis, the information group manager at a Hudson, Massachusetts, division of America's largest printer, R. R. Donnelley & Sons. Since her division began using self-managed teams, Zalentatis found that her job has become one of teaching, cajoling, and comforting 40 others until they feel confident enough to handle many of her responsibilities. She sees her job now as being more of an internal consultant than a traditional manager.

As described in Chapter 8, this is typical of the behaviors of people supervising self-directed teams.

If the practices we've been describing here don't square with your experiences, don't feel bad. The empowered employee is still in the minority in the vast majority of today's organizations—but, experts predict a change in that direction is coming, and fast. According to management consultant James Champey, "We won't see them in great numbers for another five to ten years. But corporate America is definitely moving in that direction."[26] If this prognostication is correct, as we believe it is, we can look forward to significant changes in the way people will use power in organizations.

■ **Figure 12-6**
Empowerment: One Success Story
This team at the Davidson Interiors division of Textron created "Flexible Bright," a coating used in the grilles of the Lincoln Mark VIII. This successful product, which looks like chrome, but which won't crack, chip, or rust, was developed by a team based in Dover, New Hampshire, that was empowered to do the variety of tasks needed to bring the product to reality.

Group or Subunit Power: Structural Determinants

Thus far, this chapter has examined the uses of power by individuals. However, in organizations, it is not only people acting alone, but also groups, who wield power.[27] Organizations are frequently divided into subunits given responsibility for different functions such as finance, human resource management, marketing, and research and development. The formal departments devoted to these various organizational activities often must direct the activities of other groups, requiring them to have power. What are the sources of such power? By what means do formal organizational groups successfully control the actions of other groups? Two theoretical models have been proposed to answer these questions—the *resource-dependency model* and the *strategic contingencies model*. Our review of these approaches will help identify the factors responsible for subunit power and describe how they operate.

The Resource-Dependency Model: Controlling Critical Resources

It is not difficult to think of an organization as a complex set of subunits that are constantly exchanging resources with each other. By this, we mean that formal organizational departments may be both giving to and receiving from other departments such valued commodities as money, personnel, equipment, supplies, and information. These critical resources are necessary for the successful operation of organizations.

Various subunits often depend on others for such resources. To illustrate this point, imagine a large organization that develops, produces, and sells its products. The Sales Department provides financial resources that enable the Research and Development Department to create new products. Of course, it cannot do so effectively without information from the Marketing Department about what consumers are interested in buying and how much they would be willing to pay. The Production Department has to do its part by manufacturing the goods on time, but only if the Purchasing Department can supply the needed raw materials—and at a price the Finance Department accepts as permitting the company to turn a profit.

It is easy to see how the various organizational subunits are involved in a complex set of interrelationships with others. To the extent that one subunit controls the resources on which another subunit depends, it may be said to have power over it. After all, controlling resources allows groups to influence the actions of other groups successfully. Subunits that control more resources than others may be considered more powerful in the organization. Indeed, such imbalances, or *asymmetries*, in the pattern of resource dependencies occur normally in organizations. The more one group depends on another for needed resources, the less power it has (see Figure 12-7).

resource-dependency model
The view according to which power resides within subunits that are able to control the greatest share of valued organizational resources.

In proposing their **resource-dependency model**, Pfeffer and Salancik note that a subunit's power is based on the degree to which it controls the resources required by other subunits.[28] Thus, although all subunits may contribute something to an organization, the most powerful ones are those that contribute the most important resources. Controlling the resources other departments need puts a subunit in a better position to bargain for the resources it requires. To illustrate this point, let's consider an important study by Salancik and Pfeffer.[29] Within a university, the various academic departments may be very unequal with respect to the power they possess. For example, some may have more students, be more prestigious in their national reputation, receive greater grant support, and have more representatives on important university committees than others. As such, they would be expected to have greater control over valued resources. This was found to be the case within the large state university studied by Salancik and Pfeffer. The more powerful departments proved to be

The resource-dependency model *of or-ganizational power explains that sub-units acquire power when they control critical resources needed by other sub-units. In this example, the accounting department would be considered more powerful than either the production de-partment or the marketing department.*

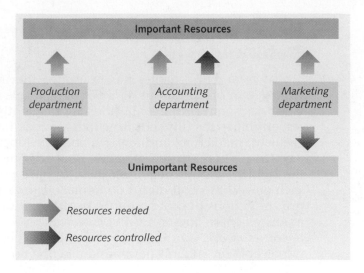

those that were most successful in gaining scarce and valued resources from the university (e.g., funds for graduate student fellowships, faculty research grants, and summer faculty fellowships). As a result, they became even more power-ful, suggesting that within organizations, the rich subunits get richer.

A question that follows from this conclusion is: How do various organiza-tional subunits come to be more powerful to begin with? That is, why might certain departments come to control the most resources when an organization is newly formed? Insight into this question is provided by Boeker's fascinat-ing study of the semiconductor industry in California.[30] Boeker used personal interviews, market research data, and archival records as the main sources of data for this investigation. Results indicated that two main factors accounted for how much power an organizational subunit had: (1) the period within which the company was founded, and (2) the background of the entrepreneur starting the company. For example, because research and development func-tions were critical among the earliest semiconductor firms (founded in 1958–1966, when semiconductors were new), this department had the most power among the oldest firms. Hence, the importance of the area of corporate activity at the time the company began dictated the relative power of that area years later (in 1985, when the study was done). It also was found that the most powerful organizational subunits tended to be those that represented the founder's area of expertise (see Figure 12-8). Thus, for example, the Marketing and Sales departments of companies founded by experts in marketing and sales tended to have the greatest amounts of power. This research provides an im-portant missing link in our understanding of the attainment of subunit power within organizations.

The resource-dependency model suggests that a key determinant of sub-unit power is the control of valued resources. However, as we will now illus-trate, it is not only control over resources that dictates organizational power, but also control over the activities of other subunits.

The Strategic Contingencies Model: Power through Dependence

The use of the contingency ap-proach was described in Chapter 1 as one of the major orientations of the modern field of OB. As its name implies, the strategic contin-gencies *model utilizes this ap-proach.*

The Accounting Department of a company might be expected to have re-sponsibility over the approval or disapproval of funds requested by various de-partments. If it does, its actions greatly affect the activities of other units, who depend on its decisions—that is, other departments' operations are *contingent* on what the Accounting Department does. To the extent that a department is able to control the relative power of various organizational subunits by virtue of its actions, it is said to have control over *strategic contingencies*. For exam-ple, if the Accounting Department consistently approved the budget requests

■ **Figure 12-8**
Company Founders: Important Influences on Subunit Power
Those functional areas within which company founders specialize tend to be the ones that have the most power. For example, Henry Ford, the founder of the Ford Motor Company (pictured at the top), was a specialist in manufacturing technology, which is still a powerful department at Ford. William Gates, the founder of Microsoft (pictured below, and described in this chapter's PREVIEW CASE*) is a specialist in developing computer software, a powerful department at Microsoft.*

strategic contingencies model A view explaining power in terms of a subunit's capacity to control the activities of other subunits. A subunit's power is enhanced when (1) it can reduce the level of uncertainty experienced by other subunits, (2) it occupies a central position in the organization, and (3) its activities are highly indispensable to the organization.

of the Production Department but rejected the budget requests of the Marketing Department, it would be making the Production Department more powerful.

Where do the strategic contingencies lie within organizations? In a classic study Lawrence and Lorsch found out that power was distributed in different departments in different industries.[31] They found that within successful firms, the strategic contingencies were controlled by the departments that were most important for organizational success. For example, within the food processing industry, where it was critical for new products to be developed and sold, successful firms had strategic contingencies controlled by the Sales and Research departments. In the container manufacturing field, where the timely delivery of high-quality goods is a critical determinant of organizational success, successful firms placed most of the decision-making power in the Sales and Production departments. Thus, successful firms focused the control over strategic contingencies within the subunits most responsible for their organization's success.

What factors give subunits control over strategic contingencies? The **strategic contingencies model** of Hickson and his associates suggests several key considerations.[32] Refer to the summary of these factors in Figure 12-9.

■ Figure 12-9
Strategic Contingencies Model:
Identifying Sources of Subunit
Power
The strategic contingencies model
explains intraorganizational power in
terms of the capacity of some subunits
to control the actions of others. Subunit
power may be enhanced by the factors
shown here.

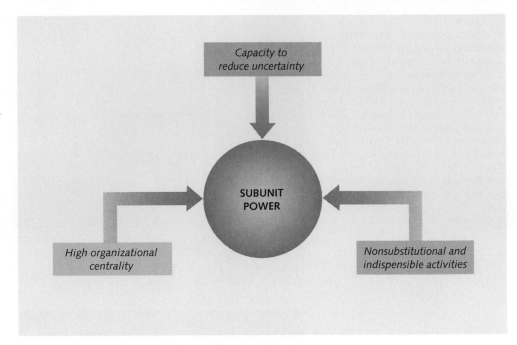

Power may be enhanced by subunits that can help reduce the levels of uncertainty faced by others. Any department that can shed light on the uncertain situations organizations may face (e.g., those regarding future markets, government regulation, availability of needed supplies, financial security) can be expected to wield the most organizational power. Accordingly, the balance of power within organizations may be expected to change as organizational conditions change. Consider, for example, changes that have taken place over the years in public utility companies. Studying the strategic contingencies in such organizations, Miles noted that a shift has occurred.[33] When public utilities first began, the engineers tended to wield the most power. But now that these companies have matured and face problems of litigation and governmental regulation (particularly over nuclear power), the power has shifted to lawyers. A similar shift toward the power of the Legal Department has occurred in recent years in the area of human resource management, where a complex set of laws and governmental regulations have created a great deal of uncertainty for organizations. Powerful subunits are those that can help reduce organizational uncertainty.

That more powerful subunits are ones that have *a high degree of centrality in the organization* also has been established. Some organizational subunits perform functions that are more central, and others, more peripheral. For example, some departments—such as Accounting—may have to be consulted by most others before any action can be taken, giving them a central position in their organizations. Centrality is also high when a unit's duties have an immediate effect on an organization. For example, the effects would be much more dramatic on an auto manufacturer if the production lines stopped than if market research activities ceased. The central connection of some departments to organizational success dictates the power they wield.

Third, a subunit controls power when its *activities are nonsubstitutable and indispensable.* If any group can perform a certain function, subunits responsible for controlling that function may not be particularly powerful. In a hospital, for example, personnel on surgical teams are certainly more indispensable than personnel in the maintenance department because fewer individuals have the skills needed to perform their unit's duties. Because an organization can easily replace some employees with others either within or outside it, subunits composed of individuals who are most easily replaced tend to wield very little organizational power.

The strategic contingencies model has been tested and supported in organizational studies.[34] For example, one investigation conducted in several companies found that a subunit's power within an organization was higher when it could reduce uncertainty, occupied a central place in the work flow, and performed functions that other subunits could not perform.[35] The strategic contingencies model should be considered a valuable source of information about the factors that influence the power of subunits within organizations.

Organizational Politics: Power in Action

Our discussion of power focused on the potential to influence others successfully. When this potential is realized, put into action to accomplish desired goals, we are no longer talking about power, but *politics*.[36] It is quite easy to imagine situations in which someone does something to accomplish his or her own goals, which do not necessarily agree with the goals of the organization. This is what *organizational politics* is all about—actions not officially approved by an organization taken to influence others to meet one's personal goals.[37]

If you think we're describing something that is a bit selfish and appears to be an abuse of organizational power, you are correct. Organizational politics does involve placing one's self-interests above the interests of the organization. Indeed, this element of using power to foster one's own interests distinguishes organizational politics from uses of power that are approved and accepted by organizations.[38] Not surprisingly, business people often look down upon those who engage in organizational politics. For example, as the outspoken billionaire and sometime presidential candidate H. Ross Perot put it, "I don't want any corporate politicians, any upwardly mobile corporate gypsies, I don't want some guy that wants to move ahead at the expense of others."[39]

Political Tactics: What Forms Does It Take?

To understand organizational politics, one must recognize the various forms political behavior can take in organizations. In other words, what are the techniques of organizational politics? Six techniques are used most often.[40]

Controlling access to information. Information is the lifeblood of organizations. Therefore, controlling who knows and doesn't know certain things is one of the most important ways to exercise power in organizations. Although outright lying and falsifying information may be used only rarely in organizations (in part because of the consequences of getting caught), there are other ways of controlling information to enhance one's organizational position. For example, you might (1) withhold information that makes you look bad (e.g., negative sales information), (2) avoid contact with those who may ask for information you would prefer not to disclose, (3) be very selective in the information you disclose, or (4) overwhelm others with information that may not be completely relevant. These are all ways to control the nature and degree of information people have at their disposal. Such information control can be critical.

As we noted in Chapter 10, information is the key to successful decision making in organizations.

An analysis of the organizational restructuring of AT&T's Phone Stores revealed that control was transferred through the effective manipulation, distortion, and creation of information.[41] A vice president's secret plan to feed incomplete and inaccurate information to the CEO was responsible for that vice president's winning control over the stores.

Cultivating a favorable impression. People interested in enhancing their organizational control commonly engage in some degree of image building— an attempt to enhance the goodness of their impressions on others. Such efforts may take many forms, such as (1) "dressing for success," (2) associating oneself with the successful accomplishments of others (or, in extreme cases, taking credit for others' successes), or (3) simply drawing attention to one's own successes and positive characteristics.[42]

Recall from Chapter 3 that impression management involves the processes of social perception and attribution.

With this in mind, Ferris and King identified those individuals who worked hard to fit into their organizations as *organizational chameleons*.[43] Such individuals figure out what behaviors they believe are considered generally appropriate in their organization and then go out of their way to make sure that others are aware that they behaved in such a manner. These are all ways of developing the "right image" to enhance one's individual power in organizations.

Developing a base of support.

To influence people successfully it is often useful to gain the support of others within the organization. Managers may, for example, lobby for their ideas before they officially present them at meetings, ensuring that others are committed to them in advance and thereby avoiding the embarrassment of public rejection. They also may "scatter IOUs" throughout the organization by doing favors for others who may feel obligated to repay them in the form of supporting their ideas. The norm of *reciprocity* is very strong in organizations, as evidenced by the popular phrases, "You scratch my back, and I'll scratch yours" and "One good turn deserves another." After all, when someone does a favor for you, you may say, "I owe you one," suggesting that you are aware of the obligation to reciprocate that favor. "Calling in" favors is a well-established and widely used mechanism for developing organizational power.

Blaming and attacking others.

One of the most popularly used tactics of organizational politics involves blaming and attacking others when bad things happen. A commonly used political tactic is finding a *scapegoat*, someone who could take the blame for some failure or wrongdoing. A supervisor, for example, may explain that the failure of a sales plan she designed was based on the serious mistakes of one of her subordinates—even if this is not entirely true. Explaining that "it's his fault," that is, making another "take the fall" for an undesirable event, gets the real culprit "off the hook" for it.

Finding a scapegoat can allow the politically astute individual to avoid (or at least minimize) association with the negative situation. For example, research has found that when corporate performance drops, powerful chief executives often resort to placing the blame onto a lower-ranking individual, protecting themselves from getting fired while their subordinate gets the ax.[44]

Aligning oneself with more powerful others.

One of the most direct ways to gain power is by connecting oneself with more powerful others. There are several ways to accomplish this. For example, a lower-power person may become more powerful if she has a very powerful mentor, a more powerful and better-established person who can look out for and protect her interests. As another example, people may also agree in advance to form *coalitions*—groups that band together to achieve some common goal (e.g., overthrowing a current corporate CEO).[45] Research has shown that the banding together of relatively powerless groups is one of the most effective ways they have to gain organizational power.[46] Two relatively powerless individuals or groups may become stronger if they agree to act together, forming a coalition. People may also align themselves with more powerful others by giving them "positive strokes" in the hope of getting more powerful people to like them and help them, a process known as *ingratiation*.[47] Agreeing with someone more powerful may be an effective way of getting that person to consider you an ally. Such an alliance, of course, may prove indispensable when you are looking for support within an organization. To summarize, having a powerful mentor, forming coalitions, and using ingratiation are all potentially effective ways of gaining power by aligning oneself with others.

In Chapter 7 we fully discuss the role of mentorship as a process facilitating career development.

Playing political games.

One expert in the field of organizational power and politics, Henry Mintzberg, has suggested that political behavior is a collection of games going on in a multiring circus.[48] His idea is that many people or groups may be trying to influence many other people or groups simultaneously, as in playing a game. What, then, are the political games that unfold in organizations? Mintzberg has identified four major categories of political games. As we describe them, refer to our summary in Table 12-1.

- AUTHORITY GAMES. Some games, known as *insurgency games*, are played to resist authority. Others, known as *counterinsurgency games*, are played to counter such resistance to authority. Insurgency can take forms ranging from quite mild (such as intentionally not doing what is asked) to very severe (such as organizing workers to mutiny or sabotage their workplaces).[49] Companies may try to fight back with counterinsurgency moves. One way they may do so is by invoking stricter authority and control over subordinates. Often unproductive for both sides, such games frequently give way to the more adaptive techniques of bargaining and negotiation.

- POWER BASE GAMES. These games are played to enhance the degree and breadth of one's organizational power. For example, the *sponsorship game* is played with superiors. It involves attaching oneself to a rising or established star in return for a piece of the action. A relatively unpowerful subordinate, for example, may agree to help a more established person (such as his boss) by loyally supporting him in exchange for getting advice and information from him, as well as some of his power and prestige. Both benefit as a result. Similar games may be played among peers, such as the *alliance game*. Here, workers at the same level agree in advance to support each other mutually, gaining strength by increasing their joint size and power. One of the riskiest power base games is known as *empire building*. In this game, an individual or group attempts to become more powerful by gaining responsibility for more and more important organizational decisions. Indeed, a subunit may increase its power by attempting to gain control over budgets, space, equipment, or any other scarce and desired organizational resource.

- RIVALRY GAMES. Some political games are designed to weaken one's opponents. For example, in the *line versus staff game* managers on the "line," who are responsible for the operation of an organizational unit, clash

■ TABLE 12-1   POLITICAL GAMES: A SUMMARY OF SOME EXAMPLES

Many political games are played in organizations, each involving different individuals playing for different political goals.

Game	Typical Major Players	Purpose
Authority Games		
Insurgency game	Lower-level managers	To resist former authority
Counterinsurgency game	Upper-level managers	To counter resistance to formal authority
Power Base Games		
Sponsorship game	Any subordinate employee	To enhance base of power with superiors
Alliance game	Line managers	To enhance base of power with peers
Empire building	Line managers	To enhance base of power with subordinates
Rivalry Games		
Line versus staff game	Line managers and staff personnel	To defeat each other in the quest for power
Rival camps game	Any groups at the same level	To defeat each other in the quest for power
Change Games		
Whistle-blowing game	Lower-level managers	To correct organizational wrongdoings
Young Turks game	Upper-level managers	To seize control over the organization

SOURCE: Adapted from Mintzberg, 1983: see Note 3.

■ Figure 12-11
Guidelines for Determining Ethical Action
Although assessing the ethicality of a behavior is a complex matter, answers to the three questions shown here can provide a good indication. This flow-chart shows the path that must be taken to achieve ethical action.

(**Source:** Based on suggestions by Velasquez, Moberg, & Cavanaugh, 1983; see Note 66.)

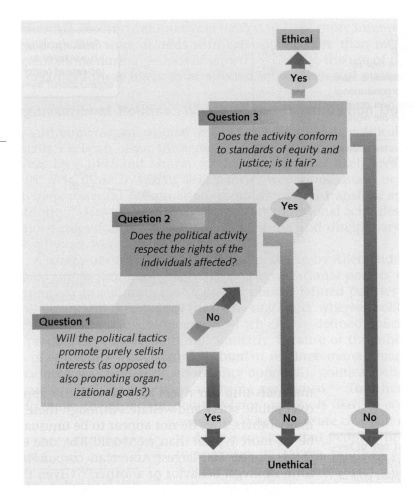

cause of this that society often entrusts such decisions to high courts charged with the responsibility for considering both individual rights and the rights and benefits of the community at large.

Velasquez and his associates also identified a third consideration in assessing the ethics of political action: Does the activity conform to standards of equity and justice; is it fair? Any political behavior that unfairly benefits one party over another may be considered unethical. Paying one person more than another similarly qualified person is one example. Standards regarding the fair treatment of individuals are often unclear. Not surprisingly, more powerful individuals often use their power to convince others (and themselves) that they are taking action in the name of justice. That is, they seek to implement seemingly fair rules that benefit themselves at the expense of others.[67] This, of course, represents an abuse of power.

However, we must sometimes consider instances in which violating standards of justice may be considered appropriate. For example, it has been found that managers may sometimes give poorly performing employees higher pay than they deserve in the hope of stimulating them to work at higher levels.[68] Although the principle of equity is violated in this case (people should be paid in proportion to their job contributions), the manager may argue that the employee and the organization benefit as a result. Of course, the result may be considered unfair to the other individuals who are not so generously treated. Obviously, we will not be able to settle this complex issue here. Our point is that although ethical behavior involves adhering to standards of justice, there may be instances in which violations of these standards may be considered ethically acceptable.

As you can probably tell by now, most matters involving the resolution of moral and ethical issues are quite complex. Each time a political strategy is considered, its potential effects should be evaluated in terms of the questions outlined here. If the practice appears to be ethical based on these considerations, it may be acceptable in that situation. If ethical questions arise, however, alternative actions should be seriously considered. Unfortunately, many unethical political practices are followed in organizations despite their obvious violations of moral standards. We will now consider some of the underlying reasons for this.

More than 1,000 professionals in the field of human resources management were surveyed concerning their feelings about the ethics of various managerial practices.[69] Interestingly, among the ethical situations considered most serious were several practices that dealt with political activities reflecting an abuse of power. These included practices such as "making personnel decisions based on favoritism instead of job performance," and "basing differences in pay on friendship." In fact, these were the two most frequently cited types of unethical situations faced by human resource managers (with almost 31 percent of the sample indicating that each was among *the* most serious violations).

Another type of unethical political behavior (indicated as being most serious by over 23 percent of the sample) was "making arrangements with vendors or consulting agencies leading to personal gain." As shown in Figure 12-12, these actions are in addition to various other types of unethical behavior that represent bias, but that are not so clearly self-serving as to constitute political acts.

Given that so many critical ethics violations appear to be politically motivated, self-serving actions, it is not surprising that these happened to be the very behaviors that managers had the greatest difficulty addressing. In fact,

■ **Figure 12-12**
Political Antics Top the "Most Unethical List": Survey Results
Among the most widely reported sources of unethical behaviors noted in a survey of human resources managers are those dealing with political behaviors—actions that benefit oneself as opposed to the organization.

(**Source:** Based on data reported by the Commerce Clearing House, 1991; see Note 69.)

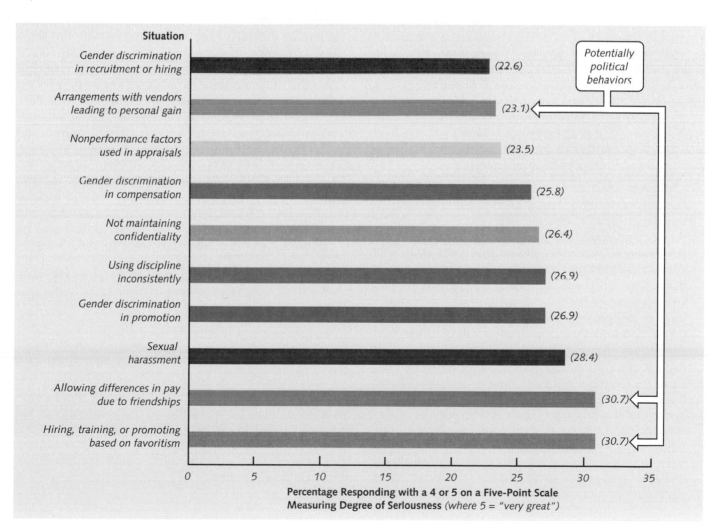

only about half of the managers surveyed reported having any success in minimizing a problem such as hiring based on favoritism. The very fact that such behaviors benefit oneself makes them difficult to eliminate. In contrast, it is easier to combat unethical behaviors based on insensitivity (e.g., lack of attention to privacy) because these serve no beneficial functions for the person doing the violating.

Managers tend to be relatively unaware of the political biases underlying their unethical actions, however. Instead, they attribute their actions to the attitudes and behaviors of senior management. Specifically, whereas only 10 percent of the participants attributed unethical behaviors to political pressures, 56 percent attributed unethical behaviors to the attitudes and behaviors of senior management. They blamed top management most frequently for instances

THE QUEST FOR QUALITY

Coping with Organizational Politics: Some Techniques

Given how fundamental the need for power appears to be among people, and how differences in power between employees are basic to organizations, it is safe to say that organizational politics is inevitable. This is not good news, however, as many of the effects of organizational politics are quite negative. Indeed, lowered corporate morale and diversion from key organizational goals (as employees pay closer attention to planning their attacks on others than to doing their jobs) are expected to result from political activity. The more organizational politics is recognized as going on, the less trust and more alienation people are likely to feel.[70] And this can only threaten the quality of organizational performance.[71]

In view of this, managers must consider ways to minimize the effects of political behavior. Although it may be impossible to abolish organizational politics, managers can do several things to limit its effects.

1. *Clarify job expectations.* You will recall that political behavior is nurtured by highly ambiguous conditions. To the extent that managers help reduce uncertainty, they can minimize the likelihood of political behavior. For example, managers should give very clear, well-defined work assignments. They should also clearly explain how work will be evaluated. Employees who know precisely what they are supposed to do and what level of performance is acceptable will find political games to assert their power unnecessary. Under such conditions, recognition will come from meeting job expectations, instead of from less acceptable avenues.

2. *Open the communication process.* People have difficulty trying to foster their own goals at the expense of organizational goals when the communication process is open to scrutiny by all. Compare, for example, a department manager who makes budget allocation decisions in a highly open fashion (announced to all) and one who makes the same decisions in secret. When decisions are not openly shared and communicated

to all, conditions are ideal for unscrupulous individuals to abuse their power. Decisions that can be monitored by all are unlikely to allow any one individual to gain excessive control over desired resources.

3. *Be a good role model.* It is well established that higher-level personnel set the standards by which lower-level employees operate. As a result, any manager who is openly political in her use of power is likely to create a climate in which her subordinates behave the same way. Engaging in dirty political tricks teaches subordinates not only that such tactics are appropriate, but also that they are the desired way of operating within the organization. Managers will certainly find it difficult to constrain the political actions of their subordinates unless they set a clear example of honest and reasonable treatment of others in their own behavior.

4. *Do not turn a blind eye to game players.* Suppose you see one of your subordinates attempting to gain power over another by taking credit for that individual's work. Immediately confront this individual and do not ignore what he did. If the person believes he can get away with it, he will try to do so. What's worse, if he suspects that you are aware of what he did but didn't do anything about it, you are indirectly reinforcing his unethical political behavior—showing him that he can get away with it.

In conclusion, it is important for practicing managers to realize that because power differences are basic to organizations, attempts to gain power advantages through political maneuvers are to be expected. However, a critical aspect of a manager's job is to redirect these political activities away from any threats to the integrity of the organization. Although expecting to eliminate dirty political tricks would be unrealistic, we believe the suggestions offered here provide some useful guidelines for minimizing their impact.

of unethical behavior, but they also recognized that top management of organizations tends to be committed to ethical conduct. Despite such commitment, company officials tend to overlook the capacity of human resources managers to help promote their company's ethical values. Too often, they tend to concentrate on using human resources managers for maintaining up-to-date legal information about personnel matters. But, ethics goes well beyond mere compliance with the law, and society expects companies to go well beyond the ethical minimums. For these reasons—not to mention the long-term success of companies themselves—it is essential for human resource officials to help institute policies that encourage basing personnel-related decisions on job performance instead of favoritism. In view of the potential problems that may arise in organizations in which the amount of political activity is high, it is necessary to consider ways of curbing such behavior. For a look at several ways of doing so, see the QUEST FOR QUALITY section.

SUMMARY AND REVIEW

Social Influence

When someone attempts to affect another in a desired fashion, that person is said to be using **social influence**. People generally prefer to use open, consultative forms of influence (e.g., rational persuasion, inspirational appeal) rather than coercive methods (e.g., pressure, coalition building).

Individual Power

The concept of **power** refers to the capacity to change the behavior or attitudes of others in a desired manner. One major type of power, known as **position power**, resides within one's formal organizational position. It includes: (1) **reward power** and (2) **coercive power**, the capacity to control valued rewards and punishments, respectively; (3), **legitimate power**, the recognized authority that an individual has by virtue of his or her organizational position; and (4) **information power**, the power that stems from having special data and knowledge.

Another major type of power, known as **personal power**, resides within an individual's own unique qualities or characteristics. It includes: (1) **rational persuasion**, using logical arguments and factual evidence to convince others that an idea is acceptable; (2) **expert power**, the power an individual has because he or she is recognized as having some superior knowledge, skill, or expertise; (3) **referent power**, influence based on the fact that an individual is admired by others; and (4) **charisma**, having an engaging and magnetic personality.

Research has shown that differences in the use of power depend on the specific situations faced (e.g., facing others who have counterpower). For example, people tend to use rational persuasion when communicating with superiors.

There has been a recent trend toward **empowerment**, the shifting of power away from managers and into the hands of subordinates. Empowerment occurs in varying degrees in different organizations.

Group or Subunit Power

Power also may reside within work groups, or subunits. The **resource-dependency model** asserts that power resides within the subunits that control the greatest share of valued organizational resources.

The **strategic contingencies model** explains power in terms of a subunit's capacity to control the activities of other subunits. Such power may be enhanced by the capacity to reduce the level of uncertainty experienced by another unit, having a central position within the organization, or performing functions that other units cannot perform.

Organizational Politics

Behaving in a manner that is not officially approved by an organization to meet one's own goals by influencing others is known as **organizational politics**. Political tactics may include blaming and attacking others, controlling access to information, cultivating a favorable impression, developing an internal base of support, and aligning oneself with more powerful others. This may involve the playing of political games, such as asserting one's authority, enhancing one's power base, attacking one's rivals, and trying to foster organizational change.

Such activities typically occur under ambiguous conditions (such as in areas of organizational functioning in which clear rules are lacking). Furthermore, politics is likely to occur under conditions in which organizational uncertainty exists, important decisions involving large amounts of scarce resources are made, and the groups involved have conflicting interests but are approximately equal in power. Specifically, political activity is expected to be high when it comes to matters of human resource management and during an organization's mature stage of development (as opposed to its early and declining stages).

Although there are exceptions, political behavior may be considered ethical to the extent that it fosters organizational

JIM BARKSDALE: NETTING IT BIG AT NETSCAPE

He has no MBA, but he heads the fastest-growing software company in history. The man is Jim Barksdale, and the company is Netscape Communications, the Mountain View, California–based developer of software for browsing and authoring pages on the Internet (including the popular, Netscape Navigator). As president and CEO of Netscape, Barksdale has led the company on an odyssey of unparalleled proportions.

When Barksdale was handed the reins in January 1995, he found Netscape to be in chaos. Product development deadlines were in danger of being missed, and no clear strategy guided the company. A Netscape engineer, one of only 100 employees at the time, characterized the company as "spinning like a tornado" and "desperate for leadership." Co-founder, Silicon Valley entrepreneur Jim Clark had imposed a hiring freeze to keep the company from running out of money.

The first thing Barksdale did was to lift that freeze in an effort to expand the company's research and development activities. At the same time, he cut prices, opened offices in foreign countries, and broadened the company's target markets. Barksdale likened Netscape to a rocket: It had to go full speed to reach its velocity or crash. With low barriers to entry and giant competitors like Microsoft peering over its shoulder, he knew that establishing a presence in the market was key to Netscape's success—indeed, its survival.

Barksdale realized that this strategy was a gamble, but this fear of failure only energized him more. The challenge of taking the company from a small upstart to a big-time player was infectious. Netscape employees loved watching Barksdale go for broke, and the troops rallied around him. Soon Netscape entered into deals with Sun Microsystems, Silicon Graphics, Digital Electronic Corporation, and other companies for whom it develops Web server systems and encryption products. Barksdale's charm won over not only Netscape employees, but founders Jim Clark and John Doerr. The very day the two met, Clark told Barksdale, "You gotta take the job, Jim." In fact, Clark has attributed Netscape's success to Barksdale's winning ways, claiming, "A huge portion of what Netscape is worth is Jim Barksdale telling investors it's going to work. He has this great ability to convey confidence and give comfort."

There's no doubt that Clark's gamble on Barksdale, and Barksdale's gamble for Netscape paid off—and big. In the summer of 1995, after only a year of being formed, the company went public. Its stock took off immediately, and within a few months it quintupled. This made Barksdale's 11 percent stake in the company worth some $500 million. Netscape was so flushed with cash that it soon began acquiring other companies, further extending its reach into cyberspace.

There are very few corporate leaders who have had the same success and impact as Jim Barksdale. John D. Rockefeller at Standard Oil, Tom Watson at IBM, and Alfred Sloan at General Motors also come to mind as some of the most visible examples of business leaders whose achievements have been well publicized. But these well-known leaders simply mirror the accomplishments of thousands of unsung leaders who toil in the trenches of businesses both large and small on a daily basis (see Figure 13-1). If you asked 100 executives to name the single most important factor in determining organizational success, chances are good that many would reply "effective leadership." This answer reflects the general belief in the world of business that *leadership* is a key ingredient in corporate effectiveness. And this view is by no means restricted to organizations; leadership also plays a central role in politics, sports, and many other human activities.

Is this view justified? Do leaders really play such a crucial role in shaping the fortunes of organizations? Almost a century of research on this topic sug-

■ **Figure 13-1**
***Doug Cahill: A Successful Leader
You Never Heard Of***

*Doug Cahill is general manager of Olin
Pool Products, a company that makes
dry sanitizer, a water treatment product
for swimming pools. As sales started
heading down the drain a few years ago,
he initiated several changes in the organization that revitalized the company and
helped it regain its dominance in the
market. Although Mr. Cahill is not a famous leader in the eyes of the world, he
is a good example of the hard-working
and talented people on whom organizations depend for leadership.*

leadership The process
whereby one individual influences
other group members toward the
attainment of defined group or
organizational goals.

gests that they do.[1] Effective leadership, it appears, is indeed a key factor in organizational success.[2] Given this fact and its relevance to the field of organizational behavior, it seems appropriate for us to consider the topic of leadership in some detail. In this chapter, therefore, we will summarize current information about this complex process. One review of research on leadership published a few years ago cited more than 10,000 separate articles and books on this topic.[3] Not surprisingly, leadership is considered the most studied concept in the social sciences.[4]

Obviously, there is quite a lot of ground to cover. To make the task of summarizing this wealth of information more manageable, we will proceed as follows. First, we will consider some basic points about leadership—what it is and why being a leader is not necessarily synonymous with being a manager. Second, we will examine views of leadership focusing on the traits of leaders and on their behaviors. Third, we will examine several major theories of leadership that focus on the relationship between leaders and their followers. Finally we will review several contrasting theories dealing with the conditions under which leaders are effective or ineffective in their important role.

Leadership: Its Basic Nature

In a sense, *leadership* resembles love: It is something most people believe they can recognize but often find difficult to define. What, precisely, is it? And how does being a leader differ from being a manager? We will now focus on these questions.

Leadership: A Working Definition

Imagine that you have accepted a new job and entered a new work group. How would you recognize its *leader*? One possibility, of course, is through the formal titles and assigned roles each person in the group holds. In short, the individual designated as department head or project manager would be the one you would identify as the group's leader. But imagine that during several staff meetings, you noticed that this person was really not the most influential. Although she or he held the formal authority, these meetings were actually dominated by another person, who, ostensibly, was the top person's subordinate. What would you conclude about leadership then? Probably that the real leader of the group was the person who actually ran things—not the one with the fancy title and the apparent authority.

In many cases, of course, the disparity we have just described does not exist. The individual possessing the greatest amount of formal authority is also the most influential. In some situations, however, this is not so. And in such cases, we typically identify the person who actually exercises the most influence over the group as its leader. These facts point to the following working definition of leadership—one accepted by many experts on this topic: **Leadership** is the process whereby one individual influences other group members toward the attainment of defined group or organizational goals.[5]

Note that according to this definition, leadership is primarily a process involving influence—one in which a leader changes the actions or attitudes of several group members or subordinates. As we saw in Chapter 12, many techniques for exerting such influence exist, ranging from relatively coercive ones—the recipient has little choice but to do what is requested—to relatively noncoercive ones—the recipient can choose to accept or reject the influence offered. In general, leadership refers to the use of relatively noncoercive influence techniques. This characteristic distinguishes a leader from a *dictator*. Whereas dictators get others to do what they want by using physical coercion or by threats of physical force, leaders do not.[6] As Mao Zedong (founder of the

Leaders and Followers

Thus far in this chapter, we have focused on leaders—their traits and their behaviors. Followers, by and large, have been ignored. But note: In a crucial sense, followers are the essence of leadership. Without them, there really is no such thing as leadership (see Figure 13-5). As Lee put it, "Without followers leaders cannot lead. . . . Without followers, even John Wayne becomes a solitary hero, or, given the right script, a comic figure, posturing on an empty stage."[30]

The importance of followers, and the complex, reciprocal relationship between leaders and followers, is widely recognized by organizational researchers. Indeed, major theories of leadership, such as those we will consider in this section, note—either explicitly or implicitly—that leadership is really a two-way street. We will now consider four such approaches: the *leader-member exchange model*, the *attribution approach* to leadership, *charismatic leadership*, and *transformational leadership*. After reviewing these approaches we will end this section by discussing the changing nature of the relationship between leaders and followers—special issues involved in the leadership of teams.

The Leader-Member Exchange (LMX) Model: The Importance of Being in the "In-Group"

Do leaders treat all their subordinates in the same manner? Informal observation suggests that, clearly, they do not. Yet, many theories of leadership ignore this fact. They discuss leadership behavior in terms that suggest similar actions toward all subordinates. The importance of potential differences in this respect is brought into sharp focus by the **leader-member exchange (LMX) model** developed by Graen and his associates.[31]

This theory suggests that for various reasons leaders form different kinds of relationships with various groups of subordinates. One group, referred to as the *in-group* is favored by the leader. Members of in-groups receive considerably more attention from the leader and larger shares of the resources they have to offer (such as time and recognition). By contrast, other subordinates fall into the *out-group*. These individuals are disfavored by leaders. As such, they receive fewer valued resources from their leaders. Leaders distinguish between in-group and out-group members very early in their relationships with them—and, on the basis of surprisingly little information. Sometimes, perceived similarity with respect to personal characteristics such as age, gender, or personality, is sufficient to categorize followers into a leader's in-group.[32] Similarly, a particular follower may be granted in-group status if the leader believes that person to be especially competent at performing his or her job.[33]

leader-member exchange (LMX) model A theory suggesting that leaders form different relations with various subordinates and that the nature of such exchanges can exert strong effects on subordinates' performance and satisfaction.

■ **Figure 13-5**
Leaders: Nothing without Followers
Like all leaders, this one probably would be unsuccessful without "support" from his followers. Recognizing this, several theories of leadership have focused on the relationship between leaders and followers.

(**Source:** Copyright © 1994 by Leo Cullum.)

"Naturally, I can't take all the credit. I have a wonderful support group."

The LMX model is based on principles of group dynamics discussed in Chapter 8.

Research has supported the idea that leaders favor members of their in-groups. For example, one study found that supervisors inflated the ratings they gave poorly performing employees when these individuals were members of the in-group, but not when they were members of the out-group.[34] Given the favoritism shown toward in-group members, it follows that such individuals would perform their jobs better and hold more positive attitudes toward their jobs than members of out-groups. In general, research has supported this prediction. For example, it has been found that in-group members are more satisfied with their jobs and more effective in performing them than out-group members.[35] In-group members are also less likely to resign from their jobs than our-group members.[36] And, as you might imagine, members of in-groups tend to receive more mentoring from their superiors than do members of out-groups, helping them become more successful in their careers.[37]

Together, these studies provide good support for LMX model. Such findings suggest that attention to the relations between leaders and their followers can be very useful. The nature of such relationships can strongly affect the morale, commitment, and performance of employees. Helping leaders to improve such relations, therefore, can be extremely valuable in several respects.

The Attribution Approach: Leaders' Explanations of Followers' Behavior

attribution approach (to leadership) The approach to leadership that focuses on leaders' attributions of followers' performance—that is, their perceptions of its underlying causes.

The general nature of the attribution process, as it applies to organizations, is considered in depth in Chapter 3.

As we have just noted, leaders' relationships with individual subordinates can play an important role in determining the performance and satisfaction of these individuals. One specific aspect of such exchanges serves as focus of another contemporary perspective on leadership—the **attribution approach**.[38] This theory emphasizes the role of leaders' attributions concerning the causes behind followers' behavior—especially, the causes of their job performance.

Leaders observe the performance of their followers and then attempt to understand why this behavior met, exceeded, or failed to meet their expectations. Since poor performance often poses greater difficulties than effective performance, leaders are more likely to engage in a careful attributional analysis when confronted with the former. When they are, they examine the three kinds of information described in Chapter 3 (consensus, consistency, and distinctiveness), and on the basis of such information form an initial judgment as to whether followers' performance stemmed from internal causes (e.g., low effort, commitment, or ability) or external causes (factors beyond their control, such as faulty equipment, unrealistic deadlines, or illness). Then, on the basis of such attributions, they formulate specific actions designed to change the present situation, and perhaps improve followers' performance. Attribution theory suggests that such actions are determined, at least in part, by leaders' explanations of followers' behavior. For example, if they perceive poor performance as stemming from a lack of required materials or equipment, they may focus on providing such items. If, instead, they perceive poor performance as stemming mainly from a lack of effort, they may reprimand, transfer, or terminate the person involved (for a summary example, see Figure 13-6).

Evidence for the accuracy of these predictions has been reported in several studies.[39] In perhaps the best known of these, Mitchell and Wood presented nursing supervisors with brief accounts of errors committed by nurses.[40] The incidents suggested that the errors stemmed either from internal causes (lack of effort or ability) or from external causes (e.g., overdemanding work environment). After reading about the incidents, supervisors indicated what kind of action they would be likely to take in each situation. Results showed that they were more likely to direct corrective action toward the nurses when they perceived the errors as stemming from internal causes (e.g., showing them how to do something), but more likely to direct action toward the environment

this framework, charismatic leadership rests more on specific types of reaction by followers than on traits possessed by leaders. That is to say, leaders are considered charismatic by virtue of their effects on followers. Such reactions include: (1) levels of performance beyond those that would normally be expected;[44] (2) high levels of devotion, loyalty, and reverence toward the leader;[45] and (3) enthusiasm for and excitement about the leader and the leader's ideas.[46] In short, charismatic leadership involves a special kind of leader-follower relationship, in which the leader can, in the words of one author, "make ordinary people do extraordinary things in the face of adversity."[47]

The effects of charismatic leadership—both good and bad. As you might imagine, charismatic leaders can have dramatic effects on the behavior of their followers. Indeed, studies have shown that charismatic leadership is positively correlated with job performance.[48] And, because these leaders are perceived as being so heroic, followers are very pleased with them—satisfaction that generalizes to perceptions of the job itself. In short, people enjoy working for charismatic leaders and do well under their guidance. On a larger scale, research by House and his associates has found that U.S. presidents believed to be highly charismatic (as suggested by biographical accounts of their personalities and their reactions to world crises) received higher ratings by historians of their effectiveness as president.[49] In short, evidence suggests that charismatic leadership can have some very beneficial effects.

It is important to caution, however, that being charismatic does not necessarily imply being virtuous. There appears to be a "dark side" of charisma as well.[50] After all, several of history's most infamous people, dictator Adolph Hitler, cult leaders David Koresh and Charles Manson, were very charismatic. Indeed, it was their clear visions of different worlds, misguided though they may have been, that led them to have such profound effects on their followers.

It is important to note that there is not always a place for charismatic leaders in organizations. They tend to be needed most under circumstances in which there is some crisis.[51] For example, charismatic leaders tend to emerge under wartime conditions, such as in 1991 when U.S. General Norman

THE ETHICS ANGLE

Northrop Keeps Tabs on Leaders' Ethics

Northrop Corporation, the large defense contractor, has had its share of ethical scandals. The company was charged with bribery when it was found making illegal payments to the 1972 campaign of President Richard M. Nixon. Then, in 1990, Northrop was required to pay a $17 million fine after pleading guilty to falsifying test results on government projects.[52] Naturally, such events can be quite harmful to a company's reputation as an honest provider of goods in a vital industry.

In an attempt to avoid such scandals in the future, Northrop has instituted a program, the Northrop Leadership Inventory, designed to make the company's leaders accountable for adhering to ethical values.[53] Employees annually complete a questionnaire in which they evaluate their leaders with respect to the degree to which they are acting in accord with the company's ethical values

(e.g., doing the right thing instead of the easy thing). This questionnaire is then returned to the leaders along with feedback about how well others, in general, have scored. Leaders—all 3,200 of them—are then given an opportunity to discuss this feedback with counselors from outside the company. During these sessions they discuss things that may require attention and ways of going about acting more ethically.

Each year, employees are asked if they have noted changes in those areas marked as needing attention. In December 1993, CEO Kent Kresa sent Northrop leaders a memo congratulating them on improving: Between the first and second administrations of the survey, leaders received ratings that were 12.5 percent higher. The feedback provided by Northrop's Leadership Inventory appears to be telling a positive story.

Schwartzkopf expressed a vision of victory over Iraq and led his troops to victory in Operation Desert Storm. A crisis, such as the Great Depression, led to the election of President Franklin D. Roosevelt, the individual who would lead the United States out of the depression. And, as noted earlier, the economic crisis at Chrysler during the 1970s led to the emergence of Lee Iacocca, the man who saved the company. By the same token, it is easy to imagine that under everyday conditions, leaders who approach others with such overwhelming levels of arrogance and self-confidence that they ignore others may be more of a liability than an asset. Such was the case, for example, at Borland International, the world's largest database software provider.[54] When the company faced financial crises in the late 1980s, charismatic president and CEO Philippe R. Kahn was most helpful in turning things around. Interestingly, however, as the company emerged from crisis, Kahn's "Barbarian" approach to leadership, only interfered with the company's operations.

In closing, we should point out a particularly interesting thing about charismatic leaders: People's reactions to them tend to be highly polarized. That is, people either love them (as is the case most of the time) or hate them. With this in mind, it is not surprising that some of the world's most charismatic leaders, such as John F. Kennedy and Israeli leader Itzak Rabin have fallen victim to assassination. Less visionary leaders certainly would have done little to inspire would-be assassins from attempting to leave their marks on the world in such clearly inappropriate ways.

Transformational Leadership: Beyond Charisma

If you're thinking that charismatic leaders are really something special, we're inclined to agree. But being charismatic is only the beginning of doing what it takes to get followers to be their most effective. Theorists have recognized that although charisma is important, the most successful leaders also do things that revitalize and transform their organizations. Accordingly, their orientation is referred to as **transformational leadership**.

Transformational leaders may be described according to several characteristics. First, as we said, they have *charisma*. That is, they provide a strong vision and a sense of mission for the company. As leadership theorist Jay Conger put it, "If you as a leader can make an appealing dream seem like tomorrow's reality, your subordinates will freely choose to follow you."[55] Consider, for example, the great visions expressed by the highly charismatic leaders, Dr. Martin Luther King Jr., when he shared his vision of world peace in his "I have a dream" speech, and President John F. Kennedy, when he shared his vision of landing a man on the moon and returning him safely to earth before 1970.

But charisma alone is insufficient for changing the way an organization operates. For this to occur, transformational leaders also must provide *intellectual stimulation*. That is, they help their followers recognize problems and ways of solving them. Furthermore, they provide *individualized consideration* by giving followers the support, encouragement, and attention they need to perform their jobs well. Finally, transformational leaders are said to provide *inspirational motivation*. That is, they clearly communicate the importance of the company's mission and rely on symbols (e.g., pins and slogans) to help focus their efforts.

Transformational leaders arouse strong emotions and identification with the leader. They also help transform their followers by teaching them, often by serving as mentors.[56] In so doing, transformational leaders seek to encourage followers to "do their own thing." By contrast, charismatic leaders may keep their followers weak and highly dependent on them. A charismatic leader may be the whole show, whereas a transformational leader does a good job of inspiring change in the whole organization. Many celebrities, be they musicians, actors, or athletes, tend to be highly charismatic, but they do not necessarily have any transformational effects on their followers. As such, although

transformational leadership
Leadership in which leaders have charisma, provide intellectual stimulation, individualized consideration, and inspirational motivation.

Mentorship, as described in Chapter 7, is an important tool in the development of careers.

■ **Figure 13-8**
Mary Kay Ash: A Transformational Leader
Beyond being charismatic, Mary Kay Ash is a transformational leader. The founder of the cosmetics empire that bears her name is highly regarded among her associates for the considerable inspiration she provides and the warm personal consideration she shows them.

These work-related attitudes are described more fully in Chapter 6.

some people may idolize certain rock stars and dress like them, these musicians' charisma is unlikely to stimulate their fans into making sacrifices that revitalize the world. When you think of it this way, it's easy to see how charisma is just a part of transformational leadership.

A good example of a transformational leader is Mary Kay Ash, founder of the large cosmetics empire that bears her name (see Figure 13-8).[57] For a close-up look at this highly transformational leader and what she has done to revitalize the lives of so many of her associates, see the CASE IN POINT at the end of this chapter (p. 464).

Chairman and CEO of General Electric (GE) Jack Welch is another good example of a transformational leader. Under Welch's leadership, GE has undergone a series of changes with respect to the way it does business.[58] At the individual level, GE has abandoned its highly bureaucratic ways and now does a better job of listening to its employees. Not surprisingly, GE has consistently ranked among the most admired companies in its industry in *Fortune* magazine's annual survey of corporate reputations.[59] In the 1980s, Welch bought and sold many businesses for GE, using as his guideline the fact that GE would only keep a company if it placed either number one or number two in market share. If this meant closing plants, selling assets, and laying off personnel, he did it, and got others to follow suit. Not surprisingly, he earned the nickname, "Neutron Jack." Did Welch transform and revitalize GE? Having added $52 billion of value to the company, there can be no doubt about it.[60]

Scientists measure transformational leadership by using a questionnaire known as the Multifactor Leadership Questionnaire (MLQ). In completing this instrument, subordinates answer a series of questions in which they describe the behavior of their superiors. It consists of items tapping the four aspects of transformational leadership described above. So, for example, agreeing with an item such as "My leader makes me feel proud to be associated with him/her" is taken as an indication of the leader's transformational ways. The more subordinates agree with such statements as they describe the leader in question, the more highly that leader is scored as being transformational.

Using this questionnaire, researchers have found that transformational leaders tend to be very effective in making their organizations highly successful. For example, in a recent study Kohl, Steers and Terborg gave the MLQ to teachers in various secondary schools in Singapore and asked them to complete it with their school principals in mind.[61] They found that the more highly transactional the principals were described using the MLQ, the more the teachers engaged in organizational citizenship behavior, the more they were satisfied with their jobs and the more strongly they were committed to their organizations. The principals' transformational leadership scores also predicted how well the schools' students performed, although this connection was much weaker. Likewise, additional research has shown managers at FedEx who are rated by their subordinates as being highly transformational tend to be higher performers and are recognized by their superiors as being highly promotable.[62] These and other studies suggest that the benefits of being a transformational leader may be considerable.

With this in mind, it certainly would be useful to consider ways in which people might go about developing ways of transforming their organizations through their leadership. We have summarized several key guidelines in Table 13-3. Although you may find it easier to understand than to carry out some of these suggestions, the evidence regarding the effectiveness of transformational leadership suggests that the effort may be worthwhile.

Leading Teams: Special Considerations

When most people think of leaders, they tend to think of individuals who make strategic decisions on behalf of followers, who are responsible for carrying them out. In many of today's organizations, however, where the

Being a transformational leader is not easy, but following the suggestions outlined here may help leaders transform and revitalize their organizations.

Suggestion	Explanation
Develop a vision that is both clear and highly appealing to followers.	A clear vision will guide followers toward achieving organizational goals and make them feel good about doing so.
Articulate a strategy for bringing that vision to life.	Don't present an elaborate plan; rather, state the best path toward achieving the mission.
State your vision clearly and promote it to others.	Visions must not only be clear but made compelling, such as by using anecdotes.
Show confidence and optimism about your vision.	If a leader lacks confidence about success, followers will not try very hard to achieve that vision.
Express confidence in followers' capacity to carry out the strategy.	Followers must believe that they are capable of implementing a leader's vision. Leaders should build followers' self-confidence.
Build confidence by recognizing small accomplishments toward the goal.	If a group experiences early success, it will be motivated to continue working hard.
Celebrate successes and accomplishments	Formal or informal ceremonies are useful for celebrating success, thereby building optimism and commitment.
Take dramatic action to symbolize key organizational values.	Visions are reinforced by things leaders do to symbolize them. For example, one leader demonstrated concern for quality by destroying work that was not up to standards.
Set an example; actions speak louder than words.	Leaders serve as role models. If they want followers to make sacrifices, for example, they should do so themselves.

SOURCE: Based on suggestions by Yukl, 1994; see Note 1.

The use of self-managed work teams, as described in Chapter 8, is growing in popularity in today's organizations.

movement toward *self-managed teams* predominates, it is less likely than ever that leaders are responsible for getting others to implement their orders to help fulfill their visions. Instead, team leaders may be called upon to provide special resources to groups empowered to implement their own missions in their own ways. They don't call all the shots but help subordinates take responsibility for their own work (see Figure 13-9). This suggests that the role of team leader is clearly very different than the traditional "command and control" leadership role we have been discussing.[63] With this in mind, here are a few guidelines that may be followed to achieve success as a team leader.

- First, instead of directing people, team leaders work at *building trust and inspiring teamwork*. One way this can be done is by encouraging interaction between all members of the team as well as between the team and its customers and suppliers. Another key ingredient involves taking initiatives to make things better. Instead of taking a reactive, "if it ain't broke, don't fix it" approach, teams may be lead to success by individuals who set a good example for improving the quality of their team's efforts.
- Second, instead of focusing simply on training individuals, effective team leaders concentrate on *expanding team capabilities*. In this connection, team leaders function primarily as coaches, helping team members by providing all members with the skills needed to perform the task, removing barriers that might interfere with task success, and finding the necessary resources required to get the job done. Likewise, team leaders work at building the confidence of team members, cultivating their untapped potential.

■ Fig
Cindy
at Cl
Under
100 w
Fairfiel
comple
ations.
work, :
needs
plant v
improv
housek

of commitment among subordinates needed for its implementation. For example, with respect to decision quality, a leader should ask questions such as: Is a high-quality decision required? Do I have enough information to make such a decision? Is the problem well structured? With respect to decision acceptance, he or she should ask: Is it crucial for effective implementation that subordinates accept the decision? Do subordinates share the organizational goals that will be reached through solution of this problem?

According to normative decision theory, answering such questions, and applying specific rules such as those shown in Table 13-5, eliminates some of the potential approaches to reaching a given decision. Those that remain constitute a feasible set that can, potentially, be used to reach the necessary decision.

To simplify this process, Vroom and Yetton recommend using a decision tree such as the one shown in Figure 13-13. To apply this diagram, a manager begins on the left side and responds, in turn, to the questions listed under each letter (A, B, C, and so on). As the manager replies to each question, the set of feasible approaches narrows. For example, imagine that the manager's answers are as follows:

- Question A: Yes—a high-quality decision is needed.
- Question B: No—the leader does not have sufficient information to make a high quality decision alone.
- Question C: No—the problem is not structured.
- Question D: Yes—acceptance by subordinates is crucial to implementation.
- Question E: No—if the leader makes the decision alone, it may not be accepted by subordinates.
- Question F: No—subordinates do not share organizational goals.
- Question G: Yes—conflict among subordinates is likely to result from the decision.

As you can see, these replies lead to the conclusion that only one decision-making approach is feasible: full participation by subordinates. (The path leading to this conclusion is shown in gold in Figure 13-13.) Of course, different answers to any of the seven key questions would have led to different conclusions.

The Vroom and Yetton model is highly appealing because it takes full account of the importance of subordinates' participation in decisions and offers leaders clear guidance for choosing among various methods for reaching decisions. As with any theory, though, the key question remains: Is it valid? Are its suggestions concerning the most effective style of decision making under various conditions really accurate? The results of several studies designed to test the model have been encouraging.

In Chapter 1 we described the characteristics of a good theory.

For example, it has been found that practicing managers rate their own past decisions as more successful when they are based on procedures falling within the set of feasible options identified by the model than when they fall outside this set of methods.[79] Similarly, when small groups reach decisions through methods falling within the feasible set identified by the model, these decisions are judged to be more effective by outside raters than when they are made using other methods.[80] However, all studies have not supported the theory. For example, studies have found that the most effective path is based on considerations that go beyond the model, such as differences in the perspectives of leaders and subordinates and the personal skills or traits of leaders.[81] Such findings suggest that the theory may need to be modified, and indeed, in recent years it has.[82] The latest version of the theory is more complex: Instead of seven contingency questions there are twelve, and instead of answering questions with a simple "yes" or "no," there are now five response options. This revised model is so highly complex that a computer program is used instead of a decision tree to help find the most appropriate leadership style. Preliminary evidence suggests that the resulting theory is more valid than the original, although it is far too complex to present here.

In Chap
eral nat
approac
tional b
represer

450   458   PART 5 Influencing Others

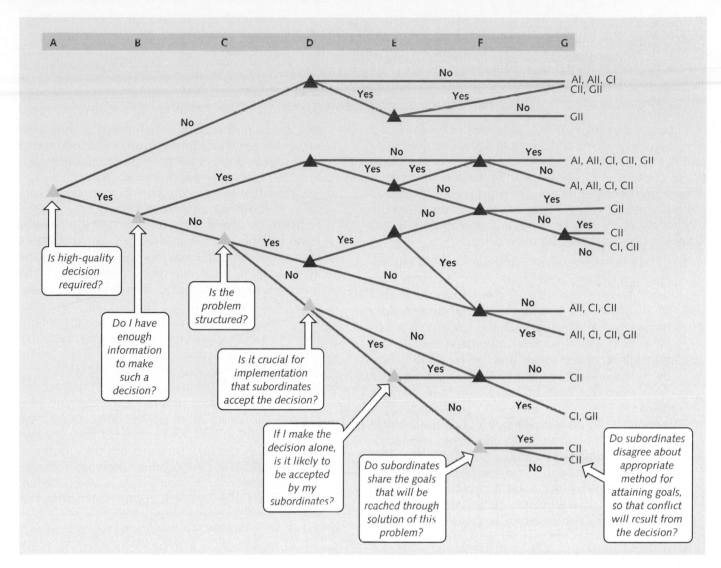

A   B   C   D   E   F   G

■ Figure 13-13
Normative Decision Theory:
An Example

By answering the questions listed here and tracing a path through this decision tree, leaders can identify the most effective approaches to making decisions in a specific situation. Note: The path suggested by the answers to questions A through G (see page 458) is shown by the gold-colored triangles.

(**Source:** Based on suggestions by Vroom & Yetton, 1973; see Note 78.)

Whether we're talking about the more sophisticated version or the original version of normative decision theory, it is clear that this formulation makes an important contribution to our understanding of leadership. Insofar as there is widespread current interest in allowing subordinates to participate in decision making, normative decision theory is useful because it gives leaders clear guidance as to when such a move may be expected to improve task performance. Despite this guidance, leaders will be ineffective at consulting subordinates unless they are willing to participate in the decision-making process. Some guidelines for encouraging participation are described in the QUEST FOR QUALITY section.

Substitutes for Leadership: When Leaders Are Superfluous

Throughout this chapter, we have emphasized that leaders are important. Their style, actions, and degree of effectiveness all exert major effects on subordinates and, ultimately, on organizations. In many cases, this is certainly true. Yet, almost everyone has observed or been part of groups in which the designated leaders actually had little influence—groups in which these people were mere figureheads with little impact on subordinates. One explanation for such situations involves the characteristics of the leaders in question: They are simply weak and unsuited for their jobs. Another, and in some ways more intriguing, possibility is that in some contexts, other factors may actually sub-

HOW TO ENCOURAGE PARTICIPATION: SOME GUIDELINES

*I*t is one thing to say that people should be consulted in decision making under certain situations, and quite another to see that it actually occurs. To reap the benefits of consultation, people must be actively involved in expressing their preferences, coming up with ideas, and voicing their concerns. What can leaders do to ensure that followers are ready, willing, and able to participate? Several suggestions may be offered.[83]

1. It has been recommend that leaders *consult with followers before making changes that affect them.* If an organizational change is in the works, it is helpful to ensure that it is understood and accepted by those who are affected. With this in mind, it is useful to hold special meetings to outline the changes that will occur and things that can be done to help them through it. People are likely to accept decisions when they have had a voice in implementing them.

2. It is helpful to *present proposals as tentative.* People are unlikely to participate in discussions in which a plan is presented to them as a *fait accompli,* a done deal. If a plan appears to be complete, people may feel reluctant to challenge it. However, they are more likely to participate in discussions about plans that are presented as tentative and in need of improvement.

3. It is a good idea to *keep a record of ideas and suggestions.* We all feel badly when our ideas are ignored. If these are written down on a blackboard or flipchart, or even in written minutes of meetings, they are less likely to be forgotten.

4. Attempt to *build upon existing ideas and suggestions.* Suppose you propose an idea, only to have it shot down without much consideration. If you're like most people, you would probably feel reluctant to participate in any further deliberations. If you're turned off in this way, the group will be unlikely to reap the benefits of what you bring to it. To avoid this, try to find ways in which every idea may be expanded upon and turned into a better one rather than rejected out of hand. Work to consider ways in which ideas may be improved upon.

5. It is important to *be tactful when expressing your concerns.* If you don't agree with something someone has said, no one is likely to benefit if you were to stand up and say, "That idea really stinks!" Rather than make the individual feel bad by rejecting the idea outright, raise questions that will get the speaker to realize himself or herself what problems might exist. You might say, for example, "I like your idea, but I am concerned about the cost. Might there be a less expensive way of bringing it about?" The trick is to get people to understand the limitations of their ideas, but not turn them off.

6. It is essential to *listen to dissenting ideas without getting defensive.* It hurts us all to listen to those who oppose our ideas. But, if we get defensive and fail to pay attention, we may miss what they are saying. After all, the goal is not to win the argument, but to make the best possible decision. To make sure you understand what someone else is saying, try to restate their concerns in your own words. This will help you consider it objectively.

7. Although it should go without saying, it is important to *show appreciation for suggestions.* If it is important for someone to cooperate in making decisions, it is important for their contributions to be reinforced. Complimenting people for their ideas and suggestions makes them feel good about participating and makes them likely to lend their insight again.

We realize that it may take a concerted effort to follow these suggestions. After all, most people are not inclined to do what it takes to get others to participate in decision making. For leaders to be effective, however, these skills must be mastered.

---

substitutes for leadership
The view that high levels of skill among subordinates or certain features of technology and organizational structure sometimes serve as substitutes for leaders, rendering their guidance or influence superfluous.

stitute for a leader's influence, making it superfluous, or neutralize the effects of the leader's influence. Kerr and Jermier propose this idea formally in their **substitutes for leadership** framework.[84]

According to this conceptualization, leadership may be irrelevant because various factors make it impossible for leaders to have any effect on subordinates—that is, they *neutralize* the effects of leadership. For example, people who are indifferent to the rewards a leader controls are unlikely to be influenced by those rewards. As a result, the leader's influence is likely to be negated. Leadership also may be irrelevant because conditions make a leader's influence unnecessary. That is various factors *substitute for* leadership. For example, leadership may be superfluous when individuals have a highly professional orientation and find their work to be intrinsically satisfying. When the leader's impact is either neutralized or substituted for by various conditions, his or her impact is limited, at best.

Specifically, many different variables can produce such effects. Thus, we may ask: Under what conditions are leaders expected to have limited impact on task performance? The answers fall into three different categories. First, leadership may be unnecessary because of various individual characteristics. For example, a high level of knowledge, commitment, or experience on the part of subordinates may make it unnecessary for anyone to tell them what to do or how to proceed. Second, leadership may be unnecessary because jobs themselves may be structured in ways that make direction and influence from a leader redundant. For example, highly routine jobs require little direction, and jobs that are highly interesting also require little in the way of outside leadership stimulation. Third, various characteristics of organizations may make leadership unnecessary. For example, various work norms and strong feelings of cohesion among employees may directly affect job performance and render the presence of a leader unnecessary. Similarly, the technology associated with certain jobs may strongly determine the decisions and actions of people performing them, and so leave little room for input from a leader.

Evidence for these assertions has been obtained in several recent studies.[85] For example, in a recent investigation Podsakoff, Niehoff, MacKenzie, and Williams examined the work performance and attitudes of a broad sample of workers (including building service employees, administrative and clerical employees, and managers) who completed scales measuring their perceptions of the extent to which various leadership behaviors and substitutes for leadership were exhibited on their jobs.[86] Consistent with the theory, they found that job performance and attitudes were more strongly associated with the various substitutes than with the leadership behaviors themselves.

If leaders are superfluous in many situations, why has this fact often been overlooked? One possibility, suggested by Meindl and Ehrlich, is that we have a strong tendency to *romanticize* leadership—to perceive it as more important and more closely linked to performance in many contexts than it actually is.[87] To test this suggestion, they presented MBA students with detailed financial information about an imaginary firm, including a paragraph describing the firm's key operating strengths. The content of this paragraph was varied, so that four different groups of subjects received four different versions. These attributed the firm's performance either to its top-level management team, the quality of its employees, changing patterns of consumer needs and preferences, or federal regulatory policies, respectively.

After reading one of these paragraphs and examining other information about the firm, subjects rated two aspects of its overall performance: profitability and risk. Meindl and Ehrlich reasoned that because of the tendency to overestimate the importance of leadership, subjects would rate the firm more favorably when its performance was attributed to top-level management than when it was attributed to any of the other factors. As you can see in Figure 13-14, this was precisely what occurred. The imaginary company was rated as higher in profitability and lower in risk when subjects had read the leadership-based paragraph than when they had read any of the others.

These findings, plus others obtained by the same researchers, help explain why leaders are often viewed as important and necessary even when, to a large degree, they are superfluous. Note: This in no way implies that leaders are usually unimportant. On the contrary, they often do play a key role in work groups and organizations. However, because this is not always so, their necessity should never be taken for granted.

■ **Figure 13-14**
Evidence of the Tendency to Overestimate the Importance of Leadership
People who received information suggesting that an imaginary company's past success was attributable to its top management rated the company more favorably (higher in profitability, lower in risk) than those who received information suggesting that the identical record resulted from other causes. These findings suggest that people *romanticize* leadership, overestimating its impact in many situations.

(**Source:** Based on data reported by Meindl & Ehrlich, 1987; see Note 87.)

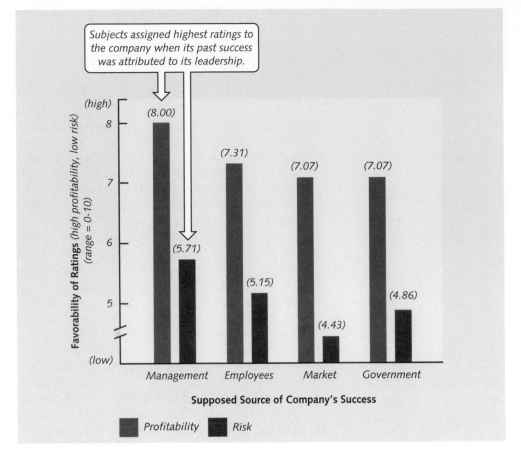

SUMMARY AND REVIEW

Leadership: Some Basic Issues

Leadership is the process whereby one individual influences other group members toward the attainment of defined group or organizational goals. **Leaders** generally use noncoercive forms of influence and are influenced, in turn, by their followers. Whereas *leaders* create the group's or organization's mission and outline the strategy for attaining it, *managers* are responsible for implementing that mission. In practice, however, many leaders are also responsible for managerial tasks. Thus, although there is a distinction between leaders and managers, it is often blurred in practice.

Leader Traits and Behaviors

Early efforts to identify key traits that set leaders apart from other people—the **great person theory**—generally failed. However, recent evidence suggests that leaders do, in fact, differ from followers in certain respects. They are higher in leadership motivation, drive, honesty, self-confidence, and several other traits. In addition, successful leaders appear to be high in *flexibility*—the ability to adapt their style to the followers' needs and to the requirements of specific situations.

Leaders differ greatly in their style or approach to leadership. One key dimension involves the extent to which leaders are *directive* or *permissive* toward subordinates—to the extent to which they tell subordinates how to do their jobs. Another involves the extent to which they are *autocratic* or *democratic* in their decision making—to the extent to which they permit subordinates to make decisions. Leaders also vary along two other key dimensions: concern with, and efforts to attain, successful task performance (**initiating structure**) and concern with maintaining favorable personal relations with subordinates (**consideration**). **Grid training** focuses on efforts to improve managers' concern for people and their concern for production by training them in communication skills and planning skills.

Leaders and Followers

Several approaches to leadership focus on the relationships between leaders and their followers. Graen's **leader-member exchange (LMX) model** specifies that leaders favor members of some groups—referred to as *in-groups*—more than others—referred to as *out-groups*. As a result, in-groups perform better than out-groups.

The **attributional approach** focuses on leaders' attributions of followers' performance—that is, its underlying causes. When leaders perceive that their subordinates' poor performance is caused by internal factors, they react by helping him or her to improve. However, when poor performance is attributed to external sources, leaders direct their attention toward changing aspects of the work environment believed to be responsible for the poor performance.

Some leaders—known as **charismatic** leaders—exert profound effects on the beliefs, perceptions, and actions of their followers. Such leaders have a special relationship with their followers, in which they can inspire exceptionally high levels of performance, loyalty, and enthusiasm. Charismatic leaders tend to have high amounts of self-confidence, present a clearly articulated vision, behave in extraordinary ways, are recognized as change agents, and are sensitive to the environmental constraints they face. Although many leaders use their charisma for beneficial purposes, others do not.

Transformational leaders are also very charismatic, but they also do things that transform and revitalize their organizations. They provide intellectual stimulation, individualized consideration, and inspirational motivation. Transformational leaders tend to be very effective.

Special considerations are involved when it comes to leading self-managed teams. Notably, instead of directing people, team leaders should work at building trust and inspiring teamwork, expanding team capabilities, creating a team identity, making the most of differences between team members, and foreseeing and influencing change.

Contingency Theories of Leader Effectiveness

Contingency theories of leadership assume that there is no one best style of leadership and that the most effective style of leadership depends on the specific conditions or situations faced. For example, Fiedler's **LPC contingency theory** suggests that both a leader's characteristics and situational factors are crucial. Task-oriented leaders (termed *low LPC leaders*) are more effective than people-ori-

ented leaders (termed *high LPC leaders*) under conditions in which the leader has either high or low control over the group in question. In contrast, people-oriented leaders are more effective under conditions where the leader has moderate control.

The **situational leadership theory** proposed by Hersey and Blanchard suggests that the most effective style of leadership—either delegating, participating, selling, or telling—depends on the extent to which followers require guidance, direction, and emotional support. Effective leaders are required to diagnose the situations they face and implement the appropriate behavioral style for that situation.

House's **path-goal theory** of leadership suggests that leaders' behavior will be accepted by subordinates and will enhance their motivation only to the extent that it helps them progress toward valued goals and provides guidance or clarification not already present in work settings.

Vroom and Yetton's **normative decision theory** focuses on decision making as a key determinant of leader effectiveness. According to this theory, different situations call for different styles of decision making (e.g., autocratic, consultative, participative) by leaders. Decisions about the most appropriate style of decision making for a given situation are made on the basis of answers to questions regarding the quality of the decision required and the degree to which it is important for followers to accept and be committed to the decisions made. Complex decision trees are used to guide managers to the most appropriate styles of leadership.

Finally, the **substitutes for leadership** approach suggests that leaders are unnecessary in situations in which other factors can have just as much influence. For example, leaders are superfluous when (1) subordinates have exceptionally high levels of knowledge and commitment, (2) jobs are highly structured and routine, and (3) the technology used strongly determines individuals' behavior.

QUESTIONS FOR DISCUSSION

1. What are the major differences between leaders, dictators, and managers?
2. It has often been said that "great leaders are born, not made." Do you agree? If so, why? If not, why?
3. Argue for or against the following statement: "The best leaders encourage participation from their subordinates."
4. In your experience, do most leaders have a small in-group? If so, what are the effects of this clique on other group members?

5. Explain how the process of attribution is involved in organizational leadership.
6. Consider all the people who have been president of the United States during your lifetime. Which of these (if any) would you describe as charismatic? Which of these (if any) would you describe as transformational? Why?
7. Concern for people and concern for production are two recurring themes in the study of leadership. Describe the way they manifest themselves in various theories of leadership.

Mary Kay Cosmetics: Where Success Is Not Merely Cosmetic

There are "rags-to-riches stories," and then there's Mary Kay Ash, the founder of the wildly successful Mary Kay Cosmetics empire. At age 45, in the early 1960s, she became disenchanted with the limited opportunities for women in business, and with only the help of her children she gambled her life savings of $5,000 on a cosmetics business. Some three decades later this investment has grown into a giant corporation with annual sales over $613 million and a sales force some 300,000 strong. Not surprisingly, the woman behind all this has been considered one of the best business leaders in the United States.

Many attribute the company's success in large part to Mary Kay's special touches. By giving her employees, most of whom are women, opportunities to succeed and recognizing their success, she motivates and inspires them. At its annual "Seminar" in Dallas, for example, Mary Kay representatives are awarded such forms of recognition as pink Cadillacs (some $90 million worth have been given away already), first-class trips abroad, gold bracelets studded in diamonds spelling out "$1,000,000" (for selling that amount of cosmetics), and lapel pins and ribbons denoting other sales milestones. These lavish forms of recognition are matched only by the opulent, Las Vegas–style productions in which they are presented—fetes that take on the noise level and excitement of political conventions.

One of the things Mary Kay executives pride themselves in doing is helping women become financially successful and feel good about themselves. "Give me a hard-working waitress," says national sales director, Shirley Hutton, "and in a year I'll turn her into a director making $35,000." Many do better—much better. Indeed, 74 sales consultants have earned commissions of over $1 million during their careers. (Hutton earned approximately that amount in 1993 alone.)

Mary Kay is recognized for her sincerity and concern for her employees' well-being. According to Gloria Hilliard Mayfield, a relatively new sales consultant, she is surprisingly approachable. "You wouldn't just walk over to, say, John Akers [CEO of IBM]," she explains. "But Mary Kay calls you her daughter and looks you dead in the eye. She makes you feel you can do anything. She's sincerely concerned about your welfare." When Hutton's daughter was ill, for example, Mary called her several times to cheer her up. Such expressions of personal interest are contagious: Many sales consultants treat their customers the same way—sending them birthday cards and showing they're interested in them. *This*, they are convinced, sells makeup.

Recognition from Mary is considered the ultimate form of recognition. At each year's Seminar, she personally crowns four "Queens of Seminar" in recognition of their sales accomplishments. She kisses them, gives them roses, and pats their hands. This personal touch is so important that one year when she was ill, she made an appearance from her sickbed via a closed-circuit television hook-up—just to make her presence felt.

What will happen to Mary Kay, the company, after Mary Kay Ash, the woman, is gone? "There will be a flood of tears unlike anything you've ever seen," says the husband of a sales consultant. "I'd love to have the tissue concession." But no one doubts that the company will continue without it's charismatic leader—her legacy is too strong to ever vanish.

Critical Thinking Questions

1. What does Mary Kay Ash do that makes her not only a charismatic leader but a transformational leader?
2. What do followers attribute to Mary Kay that makes her so effective as a leader?
3. What leadership characteristics does Mary Kay exhibit?

SKILLS PORTFOLIO

Experiencing Organizational Behavior

Determining Your Leadership Style

As noted on pp. 453–454, *situational leadership theory* identifies four basic leadership styles. To be able to identify and enact the most appropriate style of leadership in any given situation, it is first useful to understand the style to which you are most predisposed. This exercise will help you gain such insight into your own leadership style.

Directions

Below are eight hypothetical situations in which you have to make a decision affecting you and members of your work group. For each, indicate which of the following actions you are most likely to take by writing the letter corresponding to that action in the space provided.

A. Let the members of the group decide themselves what to do.
B. Ask the members of the group what to do but make the final decision yourself.
C. Make the decision yourself but explain your reasons.
D. Make the decision yourself, telling the group exactly what to do.

_____**1.** In the face of financial pressures, you are forced to make budget cuts for your unit. Where do you cut?

_____**2.** To meet an impending deadline, someone in your secretarial pool will have to work late one evening to finish typing an important report. Who will it be?

_____**3.** As coach of a company softball team, you are required to trim your squad to 25 players from 30 currently on the roster. Who goes?

_____**4.** Employees in your department have to schedule their summer vacations so as to keep the office appropriately staffed. Who decides first?

_____**5.** As chair of the social committee, you are responsible for determining the theme for the company ball. How do you do so?

_____**6.** You have an opportunity to buy or rent an important piece of equipment for your company. After gathering all the facts, how do you make the choice?

_____**7.** The office is being redecorated. How do you decide on the color scheme?

_____**8.** Along with your associates you are taking a visiting dignitary to dinner. How do you decide what restaurant to go to?

Scoring

1. Count the number of situations to which you responded by marking A. This is your _delegating_ score.

2. Count the number of situations to which you responded by marking B. This is your _participating_ score.

3. Count the number of situations to which you responded by marking C. This is your _selling_ score.

4. Count the number of situations to which you responded by marking D. This is your _telling_ score.

Questions for Discussion

1. Based on this questionnaire, what was your most predominant leadership style? Is this consistent with what you would have predicted in advance?

2. According to situational leadership theory, in what kinds of situations would this style be most appropriate? Have you ever found yourself in such a situation, and if so, how well did you do?

3. Do you think that it would be possible for you to change this style if needed?

4. To what extent were your responses to this questionnaire affected by the nature of the situations described? In other words, would you have opted for different decisions in different situations?

Working in Groups — Identifying Great Leaders in All Walks of Life

A useful way to understand the _great person theory_ is to identify those individuals who may be considered great leaders and then to consider what it is that makes them so great. This exercise is designed to guide a class in this activity.

Directions

1. Divide the class into four equal-sized groups, arranging each in a semicircle.

2. In the open part of the semicircle, one group member—the recorder—should stand at a flip chart, ready to write down the group's responses.

3. The members of each group should identify the five most effective leaders they can think of—living or dead, real or fictional—in one of the following fields: business, sports, politics/government, humanitarian endeavors. One group should cover each of these domains. If more than five names come up, the group should vote on the five best answers. The recorder should write down the names as they are identified.

4. Examining the list, group members should identify the traits and characteristics that the people on the list have in common but that distinguish them from others who are not on the list. In other words, what is it that makes these people so special? The recorder should write down the answers.

5. One person from each group should be selected to present his or her group's responses to members of the class. This should include both the names, and the underlying characteristics.

Questions for Discussion

1. How did the traits identified in this exercise compare to the ones described in this chapter as important determinants of leadership? Were they similar or different? Why?

2. To what extent were the traits identified in the various groups different or similar? In other words, were different characteristics associated with success in different walks of life? Or were the ingredients for success more universal?

3. Were there some traits identified that you found surprising, or were they all expected?

4. Is it possible to change the traits identified in this exercise, or are they immutable?

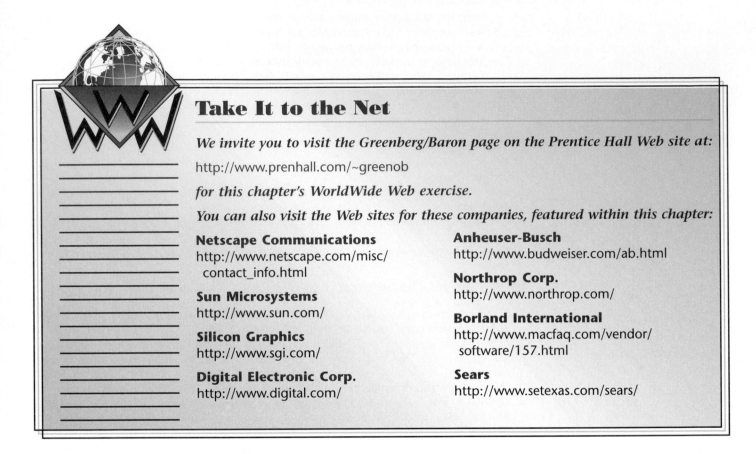

Take It to the Net

We invite you to visit the Greenberg/Baron page on the Prentice Hall Web site at:

http://www.prenhall.com/~greenob

for this chapter's WorldWide Web exercise.

You can also visit the Web sites for these companies, featured within this chapter:

Netscape Communications
http://www.netscape.com/misc/
  contact_info.html

Sun Microsystems
http://www.sun.com/

Silicon Graphics
http://www.sgi.com/

Digital Electronic Corp.
http://www.digital.com/

Anheuser-Busch
http://www.budweiser.com/ab.html

Northrop Corp.
http://www.northrop.com/

Borland International
http://www.macfaq.com/vendor/
  software/157.html

Sears
http://www.setexas.com/sears/

Ben Cohen and Jerry Greenfield preside over a business empire built on indulgence. Their company, Vermont-based Ben & Jerry's Homemade, Inc., is best known for exotic flavors of super-premium ice cream. From its humble beginnings in 1978, Ben & Jerry's grew into a company with annual sales of $150 million in 1995. Ben & Jerry's success can be attributed in part to ice cream lovers' collective passion for sinfully rich desserts and in part to the co-founders' shared sense of social responsibility and environmental awareness. This attitude is spelled out in Ben & Jerry's three-part mission statement. The product mission, for instance, states that the company will manufacture and market innovative ice cream flavors made from the highest-quality, all-natural Vermont dairy products. The social mission declares that the role of business in society is to improve the quality of life at the local, national, and international levels.

The third part of the mission statement addresses Ben & Jerry's economic mission, which is to operate in a financially sound manner and achieve profitable growth while creating career opportunities and financial rewards for employees. Cohen and Greenfield's commitment to the economic mission can be seen in their approach to compensation. The founders believe in a policy of "linked prosperity," which simply means that all employees share in the company's success. Cohen and Greenfield decided that the ratio of the salary of the highest-paid executive to that of the lowest-paid full-time employee could only be 5 to 1; in 1990, the ratio was increased to 7 to 1. Every full-time employee participates in a profit-sharing plan that distributes 5 percent of pre-tax profits according to length of service.

Emphasis on fair compensation and good deeds are just two aspects of Ben & Jerry's unique corporate culture. Cohen and Greenfield's business recipe calls for a healthy dose of fun. Indeed, one of Greenfield's favorite expressions is, "If it's not fun, why do it?" And yet, despite unorthodox policies, Ben and Jerry are focused businessmen. They realized it was time for a change when consumer preferences began to change and the company's stock, which had soared from $6.50 per share in 1990 to $32.25 in 1992, began a long slump. The partners spent much of 1995 conducting a widely publicized search for a new CEO to take over for Cohen. As Greenfield explained in a recent interview, "We manufacture ice cream on two shifts and on three different sites, and the level of complexity is such that it requires organizational, operational, and management expertise that goes beyond what Ben and I can offer." In the classic Ben & Jerry's tradition, the duo generated considerable publicity with their "Yo, I wanna be your CEO" essay contest, inviting interested persons to apply for the top job. The contest netted more than 22,000 entries.

In the end, an executive recruiting firm led Ben & Jerry's to management consultant Robert Holland Jr. Holland's base salary will be $250,000, which is low for executives in mid-sized manufacturing companies. Still, to authorize the salary, Ben & Jerry's board of directors had to make an exception to the 7 to 1 rule. Holland's first challenge is to find new growth markets. Investment banker Lewis Alton gives the new CEO high marks for his first year on the job. "Bob's done exactly the right things," says Alton. He points out, for example, that Holland has spearheaded the company's move into sorbets, a low-fat dessert that is expected to add $20 to $30 million to annual revenues. True to the Ben & Jerry's tradition, the new sorbets are likely to have fun names and fun flavors.

Video source: Sharing sweet success. (1992, May 22). *20/20*, no. 1222. *Additional sources*: Kadlec, D. (1996, January 31). Here's the scoop on Ben & Jerry's. *USA Today*, p. 4B; Bulkeley, W. M., & Lublin, J. S. (1995, January 10). Ben & Jerry's new CEO will face shrinking sales and growing fears of fat. *The Wall Street Journal*, pp. B1, B4; Dreifus, C. (1994, December 18). Passing the scoop: Ben & Jerry. *The New York Times Magazine*, pp. 38, 40–41; Laabs, J. J. (1992, November). Ben & Jerry's caring capitalism. *Personnel Journal*, pp. 50–57.

CHAPTER | Fourteen

THE WORK ENVIRONMENT: CULTURE AND TECHNOLOGY

■ OBJECTIVES

LEARNING

After reading this chapter you should be able to:

1. Define *organizational culture* and describe the role it plays in organizational functioning.

2. Distinguish between *dominant cultures* and *subcultures*, and the various types of organizational cultures that may exist within organizations.

3. Identify various mechanisms by which organizational culture is created.

4. Describe and give examples of various techniques used to transmit organizational culture.

5. Summarize the effects of organizational culture on both organizational and individual performance.

6. Explain why and how organizational culture is likely to change.

7. Identify the four major types of technology identified by Perrow.

8. Define and give examples of *automation* and explain how people are affected by the use of automation in the organizations within which they work.

9. Describe how *technology* can be used in organizations for purposes of assisting people with disabilities, monitoring job performance, improving the quality of customer service, and improving environmental quality.

THE CLASH OF THE RETAILING TITANS

What do you get when you combine two retail chains, one American and one British, each with its own established ways of operating? In 1989 we only could have guessed at the answer but were quick to learn when the venerable British department store Marks and Spencer acquired the American men's clothier Brooks Brothers, as part of its global expansion strategy. And our lesson was clear: Things don't always go smoothly when you combine two companies with an (Atlantic) ocean of differences between them.

Both stores have always been highly committed to offering attentive customer service and impeccable goods, but that's where the similarity ended. Brooks Brothers' strong suit was manufacturing fine quality traditional men's clothing, whereas Marks and Spencer had always purchased its broad inventory from a variety of suppliers. Marks and Spencer also used carefully implemented management systems (e.g., cost control and inventory management procedures), which it soon imposed on the more loosely managed Brooks Brothers. At Marks and Spencer sales staff are paid in a manner that takes into account overall store performance, an incentive to work together as a team. By contrast, Brooks Brothers employees had always been rewarded based on their own performance, with salespeople working like individual entrepreneurs—that was, until a management team from London arrived in the United States and introduced the team approach. Their lesson: What is good for the store is also good for the individual employee. The Americans grumbled, at first, and turnover resulted.

Beyond these basic differences, working together was made difficult by even the most mundane aspects of everyday communication. Marks and Spencer executives were more formal than their American counterparts at Brooks Brothers. The Americans tended to keep their office doors open and walk around, but the Marks and Spencer bosses usually sat behind closed doors and wrote memos. Employees from each company recognized what the other had to offer but felt uneasy in their quest for the common ground.

After about three years Brooks Brothers employees came to recognize that the Marks and Spencer folks were interested in working *with* them, as opposed to simply imposing their ways on them. It helped greatly for Brooks Brothers managers to spend time at the parent company's headquarters where they could be exposed to the company philosophy on a firsthand basis and learn its ways of doing things. To further demonstrate the seriousness of Marks and Spencer's investment in Brooks Brothers, it appointed to its board of directors an individual in charge of North American operations.

Although the Americans may have felt imposed upon by their new parent company, at least initially, they soon recognized that Marks and Spencer was a successful retailer that knew what it was doing. But you cannot blame them for feeling insecure. Before being acquired by Marks and Spencer, Brooks Brothers had undergone two changes of ownership in as many years—with its most recent owner unfamiliar with the world of retailing. As Brooks Brothers employees recognized that they were, in many ways, "rescued" by Marks and Spencer, they came to accept its ways.

The difficulties that Marks and Spencer and Brooks Brothers associates had in dealing with each other stemmed from their companies' different approaches to conducting business. These were fundamental differences in the shared beliefs, expectations, and core values of people in the organization— collectively referred to as *organizational culture*.[1] An organization's culture can be so deeply imbedded within the way it operates that its effects can be quite profound. In the case of Marks and Spencer, culture was reinforced by over a century's worth of successful business experience. Likewise, other companies— such as McDonald's, MCI, and the Walt Disney Company—have exceptionally

No Status Symbols for this CEO
At Intel, even CEO Andy Grove works at a small, open cubicle that makes him accessible to others. This practice fosters the kind of egalitarian organizational culture that encourages employees of the large manufacturer of computer chips to exchange ideas freely, enhancing the company's ability to introduce innovative products.

strong and effective cultures that have been credited for contributing to their success. Consider, for example, Intel, the leading developer of computer chips. A large part of its success has been linked to an organizational culture in which people are encouraged to work together and share resources as needed. To help bring people together, just about everyone works in cubicles so that they are readily accessible to others, even CEO Andy Grove (see Figure 14-1).[2]

Although the effects of organizational culture can be quite profound, it would be misleading to suggest that culture operates in a vacuum. Indeed, whereas culture influences organizations from inside, the external environments within which organizations operate also have considerable impact on their functioning. For example, economists tell us how economic forces affect corporate performance, lawyers consider the impact of legal rulings and governmental regulations, and marketers investigate the effects of competition and product demand. Specialists in organizational behavior are also sensitive to the effects of the external environmental forces acting on organizations, particularly the use of *technology*—that is, the organization's methods for transforming raw materials (whether physical entities, such as iron ore, or abstract ones, such as ideas) into various goods or services.[3]

Because these two aspects of the work environment, culture and technology, are so vital to organizational functioning, they will be the focus of this chapter.[4] Specifically, we will begin by describing the basic nature of organizational culture, including the role it plays in organizations. Then, we will describe the processes through which organizational culture is formed and maintained. Next, we will review the effects of organizational culture on individual and organizational functioning and examine when and how culture is subject to change. Following this, we will shift our attention to technology. In this regard, we will examine the role of technology in organizations, focusing especially on the way people respond to automation. Finally, we will review various ways technology is used today to improve both the quality of employees' work lives and the effectiveness of organizational functioning.

Organizational Culture: Its Basic Nature

To understand organizational culture more fully, we will begin by exploring three very fundamental issues. First, we will formally define organizational culture. Second, we will examine the role that culture plays in organizations. Finally, we will consider a key issue relevant to understanding culture: whether there is only one or many different cultures operating within organizations.

Organizational Culture: A Definition

Anyone who has worked in several different organizations knows that each is unique. Even organizations concerned with the same activities or that provide similar products or services can be very different places in which to work. For example, in the world of retailing, Wal-Mart employees are encouraged to be agents for the customer, focusing on service and satisfaction.[5] By contrast, employees of Sears, Roebuck & Co. allegedly have been pressured into meeting sales quotas, pushing customers to make unnecessary purchases.[6]

How can such similar businesses be so very different in their approaches? It's tempting to speculate that because people have different personalities, the organizations in which they work are likely to be different from each other as well. However, when you consider that entire organizations are often so consistently different from each other, it's apparent that there's more involved than simply differences in the personalities of the employees. In fact, in many organizations, employees are a constantly changing cast of characters—old ones frequently leave and new ones join. Despite such shifts, however, the organizations themselves alter slowly, if at all. In fact, it is often the new employees who themselves change rather than their organizations. In a sense, then, organizations have a stable existence of their own, quite apart from the unique combination of people of which they are composed at any given time.

What accounts for such stability? To a great extent, the answer involves the impact of **organizational culture**—a cognitive framework consisting of attitudes, values, behavioral norms, and expectations shared by organization members.[7] Once established, these beliefs, expectancies, and values tend to be relatively stable and exert strong influences on organizations and those working in them.

At the root of any organization's culture is a set of core characteristics that are collectively valued by members of an organization. Recent research by Chatman and Jehn has shown that seven elements of organizational culture may be used to describe organizations.[8] These are as follows:

1. *Innovation*: the extent to which people are expected to be creative, and generate new ideas. For example, employees of MCI Communications are encouraged to be unique and to bring fresh ideas to their work.[9] In fact, company founder Bill McGowan is so adamant about this that procedure manuals are nowhere to be found at MCI.
2. *Stability*: valuing a stable, predictable, rule-oriented environment. For example, whereas Bank of America is very conservative, making only the safest investments, buyers at The Limited are discouraged from making too many "safe" choices.[10]
3. *Orientation toward people*: being fair, supportive, and showing respect for individuals' rights. As defined in this way, FedEx is a company that has been recognized for having a highly "people-oriented" culture.[11]
4. *Results-orientation*: the strength of its concern for achieving desired results. At Motorola, for example, everything the company does is designed to take the rate of defects down to zero.
5. *Easygoingness*: the extent to which the work atmosphere is relaxed and laid back. This is certainly *not* the case at Intel, whose corporate culture has been likened to that of the Marine Corps.[12]
6. *Attention to detail*: concern for being analytical and precise. For example, one employee of Merck, the world's largest maker of prescription drugs, recognized the importance of precision in the company's work: "Here we make drugs and there's no room for error."[13]
7. *Collaborative orientation*: emphasis on working in teams, as opposed to individually. Companies in which there is a great deal of research and de-

organizational culture A cognitive framework consisting of attitudes, values, behavioral norms, and expectations shared by organization members.

ferent interaction groups. In other words, people who interacted with one another on a regular basis would come to perceive key aspects of their working world in similar terms, whereas those who did not interact regularly would come to perceive the same events differently. Results offered strong support for these predictions (see Figure 14-4).

These findings suggest that shared meanings or interpretations—a key ingredient in organizational culture—derive, at least in part, from shared experiences and from the experience of working together. Moreover, this same process seems to play a role in the development of organizational subcultures, as groups of employees who usually work together develop views somewhat different from those of other groups of employees about what is happening in their company and of the meaning of such events.

There are several practical applications from these findings. First, because different groups within an organization have somewhat different cultures, interventions designed to change job performance or work-related attitudes through shifts in culture should be customized for each important group.[25] Second, if shared expectations and values are desired across an organization, steps should be taken to increase contact and interaction between various groups. Finally, Rentsch's findings point to the fact that sometimes, seemingly small events can carry big messages. For example, one of the events described most frequently by members of the organization studied was, "Partners sometimes play golf in the afternoon." Senior partners in the company were shocked to discover that this activity, which they viewed as relatively trivial, received so much attention from others. In retrospect, however, they realized that it conveyed important meanings to other employees—meanings such as "Only senior partners have any privileges around here," or "Whatever people say, status is really important." We will return to this point in our discussion of efforts to change organizational culture. For now, we simply note that where organizational culture is concerned, actions, as they say, do indeed "speak louder than words."

Tools for Transmitting Culture

How are cultural values transmitted between people? In other words, how do employees come to learn about their organization's culture? Research has shown that there are several key mechanisms involved, most importantly: *symbols, stories, jargon, ceremonies,* and *statements of principle.*[26]

■ **Figure 14-4**
Organizational Culture as Shared Meanings
Organizational members who interacted with one another on a regular basis came to share interpretations of organizational events. Those who did not interact with one another did not share such interpretations. According to Rentsch (1991; see Note 24), such shared meanings or interpretations are an important determinant of organizational culture.

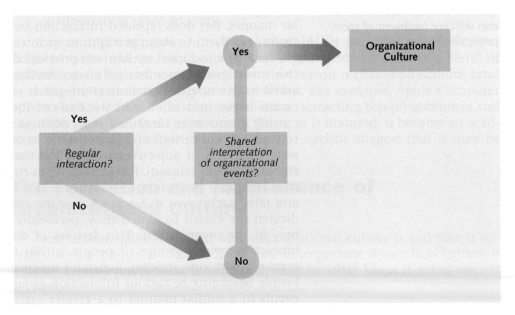

We discuss the use of status symbols in Chapter 8, and the use of power in organizations, in Chapter 12.

Symbols: Objects that say more than meets the eye. First, organizations often rely on **symbols**—material objects that connote meanings that extend beyond their intrinsic content.[27] For example, some companies use impressive buildings to convey the organization's strength and significance, signifying that it is a large, stable place.[28] Other companies rely on slogans, such as General Electric's "Progress is our most important product," or Ford's "Quality is job 1" to symbolize their values. Corporate cars (or even jets) are also used to convey information about an organization's culture, such as who wields power.

Research has shown that symbols are an important vehicle for communicating culture. For example, in an interesting study, Ornstein showed drawings of company reception areas to people and then asked them to evaluate what the companies pictured were like.[29] She found that different types of symbols projected different images of the organizations' likely cultures. For example, firms in which there were lots of plants and flower arrangements were judged to have friendly, person-oriented cultures, whereas those in which waiting areas were adorned with awards and trophies were believed to be highly interested in achieving success. These findings suggest that material symbols are potent tools for sending messages about organizational culture (see Figure 14-5).

Stories: "In the old days, we used to . . .". Organizations also transmit information about culture by virtue of the *stories* that are told in them, both formally and informally.[30] Stories illustrate key aspects of an organization's culture, and telling them can effectively introduce or reaffirm those values to employees.[31] Some of the most effective stories involve recounting *critical incidents*, important events in shaping the company's history.[32] It is important to note, however, that stories need not involve some great event, such as someone who saved the company with a single wise decision but may be small tales that become legends because they so effectively communicate a message. For example, employees at the British confectionery firm, Cadbury, are purposely told stories about the company's founding on Quaker traditions to get them to appreciate and accept the basic Quaker value of hard work.[33] Stories are also a big part of the way culture is transmitted to new employees of the Walt Disney Company.[34]

Consider this little story that has become legendary at Stew Leonard's food store, a $100 million operation that prides itself on exceptional customer service.[35] (Its motto is "Rule 1: The customer is always right. Rule 2: If the cus-

■ Figure 14-5
Symbolizing a Culture of Success
If a collection of photos of oneself with successful people symbolize one's own success, then displaying such photos in an organization may be recognized as reflecting the successfulness of the organization. Organizations regularly use such symbols to convey important aspects of their organizational culture.

(**Source:** Copyright © 1992 by Leo Cullum.)

"What we're looking for, Ted, is a guy who has pictures of himself with lots of famous people."

We will return to the topic of technology in Chapter 15, where we discuss its role in organizational design.

nology represents a potent external force to which all organizations must be responsive. It is, therefore, not surprising that top management scholars, such as Peter F. Drucker, have asserted that technology holds the key to managing tomorrow's organizations.[68]

We will now turn our attention to the matter of how technology affects individual and organizational functioning. Given how wide-reaching this topic is, it shouldn't be surprising to you that we already have had occasion to describe the effects of technology elsewhere in this book—such as in the contexts of communication and decision making, and that we will do so again later—notably, in connection with organizational structure and design. Here, we will concentrate on the more general aspects of technology. Specifically, we will begin by reviewing the basic dimensions of technology. Following this, we will explore a critical issue involving technology in today's organizations—the way people respond to automation.

Classifying Technology's Basic Dimensions

Although many organizational theorists have described the various types of technologies that exist, the most comprehensive scheme has been suggested by Charles Perrow.[69] This system is useful for categorizing the technologies of both manufacturing and service organizations.

Perrow begins by distinguishing between two basic dimensions. The first is *exceptions*, the degree to which an organization makes use of standard inputs to turn out standard outputs (i.e., makes few exceptions) or encounters many nonroutine situations (i.e., has to make many exceptions in the way it operates). Perrow's second dimension is known as *problems*—the degree to which the situations encountered are either easy to analyze, allowing for programmed decisions, or complex and difficult to analyze, requiring nonprogrammed decision making. By dichotomizing both dimensions and overlaying them onto each other, Perrow identified four distinct technological types. The resulting **matrix of technologies** is summarized in Table 14-2.

- The first technological type is known as **routine technology**. It includes operations with highly standardized inputs and outcomes, and problems that are easy to analyze. Examples include assembly-line manufacturing and vocational training, both cases in which the product or service is clearly defined. But, when exceptions occur—such as when new products are to be produced, or new subjects are to be taught—the appropriate reaction is readily apparent.
- Perrow's second technological type, **craft technology**, involves operations in which inputs and outcomes are also standardized, but problems are more difficult to analyze. For example, cabinet makers always use wood and lam-

matrix of technologies Perrow's system of categorizing technologies based on two dimensions: *exceptions*, the degree to which an organization makes use of standard inputs to turn out standard outputs; and *problems*, the degree to which the situations encountered are either easy or difficult to analyze.

routine technology Technology involving highly standardized inputs and outputs, and problems that are easy to analyze (e.g., assembly lines and vocational training) (see *matrix of technologies*).

craft technology Technology involving highly standardized inputs and outputs, and problems that are difficult to analyze (e.g., cabinet makers and public schools) (see *matrix of technologies*).

■ TABLE 14-2	PERROW'S MATRIX OF TECHNOLOGIES		
By combining two levels of exceptions (few and many) with two levels of problems (easy to analyze and difficult to analyze), Perrow identified the four technological types identified here.	Exceptions	Problems	Technological Type (and Examples)
	Few	Easy to analyze	Routine technology (e.g., assembly-line manufacturing, vocational training)
		Difficult to analyze	Craft technology (e.g., cabinet-making, public schools)
	Many	Easy to analyze	Engineering technology (e.g., heavy machinery construction, health and fitness club)
		Difficult to analyze	Nonroutine technology (e.g., research unit, psychiatric hospital)

SOURCE: Perrow, 1967; see Note 69.

inated products to create finished furniture products. Similarly, public schools focus their attention on ways of teaching the average student. In either case—such as when a special order is placed, or a student with a learning disability is encountered—the appropriate response is not entirely clear. Organizations of this type are simply not set up to handle exceptional cases where the most appropriate decisions are not clearly specified in advance.

- In contrast, Perrow's final two technological types involve industries which are better prepared to handle exceptions. For example, organizations using **engineering technology**, such as those in heavy machinery construction and health and fitness clubs, expect to encounter many exceptions in inputs or outputs, but these can be dealt with in standardized ways. For example, people come to health and fitness facilities in different physical conditions and with different goals. Some may be trying to lose weight, others may be trying to regain strength and agility after an injury, and still others may be training for a major bodybuilding contest. Although different types, amounts, and difficulty levels of exercise may be dictated on a case-by-case basis, the decision regarding exactly what the client should do to achieve his or her goal is relatively straightforward, and based on preestablished information about the effectiveness of different exercise regimes.

- Other industries also face exceptions but more difficult decisions as well. Such organizations are said to employ **nonroutine technology**. For example, research units, by their very existence, are created to tackle difficult, exceptional situations. Psychiatric hospitals also fit into this category. Not only do they encounter a wide variety of people with unique histories and combinations of mental and physical problems, but the appropriate treatment is not always obvious. Despite widespread advances in psychiatric diagnoses, treatment decisions are extremely complex and far from routine.

Automation in Today's Organizations

Traditionally, using technology on the job involved the manual or mechanical manipulation of things. People at work used chains and pulleys to help them lift heavy items and maneuver them from one place to another. Although work of this type still goes on, today's workplace is making increasing use of **high technology**, an advanced form of technology employing tools that are electronic in nature, usually relying on the use of microprocessor chips. For example, typesetters used to have to move together pieces of metal type on wooden blocks to create plates from which documents were printed. Today, this process goes on invisibly, as compositors simply enter letters onto a keyboard, just as you do word processing at home. Clearly, technology has changed the fundamental nature of work for many people.[70] Some examples of high technology used by today's organizations include:

- *Advanced manufacturing technology (AMT)*: manufacturing in which the various processes are guided by computers
- *Computer-integrated manufacturing (CIM)*: manufacturing processes that go beyond AMT by using computers to gather information and using this information to make decisions about ways in which the manufacturing process needs to be altered
- *Computer-aided design and engineering (CAD/CAE)*: the processes of using computers to build and simulate the characteristics of products and to test their effectiveness
- *Industrial robotics (IR)*: computer-controlled machines that manipulate materials and perform complex functions

engineering technology
Technology involving many exceptions in inputs or outputs and problems which are easy to analyze (e.g., heavy machinery construction and health and fitness clubs).

nonroutine technology
Technology involving many exceptions in inputs or outputs, and problems that are difficult to analyze (e.g., research units and psychiatric hospitals).

high technology The kind of technology that is electronic in nature, usually relying on the use of microprocessor chips.

Assistive Technology: Helping People with Disabilities Work Productively

assistive technology Devices and other solutions that help individuals with physical or mental problems perform the various actions needed to do their jobs.

The use of assistive technology is helpful in making it possible to further diversify the composition of the workforce, a topic discussed in Chapter 2.

If you've ever seen public telephones with volume controls, elevator signs with floor markings in Braille, and cutaway curbs on sidewalks, you are already familiar with the fact that things can be done to enable people with various handicaps to function effectively in society. However, these accommodations are just a small part of the picture when it comes to using technology to assist disabled people. In today's organizations technology is widely used to make it possible for skilled people to perform their jobs although they may be challenged by some form of physical or mental condition. (For examples of technological advances used for these purposes, refer to Table 14-3.) As a result of this technology, it is possible for people who only a few years ago could not have done so to perform mainstream jobs today. Such technology is referred to as **assistive technology**—devices and other solutions that help individuals with physical or mental problems perform the various actions needed to do their jobs.[90]

Competitive advantages. Besides the fact that it is just "the right thing to do," there are several good reasons why assistive technology is in such widespread use today. For one, the workplace is so competitive that employers simply cannot afford to overlook qualified employees just because adjustments need to be made to the way they do their jobs. According to the Job Accommodation Network, a clearinghouse of information on ways to accommodate people with disabilities, this process need not be expensive. In fact, they claim that about half the accommodations that need to be made cost under $50, and almost one-third are without any cost whatsoever.[91] For example, instead of investing in new plumbing to lower a drinking fountain so a person in a wheelchair could use it, a much cheaper alternative is possible: Simply provide a dispenser for drink cups.

Demographic imperatives. A second reason why assistive technology is in such widespread use is because of the simple demographic fact that the workforce is aging and people are living longer.[92] As people get older, even the healthiest are likely to suffer impairments in their hearing, vision, and manual dexterity. If such individuals, who are likely to be highly experienced and knowledgeable, are to leave their jobs, it would likely be prohibitively expen-

■ TABLE 14-3	ASSISTIVE TECHNOLOGY: SOME EXAMPLES

Technology can be used to assist people with various disabilities to function effectively on the job. Here are examples of devices—some sophisticated and some simple—applied to this purpose.

Device	Description
Telephone handset amplifer	Mechanism for raising the volume of telephone earpiece, enabling hearing-impaired people to use the telephone.
Voice-activated computer	Software that allows people to input words into a computer by speaking. IBM's "Speech Server" series has a 32,000-word vocabulary, and the capacity to enter 70 words per minute.
Reading machine	Hardware using simulated speech to read to visually impaired people (such as the portable unit introduced by Xerox's Kurzweil Business Unit).
Sight devices	Portable sensory guides and closed-circuit TV monitors with magnification that enable people with visual impairments to navigate their physical environments.
Mouthpicks	Stylus-like tools that quadriplegics can use to operate computers.
Gooseneck telephones	Adjustable telephone headsets that can be used by people with limited physical dexterity.

SOURCES: Tompkins, 1993, see Note 90; Anonymous, 1993, see Note 92.

sive, and possibly impossible, to replace them. Making the adjustments necessary to help these individuals perform their jobs makes good business sense.

Legal requirements. Another reason—and, for some, the major reason—why technology is being widely used to help people perform their jobs is that they are required to do so by law—specifically, the recently enacted *Americans with Disabilities Act (ADA)*. According to this law, U.S. employers must make "reasonable accommodations" for disabled people who are otherwise qualified to perform their jobs so long as this can be done without imposing an undue financial burden on the company or causing a direct threat to anyone's safety. As companies attempt to comply with ADA requirements, many new technologies have been developed, including, for wheelchair users, car-top carriers for transporting their wheelchairs, and desktops that are high enough to accommodate them while working.[93] With an eye toward publicizing the latest in assistive technology, a cable-TV network called "America's Disability Channel" headquartered in San Antonio, Texas, has gone on the air.

To help companies comply with the ADA, the federal government has several initiatives to encourage private companies to develop suitable assistive technologies. For example, the Disabled Access Credit Act gives small businesses a tax credit for investing in ways of meeting ADA requirements. Tax laws also provide credits for companies attempting to make their facilities accessible to persons with disabilities, and for hiring new employees with disabilities referred by state employment services.[94]

So intensive have been efforts to use technology to help mainstream disabled employees, that specific new positions have been created—*assistive technology coordinators*, people who help businesses and educational institutions find ways of accommodating individuals with disabilities. Laura Micklus at the Center for Independent Living of Southwestern Connecticut in Stratford, Connecticut, is one person who holds such a job.[95] Ms. Micklus has noted that the same highly automated equipment and computers earlier described as making it easier for able-bodied people to perform their jobs is often the difference between working and not working for people with disabilities. When she says this, Ms. Micklus, herself a cerebral palsy patient, knows what she's talking about. She relies on $10,000 worth of computer equipment in her office to retrieve information from a national database of ways people with handicaps can be accommodated on the job. This is not to say that Ms. Micklus is desk-bound. Making use of still more assistive technologies, she sometimes finds herself traveling to job sites around the country to analyze jobs and recommend modifications or appropriate equipment that can be used to help disabled people perform their jobs. Clearly, Ms. Micklus is a model that this can be done.

Computerized Performance Monitoring: Management by Remote Control

One of the most popular uses of technology in the workplace today comes in the form of using computers to collect, store, analyze, and report information about the work people are doing—a practice known as **computerized performance monitoring (CPM)**.[96] As this definition implies, CPM refers to a broad range of procedures that enable supervisors to "look in" on employees doing their jobs. CPM makes it possible for employees' work to be observed and quantified—particularly those who work at computer terminals (e.g., phone sales agents, data entry and word processing personnel, airline reservation agents, and telephone operators). Not all CPM systems are the same. In some, employees are monitored all the time as work is carried out; in others, observation occurs only sometimes, although the software keeps a detailed record of their work.[97] Regardless of differences between systems, all make it possible for job performance to be observed in a constant, unblinking fashion.

Within the past decade CPM systems have grown in popularity. Recent estimates are that more than 10 million employees are monitored in over

computerized performance monitoring (CPM) The practice of using computers to collect, store, analyze, and report information about the work people are doing.

70,000 companies in the United States, representing an investment in equipment of over $1 billion.[98] As one California vendor of networking software advertises, their CPM system provides a simple solution to supervisors interested in closely watching many employees at once, all from one convenient spot: "Look in on Sue's computer screen . . . In fact, Sue doesn't even know you're there! Hot key again and off you go on your rounds of the company. Viewing one screen after another, helping some, watching others. All from the comfort of your chair."[99] Clearly, CPM changes the basic nature of the supervisor-subordinate relationship.[100]

Not surprisingly, the use of CPM has been the subject of considerable debate.[101] Some have argued that it represents an invasion of employees' privacy, creates an atmosphere of distrust, and can be a source of work-related stress.[102] In fact, the U.S. Congress is considering legislation that would require employers to notify employees of their intent to monitor their performance and to somehow signal when monitoring is occurring. Proponents have countered, however, that CPM makes it possible for supervisors to gather more objective information about performance, providing a valuable source of feedback and information useful for planning training programs and workloads.[103]

What does the scientific evidence have to say about these arguments? Although there has been only limited research on the effects of CPM, what little work has been done has suggested that to some degree *both* perspectives are correct. For example, research comparing monitored and nonmonitored employees found that monitored employees were, in fact, more productive on simple tasks. However, as we described in Chapter 8, monitoring lowers performance on complex tasks. But, even if performance on simple tasks increases in response to monitoring, CPM also leads people to experience higher levels of stress and lower levels of job satisfaction.[104] Part of the problem seems to be that working in front of video display terminals all day contributes to feelings of isolation and loneliness, unpleasant conditions that are associated with stress.[105]

It is important to note that employees who are monitored with respect to specific aspects of their performance might be expected to work hard to improve those performance measures, even if doing so comes at the expense of other, possibly more important, aspects of performance. For example, Aiello reports an incident in which telephone operators were monitored by supervisors who checked to see that they did not spend longer than 22 seconds on each call.[106] The result: Operators almost always met the standard—but some, as many as 25 percent, admitted that they did so by "cheating." In instances in which customers required more than 22 seconds to help, such as when they had strong accents or hearing impediments, operators simply disconnected such callers so they could be rewarded for meeting the goal. Even those who didn't take such drastic measures lamented that they could not take the time to be as pleasant and friendly as they wanted.

Not only do employees dislike being monitored, evidence also shows that many supervisors dislike the added workload that comes from having to review constantly incoming data about employees' work performance. The problem is that monitoring raises expectations that supervisors will have to "say something" to employees about their performance, holding them to a standard that their busy schedules may not permit.[107] However, when employee performance appears to be unexpectedly poor, supervisors are able to rely on computerized records of performance as the basis for making accurate assessments of the problem.[108] Under such conditions, supervisors will surely benefit from having accurate information at their disposal to help them diagnose the problem at hand.

To summarize, it appears that although there may be some benefits associated with CPM, there are also some limitations (for a summary, see Figure 14-10). It is important to note that this particular use of technology has a long way to go before it gains widespread acceptance. By creating a whole new dy-

As you may recall from Chapter 8, the impact of CPM on performance may be explained by the process of social facilitation.

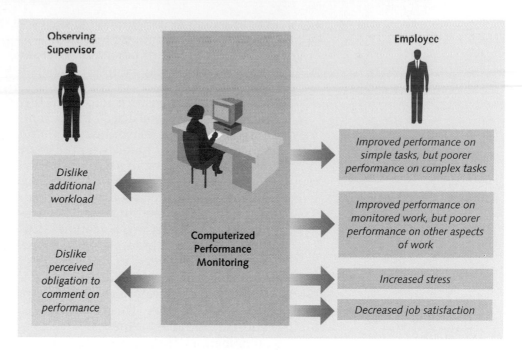

■ **Figure 14-10**
Computerized Performance Monitoring: A Mixed Bag of Results
Although computerized performance monitoring has been introduced in the hopes of improving employees' work performance, studies have found its impact to be both positive and negative in nature.

namic between superiors and subordinates, CPM—like many other new technologies that have been introduced in the workplace—appears threatening. But will it ever be completely accepted? We suspect that the answer resides in how the technique is used—or abused—in practice. If used as a tool to help improve performance, we believe CPM has a valuable role in organizations. However, if it is misused—such as for close surveillance of nonwork activities, such as bathroom trips—such invasions of privacy are sure to be rejected. In conclusion, it is not necessarily the technology itself that is either useful or harmful in practice, but the way in which people use it.

Technological Aids to Customer Service

Have you ever heard someone grumble that the service received today is "not like it was in the good old days"? For the most part, such complaints are well founded. Through the early 1950s, it was not unusual for businesses to provide high levels of courteous, personalized service. You could phone in your order to Mr. Smith's corner store, and his son would deliver your groceries to your table after school, and charge them to your account. You also could go to the corner "service" station, where Gus would pump your gas, clean your windshield, check your oil, and even install a new muffler or set of tires on your car. Today, however, Mr. Smith's place more than likely has given way to a huge, 24-hour supermarket, and Gus has been replaced by a pay-at-the-pump, self-serve operation.

Experts tell us that the depersonalization of service came about as a result of several forces. The automobile led to suburban sprawl, cities grew, and markets expanded. Increasing competition led to reduced profit margins, and the need to standardize goods and services. The result: Mom's diner surely delivered more personalized service than McDonald's, but given its economic disadvantage (e.g., the higher per unit cost of producing on a small scale), it simply couldn't afford to compete. Personal service became a casualty as a result.

Analyzing this state of affairs, Ives and Mason have pointed out that technology is now being used to revitalize customer service.[109] They note that this is occurring in three distinct ways:

1. Many of today's organizations are employing technology aimed at *delivering personalized service*. For example, computerized systems are also used to give the most appropriate coupons to shoppers who make certain purchases at their supermarket. Systems are in use in many chains in which

in-store coupons are printed on the backs of register receipts (or, in some systems, on separate printers). These coupons are customized to fit the customer's profile of purchases. For example, purchasers of one brand of breakfast cereal may be given a coupon to induce them to try another brand. Or, purchasers of peanut butter may be given coupons for products that might go with it, such as bread or jelly. Although these practices are not "personalized" in the same sense as Mr. Smith taking your grocery order and delivering it to your door, they represent forms of personalization that capitalize on the computer technology available today.

2. Technology is being used to help revitalize service by *augmenting service*. This refers to the practice of providing customers with additional support related to the product or service. How can technology be used to help provide "something extra"? Several companies have been fairly ingenious in this regard. Sometimes, the additional service is small—but quite helpful. For example, Hertz pioneered systems by which rental car customers are guided to their vehicles by signs displaying their names, and handheld devices that agents use to check in returned vehicles and print customer receipts on the spot—practices that eliminated check-in and check-out lines. This customer-friendly technology helped Hertz attract considerable business.

American Hospital Supply is another company whose business also grew because of the technology they used to help customers. Their strategy was to install terminals in the offices of clients, devices that could be used to order any of the company's 135,000 products directly from the company at any time with just a few simple keystrokes. Both examples represent extra services made available through technology that add to the benefits customers receive from dealing with those companies.

3. Ives and Mason note that technology can help by *transforming business*—that is, developing entirely new practices that better satisfy customers' needs. Specifically, today's advanced computer information systems make it possible for customized goods to be made with almost the same efficiency as standardized goods.

For example, Benjamin Moore paints uses a photospectrometer to identify the color of a customer's fabric sample and tells the computer how to match it by appropriately mixing the company's paints. In-store displays also exist today to help Hallmark customers create greeting cards, personalized with the name and message specified by the purchaser. Similarly, Warner Brothers has a system in which customers can mail order music cassettes containing their favorite songs selected from a menu of available titles. As a final example, printing technology has made it possible for magazine publishers to tailor their advertisements and editorials to different readers. As a result, swine farmers in Iowa who subscribe to the *Farm Journal* are sent a somewhat different magazine than dairy farmers in Vermont.

All these examples represent ways in which today's companies are using technology to transform their businesses to provide improved customer service.

Although some technology has led to the depersonalization of service, the above examples make it clear that technology also can be used—and, in fact, *is* being used—to vastly improve customer service. While we shouldn't look anytime soon for Mr. Smith to return to his corner grocery, or Gus to return to his service station, we can expect technology to be used to improve customer service in these, and all businesses, in a variety of different forms.

Environmentally Friendly Technology: Design for Disassembly

Problem: The earth's mineral deposits are rapidly being depleted and landfills are reaching capacity. Believe it or not, 94 percent of materials taken from the earth enters the waste stream only months later.[110] There's no mistaking the fact that the industrialized world has a long history of taking riches from the earth and returning rubbish. Scientists tell us that this cannot go on forever and that if we are to rely on the earth's natural resources in the future, we must conserve them now, using them wisely. Fortunately, a movement is afoot to make manufacturers responsible for taking back their used products and recycling them. Laws across Europe will soon be requiring manufacturers to do this. Already, in Germany companies are legally responsible for the way their packaging is used, encouraging them not only to recycle, but to come up with ingenious ways to reduce the amount of packaging they use for their products (see Figure 14-11).

The impact of the German legislation has been encouraging: Within the first two years, the "take-back" law has reduced the amount of packaging waste by 4 percent—some 600 million tons. On the heels of this success, companies are moving to reduce the amount of product they waste. One of the most effective processes in this regard is known as **design for disassembly (DFD)**. This is the process of designing and building products so that their parts can be reused several times and then safely disposed of at the end of the product's life. What this boils down to is fewer parts, fewer materials, and assembly processes designed with later disassembly in mind.

A good example of DFD can be seen in the manufacturing of automobiles: By the end of this decade, in Europe some 200,000 cars will be making "return trips." BMW is a leader in this process.[111] It is replacing glue and solder in bumpers with fasteners, making them easier to be recycled. Instrument panels are made of polyurethane foam that can be recycled in one piece. Already 80 percent of the weight of a BMW comes from recycled parts, and the company hopes to get this figure up to 95 percent. But it is not only cars that are prime candidates for DFD. Computers, telephones, and engines are also commonly designed with disassembly in mind.

Although you might not know it, if you've ever used one of Kodak's Fun Saver 35 cameras (with camera and film in a single "disposable" package), you have used a product that was designed for disassembly. But, it wasn't always that way. The first such products were simply tossed away. That was, until 1990 when Kodak was taken to task by environmentalists for putting hundreds of thousands of used cameras into landfills. Today, however, these cameras are designed so that they can be returned to Kodak by film processors, where the plastic is ground up and remolded into new parts, and the guts of the camera—the moving parts and electronics—are reused up to ten times.

design for disassembly (DFD) The process of designing and building products so that their parts can be reused several times and then safely disposed of at the end of the product's life.

■ **Figure 14-11**
Recycling Packaging: It's the Law in Germany
German law requires retailers, like this hardware store in Münster, to collect for recycling the packaging materials in which items are sold. Manufacturers are attempting to eliminate such waste by repackaging their merchandise in creative ways.

Kodak is not alone among American companies using DFD. Xerox also has been using recycled parts in its copiers, as has Hewlett-Packard in its DeskJet printers. As you might imagine, the motivation for doing so is "green," no matter what you mean by it. Whether by "green" you're talking about preserving the environment or making money, the result is the same: After retooling costs, companies find themselves saving money by using recycled parts. The Kodak Fun Saver 35 flash camera is the company's most profitable product. And Xerox has been saving about $500 million a year by remanufacturing and recycling parts. The bottom line: DFD is helping companies save both money and the earth's natural environment at the same time.

SUMMARY AND REVIEW

Organizational Culture: Its Basic Nature

Organizational culture is a cognitive framework consisting of attitudes, values, behavioral norms, and expectations shared by organization members. It serves several different functions, including providing members with a sense of identity, generating commitment to the organization's mission, and clarifying and reinforcing standards of behavior.

Typically, organizations consist of both a **dominant culture**, reflecting the organization's overall values, and various **subcultures**, separate cultures existing within selected parts of the dominant culture. Four main types of organizational culture are the *academy*, the *club*, the *baseball team*, and the *fortress*.

The Formation and Maintenance of Organizational Culture

The emergence of organizational culture can be traced to several different factors. Among these are the influence of founders, the organization's experiences with the external environment, and contact between various people within the organization. Culture is transmitted via various mechanisms, including: **symbols**, *stories*, *jargon*, *ceremonies*, and *statements of principle* (including *codes of ethics*).

Organizational Culture: Its Consequences and Capacity to Change

Although it is popularly believed that certain types of organizational culture are associated with more successful organizational performance, scientific evidence does not support this claim. However, the voluntary turnover of individuals is related to organizational culture: People remain employed longer in cultures that stress pleasant interpersonal relationships than those emphasizing hard work. Turnover is also lower among individuals whose personal values more closely match those of the organizations in which they are employed than those for whom personal and organizational values are less closely matched.

Organizational culture is likely to change due to a variety of factors. Among these are changes in the composition of the workforce (over time, different people bring different values into the organization), mergers and acquisitions (adjustments have to be made to accommodate the "marriage" between companies), and planned change (deliberate decisions to alter the organization's structure or its basic operations).

The Role of Technology in Organizations

Technology refers to the physical and mental processes used to transform inputs into usable outputs. According to Perrow's **matrix of technologies**, four different classes of technology may be identified: **routine technology**, **craft technology**, **engineering technology**, and **nonroutine technology**.

Today's organizations frequently rely on the use of such **high technology** tools as **automation**—the process of using machines to perform tasks that might otherwise be done by people. Not only is automation extremely expensive to employ, but it sometimes also leads to high levels of unemployment. When people remain employed in automated work environments, their work is typically either extremely dull (e.g., monitoring machines that do all the work) or highly challenging and involving a great deal of training (e.g., programming and maintaining the machines). Economic competition is making the shift to automation a reality in a growing number of manufacturing and service organizations.

Modern Uses of Technology

Technology is used in many different ways in today's organizations. For example, **assistive technology** focuses on the task of helping people with handicaps perform their jobs. Such efforts are stimulated both by law (e.g., the *Americans with Disabilities Act*), and economic forces (e.g., the need to keep qualified employees who happen to be disabled).

Computerized performance monitoring (CPM) is used to observe and record the performance of employees, particularly those working at computer terminals. Although this practice may lead to performance improvement, it is also highly stress-provoking, and generally disliked by employees. Technology is also frequently used to improve customer service. Computers are being used in various ways to deliver not only more personalized service but also to add new and improved services to those currently performed.

Finally, technology known as **design for disassembly** is being used to allow products to be reused, and waste to be reduced, thereby preserving the physical environment.

1. Characterize the culture of any organization with which you may be familiar by describing the core characteristics collectively valued by its members. Would you consider it an academy, club, baseball team, or fortress?
2. Suppose you are founding a new company. Describe how you might either intentionally or unintentionally affect its culture. How might your influences linger within the organization long after you have left it?
3. What kinds of events might be responsible for the changing of organizational culture? Explain why these events are likely to be so influential.
4. Select a major business close to where you live. Then, using Perrow's system for classifying technology, categorize the types of technology employed by this company.
5. It may be said that automation may lead to unemployment on the one hand and new opportunities for employment, on the other. Explain this apparent contradiction.
6. Describe how technology can be used to improve: (a) work opportunities for people with physical handicaps, (b) the quality of customer service delivered, and (c) the quality of the physical environment.
7. Do you think the practice of computerized performance monitoring (CPM) is ethical? Why or why not? What benefits and costs may be expected from using CPM?

CASE IN POINT

Putting the "Service" Back into United Parcel Service

When you've been in business almost 90 years, it's understandable that you might begin to feel comfortable and set in your ways. This is the position in which United Parcel Service (UPS) found itself only a few years ago—a situation that kept growth flat during the late 1980s and early 1990s, while some aggressive competitors, notably Roadway Package Systems (RPS) and Airborne Express, were increasing volume by 30 to 40 percent.

One of UPS's problems was that its pricing and service policies were highly rigid. This "we-know-what's best" approach prevailed at UPS for many years. That was until 1990, when Kent C. "Oz" Nelson, UPS's CEO overhauled the company's underlying philosophy, transforming it from an aloof and rigid approach to a highly flexible one. This "velvet revolution," as UPS insiders referred to it, reflects a whole new way of doing business. For example, Kodak found service with UPS so difficult that it almost dropped them. Now, however, UPS has a full-time service representative in place at Kodak who helps reduce shipping expenses. "It's an entirely different company," says a Kodak official, who has increased its business with UPS by 15 percent—shipping some 50,000 packages a week.

Although UPS saved Kodak from defecting to the competition, the highly aggressive RPS was successful in luring away some UPS customers with volume pricing and innovative ways of tracing and billing shipments. UPS has been a longtime believer in a single-price formula. "We'd always prided ourselves on saying your grandmother paid the same price General Motors did," says Nelson. Now, however, GM gets a break, but granny doesn't. Since 1991, UPS's commercial rates grew only 3.4 percent a year, while average residential rates have jumped 11.4 percent per year.

To ensure that UPS's corporate customers remained satisfied—and loyal—Nelson appointed a panel of senior executives to study the company's problems. With this in mind, 25,000 UPS customers were interviewed to find out what new services they required. From this effort a new three-day guaranteed delivery service was introduced in February 1993—a product for customers who wanted assured delivery but who didn't need overnight or second-day deliveries, and who were attracted by the 20 percent lower price. Other changes merely required suspending rigid policies. For example, although customers used to be told when they had to have their packages ready, high-volume shippers can now get customized pickup and delivery times.

Listening to its customers, UPS also invested heavily—some $2 billion from 1991 to 1993 alone—in the latest technology needed to pinpoint all shipments in the system. Drivers now carry computerized clipboards on which the signatures of receiving parties are stored in digital form. Using cellular phones inside their familiar brown trucks, drivers transmit delivery information back to the company's central computers. If you call about your package, UPS can tell you where it is. Although Federal Express customers were used to this service for some time, the stodgier UPS was behind the times when it came to using the latest technology to improve its tracking service.

The fact that people commonly talk about "FedExing," instead of "UPS-ing" their shipments suggests that UPS may have lost the undisputed dominance in the delivery business it had only a decade ago. But, with the changes it has made, it is apparent that "Big Brown," as it is often called, will keep on delivering—and profitably.

Critical Thinking Questions

1. In what ways has UPS's organizational culture changed? What factors stimulated these changes?
2. What barriers would you imagine UPS faced in changing as it did?
3. How has UPS used technology to improve its customer service?

ROCKWELL INTERNATIONAL: A HIGH-TECH CONGLOMERATE REBORN

Traditionally, Rockwell International has been known for its aerospace business. In fact, 70 percent of all U.S. space flights relied on engines produced by Rockwell's Rocketdyne division. And, it was Rockwell's North American aviation division that built all the space capsules that went to the moon. However, with cutbacks in the space program and defense spending, Rockwell's government business plummeted from over 60 percent of sales to under 30 percent. For the giant conglomerate this translated into some $4 billion in lost business since 1986.

Amazingly, the company's revenues have not dropped accordingly, but have remained flat. The key has been in changing its business lines by acquiring new companies—some 43 in all during the past ten years. These include such industrial manufacturing companies as Allen-Bradley, Reliance Electric, and the Swiss firm Sprecher + Schuh. Today, Rockwell's $11 billion in revenue comes from electronics and industrial automation products, automotive components, aerospace products, and printing presses. No longer is it primarily an aerospace company. Instead, it makes 80 percent of the fax and modem chips, two-thirds of the presses used to print newspapers, and two-thirds of the truck axles used today.

Despite its highly diversified business mix, Rockwell has done an outstanding job of using one division to support another—and in the process, building them all. Take, for example, Rockwell's automotive electronics division, in existence only since 1993. It has no plants of its own, but scours other divisions to come up with new high-tech products that can be created using existing technologies. Case in point: the PathMaster navigation system for cars. This is a dash-mounted navigation screen that keeps drivers from getting lost and conveniently shows them the locations of nearby ATMs and fast-food restaurants. The PathMaster system started life several years ago as a $50,000 military navigation unit. But, with technical innovations and mass production, Rockwell now supplies the "brains" of such units to General Motors for only $500. GM, then produces and sells the final product as an option in some of its high-end vehicles.

The PathMaster is a lesson in coordination among various Rockwell divisions. Components for the device come from all over. The semiconductor to receive satellite signals comes from Rockwell's Microelectronics Technology Center (Newbury Park, California). The Digital Communications Division (Newport Beach, California) makes the digital signal processor. The main microprocessor is a product of the Collins avionics division (Cedar Rapids, Iowa). The satellite receiver was designed at the commercial global positioning system unit (Dallas, Texas). Other assorted components come off the drawing boards at the auto electronics division (Troy, Michigan). Final assembly is handled in the manufacturing facility of the telecommunication division (El Paso, Texas). The signals themselves are bounced off satellites made by Rockwell's space systems division (Downey, California).

Rockwell officials, such as Jeff Brady, vice president of transportation systems at the Autonetics Electronic Systems division, see the synergy between the company's various high-tech divisions as the key to its transition from military and space electronics into digital-based transportation devices for the private sector. Not only are the sales of such units projected to increase almost tenfold during the next few years, but similar collaborations between high-tech and manufacturing facilities throughout Rockwell are expected to bring even more possibilities for growth. As this occurs, analysts expect Rockwell International to become even stronger than it was before the government pulled the plug on its core business.

As this case illustrates, through careful coordination between its various divisions, Rockwell International has realized spectacular gains in new business. And, given the fact that the company was courting disaster due to dramatic losses of government business, such initiatives came none too soon. At the heart of this effort were moves to purchase new companies and to set them up as divisions whose efforts were carefully coordinated to create innovative new products, such as the PathMaster. In fact, it may be said that Rockwell International is a company whose whole is greater than the sum of its parts. This suggestion raises a question about exactly how various organizational tasks should be coordinated between the various individuals and groups that make up an organization.

OB researchers and theorists have provided considerable insight into this matter by studying what is called *organizational structure*—the way individuals and groups are arranged with respect to the tasks they perform—and *organizational design*—the process of coordinating these structural elements in the most effective manner. As you probably suspect, finding the best way to structure and design organizations is not a simple matter, and Rockwell's approach may not work well for all organizations. However, insofar as understanding the structure and design of organizations is essential to appreciate their functioning fully, organizational scientists have devoted considerable energy to this topic. We will describe these efforts in this chapter.

To begin, we will identify the basic building blocks of organizations, which can be depicted by the *organizational chart*, a useful pictorial way of showing key features of organizational structure. Following this, we will examine how these structural elements can be most effectively combined into productive organizational designs. Finally, we will discuss the role of technology as a cause—and a consequence—of organizational design. In so doing, we will be highlighting some basic facts regarding the role of the environment on organizational design.

Organizational Structure: The Basic Dimensions of Organizations

Think about how a simple house is constructed. It is composed of a wooden frame positioned atop a concrete slab covered by a roof and siding materials. Within this basic structure are separate systems operating to provide electricity, water, and telephone services. Similarly, the structure of the human body is composed of a skeleton surrounded by various systems of organs, muscle, and tissue serving bodily functions such as respiration, digestion, and the like. Although you may not have thought about it much, we can also identify the structure of an organization in a similar fashion.

Consider, for example, the college or university you attend. It is probably composed of various groupings of people and departments working together to serve special functions. Individuals and groups are dedicated to tasks such as teaching, providing financial services, maintaining the physical facilities, and so on. Of course, within each group, even more distinctions can be found between the jobs people perform. For example, it's unlikely that the instructor for your organizational behavior course is also teaching seventeenth-century French literature. You also can distinguish between the various tasks and functions people perform in other organizations. In other words, an organization is not a haphazard collection of people, but a meaningful combination of groups and individuals working together purposefully to meet the goals of the organization.[1] The term **organizational structure** refers to the formal configuration between individuals and groups with respect to the allocation of tasks, responsibilities, and authority within organizations.[2]

Strictly speaking, one cannot see the structure of an organization; it is an abstract concept. However, the connections between various clusters of functions of which an organization is composed can be represented in the form of a diagram known as an **organizational chart**. In other words, an organizational chart can be considered a representation of an organization's internal structure (see Figure 15-1). As you might imagine, organizational charts may be recognized as useful tools for avoiding confusion within organizations regarding how vari

organizational structure
The formal configuration between individuals and groups with respect to the allocation of tasks, responsibilities, and authorities within organizations.

organizational chart A diagram representing the connections between the various departments within an organization; a graphic representation of organizational structure.

The Organizational Chart:
A Valuable Guide to
Organizational Structure
Organizational charts provide useful
information about the interrelationships
between various organizational units
and the basic structural elements of
organizations.

(**Source:** Copyright © 1995 by Mark Litzler.)

"*I reported to the vice president of finance until someone discovered*
it wasn't a dotted line at all... just some spilled coffee."

As noted in Chapter 9, organiza-
tional charts are also used to trace
the formal flow of communication
within organizations.

ous tasks or functions are interrelated. By carefully studying organizational charts, we can learn about some of the basic elements of organizational structure. With this in mind, we will now turn our attention to the five basic dimensions of organizational structure that can be revealed by organizational charts.

Organizational charts provide information about the various tasks performed within an organization and the formal lines of authority between them. For example, look at the chart depicting part of a hypothetical manufacturing organization shown in Figure 15-2. Each box represents a specific job, and the lines connecting them reflect the formally prescribed lines of communication between the individuals performing those jobs. To specialists in organizational structure, however, such diagrams reveal a great deal more.

Hierarchy of Authority: Up and Down the Organizational Ladder

hierarchy of authority A
configuration of the reporting relationships within organizations;
that is, who reports to whom.

In particular, the organizational chart also provides information about who reports to whom—what is known as **hierarchy of authority**. The diagram reveals which particular lower-level employees are required to report to which particular individuals immediately above them in the organizational hierarchy. In our hypothetical example in Figure 15-2, the various regional salespeople (at the bottom of the hierarchy and the bottom of the diagram) report to their respective regional sales directors, who report to the vice president of sales, who reports to the president, who reports to the chief executive officer, who reports to the members of the board of directors. As we trace these reporting relationships, we work our way up the organization's hierarchy. In this case, the organization has six levels. Organizations may have many levels, in which case their structure is considered *tall*, or only a few, in which case their structure is considered *flat*.

For an extended discussion of the
trend toward downsizing organiza-
tions, see Chapters 2 and 16.

In recent years, a great deal has appeared in the news about organizations restructuring their workforces by flattening them out.[3] Although it has not been uncommon for large companies to lay off people in low-level assembly-line jobs, these days middle managers and executives, long believed to be se-

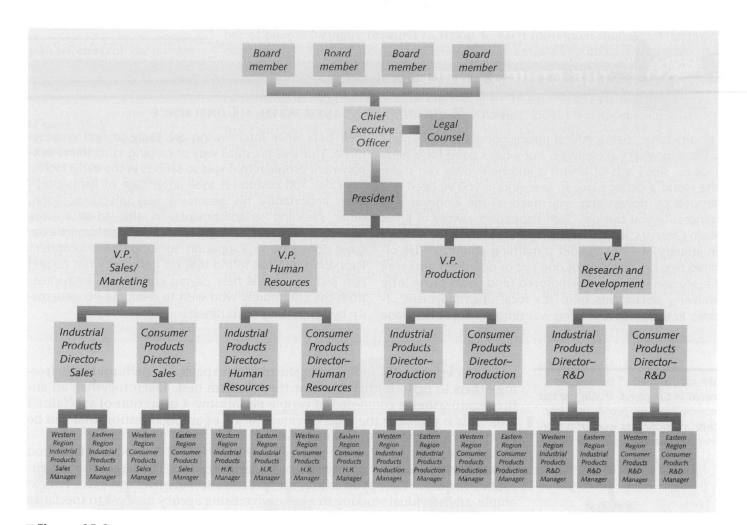

■ Figure 15-2

Organizational Chart of a Hypothetical Manufacturing Firm

An organizational chart, such as this one, identifies pictorially the various functions performed within an organization and the lines of authority between people performing those functions.

cure in their positions, find themselves unemployed as companies "downsize," "rightsize," "delayer," or "retrench" by eliminating entire layers of organizational structure.[4] In fact, it has been estimated that during the 1980s, one-quarter of middle management jobs were eliminated in American companies.[5] In 1990s the trend has continued as millions of people have lost their jobs due to the flattening of organizational hierarchies.[6] In January 1996 alone, U.S. companies eliminated 97,379 jobs due to reorganization and mergers, with the largest losses from AT&T, Apple Computer, and First Interstate Bank.[7]

The underlying assumption behind all these cutbacks is that fewer layers reduce waste and enable people to make better decisions (by moving them closer to the problems at hand), thereby leading to greater profitability. Consider an example from the auto industry. Whereas Ford has seventeen layers of management between its CEO and its employees on the factory floor, and GM has as many as twenty-two, the more profitable Toyota has only seven.[8] Although this is hardly conclusive evidence of the benefits of reducing the size of an organizational hierarchy, the differences are remarkable. In general, most management experts claim that although some hierarchy is necessary, too many layers of hierarchy can be hazardous to a company's bottom line.[9]

Division of Labor: Carving Up the Jobs Done

The standard organizational chart makes clear that the many tasks to be performed within an organization are divided into specialized jobs, a process known as the **division of labor**. The more that tasks are divided into separate jobs, the more those jobs are *specialized* and the narrower the range of activities that job incumbents are required to perform. In theory, the fewer tasks

division of labor The process of dividing the many tasks performed within an organization into specialized jobs.

there are many layers in the hierarchy and the span of control is relatively narrow (i.e., the number of people supervised is low). By contrast, the diagram at the bottom of Figure 15-3 shows a *flat* organization—one in which there are only a few levels in the hierarchy and the span of control is relatively wide. Note that both organizations depicted here have the same number of positions, but these are arranged differently.

The organizational chart may not reflect perfectly a manager's actual span of control. Other factors not immediately forthcoming from the chart itself may be involved. For example, managers may have additional responsibilities that do not appear on the chart—notably, assignments on various committees. Moreover, some subordinates (e.g., new people to the job) might require more attention than others. Also, the degree of supervisory control needed may increase (e.g., when jobs change) or decrease (e.g., when subordinates become more proficient). In fact, it is not readily possible to specify the "ideal" span of control that should be sought. Instead, it makes better sense to consider what form of organization is best suited to various purposes. For example, because supervisors in a military unit must have tight control over subordinates and get them to respond quickly and precisely, a narrow span of control is likely to be effective. As a result, military organizations tend to be extremely tall. In contrast, people working in a research and development lab must have an open exchange of ideas and typically require little managerial guidance to be successful. Units of this type tend to have very flat structures.

Line versus Staff Positions: Decision Makers versus Advisers

The organizational chart shown in Figure 15-2 reveals an additional distinction that deserves to be highlighted—that between *line positions* and *staff positions*. People occupying **line positions** (e.g., the various vice presidents and managers) have decision-making power. However, the individual shown in the pink box—the legal counsel—cannot make decisions but provides advice and recommendations to be used by the line managers. Such an individual may be said to occupy a **staff position**. For example, a corporate attorney may help corporate officials decide whether a certain product name can be used without infringing on copyright restrictions. In many of today's organizations, human resources managers may be seen as occupying staff positions because they may provide specialized services regarding testing and interviewing procedures as well as information about the latest laws on personnel discrimination. However, the ultimate decisions on personnel selection might be made by more senior managers in specialized areas—that is, line managers.

Differences between line and staff personnel are not unusual. Such differences may be conflict-arousing, or even may be used to create intentional sources of conflict. For example, when Harold Green was the CEO of ITT, staff specialists in the areas of planning and strategy were regularly brought in from headquarters to challenge the decisions made by line managers in an attempt to "keep them on their toes."[14] Sociologists have noted that staff managers tend to be younger, better educated, and more committed to their fields than to the organizations employing them.[15] Line managers might feel more committed not only because of the greater opportunities they have to exercise decisions, but also because they are more likely to perceive themselves as part of a company rather than as an independent specialist (whose identity lies primarily within his or her specialty area).

Decentralization: Delegating Power Downward

During the first half of the twentieth century, as companies grew larger and larger, they shifted power and authority into the hands of a few upper-echelon administrators—executives whose decisions influenced the many people below them in the organizational hierarchy. In fact, it was during the 1920s

line positions Positions in organizations in which people can make decisions related to doing its basic work.

staff positions Positions in organizations in which people make recommendations to others but are not themselves involved in making decisions concerning the organization's day-to-day operations.

decentralization The extent to which authority and decision making are spread throughout all levels of an organization rather than being reserved for top management (centralization).

We discuss centralization in the process of decision making in Chapter 10 and the bases of social power in Chapter 12.

In Chapter 5—when describing growth need strength *as a moderator of the job characteristics model—we discuss the idea that people differ in the extent to which they may seek responsibility for making decisions on the job.*

that Alfred P. Sloan Jr., then the president of General Motors, introduced the notion of a "central office," the place where a few individuals made policy decisions for the entire company.[16] As part of Sloan's plan, decisions regarding the day-to-day operation of the company were pushed lower and lower down the organizational hierarchy, allowing those individuals who were most affected to make the decisions. This process of delegating power from higher to lower levels within organizations is known as **decentralization**. It is the opposite, of course, of *centralization*, the tendency for just a few powerful individuals or groups to hold most of the decision-making power.

Recent years have seen a marked trend toward increasingly greater decentralization. As a result, organizational charts might show fewer staff positions, as decision-making authority is pushed farther down the hierarchy (see Figure 15-4). Many organizations have moved toward decentralization to promote managerial efficiency and to improve employee satisfaction (the result of giving people greater opportunities to take responsibility for their own actions). For example, in recent years, thousands of staff jobs have been eliminated at companies such as 3M, Eastman Kodak, AT&T, and GE as these companies have decentralized.[17]

Decentralization is not always an ideal step for organizations to take. In fact, for some types of jobs, it actually may be a serious hindrance to productivity. Consider production-oriented positions, like assembly line jobs. In a classic study, Lawrence and Lorsh found that decentralization improved the performance on some jobs—notably, the work of employees in a research lab—but interfered with the performance of people performing more routine, assembly-line jobs.[18] These findings make sense once you consider that people working in research and development positions are likely to enjoy the autonomy to make decisions that decentralization allows, whereas people working on production jobs are likely to be less interested in taking responsibility for decisions and may enjoy not having to take such responsibility. With this in mind, many of today's companies heavily involved in research and development—including parts of Hewlett-Packard, Intel Corporation, Philips Electronics, and AT&T's Bell Laboratories—have shifted to more decentralized designs.[19,20]

In contrast, under some conditions, such as when only a few individuals are in a position to judge what's best for the company, highly centralized authority makes the most sense. For example, at Delta Airlines, CEO Ronald W. Allen must personally approve every expenditure over $5,000 (except jet fuel).[21] By so doing, he can very carefully monitor the company's expenses and keep it afloat during difficult times. Despite the possible benefits likely to

■ **Figure 15-4**
The Trend toward Decentralization: Pushing Decision-Making Authority Downward
Howard Fuller, superintendent of the Milwaukee public school system—shown here with some of the system's students—has been a crusader for decentralization. *He has fought to improve public education by loosening the tight grip of government bureaucrats and shifting control over the curriculum to those closest to the students— namely, teachers and parents. Fuller complains that the system still relies on a heavily centralized bureaucratic structure that many private industries have discarded.*

Various benefits are associated with low decentralization (high centralization) and high decentralization (low centralization) within organizations.	Low decentralization (High centralization)	High decentralization (Low centralization)
	Eliminates the additional responsibility not desired by people performing routine jobs	Can eliminate levels of management, making a leaner organization
	Permits crucial decisions to be made by individuals who have the "big picture"	Promotes greater opportunities for decisions to be made by people closest to problems

result from relieving Allen of these chores, he believes that it is necessary to enforce tightly the decisions made at times when the margin for error is small. To conclude, although the potential exists to derive considerable benefits from decentralization, the process should be avoided under certain conditions (see the summary in Table 15-2).

The five elements of structure described thus far—hierarchy of authority, division of labor, span of control, line versus staff positions, and decentralization—are the building blocks of organizational structure. They represent key dimensions along which organizations differ.

Departmentalization: Ways of Structuring Organizations

Thus far, we have been talking about "the" organizational chart of an organization. Typically, such charts, like the one shown in Figure 15-2, divide the organization according to the various functions performed. However, as we will explain in this section, this is only one option. Organizations can be divided up not only by function, but also by product or market, and by a special blend of function and product or market known as the matrix form. We will now take a closer look at these various ways of breaking up organizations into coherent units—that is, the process of **departmentalization**.

departmentalization The process of breaking up organizations into coherent units.

Functional Organizations: Departmentalization by Task

Because it is the form organizations usually take when they are first created, and because it is how we usually think of organizations, the **functional organization** can be considered the most basic approach to departmentalization. Essentially, functional organizations departmentalize individuals according to the nature of the functions they perform, with people who perform similar functions assigned to the same department. For example, a manufacturing company might consist of separate departments devoted to basic functions such as production, sales, research and development, and accounting (see Figure 15-5).

functional organization The type of departmentalization based on the activities or functions performed (e.g., sales, finance).

Naturally, as organizations grow and become more complex, additional departments are added or deleted as the need arises. As certain functions become centralized, resources can be saved by avoiding duplication of effort, resulting in a higher level of efficiency. Not only does this form of organizational structure take advantage of economies of scale (by allowing employees performing the same jobs to share facilities and not duplicating functions), but in addition it allows individuals to specialize, thereby performing only those tasks at which they are most expert. The result is a highly skilled workforce, a direct benefit to the organization.

Partly offsetting these advantages, however, are several potential limitations. The most important of these stems from the fact that functional organizational structures encourage separate units to develop their own narrow

■ **Figure 15-5**
*Functional Organization of
a Typical Manufacturing Firm*
Functional organizations are ones in
which departments are formed on the
basis of common functions performed.
In the hypothetical manufacturing firm
shown in this simplified organizational
chart, four typical functional departments are identified. In specific organizations the actual functions may differ.

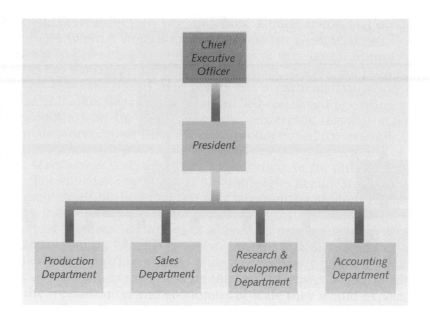

perspectives and to lose sight of overall organizational goals. For example, in a manufacturing company, an engineer might see the company's problems in terms of the reliability of its products and fail to consider other key factors, such as market trends, overseas competition, and so on. Such narrow-mindedness is the inevitable result of functional specialization—the downside of people seeing the company's operations through a narrow lens. A related problem is that functional structures discourage innovation because they channel individual efforts toward narrow, functional areas and do not encourage coordination and cross-fertilization of ideas between areas. As a result, functional organizations are slow to respond to the challenges and opportunities they face from the environment (such as the need for new products and services). In summary, although functional organizations are certainly logical in nature and have proven useful in many contexts, they are by no means the perfect way to departmentalize people in organizations.

Product Organizations: Departmentalization by Type of Output

Organizations—at least successful ones—do not stand still; they constantly change in size and scope. As they develop new products and seek new customers, they might find that a functional structure doesn't work as well as it once did. Manufacturing a wide range of products using a variety of different methods, for example, might put a strain on a manufacturing division of a functional organization. Similarly, keeping track of the varied tax requirements for different types of business (e.g., restaurants, farms, real estate, manufacturing) might pose quite a challenge for a single financial division of a company. In response to such strains, a **product organization** might be created. This type of departmentalization creates self-contained divisions, each of which is responsible for everything to do with a certain product or group of products. (For a look at the structure of a product organization, see Figure 15-6.)

product organization The type of departmentalization based on the products (or product lines) produced.

When organizations are departmentalized by products, separate divisions are established, each of which is devoted to a certain product or group of products. Each unit contains all the resources needed to develop, manufacture, and sell its products. The organization is composed of separate divisions, operating independently, the heads of which report to top management. Although some functions might be centralized within the parent company (e.g., human resource management or legal staff), on a day-to-day basis each division operates autonomously as a separate company or, as accountants call them, "cost centers" of their own.

For boundaryless organizations to function effectively, they must meet many of the same requirements as successful teams. For example, there must be high levels of trust between all parties concerned. Also, everyone involved must have such high levels of skill that they can operate without much, if any, managerial guidance. Insofar as the elimination of boundaries weakens traditional managerial power bases, some executives may find it difficult to give up their authority, leading to political behavior. However, to the extent that the elimination of boundaries leverages the talents of all employees, such limitations are worth striving to overcome.

For a discussion of the factors that contribute to the success of teams, see Chapter 8.

The boundaryless organizations we have been describing involve breaking down both internal and external barriers. As a result, they are sometimes referred to as *barrier-free organizations*. However, there are variations of the boundaryless organization involving only the elimination of external boundaries.[35] These are known as *modular organizations* and *virtual organizations*. Although the key aspects of both types of organizations have been described earlier in this text (see Chapter 2), they deserve to be reiterated here for purposes of identifying them as specific forms of boundaryless organizations.

Modular organizations. As we described in Chapter 2, many of today's organizations outsource noncore functions to other companies while retaining full strategic control over their core business. Such companies may be thought of as having a central hub surrounded by networks of outside specialists that can be added or subtracted as needed. As such, they are referred to as **modular organizations**.[36]

modular organization An organization that surrounds itself by a network of other organizations to which it regularly outsources noncore functions.

As a case in point, you surely recognize Nike and Reebok as major designers and marketers of athletic shoes. However, you probably didn't realize that Nike's production facilities are limited, and that Reebok doesn't even have any plants of its own. Both organizations contract all their manufacturing to companies in countries such as Taiwan and South Korea where labor costs are low. In so doing, not only can they avoid making major investments in facilities, but they can concentrate on what they do best—tapping the changing tastes of their customers. While doing this, their suppliers can focus on rapidly retooling to make the new products.[37] Similarly, such popular computer companies as Dell, Gateway, and CompuAdd buy computer components made by other companies and perform only the final assembly themselves (as ordered by customers). These apparel and computer companies are both examples of modular organizations.

Toyota, one of the world's most successful automakers, has taken the modular form to the extreme. Its network of 230 suppliers (two of which are owned by Toyota itself) do just about everything the company needs, from making molds for machine parts, to general contracting.[38] The key to the success of this arrangement is Toyota's very close ties to its suppliers—providing assurances that they will meet its stringent quality standards. Of course, companies that outsource any proprietary work (e.g., high-tech breakthroughs) must be assured that their trade secrets will not be compromised.

Virtual organizations. Another approach to the boundaryless organization is the **virtual organization**. You will recall from Chapter 2 that such an organization is composed of a continually evolving network of companies (e.g., suppliers and customers) that are linked together to share skills, costs, and access to markets. They form a partnership to capitalize on their existing skills, pursuing common objectives. Then, after these objectives have been met, they disband.[39] Unlike modular organizations, which maintain close control over the companies with which they do outsourcing, virtual organizations give up some control and become part of a new organization, at least for a while.

virtual organization A highly flexible, temporary organization formed by a group of companies that join forces to exploit a specific opportunity.

Corning, the giant glass and ceramics manufacturer, is a good example of a company that builds upon itself by developing partnerships with other companies (including Siemens, the German electronics firm, and Vitro, the largest glass manufacturer from Mexico). In fact, Corning officials see their company not as a single entity, but as "a network of organizations."[40] Although Corning's alliances tend to be long-lived, most virtual organizations are formed on a limited basis (such as the Rolling Stones' "Voodoo Lounge" Tour described in Chapter 2).

The underlying idea of a virtual organization is that each participating company contributes only its core competencies (i.e., its areas of greatest strength). By several companies mixing and matching the best of what they can offer, a joint product is created that is better than one that any single company could have created alone. Consider, for example, the new projects from the parent company that publishes this book, Paramount Communications. In today's rapidly changing entertainment industry, no one company can do it all. With this in mind, Paramount has entered into partnerships with other companies that will help create new products where none existed before. For example, Paramount has entered into an alliance with Hughes Aircraft that will allow its movies to be transferred to compact disks and distributed over a satellite system. The virtual corporation it formed is not unusual in the entertainment industry. Indeed, Time Warner also has become part of several multimedia ventures. By sharing risks, costs, and expertise, many of today's companies are finding the virtual organization to be a highly appealing type of organizational structure.

To summarize, the boundaryless organization is becoming an increasingly popular organizational form. It involves eliminating all internal boundaries (such as those between employees) and external boundaries (such as those between the company and its suppliers). A variation on this organizational form involves eliminating only external boundaries. This occurs in modular organizations (in which secondary aspects of the company's operations are outsourced) and virtual organizations (in which organizations combine forces with others on a temporary basis to form new organizations, usually only briefly). For a summary of these three organizational structures, see Figure 15-8.

This type of cooperative effort between organizations is discussed in more detail in Chapter 11.

Organizational Design: Coordinating the Structural Elements of Organizations

We began the first major section of this chapter by likening the structure of an organization to the structure of a house. Now we are prepared to extend that analogy for purposes of introducing the concept of *organizational design*. Just as a house is designed in a particular fashion by combining its structural elements in various ways, so too can an organization be designed by combining its basic elements in certain ways. Accordingly, **organizational design** refers to the process of coordinating the structural elements of organizations in the most appropriate manner.

organizational design The process of coordinating the structural elements of an organization in the most appropriate manner.

As you might imagine, this is no easy task. Although we might describe some options that sound neat and rational on the next few pages, in reality this is hardly ever the case. Even the most precisely designed organizations will face the need to change at one time or another, adjusting to the realities of technological changes, political pressures, accidents, and so on. Organizational designs might also be changed purposely in an attempt to improve operating efficiency, such as the promise by some recent U.S. presidents to streamline the huge federal bureaucracy. Our point is simple: Because organizations operate within a changing world, their own designs must be capable of changing as well. Those organizations that are either poorly designed or inflexible cannot survive. If you consider the large number of banks and airlines that have gone out of business in the last few years because of their inability to deal with rapid changes brought about by deregulation and a shift-

The Boundaryless Organization: Various Forms
The true boundaryless organization *is free of both internal barriers and external barriers. Variants, such as the* modular organization *and the* virtual organization, *eliminate only external barriers. All forms of boundaryless organizations are growing in popularity.*

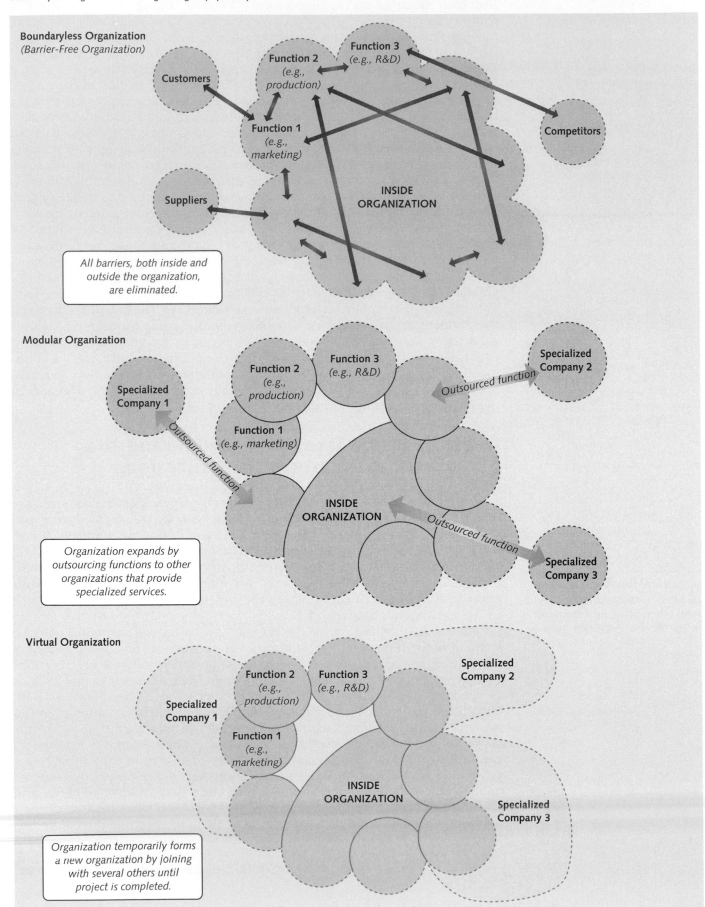

Boundaryless Organization
(Barrier-Free Organization)

Customers

Function 2
(e.g., production)

Function 3
(e.g., R&D)

Function 1
(e.g., marketing)

Competitors

INSIDE ORGANIZATION

Suppliers

All barriers, both inside and outside the organization, are eliminated.

Modular Organization

Function 2
(e.g., production)

Function 3
(e.g., R&D)

Function 1
(e.g., marketing)

Specialized Company 1

Specialized Company 2

Outsourced function

Outsourced function

Outsourced function

INSIDE ORGANIZATION

Specialized Company 3

Organization expands by outsourcing functions to other organizations that provide specialized services.

Virtual Organization

Function 2
(e.g., production)

Function 3
(e.g., R&D)

Function 1
(e.g., marketing)

Specialized Company 1

Specialized Company 2

INSIDE ORGANIZATION

Specialized Company 3

Organization temporarily forms a new organization by joining with several others until project is completed.

ing economy (see Figure 15-9), you'll get a good idea of the ultimate consequences of ineffective organizational design.

Classical and Neoclassical Approaches: The Quest for the One Best Design

The earliest theorists interested in organizational design did not operate out of awareness of the point we just made regarding the need for organizations to be flexible. Instead, they approached the task of designing organizations as a search for "the one best way." Although today we are more attuned to the need to adapt organizational designs to various environmental and social conditions, theorists in the early and middle part of the twentieth century sought to establish the ideal form for all organizations under all conditions—the universal design.

In Chapter 1, we described the efforts of organizational scholars such as Max Weber, Frederick Taylor, and Henri Fayol. These theorists believed that effective organizations were ones that had a formal hierarchy, a clear set of rules, specialization of labor, highly routine tasks, and a highly impersonal working environment. You may recall that Weber referred to this organizational form as a *bureaucracy*. This **classical organizational theory** has fallen into disfavor because it is insensitive to human needs and is not suited to a changing environment. Unfortunately, the "ideal" form of an organization, according to Weber, did not take into account the realities of the world within which it operates. Apparently, what is ideal is not necessarily what is realistic.

In response to these conditions, and with inspiration from the Hawthorne studies, the classical approach to the bureaucratic model gave way to a human relations orientation. Organizational scholars such as McGregor, Argyris, and Likert attempted to improve upon the classical model—which is why their approach is labeled **neoclassical organizational theory**—by arguing that economic effectiveness is not the only goal of an industrial organization, but also employee satisfaction.

Specifically, Douglas McGregor was an organizational theorist who objected to the rigid hierarchy imposed by Weber's bureaucratic form because it was based on negative assumptions about people—primarily that they lacked ambition and wouldn't work unless coerced (the *Theory X* approach).[41] In contrast, McGregor argued that people desire to achieve success by working and that they seek satisfaction by behaving responsibly (the *Theory Y* approach). Another neoclassical

classical organizational theory Approaches assuming that there is a single best way to design organizations.

We described the Hawthorne studies in detail in Chapter 1.

neoclassical organizational theory An attempt to improve upon the classical organizational theory which argues that economic effectiveness is not the only goal of organizational structure, but also employee satisfaction.

■ Figure 15-9
Failure to Adapt to a Changing Environment: An Extreme Example
The changing environments within which organizations operate require that their designs are capable of changing so as to adapt properly. When savings and loan institutions became less heavily regulated by the U.S. government, many found themselves unable to change rapidly enough to survive.

The Theory X *and* Theory Y *philosophies of management are contrasted in Chapter 1.*

theorist, Chris Argyris, expressed similar ideas.[42] Specifically, he argued that managerial domination of organizations blocks basic human needs to express oneself and to accomplish tasks successfully. Such dissatisfaction, he argues, would encourage turnover and lead to poor performance.

Another neoclassical theorist, Rensis Likert, shared these perspectives, arguing that organizational performance is enhanced not by rigidly controlling people's actions, but by actively promoting their feelings of self-worth and their importance to the organization.[43] An effective organization, Likert proposed, was one in which individuals would have a great opportunity to participate in making organizational decisions—what he called a *System 4 organization*. Doing this, he claimed, would enhance employees' personal sense of worth, motivating them to succeed. Likert called the opposite type of organization *System 1*, the traditional form in which organizational power is distributed in the hands of a few top managers who tell lower-ranking people what to do. (*System 2* and *System 3* are intermediate forms between the System 1 and System 4 extremes.)

The organizational design implications of these neoclassical approaches are clear. In contrast to the classical approach, calling for organizations to be designed with a rigid, tall hierarchy, and with a narrow span of control (allowing managers to maintain close supervision over their subordinates), the neoclassical approach argues for designing organizations with flat hierarchical structures (minimizing managerial control over subordinates) and a high degree of decentralization (encouraging employees to make their own decisions). Indeed, such design features may well serve the underlying neoclassical philosophy.

Like the classical approach, the neoclassical approach also may be faulted on the grounds that it is promoted as "the one best approach" to organizational design. Although the benefits of flat, decentralized designs may be many, to claim that this represents the universal, ideal form for all organizations would be naive. In response to this criticism, more contemporary approaches to organizational design have given up on finding the one best way to design organizations in favor of finding designs that are most appropriate to various circumstances and contexts within which organizations operate.

The Contingency Approach: Design According to Environmental Conditions

The idea that the best design for an organization depends on the nature of the environment in which the organization is operating lies at the heart of the modern **contingency approach** to organizational design. We use the term "contingency" here in a manner similar to the way we used it in our discussion of leadership. But rather than considering the best approach to leadership for a given situation, we are considering the best way to design an organization given the environment within which the organization functions.

The external environment: Its connection to organizational design. It is widely assumed that the most appropriate type of organizational design depends on the organization's *external environment*. In general, the external environment is the sum of all the forces impinging on an organization with which it must deal effectively if it is to survive.[44] These forces include general work conditions, such as the economy, geography, and national resources, as well as the specific task environment within which the company operates—notably, its competitors, customers, workforce, and suppliers.

Let's consider some examples. Banks operate within an environment that is highly influenced by the general economic environment (e.g., interest rates and government regulations) as well as a task environment sensitive to other banks' products (e.g., types of accounts) and services (e. g., service hours, access to account information by computers and/or telephone), the needs of the customer base (e.g., direct deposit for customers), the availability of trained

contingency approach
The approach that recognizes that the best organizational design is the one that best fits with the existing environmental conditions.

The contingency approach *is described as a general orientation to the study of OB in Chapter 1, and as a specific theory of leadership in Chapter 13.*

personnel (e.g., individuals suitable for entry-level positions), as well as the existence of suppliers providing goods and services (e.g., automated teller equipment, surveillance equipment, computer workstations) necessary to deliver requisite services. Analogous examples can be found in other industries as well. For example, think about the environmental forces faced by the airlines, the computer industry, and automobile manufacturers. It's easy to recognize the features of their environments that must be taken into account when considering how organizations in these industries could be designed.

Although many features of the environment may be taken into account when considering how an organization should be designed, a classic investigation by Burns and Stalker provides some useful guidance.[45] These scientists interviewed people in 20 industrial organizations in the United Kingdom to determine the relationship between managerial activities and the external environment. In so doing, they distinguished between organizations that operated in highly *stable*, unchanging environments, and those that operated in highly *unstable*, turbulent environments. For example, a rayon company in their sample operated in a highly stable environment: The environmental demands were predictable, people performed the same jobs in the same ways for a long time, and the organization had clearly defined lines of authority that helped get the job done. In contrast, a new electronics development company in their sample operated in a highly turbulent environment: Conditions changed on a daily basis, jobs were not well defined, and no clear organizational structure existed.

Burns and Stalker noted that many of the organizations studied tended to be described in ways that were appropriate for their environments. For example, when the environment is stable, people can do the same tasks repeatedly, allowing them to perform highly specialized jobs. However, in turbulent environments, many different jobs may have to be performed, and such specialization should not be designed into the jobs. Clearly, a strong link exists between the stability of the work environment and the proper organizational form. It was Burns and Stalker's conclusion that two different approaches to management existed and that these are largely based on the degree of stability within the external environment. These two approaches are known as *mechanistic organizations* and *organic organizations*.

Mechanistic versus organic organizations: Designs for stable versus turbulent conditions.

If you've ever worked at a McDonald's, you probably know how highly standardized each step of the most basic operations must be.[46] Boxes of fries are to be stored two inches from the wall in stacks one inch apart. Making those fries is another matter—one that requires 19 distinct steps, each clearly laid out in a training film shown to new employees. The process is the same, whether it's done in Moscow, Idaho, or in Moscow, Russia. This is an example of a highly mechanistic task. Organizations can be highly mechanistic when conditions don't change. Although the fast-food industry has changed a great deal in recent years (with the introduction of new, healthier menu items, competitive pricing, and the like), the making of fries at McDonald's has not changed. The key to using mechanization is the lack of change. If the environment doesn't change, a highly mechanistic organizational form can be very efficient. A **mechanistic organization** exists under stable conditions.

An environment is considered stable whenever there is little or no unexpected change in product, market demands, technology, and the like. Have you ever seen an old-fashioned-looking bottle of E. E. Dickinson's witch hazel (a topical astringent used to cleanse the skin in the area of a wound)? Since the company has been making the product following the same distillation process since 1866, it is certainly operating in a relatively stable manufacturing environment.[47] As we described earlier, stability affords the luxury of high

mechanistic organization
An organizational structure in which people perform specialized jobs, many rigid rules are imposed, and authority is vested in a few top-ranking officials.

Mechanistic and organic designs differ along several key dimensions identified here. These represent extremes; organizations can be relatively organic, relatively mechanistic, or somewhere in between.

| | Structure | |
Dimension	Mechanistic	Organic
Stability	Change unlikely	Change likely
Specialization	Many specialists	Many generalists
Formal rules	Rigid rules	Considerable flexibility
Authority	Centralized in few top people	Decentralized, diffused throughout the organization

employee specialization. Without change, people can easily specialize. When change is inevitable, specialization is impractical.

Mechanistic organizations can be characterized in several additional ways (for a summary, see Table 15-3). Not only do mechanistic organizations allow for a high degree of specialization, but they also impose many rules. Authority is vested in a few people located at the top of a hierarchy who give direct orders to their subordinates. Mechanistic organizational designs tend to be most effective under conditions in which the external environment is stable and unchanging.

Now think about high-technology industries, such as those dedicated to computers, aerospace products, and biotechnology. Their environmental conditions are likely to be changing all the time. These industries are so prone to change that as soon as a new way of operating could be introduced into one of them, it would have to be altered. It isn't only technology, however, that makes an environment turbulent. Turbulence also can be high in industries in which adherence to rapidly changing regulations is essential. For example, times were turbulent in the hospital industry when new Medicaid legislation was passed, and times were turbulent in the nuclear power industry when governmental regulations dictated the introduction of many new standards that had to be followed. With the dominance of foreign automobiles in the United States, the once-stable American auto industry has faced turbulent times of late. Unfortunately, in this case, the design of the auto companies could not rapidly accommodate the changes needed for more organic forms (since the American auto industry was traditionally highly mechanistic). An **organic organization** exists under turbulent conditions.

The pure organic form of organization may be characterized in several different ways (see Table 15-3). The degree of job specialization possible is very low; instead, a broad knowledge of many different jobs is required. Very little authority is exercised from the top. Rather, self-control is expected, and an emphasis is placed on coordination between peers. As a result, decisions tend to be made in a highly democratic, participative manner. Be aware that the mechanistic and organic types of organizational structure described here are ideal forms. The mechanistic-organic distinction should be thought of as opposite poles along a continuum rather than as completely distinct options for organization. Certainly, organizations may be relatively organic or relatively mechanistic compared with others, but may not be found at either extreme.

Finally, note that research supports the idea that organizational effectiveness is related to the degree to which an organization's structure (mechanistic or organic) is matched to its environment (stable or turbulent). In a classic study, Morse and Lorsch evaluated four departments in a large company—two of which manufactured containers (a relatively stable environment) and two of which dealt with communications research (a highly unstable environment).[48] One department in each pair was evaluated as being more effective than the other. It was found that for the container manufacturing departments,

In Chapter 14 we discuss the impact of introduction of high-technology into the workplace.

organic organization An internal organizational structure in which jobs tend to be very general, there are few rules, and decisions can be made by lower-level employees.

the more effective unit was the one structured in a highly mechanistic form (roles and duties were clearly defined). In contrast, the more effective communications research department was structured in a highly organic fashion (roles and duties were vague). Additionally, the other, less effective departments were structured in the opposite manner (i.e., the less effective manufacturing department was organically structured, and the less effective research department was mechanistically structured) (see Figure 15-10). Taken together, the results made it clear that departments were most effective when their organizational structures fit their environments. This notion of "which design is best under which conditions?" lies at the heart of the modern orientation—the contingency approach—to organizational structure. Rather than specifying *which* structure is best, the contingency approach specifies *when* each type of organizational design is most effective.

Mintzberg's Framework: Five Organizational Forms

Although the distinction between mechanistic and organic designs is important, it is not terribly specific with respect to exactly how organizations should be designed. Filling this void, however, is the work of contemporary organizational theorist, Henry Mintzberg.[49] Specifically, Mintzberg claims that organizations are composed of five basic elements, or groups of individuals, any of which may predominate in an organization. The one that does will determine the most effective design in that situation. The five basic elements are:

- *The operating core*: employees who perform the basic work related to the organization's product or service. Examples include teachers (in schools) and chefs and waiters (in restaurants).
- *The strategic apex*: top-level executives responsible for running the entire organization. Examples include the entrepreneur who runs her own small business and the general manager of an automobile dealership.
- *The middle line*: managers who transfer information between the strategic apex and the operating core. Examples include middle managers, such as regional sales managers (who connect top executives with the sales

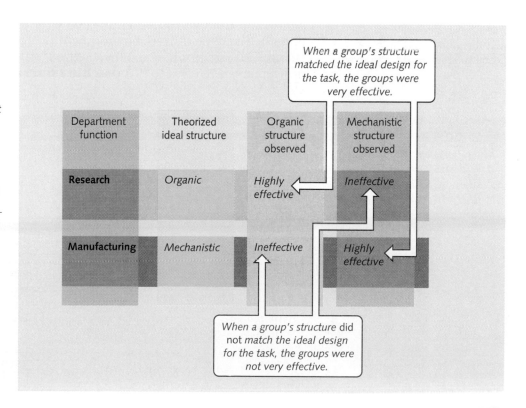

■ **Figure 15-10**
Matching Organizational Design and Industry: The Key to Effectiveness
In a classic study, Morse and Lorsch evaluated the performance of four departments in a large company. The most effective units were ones in which the way the group was structured (mechanistic or organic) matched the most appropriate form for the type of task performed (i.e., organic for research work and mechanistic for manufacturing work).

(**Source:** Based on suggestions by Morse & Lorsch, 1970; see Note 48.)

force), and the chair of an academic department in a college or university (an intermediary between the dean and the faculty).

■ *The technostructure*: those specialists responsible for standardizing various aspects of the organization's activities. Examples include accountants, auditors, and computer systems analysts.

■ *The support staff*: individuals who provide indirect support services to the organization. Examples include consultants on technical matters and corporate attorneys.

What organizational designs best fit under conditions in which each of these five groups dominate? Mintzberg has identified five specific designs: *simple structure, machine bureaucracy, professional bureaucracy*, the *divisionalized structure*, and the *adhocracy* (see summary in Table 15-4).

Simple structure. Imagine that you open up an antique shop and hire a few people to help you out around the store. You have a small, informal organization in which there is a single individual with the ultimate power. There is little in the way of specialization or formalization, and the overall structure is organic in nature. The hierarchy is quite flat, and all decision-making power is vested in a single individual—you. An organization so described, simple in nature, with the power residing at the strategic apex, is referred to by Mintzberg as having a **simple structure**. As you might imagine, organizations with simple structure can respond quickly to the environment and be very flexible. For example, the chef-owner of a small, independent restaurant can change the menu to suit the changing tastes of customers whenever needed, without first consulting anyone else. The down side of this, however, is that the success or failure of the entire enterprise is dependent on the wisdom and health of the individual in charge. Not surprisingly, organizations with simple structure are risky ventures.

Machine bureaucracy. If you've ever worked for your state's department of motor vehicles, you probably found it to be a very large place, with numerous rules and procedures for employees to follow. The work is highly specialized (e.g., one person gives the vision tests, and another completes the registration forms), and decision making is concentrated at the top (e.g., you need to get permission from your supervisor to do anything other than exactly what's expected). This type of work environment is highly stable, and does not have to change. An organization so characterized, where power resides with the technostructure, is referred to as a **machine bureaucracy**. Although machine bu-

---

simple structure An organization characterized as being small and informal, with a single powerful individual, often the founding entrepreneur, who is in charge of everything.

machine bureaucracy An organizational form in which work is highly specialized, decision making is concentrated at the top, and the work environment is not prone to change (e.g., a government office).

■ TABLE 15-4	MINTZBERG'S FIVE ORGANIZATIONAL FORMS: A SUMMARY			
Mintzberg has identified five distinct organizational designs, each of which is likely to occur in organizations in which certain groups are in power.	**Design**	**Description**	**Dominant Group**	**Example**
	Simple structure	Simple, informal, authority centralized in a single person	Strategic apex	Small, entrepreneurial business
	Machine bureaucracy	Highly complex, formal environment with clear lines of authority	Technostructure	Government offices
	Professional bureaucracy	Complex, decision-making authority is vested in professionals	Operating core	Universities
	Divisionalized structure	Large, formal organizations with several separate divisions	Middle line	Multidivision businesses such as General Motors
	Adhocracy	Simple, informal, with decentralized authority	Support staff	Software development firm

SOURCE: Based on suggestions by Mintzberg, 1983; see Note 49.

This is consistent with our description of Max Weber's description of bureaucracy in Chapter 1.

professional bureaucracy
Organizations (e.g., hospitals and universities) in which there are lots of rules to follow, but employees are highly skilled and free to make decisions on their own.

For a discussion of several other sources of conflict in organizations, see Chapter 11.

divisional structure The form used by many large organizations, in which separate autonomous units are created to deal with entire product lines, freeing top management to focus on larger-scale, strategic decisions.

adhocracy A highly informal, organic organization in which specialists work in teams, coordinating with each other on various projects (e.g., many software development companies).

reaucracies can be highly efficient at performing standardized tasks, they tend to be dehumanizing and very boring for the employees.

Professional bureaucracy. Suppose you are a doctor working at a large city hospital. You are a highly trained specialist with considerable expertise in your field. You don't need to check with anyone else before authorizing a certain medical test or treatment for your patient; you make the decisions as they are needed, when they are needed. At the same time, the environment is highly formal (e.g., there are lots of rules and regulations for you to follow). Of course, you do not work alone; you also require the services of other highly qualified professionals such as nurses and laboratory technicians. Organizations of this type—and these include universities, libraries, and consulting firms as well as hospitals—maintain power with the operating core, and are called **professional bureaucracies**. Such organizations can be highly effective because they allow employees to practice those skills for which they are best qualified. However, sometimes specialists become so overly narrow that they fail to see the "big picture," leading to errors and potential conflict between employees.

Divisional structure. When you think of large organizations, such as General Motors, Du Pont, Xerox, and IBM, the image that comes to mind is probably closest to what Mintzberg describes as **divisional structure**. Such organizations consist of a set of autonomous units coordinated by a central headquarters (i.e., they rely on departmental structure based on products, as described on pages 513–515). In such organizations, because the divisions are autonomous (e.g., a General Motors employee at Buick does not have to consult with another at Chevrolet to do his or her job) division managers (the *middle line* part of Mintzberg's basic elements) have considerable control. Such designs preclude the need for top-level executives to think about the day-to-day operations of their companies and free them to concentrate on larger scale, strategic decisions. At the same time, companies organized into separate divisions frequently tend to have high duplication of effort (e.g., separate order processing units for each division). Having operated as separate divisions for the past 70 years, General Motors is considered the classic example of divisional structure.[50] Although the company has undergone many changes during this time—including the addition of the Saturn Corporation—it has maintained its divisional structure.

Adhocracy. After graduating from college, where you spent years learning how to program computers, you take a job at a small software company. Compared to your friends who found positions at large accounting firms, your professional life is much less formal. You work as a member of a team developing a new time-management software product. There are no rules, and schedules are made to be broken. You all work together, and although there is someone who is "officially" in charge, you'd never know it. Using Mintzberg's framework, you work for an **adhocracy**—an organization in which power resides with the support staff. Essentially, this is the epitome of the organic structure identified earlier. Specialists coordinate with each other not because of their shared functions (e.g., accounting, manufacturing), but as members of teams working on specific projects.

The primary benefit of the adhocracy is that it fosters innovation. Some large companies, such as Johnson & Johnson (see this chapter's CASE IN POINT on p. 540), nest within their formal divisional structure units that operate as adhocracies. In the case of J&J, it's the New Products Division, a unit that has been churning out an average of 40 products per year during recent years.[51] As in the case of all other designs there are disadvantages. In this case, the most serious limitations are their high levels of inefficiency (they are the opposite of machine bureaucracies in this regard) and the potential for disruptive conflict. All the organizational designs we've discussed thus far may be seen as taking

THE ORGANIZATION OF THE FUTURE

INTERNAL MARKETS: DESIGN FOR THE INFORMATION AGE

A century ago, during the *industrial age*, it made sense for organizations to be designed around rigid hierarchies. Work involved routine manufacturing, and the workforce was largely uneducated and unskilled. Hierarchies made things predictable and helped keep people under control. Today, however, the *information age* is upon us, and we are seeing the end of the hierarchy. Indeed, hierarchies are flattening as companies are cutting the middle sections out of their organizational charts. With it, people are experiencing greater autonomy than ever before. However, we still see vestiges of the hierarchy that has served us so well for so long. According to management scholar William E. Halal, its days are numbered.[52] In fact, he predicts that with the full arrival of the information age, by the year 2000, organizational hierarchies as we know them (and have described them in this book) will be gone for good.

Replacing hierarchies will be organizations modeled after the free-enterprise system, with organizational units operating as individual companies (or "profit centers") within the company. In such an **internal market system**, all organizational units must function effectively—hence, profitably—if they are to survive. That is, they must "earn their keep." This parallels the free-market economy that operates outside organizations.

In part, this process involves transforming hierarchies into *internal enterprise units*. When this occurs, traditional "divisions" or "departments" become "internal enterprises," separate entrepreneurial businesses. Hewlett-Packard (HP) provides a good illustration. Each unit at HP is accountable for its own financial results, but its employees are free to decide how to go about being profitable (while also meeting high standards of product quality and customer satisfaction). HP units run their own separate business: They plan their own strategies, select their own suppliers and customers, and even reinvest their own profits. At some companies, such as Alcoa, units are even encouraged to do business outside their own company. IBM, DEC, and NCR go as far as selling their excess plant capacity to their competitors. In fact, some IBM offices have become so cost-conscious that they purchase less expensive IBM clones rather than use their own company's more expensive computers.

Under an internal market system, executives are expected to foster an entrepreneurial culture. At MCI Communications, for example, employees are encouraged to start their own ventures within the company—an environment that has been responsible for MCI's successful "Friends & Family" calling plan. At HP, units are expected to compete against each other if necessary. In fact, when HP introduced its successful LaserJet line of printers, they competed with the company's own, more expensive printers. At IBM, this never would have been tolerated, whereas at HP it was encouraged. Today, LaserJet printers account for 40 percent of HP's sales. At the same time, HP employees also are expected to cooperate with each other, lending help, and working together on projects as needed. Executives are not expected to intervene but to facilitate cooperation. In the words of Lewis Platt, HP's CEO, "The best thing I can do is bring people together and hope they mate."[53]

Although the shift to internal market structures is just beginning, signs are clear that it will be one of the most popular ways of designing organizations in the years ahead. As Professor Halal put it, the internal market approach will harness "the abundant entrepreneurial talent now languishing beneath the layers of today's bureaucracies."[54] If the successes of HP, Alcoa, and MCI are any indication, he is undoubtedly correct.

---

internal market system
An organizational design in which rigid hierarchies are eliminated, and individual organizational units are allowed to compete as separate, profitable independent businesses.

different approaches to the question of how to best arrange the boxes in an organizational chart. For a novel approach to this issue, and one that is growing in popularity, see the ORGANIZATION OF THE FUTURE section.

Interorganizational Designs: Going Beyond the Single Organization

All the organizational designs we have examined thus far have concentrated on the arrangement of units within an organization—what may be termed *intraorganizational designs*. However, sometimes at least some parts of different organizations must operate jointly. To coordinate their efforts on such projects, organizations must create *interorganizational designs*, plans by which two or more organizations come together. Two such designs are commonly found: *conglomerates* and *strategic alliances*.

Conglomerates: Diversified "Megacorporations"

conglomerate A form of organizational diversification in which an organization (usually a very large, multinational one) adds an entirely unrelated business or product to its organizational design.

When an organization diversifies by adding an entirely unrelated business or product to its organizational design, it may be said to have formed a **conglomerate**. Some of the world's largest conglomerates may be found in Asia. For example, in Korea, companies such as Samsung and Hyundai produce home electronics, automobiles, textiles, and chemicals in large, unified conglomerates known as *chaebols*.[55] These are all separate companies overseen by the same parent company leadership. In Japan, the same type of arrangement is known as a *keiretsu*.[56] A good example of a keiretsu is the Matsushita Group.[57] This enormous conglomerate consists of a bank (Asahi Bank), a consumer electronics company (Panasonic), and several insurance companies (e.g., Sumitomo Life, Nippon Life). These examples are not meant to suggest that conglomerates are unique to Asia. Indeed, many large U.S.-based corporations, such as IBM and Tenneco, are also conglomerates. So too is Johnson & Johnson, which we describe in our CASE IN POINT on p. 540.

Companies form conglomerates for several reasons. First, as an independent business, the parent company can enjoy the benefits of diversification. Thus, as one industry languishes, another may excel, allowing for a stable economic outlook for the parent company. In addition, conglomerates may provide built-in markets and access to supplies, since companies typically support other organizations within the conglomerate. For example, General Motors cars and trucks are fitted with Delco radios, and Ford cars and trucks have engines with Autolite spark plugs, separate companies that are owned by their respective parent companies. In this manner conglomerates can benefit by providing a network of organizations that are dependent on each other for products and services, thereby creating considerable advantages.

In recent years, however, many large conglomerates have been selling off parts of themselves in a move to concentrate on their core business.[58] For example, the giant Korean chaebol, Hyundai (which accounts for 10 percent of Korea's gross national product), has recently dismantled parts of its sprawling corporate structure, selling controlling interests in its heavy manufacturing and shipping companies, and severing all ties with its hotel, insurance, and department store companies.[59] In other words, compared to the 1960s, which was a period of growth for many conglomerates, the 1990s appears to be a period of decline.

Strategic Alliances: Joining Forces for Mutual Benefit

strategic alliance A type of organizational design in which two or more separate companies combine forces to develop and operate a specific business.

A **strategic alliance** is a type of organizational design in which two or more separate firms join their competitive capabilities to operate a specific business. The goal of a strategic alliance is to provide benefits to each individual organization that could not be attained if they operated separately. Strategic alliances are low-risk ways of diversifying (adding new business operations) and entering new markets. Some companies, such as GE and Ford have strategic alliances with many others. Some alliances last only a short time, whereas others have remained in existence for well over 20 years, and are still going strong.[60]

mutual service consortia A type of strategic alliance in which two similar companies from the same or similar industries pool their resources to receive a benefit that would be too difficult or expensive for either to obtain alone.

The continuum of alliances. In a recent study of 37 strategic alliances from throughout the world, Kanter and her associates found that three types of cooperative arrangements between organizations could be identified.[61] These may be arranged along a continuum ranging from those alliances that are weak and distant, at one end, to those that are strong and close, at the other end. As shown in Figure 15-11, at the weak end of the continuum are strategic alliances known as **mutual service consortia**. These are arrange-

■ Figure 15-11
Strategic Alliances: A Continuum of Interorganizational Relationships
The three types of strategic alliances identified here may be distinguished with respect to their location along a continuum ranging from weak and distant to strong and close.

(**Source:** Based on suggestions by Kanter, 1994; See note 60.)

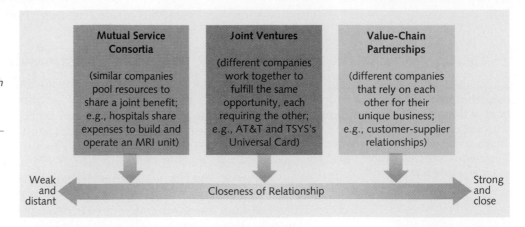

ments between two similar companies from the same or similar industries to pool their resources to receive a benefit that would be too difficult or expensive for either to obtain alone. Often, the focus is some high-tech capacity, such as an expensive piece of diagnostic equipment that might be shared by two or more local hospitals (e.g., a magneto-resonance imaging, or MRI unit).

At the opposite end of the scale are the strongest and closest type of collaborations, referred to as **value-chain partnerships**. These are alliances between companies in different industries that have complementary capabilities. Customer-supplier relationships are a prime example. In such arrangements one company buys necessary goods and services from another so that it can do business. Because each company greatly depends on the other, each party's commitment to their mutual relationship is high. As noted earlier, Toyota has a network of 230 suppliers with whom it regularly does business. The relationship between Toyota and these various companies represents value-chain partnerships.

Between these two extremes are **joint ventures**. These are arrangements in which companies work together to fulfill opportunities that require the capabilities of the other. For example, two companies might enter into a joint venture if one has a valuable technology and the other has the marketing knowledge to help transform that technology into a viable commercial product. For a description of a highly successful joint venture, see the QUEST FOR QUALITY section.

As our descriptions of these types of alliances illustrate, there are clear benefits to be derived from forming alliances. These primarily come in the form of improved technology, widened markets, and greater economies of scale (e.g., sharing functional operations across organizations). However, as you might imagine, for these benefits to be realized, a high degree of coordination and fit must exist between the parties, each delivering on its promise to the other.

As you might imagine, not all strategic alliances are successful. For example, AT&T and Olivetti tried unsuccessfully to work together on manufacturing personal computers. Strong differences in management styles and organizational culture were cited as causes. Similarly, a planned alliance between Raytheon and Lexitron, a small word processing company, failed because of clashes between the rigid culture of the much larger Raytheon, and the more entrepreneurial style of the smaller Lexitron. Clearly, for strategic alliances to work, the companies must not only be able to offer each other something important, but they also must be able to work together to make it happen.

Strategic alliances in the global economy. Strategic alliances with companies in nations with transforming economies (such as China and eastern Europe) provide good opportunities for those nations' economies to develop.[62] Given the rapid move toward globalization of the economy, we may expect to see many companies seeking strategic alliances in the future as a means for

value-chain partnerships
Strategic alliances between companies in different industries that have complementary capabilities.

joint ventures Strategic alliances in which several companies work together to fulfill opportunities that require the capabilities of one another.

Recall our discussion in Chapter 1 of how the global nature of the economy influences the study of organizations.

THE JOINT VENTURE BETWEEN UNIVERSAL CARD
AND TSYS: LESSONS LEARNED

*I*f you have a credit card, chances are pretty good that it's an AT&T Universal Card. After all, there are over 19 million such card holders, making it second only to Citicorp in the number of cards issued.[63] What makes this particularly impressive is that the Universal Card has only been in existence since 1990, and also that AT&T is not in the banking business.

AT&T officials thought that entering the credit card business would not only be another good source of income, but also a useful way to extend its traditional calling card business. To help, it entered into a joint venture with Total System Services, Inc. (TSYS), a firm with a successful track record with respect to credit cards and large volume data processing. Combined with AT&T's brand name, superiority as a long distance carrier, and access to a gigantic mailing list, the prospect of combining forces on the Universal Card seemed promising. And, history proved them right. The Universal Card was carried by over a million people within the first 72 days of the company's existence, and over 10 million within the first two years.

This venture worked well for several reasons. First, it was based on the strengths of each partner. AT&T's outstanding reputation paired with TSYS's leadership in the technology of data processing allowed each to do what it does best. Second, both parties have benefited financially. AT&T found the card to be profitable after only three years, and the added volume helped TSYS re-duce its per-unit costs of processing accounts. Third, the cultures of both companies meshed nicely. Executives of both companies have a very conservative, businesslike style common among telephone companies and banks. Fourth, the companies complement each other's strategic interests. Both companies are driven by the desire to give the best possible customer service. The joint venture helped each achieve this objective.

Beyond simply helping both companies achieve their strategic goals, the joint venture between AT&T and TSYS helped each improve what it already does well—and, in several ways. First, it has raised both companies' quality standards, making them higher than ever before. For example, in the area of customer service, representatives are now available around the clock to answer questions, as is an automated voice response system that allows customers to access information about their accounts at any time. Second, the venture has helped each company develop state-of-the-art facilities in which to operate. Finally, and very importantly, the venture has benefited both companies such that their core businesses are enhanced. AT&T's calling card revenues have increased (40 percent in the Universal Card's first year, alone), as has TSYS's capacity to develop more effective hardware and software for processing credit cards. The fact that the parent companies have added value to each other's operations keeps the partnership alive and well.

gaining or maintaining a competitive advantage.[64] Frequently, companies form strategic alliances with foreign firms to gain entry into that country's market (see Figure 15-12). The company in the host country also may benefit by the influx of foreign expertise and capital. For example, Florida's Orlando Helicopter Airway Company and China's Guangdung No. 3 Machine Tools Factory formed a strategic alliance in 1986 to make the first helicopters available in Guangdung Province, China.[65] Such arrangements also may allow for an exchange of technology and manufacturing services. For example, Korea's Daewoo receives technical information and is paid to manufacture automobiles for companies with which it has entered into alliances, such as General Motors, as well as Germany's Opel and Japan's Isuzu and Nissan.[66] Some companies, such as the telecommunications giant MCI, are actively involved in several strategic alliances, including one in Canada and several in New Zealand.[67]

In addition to the financial incentives (circumventing trade and tariff restrictions) and marketing benefits (access to internal markets) associated with strategic alliances, direct managerial benefits also are associated with extending one company's organizational chart into another's. These benefits primar-

■ Figure 15-12
Strategic Alliances as the Key to Growth in Foreign Markets
These employees of the Korean company Samsung Electronics might not know it, but their CEO, Kim Kwang-Ho is hoping to develop their organization into a global electronics giant by establishing strategic alliances with partners in other countries. With this in mind, Samsung has been building its technological strength and market penetration by partnering with Japanese firms (such as Toshiba and Fujitsu) and American firms (such as AT&T and Motorola).

ily come from improved technology and greater economies of scale (e.g., sharing functional operations across organizations). For these benefits to be derived, a high degree of coordination and fit must exist between the parties, each delivering on its promise to the other.

Technology: A Major Cause— and Consequence—of Design

Organizations differ tremendously with respect to *technology*—the means by which they transform inputs into outputs. These can vary from the simplest of tools used by single individuals to huge machines and complex, automated equipment. Clearly, the technology employed by a given organization is closely linked to the work it performs and the major tasks it seeks to accomplish. But growing evidence indicates that this relationship, too, is something of a two-way street. Organizations not only choose the technology they will employ; they are also affected by such tools once they are selected.

In short, just as the design of a specific building reflects the activities that take place within it, the structure of many organizations, too, tends to mirror the technologies they employ. In the discussion that follows, we will describe several major studies that point to this conclusion. As you will soon see, these investigations classify technology in contrasting ways and focus on a wide range of issues. Thus, their findings are often difficult to compare in a simple or direct manner. Generally, though, all point to the same basic conclusion: Technology plays an important role in shaping both the design and performance of many organizations.

You may wish to refer to our more general discussion of technology in Chapter 14.

Technology and Structure in Manufacturing Companies: The Woodward Studies

Perhaps the best-known study on the effects of technology is one conducted in England during the 1960s by Woodward and her associates.[68] To determine the relationship between various structural characteristics (e.g., span of control, decentralization) and organizational performance (e.g., profitability, market share), these investigators gathered data about 100 manufacturing firms. In keeping with the classical view of management (described on page 521), they initially expected that organizations classified as highly successful would share similar structural characteristics, and those classified as relatively unsuccessful would share other characteristics. Surprisingly, this was not the case. Instead, various aspects of organizational structure appeared to be just as common in successful and unsuccessful companies. Thus, there was little if any support for the accuracy of universal principles of management.

Instead, Woodward and her colleagues found that the organization's success depended on the degree to which it was structured in the most appropriate way given the technology used. Specifically, they compared organizations using each of three different types of technology in popular use at the time. In the first, labeled **small-batch production**, custom work was the norm. Capital equipment (machinery) was not highly mechanized, and the companies involved typically produced small batches of products to meet specific orders from customers. Employees were either skilled or unskilled, depending on the tasks they performed. Firms included in this category made items such as specialized construction equipment or custom-ordered electronic items. Other examples include dressmaking and printing.

Companies in the second category, known as **large-batch** or **mass production**, used basic assembly-line procedures. These organizations typically engaged in long production runs of standardized parts or products. Their output then went into inventory from which orders were filled on a continuous basis. Employees were mainly unskilled or semiskilled, with a sprinkling of research and engineering personnel.

The third category, known as **continuous-process production**, was the most technologically complex. Here, there was no start and no stop to production, which was automated and fully integrated. Employees were skilled workers or engineers. Among the organizations employing such advanced technology were oil refining and chemical companies.

When companies using these various types of technology were compared, important differences were noted. First, as expected, they demonstrated contrasting internal structures. For example, the span of control (of first-level supervisors) and centralization were higher in companies employing mass production than in ones using small-batch or continuous-process technologies. Similarly, chains of command were longest in organizations using continuous-process production, and shortest in those using small-batch methods. In short, the type of technology employed in production appeared to be an important variable in shaping organization structure. As Woodward herself put it, "Different technologies imposed different kinds of demands on individuals and organizations, and those demands had to be met through an appropriate structure."[69]

Perhaps even more important than these findings was the fact that the characteristics distinguishing highly successful from unsuccessful companies also varied with technology. At the low and high ends of the technology dimension described above, an *organic* management approach seemed best; companies showing this strategy were more successful than those demonstrating a *mechanistic* approach. In contrast, in the middle of the technology dimension (mass production), the opposite was true. Here, companies adopting a mechanistic approach tended to be more effective (see Figure 15-13). Another finding was that successful firms tended to have structures suited to their level of technology. Specifically, those with above average performance showed structural characteristics similar to most other firms using the same type of production methods; in contrast, those with below-average records tended to depart from the median structure shown by companies in the same technology category. In summary, the results of Woodward's study indicated that important links exist between technology and performance.

Additional support for these conclusions was later obtained in several other studies. For example, in a project involving 55 U.S. firms, Zwerman found that

small-batch production A technology in which products are custom-produced in response to specific orders from customers.

large-batch (mass) production Technology based on long production runs of standardized parts or products.

continuous-process production A highly automated form of production that is continuous in nature and highly integrated in terms of component steps and processes.

The Woodward Studies: The Relationship between Technology and Design
In a classic study, Woodward found that organic organizations were most effective when performing small-batch production and continuous-batch production jobs, whereas mechanistic organizations were most effective when performing large-batch production jobs.

(**Source:** Based on findings by Woodward, 1965; see Note 68.)

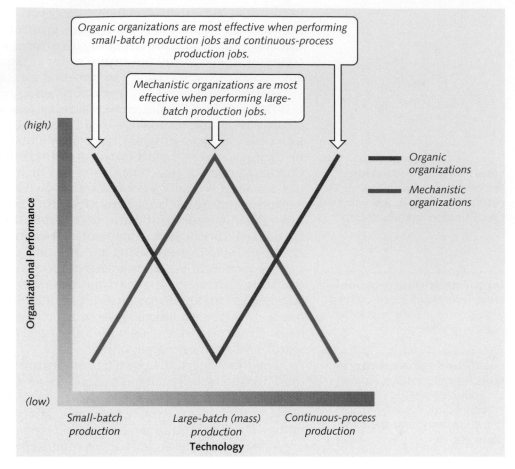

organizations employing small-batch or continuous-process technology tended to adopt an organic management approach.[70] Those employing mass production generally showed a mechanistic approach. In general, research has shown that the more sophisticated technology is used, the greater are the opportunities for organizations to thrive when authority is decentralized (in essence, because the "smart" technology is making the decisions, eliminating the need for some people in the hierarchy).[71] Woodward's findings are valuable because they were among the first that recognized the value of the contemporary, contingency approach to organizational structure.

As you might imagine, we have learned a great deal about organizational design since Woodward's time—if for no other reason than technology has changed so very much. In addition to the three types of technology studied by Woodward, today some organizations produce highly customized, high-performance products in relatively small runs. However, because these products are technologically advanced and complex, they are produced by highly automated, computer-controlled equipment. Moreover, the people involved in their manufacture must often possess a high level of professional or technical knowledge. In short, such companies share some characteristics with the traditional small-batch firms studied by Woodward, but share others with the technologically advanced continuous-process firms at the other end of her continuum.

What type of internal structure do such technical batch organizations demonstrate? Evidence on this issue has been provided by Hull and Collins.[72] These researchers examined the internal structure of 110 separate companies operating in the United States. On the basis of careful examination of their methods of production, Hull and Collins divided these organizations into four categories: traditional batch, technical batch, mass production, and process production. Then they compared the companies' internal structures along several key dimensions (e.g., supervisory span of control, occupational specialization, decentralization, formalization). As the examples in Figure 15-14 show, the types differed in various ways.

Consistent with predictions, organizations classified as traditional batch or technical batch in their methods of production showed contrasting structure in several respects. For example, the traditional batch companies possessed a larger supervisory span of control. In contrast, the technical batch companies showed a greater degree of occupational specialization and more decentralization. Further, and perhaps most important, the technical batch companies showed a much higher level of innovative activity (e.g., a higher percentage of employees involved in research and development activities).

In summary, expanding Woodward's original categories to reflect recent developments in methods of production yielded additional evidence for the powerful impact of technology on internal structure. Additional research along similar lines may help us to sharpen our knowledge of this important relationship still further.

Work-Flow Integration: The Aston Studies

As the heading of the preceding section suggests, Woodward's project, and several subsequent investigations, focused primarily on the links between technology and structure in manufacturing companies. Thus, as thorough as this work was, it left a basic issue unresolved: Would similar findings be observed in other types of companies as well?

Evidence on this question was provided by another team of British researchers affiliated with the University of Aston.[73] After studying a wide range of both manufacturing and service organizations (e.g., savings banks, insurance companies, department stores), these researchers concluded that technology can be described in terms of three basic characteristics: *automation of equipment*—the extent to which work activities are performed by machines; *work-flow rigidity*—the extent to which the sequence of work activities is inflexible;

■ **Figure 15-14**
Technology and Structure: Evidence of Linkages
Organizations employing technical batch technology differ in several respects from those employing traditional batch technology.

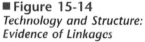

(**Source:** Based on data from Hull & Collins, 1987; see Note 72.)

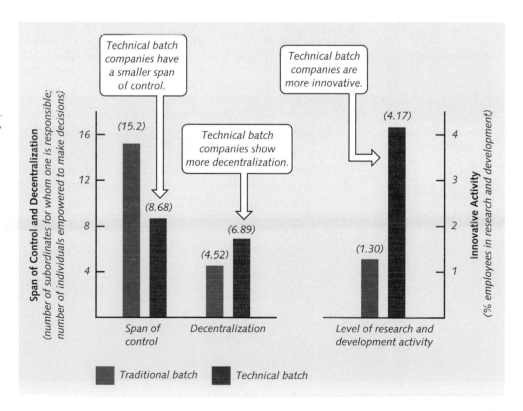

and *specificity of evaluation*—the degree to which work activities can be assessed by specific, quantitative means. Since these three factors appeared to be highly associated, they were combined into a single-scale labeled **work-flow integration**. The higher an organization's score on this scale, the more likely it was to employ automation, rigid task sequences, and quantitative measurement of its operations. The work-flow integration scores obtained by various companies are shown in Table 15-5. As you can see from this table, manufacturing firms generally score higher than those whose primary output is service.

When work-flow integration was related to structural characteristics in the organizations studied, no strong or general links were uncovered. Thus, at first glance, findings seemed contradictory to those reported by Woodward. Closer analysis of the data obtained, however, revealed that technological complexity *was* related to structural features, in at least some ways. For example, as work-flow integration increased, so did specialization, standardization, and decentralization of authority. The magnitude of these findings was small, and they seemed to involve mainly those aspects of structure closely connected to actual work flow. Moreover, *size* exerted stronger effects on several aspects of structure than technology.

These findings, plus those obtained in later studies, point to two conclusions. First, although technology does indeed seem to affect the internal structure of organizations, it is only one of several influences. As a result, the so-called *technological imperative*—the view that technology always has a compelling influence on organizational structure—clearly overstates the case.[74] Second, technology probably exerts stronger effects on structure in small organizations, where such characteristics impinge directly on work flow, than in large ones, where structure is complex and often far removed from actual production. In any case, taken as a whole, the findings of the Aston studies can be interpreted as indicating that the impact of technology on organizational structure is not restricted to manufacturing concerns. Under certain conditions, it can be observed in other types of companies as well.

YOU BE THE CONSULTANT

Fabricate-It, Inc., is a medium-sized manufacturing company that uses standard assembly lines to produce its products. Its employees tend to be poorly educated and perform monotonous work. Think-It, Inc., is a software design firm that writes cutomized programs to solve its customers' problems. Its employees tend to be highly educated and perform highly creative work. Both are reconsidering their present organizational designs.

1. What type of organizational design would you imagine would best suit the needs of Fabricate-It? Explain your decision.
2. What type of organizational design would you imagine would best suit the needs of Think-It? Explain your decision.

■ TABLE 15-5	WORKFLOW INTEGRATION IN DIFFERENT ORGANIZATIONS	

Manufacturing firms generally score higher on work-flow integration than do service organizations (e.g., banks, stores).

Organization	Classification (Manufacturing or Service)	Workflow Integration Score
Vehicle manufacturer	Manufacturing	17
Metal goods manufacturer	Manufacturing	14
Tire manufacturer	Manufacturing	12
Printer	Service	11
Local water department	Service	10
Insurance company	Service	7
Savings bank	Service	4
Department stores	Service	2
Chain of retail stores	Service	1

SOURCE: Based on data from Hickson, Pugh & Pheysey, 1969; see Note 73.

Technology and Interdependence: Thompson's Framework

interdependence The extent to which the units or departments within an organization depend on each other to accomplish tasks.

Another aspect of technology with important implications for organizational structure is **interdependence**. This refers to the extent to which individuals, departments, or units within a given organization depend on each other in accomplishing their tasks. Under conditions of low interdependence, each person, unit, or group can carry out its functions in the absence of assistance or input from others. Under high interdependence, in contrast, such coordination is essential. A framework proposed by Thompson helps clarify the various types of interdependence possible in organizations, and also the implications of this factor for effective structural design.[75]

pooled interdependence A relatively low level of interdependence in which units within an organization operate in a largely independent manner.

The lowest level within this framework is known as **pooled interdependence**. Under such conditions, departments or units are part of an organization, but work does not flow between them. Rather, each carries out its tasks independently. One example of pooled interdependence is provided by the branch stores of a clothing retailer in many large shopping malls. Each contributes to the total earnings of the parent company, but there is little, if any, contact or coordination between them.

sequential interdependence An intermediate level of interdependence in which the output of one unit serves as input for another.

The next higher level suggested by Thompson is **sequential interdependence**. Here, the output of one department or subunit becomes the input for another. For example, the marketing department of a food company cannot proceed with promotional campaigns until it receives information about new products from the product development unit. Similarly, in a company that manufactures electronic toys, final assemblers cannot perform their jobs unless they receive a steady supply of component parts from other work units or outside suppliers. Note that in sequential interdependence, information, products, and components flow in one direction. Thus, units farther along the chain of production are dependent on ones that precede them, but the reverse is not true.

reciprocal interdependence A high level of interdependence in which the output of each unit within an organization serves as the input for others, and vice versa.

The highest level in Thompson's model is known as **reciprocal interdependence**. Here the output of each department or unit serves as the input for other departments or units in a reciprocal fashion. Thus, the output of Department A provides input for Department B, and the output of Department B serves as the input for Department A. An example of such reciprocal interdependence is provided by the operations of the marketing and production departments of many companies. Marketing, through appropriate surveys, may develop a profile of new products or product innovations attractive to potential customers. This serves as input for Production, which considers the feasibility of actually making such products and suggests modifications. The appeal of these modifications is then assessed by Marketing and the results obtained serve as the basis for further planning by Production. This process may be repeated until a plan for product innovations acceptable to both units is devised (see Figure 15-15).

■ **Figure 15-15**
Reciprocal Interdependence: An Example
Under conditions of reciprocal interdependence, *the output of two or more departments serves as the input for each other in a reciprocal fashion.*

(**Source:** Based on suggestions by Thompson, 1967; see Note 75.)

Marketing Department

Profile of desirable product innovations

Feasibility of producing innovative products

Marketability of modified innovations

Requirements for revised product

Production Department

articles in the popular literature that describe something about the structure and design of any organizations within their assigned industry. (Feel free to focus on any aspects of design and structure described in this chapter. For example, articles may be found on the tendency for some companies to be eliminating middle management.) Computerized databases that allow you to search for stories about companies by name will be very useful.

4. After completing their research, students within the four groups should meet to discuss the structural characteristics of the organizations described by the various teams.

5. Gather as a class to compare the findings of the various groups.

Questions for Discussion

1. What major trends were found with respect to organizational structure and design? For example, were organizations eliminating levels of management?

2. Did you find that there were differences between companies with respect to key aspects of organizational structure and design? For example, were spans of control different at different organizational levels? If so, how?

3. Did the class find structural similarities between companies in various industries and differences between companies in different industries? If so, what were these? For example, were spans of control generally broader in some industries and narrower in others?

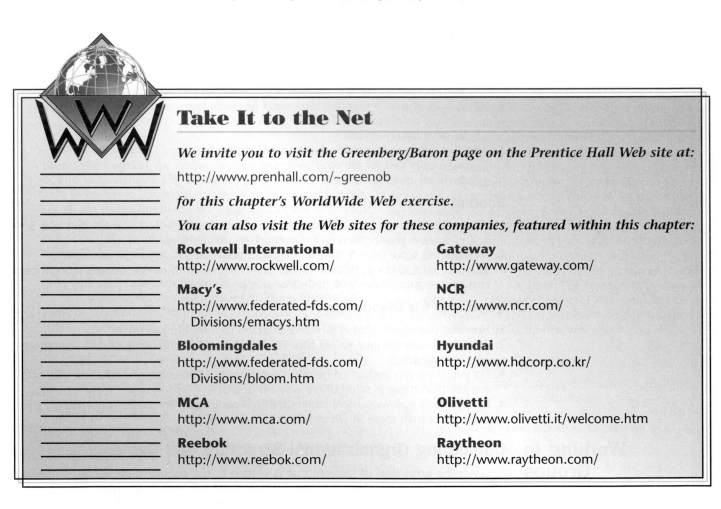

Take It to the Net

We invite you to visit the Greenberg/Baron page on the Prentice Hall Web site at:

http://www.prenhall.com/~greenob

for this chapter's WorldWide Web exercise.

You can also visit the Web sites for these companies, featured within this chapter:

Rockwell International
http://www.rockwell.com/

Gateway
http://www.gateway.com/

Macy's
http://www.federated-fds.com/
    Divisions/emacys.htm

NCR
http://www.ncr.com/

Bloomingdales
http://www.federated-fds.com/
    Divisions/bloom.htm

Hyundai
http://www.hdcorp.co.kr/

MCA
http://www.mca.com/

Olivetti
http://www.olivetti.it/welcome.htm

Reebok
http://www.reebok.com/

Raytheon
http://www.raytheon.com/

CHAPTER Sixteen

ORGANIZATIONAL CHANGE AND DEVELOPMENT

■ OBJECTIVES

LEARNING

After reading this chapter you should be able to:

1. Identify why it is important for organizations to change.
2. Describe the forces behind *organizational change*.
3. Identify the conditions under which organizational change is likely to occur.
4. Explain the major factors making people resistant to organizational change—and some ways of overcoming them.

5. Describe the major techniques of *organizational development*.
6. Evaluate the effectiveness of organizational development efforts.
7. Debate the idea that organizational development is inherently unethical.

CASE Preview

ZALES BECOMES A GEM OF A CHAIN

Robert DiNicola has a history of shaking things up at the department stores he has run. Not surprisingly, it sparked curiosity when in April 1994 DiNicola took over as chief executive of Zale Corp., a chain of 1,200 jewelry stores (most operating under the Zales and Gordon's names). Zale's board of directors was not looking for someone with jewelry experience; they had that in company president Larry Pollack. Rather, they wanted someone who could help the stores regain the glory—and profitability—they enjoyed before serious financial troubles in the early 1990s left the company drifting aimlessly in a sea of red ink.

DiNicola took no time to show that he was up to the challenge of turning things around. No sooner did he find his new office than he began stirring the pot by inquiring about plans for Memorial Day sales. Store officials had all they could do to contain their surprise at their new boss's naiveté about the jewelry business. After all, jewelry is traditionally purchased for special occasions, such as weddings and anniversaries, and not on impulse in response to attractive sale prices. Or, at least, that *was* the case. On Memorial Day 1994, Zales kept their doors open late to accommodate the throngs of holiday shoppers who were lured by attractive prices for clearance goods.

Based on that experience, DiNicola completely revamped Zales' approach to doing business. He identified their 100 best-selling items (such as diamond tennis bracelets and anniversary bands), purchased them in large quantities, and then promoted them heavily in radio and TV ads. After only a few months, these items, which had represented 30 per-

cent of total sales, rose to 40 percent. Advertising low prices for popular items quickly became part of the way Zales does business.

In another move, DiNicola positioned Zales as a value leader. Dropping its long-standing 60 percent profit margin, he traded lower margins for higher volume. Case in point: Instead of selling a bracelet at $1,295, and moving only 300 of them, Zales now sells the same product at $799 and watches ten times as many fly out the door. DiNicola also has renovated Zales stores and standardized their inventory and advertising at the national level (subject to minor regional variations), following the time-tested McDonald's formula for success.

As far as DiNicola is concerned, this is only the beginning of things to come for Zales. He has several new ideas up his sleeve—among them, increasing the chain's presence by opening 250 stores over the next three years. In the fall of 1995, the company experienced success with its first mail-order campaign. Other shop-at-home ideas DiNicola is pondering include a Zales home shopping channel and a Zales Internet site. If there's jewelry to be sold, chances are good that Zales will be involved.

There can be little doubt that DiNicola has made Zales a very different chain of jewelry stores than it was when he took over. It is a more profitable place as well. In 1995 Zale Corp. enjoyed a 46 percent increase in earnings ($31.5 million) from a 13 percent increase in sales ($1.04 billion) compared to 1994. And, with numbers like these, DiNicola appears to have the Midas touch.

When you picture a large chain of spacious stores packed with showcases brimming with diamonds and jewels, you probably don't think of a business fighting for its existence. Yet, in the wake of some failed business dealings, Zale Corp. had an uncertain future when DiNicola took over. Faced with pressures to boost sales, DiNicola altered Zale's approach to selling jewelry. Customers now enjoy better values than ever before, and the company's financial picture has improved. Of course, whether DiNicola's strategy comes as too little too late or marks a successful rebirth for Zale Corp., one thing is for certain: A great deal of *change* has occurred.

544   **PART 6** Organizational Processes

"*Today the secret ingredients for Mom's Apple Pie were sold to the Japanese for sixty-eight million dollars.*"

The pressure for change in the world of organizations is enormous, and not just at Zales. Think of the changes you may have seen in recent years in the way different businesses operate. The prices of many fast-food items have dropped, some auto dealerships have adopted no-haggle pricing policies, accommodations for people with handicaps have appeared, just about everything you can imagine has become computerized, and companies are buying up other companies in foreign lands (see Figure 16-1). Clearly, signs of *organizational change* can be found everywhere. Examining both the causes and consequences of change is one of the key missions of this chapter.

Most people have difficulty accepting that they may have to alter their work methods. After all, if you're used to working a certain way, a sudden change can be very unsettling. Fortunately, social scientists have developed various methods, known collectively as *organizational development* techniques, that are designed to implement needed organizational change in a manner that both is acceptable to employees and enhances the effectiveness of the organizations involved.[1] We will examine these techniques and critical issues surrounding them in this chapter. Before doing so, however, we will take a closer look at the process of organizational change by chronicling different forces for change acting on organizations. Then we will explore some major issues involved in the process of organizational change, such as what is changed, when change will occur, why people are resistant to change, and how this resistance may be overcome.

Organizational Change: An Ongoing Process

A century ago, advances in machine technology made farming so highly efficient that fewer hands were needed to plant and reap the harvest. The displaced laborers fled to nearby cities, seeking jobs in newly opened factories—ironically, taking advantage of opportunities created by some of the same technologies that displaced them from the farm. The economy shifted from agrarian to manufacturing, and the *industrial revolution* was under way. With it came drastic shifts in where people lived, how they worked, how they spent their leisure time, how much money they made, and how they spent it.

Today's business analysts claim that we are currently experiencing *another* industrial revolution—one driven by a new wave of economic and technological forces.[2] As one observer put it, "This workplace revolution . . . may be remembered as a historic event, the Western equivalent of the collapse of com-

For discussions of the ways in which technology influences the way people work, see Chapters 14 and 15.

organizational change

Planned or unplanned transformations in an organization's structure, technology, and/or people.

munism."[3] Not surprisingly, a great deal of **organizational change** is occurring—that is, planned or unplanned transformations in an organization's structure, technology, and/or people.

Change Is a Global Phenomenon

Interestingly, the forces for organizational change are not isolated to the United States; they appear to be global in nature. To illustrate this point, consider the findings of a survey of 12,000 managers in 25 different countries conducted a few years ago.[4] When asked to identify the changes they've experienced in the past two years, respondents reported that major restructurings, mergers, divestitures and acquisitions, reductions in employment, and international expansion had occurred in their organizations.

Figure 16-2 shows the percentage reporting each of these activities in six selected nations. Although some forms of change were more common in some countries than others, organizations in all countries were actively involved in each of these change efforts. This evidence suggests that organizational change is occurring throughout the world. Although different forces may be shaping change at different rates in different places, the conclusion is apparent: Change is a universal fact of life for organizations.

The Message Is Clear: Change or Disappear!

It's shocking when you think of all the once well-known companies, or parts of them, that have gone out of business in the past few decades. Even the Sears Catalogue, a longtime icon of the business world, is now just a memory

■ **Figure 16-2**

Organizational Change: An International Phenomenon

A large cross-national survey found that various forms of organizational change were reported to occur throughout the world. Shown here are the percentages of respondents in six countries indicating that each of four different forms of change occurred in organizations within their country in the past two years. Major restructuring was found to be the most widely encountered form of change in most countries.

(**Source:** Based on data reported by Kanter, 1991; see Note 4.)

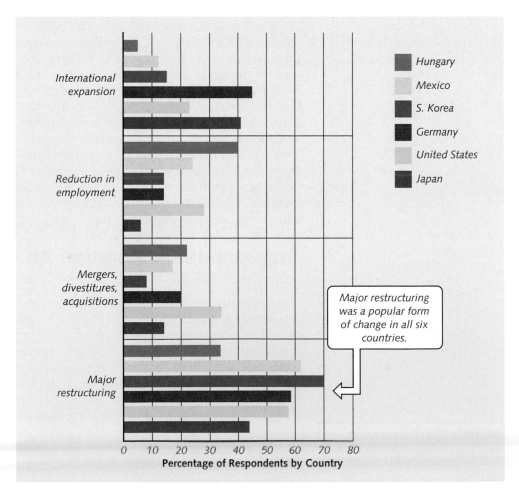

of a bygone era. No organization is immune. Even industry leaders are vulnerable to failure if they do not adapt to changing times.

Consider just the computer industry. Although it invented desktop word processing, Wang Laboratories was forced into bankruptcy when it failed to shift its emphasis from mainframes to PCs. Even Digital Equipment, which was once one of the world's major computer companies, is now in trouble, in large part because it too failed to jump onto the PC bandwagon.[5] When the authors started using personal computers in the mid-1980s, products such as Multimate and WordStar resided on their hard drives. "What are they?" you ask. Believe it or not, these were the premier word processing programs of their day. The very fact that they are now unfamiliar to you makes the point: Those companies that fail to change when required find themselves out of business as a result.[6] In fact, fully 62 percent of new ventures fail to last as long as five years, and only 2 percent make it as long as fifty years.[7]

In view of this, it is particularly impressive that some American companies have beaten the odds—so soundly, in fact, that they have remained in business for well over 200 years (see Table 16-1 for a summary of these "corporate Methuselahs").[8] As you might imagine, these companies have undergone *many* changes during their years of existence. For example, the oldest U.S. company, J. E. Rhoads & Sons, now makes conveyer belts, although it originally started out in 1702 making buggy whips. Another company, Dexter, in Windsor Locks, Connecticut, began in 1767 as a grist mill. Not surprisingly, it no longer does that; it now makes adhesives and coatings for aircraft. Earlier, it manufactured specialty papers for stationery and for tea bags. Obviously, this company is very willing to change. According to Dexter spokesperson Ellen Cook, "We have no traditions, whatsoever. None."[9]

In recent years, just about all companies you can think of have made adjustments in the ways they operate, some more pronounced than others. (One example may be seen in our PREVIEW CASE about Zales.) The changes that organizations make differ in scope; some are only minor, whereas others are major. Change that is continuous in nature, and involves no major shifts in the way an organization operates, is known as **first-order change**. Changes of this type are apparent in the very deliberate, incremental changes that Toyota has been making in continuously improving the efficiency of its production process.[10] Similarly, a restaurant may be seen as making first-order changes as

first-order change Change that is continuous in nature and involves no major shifts in the way an organization operates.

■ TABLE 16-1	THE TEN OLDEST COMPANIES IN AMERICA			
Very few companies continue to exist as long as the ones shown here. As you might expect, all have undergone considerable changes in their 200 to 300 years.	Rank	Year Founded	Name	Current Business
	1	1702	J. E. Rhoads & Sons	Conveyer belts
	2	1717	Covenant Life Insurance	Insurance
	3	1752	Philadelphia Contributorship	Insurance
	4	1767	Dexter	Adhesives and coatings
	5	1784	D. Landreth Seed	Seeds
	6	1784	Bank of New York	Banking
	7	1784	Mutual Assurance	Insurance
	8	1784	Bank of Boston	Banking
	9	1789	George R. Ruhl & Sons	Bakery supplies
	10	1790	Burns & Russell	Building materials

it gradually adds new items to its menu and gauges their success before completely revamping its concept.

As you might imagine, however, other types of organizational change are far more complex. **Second-order change** is the term used to refer to more radical change, major shifts involving many different levels of the organization and many different aspects of business.[11] Citing only some of the most publicized examples of second-order change from recent years, General Electric, Allied Signal, Ameritech, and Tenneco have radically altered the ways they operate, their culture, the technology they use, their structure, and the nature of their relations with employees.[12] For a close-up example of one company's second-order change, see the CASE IN POINT describing Boeing at the end of Chapter 5 (see p. 172).

(see p. 172)

second-order change Radical change; major shifts involving many different levels of the organization and many different aspects of business.

The Learning Organization: Benefiting from Change

Our discussion thus far makes it clear that the most successful organizations are those that focus on doing whatever it takes to adapt to changing conditions. Such an organization has been referred to as a **learning organization**—one that is successful at acquiring, cultivating, and applying knowledge that can be used to help it adapt to change.[13] Learning organizations are skilled at experimenting with new approaches to doing things. They do a particularly good job of learning from the experiences and best practices of others, and disseminating this informaton throughout the organization.[14]

In Chapter 3 we described the process of individual learning as one that focuses on changes in behavior. Recently, organizational scientists have found it useful to conceive of changes at the organizational level as the result of an analogous learning process. Specifically, organizations "learn" by following four basic steps (see summary in Figure 16-3):[15]

1. *Knowledge acquisition*: This is the process by which organizations tap the expertise of their employees to create a pool of knowledge upon which it can draw. For example, professional and technical information is shared on a computer network by the 110 corporate officers belonging to the Chicago Research and Planning Group.[16] In fact, computer programs known as *groupware* are becoming increasingly popular tools for aquiring and sharing information within organizations.[17] (These are software pro-

learning organization An organization that is successful at acquiring, cultivating, and applying knowledge that can be used to help it adapt to change.

■ **Figure 16-3**
Becoming a Learning Organization: Basic Steps
A learning organization *is one that is successful at acquiring, cultivating, and applying knowledge that helps it adapt to change. Some of the key steps in this process are summarized here.*

(**Source:** Based on suggestions by Huber, 1991; see Note 15.)

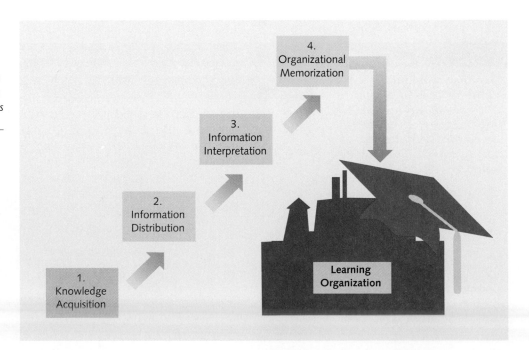

grams that enable several people to work together on the same project and have access to the same information.)

2. *Information distribution*: For information to be used as the basis for change, it must be distributed to and understood by those who require it. For example, at the Boston Market restaurant chain, employees are connected via a computer network to an electronic bulletin board in which information is posted on-line about sales figures, cost breakdowns, and even customer complaints.[18] By doing this, company officials hope to provide managers and lower-level employees opportunities to benefit from the experiences of others—thereby helping them better understand their own behavior.

3. *Information interpretation*: For learning to bring effective change, knowledge must be not only thoroughly collected, but also accurately interpreted. With this in mind, organizations are taking steps to ensure that employees can make the best possible use of the information they have gathered. Information technology has proven useful in this regard. For example, at the M.D. Anderson Cancer Center in Houston, systems analysts used software to track their earlier informational sessions to help them draw conclusions about the nature of the software they needed to design for managing their facility.[19] Interpreting their electronic discussions would have been far more difficult without this assistance.

4. *Organizational memorization*: This refers to the means by which knowledge from an organization's history is stored so that it can be tapped when needed to initiate change.[20] When people leave an organization, or a part of it, they take with them important lessons of history and knowledge that may be valuable to others. As a result, it is considered important to store the accumulated wisdom of the past in a readily accessible form. Without doing so, present generations will be unable to learn from past generations, providing a distinct disadvantage.

An example may be seen in the practice of using computerized files to record and keep track of customers' inquiries. Bankers Trust does this in its New York office so that any customer service agent can field a customer's inquiry at a later time, even if the individual who originally helped is out of the office.[21] The idea is that careful records are kept of key experiences so that they may be used as needed in the future. In so doing, the organization is not dependent on the presence—and memory—of any single individual. Rather, key events are made part of "institutional memory."

Most organizations fail to take these steps and cannot be considered learning organizations. They are rather unsystematic about gathering and using information that may facilitate change. However, a growing number of today's organizations—notably, Clorox, Ford, Corning, and General Electric—are attempting to ensure their long-term viability by taking the steps needed to adapt to a changing world, even if these are dramatic (e.g., redesigning their organizational structure and reshaping organizational culture). By collecting and using information, these organizations are learning to make changes that will help them adapt—and survive—in the future.

Now that we have described the prevalence and importance of change in organizations we will turn our attention to another basic issue: Why do organizations change? In other words, what factors lead organizations to change?

Forces Behind Change in Organizations

If you think about it, it's clear that organizations change either because they want to or because they have to. In our PREVIEW CASE, Zales saw the handwriting on the wall and its message was clear: Change or else! Organizations

In the face of changing conditions, organizations frequently require fewer employees than they currently have. So as to avoid large-scale layoffs that harm large numbers of employees, several alternative practices are being used.

Practice	Description	Example
Temporary salary cuts	Reducing the pay of all employees—either by an equal percentage, or in reverse proportion to salary	Intel temporarily cut employees' pay in amounts ranging up to 10% for its highest-paid employees
Layoff rotations	Workers take turns spending time on and off the job	Miners at Climax Molybdenum rotated two weeks on and two weeks off their jobs during a period of decreased demand for steel
Shortened work week	Reducing the number of days worked, with pay reductions to match	Nucor Corp. puts employees on four-day work weeks during slack periods
Flexible employment	Employees get to perform temporary jobs during slow periods	At Worthington Industries, production workers perform maintenance jobs at the factory while their regular services are not required
Early retirement	Offering financial incentives to employees who agree to retire ahead of schedule	Northwest Airlines offered senior flight attendants lump-sum payments of $20,000 along with fringe benefits
Delaying projects	By delaying the completion of projects, employees nearing retirement could be kept on the payroll	Anheuser Busch kept senior employees on the job by delaying the completion of projects until those individuals were ready to retire
Tin parachutes for employees	Money is put aside to ease transitions should a hostile takeover result in new management which cuts people	Kodak promises severance pay, insurance benefits, and outplacement help to its hourly employees in the event of a takeover
Invite employees back	Hire former employees as conditions improve	Super Value Stores makes an effort to rehire former employees who were laid off during slow periods

SOURCE: Based on suggestions by Rosen & Berger, 1991; see Note 30.

Organizational designs of this type are described in detail in Chapter 15.

dual-core model The theory recognizing that changes in the administration of organizations come from upper management (i.e., from the top down), whereas changes in the work performed come from the technical specialists within organizations (i.e., from the bottom up).

A discussion of the distinction between mechanistic and organic organizations appears in Chapter 15.

by PepsiCo to structurally reorganize.[34] For many years, PepsiCo had a separate international food service division, which included the operation of 62 foreign locations of the company's Pizza Hut and Taco Bell restaurants. Because of the great profit potential of these foreign restaurants, PepsiCo officials decided to reorganize, putting these restaurants directly under the control of the same executives responsible for the successful national operations of Pizza Hut and Taco Bell. This type of departmentalization allows the foreign operations to be managed under the same careful guidance as the national operations.

Typically, the pressure to bring about changes in the administration of organizations (e.g., to coordinate activities, set goals and priorities) comes from upper management—that is, from the top down. In contrast, pressure to change the central work of the organization (i.e., the production of goods and services) comes from the technical side of the organization, from the bottom upward.[35] This is the idea behind the **dual-core model** of organizations. Many organizations, especially medium-sized ones, may be characterized by potential conflicts between the administrative and the technical cores—each faction wishing to change the organization according to its own vested interests. Which side usually wins? Research suggests that the answer depends on the design of the organization in question. Organizations that are highly *mecha-*

nistic as opposed to *organic* in their approach (i.e., they are highly formal and centralized) tend to be more successful in introducing administrative changes.[36] The high degree of control wielded by the administrative core paves the way for introducing administrative change.

Introduction of new technologies: From slide rules to computers. As described in Chapter 14, advances in technology have produced changes in the way organizations operate. Senior scientists and engineers, for example, can probably tell you how their work was drastically altered in the mid-1970s, when their ubiquitous plastic slide rules gave way to powerful pocket calculators. Things changed again only a decade later, when calculators were supplanted by powerful desktop microcomputers, which have revolutionized the way documents are prepared, transmitted, and filed in an office. Manufacturing plants have also seen a great deal of growth recently in the use of computer-automated technology and robotics. Technology is used widely to ensure the quality of manufactured goods (see Figure 16-4). Each of these examples represents an instance in which technology has altered the way people do their jobs.

The use of computer technology has been touted as one of the major revolutions occurring in the business world today. Not only are personal computers found in 30 percent of American homes, but they also are used by people in practically every job you can think of, from package deliverer to bill collector.[37] During the earliest years in which computers were used in the workplace, they failed to fulfill the promise of increased productivity that was used to usher them in. The hardware and software technology was not only too primitive, but also the users were too unprepared. Today, however, this has finally changed. According to William Wheeler, a consultant at Coopers & Lybrand, "For the first time the computer is an enabler of productivity improvement rather than a cause of lack of productivity.[38]

In Chapter 14 we describe the role of information technology in organizations.

The key is that technology gives people access to vast amounts of information faster and more widely than ever before. As a result, it is not necessary to configure work in the same old way. For example, ten years ago General Electric Lighting had 34 warehouses and 25 customer service centers. Today, using a vast computer network linked to a database, the company needs only 8 warehouses and one customer service center to do the same amount of work even more efficiently. Indeed, information technology is reducing the need for expensive investments in physical assets such as factories and warehouses. Seeing this handwriting on the wall, companies are now investing more money on equipment to manage information (e.g., computers and telecommunications hardware) than on such traditional capital expenses as industrial equipment.[39] As we have noted throughout this book, this trend represents a major change in the way work is done. One of the most important sources of information that organizations use as the basis for making changes is information regarding what one's competitors are doing. For a closer look at an intriguing way such information is gathered, see the QUEST FOR QUALITY section.

■ **Figure 16-4**
Technology: A Key to Quality
A Mattel technician performs tests on a Barbie doll to see whether she'll swim nonstop for 15 hours and if her batteries will remain dry. Work of this type is used to ensure that only quality products make it to the market.

COMPETITIVE INTELLIGENCE: PLANNING CHANGE BY LEARNING ABOUT THE COMPETITION

Only about 10 percent of American companies do it, and the other 90 percent probably should. What, you ask? The answer is **competitive intelligence (CI)**—the process of gathering information about one's competitors that can be used as the basis for planning organizational change. CI is a search for clues about what one's competitor is actually doing or considering doing. To stay competitive, some of the biggest companies—especially those in rapidly changing, high-tech fields, such as General Electric, Motorola, Microsoft, Hewlett-Packard, IBM, AT&T, and Intel—engage in CI all the time. In fact, Gary Costley, former president of Kellogg Co. North America says that managers who don't engage in CI are "incompetent" insofar as it is "irresponsible to not understand your competitors."[40]

Before you dismiss CI on the grounds that it is unethical, it's important to note that we're not talking about doing anything illegal. Rather, CI efforts usually involve gathering readily available information, such as that contained in public records. Companies are required to disclose information on their finances, inventories, and compliance with various legal regulations. Documents containing this information are available to anyone, and growing numbers of competitors are availing themselves of them. Valuable information also may be obtained by interviewing people who work for competing companies. It's amazing what loose-lipped employees may tell you without prying it out of them. Sometimes, all you have to do to gather competitive information is be observant. Case in point: Years before he became president of Kellogg, Costley simply stood on a public street and watched as a competitor, General Foods, unloaded a new extruding machine onto the loading dock of its Post cereal plant (which was located across the street from his own company). Costley later used what he saw as the basis for convincing his bosses to switch to that machine.

Although most companies do not gather and use competitive information, a few go out of their way to put such information to good use. For example, in the mid-'80s Motorola sent someone to Japan to research the budgets of companies that might compete with its electronics market in Europe. Discovering that several Japanese firms planned to sell semiconductors in Europe, Motorola immediately strengthened its business in that area (such as by starting strategic alliances with other companies). When the Japanese did enter the market, their impact was far less than it would have been had Motorola not struck first. Competitive intelligence also helped the Adolph Coors Co. avoid a failure in the wine cooler market. It sent a team to study its competitor, Gallo to see exactly what they did right. What they learned was that Gallo could make the product for much less because it owned its own vineyards. Deciding that it couldn't beat Gallo, Coors dropped its plans.

Knowing how effective a little detective work may be, some of the most careful companies go out of their way to make sure that they do not become easy targets for their own competitors who may be trying their hands at CI. In fact, they sometimes hire people to try to crack their own security. If these counterspies can get valuable information, they plug the leak before there's any real harm done. Of course, we're not talking about information that *must* be disclosed by law, but information that is disclosed for no good reason. For example, some companies provide too much information on the forms they fill out. Some executives divulge too much in speeches they give or in press releases without ever thinking that what they say may be getting into the wrong hands. Not surprisingly, the companies that are most sophisticated in matters of CI not only engage in it, but go out of their way to make sure that they don't become targets themselves. Experts advise: Play it safe; assume your competitors are better at CI than you.

There's no mistaking the fact that competitive intelligence has become an important source of profit for many companies. As just one example, Robert Flynn, the former CEO of the NutraSweet division of Monsanto, has claimed that CI was worth some $50 million to his company (in terms of revenues gained and revenues not lost to competitors). With figures like these, it's easy to make the case that companies cannot afford *not* to make CI a key part of their strategic change plans.

---

competitive intelligence (CI) The process of gathering information about one's competitors that can be used as the basis for planning organizational change.

Unplanned Change

Until now, the forces for change we've discussed represent planned attempts to improve the way organizations operate. However, not all forces for change are deliberate in nature. Indeed, organizations must often be responsive to changes that are unplanned. One of the greatest challenges faced by an organization is its ability to respond to changes from the outside world over which it has little or no control. As the environment changes, organizations must follow suit. In fact, research has shown that organizations that can best adapt to changing conditions tend to survive.[41]

We already have identified some major determinants of unplanned organizational change. For example, in Chapter 2, we explained that today's organizations have been forced to adapt to shifts in the demographic makeup of the workplace. They also must be responsive to the growing trend toward globalization. Three additional forces for unplanned change deserve to be mentioned: governmental regulation, economic competition, and performance gaps.

Government regulation. One of the most commonly witnessed unplanned organizational changes results from government regulations. For example, in the late 1980s, restaurant owners in the United States had to alter the way they report the income of waiters and waitresses to the federal government for purposes of collecting income taxes. In recent years, the U.S. federal government has been involved in both imposing and eliminating regulations in industries such as commercial airlines (e.g., mandating inspection schedules, but no longer controlling fares) and banking (e.g., restricting the amount of time checks can be held before clearing, but no longer regulating interest rates). Such activities have greatly influenced the way business is conducted in these industries.

An excellent example of how government activities drive organizational change is provided by the 1984 divestiture of AT&T. A settlement of antitrust proceedings dramatically rearranged the activities of almost 1 million employees of the Bell System. Among other things, the agreement led to the creation of seven new independent companies. At Southwestern Bell, CEO Zane Barnes remarked that the divestiture forced them to "rethink the functions of some 90,000 employees," a process likened to "taking apart and reassembling a jumbo jet while in flight."[42] Not surprisingly, the company relied on its expertise in satellite and communications technology to provide information about the change process to its employees in 57 locations.

Government regulations are often imposed on organizations following some crisis of public health or safety. For example, following the March 22, 1990, sinking of a crab fishing boat, the *Aleutian Enterprise*, off the coast of Alaska, the National Transportation Safety Board stiffened regulations regarding the condition of ships and the procedures used to bring in the catch.[43] Similarly, following the 1979 accident at Three Mile Island, the Nuclear Regulatory Commission imposed safety standards on all nuclear power plants.[44] To the extent that the government imposes regulations on organizations, they are forced to make changes to accommodate them.

Organizations often agree to regulate themselves in response to governmental pressure to change. For example, in 1996 executives from the television industry agreed to introduce a rating system that identifies for viewers program content that they might find objectionable due to sexual content or violence. Although these individuals took steps to regulate their industry, they did so only after confronting the reality that if they did not do so, the government would do it for them. So, rather than accepting imposed control, they heeded the message to impose their own control. Either way, the imposition of controls of this type leads to unplanned organizational change.

Economic competition. It happens every day: Someone builds a better mousetrap—or at least a cheaper one. As a result, companies often must fight to maintain their share of the market, advertise more effectively, and produce products more inexpensively. This kind of economic competition not only forces organizations to change, but also demands that they change effectively if they are to survive (see Figure 16-5).

On some occasions, competition can become so fierce that the parties involved would actually be more effective if they dropped their swords and joined forces. It was this "if you can't beat 'em, join 'em" reasoning that was responsible for the announced alliance between arch rivals IBM and Apple Computer in the summer of 1991, an alliance dubbed "the deal of the decade" by one financial analyst.[45]

Performance gaps. Traditionally, organizations have operated under the philosophy, "If it's not broken, don't fix it." That is, they focused on *performance gaps*, disparities between actual and expected levels of performance. A product line that isn't moving, a vanishing profit margin, a level of sales that isn't up to corporate expectations are examples. Few things force change more than sudden and unexpected information about poor performance.

Historically, organizations have stayed with winning courses of action and changed only in response to failure; in other words, they followed a *win-stay/lose-change rule*. Indeed, several studies have shown that a performance gap is one of the key factors providing an impetus for organizational innovation.[46] Those organizations that are best prepared to mobilize change in response to unexpected downturns are expected to be the ones that succeed.

The Process of Organizational Change: Some Basic Issues

As you might imagine, the process of changing organizations is not haphazard; rather, it proceeds according to some well-established, orderly fashion. It is well known, for example, what the targets of organizational change efforts may be, and when organizational change is likely to occur. We will address these basic issues in this section.

Targets of Organizational Change: What Is Changed?

Imagine that you are an engineer responsible for overseeing the maintenance of a large office building. The property manager has noted a dramatic increase in the use of heat in the building, causing operating costs to skyrocket. In other words, a need for change exists—specifically, a reduction in the building's heat usage. You cannot get the power company to lower its rates, so you realize you must bring about changes in the use of heat. But how? One possibility is to rearrange job responsibilities so that only maintenance personnel are permitted to adjust thermostats. Another option is to put timers on all thermostats so that the building temperature is automatically lowered during periods of nonuse. Finally, you consider the idea of putting stickers next to the thermostats, requesting that occupants do not adjust them. These three options represent excellent examples of the three potential targets of organizational change we will consider—changes in *organizational structure*, *technology*, and *people* (see Figure 16-6).

Changes in organizational structure. In Chapter 15 we described the key characteristics of organizational structure. Here we note that altering the structure of an organization may be a reasonable way of responding to a need for change. In the above example, a structural solution to the heat regulation problem came in the form of reassigning job responsibilities. Indeed, modifying rules, responsibilities, and procedures may be an effective way to manage change. Changing the responsibility for temperature regulation from a highly decentralized system (whereby anyone can make adjustments) to a centralized one (in which only maintenance personnel may do so) is one way of implementing organizational change in response to a problem. This particular structural solution called for changing the power structure (i.e., who was in charge of a particular task).

Different types of structural changes may take other forms.[47] For example, changes can be made in an organization's span of control, altering the number of employees for which supervisors are responsible. Structural changes also may take the form of revising the basis for creating departments—such as from product-based departments to functional departments. Other structural changes may be much simpler, such as clarifying someone's job description or the written policies and procedures followed.

■ **Figure 16-6**
Organizational Change Targets: Structure, Technology, People
To create change in organizations, one can rely on altering organizational structure, technology, and/or people. Changes in any one of these areas may necessitate changes in the others.

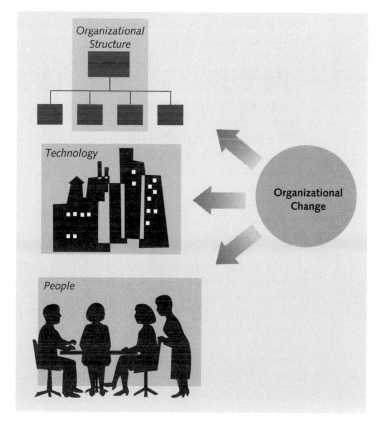

Structural changes are not uncommon in organizations. Consider, for example, some changes reported in recent years at the huge consumer products company Procter & Gamble.[48] In response to growing competition, the company was forced to make a number of changes that streamlined its highly bureaucratic organizational structure. For example, the decision-making process used to be so centralized that many decisions that could have been made at lower levels were being made by top corporate personnel (such as the color of the cap on the can of decaffeinated instant Folgers coffee!). Now decentralized business teams have been instituted and are permitted to make all the decisions about developing, manufacturing, and marketing products.

Changes in technology.   In our thermostat example, we noted that one possible solution would be to use thermostats that automatically reduce the building's temperature while it is not in use. This is an example of a technological approach to the need to conserve heat in the building. Placement of regulating devices on the thermostats that would thwart attempts to raise the temperature also would be possible. The thermostats also could be encased in a locked box, or simply removed altogether. A new, modern, energy-efficient furnace could be installed in the building. All of these suggestions represent technological approaches to the need for change.

The underlying idea is that technological improvements can lead to more efficient work. Indeed, if you've ever prepared a term paper on a typewriter, you know how much more efficient it is to do the same job using a word processor. Technological changes may involve a variety of alterations, such as changing the equipment used to do jobs (e.g., robots), substituting microprocessors for less reliable mechanical components (e.g., on airline equipment), or simply using better-designed tools (e.g., hand tools with better grips). Each of these changes may be used to bring about improvements in organizational functioning.

The means by which technology can help enhance the efficiency of work are described in Chapter 14.

Changes in people.   You've probably seen stickers next to light switches in hotels and office buildings asking the occupants to turn off the lights when not in use. These are similar to the suggestion in our opening example to affix signs near thermostats asking occupants to refrain from adjusting the thermostats. Such efforts represent attempts to respond to the needed organizational change by altering the way people behave. The basic assumption is that the effectiveness of organizations is greatly dependent on the behavior of the people working within them.

As you might imagine, the process of changing people is not easy—indeed, it lies at the core of most of the topics discussed in this book. However, theorists have identified three basic steps that summarize what's involved in the process of changing people.[49,50] The first step is known as *unfreezing*. This refers to the process of recognizing that the current state of affairs is undesirable and in need of change. Realizing that change is needed may be the result of some serious organizational crisis or threat (e.g., a serious financial loss, a strike, or a major lawsuit), or simply becoming aware that current conditions are unacceptable (e.g., antiquated equipment, inadequately trained employees).

In recent years, some executives have gotten employees to accept the need to change while things are still good by creating a sense of urgency. They introduce the idea that there is an impending crisis although conditions are, in fact, currently acceptable—an approach referred to as **doomsday management**.[51] This process effectively unfreezes people, stimulating change before its too late to do any good. Before rejecting this practice as overly deceptive, consider this analogy. People usually switch to healthier diets only after they've suffered heart attacks, although they may have been able to prevent them altogether had their doctors emphasized the urgency of adapting a healthier lifestyle beforehand.

doomsday management The practice of introducing change by suggesting that an impending crisis is likely.

After unfreezing, *changing* may occur. This step occurs when some planned attempt is made to create a more desirable state for the organization and its members. Change attempts may be quite ambitious (e.g., an organization-wide restructuring) or only minor (e.g., a change in a training program). (A thorough discussion of such planned change techniques will be presented in the next major part of this chapter.)

Finally, *refreezing* occurs when the changes made are incorporated into the employees' thinking and the organization's operations (e.g., mechanisms for rewarding behaviors that maintain the changes are put in place). Hence, the new attitudes and behaviors become a new, enduring aspect of the organizational system. For a summary of these three steps in the individual change process, see Figure 16-7. Despite the simplicity of this model, it does a good job of identifying some of the factors that make people willing to change their behavior—thereby potentially improving organizational effectiveness.

Readiness for Change: When Will Organizational Change Occur?

As you might imagine, there are times when organizations are likely to change, and times during which change is less likely. Even if the need for change is high and resistance to change is low (two important factors), organizational change does not automatically occur. Other factors are involved, and we have summarized some of the key variables in Figure 16-8.[52]

As Figure 16-8 summarizes, change is likely to occur when the people involved believe that the benefits associated with making a change outweigh the costs involved. The factors contributing to the benefits of making a change are (1) the amount of dissatisfaction with current conditions, (2) the availability of a desirable alternative, and (3) the existence of a plan for achieving that alternative. Theorists have claimed that these three factors combine multiplicatively to determine the benefits of making a change.[53] Thus, if any one of these factors is very low (or zero), the benefits of making a change, and the likelihood of change itself, are very low (or zero).

If you think about it, this should make sense to you. After all, people are unlikely to initiate change if they are not at all dissatisfied, or if they don't have any desirable alternative in mind (or any way of attaining that alternative, if they do have one in mind). Of course, for change to occur, the expected benefits must outweigh the likely costs involved (e.g., disruption, uncertainties). Professionals in the field of organizational development pay careful attention to these factors before they attempt to initiate any formal, ambitious

■ **Figure 16-7**
Changing People: Some Basic Steps
The process of changing people involves the three basic steps outlined here: unfreezing, changing, and refreezing.

(**Sources:** Based on suggestions by Lewin, 1951; see Note 49; and Schein, 1968; see Note 50.)

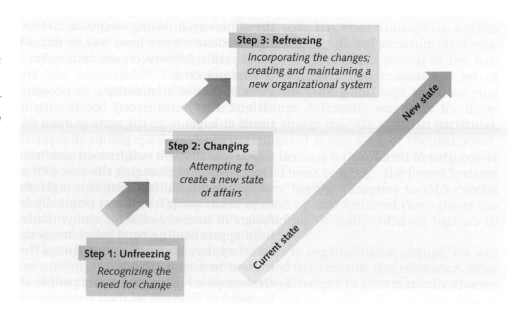

Step 3: Refreezing
Incorporating the changes; creating and maintaining a new organizational system

New state

Step 2: Changing
Attempting to create a new state of affairs

Step 1: Unfreezing
Recognizing the need for change

Current state

to employees, such as organizational climate, leadership style, and job satisfaction. This may take the form of intensive interviews or structured questionnaires, or both. Because it is important that this information be as unbiased as possible, employees providing feedback should be assured that their responses will be kept confidential. For this reason, this process is usually conducted by outside consultants.

The second step calls for reporting the information obtained back to the employees during small group meetings. Typically, this consists of summarizing the average scores on the attitudes assessed in the survey. Profiles are created of feelings about the organization, its leadership, the work done, and related topics. Discussions also focus on why the scores are as they are, and what problems are revealed by the feedback.

The final step involves analyzing problems dealing with communication, decision making, and other organizational processes to make plans for dealing with them. Such discussions are usually most effective when they are carefully documented and a specific plan of implementation is made, with someone put in charge of carrying it out.

Survey feedback is a widely used organizational development technique.[72] This is not surprising in view of the advantages it offers. It is efficient, allowing a great deal of information to be collected relatively quickly. Also, it is very flexible and can be tailored to the needs of different organizations facing a variety of problems. However, the technique can be no better than the quality of the questionnaire used—it must measure the things that really matter to employees. Of course, to derive the maximum benefit from survey feedback, it must have the support of top management. Specifically, the plans developed by the small discussion groups must be capable of being implemented with the full approval of the organization. When these conditions are met, survey feedback can be a very effective OD technique.

Sensitivity Training: Developing Personal Insight

The method by which small, face-to-face group interaction experiences are used to give people insight into themselves (e.g., who they are, the way others respond to them) is known as **sensitivity training**. Developed in the 1940s, sensitivity training groups (also referred to as *encounter groups, laboratory groups*, or *T-groups*) were among the first organizational development techniques used in organizations (such as Standard Oil and Union Carbide).[73] The rationale behind sensitivity training is that people are usually not completely open and honest with each other, a condition that thwarts insights into oneself and others. However, when people are placed in special situations within which open, honest communication is allowed and encouraged, personal insights may be gained. To do this, small groups (usually about eight to fifteen in number) are created and meet away from the pressures of the job site for several days. An expert trainer (referred to as the *facilitator*) guides the group at all times, helping assure that the proper atmosphere is maintained.

The sessions themselves are completely open with respect to what is discussed. Often, to get the ball rolling, the facilitator will frustrate the group members by not getting involved at all, appearing to be passively goofing off. As members sit around and engage in meaningless chit-chat, they begin to feel angry at the change agent for wasting their time. Once these expressions of anger begin to emerge, the change agent has created the important first step needed to make the session work—he or she has given the group a chance to focus on a current event. At this point, the discussion may be guided into how each of the group members expresses his or her anger toward the others. They are encouraged to continue discussing these themes openly and honestly, and not to hide their true feelings as they would often do on the job. So, for example, if you think someone is relying too much on you, this is the time to

sensitivity training An OD technique that seeks to enhance employees' understanding of their own behavior and its impact on others.

say so. Participants are encouraged to respond by giving each other *immediate feedback* to what was said. By doing this, it is reasoned, people will learn more about how they interrelate with others and will become more skilled at interpersonal relations. These are among the major goals of sensitivity groups.

It probably comes as no surprise to you that the effectiveness of sensitivity training is difficult to assess. After all, measuring insight into one's own personality is clearly elusive. Even if interpersonal skills seem to be improved, people will not always be able to transfer successfully their newly learned skills when they leave the artificial training atmosphere and return to their jobs.[74] As a result, sensitivity training tends not to be used extensively by itself for OD purposes. Rather, as we will see, it is often used in conjunction with, or as part of, other OD techniques.

Team Building: Creating Effective Work Groups

team building An OD technique in which employees discuss problems related to their work group's performance. On the basis of these discussions, specific problems are identified and plans for solving them are devised and implemented.

The important role of teams within organizations is emphasized in Chapter 8.

The technique of **team building** applies the techniques and rationale of sensitivity training to work groups. The approach attempts to get members of a work group to diagnose how they work together and to plan how this may be improved.[75] Given the importance of group efforts in effective organizational functioning, attempts to improve the effectiveness of work groups are likely to have profound effects on organizations. If one assumes that work groups are the basic building blocks of organizations, it follows that organizational change should emphasize changing groups instead of individuals.[76]

Team building begins when members of a group admit that they have a problem and gather data to provide insight into it. The problems that are identified may come from sensitivity training sessions or more objective sources, such as production figures or attitude surveys. These data are then shared, in a *diagnostic session*, to develop a consensus regarding the group's current strengths and weaknesses. From this, a list of desired changes is created, along with some plans for implementing these changes. In other words, an *action plan* is developed—some task-oriented approach to solving the group's problems as diagnosed. Following this step, the plan is carried out, and its progress is evaluated to determine whether the originally identified problems remain. If the problems are solved, the process is completed and the team may stop meeting. If not, the process should be restarted. (See Figure 16-10 for a summary of these steps.)

Work teams have been used effectively to combat a variety of important organizational problems.[77] For these efforts to be successful, however, all group members must participate in the gathering and evaluating of information as well as the planning and implementing of action plans. Input from group members is also especially crucial in evaluating the effectiveness of the team building program.[78] Keep in mind that because the team building approach is highly task-oriented, interpersonal problems between group members may be disruptive and need to be neutralized by an outside party. With interpersonal strain out of the way, the stage is set for groups to learn to solve their own problems effectively. However, this does not happen overnight. To be effective, team building should *not* be approached as a onetime exercise undertaken during a few days away from the job. Rather, it should be thought of as an ongoing process that takes several months (or even years) to develop. Given the great impact effective teams can have on organizational functioning, efforts to build effective work teams seem quite worthwhile.

In Chapter 8 we describe work teams and the factors that make them so effective in organizations.

A successful team building program has been in use at the France-based multinational corporation, Groupe Bull.[79] Instead of using team building exercises exclusively among top leaders (who presumably have already bought into the company's philosophies), lower-level executives and managers from companies on several different continents are brought together for several two- to three-week sessions in which they try to solve problems of mutual interest.

Team Building: Its Basic Steps
Team building, *a popular technique of
organizational development, follows the
steps outlined here.*

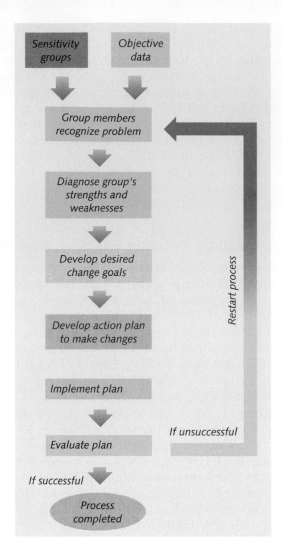

Some techniques used in team building exercises for attaining high levels of interpersonal trust are a bit more unorthodox. For example, as part of many team building exercises, group members are put into highly challenging real-life situations that are metaphors for how they have to pull together to meet challenges on the job. The idea is that by facing these difficult off-the-job challenges successfully, they will develop the skills needed for working together effectively on the job. Group Bull executives so strongly believe in this idea that their team building exercises have taken them on an adventurous white water rafting trip in the swirling waters of the river Spey in the mountains of Scotland (see Figure 16-11).[80] Other companies have sent their executives off on such challenges as mountain climbing expeditions and dog sled trips.[81]

Why the exotic adventures? In theory, learning to work together on navigating the treacherous river while staying afloat can help team members recognize how they interact with each other while navigating the rough waters of international business. But, does it work? Obviously, the effectiveness of such an approach depends on the extent to which participants come away from the experience with the type of insight desired and translate these newfound ideas into meaningful work-related activities. By itself, some rafting or mountain climbing expeditions are not likely to make executives become a cohesive team. However, such adventures can be an effective part of an ongoing program of regular team development.

Physical Challenges: Do They Help with Teamwork on the Job?
Some team building exercises put people in physically challenging conditions. The rationale is that learning to overcome these obstacles will teach team members how to work together cooperatively. The value of the exercises is realized only when the principles of teamwork learned during the training are applied back on the job.

Quality of Work Life Programs: Humanizing the Workplace

When you think of work, do you think of drudgery? Although many people believe these two terms go together naturally, it has grown increasingly popular to improve systematically the quality of life experienced on the job. As more people demand satisfying and personally fulfilling places to work, OD practitioners have attempted systematically to create work conditions that enhance employees' motivation, satisfaction, and commitment—factors that may contribute to high levels of organizational performance. Such efforts are known collectively as **quality of work life (QWL)** programs. Specifically, such programs are ways of increasing organizational output and improving quality by involving employees in the decisions that affect them on their jobs. Typically, QWL programs support highly democratic treatment of employees at all levels and encourage their participation in decision making. Although many approaches to improving the quality of work life exist, they all share a common goal: humanizing the workplace.[82]

One popular approach to improving the quality of work life involves *work restructuring*—the process of changing the way jobs are done to make them more interesting to workers.[83] If this sounds familiar to you, it is because we already discussed several such approaches to redesigning jobs—including *job enlargement, job enrichment*, and the *job characteristics model*—in our discussion of motivation in Chapter 5. In the present context, note that such techniques also represent effective ways of improving the quality of work life for employees.

Another approach to improving the quality of work life calls for using **quality circles (QCs)**. These are small groups of volunteers (usually around ten) who meet regularly (usually weekly) to identify and solve problems related to the quality of the work they perform and the conditions under which people do their jobs.[84] An organization may have several QCs operating at once, each dealing with a particular work area about which it has the most expertise. To help them work effectively, the members of the circle usually receive some form of training in problem solving. Large companies such as Westinghouse, Hewlett-Packard, and Eastman Kodak, to name only a few, have included QCs as part of their QWL efforts.[85] Groups have dealt with issues such as how to reduce vandalism, how to create safer and more comfortable working environments, and how to improve product quality. Research has shown that although quality circles are very effective at bringing about short-term improvements in quality of work life (i.e., those lasting up to 18 months), they are less effective at creating more permanent changes.[86]

As you might imagine, a variety of benefits (even if short-term ones) might result from QWL programs. These fall into three major categories.[87] The most

quality of work life (QWL) An OD technique designed to improve organizational functioning by humanizing the workplace, making it more democratic, and involving employees in decision making.

quality circles (QCs) An approach to improving the quality of work life, in which small groups of volunteers meet regularly to identify and solve problems related to the work they perform and the conditions under which they work.

direct benefit is usually *increased job satisfaction, organizational commitment, and reduced turnover* among the workforce.[88,89] A second benefit is *increased productivity*. In fact, a recent study comparing the performance of employees who participated in a QC program with a control group (an equivalent group that had not participated in such a program) revealed that in the year following the group involvement, those who had participated received higher job performance ratings and were more likely to get promoted than those who had not participated in the QC program.[90] Related to these first two benefits is a third—namely, *increased organizational effectiveness* (e.g., profitability, goal attainment). Many companies, including industrial giants such as Ford, General Electric, and AT&T, have active QWL programs and are reportedly quite pleased with their results.[91]

Achieving these benefits is not automatic, however. Two major potential pitfalls must be avoided for QWL programs to be successfully implemented. First, both management and labor must cooperate in designing the program. Should any one side believe that the program is really just a method of gaining an advantage over the other, it is doomed to fail. Second, the plans agreed to by all concerned parties must be fully implemented. It is too easy for action plans developed in QWL groups to be forgotten amid the hectic pace of daily activities.[92] It is the responsibility of employees at all levels—from the highest-ranking manager to the lowest-level laborer—to follow through on their part of the plan.

Management by Objectives: Clarifying Organizational Goals

In Chapter 5 we detailed the positive motivational benefits of setting specific goals. As you might imagine, not only individuals, but entire organizations stand to benefit from setting specific goals. For example, an organization may strive to "raise production" and "improve the quality" of its manufactured goods. These goals, noble and well intentioned though they may be, may not be as useful to an organization as more specific ones, such as "increase production of widgets by 15 percent" or "lower the failure rate of widgets by 25 percent." After all, as the old saying goes, "It's usually easier to get somewhere if you know where you're going." Peter Drucker consulting for General Electric during the early 1950s, was well aware of this idea and is credited with promoting the benefits of specifying clear organizational goals—a technique known as **management by objectives (MBO)**.[93]

management by objectives (MBO) The technique by which managers and their subordinates work together to set and then meet organizational goals.

The MBO process, summarized in Figure 16-12, consists of three basic steps. First, goals are selected that employees will try to attain to best serve the needs of the organization. The goals should be selected by managers and their subordinates together. The goals must be set mutually rather than be imposed on subordinates by their managers. Further, these goals should be directly measurable and have some time frame attached to them. Goals that cannot be measured (e.g., "make the company better"), or that have no time limits, are useless. As part of this first step, it is crucial that managers and their subordinates work together to plan ways of attaining the goals they have selected—what is known as an *action plan*.

Once goals are set and action plans have been developed, the second step calls for *implementation*—carrying out the plan and regularly assessing its progress. Is the plan working? Are the goals being approximated? Are there any problems being encountered in attempting to meet the goals? Such questions need to be considered while implementing an action plan. If the plan is failing, a midcourse correction may be in order—changing the plan, the way it's carried out, or even the goal itself.

Finally, after monitoring progress toward the goal, the third step may be instituted: *evaluation*—assessing goal attainment. Were the organization's goals reached? If so, what new goals should be set to improve things still further?

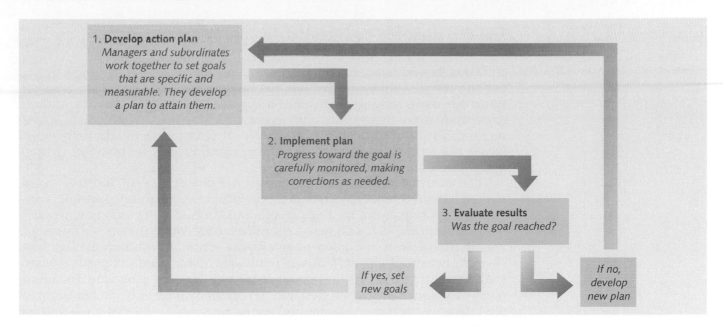

■ **Figure 16-12**
Management by Objectives: Developing Organizations through Goal Setting
The organizational development technique of management by objectives requires managers and their subordinates to work together on setting and trying to achieve important organizational goals. The basic steps of the process are outlined here.

If not, what new plans can be initiated to help meet the goals? Because the ultimate assessment of the extent to which goals are met helps determine the selection of new goals, MBO is a continuous process.

MBO represents a potentially effective source of planning and implementing strategic change for organizations. Individual efforts designed to meet organizational goals get the individual employee and the organization itself working together toward common ends. Hence, systemwide change results. Of course, for MBO to work, everyone involved has to buy into it. Because MBO programs typically require a great deal of participation by lower-level employees, top managers must be willing to accept and support the cooperation and involvement of all. Making MBO work also requires a great deal of time—anywhere from three to five years.[94] Hence, MBO may be inappropriate in organizations that do not have the time to commit to making it work.

Despite these considerations, MBO has become one of the most widely used techniques for affecting organizational change in recent years. It not only is used on an ad hoc basis by many organizations, but also constitutes an ingrained element of the organizational culture in some companies, such as Hewlett-Packard and IBM. An MBO program was used effectively by Northwest Airlines in 1989 to help improve various areas of performance in its Atlanta-based crew.[95] The program was reportedly effective in meeting these and other vital goals, thereby helping to improve Northwest's overall safety and performance record. Given the success MBO has experienced, its widespread use is not surprising.[96]

YOU BE THE CONSULTANT

You are supervising a team of ten employees who are not getting along. Their constant fighting is interfering with their job performance. They are spending so much time bickering with each other that they are not getting their work done. You decide to use organizational development techniques to address this problem.

1. What technique or techniques would you use? Why?
2. Describe the steps you would take to implement these techniques in this specific situation.
3. What problems would you expect to encounter in the process of implementing change via these OD techniques?

Critical Issues in Organizational Development

No discussion of organizational development would be complete without addressing three very important questions—Do the techniques work, what should be their main focus, and are they ethical? We will now direct our attention to these issues.

The Effectiveness of Organizational Development: Does It Really Work?

Thus far, we have described some of the major techniques used by OD practitioners to improve organizational functioning. As is probably clear, carrying out these techniques requires a considerable amount of time, money, and effort. Accordingly, it is appropriate to ask if the investment in implementing OD interventions is worth it. In other words, does OD really work? Given the growing popularity of OD in organizations, the question is more important than ever.[97]

Research has revealed that the answer is a qualified "yes." In other words, although many studies have revealed beneficial effects associated with OD programs, the findings are far from unanimous. Consider, for example, research on quality circles. Although many researchers have found that QCs help reduce organizational costs and improve employees' attitudes, other studies reported no such beneficial effects.[98] Mixed results also have been obtained in many studies assessing the effectiveness of sensitivity training programs. For example, whereas such programs often lead to temporary differences in the way people interact with others, the results tend to be short-lived on the job and are not related to permanent changes in the way people behave.[99] Thus, whereas OD may have many positive effects, not all desired outcomes may be realized.

A review by Porras and Robertson compared the results of 49 OD studies published between 1975 and 1986.[100] Among the different types of OD interventions studied were those we described: MBO, QWL, survey feedback, sensitivity groups, and team building. The investigators categorized the research with respect to whether they found the effects of the interventions to be beneficial, harmful, or nonexistent. The outcomes studied were both individual (e.g., job satisfaction) and organizational (e.g., profit, productivity) in nature. The results, summarized in Figure 16-13 reveal that a sizable percentage of the studies found effects of the various interventions beneficial. However, these beneficial results were not as impressive for individual outcomes (where the vast majority of the studies demonstrated no effects of any of the interventions) as they were for organizational outcomes (where many studies found positive effects). Clearly, the benefits of OD techniques are more firmly established with respect to improving organizational functioning than with respect to improving individuals' job attitudes.

■ **Figure 16-13**
Organizational Development: How Effective Is It?

In reviewing 49 studies using organizational development techniques, Porras and Robertson found a greater percentage reporting improvement among organizational outcomes (e.g., profit) than individual outcomes (e.g., job satisfaction).

(**Source:** Based on data reported by Porras & Robertson, 1992; see Note 67.)

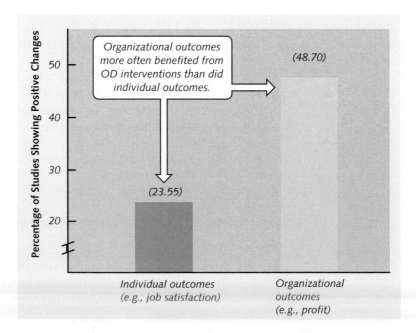

We hasten to add that any conclusions about the effectiveness of OD should be qualified in several important ways. First, research has shown that OD interventions tend to be more effective among blue-collar employees than among white-collar employees.[101] Second, it has been found that the beneficial effects of OD can be enhanced by using several techniques instead of just one. Specifically, studies in which four or more OD programs were used together yielded positive findings more frequently than those in which fewer techniques were used.[102] Thus, it appears that the effectiveness of OD efforts can be enhanced by relying not on any one single technique, but rather on a combination of several.[103] Finally, research has shown that the effectiveness of OD techniques depends on the degree of support they receive from top management: The more programs are supported from the top, the more successful they tend to be.[104]

Despite the importance of attempting to evaluate the effectiveness of OD interventions, a great many of them go unevaluated. Although there are undoubtedly many reasons for this, one key factor is the difficulty of assessing change. Because many factors can cause people to behave differently in organizations, and because such behaviors may be difficult to measure, many OD practitioners avoid the problem of measuring change altogether. In a related vein, political pressures to justify OD programs may discourage some OD professionals from honestly and accurately assessing their effectiveness. After all, in doing so, one runs the risk of scientifically demonstrating one's wasted time and money.

These temporary improvements may well be due to the Hawthorne effect described in Chapter 1.

In cases where the effects of OD have been studied, however, the research is more often than not conducted in a manner that leaves its conclusions seriously open to question.[105] In particular, it is often very difficult to isolate exactly which aspects of an organizational intervention were responsible for the changes noted. Also, because OD practices are a novelty to most employees, they may have a tendency to produce temporary improvements.[106] In other words, serious questions may be raised about the true effectiveness of organizational development efforts as revealed in existing research. (As noted in the GLOBALIZATION AND DIVERSITY section, further limitations may be identified when OD techniques are used in different nations.)

We may conclude that despite some limitations, organizational development is an approach that shows considerable promise in its ability to benefit organizations and the individuals working within them. These benefits notwithstanding, some have raised questions about the ethics of OD practice.

What Should Be the Main Focus of OD: Process or Results?

For the most part, the OD techniques we've described have focused on *how* to get things done (e.g., using certain exercises ranging from simple group discussions to elaborate treks in the wilderness) more so than exactly *what* should be accomplished. Although, some general goals are often stated, the emphasis is generally on using the techniques assuming that they will sometime yield benefits. OD *is* by definition results-oriented, and practitioners appear to have become more preoccupied by the processes themselves than by the hopes of achieving any specific results. Indeed, OD activities frequently become management fads; as one company uses a technique, others quickly jump on the bandwagon for fear of not remaining competitive. Management scholars Mitroff and Mohrman expressed this situation clearly by noting that, "U.S. business easily fell prey to every new management fad promising a painless solution, especially when it was presented in a neat, bright package. But all simple formulas are eventually bound to fail."[107]

In agreement with this pessimistic observation are management consultants Robert H. Schaffer and Harvey A. Thomson, who have countered the process orientation of OD by arguing that successful change programs should begin with results and not with an assortment of activities.[108] They call existing

Is OD Universally Effective?
Cultural Barriers to Effective OD Interventions

Warren Bennis, an expert in organizational development, recounts an incident in which a large Swiss company terminated an OD program after the company president found that it stressed egalitarian values. It seems that egalitarianism was inconsistent with a key value of the president's Swiss Army training—that authority is based on one's position in an organizational hierarchy.[109] This example raises an interesting question about the extent to which the effectiveness of OD interventions may be dependent upon the national cultures within which the organizations are located.

In analyzing this question, Jaeger relied on the four dimensions of culture identified by Hofstede (described in Chapter 2)—power distance, uncertainty avoidance, individualism-collectivism, and masculinity-femininity.[110] Overall, OD techniques may be understood as placing a low value on power distance (i.e., unequal power is not favored), a low value on uncertainty avoidance (i.e., ambiguous situations are nonthreatening), a high value on femininity (i.e., willingness to show sensitivity and concern for others' welfare), and a moderate value on individualism (i.e., interest in balancing concern for oneself with concern for one's group). Jaeger reasoned that countries whose national values come closest to this pattern (e.g., Scandinavian nations) may be the most successful in using OD techniques, whereas those that are highly different (e.g., most Latin American nations) may be most unsuccessful. The United States would fit between these two extremes.

Because not all OD techniques are alike, Jaeger analyzed specific intervention techniques with respect to their underlying cultural values. For example, MBO, a very popular OD technique in the United States may have caught on because it promotes the American values of willingness to take risks and to work aggressively at attaining high performance. However, because MBO also encourages superiors and subordinates to negotiate freely with each other, the technique has been generally unsuccessful in France, where high power distance between superiors and subordinates is culturally accepted.[111] Following similar reasoning, one may expect the OD techniques of survey feedback to be successful in the Southeast Asian nation of Brunei, where the prevailing cultural value is such that problems are unlikely to be confronted openly.[112] These examples illustrate an important point: The effectiveness of OD techniques depend, in part, on the extent to which the values of the technique match the underlying values of the national culture in which it is employed.

Given this, we may conclude that OD practitioners must fully appreciate the cultural norms of the nations where they are operating. Failure to do so not only may make OD interventions unsuccessful, but may even have negative consequences. Therefore, as part of planning an OD intervention, OD practitioners are strongly advised to match carefully the techniques they use to the values of the host culture. The most rigidly held values of a culture should never be challenged by the OD techniques. Remember, those techniques are designed to improve the functioning of the organization *within its culture*. Any techniques that clash with prevailing cultural norms should be avoided.

OD programs "corporate rain dances" in that they *may* yield positive results, although not necessarily as a result of the programs themselves. Schaffer and Thomson's prescription calls for using results-driven programs—those that lead to specific, measurable improvements in a short period of time. (If this idea sounds familiar it's probably because it follows from the basic tenet of goal setting described in Chapter 5—namely, to set *specific* goals. Unfortunately, when applied to MBO programs, sometimes the goals set are far too general to be useful.) A problem noted about OD techniques is that they too often define effort in a general, long-term fashion (e.g., "we're going to be considered to have the best quality production in the industry") as opposed to measurable, short-term goals for improvement (e.g., "by two months from today, we will settle 95 percent of all claims within one week").

As an example of their approach in action, Schaffer and Thomson describe an automotive parts plant plagued by problems of poor quality. The plant superintendent asked the manager on one assembly line to work with the employees and the plant engineers to reduce their most prevalent defect by 30 percent within two months. This goal was met on time, and the effort soon was extended to other assembly lines, where the effects were equally positive. In essence, "The results-driven path strikes out specific targets and matches resources, tools, and action plans to the requirements of reaching those targets. As a consequence, managers know what they are trying to achieve and when it should be done, and how it can be evaluated."[113]

Clearly, Schaffer and Thomson's approach makes good sense. (Indeed, it is founded on one of the best established principles of OB described in this text.) Their approach, however, does not necessarily make OD techniques obsolete, because these tools are not necessarily designed to have an immediate impact on organizational functioning. In fact, by definition, a *development* tool is meant to have the long-term benefit of developing managerial talent for the long run (as opposed to *training* people to solve immediate problems). If you think of OD as a long-term investment in improving the insight and managerial skills of supervisory personnel, it's difficult to accept Schaffer and Thomson's approach as a substitute for OD. Instead, it appears that *both* long-term (process-oriented) and more immediate (results-oriented) techniques may have their place in the toolbox of today's organizational practitioner. Just as a physician may encourage patients to lead a healthy lifestyle marked by good nutrition and exercise, it would be misleading to condemn this advice simply because it does not also provide relief from an immediate ailment. Here, too, both long-term, healthy development is important as well as seeking solutions to immediate problems that present themselves.

Is Organizational Development Inherently Unethical? A Debate

By its very nature, OD applies powerful social science techniques in an attempt to change attitudes and behavior. From the perspective of a manager attempting to accomplish various goals, such tools may be very useful. However, if you think about it from the perspective of the individual being affected, several ethical issues arise.

For example, it has been argued that OD techniques impose the values of the organization on the individual without taking the individual's own attitudes into account.[114] OD is a very one-sided approach, reflecting the imposition of the more powerful organization on the less powerful individual. A related issue is that the OD process does not provide any free choice on the part of the employees.[115] As a result, it may be seen as *coercive* and *manipulative*. When faced with a "do it, or else" situation, employees tend to have little free choice and are forced to allow themselves to be manipulated, a potentially degrading prospect.

Another issue is that the unequal power relationship between the organization and its employees makes it possible for the true intent of OD techniques to be misrepresented. As an example, imagine that an MBO technique is presented to employees as a means of allowing greater organizational participation, whereas in reality it is used as a means for holding individuals responsible for their poor performance and punishing them as a result. Although such an event might not happen, the potential for abuse of this type does exist, and the potential to misuse the technique—even if not originally intended—might later prove to be too great a temptation.

Despite these considerations, many professionals do not agree that OD is inherently unethical. Such a claim, it has been countered, is to say that the practice of management is itself unethical. After all, the very act of going to work for an organization requires one to submit to the organization's values and the overall values of society at large.[116] One cannot help but face life situations in which others' values are imposed. This is not to say that organizations have the right to impose patently unethical values on people for the purpose of making a profit (e.g., stealing from customers). Indeed, because they have the potential to abuse their power (such as in the MBO example above), organizations have a special obligation to refrain from doing so.

Although abuses of organizational power are all too common, OD itself is not necessarily the culprit. Indeed, like any other tool, OD is not inherently good or evil. Instead, *whether the tool is used for good or evil will depend on the individual using it*. With this in mind, the ethical use of OD interventions will require that they be supervised by professionals in an organization that places a high value on ethics. To the extent that top management officials embrace ethical values and behave ethically themselves, norms for behaving ethically are likely to develop in organizations. When an organization has a strong ethical culture, it is unlikely that OD practitioners would even think of misusing their power to harm individuals. The need to develop such a culture has been recognized as a way for organizations to take not only moral leadership in their communities, but financial leadership as well. (For a summary of this debate, see Figure 16-14.)

After considering both sides of this issue, you will probably wish to draw your own conclusions about this matter. The only thing we can be sure about here is that the debate is not settled, and it is likely to remain a key question for years to come. One reason the issue might not be put to rest anytime soon is that executives are becoming increasingly concerned about the importance of ethics in their organizations. Given corporations' ongoing concerns about being competitive, it is also likely that OD interventions will remain popular in the years to come.

■ **Figure 16-14**
The Ethics of OD: Summary of the Debate
Some have claimed that OD is an inherently unethical practice while others have countered that it is not. The arguments for each side are summarized here.

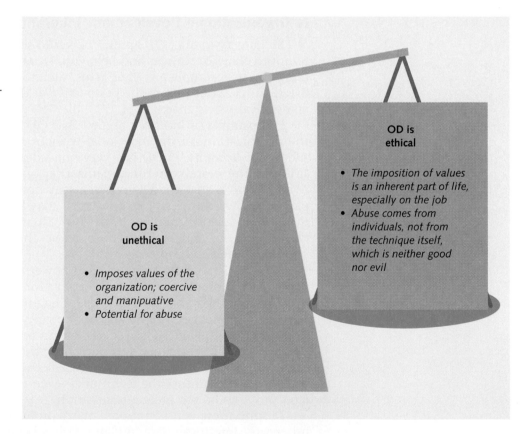

OD is
ethical

- *The imposition of values is an inherent part of life, especially on the job*
- *Abuse comes from individuals, not from the technique itself, which is neither good nor evil*

OD is
unethical

- *Imposes values of the organization; coercive and manipuative*
- *Potential for abuse*

Organizational Change: An Ongoing Process

Organizational change refers to planned or unplanned transformations in an organization's structure, technology, and/or people. It occurs in organizations throughout the world and is required for their long-term survival. The **learning organization** is one that is successful at acquiring, cultivating, and applying knowledge that can be used to help it adapt to change. Organizations learn by acquiring knowledge, distributing information, interpreting information, and taking steps to ensure that this informaton is "memorized" by the organization.

Forces behind Organizatonal Change

Changes in organizations may be either planned or unplanned. Planned changes may include changes in products or services, changes in organizational size and structure, changes in administrative systems, and the introduction of new technologies. Unplanned changes include governmental regulation, economic competition, and performance gaps.

The Process of Organizational Change and Resistance to Change

Organizations may change with respect to their organizational structure (responsibilities and procedures used), the technology used on the job and the people who perform the work. Change is likely to occur whenever the benefits associated with making a change (i.e., dissatisfaction with current conditions, the availability of desirable alternatives, and the existence of a plan for achieving that alternative) outweigh the costs involved.

In general, people are resistant to change because of individual factors (e.g., economic insecurity, fear of the unknown) and organizational factors (e.g., the stability of work groups, threats to the existing balance of power). However, resistance to change can be overcome in several ways, including educating the workforce about the effects of the changes and involving employees in the change process.

Techniques of Organizational Development

Techniques for planning organizational change in order to enhance personal and organizational outcomes are collectively known as **organizational development** prac-

tices. For example, **survey feedback** uses questionnaires and/or interviews as the basis for identifying organizational problems, which are then addressed in planning sessions. **Sensitivity training** is a technique in which group discussions are used to enhance interpersonal awareness and reduce interpersonal friction. **Team building** involves using work groups to diagnose and develop specific plans for solving problems with respect to their functioning as a work unit. **Quality of work life** programs attempt to humanize the workplace by involving employees in the decisions affecting them (e.g., through quality circle meetings) and by restructuring the jobs themselves. Finally, **management by objectives** focuses on attempts by managers and their subordinates to work together at setting important organizational goals and developing a plan to help meet them. The rationale underlying all five of these techniques is that they may enhance organizational functioning by involving employees in identifying and solving organizational problems.

Critical Issues in Organizational Development

The effectiveness of most organizational development programs is not systematically assessed in practice, and the few studies that do attempt to measure the success of such programs are not carefully conducted. However, those studies that have systematically evaluated organizational development programs generally find them to be successful in improving organizational functioning and, to a lesser degree, individual satisfaction.

OD, as a whole, has been criticized on the grounds that it focuses too much on processes and not enough on outcomes. However, experts have argued that both orientations are necessary.

Some have argued that OD is unethical for several reasons, most notably because it has the potential to be used for illegitimate purposes. However, others counter that OD is just a tool and that it is people who are at fault for using it inappropriately.

1. Some changes in organizations are unplanned, whereas others are the result of deliberate, planned actions. Give examples of each of these varieties of change and explain their implications for organizational functioning.
2. Suppose you are having difficulty managing a small group of subordinates who work in an office 1,000 miles away from your home base. What kinds of changes in structure, technology, and people can be implemented to supervise these distant employees more closely?
3. Under what conditions will people be most willing to make changes in organizations? Explain your answer and give an example.

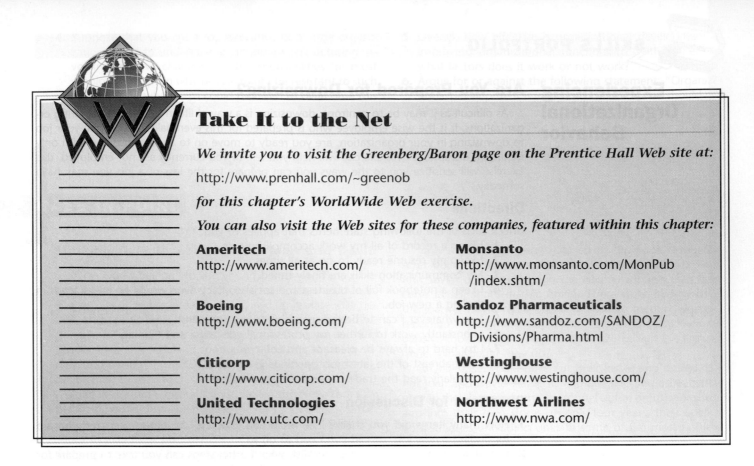

Take It to the Net

We invite you to visit the Greenberg/Baron page on the Prentice Hall Web site at:

http://www.prenhall.com/~greenob

for this chapter's WorldWide Web exercise.

You can also visit the Web sites for these companies, featured within this chapter:

Ameritech
http://www.ameritech.com/

Boeing
http://www.boeing.com/

Citicorp
http://www.citicorp.com/

United Technologies
http://www.utc.com/

Monsanto
http://www.monsanto.com/MonPub
/index.shtm/

Sandoz Pharmaceuticals
http://www.sandoz.com/SANDOZ/
Divisions/Pharma.html

Westinghouse
http://www.westinghouse.com/

Northwest Airlines
http://www.nwa.com/

When the "Blizzard of 1996" blanketed the east coast of the US with more than two feet of snow, many employees put in full days worth of work without ever leaving their homes. Armed with personal computers, modems, and fax machines, employees logged onto the Internet, swapped e-mail messages and took conference calls. Some observers expect that *telecommuting*—working from home or from satellite office centers—will gain momentum as a result of the storm. Noted Eric Goldman of Telecommute America, "When the top brass of *Fortune* 500 companies can't get out of their own driveways, they'll look more seriously at the issue."

Tom Miller, a market researcher with Find/SVP, estimates that 8.1 million people telecommute at least one day per month. The number of telecommuters has doubled since 1990, and experts predict that by the year 2000, 25 million American workers will telecommute each year. Organizations benefit from better employee productivity, improved customer satisfaction, and quicker market responses. For employees, benefits include lowered stress resulting from a less hectic pace. Telecommuters also report increased job satisfaction because they are better able to manage their work and personal lives. Satellite office centers enable employees to work in outlying suburban communities instead of fighting rush-hour traffic to and from crowded downtown offices.

Pacific Bell began its telecommuting program in 1984; since that time, employees have consistently reported 100 percent increases in productivity. In 1994, 1,300 of Pacific Bell's 57,000 employees telecommuted. Says human resources manager Gary Fraundorfer: "They tell us that this fits into family and flexibility issues and that they enjoy working for the company more than ever before." Telecommuting has allowed IBM's Midwest division to reduce required real estate by 55 percent. IBM has equipped employees with ThinkPad computers, fax and e-mail modems, and cellular phones. An IBM survey showed that 83 percent of those who had tried telecommuting did not want to go back to a traditional office environment.

Despite its popularity, there are problems associated with telecommuting. In Washington state, for example, where 25 employers participated in a telecommuting project, telecommuters' most often-voiced concern was lost visibility and career momentum. In other words, even though telecommuters may be producing results, those with strong advancement ambitions may not tolerate the inability to network and rub elbows with upper management on a day-to-day basis. Another obstacle to telecommuting is convincing management that it can be beneficial for all involved. Telecommuters may have to fight the perception—from both bosses and co-workers—that if they aren't being supervised, they aren't working. As founder of the Telecommuting Research Institute and author of *The Telecommuting Handbook*, Jack Nilles has worked in the field for 20 years. Managers, he admits, "usually have to be dragged kicking and screaming into this. They always ask, 'How can I tell if someone is working when I can't see them?' That's based on the erroneous assumption that if you *can* see them they *are* working."

Judy Rapp-Guadagnoli, telecommuting program manager for the city and county of Denver, sums it up: "In the next 10 years, the way people do their work is going to change radically. Offices are decentralizing, and more and more workers are going to be at home or in satellite offices, not at company headquarters. Telecommuting is a bulldozer—and it's coming through."

Video source: Telecommuting. (1991, February). *Business World*. *Additional sources*: Maney, K. (1996, January 9). Many, snowed in, plugged in: Telecommuters bypass the blizzard of '96. *USA Today*, p. 1A; Dumas, L. S. (1994, July). Home work: The telecommuting option. *Working Mother*, pp. 22, 24, 26; Greengard, S. (1994, September). Making the virtual office a reality. *Personnel Journal*, pp. 66–79; Sharpe, P. 1994, February). Workforce revolution. *Self*, pp. 82, 84, 86; Shellenbarger, S. (1994, December 14). Some thrive, but many wilt working at home. *The Wall Street Journal*, pp. B1, B10.

360° feedback The practice of collecting performance feedback from multiple sources at a variety of organizational levels (p. 95).

abilities Mental and physical capacities to perform various tasks (p. 127).

achievement motivation The strength of an individual's desire to excel—to succeed at difficult tasks and to do them better than other persons (p. 123).

additive tasks Types of group tasks in which the individual efforts of several people are added together to form the group's product (p. 266).

adhocracy A highly informal, organic organization in which specialists work in teams, coordinating with each other on various projects (e.g., many software development companies) (p. 527).

administrative model A model of decision making that recognizes the bounded rationality that limits the making of optimally rational-economic decisions (p. 341).

affective commitment The strength of a person's desire to work for an organization because he or she agrees with it and wants to do so (p. 191).

affiliation motivation The strength of an individual's desire to have close, friendly relations with others (p. 124).

arbitration A form of third-party intervention in disputes in which the intervening person has the power to determine the terms of an agreement (p. 389).

assistive technology Devices and other solutions that help individuals with physical or mental problems perform the various actions needed to do their jobs (p. 491).

attitudes Stable clusters of feelings, beliefs, and behavioral intentions toward specific objects, people, or institutions (p. 178).

attribution approach (to leadership) The approach to leadership that focuses on leaders' attributions of followers' performance—that is, their perceptions of its underlying causes (p. 443).

attribution The process through which individuals attempt to determine the causes of others' behavior (p. 73).

autocratic (leadership style) A style of leadership in which the leader makes all decisions unilaterally (p. 437).

automation The process of using machines to perform tasks that might otherwise be done by people (p. 488).

availability heuristic The tendency for people to base their judgments on information that is readily available to them although it may be potentially inaccurate, thereby adversely affecting decision quality (p. 311).

awareness-based diversity training A type of diversity management program designed to make people more aware of diversity issues in the workplace and to get them to recognize the underlying assumptions they make about people (p. 202).

baby boom generation The large group of people born in the United States in the years following World War II (p. 48).

bargaining (or negotiation) A process in which two or more parties in a dispute exchange offers, counteroffers, and concessions in an effort to attain a mutually acceptable agreement (p. 386).

behavioral sciences Fields such as psychology and sociology that seek knowledge of human behavior and society through the use of the scientific method (p. 3).

benchmarking The process of seeking to improve quality by comparing one's own products or services with the best products or services of others (p. 58).

"big five" dimensions of personality Five basic dimensions of personality that are assumed to underlie many specific traits (p. 111).

boundaryless organization An organization in which chains of command are eliminated, spans of control are unlimited, and rigid departments give way to empowered teams (p. 517).

bounded discretion Limitations imposed on decisions due to moral and ethical constraints (p. 348).

bounded rationality The major assumption of the administrative model—that organizational, social, and human limitations lead to the making of *satisficing* rather than optimal decisions (p. 341).

brainstorming A technique designed to foster group productivity by encouraging interacting group members to express their ideas in a noncritical fashion (p. 353).

bureaucracy An organizational design developed by Max Weber that attempts to make organizations operate efficiently by having a clear hierarchy of authority in which people are required to perform well-defined jobs (p. 15).

burnout A syndrome resulting from prolonged exposure to stress, consisting of physical, emotional, and mental exhaustion plus feelings of a lack of personal accomplishment (p. 236).

cafeteria-style benefit plans Incentive systems in which employees have an opportunity to select the fringe benefits they want from a menu of available alternatives (p. 161).

career The evolving sequence of a person's work experience over time (p. 219).

case method A qualitative research method in which a particular organization is studied in detail, usually in the hopes of being able to learn about organizational functioning in general (p. 28).

centralization The degree to which information must flow through a specific central member of a communication network (p. 305).

centralized networks Communication networks that have central members through which all information must pass to reach other members (e.g., the Y, the wheel, and the chain) (p. 305).

charisma An attitude of enthusiasm and optimism that is contagious; an aura of leadership (p. 409).

charismatic leaders Leaders who exert especially powerful effects on followers by virtue of the attributions followers make about them. Such individuals have high amounts of self-confidence, present a clearly articulated vision, behave in extraordinary ways, are recognized as change agents, and are sensitive to the environmental constraints they face (p. 444).

child-care facilities Sites at or near company locations where parents can leave their children while they are working (p. 50).

classical organizational theory An early approach to the study of management that focused on the most efficient way of structuring organizations (p. 14).

classical organizational theory Approaches assuming that there is a single best way to design organizations (p. 521).

codes of ethics Documents describing what an organization stands for and the general rules of conduct expected of employees (e.g., to avoid conflicts of interest, to be honest, etc.) (p. 64).

coercive power The individual power base derived from the capacity to administer punishment to others (p. 407).

cohesiveness The strength of group members' desires to remain part of their groups (p. 259).

collectivism According to Hofstede, a characteristic of a culture that orients people toward the good of the group (p. 43).

communication The process by which a person, group, organization (the sender) transmits some type of information (the message) to another person, group, or organization (the receiver) (p. 273).

communication networks Pre-established patterns dictating who may communicate with whom (see *centralized networks* and *decentralized networks*) (p. 304).

competition A process in which individuals or groups seek to attain desired goals at the expense of others seeking the same goals (p. 374).

competitive intelligence (CI) The process of gathering information about one's competitors that can be used as the basis for planning organizational change (p. 554).

competitors Individuals who are primarily concerned with exceeding the outcomes of others (p. 377).

compressed workweeks Scheduling workweeks such that people are permitted to work fewer, but longer days (e.g., four ten-hour days), instead of five days of eight hours each (p. 49).

computerized performance monitoring (CPM) The practice of using computers to collect, store, analyze, and report information about the work people are doing (p. 493).

computerized performance monitoring The process of using computers to monitor job performance (p. 262).

confirmation candidate A decision alternative considered only for purposes of convincing oneself of the wisdom of selecting the *implicit favorite* (p. 346).

conflict A process that begins when individuals or groups perceive that others have taken or will soon take actions incompatible with their own major interests (p. 380).

conglomerate A form of organizational diversification in which an organization (usually a very large, multinational one) adds an entirely unrelated business or product to its organizational design (p. 529).

consideration Actions by a leader that demonstrate concern with the welfare of subordinates and establish positive relations with them. Leaders who focus primarily on this task are often described as demonstrating a person-oriented style (p. 439).

consortium A confederation in which organizations maintain their formal independence but agree to coordinate their activities through a central management (p. 379).

contingencies of reinforcement The various relationships between one's behavior and the consequences of that behavior—positive reinforcement, negative reinforcement, punishment, and extinction (p. 89).

contingency approach The approach that recognizes that the best organizational design is the one that best fits with the existing environmental conditions (p. 522).

contingency approach A perspective suggesting that organizational behavior is affected by a large number of interacting factors. How someone will behave is said to be contingent upon many different variables at once (p. 9).

contingency theories (of leadership) Any of several theories which recognize that certain styles of leadership are more effective in some situations than others (p. 450).

contingent workforce People hired by or-

ganizations temporarily to work as needed for finite periods of time (p. 53).

continuance commitment The strength of a person's desire to continue working for an organization because he or she needs to do so and cannot afford to do otherwise (see *side-bets orientation*) (p. 191).

continuous reinforcement A schedule of reinforcement in which all desired behaviors are reinforced (p. 89).

continuous-process production A highly automated form of production that is continuous in nature and highly integrated in terms of component steps and processes (p. 533).

convergence hypothesis The biased assumption that principles of good management are universal and that the best management practices are ones that work well in the United States (p. 42).

cooperation A process in which individuals or groups work together to attain shared goals (p. 368).

cooperators Individuals who are primarily concerned with maximizing joint outcomes (p. 377).

core competency The main things that an organization does best; those activities most central to its mission (p. 52).

corporate image The impressions that people have of an organization (p. 85).

correlation coefficient A statistical index indicating the degree to which two or more variables are related (p. 22).

correlational research An empirical research technique in which variables of interest are identified and carefully measured. These measures are then analyzed statistically to determine the extent to which they are related to one another (p. 21).

correspondent inferences Judgments made about what someone is like based on observations of his or her behavior (p. 73).

craft technology Technology involving highly standardized inputs and outputs, and problems that are difficult to analyze (e.g., cabinet makers and public schools) (see *matrix of technologies*) (p. 486).

critical incidents technique A procedure for measuring job satisfaction in which employees describe incidents relating to their work that they have found especially satisfying or dissatisfying (p. 181).

cross-functional teams Teams represented by people from different specialty areas within organizations.

cultural homogenization The tendency for people throughout the world to become culturally similar (p. 39).

cultural pluralism The idea that people's separate cultural identities should be maintained and accepted by others as they work alongside each other (p. 45).

culture shock The tendency for people to become confused and disoriented as they find it difficult to become adjusted to a new culture (p. 41).

culture The set of values, customs, and beliefs that people have in common with other members of a social unit (e.g., a nation) (p. 40).

daily hassles Problems of everyday life that

serve as important causes of stress (p. 234).

decentralization The extent to which authority and decision making are spread throughout all levels of an organization rather than being reserved for top management (centralization) (p. 511).

decentralized networks Communication networks in which all members play an equal role in the transmittal of information (e.g., *the circle and the comcon*) (p. 305).

decision style model The conceptualization according to which people use one of four predominant decision styles: *directive, analytical, conceptual, and behavioral* (p. 334).

decision making The process of making choices from among several alternatives (p. 331).

decision style Differences between people with respect to their orientations toward decisions (p. 334).

decision support systems (DSS) Computer programs in which information about organizational behavior is presented to decision makers in a manner that helps them structure their responses to decisions (p. 333).

decoding The process by which a receiver of messages transforms them back into the sender's ideas (p. 291).

Delphi technique A method of improving group decisions using the opinions of experts, which are solicited by mail and then compiled. The expert consensus of opinions is used to make a decision (p. 358).

departmentalization The process of breaking up organizations into coherent units (p. 512).

dependent variable The variable in an experiment that is measured, affected by the impact of the independent variable (p. 25).

design for disassembly (DFD) The process of designing and building products so that their parts can be reused several times and then safely disposed of at the end of the product's life (p. 497).

developmental opportunities Jobs or assignments that can contribute to employees' competence and skills (p. 223).

discipline The process of systematically administering punishments (p. 98).

discrimination The behavior consistent with a prejudicial attitude; the act of treating someone negatively because of his or her membership in a specific group (p. 196).

distraction-conflict model A conceptualization explaining social facilitation in terms of the tendency for others' presence to cause a conflict between directing attention to others versus the task at hand (p. 262).

distribution A basic dimension of conflict situations, referring to the extent to which individuals show concern for their own outcomes (p. 381).

divergence hypothesis The assumption that there may be many possible ways to manage effectively and that these will depend greatly on the individual culture in which people live (p. 42).

diversity management programs Programs in which employees are taught to celebrate the differences between people and in which organizations create supportive work environments for women and minorities (p. 202).

diversity training The process of training employees not only to recognize and accept others who are different from themselves, but also to value these differences (p. 48).

division of labor The process of dividing the many tasks performed within an organization into specialized jobs (p. 507).

divisional structure The form used by many large organizations, in which separate autonomous units are created to deal with entire product lines, freeing top management to focus on larger-scale, strategic decisions (p. 527).

dominant culture The overall culture of an organization, reflected by core values that are shared throughout the organization (p. 473).

doomsday management The practice of introducing change by suggesting that an impending crisis is likely (p. 558).

downsizing The process of adjusting downward the number of employees required to perform jobs in newly designed organizations (p. 52).

drive theory of social facilitation The theory according to which the presence of others increases arousal, which increases people's tendencies to perform the dominant response. If that response is well learned, performance will improve. But, if it is novel, performance will be impaired (p. 261).

dual-core model The theory recognizing that changes in the administration of organizations come from upper management (i.e., from the top down), whereas changes in the work performed come from the technical specialists within organizations (i.e., from the bottom up) (p. 552).

elder-care facilities Sites at or near company locations where, while working, employees can leave their elderly relatives (e.g. parents and grandparents) for whom they may serve as caretakers (p. 50).

electronic mail (e-mail) A system whereby people use personal computer terminals to send and receive messages between each other (p. 296).

electronic meeting systems The practice of bringing individuals from different locations together for a meeting via telephone or satellite transmissions, either on television monitors or via shared space on a computer screen (p. 360).

emotional intelligence The ability to perceive and control emotions (p. 129).

employee assistance programs (EAPs) Plans that provide employees with assistance in meeting various problems (e.g., substance abuse, career planning, financial and legal problems) (p. 241).

employee handbook A document describing to employees basic information about a company; a general reference regarding a company's background, the nature of its business, and its rules (p. 293).

employee withdrawal Actions, such as chronic absenteeism and voluntary turnover (i.e., quitting one's job), that enable employees to escape from adverse organizational situations (p. 186).

empowered decision The practice of vesting power for making decisions in the hands of employees themselves (p. 339).

empowerment The passing of responsibility and authority from managers to employees (p. 411).

encoding The process by which an idea is transformed so that it can be transmitted to, and recognized by, a receiver (e.g., a written or spoken message) (p. 290).

engineering technology Technology involving many exceptions in inputs or outputs and problems which are easy to analyze (e.g., heavy machinery construction and health and fitness clubs) (p. 487).

entry shock The confusion and disorientation experienced by many newcomers to an organization (p. 215).

equalizers Individuals primarily concerned with assuring equality of outcomes among all people who work together on joint projects (p. 377).

equitable payment The state in which one person's outcome/input ratio is equivalent to that of another person with whom this individual compares himself or herself (p. 155).

equity theory The theory stating that people strive to maintain ratios of their own outcomes (rewards) to their own inputs (contributions) that are equal to the outcome/input ratios of others with whom they compare themselves (p. 154).

ERG theory An alternative to Maslow's need hierarchy theory proposed by Alderfer, which asserts that there are three basic human needs: existence, relatedness, and growth (p. 147).

escalation of commitment phenomenon The tendency for individuals to continue to support previously unsuccessful courses of action (p. 346).

ethics audit The practice of regularly assessing the morality of a company's employees' behavior so as to identify incidents of dubious ethical value (p. 64).

evaluation apprehension The fear of being evaluated or judged by another person (p. 262).

evening persons Individuals who feel most energetic and alert late in the day (p. 127).

expatriates People who are citizens of one country but who are living in another country (p. 38).

expectancy theory The theory that asserts that motivation is based on people's beliefs about the probability that effort will lead to performance (expectancy), multiplied by the probability that performance will lead to reward (instrumentality), multiplied by the perceived value of the reward (valence) (p. 159).

expectancy The belief that one's efforts will positively influence one's performance (p. 159).

experimental method An empirical research method in which one or more variables are systematically varied (the independent variables) to determine if such changes have any impact on the behavior of interest (the dependent variables) (p. 23).

expert power The individual power base derived from an individual's recognized superior skills and abilities in a certain area (p. 408).

exploitative mentality The view that encourages "using" people in a way that promotes stereotypes and undermines empathy and compassion (p. 63).

extinction The process through which responses that are no longer reinforced tend to gradually diminish in strength (p. 88).

false-consensus effect The general tendency for people to believe that certain actions are more common than they really are (p. 406).

family-supportive policies Policies adopted by an organization that help reduce the conflict between family and work obligations (p. 240).

feedback Knowledge about the impact of messages on receivers (p. 291).

feedback Knowledge of the results of one's behavior (p. 94).

feminine culture According to Hofstede, the cultural orientation in which people emphasize concern for others and the relationships among people (p. 44).

first-impression error The tendency to base our judgments of others on our earlier impressions of them (p. 78).

first-order change Change that is continuous in nature and involves no major shifts in the way an organization operates (p. 547).

fixed interval schedules Schedules of reinforcement in which a fixed period of time must elapse between the administration of reinforcements (p. 89).

fixed ratio schedules Schedules of reinforcement in which a fixed number of responses must occur between the administration of reinforcements (p. 90).

fixed-sum error The perception on the part of bargainers that the other party places the same importance or priority as they do on each issue (p. 387).

flexplace policies Policies that allow employees to spend part of their regular working hours performing their jobs while at home (see telecommuting) (p. 50).

flextime programs Policies that give employees some discretion over when they can arrive and leave work, thereby making it easier to adapt their work schedules to the demands of their personal lives (p. 49).

formal groups Groups that are created by the organization, intentionally designed to direct its members toward some organizational goal (p. 251).

framing In the context of bargaining, refers to the cognitive set or focus adopted by bargainers (p. 386).

framing The presentation of a problem to an individual, either in negative terms (leading to risk-seeking) or positive terms (leading to risk-aversion) (p. 343).

functional organization The type of departmentalization based on the activities or functions performed (e.g., sales, finance) (p. 512).

fundamental attribution error The tendency to attribute others' actions to internal causes (e.g., their traits) while largely ignoring external factors that also may have influenced their behavior (p. 77).

glass ceiling A barrier preventing females from reaching top positions in many organizations (p. 227).

globalization The process of interconnecting the world's people with respect to the cultural, economic, political, technological, and environmental aspects of their lives (p. 37).

goal commitment The degree to which people accept and strive to attain goals (p. 151).

goal setting The process of determining specific levels of performance for workers to attain (p. 150).

goal-congruence orientation An approach to organizational commitment according to which the degree of agreement between an individual's personal goals and those of the organization is a determinant of organizational commitment (p. 191).

grapevine An organization's informal channels of communication, based mainly on friendship or acquaintance (p. 308).

great person theory The view that leaders possess special traits that set them apart from others and that these traits are responsible for their assuming positions of power and authority (p. 435).

grid training A technique designed to strengthen leaders' concerns for people and their concerns for production (p. 440).

group A collection of two or more interacting individuals who maintain stable patterns of relationships, share common goals, and perceive themselves as being a group (p. 249).

group dynamics The social science field focusing on the nature of groups—the factors governing their formation and development, the elements of their structure, and their interrelationships with individuals, other groups, and organizations (p. 249).

group structure The pattern of interrelationships between the individuals constituting a group; the guidelines of group behavior that make group functioning orderly and predictable (p. 254).

groupthink The tendency for members of highly cohesive groups to conform to group pressures regarding a certain decision so strongly that they fail to think critically, rejecting the potentially correcting influences of outsiders (p. 353).

halo effect The tendency for our overall impressions of others to affect objective evaluations of their specific traits; perceiving high correlations between characteristics that may be unrelated (p. 77).

heuristics Simple decision rules (rules of thumb) used to make quick decisions about complex problems (see *availability heuristic* and *representativeness heuristic*) (p. 344).

hierarchy of authority A configuration of the reporting relationships within organizations; that is, who reports to whom (p. 506).

high technology The kind of technology that is electronic in nature, usually relying on the use of microprocessor chips (p. 487).

high-performance teams Teams whose members are deeply committed to one another's personal growth and success (p. 272).

human relations movement A perspective on organizational behavior that recognizes the importance of social processes in work settings (p. 12).

HURIER model The conceptualization that describes effective listening as made up of the following six components: *hearing, understanding, remembering, interpreting, evaluating,* and *responding* (p. 318).

hypothesis An unverified prediction concerning the relationships between variables. These propositions may be derived from previous research, existing theory, or informal observation (p. 21).

image theory A theory of decision making that recognizes that decisions are made in an automatic, intuitive fashion. According to the theory, people will adopt a course of action that best fits their individual principles, current goals, and plans for the future (p. 342).

implicit favorite One's preferred decision alternative, selected even before all options have been considered (p. 346).

impression management Efforts by individuals to improve how they appear to others (p. 83).

incompatibility error The perception on the part of bargainers that their own interests and that of the other side are completely incompatible (p. 387).

independent variable The factor in an experiment that is systematically varied by the experimenter to determine its impact on behavior (the dependent variable) (p. 25).

individualism-collectivism A dimension of cultures relating to the extent to which individuals in these cultures attach primary importance to their own interests or to those of groups to which they belong (p. 377).

individualism According to Hofstede, a characteristic of culture in which people emphasize taking care of themselves and members of their immediate families (p. 43).

individualists People primarily concerned with maximizing their own outcomes (p. 377).

informal groups Groups that develop naturally among people, without any direction from the organization within which they operate (p. 251).

informate The process by which workers manipulate products by "inserting data" between themselves and those objects instead of doing so physically (p. 52).

information power The extent to which one has access to information that makes him or her especially influential (p. 407).

initiating structure Activities by a leader designed to enhance productivity or task performance. Leaders who focus primarily on these goals are described as demonstrating a task-oriented style (p. 438).

inputs People's contributions to their jobs, such as their experience, qualifications, or the amount of time worked (p. 154).

instrumentality An individual's beliefs regarding the likelihood of being rewarded in accord with his or her own level of performance (p. 159).

integration A basic dimension of conflict situations, referring to the extent to which individuals show concern for others' outcomes (p. 381).

interactionist perspective The view that behavior is a result of a complex interplay between personality and situational factors (p. 110).

interdependence The extent to which the units or departments within an organization depend on each other to accomplish tasks (p. 537).

internal market system An organizational design in which rigid hierarchies are eliminated, and individual organizational units are allowed to compete as separate, profitable independent businesses (p. 528).

interorganizational coordination Instances or situations in which independent organizations choose to coordinate their actions or efforts to attain mutual gains (p. 379).

jargon The specialized language used by a particular group (e.g., people within a profession) (p. 317).

Job Descriptive Index (JDI) A rating scale for assessing job satisfaction. Individuals respond to this questionnaire by indicating whether or not various adjectives describe aspects of their work (p. 181).

job characteristics model An approach to job enrichment which specifies that five core job dimensions (skill variety, task identity, task significance, autonomy, and job feedback) produce critical psychological states that lead to beneficial outcomes for individuals (e.g., high job satisfaction) and the organization (e.g., reduced turnover) (p. 166).

job design An approach to motivation suggesting that jobs can be created so as to enhance people's interest in doing them (see *job enlargement, job enrichment* and the *job characteristics model*) (p. 163).

job enlargement The practice of expanding the content of a job to include more variety and a greater number of tasks at the same level (p. 163).

job enrichment The practice of giving employees a high degree of control over their work, from planning and organization, through implementing the jobs and evaluating the results (p. 164).

job rotation Lateral transfers of employees between jobs in an organization (p. 224).

job satisfaction People's cognitive, affective, and evaluative reactions toward their jobs (p. 178).

job sharing A form of regular part-time work in which pairs of employees assume the duties of a single job, splitting its responsibilities, salary, and benefits in proportion to the time worked (p. 50).

joint ventures Strategic alliances in which several companies work together to fulfill opportunities that require the capabilities of one another (p. 530).

K.I.S.S. principle A basic principle of communication advising that messages should be as short and simple as possible (an abbreviation for keep it short and simple) (p. 317).

Kelley's theory of causal attribution The approach suggesting that people will believe others' actions to be caused by internal or external factors based on three types of information: consensus, consistency, and distinctiveness (p. 75).

knowledge workers Professional people, such as scientists and engineers, whose technical skills can contribute to the explosion in high-tech fields (p. 55).

large-batch (mass) production Technology based on long production runs of standardized parts or products (p. 533).

Law of Effect The tendency for behaviors leading to desirable consequences to be strengthened and those leading to undesirable consequences to be weakened (p. 87).

leader match The practice of matching leaders (based on their LPC scores) to the groups whose situations best match those in which they are expected to be most effective (according to LPC contingency theory) (p. 453).

leader-member exchange (LMX) model A theory suggesting that leaders form different relations with various subordinates and that the nature of such exchanges can exert strong effects on subordinates' performance and satisfaction (p. 442).

leader An individual whose primary function is to create the essential purpose of an organization and the strategy for attaining it (p. 434).

leadership motivation pattern (LMP) A pattern of personality traits involving high power motivation, low affiliation motivation, and a high degree of self-control (p. 126).

leadership motivation The desire to influence others, especially toward the attainment of shared goals (p. 436).

leadership The process whereby one individual influences other group members toward the attainment of defined group or organizational goals (p. 433).

learning organization An organization that is successful at acquiring, cultivating, and applying knowledge that can be used to help it adapt to change (p. 548).

learning A relatively permanent change in behavior occurring as a result of experience (p. 87).

legitimate power The individual power base derived from ones position in an organizational hierarchy; the accepted authority of ones position (p. 405).

line positions Positions in organizations in which people can make decisions related to doing its basic work (p. 510).

LPC contingency theory Fiedler's theory suggesting that leader effectiveness is determined both by characteristics of leaders (their LPC scores) and by the degree to which the situation encountered gives leaders control over their subordinates (p. 451).

LPC Short for "esteem for least preferred co-worker"—a personality variable distinguishing between individuals with respect to their concern for people (high LPC) and their concern for production (low LPC) (p. 451).

Machiavellianism A personality trait involving willingness to manipulate others for one's own purposes (p. 121).

machine bureaucracy An organizational form in which work is highly specialized, decision making is concentrated at the top, and the work environment is not prone to change (e.g., a government office) (p. 526).

management by objectives (MBO) The technique by which managers and their subordinates work together to set and then meet organizational goals (p. 568).

masculine culture According to Hofstede, cultures in which people are highly materialistic and value assertiveness and the acquisition of money (p. 44).

matrix of technologies Perrow's system of categorizing technologies based on two dimensions: *exceptions*, the degree to which an organization makes use of standard inputs to turn out standard outputs; and *problems*, the degree to which the situations encountered are either easy or difficult to analyze (p. 486).

matrix organization The type of departmentalization in which a product or project form is superimposed on a functional form (p. 515).

mechanistic organization An organizational structure in which people perform specialized jobs, many rigid rules are imposed, and authority is vested in a few top-ranking officials (p. 523).

mediation A form of third-party intervention in disputes in which the intervener does not have the authority to dictate an agreement (p. 388).

meditation A technique for inducing relaxation in which individuals clear disturbing thoughts from their minds by repeating a single syllable (p. 239).

melting pot The principle that people from different racial, ethnic, and religious backgrounds are transformed into a common American culture (p. 45).

mentor A more experienced employee who offers advice, assistance, and protection to a younger and less experienced one (a protégé) (p. 216).

mentoring The process of serving as a mentor (p. 216).

midlife crisis A period of great emotional turmoil and uncertainty, supposedly experienced by many individuals during middle age (p. 228).

Minnesota Satisfaction Questionnaire (MSQ) A rating scale for assessing job satisfaction in which people indicate the extent to which they are satisfied with various aspects of their jobs (p. 181).

mission statements Documents in which organizations formally state their basic values and purpose (p. 195).

modular organization An organization that surrounds itself by a network of other organizations to which it regularly outsources noncore functions (p. 518).

morning persons Individuals who feel most energetic and alert early in the day (p. 127).

motivating potential score (MPS) A mathematical index describing the degree to which a job is designed so as to motivate people, as suggested by the *job characteristics model*. It is computed on the basis of a questionnaire known as the Job Diagnostic Survey (JDS). The higher the MPS, the more the job may stand to benefit from redesign (p. 168).

motivation The set of processes that arouse, direct, and maintain human behavior toward attaining some goal (p. 142).

multicultural society A society within which there are many racial, ethnic, socioeconomic, and generational groups, each with its own culture (p. 40).

multinational corporations (MNCs) Organizations that have significant operations spread throughout various nations but are headquartered in a single nation (p. 37).

multiple regression A statistical technique indicating the extent to which each of several variables contributes to accurate predictions of another variable (p. 23).

MUM effect The reluctance to transmit bad news, shown either by not transmitting the message at all, or by delegating the task to someone else (p. 315).

mutual service consortia A type of strategic alliance in which two similar companies from the same or similar industries pool their resources to receive a benefit that would be too difficult or expensive for either one to obtain alone (p. 529).

naturalistic observation A qualitative research technique in which an investigator observes events occurring in an organization while attempting not to affect those events by being present (p. 27).

need hierarchy theory Maslow's theory specifying that there are five human needs (physiological, safety, social, esteem, and self-actualization) and that these are arranged such that lower, more basic needs must be satisfied before higher-level needs become activated (p. 144).

negative affectivity The tendency to experience negative moods in a wide range of settings and under many different conditions (p. 113).

negative correlation A relationship between variables such that more of one variable is associated with less of another (p. 22).

negative reinforcement (or avoidance) The process by which people learn to perform acts that lead to the removal of undesired events (p. 88).

neoclassical organizational theory An attempt to improve upon the classical or ganizational theory which argues that economic effectiveness is not the only goal of organizational structure, but also employee satisfaction (p. 521).

newsletters Regularly published internal documents describing information of interest to employees regarding an array of business and nonbusiness issues affecting them (p. 293).

noise Factors capable of distorting the clarity of messages at any point during the communication process (p. 291).

nominal group technique (NGT) A technique for improving group decisions in which small groups of individuals systematically present and discuss their ideas before privately voting on their preferred solution. The most preferred solution is accepted as the group's decision (p. 359).

nonprogrammed decisions Decisions made about a highly novel problem for which there is no prespecified course of action (p. 336).

nonroutine technology Technology involving many exceptions in inputs or outputs, and problems that are difficult to analyze (e.g., research units and psychiatric hospitals) (p. 487).

nonverbal communication The transmission of messages without the use of words (e.g., by gestures, the use of space) (p. 297).

normative commitment The strength of a person's desire to continue working for an organization because he or she feels obligations from others to remain there (p. 191).

normative decision theory A theory of leader effectiveness focusing primarily on strategies for choosing the most effective approach to making decisions (p. 456).

norms Generally agreed on informal rules that guide group members' behavior (p. 256).

North American Free Trade Agreement (NAFTA) An agreement between the United States, Canada, and Mexico, ratified on January 1, 1994, which eliminates tariffs between these nations (p. 39).

objective tests Questionnaires and inventories designed to measure various aspects of personality (p. 131).

observational learning (or modeling) The form of learning in which people acquire new behaviors by systematically observing the rewards and punishments given to others (p. 90).

open systems Self-sustaining systems that transform input from the external environment into output, which the system then returns to the environment (p. 8).

operant conditioning (or instrumental conditioning) The form of learning in which people associate the consequences of their actions with the actions themselves. Behaviors with positive consequences are acquired; behaviors with negative consequences tend to be eliminated (p. 87).

organic organization An internal organizational structure in which jobs tend to be very general, there are few rules, and decisions can be made by lower-level employees (p. 524).

organization A structured social system consisting of groups and individuals working together to meet some agreed-upon objectives (p. 8).

organizational behavior management (also known as organizational behavior modification or OB Mod) The practice of altering behavior in organizations by systematically administering rewards (p. 95).

organizational behavior The field that seeks increased knowledge of all aspects of behavior in organizational settings through the use of the scientific method (p. 4).

organizational change Planned or unplanned transformations in an organization's structure, technology, and/or people (p. 546).

organizational chart A diagram representing the connections between the various departments within an organization; a graphic representation of organizational structure, indicating who is to communicate with whom (pp. 311, 505).

organizational citizenship behavior (OCB) Actions by organization members that exceed the formal requirements of their job and are, therefore, above and beyond the call of duty (p. 370).

organizational commitment The extent to which an individual identifies and is involved with his or her organization and/or is unwilling to leave it (see *effective commitment* and *continuance commitment*) (p. 190).

organizational culture A cognitive framework consisting of attitudes, values, behavioral norms, and expectations shared by organization members (p. 471).

organizational design The process of coordinating the structural elements of an organization in the most appropriate manner (p. 519).

organizational development (OD) A set of social science techniques designed to plan change in organizational work settings for purposes of enhancing the personal development of individuals and improving the effectiveness of organizational functioning (p. 563).

organizational politics (or **politics**) Unauthorized uses of power that enhance or protect one's own or one's group's personal interests (p. 403).

organizational socialization The process through which newcomers to an organization become full-fledged members who share its major values and understand its policies and procedures (p. 214).

organizational spontaneity Prosocial behavior within an organization that may or may not be recognized by the formal reward system (p. 370).

organizational structure The formal configuration between individuals and groups with respect to the allocation of tasks, responsibilities, and authorities within organizations (p. 505).

organizational structure The formally prescribed pattern of interrelationships existing between the various units of an organization (p. 311).

outcomes The rewards employees receive from their jobs, such as salary and recognition (p. 154).

outplacement services Assistance in finding new jobs that companies provide to employees they lay off (p. 148).

outsourcing The practice of eliminating nonessential aspects of business operations by hiring other companies to perform these tasks (p. 52).

overload The condition in which a unit of an organization becomes overburdened with too much incoming information (p. 320).

overpayment inequity The condition, resulting in feelings of guilt, in which the ratio of one's outcomes to inputs is more than the corresponding ratio of another person with whom that person compares himself or herself (p. 154).

partial (or intermittent) **reinforcement** A schedule of reinforcement in which only some desired behaviors are reinforced. Types include: *fixed interval, variable interval, fixed ratio,* and *variable ratio* (p. 89).

participant observation Naturalistic observations of an organization made by individuals who have been hired as employees (p. 28).

participation Active involvement in the process of learning; more active participation leads to more effective learning (p. 94).

path-goal theory A theory of leadership suggesting that subordinates will be motivated by a leader only to the extent they perceive this individual as helping them to attain valued goals (p. 455).

Pay Satisfaction Questionnaire (PSQ) A questionnaire designed to assess employees' level of satisfaction with various aspects of their pay (e.g., its overall level, raises, benefits) (p. 188).

pay-for-performance plan A payment system in which employees are paid differentially, based on the quantity and quality of their performance. Pay-for-performance plans strengthen *instrumentality beliefs* (p. 161).

perception The process through which we select, organize, and interpret information gathered by our senses in order to understand the world around us (p. 72).

perceptual biases Predispositions that people have to misperceive others in various systematic ways (p. 76).

performance appraisal The process of evaluating employees on various work-related dimensions (p. 82).

permissive (leadership style) A style of leadership in which the leader permits subordinates to take part in decision making and also gives them a considerable degree of autonomy in completing routine work activities (p. 437).

person-job fit The extent to which individuals possess the traits and competencies required to perform specific jobs (p. 110).

personal communication style The consistent ways people go about communicating with others (e.g., the *Noble, the* Socratic, the *Reflective, the* Magistrate, the *Candidate, and the* Senator) (p. 300).

personal power The power that one derives because of his or her individual qualities or characteristics (p. 407).

personal support policies Widely varied practices (e.g., helping with transportation to and from the job) that assist employees in meeting the demands of their family lives, freeing them to concentrate on their work (p. 51).

personality The unique and relatively stable patterns of behavior, thoughts, and emotions shown by individuals (p. 109).

planned change Activities that are intentional and purposive in nature and designed to fulfill some organizational goals (p. 550).

pooled interdependence A relatively low level of interdependence in which units within an organization operate in a largely independent manner (p. 537).

position power Power based on one's formal position in an organization (p. 405).

positive affectivity The tendency to experience positive moods and feelings in a wide range of settings and under many different conditions (p. 113).

positive correlation A relationship between variables such that more of one variable is associated with more of another (p. 22).

positive reinforcement The process by which people learn to perform behaviors that lead to the presentation of desired outcomes (p. 87).

power distance According to Hofstede, the degree to which the unequal distribution of power is accepted by people in a culture (high power distance) or rejected by them (low power distance) (p. 43).

power motivation The strength of an individual's desire to be in charge, to be able to exercise control over others (p. 124).

power The capacity to change the behavior or attitudes of others in a desired manner (p. 402).

predecision A decision about what process to follow in making a decision (p. 333).

prejudice Negative attitudes toward the members of specific groups, based solely on the fact that they are members of those groups (e.g., age, race, sexual orientation) (p. 196).

proactive personality A personality trait reflecting the extent to which individuals seek to change the environment to suit their purposes and to capitalize on various opportunities (p. 115).

procedural justice Perceptions of the fairness of the procedures used to determine outcomes (p. 159).

product organization The type of departmentalization based on the products (or product lines) produced (p. 513).

professional bureaucracy Organizations (e.g., hospitals and universities) in which there are lots of rules to follow, but employees are highly skilled and free to make decisions on their own (p. 527).

programmed decisions Highly routine decisions made according to preestablished organizational routines and procedures (p. 336).

progressive discipline The practice of gradually increasing the severity of punishments for employees who exhibit unacceptable job behavior (p. 99).

projective tests Methods for measuring personality in which individuals respond to ambiguous stimuli. Their responses provide insights into their personality traits (p. 132).

prosocial behavior Actions that benefit others within an organization (p. 369).

protégé A less experienced (often new) employee whose organizational socialization is facilitated by working with a mentor (p. 216).

punishment Decreasing undesirable behavior by following it with undesirable consequences (p. 88).

qualitative overload The belief among employees that they lack the skills or abilities needed to perform their jobs (p. 231).

qualitative underload The lack of mental stimulation that accompanies many routine, repetitive jobs (p. 232).

quality circles (QCs) An approach to improving the quality of work life, in which small groups of volunteers meet regularly to identify and solve problems related to the work they perform and the conditions under which they work (p. 567).

quality control audits Careful examinations of how well a company is meeting the standards of quality toward which it is striving (p. 58).

quality of work life (QWL) An OD technique designed to improve organizational functioning by humanizing the workplace, making it more democratic, and involving employees in decision making (p. 567).

quantitative overload A situation in which individuals are required to do more work than they can actually accomplish in a given period of time (p. 231).

quantitative underload A situation in which individuals have so little to do that they spend much of their time doing nothing (p. 231).

rational decisions Decisions that maximize the chance of attaining an individual's, group's, or organization's goals (p. 340).

rational persuasion Using logical arguments and factual evidence to convince others that an idea is acceptable (p. 407).

rational-economic model The model of decision making according to which decision makers consider all possible alternatives to problems before selecting the optimal solution (p. 340).

realistic job previews Accurate information concerning the conditions within an organization or job provided to potential employees prior to their decision to join an organization (p. 215).

reciprocal interdependence A high level of interdependence in which the output of each unit within an organization serves as the input for others, and vice versa (p. 537).

reciprocity The tendency to treat others as they have treated us (p. 374).

reengineering The fundamental rethinking and radical redesign of business processes to achieve drastic improvements in performance (p. 60).

referent power The individual power base derived from the degree to which one is liked and admired by others (p. 408).

relaxation training Procedures through which individuals learn to relax in order to reduce anxiety or stress (p. 239).

reliability The extent to which a test yields consistent scores on various occasions, and the extent to which all of its items measure the same underlying construct (p. 132).

repatriation The process or readjustment associated with returning to one's native culture after spending time away from it (p. 41).

repetition The process of repeatedly performing a task so that it may be learned (p. 94).

representativeness heuristic The tendency to perceive others in stereotypical ways if they appear to be typical representatives of the category to which they belong (p. 345).

resistance to change The tendency for employees to be unwilling to go along with organizational changes, either because of individual fears of the unknown or organizational impediments (such as *structural inertia*) (p. 560).

resource-dependency model The view according to which power resides within subunits that are able to control the greatest share of valued organizational resources (p. 413).

reward power The individual power base derived from an individual's capacity to administer valued rewards to others (p. 406).

rightsizing See *downsizing* (p. 52).

role The typical behavior that characterizes a person in a specific social context (p. 254).

role ambiguity Confusion arising from not knowing what one is expected to do as the holder of a role (p. 255).

role ambiguity Uncertainty among employees about the key requirements of their jobs (p. 231).

role conflict Incompatible demands made on an individual by different groups or persons (p. 231).

role differentiation The tendency for various specialized roles to emerge as groups develop (p. 255).

role expectations The behaviors expected of someone in a particular role (p. 254).

role incumbent A person holding a particular role (p. 254).

routine technology Technology involving highly standardized inputs and outputs, and problems that are easy to analyze (e.g., assembly lines and vocational training) (p. 486).

rumors Information with little basis in fact, often transmitted through informal channels (see *grapevine*) (p. 310).

sandwich generation The generation of people who face economic pressures associated with taking care of their own children and their elderly parents, both of whom who live with them (p. 48).

satisficing decisions Decisions made by selecting the first minimally acceptable alternative as it becomes available (p. 341).

saturation The amount of information a single member of a communication network must handle (p. 306).

schedules of reinforcement Rules governing the timing and frequency of the administration of reinforcement (p. 90).

scientific management An early approach to management and organizational behavior emphasizing the importance of designing jobs as efficiently as possible (p. 11).

second-order change Radical change; major shifts involving many different levels of the organization and many different aspects of business (p. 548).

selective perception The tendency to focus on some aspects of the environment while ignoring others (p. 79).

self-actualization The need to discover who we are and to develop ourselves to the fullest potential (p. 146).

self-efficacy Individuals' beliefs concerning their ability to perform specific tasks successfully (p. 117).

self-managed work teams Teams whose members are permitted to make key decisions about how their work is done (p. 273).

self-monitoring A personality trait involving the extent to which individuals adapt their behavior to the demands of specific situations, primarily to make the best possible impression on others (p. 120).

sequential interdependence An intermediate level of interdependence in which the output of one unit serves as input for another (p. 537).

sexual harassment Unwanted contact or communication of a sexual nature (p. 232).

shaping The process of selectively reinforcing behaviors that approached a desired goal behavior (p. 97).

shared-screen conferencing The process of connecting computer workstations so as to provide concurrent displays of information and interaction between several individuals (p. 264).

side-bets orientation The view of organizational commitment that focuses on the accumulated investments an individual stands to lose if he or she leaves the organization (see *continuance commitment*) (p. 191).

similar-to-me effect The tendency for people to perceive in a positive light others who are believed to be similar to themselves in any of several different ways (p. 77).

simple structure An organization characterized as being small and informal, with a single powerful individual, often the founding entrepreneur, who is in charge of everything (p. 526).

situational leadership theory A theory suggesting that the most effective style of leadership—either delegating, participating, selling, or telling—depends on the extent to which followers require guidance, direction, and emotional support (p. 453).

skills-based diversity training An approach to diversity management that goes beyond *awareness-based diversity training* and is designed to develop people's skills with respect to managing diversity (p. 202).

small-batch production A technology in which products are custom-produced in response to specific orders from customers (p. 533).

social facilitation The tendency for the presence of others sometimes to enhance an individual's performance and at other times to impair it (p. 261).

social impact theory The theory that explains social loafing in terms of the diffused responsibility for doing what is expected of each member of a group (see *social loafing*). The larger the size of a group, the less each member is influenced by the social forces acting on the group (p. 266).

social influence Attempts to affect another in a desired fashion (p. 402).

social loafing The tendency for group members to exert less individual effort on an additive task as the size of the group increases (p. 266).

social perception The process through which individuals attempt to combine, integrate, and interpret information about others (p. 73).

span of control The number of subordinates in an organization who are supervised by managers (p. 508).

staff positions Positions in organizations in which people make recommendations to others but are not themselves involved in making decisions concerning the organization's day-to-day operations (p. 510).

status The relative prestige, social position, or rank given to groups or individuals by others (p. 258).

status symbols Objects reflecting the position of any individual within an organization's hierarchy of power (p. 258).

stepladder technique A technique for improving the quality of group decisions that minimizes the tendency for group members to be unwilling to present their ideas by adding new members to a group one at a time and requiring each to present his or her ideas independently to a group that already has discussed the problem at hand (p. 361).

stereotypes Beliefs that all members of specific groups share similar traits and are prone to behave the same way (p. 80).

strain Deviations from normal states or functioning resulting from stress (p. 230).

strategic alliance A type of organizational design in which two or more separate companies combine forces to develop and operate a specific business (p. 529).

strategic contingencies model A view explaining power in terms of a subunit's capacity to control the activities of other subunits. A subunit's power is enhanced when (1) it can reduce the level of uncertainty experienced by other subunits, (2) it occupies a central position in the organization, and (3) its activities are highly indispensable to the organization (p. 415).

strategic decisions Nonprogrammed decisions typically made by high-level executives regarding the direction their organization should take to achieve its mission (p. 336).

stress management programs Systematic efforts by organizations designed to help employees reduce and/or prevent stress (p. 241).

stress The pattern of emotional states, cognitions, and physiological reactions occurring in response to stressors (p. 230).

stressors Various factors in the external environment that induce stress among people exposed to them (p. 230).

structural inertia The organizational forces acting on employees encouraging them to perform their jobs in certain ways (e.g., training, reward systems), thereby making them resistant to change (p. 561).

subculture Smaller cultural groups operating within larger, primary cultural groups, each of which may have its own highly defined culture (p. 40).

subcultures Cultures existing within parts of organizations rather than entirely through them. Members of subcultures share values in addition to the core values of their organization as a whole (p. 473).

substitutes for leadership The view that high levels of skill among subordinates or certain features of technology and organizational structure sometimes serve as substitutes for leaders, rendering their guidance or influence superfluous (p. 459).

superordinate goals Goals shared by the parties in a conflict or dispute (p. 389).

survey feedback An OD technique in which questionnaires and interviews are used to collect information about issues of concern to an organization. This information is shared with employees and then used as the basis for planning organizational change (p. 563).

surveys Questionnaires designed to measure people's perceptions of some aspect of organizational behavior (p. 20).

symbols Material objects that connote meanings extending beyond their intrinsic content (p. 477).

team A group whose members have complementary skills and are committed to a common purpose or set of performance goals for which they hold themselves mutually accountable (p. 270).

team building An OD technique in which employees discuss problems related to their work group's performance. On the basis of these discussions, specific problems are identified and plans for solving them are devised and implemented (p. 565).

teamwork The practice of working in teams (see *team*) (p. 249).

technology The physical and mental processes used to transform inputs into usable outputs (p. 484).

telecommuting The practice of using communications technology so as to enable work to be performed from remote locations, such as the home (see *flexplace*) (p. 56).

Theory X A traditional philosophy of management suggesting that most people are lazy and irresponsible and will work hard only when forced to do so (p. 6).

Theory Y A philosophy of management suggesting that under the right circumstances, people are fully capable of working productively and accepting responsibility for their work (p. 7).

theory Efforts by scientists to explain why various events occur as they do. Theories consist of basic concepts and assertions regarding the relationship between them (p. 18).

time-and-motion study A type of applied research designed to classify and streamline the individual movements needed to perform jobs with the intent of finding the most efficient way of doing them (p. 12).

top-down decision making The practice of vesting decision-making power in the hands of superiors as opposed to lower-level employees (p. 339).

total quality management (TQM) An organizational strategy of commitment to improving customer satisfaction by developing techniques to carefully manage output quality (p. 58).

training The process of systematically teaching employees to acquire and improve job-related skills and knowledge (p. 92).

transfer of training The degree to which the skills learned during training sessions may be applied to performance of one's job (p. 94).

transformational leadership Leadership in which leaders have charisma, provide intellectual stimulation, individualized consideration, and inspirational motivation (p. 447).

trust The belief among employees that they will be treated fairly by their organization and, more specifically, by their immediate supervisor (p. 375).

two-factor theory (of job satisfaction) A theory, devised by Herzberg, suggesting that satisfaction and dissatisfaction stem from different groups of variables (*motivators* and *hygienes*, respectively) (p. 183).

two-tier wage structures Payment systems in which newer employees are paid less than employees hired at earlier times to do the same work (p. 157).

Type A behavior pattern A pattern of behavior involving high levels of competitiveness, time urgency, and irritability (p. 113).

Type B behavior pattern A pattern of behavior characterized by a casual, laid-back style; the opposite of the Type A behavior pattern (p. 113).

uncertainty avoidance According to Hofstede, the degree to which people in a culture feel threatened by, and attempt to avoid, ambiguous situations (p. 44).

underpayment inequity The condition, resulting in feelings of anger, in which the ratio of one's outcomes to inputs is less than the corresponding ratio of another person with whom that person compares himself or herself (p. 154).

unplanned change Shifts in organizational activities due to forces that are external in nature, those beyond the organization's control (p. 550).

valence The value a person places on the rewards he or she receives from an organization (p. 159).

validity The extent to which a test actually measures what it claims to measure (p. 133).

value theory (of job satisfaction) A theory, devised by Locke, suggesting that job satisfaction depends primarily on the match between the outcomes individuals value in their jobs and their perceptions about the availability of such outcomes (p. 184).

value-chain partnerships Strategic alliances between companies in different industries that have complementary capabilities (p. 530).

valuing diversity Encouraging awareness of and respect for different people in the workplace (p. 45).

variable interval schedules Schedules of reinforcement in which a variable period of time (based on some average) must elapse between the administration of reinforcements (p. 89).

variable ratio schedules Schedules of reinforcement in which a variable number of responses (based on some average) must occur between the administration of reinforcements (p. 90).

verbal communication The transmission of messages using words, either written or spoken (p. 292).

videoconferencing The practice of using technology to provide audio and video links (either limited or full-motion) between work sites, allowing visual communication between people who are not physically present (p. 264).

virtual corporation A highly flexible, temporary organization formed by a group of companies that join forces to exploit a specific opportunity (p. 56).

virtual organization A highly flexible, temporary organization formed by a group of companies that join forces to exploit a specific opportunity (p. 518).

voice messaging (voice mail) A system that uses a computer to convert human speech into digital information saved on a hard disk for playback later by the receiver at any time from any touch-tone telephone (p. 297).

voluntary reduced work time (V-time) programs Programs that allow employees to reduce the amount of time they work by a certain amount (typically 10 or 20 percent), with a proportional reduction in pay (p. 50).

whistle-blowing Calling attention to actions or practices that are inconsistent with established organizational norms or policies (p. 372).

work-flow integration A measure of technology that takes account of the degree of automation, work-flow rigidity, and specificity of evaluation within an organization (p. 536).

work-related attitudes Attitudes relating to any aspect of work or work settings (p. 178).

workplace aggression Efforts by individuals to harm other members of their organization, persons with whom they previously worked, or their organization itself (p. 391).

workplace violence Direct physical assaults by present or former employees against other persons in their organizations (p. 389).

CHAPTER 1

Preview Case Sources

Labich, K. (1994, May 2). Is Herb Kelleher America's best CEO? *Fortune*, pp. 44–47, 50, 52. Woodbury, R. (1993, January 25). Prince of midair. *Time*, p. 55. Southwest Airlines' Herb Kelleher: Unorthodoxy at work. (1995, January). *Management Review*, pp. 9–12.

Chapter Notes

1. Greenberg, J. (Ed.). (1994). *Organizational behavior: The state of the science*. Hillsdale, NJ: Erlbaum.

2. Elden, M., & Chisholm, R. F. (1993). Emerging varieties of action research: Introduction to the special issue. *Human Relations, 46*, 121–142.

3. Case, J. (1993, April). A company of businesspeople. *Inc.*, pp. 79–84, 86–87, 90, 92–93.

4. McGregor, D. (1960). *The human side of enterprise*. New York: McGraw-Hill.

5. Katz, D., & Kahn, R. (1978). *The social psychology of organizations*. New York: Wiley.

6. Pennings, J. M. (1992). Structural contingency theory: A reappraisal. In B. M. Staw & L. L. Cummings (Eds.), *Research in organizational behavior* (Vol. 14, pp. 267–310). Greenwich, CT: JAI Press.

7. Jackson, S. E., & Alvarez, E. B. (1992). Working through diversity as a strategic imperative. In S. E. Jackson (Ed.), *Diversity in the workplace* (pp. 13–29). New York: Guilford Press.

8. Towers Perrin, & Hudson Institute. (1990). *Workforce 2000: Competing in a seller's market*. Valhalla, NY: Towers Perrin.

9. Maruyama, M. (1992). Changing dimensions in international business. *Academy of Management Executive, 6*, 88–96.

10. Teagarden, M. B., Von Glinow, M. A., Bowen, D. E., Frayne, C. A., Nason, S., Huo,
P., Milliman, J., Arias, M. E., Butler, M. C., Geringer, J. M., Kim, N. Scullion, H., Lowe, K. B., & Drost, E. A. (1995). Toward a theory of comparative management research: An idiographic case study of the best international human resources management project. *Academy of Management Journal, 38*, 1261–1287.

11. Warner, M. (1994). Organizational behavior revisited. *Human Relations, 47*, 1151–1166.

12. Kennedy, C. (1991). *Instant management*. New York: William Morrow.

13. Taylor, F. W. (1947). *Scientific management*. New York: Harper & Row.

14. Drucker, P. F. (1974). *Management: Tasks, responsibilities, practices*. New York: Harper & Row.

15. Münsterberg, H. (1913). *Psychology and industrial efficiency*. New York: Houghton Mifflin.

16. Metcalf, H., & Urwick, L. F. (Eds.). (1942). *Dynamic administration: The collected papers of Mary Parker Follett*. New York: Harper & Row.

17. Bedian, A. (1976, June). Finding the one best way: An appreciation of Frank B. Gilbreth, the father of motion study. *Conference Board Record*, pp. 37–39.

18. Gotcher, J. M. (1992). Assisting the handicapped: The pioneering efforts of Frank and Lillian Gilbreth. *Journal of Management, 18*, 5–13.

19. Mayo, E. (1933). *The human problems of an industrial civilization*. London: Macmillan.

20. Roethlisberger, F. J., & Dickson, W. J. (1939). *Management and the worker*. Cambridge, MA: Harvard University Press.

21. Baron, R. A., Rea, M. S., & Daniels, S. G. (1992). Lighting as a source of environmentally-
generated positive affect in work settings: Impact on cognitive tasks and interpersonal behavior. *Motivation and Emotion, 15*, 1–34.

22. Fayol, H. (1949). *General and industrial management*. London: Pittman.

23. Weber, M. (1921), *Theory of social and economic organization* (A. M. Henderson & T. Parsons, Trans.), London: Oxford University Press.

24. Flexner, S. B. (1976). *I hear America talking*. New York: Van Nostrand Reinhold.

25. Lawrence, P. R. (1987). Historical development of organizational behavior. In J. W. Lorsch (Ed.), *Handbook of organizational behavior* (pp. 1–9). Englewood Cliffs, NJ: Prentice-Hall.

26. Gardner, B., & Moore, G. (1945). *Human relations in industry*. Homewood, IL: Irwin.

27. See note 26.

28. Gordon, R. A., & Howell, J. E. (1959). *Higher education for business*. New York: Columbia University Press.

29. Cooper, H., & Hedges, L. V. (1994). *The handbook of research synthesis*. New York: Russell Sage Foundation.

30. Van Mannen, J., Dabbs, J. M., Jr., & Faulkner, R. R. (1982). *Varieties of qualitative research*. Beverly Hills, CA: Sage Publications.

31. Greenberg, J., & Folger, R. (1988). *Controversial issues in social research methods*. New York: Springer-Verlag.

32. Eisenhardt, K. M. (1989). Building theories from case study research. *Academy of Management Review, 14*, 532–550.

Case In Point Source

Ettorre, B. (1995, September). GE brings a new washer to life. *Management Review*, pp. 33–38.

CHAPTER 2

Preview Case Source

Paton, S. M. (1995, September/October). Diversity at Texas Instruments. *Quality Digest*, pp. 26–28, 30, 32–33.

Chapter Notes

1. Cascio, W. F. (1995). Whither industrial and organizational psychology in a changing world of work? *American Psychologist, 50*, 928–939.

2. See Note 1 (quote, p. 928).

3. Gwynne, S. C. (1992, September 28). The long haul. *Time*, pp. 34–38.

4. Investing in people and prosperity. (1994, May). U.S. Department of Labor, Washington, DC, p. 7.

5. See Note 4.

6. Brown, L. R., Kane, H., & Ayres, E. (1994). *Vital signs*. New York: Norton.

7. See Note 6.

8. Lodge, G. C. (1995). *Managing globalization in the age of interdependence*. San Diego, CA: Pfeffer.

9. See Note 8.

10. A survey of multinationals. (1993, March 27). *The Economist*, p. 6.

11. "Cross-border investment is high." (1993, September 15). *Chemical Week*, p. 5.

12. Ronen, S. (1986). *Comparative multinational management*. New York: Wiley.

13. See Note 8.

14. See Note 8.

15. Huntington, S. P. (1993, summer). The clash of civilizations. *Foreign Affairs*, pp. 22–49.

16. Duerr, M. G. (1986, October). International business management: Its four tasks. *Conference Board Record*, pp. 42–45 (quote, p. 43).

17. Earley, P. C., & Singh, H. (1995). International and inter-

cultural management research: What's next? *Academy of Management Journal, 38,* 327–340.

18. Ogbonna, E. (1993). Managing organizational culture: Fantasy or reality? *Human Resource Management Journal, 3(2),* 42–54.

19. DeCieri, H., & Dowling, P. J. (1995). Cross-cultural issues in organizational behavior. In C. L. Cooper & D. M. Rousseau (Eds.), *Trends in organizational behavior* (Vol. 2, pp. 127–145). New York: John Wiley & Sons.

20. Hesketh, B., & Bochner, S. (1994). Technological change in a multicultural context: Implications for training and career planning. In H. C. Triandis, M. D. Dunnette, & L. Hough (Eds.), *Handbook of industrial and organizational psychology* (Vol. 4, pp. 190–240). Palo Alto, CA: Consulting Psychologists Press.

21. Janssens, M. (1995). Intercultural interaction: A burden on international managers? *Journal of Organizational Behavior, 16,* 155–167.

22. See Note 19.

23. Hofstede, G. (1980). *Culture's consequences: International differences in work related values.* Beverly Hills, CA: Sage.

24. Carnevale, A. P., & Stone, S. C. (1995). *The American mosaic: An in-depth report on the future of diversity at work.* New York: McGraw-Hill.

25. Garraty, J. A., & McCaughey, R. A. (1987). *The American nation: A history of the United States* (6th ed.). New York: Harper & Row.

26. Boyett, J. H., & Boyett, J. T. (1995). *Beyond workplace 2000.* New York: Dutton.

27. See Note 26.

28. See Note 24.

29. See Note 26.

30. See Note 26.

31. See Note 24.

32. See Note 24

33. See Note 26.

34. See Note 26.

35. Cox, T. C., Jr. (1994). *Cultural diversity in organizations.* San Francisco: Berrett-Kohler.

36. Cohen, A. R., & Gadon, H. (1980). *Alternative work sched-*

ules. Reading, MA: Addison-Wesley.

37. Galen, M., Palmer, A. T., Cuneo, A., & Maremont, M. (1993, June 28). Work & family. *Business Week,* pp. 80–84, 86, 88.

38. Olmsted, B., & Smith, S. (1994). *Creating a flexible workplace* (2nd ed.). New York: AMACOM.

39. Meier, L., & Meagher, L. (1993, September). Teaming up to manage. *Working Woman,* pp. 31–32, 108.

40. See Note 38.

41. See Note 38.

42. Mason, J. C. (1993, July). Working in the family way. *HRMagazine,* pp. 25–28.

43. Shellenbarger, S. (1994, February 16). The aging of America is making "elder care" a big workplace issue. *Wall Street Journal,* p. A1.

44. Fenn, D. (1993, July) Bottoms up. *Inc.,* pp. 57–60.

45. Martinez, M. N. (1993). Family support makes business sense. *HRMagazine,* pp. 38–43.

46. See Note 39.

47. See Note 42.

48. See Note 42.

49. See Note 39.

50. Zuboff, S. (1988). *In the age of the smart machine.* New York: Basic Books.

51. Bridges, W. (1994). *Job shift: How to prosper in a workplace without jobs.* Reading, MA: Addison-Wesley.

52. See Note 51.

53. Tomasko, R. M. (1990). *Downsizing: Reshaping the corporation for the future.* New York: AMACOM.

54. Hendricks, C. F. (1992). *The rightsizing remedy.* Homewood, IL: Business One Irwin.

55. Fierman, J. (1994, January 24). The contingency work force. *Fortune,* pp. 30–34, 36.

56. Szwergold, J. (1993, December). Downsizing: Down, but not out. *Management Review,* p. 6.

57. Richman, L. S. (1993, September 20). When will the layoffs end? *Fortune,* pp. 54–56.

58. Tomasko, R. M. (1993). *Rethinking the corporation,* New York: AMACOM.

59. See Note 58.

60. Lusk, A. (1992, May). New business from old clients. *Working Woman,* pp. 26, 28.

61. Bettis, R. A., Bradley, S. P., & Hamel, G. (1992). Outsourcing and industrial decline. *Academy of Management Review, 6,* 7–22.

62. Haapaniemi, P. (1993, winter). Taking care of business. *Solutions,* pp. 6–8, 10–13.

63. See Note 58.

64. Stewart, T. A. (1993, December 13). Welcome to the revolution. *Fortune,* pp. 66–68, 70, 72, 76, 78.

65. Fierman, J. (1994, January 24). The contingency workforce. *Fortune,* pp. 30–34, 36.

66. Brotherton, P. (1995, December). Staff to suit. *HRMagazine,* pp. 50–55.

67. Aley, J. (1995, September 18). Where the jobs are. *Fortune,* pp. 53–54, 56.

68. See Note 66.

69. Handy, C. (1994). *The age of paradox.* New York: Morrow.

70. Beard, K. M., & Edwards, J. R. (1995). Employees at risk: Contingent work and the psychological experience of contingent workers. In C. L. Cooper & D. M. Rousseau (Eds.), *Trends in organizational behavior* (Vol. 2, pp. 109–126). London: John Wiley & Sons.

71. See Note 65 (quote, p. 36).

72. Bridges, W. (1994, September 19). The end of the job. *Fortune,* pp. 62–64, 68, 72, 74.

73. Nollen, S., & Axel, H. (1995). *The contingent workforce.* New York: AMACOM.

74. Sasseen, J. A., Neff, R., Hattangadi, S., & Sasoni, S. (1994, October 17). The winds of change blow everywhere. *Business Week,* pp. 92, 94.

75. Byrne, J. A., Brandt, R., & Port, O. (1993, February 8). The virtual corporation: The company of the future will be the ultimate in adaptability. *Business Week,* pp. 98–102.

76. Lander, M. (1994, October 10). It's not only rock 'n' roll. *Business Week,* pp. 83–84.

77. O'Connell, S. E. (1996, March). The virtual workplace moves at warp speed. *HR Magazine,* pp. 50–57.

78. Davidow, W. H., & Malone, M. S. (1992). *The virtual corporation.* New York: Harper Business. (quote, p. 99).

79. Greengard, S. (1994, September). Workers go virtual. *Personnel Journal,* p. 71.

80. Kugelmass, J. (1995). *Telecommuting: A manager's guide to flexible work arrangements.* New York: Lexington Books.

81. DuBrin, A. J. (1994). *Contemporary applied management: Skills for managers* (4th ed.). Burr Ridge, IL: Irwin.

82. Walton, M. (1990). *The Demming management method at work.* New York: Perigree.

83. Hart, C. W. L. & Bogan, C. E. (1992). *The Baldridge.* New York: McGraw Hill.

84. Hodgetts, R. M. (1993). *Blueprints for continuous improvement: Lessons from the Baldridge winners.* New York: AMACOM.

85. Boyett, J. H., Schwartz, S., Osterwise, L., & Bauer, R. (1993). *The quality journey: How winning the Baldridge sparked the remaking of IBM.* New York: Dutton.

86. Stewart, T. A. (1993, August 23). Reengineering: The hot new managing tool. *Fortune,* pp. 40–43, 46, 48.

87. The promise of reengineering. (1993, May 3). *Fortune,* pp. 94–97.

88. Ferrell, O. C., & Fraedrich, J. (1994). *Business ethics: Ethical decision making and cases* (2nd ed.). Boston: Houghton Mifflin.

89. Henderson, V. E. (1992). *What's ethical in business?* New York: McGraw-Hill.

90. Jansen, E., & Von Glinow, M. A. (1985). Ethical ambivalence and organizational reward systems. *Academy of Management Review, 10,* 814–822.

91. Wolfe, D. M. (1988). Is there integrity in the bottom line: Managing obstacles to executive integrity. In S. Srivastava (Ed.), *Executive integrity: The search for high human values in organizational life* (pp. 140–171). San Francisco: Jossey-Bass.

92. Rosen, R. H. (1991). *The healthy company.* New York: Jeremy P. Tarcher/Perigee.

93. See Note 81.

94. Manley, W. W., II. (1991). *Executive's handbook of model business conduct codes.* Englewood Cliffs, NJ: Prentice Hall.

95. Treviño, L. K., & Nelson, K. A. (1995). *Managing business ethics*. New York: Wiley.

Case in Point Source

Schlender, B. (1995, September 19). Steve Jobs' amazing movie adventure. *Fortune*, pp. 155–156, 160, 164, 168, 172.

CHAPTER 3

Preview Case Source

Stewart, T. A. (1995, September 4). How a little company won big by betting on brainpower. *Fortune*, pp. 121–122.

Chapter Notes

1. Schiffman, H. R. (1993). *Sensation and perception* (4th ed.). New York: Wiley.

2. Kenny, D. A. (1994). Interpersonal perception. New York: Guilford.

3. Weiner, B. (1995). *Judgments of responsibility*. New York: Guilford.

4. Jones, E. E., & McGillis, D. (1976). Correspondent inferences and the attribution cube: A comparative reappraisal. In J. H. Harvey, W. J. Ickes, & R. F. Kidd (Eds.), *New directions in attribution research* (Vol. 1, pp. 389–420). Hillsdale, NJ: Lawrence Erlbaum Associates.

5. Kelley, H. H. (1972). Attribution in social interaction. In E. E. Jones, D. E. Kanous, H. H. Kelley, R. E. Nisbett, S. Valins, & B. Weiner (Eds.), *Attribution: Perceiving the causes of behavior* (pp. 1–26). Morristown, NJ: General Learning Press.

6. Burger, J. M. (1991). Changes in attribution errors over time: The ephemeral fundamental attribution error. *Social Cognition, 9*, 182–193.

7. Murphy, K. R., Jako, R. A., & Anhalt, R. L. (1993). Nature and consequences of halo error: A critical analysis. *Journal of Applied Psychology, 78*, 218–225.

8. Pulakos, E. D., & Wexley, K. N. (1983). The relationship among perceptual similarity, sex, and performance ratings in manager-subordinate dyads. *Academy of Management Journal, 26*, 129–139.

9. Turban, D. B., & Jones, A. P. (1988). Supervisor-subordinate similarity: Types, effects, and mechanisms. *Journal of Applied Psychology, 73*, 228–234.

10. Dougherty, T. W., Turban, D. B., & Callender, J. C. (1994). Confirming first impressions in the employment interview: A field study of interviewer behavior. *Journal of Applied Psychology, 79*, 659–665.

11. Dearborn, D. C., & Simon, H. A. (1958). Selective perception: A note on the departmental identification of executives. *Sociometry, 21*, 140–144.

12. Waller, M. J., Huber, G. P., & Glick, W. H. (1995). Functional background as a determinant of executives' selective perception. *Academy of Management Journal, 38*, 943–974.

13. Srull, T. K., & Wyer, R. S. (1988). *Advances in social cognition*. Hillsdale, NJ: Lawrence Erlbaum Associates.

14. Mohrman, A. M., Jr., Resnick-West, S. M., & Lawler, E. E., III. (1989). *Designing performance appraisal systems*. San Francisco: Jossey-Bass.

15. Ilgen, D. R., Major, D. A., & Tower, S. L. (1994). The cognitive revolution in organizational behavior. In J. Greenberg (Ed.), *Organizational behavior: The state of the science* (pp. 1–22). Hillsdale, NJ: Lawrence Erlbaum Associates.

16. Hogan, E. A. (1987). Effects of prior expectations on performance ratings: A longitudinal study. *Academy of Management Journal, 30*, 354–368.

17. Wayne, S. J., & Liden, R. C. (1995). Effects of impression management on performance ratings: A longitudinal study. *Academy of Management Journal, 38*, 232–260.

18. Fletcher, C. (1989). Impression management in the selection interview. In R. A. Giacalone & P. Rosenfeld (Eds.), *Impression management in the organization* (pp. 269–282). Hillsdale, NJ: Lawrence Erlbaum Associates.

19. Giacalone, R. A., & Rosenfeld, P. (1989). *Impression management in the organization*. Hillsdale, NJ: Lawrence Erlbaum Associates.

20. Stevens, C. K., & Kristof, A. L. (1995). Making the right impression: A field study of applicant impression management during job interviews. *Journal of Applied Psychology, 80*, 587–606.

21. Garbett, T. (1988). *How to build a corporation's identity and project its image*. Lexington, MA: Lexington Books.

22. Gatewood, R. D., Gowan, M. A., & Lautenschlager, G. J. (1993). Corporate image, recruitment image, and initial job choice decisions. *Academy of Management Journal, 36*, 414–427.

23. Jacob, R. (1995, March 6). Corporate reputations. *Fortune*, pp. 54–64.

24. Bongiorno, L. (1995, April 10). The duller the better: For 1994's annual reports, modesty is a virtue. *Business Week*, p. 44.

25. Jordan, M., & Sullivan, K. (1995, September 8). Saving face: Japanese can rent mourners, relatives, friends, even enemies to buff an image. *Washington Post*, pp. A1, A28.

26. Wick, C. W., & Leon, L. S. (1993). *The learning edge: How smart managers and smart companies stay ahead*. New York: McGraw-Hill.

27. Atkinson, R. C., Herrnstein, R. J., Lindzey, G., & Luce, R. D. (Eds.). (1988). *Stevens' handbook of experimental psychology* (2nd ed.) (Vol. 1, pp. 218–266). New York: Wiley.

28. Skinner, B. F. (1969). *Contingencies of reinforcement*. New York: Appleton-Century-Crofts.

29. Scott, W. E., & Podsakoff, P. M. (1985). *Behavioral principles in the practice of management*. New York: Wiley.

30. Bandura, A. (1986). *Social foundations of thought and action*. Englewood Cliffs, NJ: Prentice Hall.

31. Harrison, J. K. (1992). Individual and combined effects of behavior modeling and the cultural assimilator in cross-cultural management training. *Journal of Applied Psychology, 77*, 962–962.

32. Goldstein, I. L. (1991). Training in work organizations. In M. D. Dunnette & L. M. Hough (Eds.), *Handbook of industrial and organizational psychology*, (2nd ed.) (Vol. 2, pp. 507–620). Palo Alto, CA: Consulting Psychologists Press.

33. Schnake, M. E. (1986). Vicarious punishment in a work setting. *Journal of Applied Psychology, 71*, 343–345.

34. Carnevlae, A. P., & Gainer, L. J. (1989). *The learning enterprise*. Alexandria, VA: American Society for Training and Development.

35. Waller, D. C. (1992, February 28). Tailhook's lightning rod. *Newsweek*, p. 31.

36. Trevino, L. K., & Nelson, K. A. (1995). *Managing business ethics*. New York: John Wiley & Sons.

37. Del Valle, C. (1993, April 26). From high schools to high skills. *Business Week*, pp. 110, 112.

38. Webster, J., & Martocchio, J. J. (1993). Turning work into play: Implications for microcomputer software training. *Journal of Management, 19*, 127–146.

39. Gist, M. E., Stevens, C. K., & Bavetta, A. G. (1991). Effects of self-efficacy and post-training intervention on the acquisition and maintenance of complex interpersonal skills. *Personnel Psychology, 44*, 837–861.

40. O'Reilly, B. (1993, April 5). How execs learn now. *Fortune*, pp. 52–54, 58.

41. Argyris, C. (1991, May–June). Teaching smart people how to learn. *Harvard Business Review, 69*(3), 99–109.

42. Driskell, J. E., Cooper, C., & Moran, A. (1994). Does mental practice enhance performance? *Journal of Applied Psychology, 79*, 481–492.

43. Tracey, B. J., Tannenbaum, S. I., & Kavanaugh, M. J. (1995). Applying trained skills on the job: The importance of the work environment. *Journal of Applied Psychology, 80*, 239–252.

44. Tannenbaum, S. I., & Yukl, G. A. (1992). Training and development in work organizations. *Annual Review of Psychology, 43*, 399–441.

45. Hoffman, R. (1995, April). Ten reasons you should be using 360-feedback. *HRMagazine*, pp. 82–85.

46. Miller, L. (1978). *Behavior management*. New York: Wiley.

47. Brooks, S. S. (1994, April). Noncash ways to compensate employees. *HRMagazine*, pp. 38–43.

48. Smart, T., & Hayes, K. (1995). Look who's showing small fry the ropes. *Business Week Enterprise*, pp. 6–8.

49. Lawler, E. O. (1993, April). How MCI wrought a 100-day "miracle." *Business Marketing*, pp. 56–57.

50. Frederiksen, L. W. (1982). *Handbook of organizational behavior management*. New York: Wiley.

51. Beyer, J., & Trice, H. M. (1984). A field study of the use and perceived effects of discipline in controlling work performance. *Academy of Management Journal, 27,* 743–754.

52. Trahan, W. A., & Steiner, D. D. (1994). Factors affecting supervisors' use of disciplinary actions following poor performance. *Journal of Organizational Behavior, 15,* 129–139.

53. Oberle, R. J. (1978). Administering disciplinary actions, *Personnel Journal, 18*(3), 30–33.

54. Arvey, R. D., & Jones, A. P. (1985). The use of discipline in organizational settings: A framework for future research. In L. L. Cummings & B. M. Staw (Eds.), *Research in organizational behavior* (Vol. 7, pp. 367–408). Greenwich, CT: JAI Press.

55. Kiechell, W., III. (1990, May 7). How to discipline in the modern age. *Fortune,* pp. 179–180 (quote, p. 180).

56. Arvey, R. E., & Icancevich, J. M. (1980). Punishment in organizations: A review, propositions, and research suggestions. *Academy of Management Review, 5,* 123–132.

57. Trevino, L. K. (1992). The social effects of punishment in organizations: A justice perspective. *Academy of Management Review, 17,* 647–676.

58. Lussier, R. H. (1990, August). A discipline model for increasing performance. *Supervisory Management,* pp. 6–7.

59. Kerr, S. (1975). On the follow of rewarding "A" while hoping for "B." *Academy of Management Journal, 18,* 769–783.

60. Dechant, K., & Viega, J. (1995). More on the folly. *Academy of Management Executive, 9,* 15–16.

Case In Point Source

Fenn, D. (1995, March). Training: Making it part of the routine. *Inc.,* p. 113.

CHAPTER 4

Preview Case Source

Jacob, R. (1995, August). The resurrection of Michael Dell.

Fortune, 117–118, 120, 124, 128.

Chapter Notes

1. Carver, C. S., & Scheier, M. F. (1992). Perspectives on personality (2nd ed.). Boston: Allyn & Bacon.

2. Eysenk, M. W. (1994). *Individual differences.* Hillsdale, NJ: Erlbaum.

3. Mischel, W. (1973). Toward a cognitive social learning reconceptualization of personality. *Psychological Review, 80,* 252–283.

4. Friedman, H. W., Tucker, J. S. Tomlinson-Keasey, C., Schwartz, J. E. Wingard, D. L., & Criqui, M. H. (1993). Does childhood personality predict longevity? *Journal of Personality and Social Psychology, 65,* 176–185.

5. Bouchard, T. J., Jr., Lykken, D. T., McGue, M., Segal, N. L., & Tellegen, A. (1990). Sources of human psychological differences: The Minnesota study of twins reared apart. *Science, 250,* 223–228.

6. Osipow, S. H. (1990). Convergence in theories of career choice and development: Review and prospect. *Journal of Vocational Behavior, 36,* 122–131.

7. Caldwell, D. F., & O'Reilly, C. A., III (1990). Measuring person-job fit with a profile-comparison process. *Journal of Applied Psychology, 75,* 648–657.

8. Allport, G. W., & Odbert, H. S. (1936). Trait names: A psycholexical study. *Psychological Monographs, 47,* 211–214.

9. Digman, J. M. (1990). Personality structure: Emergence of the five-factor model. *Annual Review of Psychology, 41,* 417–440.

10. Funder, D. C., & Colvin, C. R. (1991). Explorations in behavioral consistency. Properties of persons, situations, and behavior. *Journal of Personality and Social Psychology, 60,* 773–794.

11. Funder, D. C., & Sneed, C. D. (1993). Behavioral manifestations of personality: An ecological approach to judgmental accuracy. *Journal of Personality and Social Psychology, 64,* 479–490.

12. Tett, R. P., Jackson, D. N., & Rothstein, M. (1991).

Personality measures as predictors of job performance: A meta-analytic review. *Personnel Psychology, 44,* 703–741.

13. Cortina, J. M., Doherty, M. L., Schmitt, N., Kaufman, G., & Smith, R. G. (1992). The big five personality factors in the IPI and MMPI: Predictors of police performance. *Personnel, Psychology, 44,* 1–26.

14. Barrick, M. R., & Mount, M. K. (1993). Autonomy as a moderator of the relationships between the big five personality dimensions and job performance. *Journal of Applied Psychology, 78,* 111–118.

15. See Note 14.

16. George, J. M., & Brief, A. P. (1992). Feeling good—doing good: A conceptual analysis of the mood at work-organizational spontaneity relationships. *Psychological Bulletin, 112,* 310–329.

17. Isen, A. M., & Baron, R. A. (1992). Positive affect as a factor in organizational behavior. In B. M. Staw & L. L. Cummings (Eds.), *Research in organizational behavior* (Vol. 13, pp. 1–54). Greenwich, CT: JAI Press.

18. Staw, B. M., & Barsade, S. G. (1993). Affect and managerial performance: A test of the sadder-but-wiser vs. happier-and-smarter hypotheses. *Administrative Science Quarterly, 38,* 304–331.

19. George, J. M. (1990). Personality, affect, and behavior in groups. *Journal of Applied Psychology, 75,* 107–116.

20. Friedman, M., & Rosenman, R. H. (1974). *Type A behavior and your heart.* New York: Knopf.

21. Lee, C., Ashford, S. J., & Jamieson, L. F. (1993). The effects of Type A behavior dimensions and optimism on coping strategy, health, and performance. *Journal of Organizational Behavior, 14,* 143–157.

22. Schauabroeck, J., Ganster, D. C., & Kemmerer, B. E. (1994). Job complexity, Type A: behavior, and cardiovascular disorder: A prospective study. *Academy of Management Journal, 37,* 426–439.

23. Glass, D. C. (1977). *Behavior patterns, stress, and coronary disease.* Hillsdale, NJ: Erlbaum.

24. Holmes, D. S., McGilley, B. M., & Houston, B. K. (1984).

Task-related arousal of Type A and Type B persons: Level of challenge and response specificity. *Journal of Personality and Social Psychology, 46,* 1322–1327.

25. Jamal, M., & Baba, V. V. (1991). Type A behavior, its prevalence and consequences among women nurse: An empirical examination. *Human Relations, 44,* 1213–1228.

26. Lee, M., & Kanungo, R. (1984). *Management of work and personal life.* New York: Praeger.

27. Berman, M., Gladue, B., & Taylor, S. (1993). The effects of hormones, Type A behavior pattern and provocation on aggression in men. *Motivation and Emotion, 17,* 125–138.

28. Baron, R. A. (1989). Personality and organizational conflict: Effects of the Type A behavior pattern and self-monitoring. *Organizational Behavior and Human Decisions Processes, 44,* 281–297.

29. Baron, R. A. , & Neuman, J. H. (Under review). Workplace violence and workplace aggression: Evidence on their relative frequency and potential causes.

30. Lyness, S. A. (1993). Predictors of differences between Type A and B individuals in heart rate and blood pressure reactivity. *Psychological Bulletin, 114,* 266–295.

31. Bateman, T. S., & Crant, J. M. (1993). The proactive component of organizational behavior. *Journal of Organizational Behavior, 14,* 103–118.

32. Crant, J. M. (1995). The proactive personality scale and objective job performance among real estate agents. *Journal of Applied Psychology, 60,* 532–537.

33. Sherman, S. (1995, December 11). Wanted: Company change agents. *Fortune,* 197–198.

34. Wood, R., Bandura, A., & Bailey, T. (1990). Mechanisms governing organizational performance in complex decision-making environments. *Organizational Behavior and Human Decision Processes, 46,* 181–201.

35. Kanger, R., & Kanfer, F. H. (1991). Goals and self-regulation: Applications of theory to work settings. *Advances in Motivation and Achievement, 7,* 287–326.

36. Gist, M. E., & Mitchell, T. R. (1992). Self-efficacy: A theoretical analysis of its determinants and malleability. *Academy of Management Review*, *17*, 183–211.

37. Mitchell, T. R., Hopper, H., Daniels, D., George-Falvy, J., & James, L. R. (1994). Predicting self-efficacy and performance during skill acquisition. *Journal of Applied Psychology*, *79*, 506–517.

38. Lord, R. G., & Maher, K. J. (1991). Cognitive theory in industrial and organizational psychology. In M. D. Dunnette & L. M. Hough (Eds.), *Handbook of industrial and organizational psychology* (Vol. 2, pp. 1–62). Palo Alto, CA: Consulting Psychologists Press.

39. Eden, D., & Aviram, A. (1993). Self-efficacy training to speed reemployment: Helping people to help themselves. *Journal of Applied Psychology*, *78*, 352–360.

40. Shamir, B. (1986). Self-esteem and the psychological impact of unemployment. *Social Psychology Quarterly*, *49*, 61–72.

41. Snyder, M. (1987). *Public appearance/private realities: The psychology of self-monitoring.* San Francisco: Freeman.

42. Caldwell, D. F., & O'Reilly, C. A., III (1982). Boundary spanning and individual performance: The impact of self-monitoring. *Journal of Applied Psychology*, *67*, 124–127.

43. Kilduff, M., & Day, D. V. (1994). Do chameleons get ahead? The effects of self-monitoring on managerial careers. *Academy of Management Journal*, *37*, 1047–1060.

44. Rosenbaum, J. E. (1979). Tournament mobility: Career patterns in a corporation. *Administrative Science Quarterly*, *24*, 220–241.

45. Sellers, P. (1996, January 15). What exactly is charisma? *Fortune*, 68–72, 74–75.

46. Scandura, T. A. (1992). Mentorship and career mobility: An empirical investigation. *Journal of Organizational Behavior*, *13*, 169–174.

47. Turban, D. B., & Dougherty, T. W. (1994). Role of protégé personality in receipt of mentoring and career success. *Academy of Management Journal*, *67*, 688–702.

48. Friedman, H. S., & Miller-Herringer, T. (1991). Nonverbal display of emotion in public and private: Self-monitoring, personality, and expressive cues. *Journal of Personality and Social Psychology*, *62*, 766–775.

49. Jamieson, D. W., Lydon, J. E., & Zanna, M. P. (1987). Attitude and activity preference similarity: Different bases of interpersonal attraction for low and high self-monitors. *Journal of Personality and Social Psychology*, *53*, 1052–1060.

50. Christie, R., & Geis, F. L. (1970). *Studies in Machiavellianism.* New York: Academic Press.

51. Schultz, C. J., II (1993). Situational and dispositional predictors of performance: A test of the hypothesized Machiavellianism × structure interaction among sales persons. *Journal of Applied Social Psychology*, *23*, 478–498.

52. McClelland, D. C. (1985). *Human motivation.* Glenview, IL: Scott, Foresman.

53. Turban, D. B., & Keon, T. L. (1993). Organizational attractiveness: An interactionist perspective. *Journal of Applied Psychology*, *78*, 184–193.

54. McClelland, D. C. (1977). Entrepreneurship and management in the years ahead. In C. A. Bramletter (Ed.), *The individual and the future of organizations* (pp. 12–29). Atlanta: Georgia State University.

55. Miller, D., & Droge, C. (1986). Psychological and traditional determinants of structure. *Administrative Science Quarterly*, *31*, 539–560.

56. McClelland, D. C. (1961). *The achieving society.* Princeton, NJ: Van Nostrand.

57. Lynn, R. (1991). *The secret of the miracle economy.* London: SAU.

58. Furnham, A., Kirkcaldy, B. D., & Lynn, R. (1994). National attitudes to competitiveness, money, and work among young people: First, second, and third world differences. *Human Relations*, *47*, 119–132.

59. de Vos, G. (1968). Achievement and innovation in culture and personality. In E. Norbeck, D. Price-Williams, & W. McCord (Eds.), *The study of personality: An interdisciplinary appraisal* (pp. 434–478). New York: Holt, Rinehart, and Winston.

60. Imai, M. (1986). *Kaizen: The key to Japan's competitive success.* New York: McGraw-Hill.

61. Holpp, L. (1989, October). Achievement motivation and kaizen. *Training and Development Journal*, pp. 53–63.

62. McClelland, D. C., & Boyatzis, R. E. (1982). Leadership motive pattern and long-term success in management. *Journal of Applied Psychology*, *67*, 737–743.

63. Guthrie, J. P., Ash, R. A., & Bandapudi, V. (1995). Additional validity evidence for a measure of *morningness.* *Journal of Applied Psychology*, *80*, 186–190.

64. Fierman, J. (1995, August 21). It's 2 A.M., Let's go to work. *Fortune*, pp. 82–86.

65. Totterdell, P., Spelten, E., Smith, L., Barton, J., & Folkard, S. (1995). Recovery from work shifts: How long does it take? *Journal of Applied Psychology*, *80*, 43–57.

66. See Note 63.

67. Wallace, B. (1993). Day persons, night persons, and variability in hypnotic susceptibility. *Journal of Personality and Social Psychology*, *64*, 827–833.

68. Flynn, J. R. (1987). Massive IQ gains in 14 nations: What IQ tests really measure. *Psychological Bulletin*, *101*, 171–191.

69. Sternberg, R. J. (1986). *Intelligence applied.* New York: Harcourt Brace Jovanovich.

70. Goleman, D. (1995) *Emotional intelligence.* New York: Bantam Doubleday

71. Farnham, A. (1996, January 15). Are you smart enough to keep your job? *Fortune*, pp. 34–37, 40, 42, 46, 48.

72. Reed, T. E., & Jensen, A. R. (in press). Conduction velocity in a brain nerve pathway of normal adults correlates with intelligence level. *Intelligence.*

73. Baddeley, A. (1990). *Human memory: Theory and practice.* Boston: Allyn & Bacon.

74. Smith, L. (1995, April 17). Memory: Why you're losing it, how to save it. *Fortune*, pp. 182–192.

75. Hultsch, D. F., & Dixon, R. A. (1990). Learning and memory in aging. In J. E. Birrens & K. W. Schaie (Eds.), *Handbook of the psychology of aging* (3rd ed., pp. 359–374). San Diego: Academic Press.

76. See Note 52.

CHAPTER 5

Preview Case Source

Case, J. (1995, October). 10 commandments of hypergrowth. *Inc.*, pp. 33–34, 36, 39–40, 42, 44.

Chapter Notes

1. Kanfer, R. (1990). Motivational theory and industrial and organizational psychology. In M. D. Dunnette & L. M. Hough (Eds.), *Handbook of industrial and organizational psychology* (2nd ed., Vol. 1, pp. 75–170). Palo Alto, CA: Consulting Psychologists Press.

2. Blau, G. (1993). Operationalizing direction and level of effort and testing their relationships to individual job performance. *Organizational Behavior and Human Decision Processes*, *55*, 152–170.

3. Nord, W. R., Brief, A. P., Atieh, J. M., & Doherty, E. M., (1988). Work values and the conduct of organizational behavior. In B. M. Staw & L. L. Cummings (Eds.), *Research in organizational behavior* (Vol. 10, pp. 1–42). Greenwich, CT: JAI Press.

4. Work still a labor of love." (1981, April 20). *The Columbus Dispatch*, p. 1.

5. Maslow, A. H. (1970). *Motivation and personality* (2nd ed.). New York: Harper & Row.

6. Mudrack, P. E. (1992). 'Work' or 'leisure'? The Protestant work ethic and participation in an employee fitness program. *Journal of Organizational Behavior*, *13*, 81–88.

7. Restructuring the family diet. (1995, September). *World Traveler*, p. 92.

8. Miller, A., & Springen, K. (1988, October 31). Forget cash, give me the TV. *Newsweek*, p. 58.

9. Porter, L. W. (1961). A study of perceived need satisfaction in bottom and middle management jobs. *Journal of Applied Psychology*, *45*, 1–10.

10. Wahba, M. A., & Bridwell, L. G. (1976). Maslow reconsidered: A review of research on the need hierarchy theory.

Organizational Behavior and Human Performance, 15, 212–240.

11. Alderfer, C. P. (1972). *Existence, relatedness, and growth.* New York: Free Press.

12. Salancik, G. R., & Pfeffer, J. (1977). An examination of need-satisfaction models of job satisfaction. *Administrative Science Quarterly, 22,* 427–456.

13. Miller, A., & Bradburn, E. (1991, July 1). Shape up—or else! *Newsweek,* pp. 42–43.

14. Tully, S. (1995, June 12). America's healthiest companies. *Fortune,* pp. 98–100, 104, 106.

15. Cronin, M. P. (1993, September). Easing workers' savings woes. *Inc.,* p. 29.

16. Leana, C. R., & Feldman, D. C. (1992). *Coping with job loss.* New York: Lexington Books.

17. Schwartz, E. L. (1991, June 17). Hot dogs, roller coasters, and complaints. *Business Week,* p. 27.

18. Jaffe, C. A. (1990, January). Management by fun. *Nation's Business,* pp. 58–60.

19. Gunsch, D. (1991). Award programs at work. *Personnel Journal, 23*(4), 85–89.

20. Miller, A., & Springen, K. (1988, October 31). Forget cash, give me the TV. *Newsweek,* p. 58.

21. Shepherd, M. D. (1993, February). Staff motivation. *U.S. Pharmacist,* pp. 82, 85, 89–93. (quote, p. 91)

22. Austin, N. K. (1994, March). Why sabbaticals make sense. *Working Woman,* pp. 19, 22, 24.

23. See Note 22 (quote p. 22).

24. See Note 22 (quote p. 22).

25. See Note 22 (quote p. 24).

26. Wood, R. A., & Locke, E. A. (1990). Goal setting and strategy effects on complex tasks. In B. M. Staw & L. L. Cummings (Eds.), *Research in organizational behavior* (Vol. 12, pp. 73–110). Greenwich, CT: JAI Press.

27. Locke, E. A., & Latham, G. P. (1990). *A theory of goal setting and task performance.* Englewood Cliffs, NJ: Prentice-Hall.

28. Mento, A. J., Locke, E. A., & Klein, H. J. (1992). Relationship of goal level to

valence and instrumentality. *Journal of Applied Psychology, 77,* 395–405.

29. Wright, P. M., O'Leary-Kelly, A. M., Cortinak, J. M., Klein, H. J., & Hollenbeck, J. R. (1994). On the meaning and measurement of goal commitment. *Journal of Applied Psychology, 79,* 795–803.

30. Klein, H. J. (1991). Further evidence on the relationship between goal setting and expectancy theories. *Organizational Behavior and Human Decision Processes, 49,* 230–257.

31. Harrison, D. A., & Liska, L. Z. (1994). Promoting regular exercise in organizational fitness programs: Health-related differences in motivational building blocks. *Personnel Psychology, 47,* 47–71.

32. Gellatly, I. R., & Meyer, J. P. (1992). The effects of goal difficulty on physiological arousal, cognition, and task performance. *Journal of Applied Psychology, 77,* 694-704.

33. Wright, P. M. (1992). An examination of the relationships among monetary incentives, goal level, goal commitment, and performance. *Journal of Management, 18,* 677–693.

34. Earley, P. C., & Litucy, T. R. (1991). Delineating goal and efficacy effects: A test of three models. *Journal of Applied Psychology, 76,* 81–98.

35. Latham, G. P., & Lee, T. W. (1986). Goal setting. In E. A. Locke (Ed.), *Generalizing from laboratory to field settings* (pp.100–117). Lexington, MA: Lexington Books.

36. Latham, G., & Baldes, J. (1975). The practical significance of Locke's theory of goal setting. *Journal of Applied Psychology, 60,* 122–124.

37. Locke, E. A., & Latham, G. P. (1984). *Goal setting: A motivational technique that works!* Englewood Cliffs, NJ: Prentice-Hall.

38. Wright, P. M., Hollenbeck, J. R., Wolf, S., & McMahan, G. C. (1995). The effects of varying goal difficulty operationalizations on goal setting outcomes and processes. *Organizational Behavior and Human Decision Processes, 61,* 28–43.

39. Bernstein, A. (1991, April 29). How to motivate workers: Don't watch 'em. *Business Week,* p. 56.

40. Stedry, A. C., & Kay, E. (1964). *The effects of goal difficulty on task performance.* General Electric Company, Behavioral Research Service.

41. Latham, G. P., Erez, M., & Locke, E. A. (1988). Resolving scientific disputes by the joint design of crucial experiments by the antagonists: Application to the Erez-Latham dispute regarding participation in goal setting. *Journal of Applied Psychology, 73,* 753–772.

42. Pritchard, R. D., Jones, S. D., Roth, P. L., Stuebing, K. K., & Ekberg, S. E. (1988). Effects of group feedback, goal setting, and incentives on organizational productivity. *Journal of Applied Psychology, 73,* 337–358.

43. Kulik, C. T., & Ambrose, M. L. (1992). Personal and situational determinants of referent choice. *Academy of Management Review, 17,* 212–237.

44. Greenberg, J. (1987). A taxonomy of organizational justice theories. *Academy of Management Review, 12,* 9–22.

45. Adams, J. S. (1965). Inequity in social exchange. In L. Berkowitz (Ed.), *Advances in experimental social psychology* (Vol. 2, pp. 267–299). New York: Academic Press.

46. Greenberg, J. (1989). Cognitive re-evaluation of outcomes in response to underpayment inequity. *Academy of Management Journal, 32,* 174–184.

47. Harder, J. W. (1992). Play for pay: Effects of inequity in a pay-for-performance context. *Administrative Science Quarterly, 37,* 321–335.

48. Greenberg, J. (1990). Employee theft as a reaction to underpayment inequity: The hidden cost of pay cuts. *Journal of Applied Psychology, 75,* 561–658.

49. Martin, J. E., & Peterson, M. M. (1987). Two-tier wage structures: Implications for equity theory. *Academy of Management Journal, 30,* 297–315.

50. Ross, I. (1985, April 29). Employers win big on the move to two-tier contracts. *Fortune,* pp. 82–92.

51. See Note 50.

52. Lawler, E. E., III. (1967). Secrecy about management compensation: Are there hidden costs? *Organizational*

Behavior and Human Performance, 2, 182–189.

53. Greenberg, J. (1990). Looking fair vs. being fair: Managing impressions of organizational justice. In B. M. Staw & L. L. Cummings (Eds.), *Research in organizational behavior,* (Vol. 12, pp. 265–301). Greenwich, CT: JAI Press.

54. Schaubroeck, J., May, D. R., & Brown, F. W. (1994). Procedural justice explanations and employee reactions to economic hardship: A field experiment. *Journal of Applied Psychology, 79,* 455-460.

55. Vroom, V. H. (1964). *Work and motivation.* New York: Wiley.

56. Porter, L. W., & Lawler, E. E., III. (1968). *Managerial attitudes and performance.* Homewood, IL: Irwin.

57. Mitchell, T. R. (1983). Expectancy-value models in organizational psychology. In N. Feather (Ed.), *Expectancy, incentive, and action* (pp. 293–314). Hillsdale, NJ: Lawrence Erlbaum Associates.

58. "Flexible-benefit plans grow." (1989, March 21) *USA Today,* p. C1.

59. Zippo, M. (1982). Flexible benefits: Just the beginning. *Personnel Journal, 17*(4), 56–58.

60. Ehrenfeld, T. (1993, July). Cashing in. *Inc.,* pp. 69–70.

61. Schuster, J. R., & Zingheim, P. K. (1992). *The new pay: Linking employee and organizational performance.* New York: Lexington Books.

62. Fierman, J. (1994, June 13). The perilous new world of fair pay. *Fortune,* pp. 57, 59, 61, 63.

63. Perry, N. J. (1992, May 4). Talk about pay for performance! *Fortune,* p. 77.

64. Stern, J. M., & Stewart, G. B., III. (1993, June). Pay for performance: Only the theory is easy. *HRMagazine,* pp. 48–49.

65. Griffin, R. W., & McMahan, G. C. (1994). Motivation through job design. In J. Greenberg (Ed.), *Organizational behavior: The state of the science* (pp. 23–44). Hillsdale, NJ: Lawrence Erlbaum Associates.

66. Rigdon, J. E. (1992, May 26). Using lateral moves to spur employees. *Wall Street Journal,* pp. B1, B9.

67. Campion, M. A., & McClelland, C. L. (1991). Interdisciplinary examination of the costs and benefits of en-

larged jobs: A job design quasi-experiment. *Journal of Applied Psychology, 76*, 186–198.

68. Campion, M. A., & McClelland, C. L. (1993). Follow-up and extension of the interdisciplinary costs and benefits of enlarged jobs. *Journal of Applied Psychology, 78*, 339–351.

69. Byrne, J. A., Bongiorno, L., & Grover, R. (1994, April 25). That eye-popping executive pay: Is anybody worth this much? *Business Week*, pp. 52–56, 58.

70. Crystal, G. S. (1992). *In search of excess: The overcompensation of American executives*. New York: W. W. Norton.

71. Minkin, B. H. (1995). *Future in sight*. New York: Macmillan.

72. Tully, S. (1993, November 1). Your paycheck gets exciting. *Fortune*, pp. 83–84, 88, 95, 98.

73. See Note 68 (quote pp. 95–98).

74. Gellenhammar, P. G. (1977). *People at work*. Reading, MA: Addison-Wesley.

75. Luthans, F., & Reif, W. E. (1974). Job enrichment: Long on theory, short on practice. *Organizational Dynamics, 2*(2), 30–43.

76. Steers, R. M., & Spencer, D. G. (1977). The role of achievement motivation in job design. *Journal of Applied Psychology, 62*, 472–479.

77. Goldman, R. B. (1976). *A work experiment: Six Americans in a Swedish plant*. New York: Ford Foundation.

78. Winpisinger, W. (1973, February). Job satisfaction: A union response. *AFL-CIO American Federationist*, pp. 8–10.

79. Hackman, J. R., & Oldham, G. R. (1980). *Work redesign*. Reading, MA: Addison-Wesley.

80. Graen, G. B., Scandura, T. A., & Graen, M. R. (1986). A field experimental test of the moderating effects of growth need strength on productivity. *Journal of Applied Psychology, 71*, 484–491.

81. Hackman, J. R., & Oldham, G. R. (1976). Motivation through the design of work: Test of a theory. *Organizational Behavior and Human Performance, 16*, 250–279.

82. Johns, G., Xie, J. L., & Fang, Y. (1992). Mediating and moderating effects in job de-sign. *Journal of Management, 18*, 657–676.

83. Orpen, C. (1979). The effects of job enrichment on employee satisfaction, motivation, involvement, and performance: A field experiment. *Human Relations, 32*, 189–217.

84. Ropp, K. (1987, October). Candid conversations. *Personnel Administrator*, p. 49.

85. Hackman, J. R. (1976). Work design. In J. R. Hackman & J. L. Suttle (Eds.), *Improving life at work* (pp. 96-162). Santa Monica, CA: Goodyear.

86. Callari, J. J. (1988, June). You can be a better motivator. *Traffic Management*, pp. 52–56.

87. Magnet, M. (1993, May 3). Good news for the service economy. *Fortune*, pp. 46–50, 52.

88. Finegan, J. (1993, July). People power. *Inc.*, pp. 62–63.

89. See Note 88.

Case in Point Source

Tully, S. (1994, November 14). Why to go for stretch targets. *Fortune*, pp. 145–146, 148, 150, 154, 158.

CHAPTER 6

Preview Case Source

Martinez, M. N. (1995, January). Equality effort sharpens bank's edge. *HRMagazine*, pp. 38–43.

Chapter Notes

1. Quarstein, V. A., McAfee, R. B., & Glassman, M. (1992). The situational occurrences theory of job satisfaction. *Human Relations, 45*, 859–873.

2. Hulin, C. L. (1991). Adaptation, persistence, and commitment in organizations. In M. D. Dunnette & L. M. Hough (Eds.), *Handbook of industrial and organizational psychology* (2nd ed.,Vol. 2, pp. 445–506). Palo Alto, CA: Consulting Psychologists Press.

3. Stone, E. F., Stone, D. L., & Dipboye, R. L. (1991). Stigmas in organizations: Race, handicaps, and physical unattractiveness. In K. Kelley (Ed.), *Issues, theory, and research in industrial/organizational psychology* (pp. 385–457). Amsterdam: Elsevier Science Publishers.

4. McGuire, W. J. (1985). Attitudes and attitude change. In G. Lindzey & E. Aronson (Eds.), *Handbook of social psy-chology* (3rd ed.,Vol. 2, pp. 233–346). New York: Random House.

5. Locke, E. A. (1976). The nature and causes of job satisfaction. In M. D. Dunnette (Ed.), *Handbook of industrial and organizational psychology* (pp. 1297–1350). Chicago: Rand McNally.

6. Thornburg, L. (1992, July). When violence hits business. *HRMagazine*, pp. 40–45.

7. Page, N. R., & Wiseman, R. L. (1993). Supervisory behavior and worker satisfaction in the United States, Mexico, and Spain. *Journal of Business Communication, 30*, 161–180.

8. Quinn, R. P., & Staines, G. L. (1979). *The 1977 quality of employment survey*. Ann Arbor, MI: Institute for Social Research.

9. Weaver, C. N. (1980). Job satisfaction in the United States in the 1970s. *Journal of Applied Psychology, 65*, 364–367.

10. Eichar, D. M., Brady, E. M., & Fortinsky, R. H. (1991). The job satisfaction of older workers. *Journal of Organizational Behavior, 12*, 609–620.

11. Bedian, A. G., Ferris, G. R., & Kacmar, K. M. (1992). Age, tenure, and job satisfaction: A tale of two perspectives. *Journal of Vocational Behavior, 40*, 33–48.

12. Lambert, S. L. (1991). The combined effect of job and family characteristics on the job satisfaction, job involvement, and intrinsic motivation of men and women workers. *Journal of Organizational Behavior, 12*, 341–363.

13. Staw, B. M., & Ross, J. (1985). Stability in the midst of change: A dispositional approach to job attitudes. *Journal of Applied Psychology, 70*, 56–77.

14. Gutek, B. A., & Winter, S. J. (1992). Consistency of job satisfaction across situations: Fact or framing artifact? *Journal of Vocational Behavior, 41*, 61–78.

15. Agho, A. O., Price, J. L., & Mueller, C. W. (1992). Discriminant validity of measures of job satisfaction, positive affectivity and negative affectivity. *Journal of Occupational and Organizational Psychology, 65*, 185–196.

16. Smith, P. C., Kendall, L. M., & Hulin, C. L. (1969). *The measurement of satisfaction in work and retirement*. Chicago: Rand McNally.

17. Weiss, D. J., Dawis, R. V., England, G. W., & Loftquist, L. H. (1967). *Manual for the Minnesota Satisfaction Questionnaire* (Minnesota Studies on Vocational Rehabilitation, Vol. 22). Minneapolis, MN: Industrial Relations Center, Work Adjustment Project, University of Minnesota.

18. Heneman, H. G., III, & Schwab, D. P. (1985). Pay satisfaction: Its multidimensional nature and measurement. *International Journal of Psychology, 20*, 129–141.

19. Judge, T. A., & Welbourne, T. M. (1994). A confirmatory investigation of the dimensionality of the Pay Satisfaction Questionnaire. *Journal of Applied Psychology, 79*, 461–466.

20. Hise, P. (1994, February). The motivational employee-satisfaction questionnaire. *Inc.*, pp. 73–75.

21. Sutton, R. I., & Callahan, A. L. (1987). The stigma of bankruptcy: Spoiled organizational image and its management. *Academy of Management Journal, 30*, 405–436.

22. Herzberg, F. (1966). *Work and the nature of man*. Cleveland: World.

23. Machungaws, P. D., & Schmitt, N. (1983). Work motivation in a developing country. *Journal of Applied Psychology, 68*, 31–42.

24. Landy, F. J. (1985) *Psychology of work behavior* (3rd ed.). Homewood, IL: Dorsey.

25. Magnet, M. (1993, May 3). Good news for the service economy. *Fortune*, pp. 46–50, 52.

26. Sundstrom, E. (1986), *Workplaces*. New York: Cambridge University Press.

27. Locke, E. A. (1984). Job satisfaction. In M. Gruenberg & T. Wall (Eds.), *Social psychology and organizational behavior* (pp. 93–117). London: Wiley.

28. McFarlin, D. B., & Rice, R. W. (1992). The role of facet importance as a moderator in job satisfaction processes. *Journal of Organizational Behavior, 13*, 41–54.

29. Dalton, D. R., & Todor, W. D. (1993). Turnover, transfer, absenteeism: An interdependent perspective. *Journal of Management, 19*, 193–219.

30. Porter, L. W., & Steers, R. M. (1973). Organizational

work and personal factors in employee turnover and absenteeism. *Psychological Bulletin, 80,* 151–176.

31. Tett, R. P., & Meyer, J. P. (1993). Job satisfaction, organizational commitment, turnover intention, and turnover: Path analyses based on meta-analytic findings. *Personnel Psychology, 46,* 259–293.

32. Mobley, W. H., Horner S. O., & Hollingsworth, A. T. (1978). An evaluation of precursors of hospital employee turnover. *Journal of Applied Psychology, 63,* 408–414.

33. Carsten, J. M., & Spector, P. E. (1987). Unemployment, job satisfaction, and employee turnover: A meta-analytic test of the Murchinsky model. *Journal of Applied Psychology, 72,* 374–381.

34. "No-Shows: A Costly Trend," (1993, August). *Executive Management Forum,* p. 3.

35. Iaffaldano, M. T., & Murchinsky, P. M. (1985). Job satisfaction and job performance: A meta-analysis. *Psychological Bulletin, 97,* 251–273.

36. Porter, L. W., & Lawler, E. E., III. (1968), *Managerial attitudes and performance.* Homewood, IL: Dorsey Press.

37. Vandenberg, R. J., & Lance, C. E. (1992). Examining the causal order of job satisfaction and organizational commitment. *Journal of Management, 18,* 153–167.

38. Becker, T. E., & Billings, R. S. (1993). Profiles of commitment: An empirical test. *Journal of Organizational Behavior, 14,* 177–190.

39. Reichers, A. E. (1985). A review and reconceptualization of organizational commitment. *Academy of Management Review, 10,* 465–476.

40. Becker, H. S. (1960). Notes on the concept of commitment. *American Journal of Sociology, 66,* 32–40.

41. Porter, L. W., Steers, R. M., Mowday, R. T., & Boulian, P. V. (1974). Organizational commitment, job satisfaction, and turnover among psychiatric technicians. *Journal of Applied Psychology, 59,* 603–609.

42. Mathieu, J. E., & Zajoc, D. M. (1990). A review and meta-analysis of the antecedents, correlates, and consequences of commitment. *Psychological Bulletin, 108,* 171–194.

43. Dunham, R. B., Grube, J. A., & Castañeda, M. B. (1994). Organizational commitment: The utility of an integrative definition. *Journal of Applied Psychology, 79,* 370–380.

44. Meyer, J. P., & Allen, N. J. (1991). A three-component conceptualization of organizational commitment. *Human Resource Management Review, 1,* 61–89.

45. Hackett, R. D., Boycio, P., & Hausdorf, P. A. (1994). Further assessments of Meyer and Allen's (1991) three-component model of organizational commitment. *Journal of Applied Psychology, 79,* 15–23.

46. Whitener, E. M., & Waltz, P. M. (1993). Exchange theory determinants of affective and continuance commitment and turnover. *Journal of Vocational Behavior, 42,* 265–281.

47. Randall, D. M. (1990). The consequences of organizational commitment: A methodological investigation. *Journal of Organizational Behavior, 11,* 361–378.

48. Somers, M. J. (1995). Organizational commitment, turnover and absenteeism: An examination of direct and interaction effects. *Journal of Organizational Behavior, 16,* 49–58.

49. Lee, T. W., Ashford, S. J., Walsh, J. P., & Mowday, R. T. (1992). Commitment propensity, organizational commitment, and voluntary turnover: A longitudinal study of organizational entry processes. *Journal of Management, 18,* 15–32.

50. Randall, D. M., Fedor, D. P., & Longenecker, C. O. (1990). The behavioral expression of organizational commitment. *Journal of Vocational Behavior, 36,* 210–224.

51. Van Dyne, L., Graham, J. W., & Dienesch, R. M. (1994). Organizational citizenship behavior: Construct redefinition, measurement, and validation. *Academy of Management Journal, 37,* 765–802.

52. Romzek, B. S. (1989). Personal consequences of employee commitment. *Academy of Management Journal, 39,* 641–661.

53. Caldwell, D. F., Chatman, J. A., & O'Reilly, C. A. (1990). Building organizational commitment: A multifirm study. *Journal of Occupational Psychology, 63,* 245–261.

54. Curry, J. P., Wakefield, D. S., Price, J. L., & Mueller, C. W. (1986). On the causal ordering of job satisfaction and organizational commitment. *Academy of Management Journal, 29,* 847–858.

55. Rosen, R. H. (1991). *The healthy company.* Los Angeles: Jeremy P. Tarcher. (quote, pp. 71–72)

56. Florkowski, G. W., & Schuster, M H. (1992). Support for profit sharing and organizational commitment: A path analysis. *Human Relations, 45,* 507–523.

57. Graham, J. W., & Havlick, W. C. (1994). *Mission statements: A guide to the corporate and nonprofit sectors.* New York: Garland.

58. Vancouver, J. B., Milsap, R. E., & Peters, P. A. (1994). Multilevel analysis of organizational goal congruence. *Journal of Applied Psychology, 79,* 666–679.

59. See Note 39.

60. Stephan, W. G. (1985). Intergroup relations. In G. Lindzey & E. Aronson (Eds.), *Handbook of social psychology* (3rd ed., Vol. 2, pp. 599–658). New York: Random House.

61. Fernandez, J. P., & Barr, M. (1993). *The diversity advantage.* New York: Lexington Books.

62. Malone, M. S. (1993, July 18). Translating diversity into high-tech gains. *New York Times,* p. B2.

63. Yang, C. (1993, June 21). In any language, it's unfair: More immigrants are bringing bias charges against employers. *Business Week,* pp. 110–112.

64. Hawkins, C. (1993, June 28). Denny's: The stain that isn't coming out: Can a pact with the NAACP help it overcome charges of bias? *Business Week,* pp. 98–99.

65. Mason, J. C. (1993, July). Knocking on the glass ceiling. *Management Review,* p. 5.

66. Solomon, C. M. (1992, July). Keeping hate out of the workplace. *Personnel Journal,* 30–36.

67. Ornstein, S. L., Sankowsky, D. (1994). Overcoming stereotyping and prejudice: A framework and suggestions for learning from groupist comments in the classroom. *Journal of*
Management Education, 18, 80–90.

68. Boyett, J. H., & Conn, H. P. (1992). *Workplace 2000.* New York: Plume.

69. Overman, S. (1993, June). Myths hinder hiring of older workers. *HRMagazine,* pp. 51–52.

70. Hassell, B. L., & Perrewe, P. L. (1995). An examination of beliefs about older workers: Do stereotypes still exist? *Journal of Organizational Behavior, 16,* 457–468.

71. Stone, E. F., Stone, D. L., & Dipboye, R. L. (1991). Stigmas in organizations: Race, handicaps, and physical unattractiveness. In K. Kelley (Ed.), *Issues, theory, and research in industrial/organizational psychology* (pp. 385–457). Amsterdam: Elsevier Science Publishers.

72. Yang, C., & Forest, S. A. (1993, April 12). Business has to find a new meaning for "fairness": The Disabilities Act means some workers get special treatment. *Business Week,* p. 72.

73. See Note 72.

74. See Note 72.

75. Martinez, M. N. (1993, June). Recognizing sexual orientation is fair and not costly. *HRMagazine,* pp. 66–68, 70, 72.

76. Williamson, A. D. (1993, July–August). Is this the right time to come out? *Harvard Business Review,* pp. 18–20, 22, 24, 26, 28.

77. See Note 76.

78. See Note 76.

79. See Note 76.

80. Fernandez, J. P., & Barr, M. (1993). *The diversity advantage.* New York: Lexington Books.

81. Yang, C. (1993, June 21). In any language, it's unfair: More immigrants are bringing bias charges against employers. *Business Week,* pp. 110–112.

82. See Note 81 (quote, p. 111).

83. See Note 81.

84. Lander, M. (1992, June 8). Corporate women. *Business Week,* pp. 74, 76–78.

85. Steinberg, R., & Shapiro, S. (1982). Sex differences in personality traits of female and male master of business administration students. *Journal of Applied Psychology, 67,* 306–310.

86. Bilmoria, D., & Piderit, S. K. (1994). Toward committee

membership: Effects of sex-based bias. *Academy of Management Journal, 37,* 1453–1477.

87. Thomas, R. R., Jr. (1992). Managing diversity: A conceptual framework. In S. E. Jackson (Ed.), *Diversity in the workplace* (pp. 306–317). New York: Guilford Press.

88. Murray, K. (1993, August 1). The unfortunate side effects of "diversity training." *New York Times,* pp. E1, E3.

89. Gottfredson, L. S. (1992). Dilemmas in developing diversity programs. In S. E. Jackson (Ed.), *Diversity in the workplace* (pp. 279–305). New York: Guilford Press.

90. Carnevale, A. P., & Stone, S. C. (1995). *The American mosaic.* New York: McGraw-Hill.

91. Battaglia, B. (1992). Skills for managing multicultural teams. *Cultural Diversity at Work, 4,* 4–12.

92. Wright, P., Ferris, S. P., Hiller, J. S., & Kroll, M. (1995). Competitiveness through management of diversity: Effects of stock price valuation. *Academy of Management Journal, 38,* 272–287.

93. Gottfredson, L. S. (1992). Dilemmas in developing diversity programs. In S. E. Jackson (Ed.), *Diversity in the workplace* (pp. 279–305). New York: Guilford Press.

94. Sessa, V. I. (1992). Managing diversity at the Xerox Corporation: Balanced workforce goals and caucus groups. In S. E. Jackson (Ed.), *Diversity in the workplace* (pp. 37–64). New York: Guilford Press.

95. Walker, B. A., & Hanson, W. C. (1992). Valuing differences at Digital Equipment Corporation. In S. E. Jackson (Ed.), *Diversity in the workplace* (pp. 119–137). New York: Guilford Press.

96. See Note 93 (quote, p. 120).

97. Roberson, L., & Gutierrez, N. C. (1992). Beyond good faith: Management diversity at Pacific Bell. In S. E. Jackson (Ed.), *Diversity in the workplace* (pp. 65–88). New York: Guilford Press.

98. See Note 88.

99. See Note 89.

100. Gardenswartz, L. & Rowe, A. (1994). *The managing diversity survival guide.* Burr Ridge, IL: Irwin.

101. See Note 90.

102. Towers, Perrin. (1992). *Workforce 2000 today.* New York: Author.

103. See Note 99 (quote, p. 1.).

104. See Note 99.

105. See Note 90.

106. Rynes, S., & Rosen, B. (1995). A field survey of factors affecting the adoption and perceived success of diversity training. *Personnel Psychology, 48,* 247–270.

Case in Point Source

Phillips, N. (1994). *Managing international teams.* Burr Ridge, IL: Irwin.

CHAPTER 7

Preview Case Source

Sellers, P. (1995). So you fail. Now bounce back! *Fortune,* May 1, 48–51, 54–55, 58, 62, 64, 66.

Chapter Notes

1. Quick, J. C., Murphy, L. R., & Hurrell, J. J., Jr. (1992). *Stress and well-being at work.* Washington, DC: American Psychological Association

2. Kahn, R. L., & Byosiere, P. (1992). Stress in organizations. In M. D. Dunnette & L. M. Hough (Eds.), *Handbook of industrial and organizational psychology* (2nd ed., Vol. 3., pp. 571–650). Palo Alto, CA: Consulting Psychologists Press.

3. Wanous, J. P. (1992). *Organizational entry: Recruitment, selection, orientation, and socialization.* Reading, MA: Addison-Wesley.

4. Kram, K. E. (1985). *Mentoring at work: Development relationships in organizational life.* Glenview, IL: Scott-Foresman.

5. Ragins, B. R., & Cotton, J. L. (1993). Gender and willingness to mentor in organizations. *Journal of Management, 34,* 939–951.

6. Van Maanen, J., & Schein, E. H. (1991). Toward a theory of organizational socialization. In B. M. Staw (Ed.), *Research in organizational behavior* (Vol. 12, pp. 209–264). Greenwich, CT: JAI Press.

7. Feldman, J. C. (1981). The multiple socialization of organization members. *Academy of Management Review, 6,* 309–318.

8. Fisher, C. D. (1986). Organizational socialization: An integrative review. In G. R. Ferris & K. M. Rowland (Eds.), *Research in personnel and human resources management* (Vol. 4, pp. 101–145). Greenwich, CT: JAI Press.

9. Wanous, J. P., Poland, T. D., Premark, S. L., & Davis, K. S. (1992). The effects of met expectations on newcomer attitudes and behavior: A review and meta-analysis. *Journal of Applied Psychology, 77,* 288–297.

10. Meglino, B. M., DeNisi, A. S., Youngblood, S. A., & Williams, K. J. (1988). Effects of realistic job previews: A comparison using an enhancement and a reduction preview. *Journal of Applied Psychology, 73,* 259–266.

11. Morrison, R. F., & Brantner, T. M. (1992). What enhances or inhibits learning a new job? A basic career issue. *Journal of Applied Psychology, 77,* 926–940.

12. See Note 3.

13. Whitely, W., Dougherty, T. M., & Dreher, G. F. (1991). Relationship of career mentoring and socioeconomic origin to managers' and professionals' early career progress. *Academy of Management Journal, 34,* 331–351.

14. Olian, J., Carroll, S., Giannantonio, D., & Feren, D. (1988). What do protégés look for in a mentor? Results of three experimental studies. *Journal of Vocational Behavior, 33,* 13–37.

15. Turban, D. B., & Dougherty, T. M. (1994). Role of protégé personality in receipt of mentoring and career success. *Academy of Management Journal, 37,* 688–702.

16. Fagenson, E. A. (1992). Mentoring—who needs it? A comparison of protégés' and nonprotégés' need for power, achievement, affiliation, and autonomy. *Journal of Vocational Behavior, 41,* 48–60.

17. Tepper, B. J. (1995). Upward maintenance tactics in supervisory mentoring and nonmentoring relationships. *Academy of Management Journal, 38,* 1191–1205.

18. Kram, K. E. (1983). Phases of the mentor relationship. *Academy of Management Journal, 26,* 608–625.

19. Baron, R. A., & Byrne, D. (In press). *Social psychology* (8th ed.). Boston: Allyn & Bacon.

20. Noe, R. A. (1988). Women and mentoring: A review and research agenda. *Academy of Management Review, 13,* 65–78.

21. Thomas, D. A. (1993). Racial dynamics in cross-race developmental relationships. *Administrative Science Quarterly, 38,* 169–194.

22. Labich, K. (1995, February 20). Kissing off corporate America. *Fortune,* pp. 44–47, 50, 52.

23. Pierce, C. A. (1995). Attraction in the workplace: An examination of antecedents and consequences of organizational romance. Unpublished Doctoral Dissertation, SUNY - Albany.

24. See Note 22.

25. Holland, J. L. (1985). *Making vocational choices: A theory of vocational personalities and work environments.* Englewood Cliffs, NJ: Prentice-Hall.

26. Meier, S. T. (1991). Vocational behavior, 1988–1990: Vocational choice, decision-making, career development interventions, and assessment. *Journal of Vocational Behavior, 39,* 131–181.

27. Chatman, J. A. (1991). Matching people and organizations: Selection and socialization in public accounting firms. *Administrative Science Quarterly, 36,* 459–484.

28. Judge, T. A., & Bretz, R. D., Jr. (1992). Effects of work values on job choice decisions. *Journal of Applied Psychology, 77,* 261–271.

29. Moss, M. K., & Frieze, I. H. (1993). Job preferences in the anticipatory socialization phase: A comparison of two matching models. *Journal of Vocational Behavior, 42,* 282–297.

30. Cascio, W. F. (1995). *Managing human resources: Productivity, quality of work life, profits* (4th ed.). New York: McGraw-Hill.

31. Stewart, T. A. (1995, March 20). Planning a career in a world without managers. *Fortune,* pp. 72–74, 75, 77, 79.

32. "The 25 hottest careers." (1993, July 6). *Working Woman,* pp. 41–51.

33. Spector, P. E. (1996). *Industrial and organizational psychology: Research and practice.* New York: John Wiley

34. Campion, M. A., Cheraskin, L., & Stevens, M. J. (1994). Career-related antecedents and outcomes of job rotation. *Academy of Management Journal, 37,* 1518–1542.

35. Goldstein, L. L. (21986). *Training in organizations; needs assessment, development, and evaluation* (2nd ed.). Monterey, CA: Brooks/Cole.

36. See Note 34.

37. Fingleton, E. (1995, March 20). Jobs for life: Why Japan won't give them up. *Fortune,* pp. 119–123, 125

38. Tharenou, P., Latimer, S., & Conroy, D. (1994). How do you make it to the top? An examination of influences on women's and men's managerial advancement. *Academy of Management Journal, 37,* 899–931.

39. Van Velsor, E., & Hughes, M. W. (1990). *Gender differences in the development of managers: How women managers learn from experience.* Technical report no. 145, Center for Creative Leadership, Greensboro, NC.

40. Ohlott, P. J., Ruderman, M. N., & McCauley, C. D. (1994). Gender differences in managers' development job experiences. *Academy of Management Journal, 37,* 46–67.

41. See Note 40.

42. U.S. Department of Labor (1991). *A report on the glass ceiling initiative.* Washington, D.C.: U.S. Department of Labor.

43. Powell, G. N., & Butterfield, D. A. (1994). Investigating the "glass ceiling" phenomenon: An empirical study of actual promotions to top management. *Academy of Management Journal, 37,* 68–86.

44. See Note 40.

45. See Note 42.

46. Morris, B. (1995, September 18). Executive women confront midlife crisis. *Fortune,* pp. 60–62, 65, 68, 72, 74, 78, 80, 84, 86.

47. Levinson, D. J. (1986). A conception of adult development. *American Psychologist, 41,* 3–13.

48. Jones, M. (1995, April). Smart cookies. *Working Woman,* 50–54.

49. See Note 45.

50. See Note 1.

51. Northwestern National Life Insurance Company. (1991). *Employee burnout: America's newest epidemic.* Minneapolis, MN: Author.

52. Lazarus, R. S., & Folkman, S. (1984). *Stress, appraisal, and coping.* New York: Springer-Verlag.

53. Evans, G. W., & Carrere, S. (1991). Traffic congestion, perceived control, and psychophysiological stress among urban bus drivers. *Journal of Applied Psychology, 76,* 658–663.

54. Selye, H. (1976). *Stress in health and disease.* Boston: Butterworths.

55. Shaw, J. B., & Riskind, J. H. (1983). Predicting job stress using data from the Position Analysis Questionnaire. *Journal of Applied Psychology, 68,* 253–261.

56. Williams, K. J., Suls, J., Alliger, G. M., Learner, S.M., & Choie, K. W. (1991). Multiple role juggling and daily mood states in working mothers: An experience sampling study. *Journal of Applied Psychology, 76,* 664–674.

57. Williams, K. J., & Alliger, G. M. (1994). Role stressors, mood spillover, and perceptions of work-family conflict in employed parents. *Academy of Management Journal, 37,* 837–868.

58. Newton, T. J., & Keenan, A. (1987). Role stress reexamined: An investigation of role stress predictors. *Organizational Behavior and Human Decision Processes, 40,* 346–368.

59. Thomas, L. T., & Ganster, D. C. (1995). Impact of family-supportive work variables on work-family conflict and strain: A control perspective. *Journal of Applied Psychology, 80,* 6–15.

60. McGrath, J. E. (1987). Stress and behavior in organizations. In M.D. Dunnette (Ed.), *Handbook of industrial and organizational psychology* (pp. 1351–1398). Chicago: Rand McNally.

61. Peterson, M. F., Smith, P. B., et al. (1995). Role conflict, ambiguity, and overload: A 21-nation study. *Academy of Management Journal, 38,* 429–452.

62. Hofstede, G. (1994). Management scientists are human. *Management Science, 40,* 4–13.

63. French, J. R. P., & Caplan, R. D. (1972). Organizational stress and individual strain. In A. J. Morrow (Ed.), *The failure of success* (pp. 68–84). New York: Amacom.

64. McClean, A. A. (1980). *Work stress.* Reading, MA: Addison-Wesley.

65. Doby, V. J., & Caplan, R. D. (1995). Organizational stress as threat to reputation: Effects on anxiety at work and at home. *Academy of Management Journal, 38,* 1105–1123.

66. Segal, T., Kelly, K., & Solomon, A. (1992, November 9). Getting serious about sexual harassment. *Business Week,* pp. 78, 82.

67. Gutek, B., Nakamura, C. Y., Gadart, M., Handschumacher, J. W., & Russell, D. (1980). Sexuality and the workplace. *Basic and Applied Social Psychology, 1,* 255–265.

68. Baron, R. A. (1994). The physical environment or work settings. Effects on task performance, interpersonal relations, and job satisfaction. In B. M. Staw & L. L. Cummings (Eds.), *Research in organizational behavior,* (Vol. 16, pp. 1–46). Greenwich, CT: JAI Press.

69. Sundstrom, E., Town, J. P., Rice, R. W., Osborn, D. P., & Brill, M. (1994). Office noise, satisfaction, and performance. *Environment and Behavior, 26,* 195–222.

70. Loeb, M. (1996, January 15). What to do if you get fired. *Fortune,* 77–78.

71. See Note 59.

72. Nelson, D. L., & Sutton, C. (1990). Chronic work stress and coping: A longitudinal study and suggested new directions. *Academy of Management Journal, 33,* 659–689.

73. Holmes, T. H., & Rahe, R. H. (1967). Social readjustment rating scale. *Journal of Psychosomatic Research, 11,* 213–218.

74. Holmes, T. H., & Masuda, M. (1974). Life change and illness susceptibility. In B. S. Dohrenwend & B. P. Dohrenwend (Eds.), *Stressful life events: Their nature and effects* (pp. 45–72). New York: Wiley.

75. Lazarus, R. S., & Folkman, S. (1984). *Stress, appraisal, and coping.* New York: Springer-Verlag.

76. Bhagat, R. S., McQuaid, S. J., Lindholm, H., & Segovis, J. (1985). Total life stress: A multi-method validation of the construct and its effects on organizationally valued outcomes and withdrawal behaviors. *Journal of Applied Psychology, 70,* 202–214.

77. See Note 59.

78. Sullivan, S. E., & Bhagat, R. S. (1992). Organizational stress, job satisfaction, and job performance: Where do we go from here? *Journal of Management, 18,* 353–374.

79. Motowidlo, S. J., Packard, H. J., & Manning, M. R. (1986). Occupational stress: Its causes and consequences for job performance. *Journal of Applied Psychology, 71,* 618–629.

80. Baumeister, R. F., & Scher, S. J. (1988). Self-defeating behavior patterns among normal individuals: Review and analysis of common self-destructive tendencies. *Psychological Bulletin, 104,* 3–22.

81. Golombiewski, R. T., Ninzenrider, R. F., & Stevenson, J. G. (1986). *Stress in organizations: Toward a phase model of burnout.* New York: Praeger.

82. Pines, A. M., Aronson, E., & Kafru, D. (1981). *Burn out: From tedium to personal growth.* New York: W. H. Freeman.

83. Gaines, J., & Jermier, J. M. (1983). Emotional exhaustion in high stress organizations. *Academy of Management Journal, 31,* 567–586.

84. Stelzer, J., & Numerof, R. E. (1986). Supervisory leadership and subordinate burnout. *Academy of Management Journal, 31,* 439–446.

85. Frese, M. (1985). Stress at work and psychosomatic complaints: A causal interpretation. *Journal of Applied Psychology, 70,* 214–238.

86. Cohen, S., & Williamson, G. (1991). Stress and infectious disease in humans. *Psychological Bulletin, 109,* 5–24.

87. Kirmeyer, S. L., & Biggers, K. (1988). Environmental demand and demand engendered behavior: An observational analysis of the Type A pattern. *Journal of Personality and Social Psychology, 54,* 997–1005.

88. Schaubroeck, J., Ganster, D. C., & Kemmerer, B. E. (1994). Job complexity, "type A" behavior, and cardiovascular disorder: A prospective study. *Academy of Management Journal, 37,* 426–439.

89. Brown, J. D. (1991). Staying fit and staying well: Physical fitness as a moderator of life stress. *Journal of Personality and Social Psychology, 60,* 555–561.

90. Sobel, D. (1993, May). Outsmarting stress. *Working woman*, pp. 83–84, 101.

91. See Note 89.

92. Benson, H. (1975). *The relaxation response*. New York: William Morrow.

93. Roskies, E. (1987). *Stress management for the healthy Type A*. New York: Guilford.

94. See Note 58.

95. Fierman, J. (1995, February 6). Winning ideas from maverick managers. *Fortune*, pp. 66–68, 70, 74, 78.

96. Reynolds, S., & Shapiro, D. A. (1991). Stress reduction in transition: Conceptual problems in the design, implementation, and evaluation of worksite stress management inventories. *Human Relations, 44*, 717–733.

97. Quick, J. C., & Quick, J. D. (1984). *Organizational stress and preventive management*. New York: McGraw-Hill.

98. Philips, S. B., & Mushinki, M. H. (1992). Configuring an employee assistance program to fit the corporation's structure: One company's design. In U. C. Quick, L. R. Murphy, & J. J. Hurrell, Jr. (1992). *Stress and well-being at work* (pp. 317–3208). Washington, DC: American Psychological Association.

CHAPTER 8

Preview Case Source

Selz, M. (1994, January 11). Testing self-managed teams, entrepreneur hopes to lose job. *Wall Street Journal*, pp. B1–B2.

Chapter Notes

1. Cartwright, D., & Zander, A. (1968). Origins of group dynamics. In D. Cartwright & A. Zander (Eds.), *Group dynamics: Research and theory* (pp. 3–21). New York: Harper & Row.

2. Bettenhausen, K. L. (1991). Five years of groups research: What we have learned and what needs to be addressed. *Journal of Management, 17*, 345–381.

3. Forsyth, D. L. (1983). *An introduction to group dynamics*. Monterey, CA: Brooks/Cole.

4. Long, S. (1984). Early integration in groups: "A group to join and a group to create." *Human Relations, 37*, 311–332.

5. Tuckman, B. W., & Jensen, M. A. (1977). Stages of small group development revisited. *Group and Organization Studies, 2*, 419–427.

6. Gersick, C. J. G. (1988). Time and transition in work teams: Toward a new model of group development. *Academy of Management Journal, 31*, 9–41.

7. Biddle, B. J. (1979). *Role theory: Expectations, identities, and behavior*. New York: Academic Press.

8. Jackson, S. E., & Schuler, R. S. (1985). A meta-analysis and conceptual critique of research on role ambiguity and role conflict in work settings. *Organizational Behavior and Human Decision Processes, 36*, 16–78.

9. Benne, K. D., & Sheats, P. (1948). Functional roles of group members. *Journal of Social Issues, 4*, 41–49.

10. Bales, R. F. (1980). *SYMLOG case study kit*. New York: Free Press.

11. Hackman, J. R. (1992). Group influences on individuals in organizations. In M. D. Dunnette & L. M. Hough (Eds.), *Handbook of industrial and organizational psychology* (2nd ed., Vol. 3, pp. 199–268). Palo Alto, CA: Consulting Psychologists Press.

12. Bettenhausen, K., & Murnighan, J. K. (1985). The emergence of norms in competitive decision-making groups. *Administrative Science Quarterly, 30*, 350–372.

13. Feldman, D. C. (1984). The development and enforcement of group norms. *Academy of Management Review, 9*, 47–53.

14. Wanous, J. P., Reichers, A. E., & Malik, S. D. (1984). Organizational socialization and group development: Toward an integrative perspective. *Academy of Management Review, 9*, 670–683.

15. Watson, T. J., Jr. (1990). *Father son & co.: My life at IBM and beyond*. New York: Bantam.

16. Wilson, S. (1978). *Informal groups: An introduction*. Englewood Cliffs, NJ: Prentice-Hall.

17. Greenberg, J. (1988). Equity and workplace status: A field experiment. *Journal of Applied Psychology, 73*, 606–613.

18. Stryker, S. & Macke, A. S. (1978). Status inconsistency and role conflict. In R. H. Turner, J. Coleman, & R. C. Fox (Eds.), *Annual review of sociology* (Vol. 4, pp. 57–90). Palo Alto, CA: Annual Reviews.

19. Jackson, L. A., & Grabski, S. V. (1988). Perceptions of fair pay and the gender wage gap. *Journal of Applied Social Psychology, 18*, 606–625.

20. Torrance, E. P. (1954). Some consequences of power differences on decision making in permanent and temporary three-man groups. *Research Studies: Washington State College, 22*, 130–140.

21. Greenberg, J. (1976). The role of seating position in group interaction: A review, with applications for group trainers. *Group and Organization Studies, 1*, 310–327.

22. Hare, A. P. (1976). *Handbook of small group research* (2nd ed). New York: Free Press.

23. Aronson, E., & Mills, J. (1959). The effects of severity of initiation on liking for a group. *Journal of Abnormal and Social Psychology, 59*, 177–181.

24. Long, S. (1984). Early integration in groups: "A group to join and a group to create." *Human Relations, 37*, 311–322.

25. Cartwright, D. (1968). The nature of group cohesiveness. In D. Cartwright & A. Zander (Eds.), *Group dynamics: Research and theory* (3rd ed., pp. 91–109). New York: Harper & Row.

26. George, J. M., & Bettenhausen, K. (1990). Understanding prosocial behavior, sales performance, and turnover: A group-level analysis in a service context. *Journal of Applied Psychology 75*, 698–709.

27. Shaw, M. E. (1981). *Group dynamics: The dynamics of small group behavior* (3rd ed.). New York: McGraw-Hill.

28. Janis, I. L. (1982). *Groupthink: Psychological studies of policy decisions and fiascoes* (2nd ed.). Boston: Houghton Mifflin.

29. Douglas, T. (1983). *Groups: Understanding people gathered together*. New York: Tavistock.

30. Geen, R. (1989). Alternative conceptualizations of social facilitation. In P. B. Paulus (Ed.), *Psychology of group influence* (2nd ed., pp. 15–51). Hillsdale, NJ: Lawrence Erlbaum Associates.

31. Zajonc, R. B. (1965). Social facilitation. *Science, 149*, 269–274.

32. Zajonc, R. B. (1980). Compresence. In P. B. Paulus (Ed.), *Psychology of group influence* (pp. 35–60). Hillsdale, NJ: Lawrence Erlbaum Associates.

33. Geen, R. B., Thomas, S. L., & Gammill, P. (1988). Effects of evaluation and coaction on state anxiety and anagram performance. *Personality and Individual Differences, 6*, 293–298.

34. Baron, R. S. (1986). Distraction/conflict theory: Progress and problems. In L. Berkowitz (Ed.), *Advances in experimental social psychology* (Vol. 19, pp. 1–40). New York: Academic Press.

35. Aiello, J. R., & Kolb, K. J. (1995). Electronic performance monitoring and social context: Impact on productivity and stress. *Journal of Applied Psychology, 80*, 339–353.

36. Aiello, J. R., & Svec, C. M. (1993). Computer monitoring of work performance: Extending the social facilitation framework to electronic presence. *Journal of Applied Social Psychology, 23*, 537–548.

37. Koelsch, F. (1995). *The infomedia revolution*. New York: McGraw-Hill.

38. See Note 37.

39. Band, W. A. (1994). *Touchstones*. New York: John Wiley & Sons.

40. Minkin, B. H. (1995). *Future insight*. New York: Macmillan.

41. See Note 40.

42. Watson, W. E., Kumar, K., & Michaelsen, K. K. (1993). Cultural diversity's impact on interaction process and performance: Comparing homogeneous and diverse task groups. *Academy of Management Journal, 36*, 590–602.

43. Steiner, I. D. (1972). *Group processes and productivity*. New York: Academic Press.

44. Shepperd, J. A. (1993). Productivity loss in performance groups: A motivation analysis. *Psychological Bulletin, 113*, 67–81.

45. Latané, B., Williams, K., & Harkins, S. (1979). Many hands make light the work: The causes and consequences of social loafing. *Journal of Personality and Social Psychology, 37*, 822–832.

46. Kravitz, D. A., & Martin, B. (1986). Ringelmann rediscovered: The original article. *Journal of Personality and Social Psychology, 50*, 936–941.

47. Karau, S. J., & Williams, K. D. (1993). Social loafing: A meta-analytic review and theoretical integration. *Journal of Personality and Social Psychology, 65,* 681–706.

48. Latané, B., & Nida, S. (1980). Social impact theory and group influence: A social engineering perspective. In P. B. Paulus (Ed.), *Psychology of group influence* (pp. 3–34). Hillsdale, NJ: Lawrence Erlbaum Associates.

49. Weldon, E., & Mustari, E. L. (1988). Felt dispensability in groups of coactors: The effects of shared responsibility and explicit anonymity on cognitive effort. *Organizational Behavior and Human Decision Processes, 41,* 330–351.

50. Earley, P. C. (1993). East meets West meets Mideast: Further explorations of collectivistic and individualistic work groups. *Academy of Management Journal, 36,* 19–348.

51. Nordstrom, R., Lorenzi, P., & Hall, R. V. (1990). A review of public posting of performance feedback in work settings. *Journal of Organizational Behavior Management, 11,* 101–123.

52. Bricker, M. A., Harkins, S. G., & Ostrom, T. M. (1986). Effects of personal involvement: Thought-provoking implications for social loafing. *Journal of Personality and Social Psychology, 51,* 763–769.

53. George, J. M. (1992). Extrinsic and intrinsic origins of perceived social loafing in organizations. *Academy of Management Journal, 35,* 191–202.

54. Albanese, R., & Van Fleet, D. D. (1985). Rational behavior in groups: The free-riding tendency. *Academy of Management Review, 10,* 244–255.

55. Miles, J. A., & Greenberg, J. (1993). Using punishment threats to attenuate social loafing effects among swimmers. *Organizational Behavior and Human Decision Processes, 56,* 246–265.

56. Katzenbach, J. R., & Smith, D. K. (1993, March–April). The discipline of teams. *Harvard Business Review, 71*(2), 111–120.

57. Harari, O. (1995, October). The dream team. *Management Review,* pp. 29–31.

58. See Note 56.

59. Mohrman, S. A. (1993). Integrating roles and structure in the lateral organization. In J. R. Galbraith & E. E. Lawler, III (Eds.), *Organizing for the future* (pp. 109–141). San Francisco: Jossey-Bass.

60. Tuckman, B. W., & Jensen, M. A. (1977). Stages of small group development revisited. *Group and Organization Studies, 2,* 419–427.

61. Ray, D., & Bronstein, H. (1995). *Teaming up.* New York: McGraw-Hill.

62. Wellins, R. S., Byham, W. C., & Wilson, J. M. (1991). *Empowered teams.* San Francisco: Jossey-Bass.

63. Manz, C. C., & Sims, H. P., Jr. (1993). *Business without bosses.* New York: John Wiley & Sons.

64. Osburn, J. D., Moran, L., Musselwhite, E., & Zenger, J. H. (1990). *Self-directed work teams.* Burr Ridge, IL: Irwin.

65. Hackman, J. R. (1987). The design of work teams. In J. W. Lorsch (Ed.), *Handbook of organizational behavior* (pp. 315–342). Englewood Cliffs, NJ: Prentice-Hall.

66. See Note 65 (quote pp. 338).

67. Sheridan, J. H. (1990, October 15). America's best plants. *Industry Week,* pp. 27–64.

68. Hoerr, J. (1989, July 10). The payoff from teamwork. *Business Week,* pp. 56–62.

69. Overman, S. (1994, May). Teams score on the bottom line. *HRMagazine,* pp. 82–84.

70. Hoerr, J. (1987, April 20). Getting man and machines to live happily ever after. *Business Week,* pp. 61–62.

71. Wellins, R. S., Byham, W. C., & Wilson, J. M. (1991). *Empowered teams.* San Francisco: Jossey-Bass.

72. Dumaine, B. (1990, May 7). Who needs a boss? *Fortune,* pp. 52–60.

73. See Note 68.

74. Ilgen, D. R., Major, D. A., Hollenbeck, & Sego, D. J. (1993). Team research in the 1990s. In M. M. Chemers & R. Ayman (Eds.), *Leadership theory and research* (pp. 245–270). San Diego: Academic Press.

75. Lawler, E. E., III, Mohrman, S. A., & Ledford, G. E., Jr. (1992). *Employee involvement and total quality management.* San Francisco: Jossey-Bass.

76. Hackman, J. R. (Ed.) (1990). *Groups that work (and those that don't).* San Francisco: Jossey-Bass.

77. See Note 63.

78. See Note 63.

79. Katzenbach, J. R., & Smith, D. K. (1993). *The wisdom of teams.* Boston: Harvard Business School Press.

80. See Note 71.

81. Osburn, J. D., Moran, L., Musselwhite, E., & Zenger, J. H. (1990). *Self-directed work teams.* Burr Ridge, IL: Irwin.

82. See Note 63.

83. Pearson, C. A. L. (1992). Autonomous workgroups: An evaluation at an industrial site. *Human Relations, 45,* 905–936.

84. Wall, T. D., Kemp, N. J., Jackson, P. R., & Clegg, C. W. (1986). Outcomes of autonomous workgroups: A long-term field experiment. *Academy of Management Journal, 29,* 280–304.

85. Smith, P. B., Peterson, M. F., & Misumi, J. (1993). Event management and work team effectiveness in Japan, Britain and USA. *Journal of Occupational and Organizational Psychology, 67,* 33–43.

86. Nahavandi, A., & Aranda, E. (1994). Restructuring teams for the re-engineered organization. *Academy of Management Executive, 8,* 58–68.

87. Stern, A. (1993, July 18). Managing by team is not always as easy as it looks. *The New York Times,* p. B14.

88. See Note 87.

89. See Note 87.

90. See Note 87.

91. See Note 87.

92. See Note 87.

93. Maginn, M. D. (1994). *Effective teamwork.* Burr Ridge, IL: Business One Irwin.

94. Dumaine, B. (1994, September 5). The trouble with teams. *Fortune,* pp. 86–88, 90, 92. (quote p. 86)

95. See Note 79.

96. Campion, M. A., & Higgs, A. C. (1995, October). Design work teams to increase productivity and satisfaction. *HRMagazine,* pp. 101–102, 104, 107.

97. Campion, M. A., Medsker, & Higgs, A. C. (1993). Relations between work group characteristics and effectiveness: Implications for designing effective work groups. *Personnel Psychology, 46,* 823–850.

98. Frangos, S. J. (1993). *Team zebra.* Essex Junction, VT: Omneo.

Case in Point Source

Case, J. (1993, September). What the experts forgot to mention. *Inc.,* pp. 66–68, 70, 72, 76, 78.

CHAPTER 9

Preview Case Source

Kerr, J. (1995, March). The informers. *Inc.,* pp. 50–52, 54, 56, 59. 61.

Chapter Notes

1. Fulk, J. (1993). Social construction of communication technology. *Academy of Management Journal, 36,* 921–950.

2. Scudder, J. N., & Guinan, P. J. (1989). Communication competencies as discriminators of superiors' ratings of employee performance. *Journal of Business Communication, 26,* 217–229.

3. Roberts, K. H. (1984). *Communicating in organizations.* Chicago: Science Research Associates (quote p. 4).

4. Weick, K. E. (1987). Theorizing about organizational communication. In F. M. Jablin, L. L. Putnam, K. H. Roberts, & L. W. Porter (Eds.), *Handbook of organizational communication* (pp. 97–122). Newbury Park, CA: Sage.

5. Barnard, C. I. (1938). *The functions of the executive.* Cambridge, MA: Harvard University Press.

6. Mintzberg, H. (1973). *The nature of managerial work.* New York: Harper & Row.

7. Baskin, O. W., & Aronoff, C. E. (1980). *Interpersonal communication in organizations.* Santa Monica, CA: Goodyear.

8. Quinn, R. E., Hildebrandt, H. W., Rogers, P. S., & Thompson, M. P. (1991). A competing values framework for analyzing presentational communication in management contexts. *Journal of*

Business Communication, 28, 213–232.

9. Lengel, R. H., & Daft, R. L. (1988). The selection of communication media as an executive skill. *Academy of Management Executive, 2*, 225–232.

10. Yates, J., & Orlikowski, W. J. (1992). Genres of organizational communication: A structurational approach to studying communication and media. *Academy of Management Review, 17*, 299–326.

11. Szwergold, J. (1993, June). Employee newsletters help fill an information gap. *Management Review*, p. 8.

12. Sibson and Company, Inc. (1989). *Compensation planning survey, 1989*. Princeton, NJ: Author.

13. Heneman, R. L. (1992). *Merit pay*. Reading, MA: Addison-Wesley.

14. Killian, C. M. (1993). *Effects of a company newsletter on perceptions of procedural justice*. Unpublished doctoral dissertation, the Ohio State University, Columbus.

15. Fenn, D. (1995, August). Keep employees informed. *Inc.*, p. 99 (quote p. 99).

16. Brady, T. (1993, June). Employee handbooks: Contracts or empty promises? *Management Review*, pp. 33–35.

17. The (handbook) handbook. (1993, November). *Inc.*, pp. 57–64.

18. See Note 17 (quote p. 64).

19. Level, D. A. (1972). Communication effectiveness: Methods and situation. *Journal of Business Communication, 28*, 19–25.

20. Klauss, R., & Bass, B. M. (1982). *International communication in organizations*. New York: Academic Press.

21. Daft, R. L., Lengel, R. H., & Treviño, L. K. (1987). Message equivocality, media selection, and manager performance: Implications for information systems. *MIS Quarterly, 11*, 355–366.

22. Zuboff, S. (1988). *In the age of the smart machine*. New York: Basic Books.

23. Ritchie, L. D. (1991). Another turn of the information revolution. *Communication Research, 18*, 412–427.

24. Martinez, M. N. (1994, July). How to avoid accidents on the electronic highway. *HRMagazine*, pp. 74–77.

25. Piller, C. (1993, July). Bosses with x-ray eyes. *Macworld*, pp. 118–123.

26. Kantrowitz, B., & McKay, B. (1993, December 20). Who holds the key to the e-mailbox? *Newsweek*, p. 108.

27. See Note 25.

28. Johnson, B. (1988, November–December). Streamlining corporate communications through voice imaging technology. *The Professional Communicator*, pp. 19–20.

29. See Note 28.

30. Reinsch, N. L., Jr., & Beswick, R. W. (1990). Voice mail versus conventional channels: A cost minimization analysis of individuals' preferences. *Academy of Management Journal, 33*, 801–816.

31. Malloy, J. T. (1990). *Dress for success*. New York: Warner Books.

32. Solomon, M. R. (1986, April). Dress for effect. *Psychology Today*, pp. 20–28.

33. Saporito, B. (1993, September 20). Unsuit yourself: Management goes informal. *Fortune*, pp. 118–120 (quote p. 118).

34. Schwartz, G. (1976). *Queuing and waiting*. Chicago: University of Chicago Press.

35. Greenberg, J. (1989). The organizational waiting game: Time as a status-asserting or status-neutralizing tactic. *Basic and Applied Social Psychology, 10*, 13–26.

36. Greenberg, J. (1988). Equity and workplace status: A field experiment. *Journal of Applied Psychology, 73*, 606–613.

37. Zweigenhaft, R. L. (1976). Personal space in the faculty office: Desk placement and student-faculty interaction. *Journal of Applied Psychology, 61*, 629–632.

38. Greenberg, J. (1976). The role of seating position in group interaction: A review, with applications for group trainers. *Group and Organization Studies, 1*, 310–327.

39. Capowski, G. S. (1993, June). Designing a corporate identity. *Management Review*, pp. 37–40.

40. Scully, J. (1987). *Odyssey: Pepsi to Apple . . . a journey of adventure, ideas, and the future*. New York: Harper & Row.

41. Carstairs, E. (1986, February). No ivory tower for Procter & Gamble. *Corporate Design and Reality*, pp. 24–30.

42. McCallister, L. (1994). "I wish I'd said that!" How to talk your way out of trouble and into success. New York: Wiley.

43. See Note 42.

44. Tannen, D. (1995). *Talking 9 to 5*. New York: Avon.

45. Tannen, D. (1995, September–October). The power of talk: Who gets heard and why. *Harvard Business Review*, pp. 138–148.

46. See Note 45 (quote p. 148).

47. Munter, M. (1993, May–June). Cross-cultural communication for managers. *Business Horizons*, pp. 75–76.

48. Mellow, C. (1995, August 17). Russia: Making cash from chaos. *Fortune*, pp. 145–146, 148, 150–151.

49. Adler, N. (1991). *International dimensions of organizational behavior* (2nd ed.). Boston: PWS/Kent.

50. Shaw, M. E. (1978). Communication networks fourteen years later. In L. Berkowitz (Ed.), *Group processes* (pp. 351–361). New York: Academic Press.

51. Forsyth, D. R. (1983). *An introduction to group dynamics*. Monterey, CA: Brooks/Cole.

52. Burgess, R. L. (1968). Communication networks: An experimental reevaluation. *Journal of Experimental Social Psychology, 4*, 324–327.

53. Harcourt, J., Richerson, V., & Wattcrk, M. J. (1991). A national study of middle managers' assessment of organization communication quality. *Journal of Business Communication, 28*, 348–365.

54. Krackhardt, D., & Hanson, J. R. (1993, July–August). Informal networks: The company behind the chart. *Harvard Business Review*, pp. 104–111.

55. Zenger, T. R., & Lawrence, B. S. (1989). Organizational demography: The differential effects of age and tenure distributions on technical communication. *Academy of Management Journal, 32*, 353–376.

56. Ibarra, H. (1992). Homophily and differential returns: Sex differences in network structure and access in an advertising firm. *Administrative Science Quarterly, 37*, 422–447.

57. Lesley, E., & Mallory, M. (1993, November 29). Inside the Black business network. *Business Week*, pp. 70–72, 77, 80–81.

58. Brass, D. J. (1985). Men's and women's networks: A study of interaction patterns and influence in an organization. *Academy of Management Journal, 28*, 327–343.

59. Krackhardt, D., & Porter, L. W. (1986). The snowball effect: Turnover embedded in communication networks. *Journal of Applied Psychology, 71*, 50–55.

60. Duncan, J. W. (1984). Perceived humor and social network patterns in a sample of task-oriented groups: A reexamination of prior research. *Human Relations, 37*, 895–907.

61. Baskin, O. W., & Aronoff, C. E. (1989). *Interpersonal communication in organizations*. Santa Monica: Goodyear.

62. Walton, E. (1961). How efficient is the grapevine? *Personnel, 28*, 45–49.

63. Thibaut, A. M., Calder, B. J., & Sternthal, B. (1981). Using information processing theory to design marketing strategies. *Journal of Marketing Research, 18*, 73–79.

64. Lesley, E., & Zinn, L. (1993, July 5). The right moves, baby. *Business Week*, pp. 30–31.

65. Schiller, Z. (1995, September 11). P&G is still having a devil of a time. *Business Week*, p. 46.

66. See Note 62.

67. Argyris, C. (1974). *Behind the front page: Organizational self-renewal in a metropolitan newspaper*. San Francisco: Jossey-Bass.

68. Hogarty, D. B. (1993, June). Who goes where? A new look at office design. *Management Review*, p. 9.

69. Papa, M. J. (1990). Communication network patterns and employee performance with new technology. *Communication Research, 17*, 344–368.

70. Miller, K. I., Ellis, B. H., Zook, E. G., & Lyles, J. S. (1990). An integrated model of communication, stress, and burnout in the workplace. *Communication Research, 17*, 300–326.

71. Hawkins, B. L., & Preston, P. (1981). *Managerial communication*. Santa Monica, CA: Goodyear.

72. Schnake, M. R., Dumler, M. P., Chochran, D. S., & Barnett, T. R. (1990). Effects of differences in superior and subordinate perceptions on superiors' communication practices. *Journal of Business Communication, 27*, 37–50.

73. Szilagyi, A. (1981). *Management and performance*. Glenview, IL: Scott, Foresman.

74. Kiechell, W., III. (1986, January 6). No word from on high. *Fortune*, pp. 19, 26.

75. Coulson, R. (1981) *The termination handbook*. New York: The Free Press.

76. Cropanzano, R., & Greenberg, J. (1997). *International review of industrial and organizational psychology*. London: Wiley.

77. Greenberg, J., Lind, E. A., Scott, K. S., & Welchans, T. D. (1995). *Perceptions of injustice and wrongful termination litigation*. Final report to the National Science Foundation.

78. Walker, C. R., & Guest, R. H. (1952). *The man on the assembly line*. Cambridge, MA: Harvard University Press.

79. Luthans, F., & Larsen, J. K. (1986). How managers really communicate. *Human Relations, 39*, 161–178.

80. Kirmeyer, S. L., & Lin, T. (1987). Social support: Its relationship to observed communication with peers and superiors. *Academy of Management Journal, 30*, 138–151.

81. Read, W. (1962). Upward communication in industrial hierarchies. *Human Relations, 15*, 3–16.

82. Glauser, M. J. (1984). Upward information flow in organizations: Review and conceptual analysis. *Human Relations, 37*, 613–643.

83. Lee, F. (1993). Being polite and keeping MUM: How bad news is communicated in organizational hierarchies. *Journal of Applied Social Psychology, 23*, 1124–1149.

84. Tesser, A., & Rosen, S. (1975). The reluctance to transmit bad news. In L. Berkowitz (Ed.), *Advances in experimental social psychology* (Vol. 8, pp. 192–232). New York: Academic Press.

85. Kiechel, W., III. (1990, June

18). How to escape the echo chamber. *Fortune*, pp. 129–130 (quote p. 130).

86. Rogers, E. M., & Rogers, A. (1976). *Communication in organizations*. New York: Free Press.

87. Fiol, C. M. (1995). Corporate communications: Comparing executives' private and public statements. *Academy of Management Journal, 38*, 522–536.

88. Alessanddra, T., & Hunksaker, P. (1993). *Communicating at work*. New York: Fireside.

89. Kanter, R. M. (1977). *Men and women of the corporation*. New York: Basic Books.

90. Borman, E. (1982). *Interpersonal communication in the modern organization* (2nd ed.). Englewood Cliffs, NJ: Prentice-Hall.

91. Cantoni, C. J. (1993). *Corporate dandelions*. New York: AMACOM.

92. Rowe, M. P., & Baker, M. (1984, May–June). Are you hearing enough employee concerns? *Harvard Business Review*, pp. 127–135.

93. Burley-Allen, M. (1982). *Listening: The forgotten skill*. New York: John Wiley & Sons.

94. Brownell, J. (1985). A model for listening instructions: Management applications. *ABCA Bulletin, 48*(3), 39–44.

95. Austin, N. K. (1991, March). Why listening's not as easy as it sounds. *Working Woman*, pp. 46–48.

96. See Note 95.

97. Seyper, B. D., Bostrom, R. N., & Seibert, J. H. (1989). Listening, communication abilities, and success at work. *Journal of Business Communication, 26*, 293–303.

98. Penley, L. E., Alexander, E. R., Jernigan, I. E., & Henwood, C. I. (1991). Communication abilities of managers: The relationship to performance. *Journal of Management, 17*, 57–76.

99. Brownell, J. (1990). Perceptions of effective listeners: A management study. *Journal of Business Communication, 27*, 401–415.

100. Nichols, R. G. (1962, winter). Listening is good business. *Management of Personnel Quarterly*, p. 4.

101. See Note 21.

102. McCathrin, Z. (1990, spring). The key to employee communication: Small group meetings. *The Professional Communicator*, pp. 6–7, 10.

103. Vernyi, B. (1987, April 26). Institute aims to boost quality of company suggestion boxes. *Toledo Blade*, p. B2.

104. Taft, W. F. (1985). Bulletin boards, exhibits, hotlines. In C. Reuss & D. Silvis (Eds.), *Inside organizational communication* (2nd ed., pp. 183–189). New York: Longman.

105. Walter, K. (1995, September). Ethics hot lines tap into more than wrongdoing. *HRMagazine*, pp. 79–85.

106. See Note 104.

107. See Note 105.

Case in Point Source

McKeand, P. J. (1990, November). GM division builds a classic system to share internal communication. *Public Relations Journal*, pp. 24–26, 41.

CHAPTER 10

Preview Case Source

Meeks, F. (1995, October 23). Catering to indulgent parents. *Forbes*, pp. 148, 150, 154–155.

Chapter Notes

1. Mintzberg, H. J. (1988). *Mintzberg on management: Inside our strange world of organizations*. New York: Free Press.

2. Allison, S. T., Jordan, A M. R., & Yeatts, C. E. (1992). A cluster-analytic approach toward identifying the structure and content of human decision making. *Human Relations, 45*, 49–72.

3. Harrison, E. F. (1987). *The managerial decision-making process* (3rd ed.). Boston: Houghton Mifflin.

4. Wedley, W. C., & Field, R. H. G. (1984). A predecision support system. *Academy of Management Review, 9*, 696–703.

5. Nutt, P. C. (1993). The formulation process and tactics used in organizational decision making. *Organization Science, 4*, 226–251.

6. Nutt, P. (1984). Types of organizational decision processes. *Administrative Science Quarterly, 29*, 414–450.

7. Cowan, D. A. (1986). Developing a process model of

problem recognition. *Academy of Management Review, 11*, 763–776.

8. Dennis, T. L., & Dennis, L. B. (1988). *Microcomputer models for management decision making*. St. Paul, MN: West.

9. Fulk, J., & Boyd, B. (1991). Emerging theories of communication in organizations. *Journal of Management, 17*, 407–446.

10. Sainfort, F. C., Gustafson, D. H., Bosworth, K., & Hawkins, R. P. (1990). Decision support systems effectiveness: Conceptual framework and empirical evaluation. *Organizational Behavior and Human Decision Processes, 45*, 232–252.

11. Stevenson, M. K., Busemeyer, J. R., & Naylor, J. C. (1990). Judgment and decision-making theory. In M. D. Dunnette & L. M. Hough (Eds.), *Handbook of industrial and organizational psychology* (2nd ed., Vol. 1, pp. 283–374). Palo Alto, CA: Consulting Psychologists Press.

12. Rowe, A. J., Boulgaides, J. D., & McGrath, M. R. (1984). *Managerial decision making*. Chicago: Science Research Associates.

13. See Note 12.

14. Adler, N. J. (1991). *International dimensions of organizational behavior*. Boston: PWS-Kent.

15. Roth, K. (1992). Implementing international strategy at the business unit level: The role of managerial decision-making characteristics. *Journal of Management, 18*, 769–789.

16. Hill, C. W., & Jones, G. R. (1989). *Strategic management*. Boston: Houghton Mifflin.

17. See Note 5.

18. Amit, R., & Wernerfelt, B. (1990). Why do firms reduce business risk? *Academy of Management Journal, 33*, 520–533.

19. Provan, K. G. (1982). Interorganizational linkages and influence over decision making. *Academy of Management Journal, 25*, 443–451.

20. Galaskiewicz, J., & Wasserman, S. (1989). Mimetic processes within an interorganizational field: An empirical test. *Administrative Science Quarterly, 34*, 454–479.

21. Parsons, C. K. (1988) Computer technology: Implications for human resources management. In G. R. Ferris & K. M. Rowland (Eds.), *Research in personnel and human resources management* (Vol. 6, pp. 1–36). Greenwich, CT: JAI Press.

22. Simon, H. A. (1987). Making management decisions: The role of intuition and emotion. *Academy of Management Executive, 1,* 57–64.

23. Kirschenbaum, S. S. (1992). Influence of experience on information-gathering strategies. *Journal of Applied Psychology, 77,* 343–352.

24. Simon, H. (1977). *The new science of management decisions* (2nd ed.). Englewood Cliffs, NJ: Prentice-Hall.

25. Case, J. (1995). *Open-book management.* New York: HarperBusiness.

26. Remdomo. M. G. (1995, April). Team effort at Maguire Group leads to ethics policy. *HRMagazine,* pp. 63–64, 66.

27. Linstone, H. A. (1984). *Multiple perspectives for decision making.* New York: North-Holland.

28. Simon, H. A. (1979). Rational decision making in organizations. *American Economic Review, 69,* 493–513.

29. March, J. G., & Simon, H. A. (1958). *Organizations.* New York: Wiley.

30. See Note 29.

31. Simon, H. A. (1957). *Models of man.* New York: Wiley.

32. Browning, E. B. (1850/1950). *Sonnets from the Portuguese.* New York: Ratchford and Fulton.

33. Mitchell, T. R., & Beach, L. R. (1990). " . . . Do I love thee? Let me count . . ." Toward an understanding of intuitive and automatic decision making. *Organizational Behavior and Human Decision Processes, 47,* 1–20.

34. Beach, L. R., & Mitchell, T. R. (1990). Image theory: A behavioral theory of image making in organizations. In B. Staw & L. L. Cummings (Eds.), *Research in organizational behavior* (Vol. 12, pp. 1–41). Greenwich, CT: JAI Press.

35. Dunegan, K. J. (1995). Image theory: Testing the role of image compatibility in progress decisions. *Organizational Behavior and*

Human Decision Processes, 62, 79–86.

36. Dunegan, K. J. (1993). Framing, cognitive modes, and image theory: Toward an understanding of a glass half full. *Journal of Applied Psychology, 78,* 491–503.

37. Gaeth, G. J., & Shanteau, J. (1984). Reducing the influence of irrelevant information on experienced decision makers. *Organizational Behavior and Human Performance, 33,* 263–282.

38. Ginrich, G., & Soli, S. D. (1984). Subjective evaluation and allocation of resources in routine decision making. *Organizational Behavior and Human Performance, 33,* 187–203.

39. Kahneman, D., & Tversky, A. (1984). Choices, values, and frames. *American Psychologist, 39,* 341–350.

40. Highhouse, S., & Yüce, P. (1996). Perspectives, perceptions, and risk-taking behavior. *Organizational Behavior and Human Decision Processes, 65,* 159–167.

41. Frisch, D. (1993). Reasons for framing effects. *Organizational Behavior and Human Decision Processes, 54,* 399–429.

42. Nisbett, R. E., & Ross, L. (1980). *Human inference: Strategies and shortcomings of social judgment.* Englewood Cliffs, NJ: Prentice-Hall.

43. Abelson, R. P., & Levi, A. (1985). Decision-making and decision theory. In G. Lindzey & E. Aronson (Eds.), *Handbook of social psychology* (3rd ed., Vol. 1, pp. 231–309). Reading, MA: Addison-Wesley.

44. Kahneman, D., & Tversky, A. (1973). On the psychology of prediction. *Psychological Review, 80,* 251–273.

45. Gaeth, G. J., & Shanteau, J. (1984). Reducing the influence of irrelevant information on experienced decision makers. *Organizational Behavior and Human Performance, 33,* 187–203.

46. Power, D. J., & Aldag, R. J. (1985). Soelberg's job search and choice model: A clarification, review, and critique. *Academy of Management Review, 10,* 48–58.

47. Soelberg, P. O. (1967). Unprogrammed decision making. *Industrial Management Review, 8,* 19–29.

48. Langer, E., & Schank, R. C. (1994). *Belief, reasoning, and decision making.* Hillsdale, NJ: Lawrence Erlbaum Associates.

49. Conlon, D. E., & Garland, H. (1993). The role of project completion information in resource allocation decisions. *Academy of Management Journal, 36,* 402–413.

50. Ross, J., & Staw, B. M. (1986). Expo '86: An escalation prototype. *Administrative Science Quarterly, 31,* 274–297.

51. Bobocel, D. R., & Meyer, J. P. (1994). Escalating commitment to a failing course of action: Separating the roles of choice and justification. *Journal of Applied Psychology, 79,* 360–363.

52. Staw, B. M. (1981). The escalation of commitment to a course of action. *Academy of Management Review, 6,* 577–587.

53. Whyte, G. (1993). Escalating commitment in individual and group decision making: A prospect theory approach. *Organizational Behavior and Human Decision Processes, 54,* 430–455.

54. Simonson, I., & Staw, B. M. (1992). Deescalation strategies: A comparison of techniques for reducing commitment to losing courses of action. *Journal of Applied Psychology, 77,* 419–426.

55. Garland, H., & Newport, S. (1991). Effects of absolute and relative sunk costs on the decision to persist with a course of action. *Organizational Behavior and Human Decision Processes, 48,* 55–69.

56. Ross, J., & Staw, B. M. (1993). Organizational escalation and exit: Lessons from the Shoreham nuclear power plant. *Academy of Management Journal, 36,* 701–732.

57. Whyte, G. (1991). Diffusion of responsibility: Effects on the escalation tendency. *Journal of Applied Psychology, 76,* 408–415.

58. Heath, C. (1995). Escalation and de-escalation of commitment in response to sunk costs: The role of budgeting in mental accounting. *Organizational Behavior and Human Decision Processes, 62,* 38–54.

59. Tan, H., & Yates, J. F. (1995). Sunk cost effects: The influences of instruction and future return estimates. *Organizational Behavior and*

Human Decision Processes, 63, 311–319.

60. Tjosvold, D. (1984). Effects of crisis orientation on managers' approach to controversy in decision making. *Academy of Management Journal, 27,* 130–138.

61. Johnson, R. J. (1984). Conflict avoidance through acceptable decisions. *Human Relations, 27,* 71–82.

62. Neustadt, R. E., & Fineberg, H. (1978). *The swine flu affair: Decision making on a slippery disease.* Washington, DC: U.S. Department of Health, Education and Welfare.

63. Shull, F. A., Delbecq, A. L., & Cummings, L. L. (1970). *Organizational decision making.* New York: McGraw-Hill.

64. Sonnenberg, F. K. (1994). *Managing with a conscience.* New York: McGraw-Hill.

65. Davis, J. H. (1992). Introduction to the special issue on group decision making. *Organizational Behavior and Human Decision Processes, 52,* 1–2.

66. Delbecq, A. L., Van de Ven, A. H., & Gustafson, D. H. (1975). *Group techniques for program planning.* Glenview, IL: Scott, Foresman.

67. Patterson, J., & Kim, P. (1991). *The day America told the truth.* New York: Plume.

68. Dubrin, A. J. (1994). *Contemporary applied management* (4th ed.). Burr Ridge, IL: Irwin.

69. Murninghan, J. K. (1981). Group decision making: What strategies should you use? *Management Review, 25,* 56–62.

70. Hill, G. W. (1982). Group versus individual performance: Are N + 1 heads better than one? *Psychological Bulletin, 91,* 517–539.

71. Wanous, J. P., & Youtz, M. A. (1986). Solution diversity and the quality of group decisions. *Academy of Management Journal, 29,* 149–159.

72. Yetton, P., & Bottger, P. (1983). The relationships among group size, member ability, social decision schemes, and performance. *Organizational Behavior and Human Performance, 32,* 145–149.

73. Michaelsen, L. K., Watson, W. E., & Black, R. H. (1989). A realistic test of individual versus group consensus decision

making. *Journal of Applied Psychology, 74,* 834–839.

74. See Note 70.

75. See Note 70.

76. Osborn, A. F. (1957). *Applied imagination.* New York: Scribner's.

77. Bouchard, T. J., Jr., Barsaloux, J., & Drauden, G. (1974). Brainstorming procedure, group size, and sex as determinants of the problem-solving effectiveness of groups and individuals. *Journal of Applied Psychology, 59,* 135–138.

78. Janis, I. L. (1982). *Groupthink: Psychological studies of policy decisions and fiascoes* (2nd ed.). Boston: Houghton Mifflin.

79. Aldag, R. J., & Fuller, S. R. (1993). Beyond fiasco: A reappraisal of the groupthink phenomenon and a new model of group decision processes. *Psychological Bulletin, 113,* 533–552.

80. Morehead, G., Ference, R., & Neck, C. P. (1991). Group decision fiascoes continue: Space shuttle Challenger and a revised groupthink framework. *Human Relations, 44,* 539–550.

81. Janis, I. L. (1988). *Crucial decisions: Leadership in policy making and crisis management.* New York: Free Press.

82. Morehead, G., & Montanari, J. R. (1986). An empirical investigation of the groupthink phenomenon. *Human Relations, 39,* 399–410.

83. Schweiger, D. M., Sandberg, W. R., & Ragan, J. W. (1986). Group approaches for improving strategic decision making: A comparative analysis of dialectical inquiry, devil's advocacy, and consensus. *Academy of Management Journal, 29,* 51–71.

84. Schweiger, D. M., Sandberg, W. R., & Rechner, P. L. (1989). Experiential effects of dialectical inquiry, devil's advocacy, and consensus approaches to strategic decision making. *Academy of Management Journal, 32,* 745–772.

85. Cosier, R. A., & Schwenk, C. R. (1990). Agreement and thinking alike: Ingredients for poor decisions. *Academy of Management Executive, 4,* 69–74.

86. Sloan, A. P., Jr. (1964). *My years with General Motors.* New York: Doubleday.

87. Bottger, P. C., & Yetton, P. W. (1987). Improving group performance by training in individual problem solving. *Journal of Applied Psychology, 72,* 651–657.

88. Wiener, E. L. (1993). Crew coordination and training in the advanced-technology cockpit. In E. L. Wiener, B. G. Kanki, & R. L. Helmreich (Eds.). *Cockpit resource management* (pp. 199–230). San Diego: Academic Press.

89. Kayten, P. J. (1993). The accident investigator's perspective. In E. L. Wiener, B. G. Kanki, & R. L. Helmreich (1993). *Cockpit resource management* (pp. 283–314). San Diego: Academic Press.

90. Lee, A. T. (1991). Aircrew decision-making behavior in hazardous weather avoidance. *Aviation, Space, and Environmental Medicine, 15,* 158–161.

91. Dalkey, N. (1969). *The Delphi method: An experimental study of group decisions.* Santa Monica, CA: Rand Corporation.

92. Van de Ven, A. H., & Delbecq, A. L. (1971). Nominal versus interacting group processes for committee decision making effectiveness. *Academy of Management Journal, 14,* 203–212.

93. See Note 92.

94. Gustafson, D. H., Shulka, R. K., Delbecq, A., & Walster, W. G. (1973). A comparative study of differences in subjective likelihood estimates made by individuals, interacting groups, Delphi groups, and nominal groups. *Organizational Behavior and Human Performance, 9,* 280–291.

95. Ulshak, F. L., Nathanson, L., & Gillan, P. B. (1981). *Small group problem solving: An aid to organizational effectiveness.* Reading, MA: Addison-Wesley.

96. Harmon, J., Schneer, J. A., & Hoffman, L. R. (1995). Electronic meetings and established decision groups: Audioconferencing effects on performance and structural stability. *Organizational Behavior and Human Decision Processes, 61,* 138–147.

97. Willis, R. E. (1979). A simulation of multiple selection using nominal group procedures. *Management Science, 25,* 171–181.

98. Van de Ven, A. H., & Delbecq, A. L. (1974). The effectiveness of nominal, Delphi, and interacting group decision making processes. *Academy of Management Journal, 17,* 605–621.

99. Stumpf, S. A., Zand, D. E., & Freedman, R. D. (1979). Designing groups for judgmental decisions. *Academy of Management Review, 4,* 589–600.

100. Rogelberg, S. G., Barnes-Farrell, J. L., & Lowe, C. A. (1992). The stepladder technique: An alternative group structure facilitating effective group decision making. *Journal of Applied Psychology, 77,* 730–737.

Case in Point Sources

Ellis, J. E. & Brown, P. B. (1985, July 29). Coke's man on the spot. Business Week, pp. 56–59. Fisher, A. B. (1985, August 5). Coke's brand-loyalty lesson. Fortune, pp. 44–46. Gelb, B. D., & Gelb, G. M. (1986, Fall). New Coke's fizzle— Lessons for the rest of us. Sloan Management Review, pp. 71–76. Greenwald, J. (1985, July 22). Coca-Cola's big fizzle. Time, pp. 48–52.

CHAPTER 11

Preview Case Source

Smith, L. (1995, October 2). Rubbermaid goes thump. *Fortune,* pp. 90–92, 96, 100, 104.

Chapter Notes

1. Argyle, M. (1991). *Cooperation: The basis of sociability.* London: Routledge.

2. Organ, D. W. (1988). *Organizational citizenship behavior.* Lexington, MA: Lexington Books.

3. Evan, W. M., & Olk, P. (1990). R&D consortia: A new U.S. organizational form. *Sloan Management Review, 31,* 37–46

4. Thomas, K. W. (1992). Conflict and negotiation processes in organizations. In M. D. Dunnette & L. M. Hough (Eds.), *Handbook of industrial and organizational psychology.* (2nd ed., Vol. 3, pp. 651–718). Palo Alto, CA: Consulting Psychologists Press.

5. Baron, R. A. (1995). Workplace aggression and workplace violence: Their nature and scope. Paper presented at the Meetings of the Academy of Management, Vancouver, British Columbia, August, 1995.

6. Spacapan, S., & Oskamp, S. (Eds.). (1992). *Helping and being helped.* Newbury Park, CA: Sage.

7. George, J. T., & Brief, A. P. (1992). Feeling good—doing good: A conceptual analysis of the mood at work-organizational spontaneity relationship. *Psychological Bulletin, 112,* 310–329.

8. See Note 1.

9. See Note 7.

10. Morrison, E. W. (1994). Role definitions and organizational citizenship behavior: The importance of employee's perspective. *Academy of Management Journal, 37,* 1543–1567.

11. Konovsky, M. A., & Pugh, S. D. (1994). Citizenship behavior and social exchange. *Academy of Management Journal, 37,* 656–689.

12. See Note 7.

13. See Note 10.

14. Ball, G. A., Trevino, K. K., & Sims, H. P., Jr. (1994). Just and unjust punishment: Influences on subordinate performance and citizenship. *Academy of Management Journal, 37,* 299–322.

15. Katz, D. (1964). The motivational basis of organizational behavior. *Behavioral Science, 9,* 131–133.

16. See Note 2.

17. Fombrun, C., & Shanley, M. (1990). What's in a name? Reputation building and corporate strategy. *Academy of Management Journal, 33,* 233–258.

18. Near, J. P., & Miceli, M. P. (1985). Organizational dissidence: The case of whistleblowing. *Journal of Business Ethics, 4,* 1–16.

19. Cited in Henkoff, R. (1995, September 4). So who is this Mark Whitacre, and why is he saying these things about ADM? *Fortune,* pp. 64–66, 68.

20. Ettorre, B. (1994, May). Whistleblowers: Who's the real bad guy? *Management Review,* 18–23.

21. Yates, R. E. (1995, July 7). Whistle-blowers pay dearly for heroics. *Chicago Tribune,* pp. 16, 18, 20.

22. Forsyth, D. R. (1983). *An introduction to group dynamics.* Monterey, CA; Brooks/Cole.

23. Ring, P. S., & Van de Ven, A. (1994). Developmental processes of cooperative interorganizational relationships. *Academy of Management Review, 19,* 90–118.

24. Tjosvold, D. (1986). *Working together to get things done.* Lexington, MA: Lexington Books.

25. Baron, R. A., & Richardson, pital system. *Academy of Management Journal, 9,* 494–504.

26. Youngs, G. A., Jr. (1986). Patterns of threat and punishment reciprocity in a conflict setting. *Journal of Personality and Social Psychology, 51,* 541–546.

27. McAllister, D. J. (1995). Affect- and cognition-based trust as foundations for interpersonal cooperation in organizations. *Academy of Management Journal, 38,* 24–59.

28. Smith, K. G., Carrol, S. J., & Ashford, S. J. (1995). Intra- and interorganizational cooperation: Toward a research agenda. *Academy of Management Journal, 38,* 7–23.

29. Korsgaard, M. A., Schweiger, D. M., & Sapienza, H. J. (1995). Building commitment, attachment, and trust in strategic decision-making teams: The role of procedural justice. *Academy of Management Journal, 38,* 60–84.

30. See Note. 27.

31. See Note 29.

32. Yamagishi, M., & Yamagishi, T. (1989). Trust, commitment, and the development of network structures. Paper presented at the Workshop for the Beyond Bureaucracy Research Project, December 18–21, Hong Kong.

33. Yamagishi, T., & Yamigishi, M. (1994). Trust and commitment in the United States and Japan. *Motivation and Emotion, 18,* 129–166.

34. Knight, G. P., & Dubro, A. F. (1984). Cooperative, competitive, and individualistic social values: An individualized regression and clustering approach. *Journal of Personality and Social Psychology, 46,* 98–105.

35. See Note 34.

36. Hofstede, G. (1980). *Culture's consequences: International differences in work-related value.* beveryly Hills, CA: Sage.

37. Wagner, J A., III. (1995). Studies on individualism-collectivism: Effects on cooperation in groups. *Academy of Management Journal, 38,* 152–172.

38. Peters, T. J., & Waterman, R. H., Jr. (1982). *In search of excellence: Lessons from America's best-run companies.* New York: Warner Books.

39. Cheng, J. L. (1983). Interdependence and coordination in organizations: A role-system analysis. *Academy of Management Journjal, 26,* 156–162.

40. Provan, K. G. (1984). Interorganizational cooperation and decision making autonomy in a consortium multihospital system. *Academy of Management Journal, 9,* 494–504.

41. Barron, J. J. (1990, June 15). Consortia: High-tech co-ops. **Byte**, pp. 15–26.

42. Browning, L. D., Beyer, J. M., & Shetler, J. C. (1995). Building cooperation in a competitive industry: Sematech and the semiconductor industry. *Academy of Management Journal, 38,* 113–151.

43. See Note 4.

44. Thomas, K. W., & Schmidt, W. H. (1976). A survey of managerial intercsts with respect to conflict. *Academy of Management Journal, 10,* 315–318.

45. Mamis, R. A. (1994, June). Partner wars: Six true confessions. *Inc.,* 36–42.

46. Walton, R. S., & McKersie, R. B. (1965). *A behavioral theory of labor negotiations: An analysis of a social interaction system.* New York: McGraw-Hill.

47. Thomas, K. W. (1976). Conflict and conflict management. In M. D. Dunnette (Ed.), *Handbook of industrial and organizational psychology* (pp. 889–935). Chicago: Rand McNally.

48. Rahim, M. A. (1983). A measure of styles of handling interpersonal conflict. *Academy of Management Journal, 26,* 368–376.

49. Ting-Toomey, S. (1988). Intercultural conflict styles: A face-negotiation theory. In Y. Kim & W. Gudykunst (Eds.), *Theories in intercultural communication* (pp. 213–235). Newbury Park, CA: Sage.

50. See Note 24.

51. Sprouse, M. (1992). *Sabotage in the American workplace.* San Francisco: Pressure Drop Press.

52. Johnson, T. E., & Rule, B. G. (1986). Mitigating circumstance information, censure, and aggression. *Journal of Personality and Social Psychology, 50,* 537–542.

53. Baron, R. A. (1988). Negative effects of destructive criticism: Impact on conflict, self-efficacy, and task performance. *Journal of Applied Psychology, 73,* 199–207.

54. Baron, R.A. (1990). Countering the effects of destructive criticism: The relative efficacy of four potential interventions. *Journal of Applied Psychology, 75,* 235–245.

55. Pescarella, P. (1993, February 1). 15 ways to win people's trust. *Nation's Business,* pp. 47–51.

56. Levering, R., & Moskowitz, M. (1993). *The 100 best companies to work for in America.* New York: Currency Doubleday.

57. Baron, R. A. (1989). Personality and organizational conflict: Effects of the type A behavior pattern and self-monitoring. *Organizational Behavior and Human Decision Processes, 44,* 281–297.

58. Hylton, R. D. (1995, July 10). Behind the fall of Rockefeller Center. *Fortune,* pp. 82–85.

59. Fodor, E. M. (1976). Group stress, authoritarian style of control and use of power. *Journal of Applied Psychology, 61,* 313–318.

60. Tjosvold, D. (1985). Implications of controversy research for management. *Journal of Management, 11,* 21–37.

61. Robbins, S. P. (1974). *Managing organizational conflict: A nontraditional approach.* Englewood Cliffs, NJ: Prentice-Hall.

62. Schwenk, C. R., & Cosier, R. A. (1980). Effects of the expert, devil's advocate, and dialectical inquiry methods of prediction performance. *Organizational Behavior and Human Decision Processes, 26,* 409–424.

63. Baron, R. A. (in press). Positive effects of conflict: Insights from social cognition. In C. K. W. deDreu & E. Van de Vliert (Eds.), *Conflict escalation and organizational perfor-*mance. Thousand Oaks, CA: Sage.

64. Cosier, R. A., & Dalton, D. R. (1990). Positive effects of conflict: A field assessment. *International Journal of Conflict Management, 1,* 81–92.

65. See Note 66.

66. Lewicki, R. J., & Litterer, J. A. (1985). *Negotiation.* Homewood, IL: Irwin.

67. Lewicki, R. J., Weiss, S. E., & Lewin, D. (1992). Models of conflict, negotiation, and third party intervention: A review and synthesis. *Journal of Organizational Behavior, 13,* 209–252.

68. Chertkoff, J. M.., & Baird, S. L. (1971). Applicability of the big lie technique and the last clear chance doctrine to bargaining. *Journal of Personality and Social Psychology, 20,* 298–303.

69. Chertkoff, J. M., & Conley, M. (1967). Opening offer and frequency of concessions as bargaining strategies. *Journal of Personality and Social Psychology, 7,* 181–185.

70. Pinkley, R., & Northcraft, G. B. (1994). Conflict frames of reference: Implications for dispute processes and outcomes. *Academy of Management Journal, 78,* 193–205.

71. Pinkley, R. (1990). Dimensions of conflict frame: Disputant interpretations of conflict. *Journal of Applied Psychology, 75,* 117–126.

72. Huber, V. L., Neale, M. A., & Northcraft, G. G. (1987). Decision bias and personnel selection strategies. *Organizational Behavior and Human Decision Processes, 40,* 136–147.

73. See Note 71.

74. Thompson, L., & Hastie, R. (1990). Social perception in negotiation. *Organizational Behavior and Human Decision Processes, 47,* 98–123.

75. See Note 76.

76. Thompson, L., & Hastie, R. (1990). Judgment tasks and biases in negotiation. In B. H. Sheppard, M. H. Bazerman, & R. J. Lewicki (Eds.), *Research on negotiation in organizations* (Vol. 2, pp. 1077–1092). Greenwich, CT: JAI Press.

77. See Note 46.

78. Tjosvold, D. (1991). *The conflict-positive organization.* Reading, MA: Addison-Wesley.

79. Thomas, K. W. (1992). Conflict and conflict management: Reflections and update. *Journal of Organizational Behavior, 13,* 265–274.

80. Overman, S. (1993). Why grapple with the cloudy elephant? *HR Magazine,* pp. 60–65.

81. See Note 79.

82. Fiske, S. T., & Taylor, S. E. (1991). *Social cognition* (2nd ed.). Reading, MA: Addison-Wesley.

83. Sherif, M., Harvey, O. J., White, B. J., Hood, W. E., & Sherif, C. W. (1961). *Intergroup conflict and cooperation: The Robbers Cave experiment.* Norman, OK: Institute of Group Relations.

84. Tully, S. (1995, February 20). Purchasing's new muscle. *Fortune,* pp. 75–76, 78–79, 82–83.

85. National Institute for Occupational Safety and Health, Center for Disease Control and Prevention. (1993) "Homicide in the workplace." Document #705003, December 5, 1993.

86. Bjorkqvist, K., Osterman, K., & Lagerspetz, K. M. J. (1994). Sex, differences in covert aggression among adults. *Aggressive Behavior, 20,* 27–33.

87. Neuman, J. H., & Baron, R. A. (in press). Aggression in the workplace. In Giacalone, R. A., & Greenberg, J. (Eds.), *Antisocial behavior in organizations.* Thousand Oaks, CA: Sage.

88. Rigdon, J. E. (1994, April 12). Companies see more workplace violence. *Wall Street Journal,* pp. B1, B9.

89. Baron, S. A. (1993). *Violence in the workplace.* Ventura, CA: Pathfinder Publishing of California.

90. Anderson, C. A., Deuser, W. E., & DeNeve, K. M. (1995). Hot temperatures, hostile affect, hostile cognition, and arousal: Tests of a general model of affective aggression. *Personality and Social Psychology Bulletin, 21,* 434–448.

91. Dodge, K. A., Price, J. M., Bachorowski, J. A., & Newman, J. P. (1990). Hostile attributional biases in severely aggressive adolescents. *Journal of Abnormal Psychology, 99,* 385–392

92. Greenberg, J., & Scott, K. S. (1995). Why do workers bite the hands that feed them? Employee theft as a social exchange process. In B. M. Staw & L. L. Cummings (Eds.), *Research in organizational behavior* (Vol. 18, pp. 1–46). Greenwich, CT: JAI Press.

93. Baron, R. A. (1994). The physical environment of work settings: Effects in task performance, interpersonal relations, and job satisfaction. In R. M. Staw & L. L. Cummings (Eds.), *Research in organizational behavior,* (Vol. 16, pp. 1–46). Greenwich, CT: JAI Press.

94. Baron, R. A., & Neuman, J. H. (1990). Workplace violence and workplace aggression: Evidence on their relative frequency and potential causes. *Aggressive Behavior, 22,* 161–173.

95. Brockner, J., Grover, S., Reed, T., & Dewitt, R. L. (1992). Layoffs, job insecurity, and survivors' work effort: Evidence of an inverted-U relationship. *Academy of Management Journal, 35,* 413–425.

96. Tsui, A., Egan, T., & O'Reilly, C. O., III. (1992). Being different: Relational demography and organizational attachment. *Administrative Science Quarterly, 37,* 549–579.

97. Folger, R., & Skarlicki, D. (1995, August). *A popcorn model of workplace violence.* Paper presented at the meetings of the Academy of Management, Vancouver, British Columbia, Canada.

98. Arvey, R. D., & Jones, A. P. (1985). The use of discipline in organizational settings: A framework for future research. In L. L. Cummings & B. M. Staw (Eds.)., *Research in organizational behavior* (Vol. 7, pp. 367–408). Greenwich, CT: JAI Press.

99. Greenberg, J. (1993b). The social side of fairness: Interpersonal and informational classes of justice. In R. Cropanzano (Ed.), *Justice in the workplace: Approaching fairness in human resource management.* Hillsdale, NJ: Lawrence Erlbaum.

100. Mantell, M., & Albrecht, S. (1994). *Ticking bombs: Defusing violence in the workplace.* New York: Irwin.

CHAPTER 12

Preview Case Source

Cusumano, M. A., & Selby, R. W. (1995). *Microsoft secrets.* New York: Free Press. Elmer-Dewitt, P. (1995, June 5). Mine, all mine. *Time,* pp. 46–64. Manes, S., & Andrews, P. (1993). *Gates.* New York: Doubleday.

Chapter Notes

1. Cobb, A. T. (1984). An episodic model of power: Toward an integration of theory and research. *Academy of Management Review, 9,* 482–493.

2. Mayes, B. T., & Allen, R. T. (1977). Toward a definition of organizational politics. *Academy of Management Review, 2,* 672–678.

3. Mintzberg, H. (1983). *Power in and around organizations.* Englewood Cliffs, NJ: Prentice-Hall.

4. Schriesheim, C. A., & Hinkin, T. R. (1990). Influence tactics used by subordinates: A theoretical and empirical analysis and refinement of the Kipnis, Schmidt, and Wilkinson subscales. *Journal of Applied Psychology, 75,* 246–257.

5. Yukl, G., & Tracey, J. B. (1992). Consequences of influence tactics used with subordinates, peers, and the boss. *Journal of Applied Psychology, 77,* 525–535.

6. Yukl, G., Falbe, C. M., & Youn, J. Y. (1993). Patterns of influence behavior for managers. *Group & Organization Management, 18,* 5–28.

7. Falbe, C. M., & Yukl, G. (1992). Consequences for managers of using single influence tactics and combinations of tactics. *Academy of Management Journal, 35,* 638–652.

8. Offermann, L. R. (1990). Power and leadership in organizations. *American Psychologist, 45,* 179–189.

9. Ansari, M. A., & Kapoor, A. (1987). Organizational context and upward influence tactics. *Organizational Behavior and Human Decision Processes, 40,* 39–49.

10. Graham, J. W., Marks, G., & Hansen, W. B. (1991). Social influence processes affecting adolescent substance abuse. *Journal of Applied Psychology, 76,* 291–298.

11. Gibbons, F. X., Helweg-Larsen, M., & Gerrard, M. (1995). Prevalence estimates and adolescent risk behavior: Cross-cultural differences in social influence. *Journal of Applied Psychology, 80,* 107–121.

12. Rebello, K., Burrows, P., & Sager, I. (1996, February 5). The fall of an American icon. *Business Week,* pp. 34–42.

13. Podsakoff, P. M., & Schriesheim, C. A. (1985). Field studies of French and Raven's bases of power: Critique, reanalysis, and suggestions for future research. *Psychological Bulletin, 97,* 387–411.

14. Huber, V. L. (1981). The sources, uses, and conservation of managerial power. *Personnel, 51*(4), 62–67.

15. Kipnis, D., Schmidt, S. M., Swaffin-Smith, C., & Wilkinson, I. (1984, winter). Patterns of managerial influence: Shotgun managers, tacticians, and bystanders. *Organizational Dynamics,* 58–67.

16. Stewart, T. (1989, November 6). CEOs see clout shifting. *Fortune,* p. 66.

17. Kahn, R. L., Wolfe, D. M., Quinn, R. P., Snoek, J. D., & Rosenthal, R. A. (1964). *Organizational stress: Studies in role conflict and ambiguity.* New York: Wiley.

18. See Note 13.

19. Symonds, W. C., & Siler, J. F. (1991, April 1). CEO disease. *Business Week,* pp. 52–60.

20. Morris, S. (1990, March 13). Abbott boss's suit points to a trend. *Chicago Tribune,* Business Section, p. 1.

21. Ford, R. C., & Fottler, M. D. (1995). Empowerment: A matter of degree. *Academy of Management Executive, 9,* 21–29.

22. Dumaine, B. (1990, May 7). Who needs a boss? *Fortune,* pp. 52–54, 56, 58, 60.

23. Shipper, F., & Manz, C. C. (1991). Employee self-management without formally designated teams: An alternative road to empowerment. *Organizational Dynamics, 20*(3), 48–61.

24. Sherman, J. (1994). *In the rings of Saturn.* New York: Oxford University Press.

25. Dumaine, B. (1993, February 22). The new non-manager managers. *Fortune,* pp. 80–84.

26. See Note 25.

27. Gresov, C., & Stephens, C. (1993). The context of interunit influence attempts. *Administrative Science Quarterly, 38,* 252–276.

28. Pfeffer, J., & Salancik, G. (1978). *The external control of organizations*. New York: Harper & Row.

29. Salancik, G., & Pfeffer, J. (1974). The bases and uses of power in organizational decision-making. *Administrative Science Quarterly, 19*, 453–473.

30. Boeker, W. (1989). The development and institutionalization of subunit power in organizations. *Administrative Science Quarterly, 34*, 388–410.

31. Lawrence, P. R., & Lorsch, J. W. (1967). *Organization and environment*. Cambridge, MA: Harvard University Press.

32. Hickson, D. J., Astley, W. G., Butler, R. J., & Wilson, D. C. (1981). Organization as power. In L. L. Cummings & B. M. Staw (Eds.), *Research in organizational behavior* (Vol. 4, pp. 151–196). Greenwich, CT: JAI Press.

33. Miles, R. H. (1980). *Macro organizational behavior*. Glenview, IL: Scott, Foresman.

34. Saunders, C. S., & Scarmell, R. (1982). Intraorganizational distributions of power: Replication research. *Academy of Management Journal, 25*, 192–200.

35. Hinings, C. R., Hickson, D. J., Pennings, J. M., & Schneck, R. E. (1974). Structural conditions of intraorganizational power. *Academy of Management Journal, 19*, 22–44.

36. See Note 2.

37. Drory, A., & Romm, T. (1990). The definition of organizational politics: A review. *Human Relations, 43*, 1133–1154.

38. Ferris, G. R., & Kacmar, K. M. (1992). Perceptions of organizational politics. *Journal of Management, 18*, 93–116.

39. Rosen, R. H. (1991). *The healthy company*. New York: Jeremy P. Tarcher/Perigree (quote, p. 71).

40. Mulder, M., de Jong, R. D., Koppelaar, L., & Verhage, J. (1986). Power, situation, and leaders' effectiveness: An organizational field study. *Journal of Applied Psychology, 71*, 566–570.

41. Feldman, S. P. (1988). Secrecy, information, and politics: An essay in organizational decision making. *Human Relations, 41*, 73–90.

42. Greenberg, J. (1990). Looking fair vs. being fair:

Managing impressions of organizational justice. In B. M. Staw & L. L. Cummings (Eds.), *Research in organizational behavior* (Vol. 12, pp. 111–157). Greenwich, CT: JAI Press.

43. Ferris, G. R., & King, T. R. (1991). Politics in human resources decisions: A walk on the dark side. *Organizational Dynamics, 20*, 59–71.

44. Boeker, W. (1992). Power and managerial dismissal: Scapegoating at the top. *Administrative Science Quarterly, 37*, 400–421.

45. Cobb, A. T. (1991). Toward the study of organizational coalitions: Participant concerns and activities in a simulated organizational setting. *Human Relations, 44*, 1057–1079.

46. Feldman, S. P. (1988). Secrecy, information, and politics: An essay in organizational decision making. *Human Relations, 41*, 73–90.

47. Liden, R. C., & Mitchell, T. R. (1988). Ingratiatory behaviors in organizational settings. *Academy of Management Review, 13*, 572–587.

48. See Note 3.

49. Sprouse, M. (1992). *Sabotage in the American workplace*. San Francisco: Pressure Drop Press.

50. Madison, D. L., Allen, R. W., Porter, L. W., Renwick, P. A., & Mayes, B. T. (1980). Organizational politics: An exploration of managers perceptions. *Human Relations, 33*, 79–100.

51. Pfeffer, J. (1992). *Managing with power*. Boston: Harvard Business School.

52. See Note 38.

53. Wayne, S. J., & Ferris, G. R. (1990). Influence tactics, affect, and exchange quality in supervisor-subordinate interactions. *Journal of Applied Psychology, 75*, 487–499.

54. See Note 43.

55. Bartol, K. M., & Martin, D. C. (1990). When politics pays: Factors influencing managerial compensation decisions. *Personnel Psychology, 43*, 599–614.

56. Gray, B., & Ariss, S. S. (1985). Politics and strategic change across organizational life cycles. *Academy of Management Review, 10*, 707–723.

57. Hannan, M. T., & Freeman, J. H. (1978). Internal politics of growth and decline. In M. W. Meyer (Ed.), *Environment and organizations* (pp. 177–199). San Francisco: Jossey-Bass.

58. See Note 43.

59. Gandz, J., & Murray, V. V. (1980). The experience of workplace politics. *Academy of Management Journal, 23*, 237–251.

60. Allen, R. W., Madison, D. L., Porter, L. W., Renwick, P. A., & Mayes, B. T. (1979). Organizational politics: Tactics and characteristics of its actors. *California Management Review, 22*, 77–83.

61. See Note 43.

62. See Note 59.

63. Kipnis, D. (1976). *The powerholders*. Chicago: University of Chicago Press.

64. Buchholz, R. A. (1989). *Fundamental concepts and problems in business ethics*. Englewood Cliffs, NJ: Prentice-Hall.

65. Gellerman, S. W. (1986, July–August). Why "good" managers make bad ethical choices. *Harvard Business Review*, pp. 85–90.

66. Velasquez, M., Moberg, D. J., & Cavanaugh, G. F. (1983). Organizational statesmanship and dirty politics: Ethical guidelines for the organizational politician. *Organizational Dynamics, 11*, 65–79.

67. See Note 42.

68. Greenberg, J. (1982). Approaching equity and avoiding inequity in groups and organizations. In J. Greenberg & R. L. Cohen (Eds.), *Equity and justice in social behavior* (pp. 389–435). New York: Academic Press.

69. Commerce Clearing House. (1991, June 26). *1991 SHRM/CCH survey*. Chicago: Author.

70. Kumar, P., & Ghadially, R. (1989). Organizational politics and its effects on members of organizations. *Human Relations, 42*, 305–314.

71. Andrews, G. (1994, September). Mistrust, the hidden obstacle to empowerment. *HRMagazine*, pp. 66–68, 70.

Case in Point Sources

Hoover, G., Campbell, A., & Spain, P. J. (1994). *Hoover's handbook of American business*.

Austin, TX: Reference Press. Vlasic, B., Kerwin, K., Naughton, K., & Woodruff, D. (1995, October 16). Fighting Bob. *Business Week*, pp. 88–90, 92, 95.

CHAPTER 13

Preview Case Sources

Green, H. (1995, November 19). Netscape chief's millions become a billion after big stock surge. *Chicago Sun-Times*, Financial section, p. 50. Sellers, P. (1996, January 15). Exactly what is charisma? *Fortune*, pp. 68–72, 74–75 (quotes, p. 70).

Chapter Notes

1. Yukl, G. (1994). *Leadership in organizations* (3rd ed.). Englewood Cliffs, NJ: Prentice-Hall.

2. House, R. J., & Podsakoff, P. M. (1995). Leadership effectiveness: Past perspectives and future directions for research. In J. Greenberg (Ed.), *Organizational behavior: The state of the science* (pp. 45–82). Hillsdale, NJ: Lawrence Erlbaum Associates.

3. Bass, B. M. (1990). *Bass and Stogdill's handbook of leadership* (3rd ed.). New York: Free Press.

4. Bennis, W. G., & Nanus, B. (1985). *Leaders: The strategies for taking charge*. New York: Harper & Row (quote, p. 4).

5. See Note 1.

6. Locke, E. A. (1991). *The essence of leadership*. New York: Lexington Books.

7. Cialdini, R. B. (1988). *Influence* (2nd ed.). Glenview, IL: Scott, Foresman.

8. Kotter, J. P. (1990). *A force for change: How leadership differs from management*. New York: The Free Press.

9. Geier, J. G. (1969). A trait approach to the study of leadership in small groups. *Journal of Communication, 17*, 316–323.

10. See Note 6.

11. See Note 4.

12. House, R. J., Shane, S. A., & Herold, D. M. (1996). Rumors of the death of dispositional research are vastly exaggerated. *Academy of Management Review, 21*, 203–224.

13. Kirkpatrick, S. A., & Locke, E. A. (1991). Leadership: Do traits matter? *Academy of Management Executive, 5*, 48–60.

14. Lord, R. G., DeVader, C. L., & Alliger, G. M. (1986). A meta-analysis of the relation between personality traits and leadership perceptions: An application of validity generalization procedures. *Journal of Applied Psychology, 61,* 402–410.

15. Zaccaro, S. J., Foti, R. J., & Kenny, D. A. (1991). Self-monitoring and trait-based variance in leadership: An investigation of leader flexibility across multiple group situations. *Journal of Applied Psychology, 76,* 308–315.

16. See Note 13 (quote, p. 58).

17. Muczyk, J. P., & Reimann, B. C. (1987). The case for directive leadership. *Academy of Management Review, 12,* 637–647.

18. Chen, C. C., & Meindl, J. R. (1991). The construction of leadership images in the popular press: The case of Donald Burr and People Express. *Administrative Science Quarterly, 36,* 521–551.

19. Likert, R. (1961). *New patterns in management.* New York: McGraw-Hill.

20. Stogdill, R. M. (1963). *Manual for the leader behavior description questionnaire, form XII.* Columbus, OH: Ohio State University, Bureau of Business Research.

21. Powell, G. N. (1993). *Women and men in management* (2nd ed.). Thousand Oaks, CA: Sage.

22. Eagly, A. H., & Karau, S. J. (1991). Gender and the emergence of leaders: A meta-analysis. *Journal of Personality and Social Psychology, 61,* 685–710.

23. Eagly, A. H., Makhijani, M. G., & Klonsky, B. G. (1992). Gender and the evaluation of leaders: A meta-analysis. *Psychological Bulletin, 108,* 3–22.

24. Melamed, T., & Bosionelos, N. (1992). Gender differences in the personality features of British managers. *Psychological Reports, 72,* 979–986.

25. Weissenberg, P., & Kavanagh, M. H. (1972). The independence of initiating structure and consideration: A review of the evidence. *Personnel Psychology, 25,* 119–130.

26. Vroom, V. H. (1976). Leadership. In M. D. Dunnette (Ed.), *Handbook of industrial-organizational psychology* (pp. 1527–1552). Chicago: Rand-McNally.

27. See Note 4.

28. Band, W. A. (1994). *Touchstones.* New York: John Wiley & Sons (quote, p. 247).

29. Blake, R. R., & Mouton, J. J. (1969). *Building a dynamic corporation through grid organizational development.* Reading, MA: Addison-Wesley.

30. Lee, C. (1991). Followership: The essence of leadership. *Training, 28,* 27–35 (quote, p. 28).

31. Graen, G. B., & Wakabayashi, M. (1994). Cross-cultural leadership-making: Bridging American and Japanese diversity for team advantage. In H. C. Triandis, M. D. Dunnette, & L. M. Hough (Eds.) *Handbook of industrial and organizational psychology* (2nd ed., Vol. 4, pp. 415–466). Palo Alto, CA: Consulting Psychologists Press.

32. Phillips, A. S., & Bedian, A. G. (1994). Leader-follower exchange quality: The role of personal and interpersonal attributes. *Academy of Management Journal, 37,* 990–1001.

33. Dunegan, K. J., Duchon, D., & Uhl-Bien, M. (1992). Examining the link between leader-member exchange and subordinate performance: The role of task analyzability and variety as moderators. *Journal of Management, 18,* 59–76.

34. Duarte, N. T., Goodson, J. R., & Klich, N. R. (1993). How do I like thee? Let me appraise the ways. *Journal of Organizational Behavior, 14,* 239–249.

35. Deluga, R. J., & Perry, J. T. (1991). The relationship of subordinate upward influencing behaviour, satisfaction and perceived superior effectiveness with leader-member exchanges. *Journal of Occupational Psychology, 64,* 239–252.

36. Ferris, G. R. (1985). Role of leadership in the employee withdrawal process: A constructive replication. *Journal of Applied Psychology, 70,* 777–781.

37. Scandura, T. A., & Schriesheim, C. A. (1994). Leader-member exchange and supervisor career mentoring as complementary constructs in leadership research. *Academy of Management Journal, 37,* 1588–1602.

38. Lord, R. G., & Maher, K. (1989). Perceptions in leadership and their implications in organizations. In J. Carroll (Ed.), *Applied social psychology and organizational settings* (Vol. 4, pp. 129–154). Hillsdale, NJ: Erlbaum.

39. Heneman, R. L., Greenberger, D. B., & Anonyuo, C. (1989). Attributions and exchanges: The effects of interpersonal factors on the diagnosis of employee performance. *Academy of Management Journal, 32,* 466–476.

40. Mitchell, T. R., & Wood, R. E. (1980). Supervisors' responses to subordinate poor performance: A test of an attribution model. *Organizational Behavior and Human Performance, 25,* 123–138.

41. Bass, B. M. (1985). *Leadership and performance beyond expectations.* New York: Free Press.

42. See Note 6.

43. House, R. J., Spangler, W. D., & Woycke, J. (1991). Personality and charisma in the U.S. presidency: A psychological theory of leader effectiveness. *Administrative Science Quarterly, 36,* 364–396.

44. See Note 41.

45. House, R. J. (1977). A 1976 theory of charismatic leadership. In J. G. Hunt & L. L. Larson (Eds.), *Leadership: The cutting edge* (pp. 189–207). Carbondale, IL: Southern Illinois University Press.

46. See Note 45.

47. Conger, J. A. (1991). Inspiring others: The language of leadership. *Academy of Management Executive, 5,* 31–45.

48. House, R. J., Woycke, J., & Fedor, E. M. (1988). Charismatic and noncharismatic leaders: Differences in behavior and effectiveness. In J. A. Conger & R. N. Kanungo (Eds.), *Charismatic leadership* (pp. 122–144). San Francisco: Jossey-Bass.

49. See Note 48.

50. House, R. J., & Howell, J. M. (1992). Personality and charismatic leadership. *Leadership Quarterly, 3(2),* 81–108.

51. See Note 1.

52. Hoover, G., Campbell, A., & Spain, P. J. (1994). *Hoover's handbook of American business.* Austin, TX: Reference Press.

53. Treviño, L. K., & Nelson, K. A. (1995). Managing business ethics. New York: Wiley.

54. Zachary, G. P. (1994, June 2). How "Barbarian" style of Philippe Kahn led Borland into jeopardy. *Wall Street Journal,* p. A1.

55. See Note 47 (quote, p. 44).

56. See Note 2.

57. Tichy, N. M. (1993). *Control your destiny or someone else will.* New York: Doubleday Currency.

58. Fisher, A. B. (1996, March 6). Corporate reputations. *Fortune,* pp. 90–98.

59. Morris, B. (1995, December 11). The wealth builders. *Fortune,* pp. 80–84, 88, 90, 94.

60. Farnham, A. (1993, September 20). Mary Kay's lessons in leadership. *Fortune,* pp. 68–69, 71, 74, 76–77.

61. Kohl, W. L., Steers, & Terborg, J. R. (1995). The effects of transformational leadership on teacher attitudes and student performance in Singapore. *Journal of Organizational Behavior, 16,* 319–333.

62. Hater, J. J., & Bass, B. M. (1988). Superiors' evaluations and subordinates' perceptions of transformational and transactional leadership. *Journal of Applied Psychology, 73,* 695–702.

63. Zenger, J. H., Musselwhite, E., Hurson, K., & Perrin, C. (1994). *Leading teams: Mastering the new role.* Homewood, IL: Business One Irwin.

64. See Note 1.

65. Fiedler, F. E. (1978). Contingency model and the leadership process. In L. Berkowitz (Ed.), *Advances in experimental social psychology* (Vol. 11, pp. 60–112). New York: Academic Press.

66. Strube, M. J., & Garcia, J. E. (1981). A meta-analytic investigation of Fiedler's contingency model of leadership effectiveness. *Psychological Bulletin, 90,* 307–321.

67. Schriesheim, C. A., Tepper, B. J., & Terault, L. A. (1994). Least preferred co-worker score, situational control, and leadership effectiveness: A meta-analysis of contingency model performance predictions. *Journal of Applied Psychology, 79,* 561–573.

68. Peters, L. H., Hartke, D. D., & Pohlman, J. T. (1985).

Fiedler's contingency theory of leadership: An application of the meta-analytic procedures of Schmidt and Hunter. *Psychological Bulletin, 97,* 274–385.

69. Ashour, A. S. (1973). The contingency model of leadership effectiveness: An evaluation. *Organizational Behavior and Human Performance, 9,* 339–355.

70. Fiedler, F. E., Chemers, M. M., Mahar, L. (1976). *Improving leadership effectiveness: The leader match concept.* New York: Wiley.

71. Fiedler, F. E., Garcia, J. E., Bell, C. H., Chemers, M. M., & Patrick, D. (1984). Increasing mine productivity and safety through management training and organization development: A comparative study. *Basic and Applied Social Psychology, 5,* 1–18.

72. Hersey, P., & Blanchard, K. H. (1988). *Management of organizational behavior.* Englewood Cliffs, NJ: Prentice-Hall.

73. Hambleton, R. K., & Gumpert, R. (1982). The validity of Hersey and Blanchard's theory of leader effectiveness. *Group and Organization Studies, 7,* 225–242.

74. Vecchio, R. P. (1987). Situational leadership theory: An examination of a prescriptive theory. *Journal of Applied Psychology, 72,* 444–451.

75. See Note 74.

76. House, R. J., & Baetz, M. L. (1979). Leadership: Some empirical generalizations and new research directions. In B. M. Staw (Ed.), *Research in organizational behavior* (Vol. 1, pp. 341–424). Greenwich, CT: JAI Press.

77. Milbank, D. (1990, March 5). Managers are sent to "Charm Schools" to discover how to polish up their acts. *Wall Street Journal,* pp. A14, B3.

78. Vroom, V. H., & Yetton, P. W. (1973). *Leadership and decision making.* Pittsburgh: University of Pittsburgh Press.

79. Vroom, V. H., & Jago, A. G. (1978). On the validity of the Vroom-Yetton model. *Journal of Applied Psychology, 63,* 151–162.

80. Field, R. H. (1982). A test of the Vroom-Yetton normative model of leadership. *Journal of Applied Psychology, 67,* 532–537.

81. Heilman, M. E., Hornstein, H. A., Cage, J. H., & Herschlag, J. K. (1984). Reactions to prescribed leader behavior as a function of role perspective: The case of the Vroom-Yetton model. *Journal of Applied Psychology, 69,* 50–60.

82. Vroom, V. H., & Jago, A. G. (1988). *The new leadership: Managing participation in organizations.* Englewood Cliffs, NJ: Prentice-Hall.

83. Kerr, S., & Jermier, J. M. (1978). Substitutes for leadership: Their meaning and measurement. *Organizational Behavior and Human Performance, 22,* 375–403.

84. See Note 1.

85. Sheridan, J. E., Vredenburgh, D. J., & Abelson, M. A. (1984). Contextual model of leadership influence in hospital units. *Academy of Management Journal, 27,* 57–78.

86. Podsakoff, P. M., Niehoff, B. P., MacKenzie, S. B., & Williams, M. L. (1993). Do substitutes for leadership really substitute for leadership? An empirical examination of Kerr and Jermier's situational leadership model. *Organizational Behavior and Human Decision Processes, 54,* 1–44.

87. Meindl, J. R., & Ehrlich, S. B. (1987). The romance of leadership and the evaluation of organizational performance. *Academy of Management Journal, 30,* 91–109.

Case in Point Source

See Note 57.

CHAPTER 14

Preview Case Source

Philips, N. (1994). *Managing international teams.* Burr Ridge, IL: Irwin.

Chapter Notes

1. Schneider, B. (1990). *Organizational climate and culture.* San Francisco: Jossey-Bass.

2. Deutschman, A. (1994, October 17). The managing wisdom of high-tech superstars. *Fortune,* pp. 197–198, 200, 202–204, 206.

3. Pennings, J. M., & Buitendam, A. (1987). *New technology as organizational innovation.* Cambridge, MA: Ballinger.

4. Zammuto, R. F. (1992). Gaining advanced manufacturing technologies' benefits: The role of organization design and culture. *Academy of Management Review, 17,* 701–728.

5. Saporito, B. (1992, August 24). A week aboard the Wal-Mart express. *Business Week,* pp. 77–81, 84.

6. Flynn, J., Del Valle, C., & Mitchell, R. (1992, August 3). Did Sears take other customers for a ride? *Business Week,* pp. 24–25.

7. Schein, E. H. (1985). *Organizational culture and leadership.* San Francisco: Jossey-Bass.

8. Chatman, J. A., & Jehn, K. A. (1994). Assessing the relationship between industry characteristics and organizational culture: How different can you be? *Academy of Management Journal, 37,* 522–533.

9. Andrews, E. L. (1989, December). Out of chaos. *Business Month,* p. 33.

10. Smith, R. C. (1993). *Comeback.* Boston: Harvard Business School Press.

11. Levering, R., & Moskowitz, M. (1993). *The 100 best companies to work for in America.* New York: Currency Doubleday.

12. See Note 11.

13. See Note 11 (quote, p. 277).

14. Quick, J. C. (1992). Crafting an organizational culture: Herb's hand at Southwest Airlines. *Organizational Dynamics, 21(2),* 45–56.

15. Martin, J., & Meyerson, D. (1988). Organizational cultures and the denial, channeling, and acknowledgment of ambiguity. In L. R. Pondy, R. J. Boland, Jr., & H. Thomas (Eds.), *Managing ambiguity and change* (pp. 93–125). New York: Wiley.

16. Schein, E. H. (1985). How culture forms, develops, and changes. In R. H. Kilmann, M. J. Saxton, & R. Serpa (Eds.), *Gaining control of corporate culture* (pp. 17–43). San Francisco: Jossey-Bass.

17. Sackmann, S. A. (1992). Cultures and subcultures: Analysis of organizational knowledge. *Administrative Science Quarterly, 37,* 140–161.

18. Sonnenfeld, J. (1988). *The hero's farewell.* New York: Oxford University Press.

19. Rebello, K., Burrows, P., & Sager, I. (1996, February 5).

The fall of an American icon. *Business Week,* pp. 34–42.

20. Martin, J., Sitkin, S. B., & Boehm, M. (1985). Founders and the elusiveness of a cultural legacy. In P. J. Frost, L. F. Moore, M. R. Louis, C. C. Lundberg, & J. Martin (Eds.), *Organizational culture* (pp. 99–124). Beverly Hills, CA: Sage.

21. Dumaine, B. (1990, January 15). Creating a new company culture. *Fortune,* pp. 127–128, 130–131.

22. Schein, E. H. (1985). How culture forms, develops and changes. In R. H. Kilmann, M. J. Saxton, & R. Serpa (Eds.), *Gaining control of corporate culture* (pp. 17–43). San Francisco: Jossey-Bass.

23. Weick, K. E. (1985). The significance of corporate culture. In P. J. Frost, L. F. Moore, M. R. Louis, C. C. Lundberg, & J. Martin (Eds.), *Organizational culture* (pp. 381–390). Beverly Hills, CA: Sage.

24. Rentsch, J. R. (1991). Climate and culture: Interaction and qualitative differences in organizational meanings. *Journal of Applied Psychology, 75,* 668–681.

25. Lundberg, C. C. (1985). On the feasibility of cultural intervention in organizations. In P. J. Frost, L. F. Moore, M. R. Louis, C. C. Lundberg, & J. Martin (Eds.), *Organizational culture* (pp. 169–186). Beverly Hills, CA: Sage.

26. Ott, J. S. (1989). *The organizational culture perspective.* Chicago: Dorsey.

27. Dandridge, T. C. (1985). The life stages of a symbol: When symbols work and when they can't. In P. J. Frost, L. F. Moore, M. R. Louis, C. C. Lundberg, & J. Martin (Eds.), *Organizational culture* (pp. 141–154). Beverly Hills, CA: Sage.

28. Walton, T. (1988). *Architecture and the corporation.* New York: Macmillan.

29. Ornstein, S. L. (1986). Organizational symbols: A study of their meanings and influences on perceived psychological climate. *Organizational Behavior and Human Decision Processes, 38,* 207–229.

30. Neuhauser, P. C. (1993). *Corporate legends and lore: The power of storytelling as a management tool.* New York: McGraw-Hill.

31. Martin, J. (1982). Stories and scripts in organizational settings. In A. Hastorf, & A. Isen (Eds.), *Cognitive social psychology* (pp. 255–306). New York: Elsevier-North Holland.

32. Gundry, L. K., & Rousseau, D. M. (1994). Critical incidents in communicating culture to newcomers: The meaning is the message. *Human Relations, 47,* 1063–1088.

33. Rowlinson, M., & Hassard, J. (1993). The invention of corporate culture: A history of the histories of Cadbury. *Human Relations, 46,* 299–326.

34. Boje, D. M. (1995). Stories of the storytelling organization: A postmodern analysis of Disney as "Tamara-land." *Academy of Management Journal, 38,* 997–1035.

35. Richman, T. (1990, January). The master entrepreneur. *Inc.,* p. 50.

36. Deal, T. E., & Kennedy, A. A. (1982). *Corporate cultures.* Reading, MA: Addison-Wesley.

37. See Note 30 (quote, p. 19).

38. Lewis, G. (1993, April 12). One fresh face at IBM may not be enough. *Business Week,* p. 33.

39. See Note 26.

40. See Note 26.

41. See Note 36 (quote, p. 63).

42. Brenner, J. G. (1992, April 19). The world according to planet Mars. *Dallas Morning News,* pp. 1H, 2H, 7H.

43. Manley, W. W., II. (1991). *Executive's handbook of model business conduct codes.* Englewood Cliffs, NJ: Prentice-Hall (quote, p. 5).

44. Hatch, M. J. (1993). The dynamics of organizational culture. *Academy of Management Review, 18,* 657–693.

45. Weiner, Y. (1988). Forms of value systems: A focus on organizational effectiveness and cultural change and maintenance. *Academy of Management Review, 13,* 534–545.

46. Treviño, L. K., & Nelson, K. A. (1995). *Managing business ethics.* New York: John Wiley & Sons.

47. Saffold, G. S., III. (1988). Culture traits, strength, and organizational performance: Moving beyond "strong" culture. *Academy of Management Review, 13,* 546–558.

48. Dennison, D. (1984). Bringing corporate culture to the bottom line. *Organizational Dynamics, 13,* 5–22.

49. Peters, T., & Waterman, R. H. (1982). *In search of excellence.* New York: Harper & Row.

50. Siehl, C., & Martin, J. (1988). *Organizational culture: A key to financial performance?* (Research Paper Series No. 998.) Stanford, CA: Stanford University, Graduate School of Business.

51. Hitt, M. A., & Ireland, R. D. (1987). Peters and Waterman revisited: The unended quest for excellence. *Academy of Management Executive, 1,* 91–98.

52. Sheridan, J. E. (1992). Organizational culture and employee retention. *Academy of Management Journal, 35,* 1036–1056.

53. O'Reilly, C. A., III, Chatman, J., & Caldwell, D. F. (1991). People and organizational culture: A profile comparison approach to assessing person-organization fit. *Academy of Management Journal, 34,* 487–516.

54. Vandermolen, M. (1992, November). Shifting the corporate culture. *Working Woman,* pp. 25, 28.

55. Walter, G. A. (1985). Culture collisions in mergers and acquisitions. In P. J. Frost, L. F. Moore, M. R. Louis, C. C. Lundberg, & J. Martin (Eds.), *Organizational culture* (pp. 301–314). Beverly Hills, CA: Sage.

56. Byrbem, J. A., Symonds, W. C., & Siler, J. F. (1991, April 1). CEO disease. *Business Week,* pp. 52–60.

57. Burrough, B., & Helyar, J. (1990). *Barbarians at the gate.* New York: Harper Collins.

58. Cartwright, S., & Cooper, C. L. (1993). The role of culture compatibility in successful organizational marriage. *Academy of Management Executive, 7,* 57–70.

59. Carroll, P. (1993). Big blues: *The unmaking of IBM.* New York: Crown.

60. Boyett, J. H., Schwartz, S., Osterwise, L., & Bauer, R. (1993). *The quality journey.* New York: Dutton.

61. Hulin, C. L., & Roznowski, M. (1985). Organizational technologies: Effects on organizations' characteristics and individuals' responses. In L. L.

Cummings, & B. M. Staw (Eds.), *Research in organizational behavior* (Vol. 7, pp. 39–86). Greenwich, CT: JAI Press.

62. Swasy, A. (1993). *Soap opera: The inside story of Procter & Gamble.* New York: Times Books.

63. Porter, M. E. (1985). *Competitive advantage.* New York: Free Press.

64. Drucker, P. F. (1992). *Managing for the future.* New York: Truman Talley Books/Dutton.

65. Guthrie, J. P., & Olian, J. D. (1990). Using psychological constructs to improve health and safety: The HRM niche. In G. R. Ferris, & K. M. Rowland (Eds.), *Research in personnel and human resources management* (Vol. 8, pp. 141–201). Greenwich, CT: JAI Press.

66. Krause, T. R. (1991). A behavior-based safety management process. In J. W. Jones, B. D. Steffy, & D. W. Bray (Eds.), *Applying psychology in business* (pp. 813–824). New York: Lexington Books.

67. Rogers, B. (1995, February). Creating a culture of safety. *HRMagzine,* pp. 85–88.

68. See Note 63 (quote, p. 87).

69. Perrow, C. (1967). A framework for the comparative analysis of organizations. *American Sociological Review, 32,* 194–208.

70. Katzell, R. (1994). Contemporary meta-trends in industrial and organizational psychology. In. H. C. Triandis, M. D. Dunnette, & L. M. Hough (Eds.), *Handbook of industrial and organizational psychology* (2nd ed., Vol. 4, pp. 1–89). Palo Alto, CA: Consulting Psychologists Press.

71. Dean, J. W., Yoon, S. J., & Susman, G. I. (1992). Advanced manufacturing technology and organization structure: Empowerment or subordination? *Organization Science, 3,* 203–229.

72. Ettlie, J. E. (1988). *Taking charge of manufacturing.* San Francisco: Jossey-Bass.

73. Valery, N. (1988). Factory of the future. In J. Gibson, J. Ivancevich, & J. Donnelly Jr. (Eds.), *Organizations close-up* (pp. 274–301). Plano, TX: Business Publications.

74. See Note 73.

75. Verity, J. W. (1995, December 4). Meet Java, the

invisible computer. *Business Week,* pp. 82–83.

76. Cortese, A., Verity, J., Rebello, K., & Hof, R. (1995, December 4). The software revolution. *Business Week,* pp. 78–83, 86, 90.

77. Weick, K. (1990). Technology as equivoque: Sensemaking in new technologies. In P. S. Goodman, & L. S. Sproull (Eds.), *Technology and organizations* (pp. 1–44). San Francisco: Jossey-Bass.

78. Office of Technology Assessment. (1985). *Automation of American offices, 1985–2000.* Washington, DC.

79. Solomon, J. S. (1987, fall). Union responses to technological change: Protecting the past or looking into the future? *Labor Studies Journal,* pp. 51–65.

80. Farnham, A. (1993, autumn). Making high tech work for you. *Fortune* (Special Issue), p. 1.

81. Bayless, A. (1986, October 16). Technology reshapes North America's lumber plants. *The Wall Street Journal,* p. 6.

82. Sherman, J. (1994). *In the rings of Saturn.* New York: Oxford University Press.

83. Neff, R. (1987, April 20). Getting man and machine to live happily ever after. *Business Week,* pp. 61–63.

84. Argote, L., Goodman, P. S., & Schkade, D. (1983, spring). The human side of robots: How workers react to a robot. *Sloan Management Review,* pp. 31–42.

85. See Note 84.

86. Katzenbach, J. R., & Smith, D. K. (1993). *The wisdom of teams.* Boston: Harvard Business School Press.

87. Carstairs, J. F. (1988, March 28). America rushes to high tech for growth. *Business Week,* pp. 84–86, 88, 90.

88. See Note 73.

89. See Note 80.

90. Tompkins, N. C. (1993, April). Tools that help performance on the job. *HRMagazine,* pp. 84, 87, 89–91.

91. See Note 90.

92. Anonymous. (1993, September). New technology and the disabled. *Information Management Forum,* pp. 1, 4.

93. See Note 90.

94. See Note 90.

95. See Note 90.

96. U.S. Congress, Office of Technology Assessment (1987). *The electronic supervisor: New technology, new tensions* (OTA-CIT-333). Washington, DC: U.S. Government Printing Office.

97. Aiello, J. R. (1993). Computer-based work monitoring: Electronic surveillance and its effects. *Journal of Applied Social Psychology, 23,* 499–507.

98. See Note 97.

99. Bylinsky, G. (1991, November). How companies spy on employees. *Fortune,* pp. 131–133, 136, 138, 140 (quote, p. 136).

100. Kipnis, D. (1991). The technological perspective. *Psychological Science, 2,* 62–69.

101. Marx, G. T., & Sherizen, S. (1986). Monitoring on the job: How to protect privacy as well as property. *Technology Review, 89,* 62–72.

102. See Note 97.

103. Kulik, C. T., & Ambrose, M. L. (1993). Category-based and feature-based processes in performance appraisal: Integrating visual and computerized sources of performance data. *Journal of Applied Psychology, 78,* 821–830.

104. Irving, R. H., Higgins, C. A., & Safayeni, F. R. (1986). Computerized performance monitoring systems: Use and abuse. *Communications of the ACM, 29,* 794–801.

105. See Note 97.

106. See Note 97.

107. Chalykoff, J., & Kochan, T. A. (1989). Computer-aided monitoring: Its influence on employee satisfaction and turnover. *Personnel Psychology, 40,* 807–834.

108. Fenner, D. B., Lerch, F. J., & Kulik, C. T. (1993). The impact of computerized performance monitoring and prior performance knowledge on performance evaluation. *Journal of Applied Social Psychology, 23,* 572–601.

109. Ives, B., & Mason, R. O. (1990). Can information technology revitalize your customer service? *Academy of Management Executive, 4,* 52–69.

110. Bylinsky, G. (1996, February 6). Manufacturing for reuse. *Fortune,* pp. 102–104, 108, 110, 112.

111. See Note 110.

Case in Point Sources

Freight carriers' technology tune: We've only just begun. (1993, June 3). *Purchasing,* p. 37. Fitzgerald, M. (1993, November 29). UPS delivers new bar-code system to public domain. *ComputerWorld,* p. 38. Hawkins, C., & Oster, P. (1993, May 31). After a U-turn, UPS really delivers. *Business Week,* pp. 92–93. Laabs, J. J. (1993, October). Community service helps UPS develop managers. *Personnel Journal,* pp. 90–92, 94, 96, 98. Margolis, N. (1993, March 1). UPS head launched for IS use. *ComputerWorld,* p. 65. Pastore, R. (1993, December 15). A measured success. *CIO,* pp. 40–45.

CHAPTER 15

Preview Case Source

Lubove, S. (1995, July 17). New-tech, old-tech. *Forbes,* pp. 58, 60, 62.

Chapter Notes

1. Miller, D. (1987). The genesis of configuration. *Academy of Management Review, 12,* 686–701.

2. Galbraith, L. R. (1987). Organization design. In J. W. Lorsch (Ed.), *Handbook of organizational behavior* (pp. 343–357). Englewood Cliffs, NJ: Prentice-Hall.

3. Hendricks, C. F. (1992). *The rightsizing remedy.* Homewood, IL: Business One Irwin.

4. Swoboda, F. (1990, May 28–June 3). For unions, maybe bitter was better. *Washington Post National Weekly Edition,* p. 20.

5. Weber, J. (1990, December 10). Farewell, fast track. *Business Week,* pp. 192–200.

6. Massie, J. (1996, February 26). The downside of downsizing. *Columbus Dispatch,* Section I, pp. 1–2.

7. Kratz, V. (1996, March–April). About those 97,000 jobs eliminated in January. *Business Ethics,* p. 4.

8. Treece, J. B. (1990, April 9). Will GM learn from its own role models? *Business Week,* pp. 62–64.

9. Lawler, E. E. (1988, summer). Substitutes for hierarchy. *Organizational Dynamics,* pp. 5–6, 15.

10. Scott, M., & Rothman, H. (1992). *Companies with a con*

science. New York: Birch Lane Press.

11. Speen, K. (1988, September 12). Caught in the middle. *Business Week,* pp. 80–88.

12. Urwick, L. F. (1956). The manager's span of control. *Harvard Business Review, 34(3),* 39–47.

13. Charan, R. (July–August, 1991). How networks reshape organizations—for results. *Harvard Business Review,* pp. 10–17.

14. Green, H., & Moscow, A. (1984). *Managing.* New York: Doubleday.

15. Dalton, M. (1950). Conflicts between staff and line managerial officers. *American Sociological Review, 15,* 342–351.

16. Chandler, A. (1962). *Strategy and structure.* Cambridge, MA: MIT Press.

17. Mitchell, R. (1987, December 14). When Jack Welch takes over: A guide for the newly acquired. *Business Week,* p. 93–97.

18. Lawrence, P., & Lorsch, J. (1967). *Organization and environment.* Boston: Harvard University.

19. Pitta, J. (1993, April 26). It had to be done and we did it. *Forbes,* pp. 148–152.

20. For best results, decentralize R&D. (1993, June 28). *Business Week,* p. 134.

21. Dumaine, B. (1990, November 5). How to manage in a recession. *Fortune,* pp. 72–75.

22. Toy, S. (1988, April 25). The Americanization of Honda. *Business Week,* pp. 90–96.

23. Uttal, B. (1985, June 29). Mettle test time for John Young. *Fortune,* pp. 242–244, 248.

24. Mee, J. F. (1964). Matrix organizations. *Business Horizons, 7(2),* 70–72.

25. Bartlett, C. A., & Ghoshal, S. (1990). Matrix management: Not a structure, a frame of mind. *Harvard Business Review, 68(3),* 138–145.

26. Wall, W. C., Jr. (1984). Integrated management in matrix organizations. *IEEE Transactions on Engineering Management, 20(2),* 30–36.

27. Davis, S. M., & Lawrence, P. R. (1977). *Matrix.* Reading, MA: Addison-Wesley.

28. Goggin, W. (1974). How the multidimensional structure works at Dow Corning. *Harvard Business Review, 56(1),* 33–52.

29. See Note 27.

30. Ford, R. C., & Randolph, W. A. (1992). Cross-functional structures: A review and integration of matrix organization and project management. *Journal of Management, 18,* 267–294.

31. See Note 30.

32. GE: Just your average everyday $60 billion family grocery store. (1994, May 2). *Industry Week,* pp. 13–18.

33. Slater, R. (1993). *The new GE.* Homewood, IL: Business One Irwin (quote, p. 257).

34. Woodruff, D., & Miller, K. L. (1993, May 3). Chrysler's Neon: Is this the small car Detroit couldn't build? *Business Week,* pp. 116–126.

35. Dees, G. D., Rasheed, A. M. A., McLaughlin, K. J., & Priem, R. L. (1995). The new corporate architecture. *Academy of Management Executive, 9,* 7–18.

36. See Note 35.

37. Tully, S. (1993, February 3). The modular corporation. *Fortune,* pp. 106–108, 110.

38. Taylor, A. (1990, November 19). Why Toyota keeps getting better and better and better. *Fortune,* pp. 72–79.

39. Byrne, J. (1993, February 8). The virtual corporation. *Business Week,* pp. 99–103.

40. Sherman, S. (1992, September 21). Are strategic alliances working? *Fortune,* pp. 77–78 (quote, p. 78).

41. McGregor, D. (1960). *The human side of enterprise.* New York: McGraw-Hill.

42. Argyris, C. (1964). *Integrating the individual and the organization.* New York: Wiley.

43. Likert, R. (1961). *New patterns of management.* New York: McGraw-Hill.

44. Duncan, R. (1979, winter). What is the right organization structure? *Organizational Dynamics,* pp. 59–69.

45. Burns, T., & Stalker, G. M. (1961). *The management of innovation.* London: Tavistock.

46. Deveney, K. (1986, October 13). Bag those fries, squirt that ketchup, fry that fish. *Business Week,* pp. 57–61.

47. Kerr, P. (1985, May 11). Witch hazel still made the old-fashioned way. *New York Times,* pp. 27–28.

48. Morse, J. J., & Lorsch, J. W. (1970). Beyond Theory Y. *Harvard Business Review, 48(3),* 61–68.

49. Mintzberg, H. (1983). *Structure in fives: Designing effective organizations.* Englewood Cliffs, NJ: Prentice-Hall.

50. Livesay, H. C. (1979). *American made: Men who shaped the American economy.* Boston: Little, Brown.

51. See Note 1.

52. Halal, W. E. (1994). From hierarchy to enterprise: Internal markets are the new foundation of management. *Academy of Management Executive, 8,* 69–83.

53. Deutschman, A. (1994, May 2). How H-P continues to grow and grow. *Fortune,* pp. 77–83 (quote p. 79).

54. See Note 52 (quote p. 82).

55. Nakarmi, L., & Einhorn, B. (1993, June 7). Hyundai's gutsy gambit. *Business Week,* p. 48.

56. Gerlach, M. L. (1993). *Alliance capitalism: The social organization of Japanese business.* Berkeley, CA: University of California Press.

57. Miyashita, K., & Russell, D. (1994). *Keiretsu: Inside the Japanese conglomerates.* New York: McGraw Hill.

58. Lubove, S. (1992, December 7). How to grow big yet stay small. *Forbes,* pp. 64–66.

59. See Note 55.

60. Kanter, R. M. (1994, July–August). Collaborative advantage: The art of alliances. *Harvard Business Review,* pp. 96–108.

61. See Note 60.

62. Newman, W. H. (1992). Focused joint ventures in transforming economies. *The Executive, 6,* 67–75.

63. Lewis, J. (1990). *Partnerships for profit: Structuring and managing strategic alliances.* New York: Free Press.

64. Sankar, C. S., Boulton, W. R., Davidson, N. W., & Snyder, C. A. (1995). Building a world-class alliance: The Universal Card-TSYS case. *Academy of Management Executive, 9,* 20–29.

65. Fletcher, N. (1988, December 10). U.S., China form joint venture to manufacture helicopters. *Journal of Commerce,* p. 58.

66. Bransi, B. (1987, January 3). South Korea's carmakers count their blessings. *The Economist,* p. 45.

67. Mason, J. C. (1993, May). Strategic alliances: Partnering for success. *Management Review,* pp. 10–15.

68. Woodward, J. (1965). *Industrial organization: Theory and practice.* London: Oxford University Press.

69. See Note 68 (quote p. 58).

70. Zwerman, W. L. (1970). *New perspectives on organizational theory.* Westport, CT: Greenwood.

71. Huber, G. P. (1990). A theory of the effects of advanced information technologies on organizational design, intelligence, and decision making. *Academy of Management Review, 15,* 47–71.

72. Hull, F. M., & Collins, P. D. (1987). High-technology batch production systems: Woodward's missing type. *Academy of Management Journal, 30,* 786–797.

73. Hickson, D., Pugh, D., & Pheysey, D. (1969). Operations technology and organization structure: An empirical reappraisal. *Administrative Science Quarterly, 26,* 349–377.

74. Singh, J. V. (1986). Technology, size and organization structure: A reexamination of the Okayama study data. *Academy of Management Journal, 29,* 800–812.

75. Thompson, J. D. (1967). *Organizations in action.* New York: McGraw-Hill.

76. Daft, R. L. (1986). *Organizational theory and design* (2nd ed.). St. Paul, MN: West.

Case in Point Sources

Johnson & Johnson cuts 3,000 jobs world-wide. (1993, August 16). *Chemical Marketing Reporter,* p. 5. Tanouye, E. (1993, August 12). Another job reduction set in drug industry. *Wall Street Journal,* p. A4. Weber. J. (1992, May 4). A big company that works. *Business Week,* pp. 124–127, 130, 132.

CHAPTER 16

Preview Case Source

Feldman, A. (1995, October 23). Shaking things up. *Forbes,* pp. 260, 262.

Chapter Notes

1. Woodman, R. W. (1989). Organizational change and development: New arenas for inquiry and action. *Journal of Management, 15,* 205–228.

2. Stewart, T. A. (1993, December 13). Welcome to the revolution. *Fortune,* pp. 66–68, 70, 72, 76, 78.

3. Sherman, S. (1993, December 13). How will we live with the tumult? *Fortune,* pp. 123–125.

4. Kanter, R. M. (1991, May–June). Transcending business boundaries: 12,000 world managers view change. *Harvard Business Review,* pp. 151–164.

5. Sloan, A. (1995, June 19). Fear of the future. *Newsweek,* p. 51.

6. Haveman, H. A. (1992). Between a rock and a hard place: Organizational change and performance under conditions of fundamental environmental transformation. *Administrative Science Quarterly, 37,* 48–75.

7. Nystrom, P. C., & Starbuck, W. H. (1984, spring). To avoid organizational crises, unlearn. *Organizational Dynamics,* 44–60.

8. Reese, J. (1993, July 26). Corporate Methuselahs. *Fortune,* pp. 14–15.

9. See Note 8 (quote p. 15).

10. Miller, K. L. (1993, May 17). The factory guru tinkering with Toyota. *Business Week,* pp. 95, 97.

11. Levy, A. (1986). Second-order planned change: Definition and conceptualization. *Organizational Dynamics, 16(1),* 4–20.

12. A master class in radical change. (1993, December 13). *Fortune,* pp. 82–84, 88, 90.

13. Senge, P. M. (1990). *The fifth discipline.* New York: Doubleday Currency.

14. Garvin, D. (1993, July–August). Building a learning organization. *Harvard Business Review,* pp. 78–89.

15. Huber, G. (1991). Organizational learning: The contributing process and the literatures. *Organization Science, 2,* 88–115.

16. Appleby, C. (1994, January 18). Chicago CIOs take notes. *Information Week,* p. 24.

17. Brennan, L. L., & Rubenstein, A. H. (1995). Applications of groupware in organizational learning. In C. L. Cooper & D. M. Rousseau (Eds.), *Trends in organizational behavior* (Vol. 2, pp. 37–49). New York: Wiley.

18. Serwer, A. (1994, August 8). Lessons from America's fastest growing companies. *Fortune,* pp. 42–60.

19. Gardner, E. (1993, July 19). At M.D. Anderson, specialists read minds before they write software. *Modern Healthcare,* p. 31.

20. Walsh, J., & Ungson, G. (1991). Organizational memory. *Academy of Management Review, 16,* 57–91.

21. Kirkpatrick, D. (1993, December 27). Groupware goes boom. *Fortune,* pp. 99–106.

22. Calonius, E. (1990, December 3). Federal Express's battle overseas. *Fortune,* pp. 137–140.

23. Daft, R. L. (1992). *Organization theory and design* (4th ed.). St. Paul, MN: West.

24. Tomasko, R. M. (1993). *Rethinking the corporation.* New York: AMACOM.

25. Tomasko, R. M. (1990). *Downsizing: Reshaping the corporation for the future.* New York: AMACOM.

26. Downs, A. (1995, October). The truth about layoffs. *Management Review,* pp. 57–61.

27. See Note 26.

28. Bumpstead, you're downsized! (1994, April 23). *Time,* p. 22.

29. See Note 26.

30. Rosen, R. H., & Berger, L. (1991). *The healthy company.* New York: Jeremy P. Tarcher/Perigree.

31. Cobb, A. T., & Marguiles, N. (1981). Organizational development: A political perspective. *Academy of Management Review, 6,* 49–59.

32. Levering, R., & Moskowitz, M. (1993). *The 100 best companies to work for in America.* New York: Currency Doubleday.

33. See Note 31 (quote p. 164).

34. McCarty, M. (1990, October 30). PepsiCo to consolidate its restaurants, combining U.S. and foreign operations. *Wall Street Journal,* p. A4.

35. Daft, R. L. (1982). Bureaucratic versus nonbureaucratic structure and the process of innovation and change. In

S. B. Bachrach (Ed.), *Research in the sociology of organizations* (Vol. 1, pp. 56–88). Greenwich, CT: JAI Press.

36. Gaertner, G. H., Gaertner, K. N., & Akinnusi, D. M. (1984). Environment, strategy, and implementation of administrative change: The case of civil service reform. *Academy of Management Journal, 27,* 525–543.

37. Stewart, T. A. (1993, December 13). Welcome to the revolution. *Fortune,* pp. 66–68, 70, 72, 76, 78.

38. See Note 37 (quote, p. 70).

39. See Note 37.

40. Ettorre, B. (1995, October). Managing competitive intelligence. *Management Review,* pp. 15–19.

41. Singh, J. V., House, R. J., & Tucker, D. J. (1986). Organizational change and mortality. *Administrative Science Quarterly, 31,* 587–611.

42. Barnes, Z. E. (1987). Change in the Bell System. *Academy of Management Executive, 1,* 43–46 (quote p. 43).

43. Saporito, B. (1993, May 31). The most dangerous job in America. *Fortune,* pp. 130–132, 134, 136, 138, 140.

44. Marcus, A. A. (1988). Implementing externally induced innovations: A comparison of rule-bound and autonomous approaches. *Academy of Management Journal, 31,* 235–256.

45. Powell, B., & Stone, J. (1991, July 15). "The deal of the decade." *Newsweek,* p. 40.

46. Wheelen, T. L., & Hunger, J. D. (1989). Strategic management and business policy (3rd ed.). Reading, MA: Addison-Wesley.

47. Glueck, W. F. (1979). *Personnel: A diagnostic approach.* Dallas: Business Publications.

48. Swasy, A. (1993). *Soap opera: The inside story of Procter & Gamble.* New York: Times Books.

49. Lewin, K. (1951). *Field theory in social science.* New York: Harper & Row.

50. Schein, E. H. (1968). Organizational socialization and the profession of management. *Industrial Management Review, 9,* 1–16.

51. Dumaine, B. (1993, June 28). Times are good? Create a crisis. *Fortune,* pp. 123–124, 126, 130.

52. Armenakis, A. A., Harris, S. G., & Mossholder, K. W. (1993). Creating readiness for organizational change. *Human Relations, 46,* 681–703.

53. Beer, M. (1980). *Organizational change and development: A systems view.* Glenview, IL: Scott, Foresman.

54. Nadler, D. A. (1987). The effective management of organizational change. In J. W. Lorsch (Ed.), *Handbook of organizational behavior* (pp. 358–369). Englewood Cliffs, NJ: Prentice-Hall.

55. Wiersma, M. F., & Bantel, K. A. (1992). Top management team demography and corporate strategic change. *Academy of Management Journal, 35,* 91–121.

56. Katz, D., & Kahn, R. L. (1978). *The social psychology of organizations* (2nd ed.). New York: Wiley.

57. Hannan, M. T., & Freeman, J. (1984). Structural inertia and organizational change. *American Sociological Review, 49,* 149–164.

58. Goodstein, J., Gautam, K., & Boeker, W. (1994). The effects of board size and diversity on strategic change. *Strategic Management Journal, 15,* 241–250.

59. Tichy, N. M. (1993). *Control your destiny or someone else will.* New York: Doubleday Currency.

60. Tichy, N. M. (1993, December 13). Revolutionize your company. *Fortune,* pp. 114–115, 118.

61. Kotter, J. P., & Schlesinger, L. A. (1979, March–April). Choosing strategies for change. *Harvard Business Review,* pp. 106–114.

62. See Note 59.

63. Farber, S. (1989, September). When employees ask: "What's in it for me?" *Business Month,* p. 79.

64. Pasmore, W. A., & Fagans, M. R. (1992). Participation, industrial development, and organizational change: A review and synthesis. *Journal of Management, 18,* 375–397.

65. Huey, J. (1993, April 5). Managing in the midst of chaos. *Fortune,* pp. 38–41, 44, 46, 48.

66. See Note 42.

67. Porras, J. I., & Robertson, P. J. (1992). Organization development: Theory, practice, and research. In M. D. Dunnette & L. M. Hough (Eds.), *Handbook of industrial and organizational psychology* (2nd ed., Vol. 3, pp. 719–822). Palo Alto, CA: Consulting Psychologists Press.

68. Sanzgiri, J., & Gottlieb, J. Z. (1992). Philosophic and pragmatic influences on the practice of organization development, 1950–2000. *Organizational Dynamics, 21(2),* 57–69.

69. Huse, E. F., & Cummings, T. G. (1985). Organization development and change (3rd ed.). St. Paul, MN: West.

70. Abrahamson, E. (1991). Managerial fads and fashions: The diffusion and rejection of innovations. *Academy of Management Review, 16,* 586–612.

71. See Note 70.

72. Franklin, J. L. (1978, May–June). Improving the effectiveness of survey feedback. *Personnel,* pp. 11–17.

73. Golombiewski, R. T. (1972). *Reviewing organizations: A laboratory approach to planned change.* Itasca, IL: Peacock.

74. Campbell, J. P., & Dunnette, M. D. (1968). Effectiveness of T-group experiences in managerial training and development. *Psychological Bulletin, 70,* 73–104.

75. See Note 53.

76. See Note 53.

77. Beckhard, R. (1972, summer). Optimizing team building efforts. *Journal of Contemporary Business,* pp. 23–32.

78. Vicars, W. M., & Hartke, D. D. (1984). Evaluating OD evaluations: A status report. *Group and Organization Studies, 9,* 177–188.

79. McClenahen, J. S. (1990, October 15). Not fun in the sun. *Industry Week,* pp. 22–24.

80. See Note 79.

81. Fisher, L. (1992, January 12). The latest word on teamwork? "Mush." *New York Times,* p. B16.

82. Burke, W. W. (1982). *Organization development: Principles and practices.* Boston: Little, Brown.

83. Hackman, J. R., & Oldham, G. R. (1980). *Work redesign.* Reading, MA: Addison-Wesley.

84. Munchus, G. (1983). Employer-employee based quality circles in Japan: Human resource implications for American firms. *Academy of Management Review, 8,* 255–261.

85. Meyer, G. W., & Scott, R. G. (1985, spring). Quality circles: Panacea or Pandora's box? *Organizational Dynamics,* 34–50.

86. Griffin, R. W. (1988). Consequences of quality circles in an industrial setting: A longitudinal assessment. *Academy of Management Journal, 31,* 338–358.

87. Suttle, J. L. (1977). Improving life at work—problems and prospects. In J. R. Hackman & J. L. Suttle (Eds.), *Improving life at work: Behavioral science approaches to organizational change* (pp. 1–29). Santa Monica, CA: Goodyear.

88. Fields, M. W., & Thacker, J. W. (1992). Influence of quality of work life on company and union commitment. *Academy of Management Journal, 35,* 439–450.

89. Buch, K. (1992). Quality circles and employee withdrawal behaviors: A cross-organizational study. *Journal of Applied Behavioral Science, 28,* 62–73.

90. Buch, K., & Spangler, R. (1990). The effects of quality circles on performance and promotions. *Human Relations, 43,* 573–582.

91. Jick, T. D., & Ashkenas, R. N. (1985). Involving employees in productivity and QWL improvements: What OD can learn from the manager's perspective. In D. D. Warrick (Ed.), *Contemporary organization development: Current thinking and applications* (pp. 218–230). Glenview, IL: Scott, Foresman.

92. Deutsch, C. H. (1991, May 26). A revival of the quality circle. *New York Times,* p. E4.

93. Drucker, P. (1954). *The practice of management.* New York: Harper & Row.

94. Kondrasuk, J. N., Flager, K., Morrow, D., & Thompson, R. (1984). The effect of management by objectives on organization results. *Group and Organization Studies, 9,* 531–539.

95. Midas, M. T., Jr., & Devine, T. E. (1991, summer). A look at continuous improvement at Northwest Airlines. *National Productivity Review, 10,* 379–394.

96. Kondrasuk, J. N. (1981). Studies in MBO effectiveness. *Academy of Management Review, 6,* 419–430.

97. French, W. L., Bell, C. H., Jr., & Zawacki, R. A. (1989). *Organization development: Theory, practice, and research* (3rd ed.). Homewood, IL: BPI/Irwin.

98. Steel, R. P., & Shane, G. S. (1986). Evaluation research on quality circles: Technical and analytical implications. *Human Relations, 39,* 449–468.

99. See Note 74.

100. See Note 67.

101. Nicholas, J. M. (1982). The comparative impact of organization development interventions on hard criteria measures. *Academy of Management Review, 7,* 531–542.

102. See Note 83.

103. Neuman, G. A., Edwards, J. E., & Raju, N. S. (1989). Organizational development interventions: A meta-analysis of their effects on satisfaction and other attitudes. *Personnel Psychology, 42,* 461–483.

104. Rodgers, R., Hunter, J. E., & Rogers, D. L. (1993). Influence of top management commitment on management program success. *Journal of Applied Psychology, 78,* 151–155.

105. Roberts, D. R., & Robertson, P. J. (1992). Positive-findings bias, and measuring methodological rigor, in evaluations of organization development. *Journal of Applied Psychology, 6,* 918–925.

106. White, S. E., & Mitchell, T. R. (1976). Organization development: A review of research content and research design. *Academy of Management Review, 1,* 57–73.

107. Mitroff, I., & Mohrman, S. (1987). The slack is gone: How the United States lost its competitive edge in the world economy. *Academy of Management Executive, 1,* 65-70.

108. Schaeffer, R. H. & Thomson, H. H. (1992, January-February). Successful change processes begin with results. *Harvard Business Review,* pp. 80–91.

109. Bennis, W. (1977). Bureaucracy and social change: An anatomy of a training failure. In P. H. Mirvis & D. N. Berg (Eds.), *Failures in organizational development and change: Cases and essays for learning* (pp. 191–215). New York: Wiley.

110. Jaeger, A. M. (1986). Organizational development and national culture: Where's the fit? *Academy of Management Review, 11,* 178–190.

111. Trepo, G. (1973, autumn). Management style *à la française. European Business, 39,* 71–79.

112. Blunt, P. (1988). Cultural consequences for organizational change in a Southeast Asian state: Brunei. *Academy of Management Executive, 2,* 235–240.

114. Schaffer, R. H., & Thomson, H. H. (1992, January–February). Successful change processes begin with results. *Harvard Business Review,* pp. 80–91.

115. Cobb, A. T. (1986). Political diagnosis: Applications in organizational development. *Academy of Management Review, 11,* 482–496.

116. White, L. P., & Wotten, K. C. (1983). Ethical dilemmas in various stages of organizational development. *Academy of Management Review, 8,* 690–697.

Case in Point Source

Morais, R. C. (1995, January 30). "If you stand still, you die." *Forbes,* pp. 44–45.

Velasquez, M., 423–24
Von Glinow, M. A., 62
Vroom, V. H., 159, 456–59

W

Wagner, J. A., 378
Walker, Frank, 223
Wall, T. D., 278
Waller, M. J., 79
Walsh, J. P., 193
Walter, G. A., 483
Walton, R. S., 388

Waterman, R. H., 480
Watson, Thomas J., Jr., 257, 432
Watson, W. E., 265, 351–52
Wayne, John, 442
Wayne, S. J., 83
Weber, Max, 15–16, 29, 521
Wedley, W. C., 330
Welch, Jack, 448, 517
Weldon, E., 267
Wellins, R. S., 278
Wheeler, William, 553
Whitacre, Mark, 373
White, John Hazen, 71

Whitmore, Key, 213
Williams, K. J., 231
Williams, M. L., 461
Wilson, Tylee, 482
Winfrey, Oprah, 444
Wiseman, R. L., 179
Wolfe, Donald M., 63
Wood, R. E., 443
Woodward, J., 532–36
Wright, P., 202–03

Y

Yamagishi, M., 376

Yamagishi, T., 376
Yetton, P. W., 356, 456–59

Z

Zajonc, Robert, 261–62
Zalentatis, Dee, 412
Ziggy, 225
Zimmerman, Richard, 479
Zuboff, S., 296
Zwerman, W. L., 533
Zyman, Sergio, 212, 239

Reciprocity, 374, 418
Recruitment process, 195
Recycling packaging, 497
"Red tape," 15
Reduction in staff, 313
Redundancy, 321
Reengineering
  defined, 60
  TQM and, 58–61
  traditional career paths and, 221
Referent power, 408
Reflective communication style, 300
Refreezing, 559
Refugees, 47
Regression, multiple, 23
Regulative tactics, 217
Reinforcement, 87–91
Relatedness needs, 147
Relations-oriented role, 255
Relaxation training, 239
Relay Room studies, 13
Reliability, 132–34
Relocation, 221
Repatriation, 41
Repetition, 94
Representativeness heuristic, 345
Research
  action, 5
  correlational, 20–23
  experimental, 23–27
  normal science, 5
  qualitative, 27–28
  survey, 20–23
  theories and, 20
Resource-dependency model, 413–14
Resources, controlling critical, 413–14
Responsibility
  ambiguity over, 382
  breadth of, 508–10
  causal attribution of, 75–76
Restructuring
  organizational, 550
  QWL and work, 567
Results
  orientation, 471
  simple experimental, 25
Retailing, culture clashes in, 469
Reward power, 406
Rewards
  for change behaviors, 562
  to eliminate social loafing, 269
  learning through, 87–90
  patterns of administering, 89–90
  pay-for-performance plans, 161
  positive valent, 162
  systems of, organizational structure and, 378
  teams and, 281–82
  value of work-related, 173
Rightsizing, 52
Risk, decision makers and, 343
Rival camps game, 420
Rivalry games, 419
RMs, 478
Robots
  industrial, 487
  people working with, 490

Role
  ambiguity, 231–32, 255
  conflict, 231
  defined, 254
  differentiation, 255
  expectations, 254
  group member's, 254–56
  incumbent, 254
  perceptions, 160
Routine technology, 486
Rumors, 308–11

S
Sabbaticals, 150
Safety
  government standards for, 555
  incentives for job, 485
  needs, 144–45
Sandwich generation, 48
Satisfaction, job. See Job satisfaction
Satisficing decisions, 341
Saturation, 306
Scalar chain, 15
Scapegoat, 418
Schedules of reinforcement, 89–91
Scientific management
  defined, 11
  economic orientation of, 12
  principle of, 163
Scientific Management (Taylor), 11
Scientific method, 4–5
Screening employees, 393
Second-chance meetings, 355
Second-order change, 548
Security, need for, 252
Selective perception, 79
Self-actualization, 146
Self-control, 126
Self-efficacy, 117–20, 150
Self-esteem, 252
Self-fulfillment, 146
Self-image, 118–21
Self-justification, 347
Self-managed teams, 272–73, 449
Self-monitoring, 118–21, 136–37, 384
Self-oriented role, 255
Self-promotion, 84
Semantic memory, 130
Semiautonomous teams, 272
Semiconductor industry, 414
Senator communication style, 301
Sender, 290
Seniority-based pay, 123
Sensitivity training, 564–65
Sequential interdependence, 537
Service
  businesses, teams in, 277
  changes in, 550
  depersonalization of, 496
  personalized, 495–96
  sectors, 17
  at UPS, 499
  use of technology to augment, 496
Sex role stereotypes, 201
Sexual harassment, 232–33, 425
Sexual orientation, 199–200

Shame, Japanese avoidance of, 86
Shaping, 97
Shared-screen conferencing, 264
Short-term memory, 130
Side-bets orientation, 191
Sign, of correlation coefficients, 22
Similar-to-me effect, 77
Simple structure, 526
Situational leadership theory, 453–55
Skills-based diversity training, 202
"Skip-level" meetings, 322
Small-batch production, 533
Snowball effect, 308
Social comparisons, 154
Social facilitation, 261–65
Social impact theory, 266
Social influence, 402–5
Social interaction, 249
Socialization
  mentoring as one-on-one, 216–19
  organizational, 213
Socialized power motivation, 436
Socializing, 148
Social loafing, 266–70, 285–86
Social needs, 145, 252
Social perception, 72–73, 76–82
Social Psychology, 17
Social systems, 13
Societal norms, 62
Society, multicultural, 40
Socio-emotional role, 255
Sociology, 17
Socratic communication style, 300
Span of control, 508–10
Spatial visualization, 129
Specificity of evaluation, 536
Sponsorship game, 419
Sportsmanship, 370
Stable environment
  of organizational culture, 471
  organizational design and, 523
Staff
  positions, 510
  support, 526
Standing committees, 251
Status
  defined, 258
  group, 254, 258–59
  symbols, 258
Stepladder technique, 361
Stereotypes, 79–81
  defined, 80
  identifying, 81, 104
  prejudice and, 196
  sex role, 201
Stigmas, 199
Stonewalling, 62
Stories, transmitting culture through, 476–77
Strain, 230
Strategic alliances, 529–32
Strategic apex, 525
Strategic contingencies model, 414–17
Strategic decisions, 336

Strength, 131
Stress
  basic nature of, 230
  burnout and, 236–37
  career development and work, 211–46
  cognitive techniques for reducing, 239
  from competing demands, 231
  defined, 230
  failure and, 213
  health and, 237
  major causes of, 230–35
  major effects of, 235–38
  managing, 238–41
  nonwork-related, 233–35
  resistance to, 238
  task performance and, 235–36
  total life, 235
  from uncertainty, 231
  work-related causes of, 230–33
Stressful life events, 234
Stress management programs, 241
Stressors, 230
Stress points, 234
Striking, 158
Structural inertia, 561
Structure
  divisional, 527
  initiating, 438
  of manufacturing companies, 532–35
  organizational, 311–16, 378. See also Organizational structure
  simple, 526
Subcontractor, 221
Subculture, 40, 45, 473
Subgroups, 355
Subjective probabilities, 338
Subordinates, initiative of, 15
Subroles, 255
Substitutes for leadership, 459–62
Subunit power, 416
Success
  proactive personality and, 116
  symbolizing culture of, 477
  See also Career success
Suggestion systems, 321
Superordinate goals, 389
Supervision, improving quality of, 188
Supervisor
  leadership style of, 237
  termination tips for, 313–14
Suppliers, as partners, 390
Support
  developing base of, 417–18
  staff, 526
  teams, 277
Survey
  defined, 20
  employee, 322
  feedback, 563–64
  research, 20–23
  See also Questionnaire
Symbols, 476–77
System 4 organization, 522
Systems analysis, 222

STUDENT'S GUIDE TO USING

Be sure to visit Greenberg/Baron's home page at:
http://www.prenhall.com/~greenob

BEHAVIOR IN ORGANIZATIONS SIXTH EDITION

We have included in this book several key features designed to help students find and understand the most important aspects of the material. To help you get the most out of this book, we thought it would be useful to introduce some of these features here.

LEARNING OBJECTIVES
Your guide to what you should know after reading this chapter.

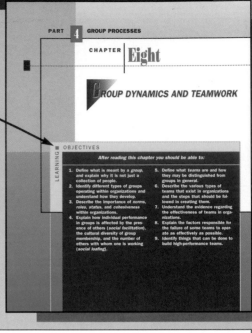

PART 4 GROUP PROCESSES

CHAPTER Eight

GROUP DYNAMICS AND TEAMWORK

OBJECTIVES

After reading this chapter you should be able to:

1. Define what is meant by a *group*, and explain why it is not just a collection of people.
2. Identify different types of groups operating within organizations and understand how they develop.
3. Describe the importance of *norms*, *roles*, *status*, and *cohesiveness* within organizations.
4. Explain how individual performance in groups is affected by the presence of others (*social facilitation*), the cultural diversity of group membership, and the number of others with whom one is working (*social loafing*).
5. Define what *teams* are and how they may be distinguished from groups in general.
6. Describe the various types of teams that exist in organizations and the steps that should be followed in creating them.
7. Understand the evidence regarding the effectiveness of teams in organizations.
8. Explain the factors responsible for the failure of some teams to operate as effectively as possible.
9. Identify things that can be done to build high-performance teams.

Key Terms
Definitions of the most important terms appear in the margins near where they are introduced.

Cross References
Other chapters where related material may be found are identified in the margins.

Summary and Review
A simplified recap of all the most important ideas in the chapter, divided into major heading.

Questions for Discussion
Useful questions for both reviewing the material and thinking about it further.

Take It to the Net
Internet addresses where Web–based information about many of the companies identified within the chapters can be found. This section also leads to the book's own home page.

Special Sections
Close-up looks at some of the most fascinating aspects of the field, focusing on such themes as ethics, quality, globalization and diversity, and future trends.

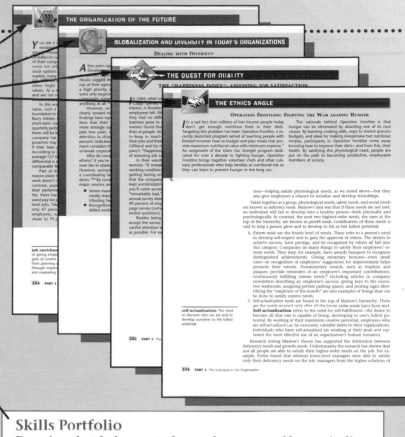

Skills Portfolio
Exercises that help you to learn about yourself as an individual (Experiencing Organizational Behavior) and to experience key ideas first hand together with others (Working in Groups).

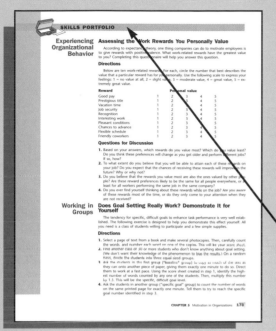

You Be the Consultant
Questions designed to get you to think about how the material may be applied to solving a typical organizational problem.

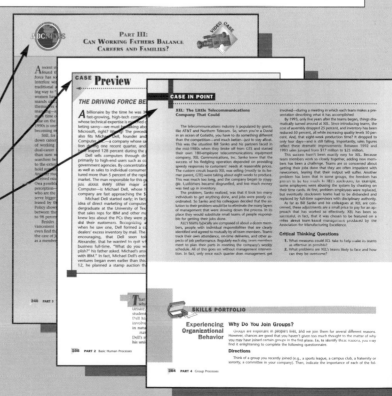

Case Studies
To demonstrate how organizational behavior is put to use, each chapter contains two cases describing actual organizations—one to help you understand the importance of the topic (Preview Case) and one to highlight how key concepts are used in practice (Case in Point). A Video Case from ABC News appears at the end of each major part of the book.